# EVELYN WAUGH
## A Biography

By the same author

FOUR STUDIES IN LOYALTY
ANSWER TO QUESTION 33
CHARACTER AND SITUATION
TWO STUDIES IN VIRTUE
A SONG OF A SHIRT
DATES AND PARTIES
ORDE WINGATE
CROSS ROADS TO ISRAEL
TROUBLED LOYALTY
*A Biography of Adam von Trott*
NANCY
*The Life of Lady Astor*

# EVELYN WAUGH

## A Biography

## CHRISTOPHER SYKES

*Illustrated*

Little, Brown and Company • Boston • Toronto

FIRST AMERICAN EDITION

Library of Congress Cataloging in Publication Data

Sykes, Christopher, 1907–
    Evelyn Waugh : a biography.

    1. Waugh, Evelyn, 1903–1966—Biography.
PR6045.A97Z83 1975      823'.9'12 [B]      75-25721
ISBN 0-316-82600-6

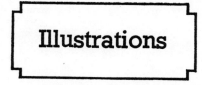

# Illustrations

TO
THE MEMORY OF OUR FRIEND
NANCY MITFORD

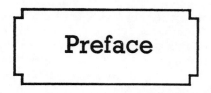

# Preface

I describe this book as *a* and not *the* biography of Evelyn Waugh because the great quantity of documentary material on which this book is based suggests to me that other biographical studies could and perhaps should be written. Until his last year Evelyn Waugh was an untiring correspondent who put his full literary skill at the disposal of his friends; one who provides striking evidence to disprove the popular myth of today that the invention of the telephone has brought to a close the art and bare practice of letter-writing. His correspondence with his friends could form the basis of a variety of books, notably (to name the largest collections) his letters to and from Alfred Duggan, Lady Diana Duff Cooper, Nancy Mitford, and Mrs Ian Fleming. To the last three above-named, and to the widow of Alfred Duggan, I owe an immeasurable debt of gratitude for fascinating material placed unconditionally at my disposal. With grief I must mention that Nancy Mitford, to whose radiant memory I dedicate this book, is no longer among the living, nor is Laura Waugh who with her eldest son Auberon Waugh was first responsible for the appearance of this portrait of Evelyn Waugh.

To Laura and Auberon I am under a heavy debt for giving me access to the whole of Evelyn Waugh's archive, most of which is now the property of the University of Texas at Austin. To that University I am much indebted for having supplied me with photostats of the original documents. Laura and Auberon furthermore gave me absolute freedom regarding the use I made of this material. To this freedom Laura made only one partial exception. She asked me to be discreet in the use of the correspondence between her and Evelyn, a large proportion of which consists of their love letters, and to consult her in cases where I felt doubt. I have been influenced by these letters in my general portrayal of Evelyn, and have quoted some phrases, but I have only quoted one letter in any fullness, the one in which he proposed marriage to her. I intended to consult Laura about using it, confident that I would receive her agreement to the publication of such a singular document, but in 1973 shortly before my intended visit to Combe Florey for the purpose and for other consultation, Laura died suddenly. In her I lost a friend to whose memory I shall always be devoted.

I am indebted to the following friends who have helped me with letters, advice and discussion: Sir Harold Acton, Lord and Lady Antrim, Lord and Lady Oxford and Asquith, the Hon. J. J. Astor, Mrs Dorothy Baker, Mr Walter Bell, the Earl of Birkenhead, Sir John and the Hon. Lady Betjeman, Mr Tom Burns, Mr Robin Campbell, the Reverend Philip Caraman S.J., Mr Dudley Carew, the late Cyril Connolly, the Reverend Martin D'Arcy S.J., Lord and Lady Donaldson, Mr and Mrs Alick Dru, Mr Tom Driberg, Colonel Brian Franks, the Hon. Mrs Fielding, Mr Graham Greene, the late Terence Greenidge, Mr Harman Grisewood, Lord and Lady Head, Sir John Heygate, Mr Christopher Hollis, Lord Kinross, the Headmaster of Lancing School, Mr Osbert Lancaster, the late Sir Robert Laycock, Lady Dorothy Lygon, Lady Mary Lygon, Sir Robert Marett, the Hon. Lady Mosley, the late A. D. Peters, Mr Anthony Powell, Mr Anthony Rhodes, Mr Robert Speaight, Professor Stephen Spender, Mr William Stirling of Keir, Mr John Sutro, Mr Douglas and the Hon. Mrs Woodruff, Dom Hubert van Zeller of Downside, the late Derek Verschoyle, Mr Alec Waugh, and to Mr John Sparrow, the Warden of All Souls College, and his fellow executors responsible for the papers of the late Sir Maurice Bowra. I am very grateful to Evelyn Waugh's youngest daughter, Mrs FitzHerbert, for her essay which occupies the last pages of this book.

I have indicated already that there is room for further publication on the subject of Evelyn Waugh so long (which I take to be a long time) as his writing commands attention. I must add my regret that I have had to deny myself the use of so much of the material open to me. I would like to have made more use of that given to me by a cherished friend, Daphne Fielding, and of her interesting remarks on Evelyn published in her book *The Nearest Way Home* (1970). I have, likewise, for the sake of literary economy, found myself compelled to neglect excellent anecdotal material given to me by Mr Robert Speaight. Even a frequently quoted authority, Sir Harold Acton, is not as abundantly represented in this book as he deserves. Great as the claims of literary economy must be, graven on the mind and heart of every biographer, indeed of every writer, as should be Voltaire's line: 'Le secret d'ennuyer, c'est celui de tout dire,' I remain regretful that I have not given anything like a full description, or full notice of the close friendship, in Evelyn's later years, that existed between himself and Dom Hubert van Zeller. As often happens to men, Evelyn became more and more difficult to please by books published in his later years. His favourite reading at the end was in some ways surprising. He refound a forgotten delight in Henry James; he regarded Georges Bernanos as the greatest of modern writers, and for lighter matter he read, among only a few others, Dom Hubert's lighter work with an enjoyment which he continually communicated to his friends.

The life of Evelyn Waugh, though centred after much uncertainty on writing, must carry his biographer into many places and interests. In his early manhood and middle age, during the years of precarious peace, he was an intrepid traveller; in time of war he was an equally intrepid soldier, one who never sought the necessary staff appointments for which he was eminently suited. My own knowledge and experience can fit out some of Evelyn's peace-time and war-time activity, but his adventures in Mexico and in Jugoslavia defeat me totally. If I have not wholly misrepresented the situations confronting him in those places in 1938, 1944 and 1945, any praise is due to Mr Walter Bell and Sir Robert Marett as regards Mexico, and to Lord Birkenhead and Mr Anthony Rhodes, the author of *The Vatican in the Age of the Dictators 1922–1945*, as regards Jugoslavia. Mr Rhodes gave me invaluable help by his research in the Public Record Office at a time when I was incapacitated by illness.

In connection with research I find myself again indebted to Mr Tom Driberg. He introduced me to Lancing and furnished me with the text of Evelyn's first serious work, *The Pre-Raphaelite Brotherhood*, now a very rare book. I am again indebted to Dorothy Baker for literary help of many kinds, including research and proof-reading. I must also express my thanks to the staffs of the London Library and of the British Museum Reading Rooms, particularly among the latter those at the Press Library at Colindale.

The bibliography which the student needs to master is not very large, unless one includes the immense volume of press articles of criticism and appreciation which have appeared in the course of the last forty years and the institution of the *Evelyn Waugh Newsletter* in the United States. From the last-named publication I have learned interesting details, but I regret to say that for the most part I have found these newsletters overloaded with pedantic debate about trifles. Most of the press comment on Evelyn in his time is ephemeral, with a few exceptions, notably Rose Macaulay's article in *Horizon* written in 1946.

Books which the researcher needs to consult include two by his brother: *The Early Years of Alec Waugh* (1962) and *My Brother Evelyn and Other Profiles* (1967). One of the best portraits of Evelyn Waugh in his young days is to be found in Sir Harold Acton's first volume of his memoirs.

The most substantial work on Evelyn Waugh is the miscellany edited by Mr David Pryce-Jones and published in 1973 under the title *Evelyn Waugh and His World*. Previous to this the chief place in Evelyn Waugh studies was held by Professor Frederick J. Stopp's book *Evelyn Waugh Portrait of an Artist*. It remains a book of considerable critical value, but, having been published in 1958, it excludes Evelyn's later work, and on this a definitive judgement must depend.

The same is more unhappily true of Edmund Wilson's comments in *Classics and Commercials*, published in New York in 1950 and in London in 1951. A knowledge of the writer's final development might have altered or qualified his hostile attitude. More balanced if less brilliant is a brief and valuable critical study by Malcolm Bradbury which appeared in 1964, as part of the *Writers and Critics* series edited by A. Norman Jeffares. It ably represents unprejudiced critical opinion of his work in Evelyn Waugh's last years.

Lady Donaldson's book *Portrait of a Country Neighbour* is the best personal document, the best-painted picture of Evelyn to date by a single hand. I have enlivened my narrative by liberal quotation from the book. Lady Donaldson sticks firmly to her subject as limited by her title: here is Evelyn as she saw him at Piers Court and at Combe Florey in the post-war years from 1948 onwards. This was when she first came to know him and, as she keeps her record strictly to personal witness, she allows herself no criticism on the work of preceding years which had made him famous. The severe limitations which she has imposed on herself stress the sincerity of the record which will remain an indispensable one to the student.

Apart from David Pryce-Jones's compilation and Lady Donaldson's all too brief memoir, the personal accounts of Evelyn to be published as books have been slight productions. Mr John St John's *To the War with Waugh*, published in 1973, with a valuable 'Introductory Memoir' by Mr Christopher Hollis, makes no pretensions to be more than a 'real life' footnote to *Men at Arms*. As such it succeeds by being interesting. Mr Dudley Carew's book *A Fragment of Friendship* was published in 1974. Unlike Mr St John's book it makes some pretensions to being considered as a serious and unbiased reassessment, but as such cannot be said to succeed. For myself, I dare to claim a detached opinion on Evelyn's literary position. I am as aware of his glaring literary errors as I am of his shining literary virtues, and I have sought to show both while not pretending to a high position in literary criticism. I do not claim the same detachment in every one of the controversial subjects which Evelyn's biographer must touch.

Last let me express my thanks to my wife for her careful scrutiny of the typescripts, and let me thank Ann Etherington for making those typescripts with such skill and judgement. I must also thank an old friend, Lady Lettice Ashley Cooper, for preparing an index.

*Swyre, Dorset*                                                    CHRISTOPHER SYKES
*January 1975*

xii

# Chapter 1

## 1903-1917

No life, unless it is an unusually dull one, can be described by a single adjective. But – a *tempestuous* life? Does that not seem to describe (roughly, of course) Evelyn Waugh's wild, frequently and often consciously shocking career? Up to a point, Lord Copper.

From his adolescence and early manhood, Evelyn Waugh lived in a state of chaotic disturbance, a state of whose chaos it is sometimes hard to distinguish the inner from the outer causes. It was a state formed by the impulses of his character, by euphoric joys and a constant melancholy, by the people with whom he mixed and among whom he made enemies and lasting friends, by the disasters of the times in which he lived. He never refused and often rejoiced in the challenge of these things, so much so that he sometimes became associated with them to a degree which the facts do not warrant. For example, the disorderly, youth-crazed, masochistically self-destroying years of the 1920s are often referred to as 'the Evelyn Waugh period'. It is forgotten that he made no impact on that period until 1928, and then a very limited one, and that though he often harked back to the scent of those years, his grown-up experience of the world hardly went back beyond 1923. He was not, in fact, a 'period piece', though he often looked like one.

In considering his personality and writing, it is remarkable how much this tempestuous life (and its tempestuousness is never to be denied) was informed by a partly fulfilled desire for the tranquillity of the opposite; for a settled routine along the accepted lines, all the more desired for being accepted; in his case that of an English gentleman living contented with his family amid his acres.

Henry Fielding's life was wilfully tempestuous, but he presented his ideal in the mild and upright character of Mr Allworthy. So far as his reader can tell, Evelyn Waugh's ideal Englishman is to be found in his portrait of the elder Crouchback, a personage as different from his inventor as can be imagined.

The resemblance to Fielding does not go far, so will not be pursued much further. Evelyn Waugh would readily have conceded that Fielding was a writer 'out of his sphere', and that comparisons of the two can only be unfair. But there is one more resemblance, and a contrast, worth noting.

Fielding's private life can provoke censure but, even from the censorious, surprised admiration also. In his younger days his conduct was licentious; as a married man he was a model of fidelity because he was essentially honest. Exactly the same can be said of Evelyn Waugh. And then the contrast. Fielding's public life was edifying throughout. In an age of low morals and open bribery, he was above all corruption in business or social dealings, though he moved in the world of the theatre which has never set an example of upright behaviour. In the larger world of Georgian England he anticipated and originated many of the most reputable features of modern social progress: enlightened magistracy; an efficient and humane police; the legal curb on mob-excitation; all these owe some and not minor debts to that great man.

Evelyn Waugh had no public life within the commonly accepted meaning. He was without any serious political or sociological interests. In politics he was without loyalties, and only had dislikes. He despised Conservatives and Liberals as moral cowards: Conservatives because they feared to act on their principles, Liberals because they curried favour with the Left, and sometimes even joined it, in the hope of appeasing its wrath. Socialists he feared and hated as people in a conspiracy to introduce Communism into Britain by means of a bloody revolution. With these negative reactions went an instinctive aversion to all the social progress of which Fielding was a herald. He saw nothing in the Welfare State except a useful lever whereby the Left hoped to prise open the gates to admit the Communist hordes.

As the last detail indicates fairly enough, age did not modify his political opinions. Rather did it increase their absurdity. Being a man of powerful intelligence, he was fully aware of the two salient and awkward facts in the case: that his political opinions were utterly ridiculous, and that while they often reflected his temperament, they almost never reflected his intelligence. In this he was not singular. The predicament is a perennial phenomenon among literary men, and Fielding's case is somewhat rare.

To open a book with a digression may be considered a grievous offence, though it is one very often committed. At least let this one be brief. There will be no further mention in this book of Henry Fielding. Some comparisons are unavoidable, but they will not be sought gratuitously, with Fielding no more than with Milton or Shakespeare. The subject of this biography will be referred to henceforth as 'Evelyn', and the first person singular will be freely employed. Apart from these I claim no other privilege, and suffer no inhibition from the fact that for many years I was his close friend, and remember him with love.

The first part of Evelyn's life has been admirably chronicled by himself, and to account for his origin, childhood, schooldays, later adolescence and early manhood needs little more than an adumbration of his own account, with a few criticisms of it. His autobiography was his last book and one of the best of his lesser writings.

His early life was not a hard one, even luxurious by comparison with that of the poor, but nevertheless one of struggle and disappointments as is usually the fate of those who enjoy exceptional talent but who lack exceptional opportunities. If he had been content to remain the successful son of a successful man in the field of publishing, he could have enjoyed security and modest riches from the beginning to the end. If he had settled for 'the little career' he could have had a desirable, not adventurous, not unpleasing, not despicable and, above all, a worry-free life. He had a great deal of talent, and some genius. The two endowments put a choice before him. The lot of the man of talent who mistakes himself for a man of genius is a familiar tale. It is not Evelyn's. The lot of those who without the needed inner fortitude thereby reject the hazards of genius is a tale rarely told because the dull ignobility of the choice leads to nothing but anticlimax, and usually the decay of the talent. 'From him that hath not, even that he hath shall be taken away from him' is an uninspiring if profoundly true theme. The story of Evelyn has an outline familiar from those of the greatest of his fellow craftsmen, that of the man who rejects the safe rewards of talent and accepts the hazards of genius for the sake of giving the best that he has to give.

In any record of life, one needs to qualify every large statement. This is true of the generalization last made, because it concerns genius, talent and craftsmanship, on which latter subject Evelyn held decided views. He was an arrogant man, often deplorably so, but he was never a conceited man. That is to say that his conceit of himself was never beyond the praise he deserved. Favourable critics and adoring admirers sometimes described him as 'a genius'. He rejected this, sometimes with needless bad temper, as adulation. It was not his opinion.

Let me illustrate the point by memories. Evelyn had large, somewhat ungainly hands. The span was enormous. Once, in conversation, he mentioned a woman friend of us both whose beauty was diminished by her rather ugly hands, and he referred to this. Perhaps to annoy him I said, 'Unlike yours,' whereupon, to my great surprise, he raised his hands and looked at them intently, saying, 'They are craftsman's hands', and he spoke without his usual irony.

That is one memory. Another of about the same date refers to a visit to him in the country by another novelist, Henry Yorke, whose work he greatly admired. Evelyn had been vexed by this friend's behaviour. 'He wore a London suit the whole time,' he complained to me, 'and he smoked at meals. And he loafed round the house as though he'd never stayed with anyone before.' Evelyn was not as easily tolerant as he should have been of the conduct in a country house of a person of humble origin to whom country visits are unfamiliar; he was extremely intolerant of the behaviour of this visitor who belonged to one of the noble families. What next! as he used to say in answer to unanswerable questions. I put in a word or two in defence of our friend. Evelyn brushed them aside, then suddenly faced me. 'Anyway, the point is this,' he said, 'Henry is a genius. I am not a genius. And,' he added with a menacing show of teeth, 'nor are you.'

A last qualifying story on this subject. Evelyn was so unappreciative of music that he was almost tone deaf. Gregorian Chant, Bach, Mozart, Beethoven, twenties jazz, it was all the same to him, a jolly background noise at the best, and a gigantic bore if you had to sit down and listen. Concerts were not for him. One day he remarked to me that he must have missed much through being 'allergic', as he described it, 'to the stuff'. I agreed that he had missed much, 'especially', I added, 'as you have perfect pianist hands'. He wanted to know what I meant. He looked at his hands. I explained that Somerset Maugham had spoiled his best story, *The Alien Corn*, by taking on trust the silly romantic view that a pianist's hands should be long lily-like things. 'Your hands', I said, 'are like the cast made of Chopin's hands. Big, muscular, with fingers that can be used as hammers. He was double-jointed, which helped. Are you?' Evelyn looked at his hands with the glow of new appreciation. 'They are craftsman's hands,' he said.


Evelyn Waugh was born on 28 October 1903. On both sides of his family he was descended from persons belonging to what used to be called 'the professional classes': the men of the four generations preceding his own included clergymen, lawyers, doctors, military men and civil servants, clergymen predominating. Some of his relations were distinguished. On his father's side he was related to Edmund Gosse, and his grandfather Dr Alexander Waugh had two female cousins who, regardless of English law as it then stood, successively married Holman Hunt. On his mother's side he was directly descended from one of the most influential and eminent of British judges, Henry, Lord Cockburn. The Waughs were of Scots origin, as was his mother's family, but they mostly lived in the south-west of England.

His interesting heredity was not a subject about which Evelyn often spoke, except as regards his fascinated interest in the connection with Holman Hunt. Though he came from many remarkable ancestors, he never showed pride in his heredity. He often affected regret that his ancestry was not aristocratic and glittering with coronets. How genuine this regret was, and how much of it was merely self-parody, is extremely difficult to say about a man who was a born actor and the son of a stage-struck father. As he says in his autobiography: 'I was early drawn to panache.' It was a true self-judgement. Let me again call on memories.

I was in Rome with Evelyn Waugh in 1951 and one day, since we were

4

Arthur Waugh

Underhill: The home of
Evelyn Waugh's childhood

Evelyn Waugh
by Henry Lamb,
probably painted in 1928

Evelyn Waugh on a motorbicycle. In later years he tried in vain
to pass the test for a licence to drive a car

bound in that direction, I planned to stop for a few minutes at a hotel where I had often stayed because an Italian valet of my father had instituted it. I wanted to ask if the old man was still alive, and if not when had he died, and to convey my respects to the family. Evelyn agreed but fell into a state of depression on the way. He became overcome by self-pity. 'My father never had an Italian valet', he whimpered. 'Well, my father never published any books, so we're quits', I replied. 'Anyone can publish books,' he moaned, 'but only the great ones of the earth have Italian valets.' I was not put out by this ridiculous farce until I was made rather uneasy by Evelyn's undisguisable joy and his grin of satisfaction when I emerged from the hotel to rejoin him, and told him that the man had evidently died or retired a long time ago as neither his name nor mine meant anything to anyone there now.

The second memory is possibly more sympathetic. He was once discussing heredity in general with my brother-in-law, Lord Antrim, and he let fall some remark of regret that he was descended from middle-class people exclusively. 'But you can always boast,' said my brother-in-law, 'that you are descended from one of the most famous lords in our history.' Evelyn shook his head sadly. 'Lord Cockburn,' he said, 'was ennobled for practical reasons. I would like to be descended from a useless Lord.'

There were numerous writers in his family tree, but in the Waugh family the only ones to achieve literary distinction before Alec and Evelyn were their father and his cousin, Sir Telford Waugh. Arthur Waugh's essays and memoirs, mostly drawn from articles of literary criticism, and his book on Tennyson, were esteemed in their time and can still be read with respectful interest. Sir Telford Waugh was an authority on the Near East and in 1930 he published a book called *Turkey: Yesterday, Today and Tomorrow.* Arthur Waugh said of it, 'Sounds like Boxing Day.'

Evelyn's father was 37 in 1903 when his second son was born. Evelyn and Alec were the only children of his marriage, Alec being five years the elder. Arthur Waugh showed his skill as a publisher from the beginning of his career, and in the year before Evelyn's birth he had, at an unusually early age, become chairman and managing director of Messrs Chapman and Hall. They were then a declining concern, having relied, it is said, too long and too slothfully on their Dickens copyright. All this was changed. In a very short time the firm was among the more forward-looking and prosperous of the publishing houses of London, thanks to the new chairman having put new life into it. Chapman and Hall were to become Evelyn's publishers twenty-six years after Arthur Waugh's appointment, but even had he had some prevision of his son's literary eminence, he would not have contemplated publishing a member of his own family. The association came about by accident, as will be told later.

There was a marvellous probity about Arthur Waugh which was inherited by Evelyn. For many years he continued to enjoy the reputation of an influential critic in the daily, weekly and monthly press. He often, it seems, wrote reviews of books he had published. In his autobiography Evelyn said: 'It is a testimony to the integrity of the period that no one, so far as I know, ever questioned the propriety of his thus doubling the role of publisher and critic.' It is a testimony, in my opinion, not to the age but to Arthur Waugh alone. His conscientious behaviour as chairman inspired G. K. Chesterton's crazy lines:

> Messrs. Chapman & Hall
> Swear not at all.
> Mr Chapman's yea is yea
> And Mr Hall's nay is nay.

Evelyn resembled his father. They grew to the same height, about 5 foot 7 inches, and in their middle years developed a tendency to corpulence. Their main physical difference was that Arthur Waugh retained remarkable facial good looks to the end of his life, whereas Evelyn, who as a youth and young man had a winning appearance which moved Harold Acton in his memoirs to describe him as a faun, lost all handsomeness in maturity and came to look gross.

In character they had much in common. Arthur Waugh has already been called 'stage-struck' in this book. The description is Evelyn's. The son was never stage-struck and took no pleasure in private theatricals, but he had inherited all his father's acting ability. It made him an incomparable story-teller and comic conversationalist. Had his inclinations been that way he would probably have enjoyed a successful career as a comedian. He once acted in an amateur film, the details of which will be given later, and the two performances which stand out are those of Evelyn and the only professional in the cast, Elsa Lanchester.

In his diary Evelyn admitted to irritation at his father's sentimentality, but he inherited this too, and it occasionally spoilt his writing. He was aware of its dangers and, unlike his father, he fought against it with ferocity. This may account for his unkindness in some part. He was on occasion very unkind to his father and, in his adolescence, the contemptuous phase in most men's lives, he came to look with contempt on him. There is no reason to doubt when he refers in his autobiography to 'a growing appreciation on my part of his quality and with it a growing pleasure in his company'. But memories of the contemptuous attitude remained with him and were used by him in his numerous pictures of fathers and sons in his novels, notably those to be found in *Work Suspended* and *Brideshead Revisited*. I knew Arthur Waugh a little, and always found him a very agreeable man to meet. Nevertheless his features are detectable in all Evelyn's fictional fathers, even in the unpleasant father of the narrator in *Brideshead Revisited*.

Of his mother, who was born Catherine Charlotte Raban, and whose mother was born Cockburn, he told far less. Nor do his readers see her reflected in his novels. I often heard Evelyn talk of his father, but I do not remember him once mentioning his mother. It can be stated with certainty that this in no way showed a want of love, only a reticence which he had inherited from her. In his autobiography he described her as 'small, neat, reticent and, until her last decade, very active. She had no special literary interests, but read a book a fortnight, always a good one. She would have preferred to live in the country and from her I learned that towns are places of exile where the unfortunate are driven to congregate in order to earn their living in an unhealthy and unnatural way.'

In a book of reminiscences and portraits his brother Alec gave some details of the mutual relations of Evelyn and his mother, and of his own with Evelyn and their father. The scene is the house that Arthur Waugh built for himself at North End, Hampstead, and to which the family moved from Hillfield Road when Evelyn was four. The new house was called Underhill. His life there as a child was one of blissful happiness. So he described it, and so did his brother Alec. In 1910, when Evelyn was seven he went to school for the first time, to a local day school called Heath Mount. In 1914, when he was between ten and eleven, he would normally have gone to a preparatory boarding-school, but he remained at home till he was close on thirteen. The financial panic following the outbreak of war was, Evelyn records, a 'decisive consideration', but he also records others: 'My evident happiness at Heath Mount and my mother's pleasure in my company.'

If the 'blissful happiness' of his early home life was in any way marred, it was by familiar psychological factors. He resented his father's prior claims over his mother, and Arthur Waugh's evening return was a moment of sorrowful wrath on the part of the young Evelyn. He also resented their pride in young Alec, which, he suspected, showed preference against him. This feeling remained strong and does all the more credit to Evelyn's affection for Alec in more crucial years ahead. More than forty years after this time, I was travelling with Evelyn in the Near East. We got an English newspaper in which Alec Waugh's name figured in the book pages. This led Evelyn on to his early memories, and of what he said I recall little except when he explained: 'I was not rejected or misprized, but Alec was their firstling and their darling lamb.' It is often the case with the first-born of whichever sex. The point to be made is that Evelyn's relations with his mother, little as he said about them, may be taken to have been exemplary as regards the natural tie between mother and son. Her letters to him are written with moving affection. Unhappily, and inescapably, it has to be said, on the authority of Alec Waugh, that in her later years Evelyn's impatience sometimes got the better of him and that in her last decade he showed to her some of his unkindness, a vice against

7

which she had warned him during those early happy years at Underhill.

The lesser experiences and events of this first period of Evelyn's life have been so enjoyably recorded by himself that for the most part they can be safely left in the pages of *A Little Learning*. It seems right, nevertheless, to recall here three items because of their later significance in Evelyn's story.

Evelyn's first and hardly conscious experience of sex was bound up with his first encounters with illness and the sense of desolation.

When he was eight Evelyn fell ill, and his condition was diagnosed as appendicitis. The operation, then one of considerable danger, was declared necessary. It was performed on the kitchen table at Underhill by a skilful surgeon, and there was no prolonged anxiety regarding Evelyn's survival. His own record is to be quoted with advantage: '. . . a strange man, not the family doctor, came into my bedroom and said: "Now I want you to smell this delicious scent," putting a gauze cone over my face, which he drenched in chloroform. It seemed to me a disgusting scent, but the next thing I knew was that I felt very sick and that my legs were strapped to my bed and that I craved water. This was denied me. Instead The Scoundrel [a hospital nurse called in for the operation] swabbed my mouth and tongue with damp cotton-wool. It was the first, and almost the last time, that I have felt really ill. They kept my legs strapped down for a week or ten days. People came with presents and praised my bravery. My idea of bravery was to cut down with a sword hordes of Pathans or Prussians. I did not feel brave at all. I did not know how else I could possibly have behaved, drugged, disembowelled, shackled as I was . . .'

There is a melancholy irony about this passage. Soon after writing it, Evelyn began to undergo the experience of feeling 'really ill' once more, and was not to recover.

Presumably the danger of the appendicitis operation in those days necessitated the patient's remaining almost completely still after it, whence the strapping of his legs to the bed. In the event this led to a complication. The strapping had somehow injured his feet and on recovery he could not walk. Electric treatment was prescribed for which his parents made odd arrangements. He was sent to stay at 'a large girls' school in the Thames estuary, then on vacation'. The only residents in the school were the headmistress, the German mistress, and 'a forlorn little girl named Daffodil, whose father was serving in India'. (Shades of Kipling and 'Saki' Munro.) 'For the first time in my life,' wrote Evelyn over fifty years later, 'I felt abandoned.' It was a feeling that was often to come over him.

There were two reasons for this exile. The location of the girls' school was considered happy as there was a belief in the curative properties of the soil in the mud-flats of the Thames estuary, in which young Evelyn was obliged to paddle 'for several hours a day' at low-water. The second reason was that in the neighbourhood of the school there lived a therapeutic electrician who three times a week applied treatment to Evelyn's feet. The combined mud and electrical regime proved effective and he could soon walk normally again. But in the meantime he enlarged his experience of life.

The therapeutic electrician was described by Evelyn as a 'stout and amiable woman', and to her he confided his 'misery in the derelict college'. She took action, wrote to Mrs Waugh, and suggested that Evelyn should be lodged with her and her family. Mrs Waugh agreed. He moved in and again found himself happy. From his very brief account it seems that this was a rather raffish household. On receiving the weekly payment, the electrician apparently took various clothes and household articles out of pawn, and the master of the house, a discharged soldier, 'got mildly drunk most evenings'. Evelyn seems to have shown no interest in poor forlorn Daffodil, but he did in Muriel, the daughter of the house. She was a little older than he was, and he records: 'Muriel from time to time exposed her private parts to me, and I mine to her.' Later in the book he says that these exposures were made only in a spirit of curiosity and he was unaware of any sexual interest. The boy and girl attended a humble school in the same street where 'the curriculum comprised a great deal of marching round the front parlour to the sound of the piano'. The two spinsters who kept the school maintained their acquaintance with Evelyn for many years, regularly sending him cards at Christmas, but after his return home Muriel seems to have passed out of his life for ever.

There is another person of his early years who should be mentioned, his young nurse, Lucy. She came from Chilcompton in Somerset, a village situated in the neighbourhood of Dr Alexander Waugh's former ministrations. Evelyn loved and respected her, and he tells how he 'lived in joyous conformity to the law of two deities, my nurse and my mother'. The last sentence makes it clear that Evelyn was in no sense one of those deprived children among the more prosperous families of the time who were forced by circumstance to find in the nurse a substitute for the parent. What he wrote about Lucy in his autobiography is moving, all the more so because of the complete absence in his portrait of the slightest trace of his accustomed irony or satire. Not that he refrained from noting oddities in Lucy's way of life. Strictly 'chapel' in religion, Lucy was a fervent reader of the Authorized Version of the Bible. Of this devout practice Evelyn wrote:

'She cannot be said to have searched the scriptures. She read undeviating, right through the genealogies, law and minor prophets, accepting them all with the same confidence in their life-giving properties. This office took her six months when she turned back to Genesis and started again. Years later during the second world war I found myself with two other bored Englishmen snowed up in Croatia in what was called "a pocket of resistance". Our few books included a Bible. One of our number was garrulous and argumentative. For the sake of quiet we offered him large bets that he could not read the whole Bible. It was a book with which he had little acquaintance. For three blessed days he was absorbed, interrupting his reading only to expound the new truths revealed to him. But Leviticus beat him. He gave up and paid up. Not so Lucy. For her the volume itself was the object of veneration, handled with especial care. No other book was ever laid upon it.'

Lucy's truthfulness was so strict that once when Evelyn and some other children in Hampstead played a hoax upon her she burst into tears, not out of chagrin at her humiliation, but because the hoax involved her little charge in conniving at a lie. From Lucy Evelyn is likely to have learned his rigid, sometimes pedantic truthfulness, from which he only swerved under the influence of self-deception. In contrast to it was his delight in fantasy, his habit of telling preposterous yarns about his friends and famous public figures. This was his novelist's instinct which he allowed to roam wildly. His fantasies were not meant to be believed, and except by great simpletons never were. But carefully contrived deceit was not in his nature. He was easily shocked by lying.

The most remarkable of the probable influences of Lucy on his mature character is to be found in his writing. He portrayed a great number of human types in his books, including a large gallery of servants. None of them escaped the satire of his hard comedy, least of all his comic or dishonest servants, with one exception. He has several nurses, of the nursery kind, in his stories, and to them he never applied parody or irony, only the gentlest comedy. Indeed, the tough-minded among fashionable critics have objected to the sentimentality with which, they allege, he fashioned these portraits. There was, as his wife said many years later, little if any sacred ground to Evelyn, but it seems that the memory of Lucy, and all she stood for, could be so described. He was a generous subscriber to charities which look after such people in old age.

As mentioned already, Evelyn did not go to boarding-school until he was thirteen. Till then from the age of seven (in 1910) he remained a day-boy at the Hampstead school of Heath Mount. The headmaster was called Mr Granville Grenfell, 'a name', remarked Evelyn, 'which would seem implausible in fiction'. Grenfell was the son of an admiral and Evelyn noted, presumably a little or perhaps much later, that 'though essentially a landsman, [he] affected many of the mannerisms of an old salt'. He noted also that in his study he kept a photograph of himself dressed in the insignia of a Grand Master of Ceremonies in the United Grand Lodge of England. Later in life Evelyn became obsessed with the delusion that Freemasons are at the heart of much of the world's evil, but he gave no indication in his autobiography that he saw anything sinister in the headmaster's devotion to this cult. He does but remark that Grenfell's Freemasonism may have accounted for the odd fact that some parents from so far away as the Channel Islands chose to send their children to this little-known school.

It was at school that Evelyn, in common with many of his compatriots, learned the vice of bullying of which he never became free. At most schools then, and probably today, bullying was only mildly rebuked. No vigorous attempt, at that time at all events, was ever made by the teachers at the majority of schools to stamp it out. It was thought to be part of the training needed by the young for the battle of life. Heath Mount seems to have been a little in advance of the vulgar morality of the time, as the following incident suggests.

Among the boys at Heath Mount there was a comely child called Cecil Beaton. 'I remember him', wrote Evelyn, 'as a tender and very pretty little boy. The tears on his long eyelashes used to provoke the sadism of youth and my cronies and I tormented him on the excuse that he was reputed to enjoy his music lessons and to hold in sentimental regard the lady who taught him. I am sure he was innocent of these charges. Our persecution went no further than sticking pins into him and we were soundly beaten for doing so.' Years after, shortly before the publication of *A Little Learning*, Evelyn told me of this first acquaintance with the famous photographer, and he seemed to find relish in these memories of young cruelty. But in most schools then boys would not have been punished for bullying.

In 1914, when he was eleven, Evelyn first became passionately interested in religion. Hitherto he had attended with Lucy Low Church services held in 'The North End Rooms' in Hampstead. The services sound grim. When Lucy left in 1914 to get married, Evelyn attended church with his parents at St Jude's in Hampstead Garden Suburb. Here he encountered religion in a very different form. St Jude's was then in the care of a 'totally preposterous parson' called Basil Bourchier. Evelyn does not say so, but a reader may suspect that this man was a brother or relative of the actor Arthur Bourchier. Basil Bourchier was at that time a famous clergyman who, as a friend of Lord Northcliffe, was frequently allowed space in the Harmsworth Press where he gave 'his wayward opinions on any subject about which he was consulted'. The theatricality of his church services seems to have been utterly extraordinary, and it drew on him the censure of all Anglican parties. The more conventional watched his extravagantly popish ritual with disgust, and the Anglo-Catholic ritualist party were angered by the caricature of their ways which he contrived: he decreed fasts or feasts according to his whim and without precedent or authority; he invented ceremonies according to his own imaginative showmanship. One of these included a novel liturgical use of salt to illustrate the Saviour's utterance concerning 'the salt of the earth'. He was a constant playgoer, but he attended the theatre in 'lay evening dress'.

Yet, hated by all parties, he never lacked for friends, thanks to Lord North-cliffe's patronage and his own journalistic ability. His church was crowded.

Attracted to panache, young Evelyn surrendered to Mr Bourchier's ecclesiastical style. This is not surprising. What is more surprising is Arthur Waugh's constant attendance which drew his son there, and ultimately led him to full acceptance of Catholicism, a thing remote from Arthur Waugh's wishes and tastes. Evelyn's father was not irreligious but held eccentric views on supernatural matters. He was a regular church-goer and, being happiest with colourful liturgy, he had for a short time taken up Anglo-Catholicism at the time of Evelyn's birth in 1903. In Victorian fashion he held family prayers for the whole household every morning, though, when the disaster of World War I came on the country in 1914, at a time when many carelessly irreligious people suddenly turned to prayer, he abandoned the custom on what Evelyn describes as 'the very curious grounds that it was "no longer any good"'. He was a convinced Protestant whose most serious objection to Catholicism was that it attempted dogmatic clarity in areas where this was inapplicable. In re-ligion he was a very typical, undecided, interested and sceptical English-man. One might wrongly suppose that his taste for colourful and theatri-cal liturgy gives sufficient explanation of his presence in St Jude's as Mr Bourchier's faithful parishioner.

Evelyn gives the real explanation with his accustomed and disconcerting directness. His father, he wrote, would never have taken a clergyman 'as a counsellor or a model'. Basil Bourchier he regarded as 'a rollicking joke' and he sat under him with unbroken regularity, never losing his enjoy-ment of 'the surprises which the services afforded'. His mother, he re-corded, 'was coldly disdainful'. The episode does illustrate the possibility of an anarchic strain in Arthur Waugh.

Evelyn's account suggests also that even at this early age he saw through Mr Bourchier's 'extravagant display', but he adds that through it he may have had 'some glimpse of higher mysteries'. Admittedly this was written when for over thirty years he had been a committed Catholic. But Mr Bourchier's influence had some effect. Soon after he had first met these religious marvels at St Jude's, he went to stay with some aunts in the little Somerset town of Midsomer Norton, near Lucy's Chilcompton, and here he met a sincere and genuinely pious Anglo-Catholic curate, a man with-out Bourchier's fame or charlatanism. He taught Evelyn to serve the Mass, according to the Anglo-Catholic version of its rite, and this made a deep impression on his latent sense of and inclination to religion.

Thereon he entered into a youthful and intense religious phase of devotional Anglicanism.

It was no more than a phase though it was a long and important one. It continued for several years till it abruptly terminated with a sudden loss of faith. It is important to note that when he did lose his faith he recognized that this also was probably a phase. He was usually a perceptive judge of himself and he recognized that in his essential being he was religious. It was not a recognition that came to him quickly. It was one with which he was not easily reconciled. In the first flush of his new religious enthusiasm, however, he conceived a wish to become a parson. His mother did not encourage this ambition which was short-lived. She also was a perceptive judge of character.

His new-found enthusiasm led him to his first serious attempt at writing. At the age of seven he had written a five hundred word novel called *The Curse of the Horse Race*. Since then he had contributed to a Boy Scoutish amateur publication called *The Pistol Troop Magazine*. He now, to quote the autobiography, 'composed a deplorable poem in the metre of Hiawatha, named *The World to Come*, describing the experiences of the soul, immediately after death. The manuscript was shown to a friend of my father's who had a printing press on which he did much fine work. He conceived the kindly idea of producing some copies on hand-made paper and binding them for my father's birthday. They were distributed within the family. I do not know how many were made or how many survive, but the existence of this work is shameful to me.'

How soon the shame set in was not mentioned by Evelyn. At all events he did not think of himself as an embryonic writer at this time, or for some years to come. He looked forward, somewhat vaguely, to a career as an artist. He had already shown some rudimentary skill as a draughtsman. His drawings had hitherto concentrated on military subjects, glittering armour and scenes of carnage in war, usually of medieval date; they were now occupied with angels and saints and representations of Jesus Christ, until there was a military revival in his art when war broke out in 1914. Then Evelyn 'drew countless pictures of German cavalry plunging among English infantry with much blood and gunpowder about'.

The family situation of the Waughs was little changed by the disaster of the outbreak of war. The two boys remained at school, Alec at Sherborne, Evelyn at Heath Mount. Mrs Waugh did hospital work in Highgate. Arthur Waugh was seized by the passions of the time, and during his phase of patriotic emotion he expressed his feelings with characteristic oddity. Evelyn accompanied him to a recruiting rally at Midsomer Norton soon after 4 August 1914, and 'in well-turned phrases and absolute sincerity he proclaimed that, if the Kaiser won, the miners of Norton would never again be allowed to play cricket'. But Arthur Waugh's heady nationalism was short-lived. After a few weeks he felt very differently about the war. He 'gave up taking in *Punch* because he disliked its style of light-hearted patriotism. His own heart grew heavier as the names appeared among the dead of boys whom a year before he had watched play cricket at Sherborne'. He became early and increasingly aware that the static battle of the interlocked armies would last long and that soon he must face the likelihood of his eldest and favourite son being drawn into the struggle, there probably to perish among thousands. He was approaching fifty in 1914 and he did not take on any war work. He fully exerted himself in managing Chapman and Hall with a depleted staff, and earning money for the family by his literary articles.

More surprising than Arthur Waugh's detachment from the war is something like the same attitude in his younger son. One would not be surprised to hear of young Evelyn indulging in every excess of youthful chauvinism. That he adopted a precociously balanced attitude was probably due to two unrelated facts.

When writing his autobiography, Evelyn omitted to do a needful piece of research into the early twentieth-century history of England. If he had done it, he would have easily discovered the answer to a question which puzzled him, namely how it came about that he and his Hampstead playmates were preoccupied long before August 1914 with the perils and likelihood of a German invasion, that this obsession turned their games towards seriousness, that they built or rather dug a redoubt on some derelict land, provisioned it with tinned food, and formed a *corps d'élite* to man the fortifications, this regiment taking the proud title of the Pistol Troop, so named after a pistol loaned to the corps by a tolerant or hysterical parent. In his book, Evelyn expressed himself as much perplexed by the origin of these patriotic manifestations, all the more so since his parents looked on the enterprise with mild, though not contemptuous amusement. Evelyn found what he believed to be an indirect origin in an early book by P. G. Wodehouse, *The Swoop*, in which a Boy Scout foils an attempted invasion.

In fact, the origins were massive and P. G. Wodehouse's book an insignificant detail of them. There had been increasing fears of a German invasion since the German Emperor had launched his naval challenge in 1897 and 1898. In England great unease was felt about the new German policy, and it found its first popular expression, not in the early Wodehouse novel but in Erskine Childers's remarkable but now almost unreadable book *The Riddle of the Sands*. (Let it be said in passing that many books, pronounced unreadable, continue to be read. Childers's book still sells in paper-back.)

*The Riddle of the Sands* came out in 1903. In 1906 there came out a now wholly forgotten book, *The Invasion of 1910*, by William Le Queux, whose publication was prodigiously and rewardingly advertised. In 1908 parliamentary concern was such that the Committee of Imperial Defence appointed a Commission of Enquiry on whether or not an invasion supported by Germany's new navy could succeed. In the next year, 1909, Henry James became nervous about the situation of his house at Rye on the south coast. 'When the German Emperor carries the next war into this country', he wrote to a friend, not quite unseriously it seems, 'my chimney pots, visible to a certain distance out at sea, may be his very first objective.' From the same date, the play by Guy du Maurier, *An Englishman's Home*, on the subject of an invasion of England by a weakly disguised Kaiser Wilhelm II, played to packed houses in London for a year and a half. It was in 1909 that Evelyn and his friends formed the Pistol Troop. The public alarm was not a swiftly passing one. 'Saki' Munro's novel *When William Came* was not to appear till 1913, and it was not ridiculed. The spiritual origins of the Pistol Troop were correctly explained by Evelyn when he wrote: 'The theme must have been much in the air', but it is surprising that he did not trouble to find out how it came to be there.

The above considerations give one obvious reason why in 1914 Evelyn was not suddenly lashed into a frenzy of patriotic excitement. The child had been through it all before. The second reason is edifying to the memory of Mr Granville Grenfell.

True to naval traditions, he placed enormous emphasis on gentlemanliness. Mr Grenfell greeted his little charges every morning as 'Gentlemen!' and consequently they called him 'Sir' with some meaning. He seems to have been a truly remarkable master of young pupils. Nothing in Evelyn's inevitably ironical account takes away from the respect of the reader.

In general British schools in 1914 gave way to xenophobia which the teachers did as little to correct as they did the related vice of bullying. At Heath Mount this was otherwise. Several of the children had German names which their families had hastened to anglicize during the summer holidays. A boy named Kaiser reappeared with the thoroughly English name of Kingsley. The change passed without remark. The boy would certainly not have got by at either of the schools where I served sentences of incarceration. There were two new boys at Heath Mount who were refugees from Belgium, and these, wrote Evelyn, 'we earnestly attempted to befriend'. No such attempts were made at my schools. The Belgians were picked out for special punishment by the masters and persecution by their fellow-inmates. At my second school a large family of Belgians were regarded, in the marvellously muddled logic of schoolboys, as German spies, and no allowance was made for their status as victims of aggression as opposed to that of conscienceless and victorious invaders. Our teachers did nothing to induce more rational ideas. At home we would have been taught a higher morality. At school we were left to that of the jungle, most of the time. Mr Grenfell seems to have been an exceptional man.

Let it not be thought that Evelyn did not show war-like spirit. Of course he showed it, although, as he wrote, 'after the first few months the war had little interest for me. I accepted it as a condition of life.' The pleasures of war were only experienced by Evelyn in the airship raids. 'An anti-aircraft gun', he related, 'was posted at the Whitestone Pond and made a great noise when Zeppelins were overhead. No bomb fell within a mile of us, but the alarms were agreeable occasions when I was brought down from bed and regaled with an uncovenanted picnic. I was quite unconscious of danger, which was indeed negligible. On summer nights we sat in the garden, sometimes seeing the thin silver rod of the enemy caught in converging search-lights. On a splendid occasion I saw one brought down, sinking very slowly in brilliant flame, and joined those who were cheering in the road outside.'

In the ordinary course of events Evelyn would have proceeded from Heath Mount to Sherborne in the later part of 1917. But certain family disturbances came to undo this plan. At Sherborne Alec Waugh became involved in a scandal concerned with the hushed abuse of most schools, homosexuality. Nothing very terrible seems to have happened, but the authorities reported that the boy should leave at the end of the summer term of 1915. So deeply inhibited were English people of that time regarding all sexual questions that Evelyn himself, by his own account, knew nothing of the scandal till the publication of his brother's autobiography in 1962. Though he was and remained devoted to Sherborne, the school seems, by Alec's own account, to have been a detestable place of education, likely to damage any young mind.

The scandal was likely to prevent Evelyn becoming a Shirburnian, but another scandal came to make prevention absolute. Alec left Sherborne in the summer of 1915 to become a cadet in the Inns of Court Officers Training Corps. He spent two years in training before being posted to a machine-gun unit in France, in time for the Passchendaele battle. In seven and a half weeks of that two years he wrote his first book, an autobiographical novel in which he expressed the love and bitterness he felt for his school. It was called *The Loom of Youth*. It was published at the same time as he was posted abroad, having been rejected by several publishing houses before acceptance and instant success. He did not ask his father to publish it, nor did his father wish to do so with his sensitive dislike of favouritism, but Arthur Waugh had read the book and immediately recognized its high quality. He also recognized that after its publication Evelyn's career as a Shirburnian would be impossibly painful.

Evelyn described the situation with his usual concision. 'There were controversies in some papers, and for my father many broken friendships. Its effect on me was that Sherborne was now barred to me. As soon as the book was accepted by its publisher, before it appeared, a new school had to be found for me in a hurry. Choice was limited by the lack of notice. My mother would have liked to keep me at home and send me to Westminster or St Paul's or the University College School in Hampstead, but these would have seemed unnatural to my father and with a minimum of deliberation his choice fell on Lancing which he had never seen and with which he had no associations.'

Let memories intrude again, less directly on the subject than hitherto. *The Loom of Youth* is a good book which has stood the test of time. It was, I believe, the first modern novel of any significance that I read. I had just swallowed *If Winter Comes* and *This Freedom* when it came my way. I had heard *The Loom of Youth* gravely discussed and gravely judged in my family circle. The considered opinion was that the facts therein exposed were not false, but that it was 'unfortunate' that they had been so precisely expressed. It was kept from me till I found a copy about four years later. It was generally forgotten that the deplorable facts fairly explicitly expressed by Alec Waugh had been as clearly indicated by the author of *Tom Brown's Schooldays*. Thomas Hughes might well have come in for all the abuse cast upon Alec Waugh, if he had written his book fifty years later. But between the years of the two books (1857 and 1917) the Public School, largely through Hughes's influence, had come to be a revered institution. To doubt, to tell the truth about British schools, was to doubt, to make faces at the Constitution and the throne. The gates of Sherborne were not closed to Evelyn, but Arthur Waugh tactfully did not knock on them.

An interesting question remains. Evelyn declared in his autobiography that he was a clever little boy, and that if he had been sent to one of the preparatory schools that specialized in such things, he might well have obtained a scholarship to Eton or Winchester. Supposing this had happened, would it have made the strange and gifted man who ultimately emerged a radically different one? As an Etonian he might have been less intolerant. As a Wykehamist he might have developed much more than he did the scholarly aptitude which he had inherited from both sides of his family. Beyond that it seems to me foolish to speculate. He was, of course, under permanent influence from the type of education he received, but he was not one of those who are overpowered by memories of school or university. He was no natural 'old boy'. Whatever his incubation he would ultimately, I believe, have resolved into the man that his friends and the world came to know: lovable for the same reasons, insufferable for the same reasons.

On 9 May 1917 Arthur Waugh took Evelyn to Lancing, near Shoreham on the south coast. It was not the heart-rending experience that such occasions usually are. Evelyn recorded that he parted from his father 'without a pang. I believed I was at the beginning of a new and exciting phase of life.'

He was thirteen.

He had reached the end of his long happy childhood.

# Chapter 2

## 1917–1921

The new and exciting phase of life that Evelyn anticipated in May 1917 proved disagreeable. Most public schools at that time, probably today too, adhered to the belief that a special degree of ill-treatment should be meted out to new arrivals. The methods varied. At some they took a crude form. The more seasoned boys formed themselves into gangs in order to bait the bewildered new boys who were also subjected to the individual ministrations of their more furious seniors. The latter had learned an acute class-consciousness governed by circumstances of age alone. It was usually expressed in great sensitiveness regarding 'lip' and 'cheek' which was detected in every failure on the part of the younger to follow obscure tribal customs; consequently kicks and insults were the usual lot of the new boy who did not have the protection of an honoured big brother.

Other schools, of which Lancing was one, applied more refined methods of persecution. For three weeks the new boys were treated as an untouchable caste, and no one, except boys selected to instruct them in the tribal lore, spoke to them. 'I had been given', wrote Evelyn in *A Little Learning*, 'some highly mysterious hints on leaving Mr Grenfell of the danger of too friendly approaches from older boys. The warning seemed singularly inappropriate to my condition.' In a grim passage, in which he speaks for many other public school men, he indicated in a few strokes the immediate psychological effects of this form of education: 'Odium was personal and something quite new to me. For thirteen years I had met only people who seemed disposed to like me. Experience has taught me that not everyone takes to me at first sight (or on close acquaintance), but I am still mildly surprised by rebuffs, such is the confidence which a happy childhood founds.' Of the less utterly miserable period which followed the preliminary persecutions he stated: 'I was too old, indeed at exactly the worst age, to accept cheerfully the sudden loss of all privacy.' Of his final, more resigned attitude, he wrote: 'I did not admire the other boys. I did not want to be like them. But, in contradiction, I wanted to be one of them. I had no aspirations to excel, still less to lead; I simply longed to remain myself and yet to be accepted as one of this distasteful mob. I cannot explain it, but I think that was what I felt.' Once more he spoke for many others.

Being a misfit, as one of the very few boys new in the summer term of 1917, he was unpopular and remained so, according to his own account, for his first two years. In his early days at Lancing he had a harrowing experience of loneliness. There was a holiday on the feast of the Ascension and all the boys went out for a day of fun, but Evelyn had no companion. To add to the misery, it began to rain. 'I wandered out', he recorded, 'with my damp pocket of food and after a time took shelter among the trees called Lancing Ring, ate a little and, for the first and last time for many years, wept. It was with comfort that late that afternoon I heard the noisy return of the holiday-makers. I have brought up my children to make a special intention at the Ascension Mass for all desolate little boys.'

He disliked games, though the diary that he kept later showed that he became proficient in some of them and joined in the common enthusiasm over house and school matches. But he only found happiness in the class-room, the library and the chapel. He had the good fortune to be under a kindly master, the 'House-tutor', whom he liked. He was called Dick Harris. The respite was short as Harris was due to leave for the army in the holidays. Under Harris's tuition he made his first adventures into modern poetry which at that time and place meant Flecker, Rupert Brooke, Ralph Hodgson and 'the Georgians'. In the library he continued his art studies with the aid of a book called *The Bible in Art*. 'My prefer-ence', he wrote, 'then, and now, was for the Quattrocento and the Pre-Raphaelites, with deviations, since corrected, towards Bouguereau and . Puvis de Chavannes. Rubens and Rembrandt seemed very ugly.'

In chapel, where 'all was ordered in the spirit of the tractarians', he continued his phase of Anglican devotion, but no longer in the ritualistic context of Anglo-Catholicism. 'The clergy were surpliced, not vested' and there was no trace of Mr Bourchier's wilful magnificence. His chief joy was in listening to the diction of the Book of Common Prayer and the Authorized Version; the main spiritual refreshment lay in 'refuge from the surrounding loneliness; contact with home and with Midsomer Norton rather than with Heaven'. The music was of a high order but was lost on Evelyn.

His devotion to that chapel remained with him for life, as did his veneration for the language of the sixteenth and seventeenth centuries which was at the centre of the services he attended there. So great was his devotion, in fact, that it led him into some indefensibly extravagant praise. 'I know', he wrote of Lancing, 'no more spectacular post-Reforma-tion ecclesiastical building in the kingdom.' He possibly wrote 'ecclesiasti-cal' in a hurried moment, in mistake for 'Gothic'. He must have been aware of St Paul's. The mistake remains interesting to my mind because it shows more eloquently than a positive statement the intensity and persistence of his love for the chapel. Nor was his admiration misplaced.

Evelyn's first holidays from Lancing were delayed by a fortnight because of an attack of mumps which overtook him during the last days of term. He spent the fortnight in the sanatorium with one of his very few friends, another new boy called Fulford minor, now better known as Roger Fulford the distinguished author. 'The woman in charge,' he recorded, 'named Sister Babcock, did nothing to mitigate our sorrow. She was by nature ill-tempered and was especially irate on this occasion at having her own holidays curtailed.'

When at length he reached home, his ecstatic joy was diminished by the anxieties of his parents. Arthur Waugh was still 'agitated by alternations of distress and exultation at the reception of *The Loom of Youth*' and hurt by the hostility of some of his Shirburnian friends on its account. But a greater distress weighed on both Evelyn's parents. Alec had graduated to the army and had been posted to the front in a machine-gun unit. From early in September he was in the battle of Ypres III, usually known by the name of Passchendaele. At Underhill every telegram was received with dread, and the casualty lists in the newspapers were scanned, with immediate relief and immediately renewed fear that one day, probably soon, Alec's would figure among those thousands of names.

'My second term', wrote Evelyn, 'was one of black misery.' Dick Harris had gone and was replaced by an elderly incompetent so that the discipline in the house fell into the hands of the House-Captains, 'martinets who . . . were too young for office'. The food, which in his first term was such as 'would have provoked mutiny in a mid-Victorian poor-house', was now noticeably worse, thanks to the U-boat campaign, and continued to worsen till the end of the war. Drilling with the Officers Training Corps became more serious, occupied more free time and began to resemble military training. Potato digging was added to the duties of the boys. Friendlessness persisted. Evelyn implored his father to take him away, but his father 'counselled endurance' so he stayed. After a short and telling indication of the miseries of that winter, and the absolute lack of freedom in a modern public school where everything is 'grimly correct', Evelyn added the following interesting note by way of summary.

'I do not seek to harrow with these mild austerities the reader who has vicariously supped full with the horrors of the concentration camp. I merely assert that *I* was harrowed. I had lived too softly for my first thirteen years.

'My brother and thousands like him, not five years my senior, were wintering in the trenches in conditions immeasurably more severe. These were dismal years for half the world. I believe it was the most dismal period in history for an English schoolboy.'

*

The Abbey Church at Downside. For many years Evelyn Waugh
attended the spiritual retreats here during Holy Week

Nancy Mitford and
Graham Greene were among
Evelyn Waugh's closest friends
in post-war years

Evelyn attached great importance to a new friendship which had begun in the Christmas holidays of 1917. This was with Barbara Jacobs, the elder daughter of W. W. Jacobs, then at the height of his abilities and fame. Alec had become engaged to Barbara a few days before embarking for the front line. Soon after, she came to lodge at Underhill from where she attended a course at a Ladies' College in Regent's Park. The Waugh and Jacobs families saw much of each other, and in his autobiography Evelyn has left a memorable portrait of the great humorist. With Barbara's younger sister, who looked up to Evelyn 'with gratifying respect', he was on terms of early and little understood sexual attraction; with Barbara his relations were wholly platonic. 'In her', he wrote, 'I found . . . the kind of friend I lacked at Lancing.' She was three years older than he was.

With Barbara he began new adventures. One was the discovery of London of which both of them had but feeble knowledge. They explored the great city from the open upper decks of the omnibuses of that day. To ride thus in the fresh air was no small pleasure on a fine day, and with others Evelyn lamented its disappearance. But these explorations do not seem to have led to any great destination. Evelyn enjoyed London but he never became one of those writers, of whom Dickens is the most character-istic and pre-eminent, for whom London is a passion. In his London fiction he did not range widely. He never described or set scenes in the poorer quarters, or in the City, or in the Law Courts and their world, or in the world of Parliament, or of the theatre, or in the life of the river. He was never in love with London.

But another adventure undertaken with Barbara had considerable results. She, like Evelyn, enjoyed painting, but, unlike him, she was instinctively drawn to the modern schools and under her influence he tried to follow her. He was not successful. 'I admired', he confessed in his autobiography, 'the worst of what Barbara showed me.' At Underhill, they 'covered the walls of the former day-nursery with what we took to be cubist paintings'. His parents in no way discouraged the new enthusi-asm and Arthur Waugh even brought a distinguished modern artist, Mark Gertler, to see and appraise the joint work. The occasion was evidently somewhat embarrassing, according to Evelyn, who wrote of it: 'Hard put to find an amiable comment, he remarked that there was originality in the way in which we had combined so many various pig-ments – enamel, oil paint, blacking and poster paint.' But they were not cast down. On the contrary, Evelyn was moved to write an essay for a magazine called *Drawing and Design* which published it in November 1917. The essay was called 'In Defence of Cubism'.

It is very short and possesses a double interest. As the work of a boy of fourteen it shows very great literary promise, and it is curious that no one in his family seems to have noticed this. The second matter of interest is to find the young Evelyn so eloquently and persuasively defending theories, personalities and arguments to which in later years he gave an absolute opposition.

No copies of the essay seem to survive except in the archives of the British Museum. Evelyn did not regret its loss. He never seems to have hunted for it in later years. In his autobiography he wrote: 'It must have been utterly fatuous for I knew nothing whatever of the theory of the movement and had seen very few of its products.'

The excitement of seeing himself in print emboldened Evelyn to send the magazine 'what I took to be a cubist drawing' which was promptly rejected, whereafter his interest waned. 'That was the end', he wrote, 'of my career as an apologist for Picasso.' He returned to his preoccupation with the art of the past. Barbara's leadership in his education gradually had an inverse effect which was permanent.

Reflection on his disparate tastes led him, when writing *A Little Learning*, to give a remarkable self-portrait, or rather a picture of his mind as it was during the years when he approached and entered adolescence.

'In the vacancies of the adolescent mind mutually contradictory principles make easy neighbours . . . I halted between two opinions and thought it more showy to express the new. Barbara, in fact, made an aesthetic hypocrite of me. It was many years before I would freely confess that the Paris school and all that derived from it were abhorrent to me. Perhaps it was Economics that Barbara read in Regent's Park. She was better informed on the subject than most girls of the time. I was totally ignorant of it and, picking up some of the jargon from her, for some years intermittently pretended to be a socialist. (At other times I advocated the restoration of the Stuarts, anarchism and the rule of a hereditary caste.) My motive was the wish to shock, of which Barbara was entirely innocent. She, the professed agnostic, was full of charity, compassion for the poor (of whom she knew little; far less than my mother), faith in the perfectibility of human nature and a longing for social equality; I, the professed Christian, merely scorned industrial and commercial capitalists and relished the arguments that proved them villains.'

The halting between two opinions to which he referred was to persist not only in his opinions but in his tastes and life until the mid-thirties. It was not until then that he was recognized as an intensely conservative character, though he was never as exclusively conservative as most of his friends and enemies believed.

To return to the last year of the Great War. His dismal life as a schoolboy at Lancing continued through 1918 with no mitigation, and in the Easter holidays his home life was further darkened by anxiety. This was the time when the last great German offensive in France had opened with preliminary success. At the end of March or the beginning of April the dreaded telegram at last arrived. Alec was 'missing'. (On 28 March his section had been surrounded by the advancing German troops.) A day or two later another telegram arrived to say that Alec was a prisoner-of-war. His father's relief was short-lived. Even when the German offensive had manifestly failed and an ultimate Allied victory became daily more evident, Arthur Waugh remained 'tormented by anxiety', because he believed that when victory came the defeated Germans would massacre their prisoners. He continued in these fears even after 11 November 1918.

Alec was home again by Christmas, 'and that holidays', recorded Evelyn, 'were the most joyous of my life'.

The end of World War I was for the most part greeted in Britain with simple joy at the success of our arms, and abundant hope that 'the world's great age' would now begin anew. The reaction of Barbara was typical of a great majority, and especially of the progressively-minded young. Evelyn wrote: 'Barbara, to whom the Russian revolution had been exhilarating, was confident that German militarism was destroyed for ever and that a Utopia would emerge.' For the most part forebodings of frightful things to come were confined to pathologically consistent pessimists.

The mood of relief, joy and hope of the first months after the German capitulation had its effect on Lancing, and when Evelyn returned to school in January 1919 he found reason to expect better days. His admired Dick Harris had been demobilized and had returned to school-mastering as Evelyn's House-tutor. With him there entered on the scene other of the younger masters who had left Lancing to serve in the war and now 'came back to civil life with zest . . . From then on both the amenities and the interests of school were increasingly enriched.' For its brief season it was a good time for most people in England and, though still enduring much unpopularity (as he was to do for the rest of his life), Evelyn began to be happy at school.

He was happy after his own peculiar fashion. He began to take on a character which he was never to lose wholly, though he sometimes fooled himself into an opposite conviction: he became a 'Bolshie', according to the 'language of the day' which he was to meet again, twenty years hence, lingering in army slang. During the spring and summer terms of 1919 his new chronic rebelliousness seems to have been held in check by his devotion to Dick Harris, but this can be no more than a guess and a deduction from *A Little Learning*; there are no surviving letters and no diary for this time. All that Evelyn had to say is that after the Armistice, with the decline in the needs of the army for young men, boys did not leave school as early as in the previous years so that the rate of promotion was retarded. This circumstance alone was conducive to rebellion, but with Evelyn it was not aimed at Palace revolution but something more essential. He recorded: 'My friends and I found ourselves for a year blocked in our advance . . . and well content to be so. In this essentially subversive stratum . . . the leaders were Fulford and I and Rupert Fremlin, a delightful mercurial fellow, whose father had been eaten by a tiger in India.'

At the end of July 1919 Alec married Barbara Jacobs. As the former has told in his autobiography the marriage was an immediate failure, but Evelyn knew nothing of this for nearly two years. Alec gives, perhaps, a somewhat exaggerated picture of the distant relationship between the two brothers, for Evelyn's diary and his early letters suggest that the younger son looked up to the gallant returned officer with something of hero-worship. The marriage made little if any difference to Evelyn's friendship with Barbara and she and Alec often went down to Brighton or Shoreham to visit him at the school.

The diary, which hitherto had been kept only for a week in August 1916, was begun again by Evelyn on the day of his return to school after the summer holidays, on 23 September 1919. The first thing that a reader notices is that the handwriting has altered radically from the childish scrawl of three years before and could be that of a much older person. (In 1919 he was approaching sixteen.) It now bears a strong, perhaps conscious resemblance to that of Alec, and is very different from the later small, elegant, occasionally illegible handwriting that his friends remember. The diary opens thus:

'Alec once said that he kept his life in "water-tight" compartments. It is very true, here I am flung suddenly into an entirely different world, different friends and different mode of life. All the comforts of home are gone but one doesn't really miss them.'

There were several checks to Evelyn's increasing happiness at school, if one should not rather say his diminishing misery. The worst was that Dick Harris was no longer the House-tutor of the Headmaster's House but had been promoted to one of his own. He was succeeded by a man referred to as Gordo (an adaptation of Gordon) whom the boys called 'Pussyfoot' and resented as untrustworthy, and utterly unworthy to step into the shoes of Harris.

When he came to write his autobiography Evelyn acknowledged the injustice of such reaction. He allowed that 'Gordo' or 'Pussyfoot' was possibly 'rather more devious than was suitable to his profession', but added that essentially he was a man of exemplary sympathy and goodwill towards his charges. What Evelyn took to be an insufferably patronizing attitude to his family turned out to be the expression of a genuine and ultimately effective wish to help a 'difficult' pupil. All this was hidden from him at the time. 'We were as pettish as a girl's school', he wrote, 'at the loss of Dick and I withheld confidence and affection.'

These setbacks and discomforts were very much more than compensated by a new influence which entered Evelyn's life and, it may be believed, never wholly left it. Among the masters who had returned to Lancing from army service in early 1919 was John Fergusson Roxburgh, always known as 'J.F.' and soon to become famous as the first headmaster of Stowe. In 1919 he was 31. During the first two terms of that year Evelyn did not meet him and 'saw little but his outward appearance and that was impressive; tall, broad, lean, slightly stooping; a fine brow, full hair, a face alive with intelligence and humour; a dandy whose numerous suits and ties we studied with respect. He had a panache of the kind to which adolescents were specially susceptible.' And especially, one may safely add, Evelyn. In the autumn term of 1919, when Evelyn and his House-mates lost Dick Harris, he found himself in J. F. Roxburgh's French class, and he was carried away with admiration. (Roxburgh was a graduate of La Sorbonne.) Evelyn wrote in his diary: 'Roxburgh's French is really a joy. It is almost worth doing the wretched subject.'

Only in his last terms at Lancing did Evelyn come to know J.F. and to become an object of his special interest, but the influence began at this time, and may be briefly recalled now. Evelyn often talked about him in later years, usually with mockery. He described to me his well-cut and well-ironed suits, his admirable watch and chain and his pompous mode of delivery and polysyllabic humour; he portrayed him as a highly ridiculous person, but I think he felt a little permanent resentment that J.F. accounted him one of Lancing's disappointments. When he came to write his autobiography Evelyn used a different tone. He wrote: 'Before the publication of Fowler's *Modern English Usage*, J.F. was inculcating in almost the same terms precision of grammar and contempt of cliché.' But Evelyn had not yet discovered that writing was his unquestionable vocation. His most serious extramural activity was in the pursuit of art, and the perfecting of himself as an artist.

He followed the unusual study which he described in much enjoyable detail when he come to write the most interesting chapter, 'Two Mentors', in his autobiography. The second mentor was a certain Francis Crease. He was a learned amateur of illuminated manuscripts and was one of the most skilled of those who, at the time, were endeavouring to revive the art after some centuries of decay. Evelyn had not for some time been interested in lettering and illumination, and his House-tutor Gordon had the good idea of introducing Evelyn to Crease in the hope that the latter would give him tuition and thus a stimulus and an interest in his life at Lancing. By and large the plan succeeded. Evelyn was introduced to Crease in December 1919.

Already he had had some success in illumination, having won an art prize at Lancing for an illuminated prayer, and in October his father, after much delay probably due to his sensitiveness to accusations of favouritism, had accepted his design for a book cover, thus giving him professional success in an allied art. He earned a guinea and dimly looked forward to a career as an artist. The diary shows that his weekly visits to

Mr Crease every Thursday were a continual refreshment, even if he was a little hurt at the contrast between his mentor's early encouragement and his later and severe criticism. Mr Crease's rooms in the farmhouse at near-by Lychpole were tasteful and comfortable, and they gave a weekly refuge to Evelyn till nearly the end of his schooldays. 'The best part', noted Evelyn in February 1920, 'is when work is put away and we have tea in his beautiful blue & white china.' He wrote enthusiastically to his mother about his progress under Mr Crease's tuition, and she was moved to invite him to stay at Underhill during the coming Easter holidays. But before then complications arose which threatened to separate Mr Crease from his new pupil. They are not mentioned in *A Little Learning*.

The whole trouble arose from Mr Crease's manner and clothes, and the fact that he could impress Evelyn, as he noted in his diary, as 'very effeminate and decadent and cultured and nice' and that he frequently visited the school and showed most interest in the better-looking boys. To many of the authorities all this was open to only one interpretation. Evelyn at sixteen remained remarkably innocent of sexual knowledge and seems to have been wholly unaware of the very fact of perversion. Consequently he misconstrued a painful event.

Evelyn's housemaster and Dick Harris discouraged boys from visiting Mr Crease, and Evelyn put this down to jealousy of his influence. Slowly he learned the real nature of their suspicions, and learned also that these scandalous rumours had reached the unfortunate Mr Crease himself. As was his wont, he was thrown into a state of violent agitation. His closest contemporary friends in Sussex were the family of the local landowner, named Tristram, to whom he may have been related, and he seems to have turned to these people with an appeal for rescue. On 31 March Evelyn wrote in his diary: 'Crease is very upset at the slander to Dick & wants to send the Tristrams to the Head to witness to his purity.' That is the last mention of the affair in the diary. Perhaps the Tristrams did go to the headmaster with the desired effect. At all events no further pressure was brought on Evelyn to discontinue his visits to Lychpole, and Mr Crease's visit to Underhill was made as arranged. It was a success, chiefly due to Mrs Waugh making a friend of him. He often stayed at Underhill after. But the suspicions about him, which Evelyn always believed to be groundless, did not wholly disappear. To quote *A Little Learning*: 'J.F. did not at all approve of Mr Crease. I was present when they met in my House-tutor's room when he said: "The Sage of Lychpole, I presume" with apparent geniality, but he would not allow boys in his house to go to Mr Crease's. Mr Crease, as I have said, was effeminate in appearance and manner; J.F. was markedly virile, but it was he who was the homosexual.'

Evelyn, in the same book, told of the subsequent but unrelated rift

26

between himself and Mr Crease. The rift was never quite healed in spite of the strong affection between Mr Crease and Evelyn's mother and Evelyn's continuing friendship. It was the Affair of the Broken Knife for cutting Quills. Evelyn's diary gives the incident in a manner which does not indicate, as does the autobiography, its gravity in Mr Crease's eyes. It seems from the contemporary document that there was merely a tiff and a reconciliation. How was it possible for young Evelyn to guess that so deep was Mr Crease's sense of injury because of the broken blade that thereafter Crease was never again to practise the art of the scribe? The affair of the knife happened in May and June of 1920.

Some sort of rift was perhaps inevitable in the case. The whole episode of Mr Crease and his pupil had been based on a misunderstanding. If it was true that Evelyn had ambitions for a career as an artist, in which he long persisted, it was quite false to suppose that he aimed at becoming supreme among the revivalists of calligraphy. The art was only one of his artistic hobbies. He did not intend to devote his life to so selfless an occupation, if only because he was not by nature selfless. But an artist he would be, and his family at this time accepted the fact. Alec was the writer. Evelyn would be something else.

But if the future novelist was showing little sign of life and growth, the opposite was true of the anarchist. He and his followers did all that they could to disrupt the working of the Officers Training Corps. An extract from the 1919 diary illustrates his success:

'It was the Certificate A candidates examination and Roxburgh's address before gave us to expect the most fearful blood of the Guards major type we get for the [general] Inspection. When we got down there we found the most blatantly risen-from-the-ranks, I've ever seen. He was not even a temporary gentleman but a Permanent Oik. As Roxburgh said he was "quite monstrous" . . . The first hour and a half was shere delight but as it grew later even the sight of dropped rifles began to pall. Candidate after candidate tried to drill us but the cry was still "They come" . . . On going into chapel a notice was found on the corps board saying that everyone had passed. How Roxburgh wangled the little grocer, God knows.'

Hooper? Trimmer? Present and correct.

Not long after this, Evelyn's rebelliousness was expressed in terms of cynical contempt for the institution in November 1919 of the 'Two Minutes' Silence' which he described as 'a disgusting idea of artificial reverence and sentimentality'.

Sometimes, as becomes a cynic, he was moved to attempt to play the melancholy disillusioned observer of the world's comedy. A result is the occasional patch of 'fine writing' in the diary, and in 1921 he wrote in that mood a reflective paragraph with a hint of blank verse rhythms, and some perhaps unconscious imitation of *As You Like It*.

'We are all painting or drawing our lives. Some draw with pencil, weakly and timidly, continually breaking the point and taking up another, continually trying to rub things out & always leaving an ugly smear. Some use ink and draw firmly and irrevocably with strong, broad lines. Some of us use colour, rich & lurid, layed on in full glowing brushfuls, with big sweeps of the wrist. Some draw a straggling haphazard design, the motive being eternally confused with unnecessary and meaningless parts. The threads pass out of the picture and are lost. The whole is an intricate incoherent maze. But some, and these are the elect, draw their design cleanly and fully. No part is unnecessary. Each twist and curl of the fanciful foliage adds to and carries on the original motive. Each part works into the whole and there is no climax or end to it.'

In keeping with this preciosity and moralizing, but transcending it, Evelyn found a new interest in 1920, and it lasted for the next year or so. This was a society founded by himself and two contemporaries: Hugh Molson (now Lord Molson) and Roger Fulford. The society was called 'The Dillettanti'.

Evelyn was active in recruiting. One youth was instantly rejected because he said that Landseer was his favourite artist. Poor boy, he got his timing wrong. Ten years later such a confession might have prompted Evelyn's profound respect. A friend of Evelyn and myself, Tom Driberg, has given me a first-hand account of Evelyn's recruiting methods. The answer of Driberg, who was Evelyn's junior by over two years, to the crucial question might have seemed much more damaging than that of the Landseer-addict. It was their first meeting. Driberg was for the first time under the scrutiny of Evelyn's 'penetrating sharp blue eyes'. At the routine question on his favourite artist, the eyes had the effect of rendering Tom's mind, so he has assured me, an absolute blank, and all names of all artists vanished from it, but seeing impatience added to the glare of the eyes, he answered at random: 'Sir John Lavery.' He was in luck and was instantly elected.

The main activity of the Dilettanti seems to have been debate. 'Once or twice,' recorded Evelyn, 'we invited visitors to address us, but that was not the prime object of our association. We did not wish to learn but to talk.'

In the summer holidays of 1920 there occurred an event of great importance in Evelyn's life. He had his first view of Oxford where he was taken by his parents in September. The entry in his diary for the 11th begins as follows:

'Our expedition to Oxford. I have never seen anything so beautiful. In places like Wells there are beautiful buildings and closes, but I have never seen anything like New College cloisters or Tom Quad or the founder's tower. Father has put my name down for New College and I am going to try for a scholarship at the House'. (In Oxford parlance Christ Church is often called 'the House'.) This was the beginning of a long love-affair to which Evelyn first gave farcical expression in his first novel, and later ardent expression in *Brideshead Revisited*.

The diary for the next term is sparse, but some of what it tells is of interest. For Sunday, 17 October there is an entry describing a day in Brighton with Alec and Barbara, who took him to lunch at the Albion. His account of the gaieties reads oddly to one who knew Evelyn's later taste in wine and how in pursuing it he sometimes erred on the side of preciosity. 'We had an excellent lunch,' he wrote, 'among other things a peculiarly good dressed crab and a glass of port. We discovered a new drink of ginger beer and Burgundy which was very good.'

Slowly and dimly Evelyn was beginning to recognize the character and direction of his talents, though full self-understanding in this respect was still far off. In the summer holidays Alec had 'offered to write a novel' if Evelyn would 'find him the plot', the reward to be a dedication. Evelyn duly found what he was asked for but nothing came of the project. However, it may be that the incident excited some further literary ambition.

In the week following Alec and Barbara's visit to Brighton there is the following intriguing entry: 'I have decided to do my first novel next holidays. I have got a scheme – the study of a man with two characters by his brother but I never realized what an immense amount of labour it entails. I have been making elaborate calculations and find that each chapter will have to be about two sections of College bumph.' A week later he wrote: 'I have not time adequately to keep a diary. All my energies are being devoted to my novel which goes fairly well.'

There is no further mention of the novel till the Christmas holidays. 'I arrived home last Friday. At last the family are beginning to take a little interest in my novel. Alec apprehensive of a rival; mother of my ruin through becoming a public figure too soon. Father likes it. Meanwhile I plod on and on at it trying to make it take some form or shape. At present it seems a mere succession of indifferently interesting conversations. However, I believe it is fairly good and I am pretty sure to be able to get it published. It's a bloody sweat however.'

Thereafter the novel languished. On 10 January 1921 he noted: '. . . my family's disapproval and my own innate sloth have led me to abandon my novel. I must set about doing it. At present Carew is nursing the abortion franticly admiring, dear fellow! My only literary achievements have been a short story on which I am still awaiting "Pan's" verdict, and some things for the Bookman competitions.'

Three weeks or so later, back at Lancing, he was moved to write a poem on 'the mute magnificence of death' which he sent to *Public School Verse*. All that can be known of it is the self-criticism in Evelyn's diary: 'The original freshness was lost as is usual in verbal inspirations and the whole was very self-conscious "mean adventurings" etc. but I hope that they take it.' The editor rejected it. The same fate befell his writings for *The*

*Bookman* (a now defunct magazine), and presumably the unidentified Pan's verdict on the short story was unfavourable. With the uncompleted novel all these juvenilia have vanished without trace. So discouraging an apprenticeship certainly delayed Evelyn's assurance that writing was his business, but he never quite lost sight of it and did not abandon his efforts to master the craft of writing good English.

The spring term of 1921 saw Evelyn rising to the higher ranks of the school. He now had one of the private rooms, of minute dimensions and slummish character which are reserved to the senior boys. They are known in Lancing parlance as the 'pits' and for some reason spelt 'pitts'. He was appointed to the staff of the library and given to understand that when the vacancy occurred he would be appointed librarian. He was elected to the Shakespeare Society in which the headmaster and his wife were active members. He was also made a sacristan. He had joined the aristocracy of the school,

His elevation posed a familiar and interesting moral problem to Evelyn: what does a Bolshevik do when he inherits a well-endowed peerage?

Evelyn decided to try to solve the problem by compromise. 'One thing I am beginning to realize', he wrote on 7 March, 'is that one must limit one's Bolshevism. It is no use leading a Loom of Youth existence ragging everything. One's attentions must be confined to certain deserving cases such as the corps. It is a great mistake to rag everything.' He took as his motto 'Limited Bolshevism'. But he found himself more and more forced into conformity.

As a schoolboy he was slowly acquiring success. It was at this time, in his eighteenth year, that he began to be the subject of J.F.'s particular interest, and an entry in the diary records his pride at having been invited for the first time to tea with this imposing man, his only reservation being a fear that he may not have shone so brightly in the conversation as his host may have expected. In his autobiography he told how from then on his reverence for Francis Crease began imperceptibly to wane, though the only indication in the diary is the increasing rarity and ulti-mate disappearance of Crease's name.

His next holidays which began on 1 April were largely occupied by Evelyn in composing a poem with which he hoped to add to his success by winning the poetry prize of Lancing known as the Scarlyn. Modelling himself, consciously or unconsciously, on Balzac, he decided to work at night, though he was in bed before the small hours. The attempt at poetry gave him a further inkling of the true nature of his talents. On 2 April he wrote: 'As sometimes walking in the middle of London one has a sudden impulse to run, I feel that I must write prose or burst.' Nevertheless he was to win the prize at the end of the year, and he continued to write poetry. (The prize poem has not survived.)

He was understandably deceived into believing that he had the makings of a poet as he evidently showed some definite promise. In June he copied into his diary a poem that he had addressed to two boys with whom he was enjoying a sentimental friendship. It was not masterly but it stands the test of time better than most such young effusions. One reference is obscure unless one knows that the Lancing school buildings are built of flint. The reader may notice a slightly derogatory reference to Mr Crease's china.

> I suppose that when I leave
> I shall think as others do,
> Storing in my memory
> Things refreshing and untrue.
>
> I shall think that I have known
> Comfort in the flint and stone
> In the light the evening shews
> When I leave, I suppose.
>
> Light on china, white and blue,
> Memories of study teas,
> I shall think that I loved these
> Just as all the others do.
>
> Fellowship, I shall believe,
> Cheered my way when I was young;
> I shall hunger for old friends,
> I suppose, when I leave.
>
> Yet I know that just you two
> Mattered out of all I knew –
> But I may lose the thought of you
> Just as all the others do.

At the time he wrote this, in June 1921, he obtained another distinction at Lancing. This was a play about public school life called *Conversion*. It was well received, so much so that a literary friend of the family sent it to the famous J. C. Squire, with the suggestion that he should print it in *The Mercury* of which he was the editor. It was not published, and like nearly all the juvenilia last mentioned has vanished. But Evelyn's success was manifestly increasing.

He was nevertheless profoundly unhappy. He was at the age (approaching eighteen) when youths generally are. It has been supposed by some that, following a usual course of events, he was in a state of emotional unease at the emergence of sex and that, as is common in public schools, he became involved in unhappy homosexual love-affairs with consequent and torturing sense of guilt. There is little if any truth in such an interpretation. There was but the mildest element of homosexualism in

Evelyn's school career. He owns in his diary to being attracted to one or two pretty boys, and reference has been made to sentimental friendships. All this was very innocent. I see no reason to doubt an assertion in his diary: 'I lead as pure a life as any Christian in the place, always excepting conversation of course.' His diary records occasions when he rebuked his cronies for 'keenness' on younger boys, and he always referred to 'cases', the Lancing euphemism then to denote homosexual relations, with disapproval. A cautionary letter from Arthur Waugh on the subject was not understood. His unhappiness came from deeper causes.

During the Easter holidays Evelyn's feelings for his father changed. He fancied that he saw through him and had discovered that the man he had loved and respected was a hollow sham. The first hint occurred early in April: 'This afternoon I went with father to hear him lecture on Dickens's women at the St Augustine gild. A good lecture but incorrigibly theatrical as usual.' At the end of the holidays he wrote as follows: 'Father has been ineffably silly the whole holidays. The extraordinary thing is that the more I see through my father the more I appreciate mother. She has been like Candida and went to father whom she must have despised, because he needed her most. I always think I am discovering some new trait in his character and find that she knew it long ago. She is a very wonderful woman.' In July his parents came down to Brighton with some family friends and gave Evelyn and his friend Dudley Carew a day of fun. 'I did not enjoy it much', recorded Evelyn.

Soon after the psychological blow of losing faith in his father he received another: he lost his religious faith.

The one contemporary to whom he confided his loss was Tom Driberg. It came about as follows: Tom also was a sacristan and one evening they were preparing the altar in the chapel for a service to be held the following morning. Tom pointed out to his friend that on his side the hanging altar cloth did not balance the other side. Evelyn replied: 'If it's good enough for me it's good enough for God.' Tom was very shocked. Evelyn then admitted to him that he was an atheist. Tom said that in that case he should no longer continue sacristan. Evelyn felt a twinge of conscience and made an appointment with the chaplain. The meeting, according to Evelyn's autobiography, was ill-devised for the recovery of a lost sheep. 'When I came into his room', he wrote, 'another master was sitting smoking with [the chaplain]. I was obliged to explain my predicament before this third person. Adolescent doubts are very tedious to the mature; I was genially assured that it was quite in order for an atheist to act as sacristan.'

Tom Driberg has told me that he doubts the authenticity of Evelyn's account of the interview. He asserts that the chaplain was a zealous clergyman incapable of indifferentism. One must remember that the account was written more than forty years after the event, and in his later years Evelyn used to complain that his memory was often exact and fallacious simultaneously. There is also the complicating factor of Evelyn's novelist's delight in mixing fact and fiction. Tom believes that Evelyn showed this impulse long before he came to write a novel worthy of publication, for which reason he, in common with many others (including myself), has come to regard the diaries as an unreliable document, to be treated with great caution. For example, Tom himself has no memory of having surprised Roxburgh in a compromising situation with another boy, as related in the diary. Had such a thing happened, he insists, it would have been unforgettable. The diary remains formidable evidence of his life. For all that it is suspect.

Evelyn asserted in his autobiography that he shed his religion without regret. The diaries suggest otherwise. 'I am sure it is only a phase,' he wrote as if to reassure himself. The phase was to last for nine years.

On 18 July Evelyn recorded the following:

'I think a lot about suicide. I really think that if I were without parents I should kill myself: as it is I owe them a certain obligation. "He has lived well who died when he wished." The other night I sat up in my window seat until one composing last letters.

'To Carew: My dear Carey, I'm afraid that the biography will be rather short but you may print this in full to swell it, if you like. Whatever happens I hope that the jury will not bring in "while temporarily insane". The supreme conceit of the living in imagining that a man must be lunatic if a deliberate train of thought leads him to the conclusion that not to be born is best. If I have ever been normal I am now. I am perhaps a little excited as one about to meet new friends but I can see everything as clearly as I ever have.

'I have no really definite cause for killing myself. I suppose it is really fear of failure. I know I have something in me. I am desperately afraid it may never come to anything. Suicide is cowardice really, you see. I am sure that if I have genius, it will survive, if not it isn't worth living anyway. Nox est perpetua una dormienda. Cheerily Evelyn.'

He wrote more flippantly to one of the friends to whom he had addressed the poem quoted above.

'I'll remember you to God if I see him but I somehow think that if he's your sort of God he'll know all about you already and if he's mine he won't much care, I'm afraid. I hope to see you on Abraham's bosom. I'm sure you'd be the first to get across the palpable obscure with a drop of water for my tongue. With love. Evelyn Waugh.'

In his autobiography Evelyn dismissed all this as tiresome affectation. He was at the age of affectation, certainly, but it is difficult to resist the impression that there is something genuine to be found in the entry, if only an expression of a deep-rooted distress.

During the Lent and summer terms Evelyn was much preoccupied with a great ambition: to win a scholarship to Oxford. An examination was to be held in December 1921, and Evelyn felt fairly confident. He and Hugh Molson put down their names and began hard work. But in his present state of unhappiness work did not come as an anodyne, and he gave vent to his feelings in a later diary entry typical of several, expressing his self-hatred.

'I am really hating this term. I am certainly making myself hateful . . . I think that too much work is making me nervously strung. Anyway I am quite conscious of behaving like a cad all the time.'

During the summer holidays before his last term at school he and Hugh Molson went to Birchington where in a dismal lodging they put in a fortnight of intensive reading. Otherwise the holiday was spent in a round of youthful festivities, dances, theatres, and many visits to the cinema. Barbara was his frequent companion, but his flirtation with her sister had come to an end. He went twice to Nigel Playfair's prodigiously successful revival of Gay's masterpiece *The Beggar's Opera*. He had first seen it in the Christmas holidays and in all went to it about ten times. In later years Evelyn was not a great theatregoer, and with his aversion to music I doubt if he ever attended a grand opera, certainly not by choice. Oddly enough, the only other theatrical entertainment which he visited very frequently was another 'musical', a Shakespeare adaptation called *Kiss Me Kate*. This was some thirty years later. Throughout life, however, he always loved the cinema, and as early as this he was an intelligent film critic. Among films showing in London in the summer of 1921 was Charlie Chaplin's *The Kid*. Evelyn detected an increasing strain of sentimentality and saw the danger to Charlie Chaplin's artistry. Among plays he saw was one that made a great stir in London then, *Abraham Lincoln*, by John Drinkwater. In his diary Evelyn took occasion to pour scorn on what he took to be his father's unintelligent reaction to this piece.

He returned to Lancing in September and found himself as dissatisfied as in the term before. He worked hard but work proved no anodyne. On 4 November the official application forms for the Oxford examination arrived. Arthur Waugh would have liked Evelyn to get a scholarship to New College, but Evelyn knew that he was not equal to it. He also remembered his father's frequent anxiety about money; so, seeing that the Hertford College scholarship was the best remunerated, he put Hertford as his first preference.

The term began to draw to an end; the fateful Oxford date in early December drew nearer. Weighed down with a sense of destiny, Evelyn wrote his last editorial for the *Lancing College Magazine*. He reprinted a large part of it in his autobiography, omitting those passages which he found excessively embarrassing. It is very revealing of Evelyn's essential character in his early manhood.

'The Youngest Generation.

'During the last few years, a new generation has grown up; between them and the young men of 1912 lies the great gulf of the war. What will they stand for and what are they going to do?

'The men of Rupert Brooke's generation are broken. Narcissus like, they stood for an instant amazedly aware of their own beauty; the war, which old men made, has left them tired and embittered. What will the young men of 1922 be? . . .' And so on.

The reference to Rupert Brooke is interesting, and had already been reflected in his entries to the diary. Throughout life he joined in the hero-worship that surrounds the names of the gifted young men who were lost in the First World War: the Grenfells, Charles Lister, Raymond Asquith, and pre-eminently at this time Rupert Brooke. Some of his contemporaries thought that his reverence was exaggerated, but he persisted in it, now and after.

On 3 December he went home for a weekend before his examination. On Monday the 5th he and Hugh Molson went to Oxford where they stayed at the Mitre. On the 10th the examination was over.

Five days after his return to Lancing the results were declared. Hugh Molson had failed for New College, but Evelyn had gained his scholarship to Hertford. The news was announced to the school by the headmaster, who in congratulating Evelyn described Hertford as 'a very rising college'. Evelyn noted the infelicitous phrase with interest.

Little has been said of the headmaster, the Reverend Henry Bowlby, a former master at Eton. He was a remote figure in young Evelyn's life, and Evelyn barely mentioned him in the diary. He described him thus in the autobiography: 'A tall, lean man, distinctly handsome except when the keen winds of the place caught and encrimsoned his narrow nose . . . He remained aloof from us, never dissembling the opinion, to which we all assented, that Lancing was a less important place than Eton.'

His ungrammatical remark on Evelyn's triumph indicates clearly enough the opinion that Hertford College was a less important place than New College.

## Chapter 3

### 1922-1924

On the day he left school Evelyn stopped keeping a diary, and did not do so again for nearly three years.

He 'commenced scholar' in the Hilary or Lent term at Hertford College, Oxford, early in the new year 1922. The great majority 'commence' in the Michaelmas term which begins in the early autumn, so it followed that Evelyn found himself one of very few 'freshmen' when he first went to Hertford. This had two opposite consequences for him: if he had 'come up' in the usual way, he would have found a number of schoolfellows coming up with him, and his emergence from a Lancing set and a Hertford College set to others would probably have been slower. As it was his premature matriculation sent him, as he told, 'into the university as a lone explorer'. He added: 'I had little choice but to rove.'

Three weeks or so after arrival he wrote to Tom Driberg: 'I am enjoying life here very well. I do no work and never go to chapel. As I am too bad to play soccer for Hertford I have joined a local hockey club which is quite a joke. There is a pleasant old world violence about the game which appeals to me strongly. Yesterday I heard Inge preach at the University church. Very witty and scholarly. Just what one wants at Oxford.

'Oxford is not yet quite itself but the aged war worn hero type is beginning to go down. It ought to be right again by the time you come up. I am well pleased with Hertford. At first I thought I could not be happy outside New College but there are really an extremely pleasant set of men here. The buildings are pretty beastly.'

His emotional bond with Lancing was made plain about a month later, in March 1922, in the course of a letter to his successor as the editor of the school magazine, Dudley Carew. He asked his friend, as he several times asked Tom Driberg, whether he was greatly disliked at Lancing 'as Good God I deserved to be', but he added: 'I am changing pretty hard and I think for the better but I am not changing my interest for Lancing and all of you.' In another letter of the same time to the same friend he wrote: 'I am very shy and a little lonely still but gradually settling down. I feel I am going to be immoderately happy. I wish I could find some congenial friends. I have at present met a gloomy scholar from some Grammar School who talked nothing, some aristocratic New College men who

36

talked winter sports and motor cars and a vociferous Carthusian who talked filth.' Before the end of his first term he had evidently made other and more rewarding friends. His love-affair with Oxford was growing in intensity as a letter to Tom Driberg written from home in his first vacation makes plain.

'After Oxford, London, and particularly Suburbia, is quite indescribably dreary and your letter came as a welcome interruption to the long back-chat of the literary cliques. There are rumours that the Times Literary Supplement is going to cease, that Catherine Mansfield is not going to die after all, that J. C. Squire has taken seriously to drink at last. No news I am afraid to match your ribald chronicle . . .

'I enjoyed last term immeasurably and left Oxford with regret and a pocket book bull of unpaid bills. I did *no* work & do not propose to do any next term so I am trying to learn a little during the vac. I have schools at the end of next term. Between whiles I read Alice in Wonderland. It is an excellent book I think.'

In the last paragraph he sends his 'love to Lancing', but the tone of the letter clearly implies that he was rapidly leaving Lancing and what it stood for behind. In a letter to Dudley Carew written from Hertford in the term time he had made this explicit. There had been some dispute about a letter he had wanted published in the school magazine and his wish had been resisted by those in authority, including Dick Harris. Eventually Evelyn conveyed his 'surrender' in a letter to Carew which contains this significant passage: 'There are things more worth defending at Oxford. You and your friends belong to Lancing & the past, you know, and it's always a mistake to try & keep up with the past. Thank you for reminding me.'

As readers may have noticed, there is evidence in these first vacation letters that the splendours of Oxford had made him a little contemptuous of his home surroundings – 'I hardly know', he wrote to Tom Driberg in another vacation letter, 'how I shall live through the next ten days until I go up. The Beggars Opera is my only comfort.' As has appeared in his relations with his father, and as is common among the awakening young, he was ruthlessly throwing away his reverence for earlier objects of worship. He wrote to Driberg in the course of the letter already quoted: 'How is the man Roxburgh? I had a letter from him recently – very insolent His sarcasm does not carry from Lancing to Oxford with advantage and his brain seems rather inconsiderable when one is daily taught by dons of real erudition.' In a later letter to his friend in the summer (or Trinity) term of 1922, Evelyn wrote of this mentor: 'I have come to the conclusion that J.F. is thoroughly second-rate.' (But in his autobiography he regretted that there had been no don at Hertford of Roxburgh's stature.)

By constrast, and perhaps as a consequence of this possibly half-hearted disillusion, Evelyn found his early admiration of Francis Crease reaffirmed.

Crease had left Sussex and was now living at Marston, then still a secluded country village near Oxford. To that village Evelyn and Hugh Molson (now studying in Oxford for the New College scholarship which he ultimately obtained) would independently and occasionally set out for a visit to this engaging man who had relieved the austerity of their younger days. As a dedicated artist, Crease still exerted influence over Evelyn. In a letter, which appears to belong to the summer of 1922, Evelyn wrote to Dudley Carew: 'A wider outlook has given me a far larger realization of Crease's designs. I am convinced now that that man is a great artist. Before, I hung my admiration on his character & did not understand his work fully. It is really great, Carey. I'm now convinced of that.'

A footnote is necessary. Unless Evelyn's memory was wholly at fault on a serious item in his life, then in 1922 he was still seeing the work Crease did in his Sussex days, for Evelyn affirmed that after the Affair of the Broken Pen, Crease never again practised as a scribe. Most likely then, Evelyn was seeing familiar things with new eyes.

He made few of his lasting friendships during his first two terms, when, as he recorded in his autobiography, he led the conventional life of the newcomer, but one friendship he made which was very strong at the time and, as with all his friendships, was never to be forgotten. This was with a man a year older than himself, Terence Greenidge, who had rooms close to his in Hertford. Greenidge was an extreme eccentric. In later life he became an actor, and as an undergraduate was abnormally stage-struck. Lionel Barrymore's film *Enemies of Women* appeared while he was in Oxford. Greenidge attended it at least once a day during its run, so Evelyn informed me once, adopted Barrymore's way of speaking and at great expense bought clothes similar to those worn by the famous actor in the film. He played uncountable practical jokes on his college and his clubs in order to disturb their routine, and had a taste for declaiming Greek tragic choruses in the quad in the middle of the night. He was also an enthusiastic athlete. All this appealed to Evelyn who had a strong vein of eccentricity, as yet hidden. Greenidge was already a leading personality of the undergraduate population and through him and James Parkes (today the eminent historian), with whom Greenidge shared rooms, Evelyn met other leading lights, the editor of the undergraduate magazine, *The Isis*, and the President of the Union. As a result he continued his journalist career from the *Lancing College Magazine* and became an occasional contributor (both of reporting paragraphs and of light verse) to *The Isis*; likewise he continued his career as a public speaker at the Union. In so far as he was known in the university, it was as a speaker at the Union where he made two other friendships which lasted the rest of his life: with Christopher Hollis and Douglas Woodruff. The main friendship of Evelyn at this time was with Greenidge. The latter's roommate, James Parkes, however, found him disagreeable and Evelyn probably made no effort to win him. He told Driberg of his aversion to the 'aged war worn hero type'. Though only twenty-six at the time, James Parkes came within this category. The hardest work Evelyn did was at his attempt to compose a Newdigate prize poem in time to be submitted for judgement in the Trinity term, but he seens to have abandoned it before completion. He began slowly to get some small reputation for draughtsmanship in which he still believed his hopes of distinction lay.

Under Greenidge's leadership Evelyn entered a frivolous world with some consequences for his future life. There was an odd and transient club in Oxford known as the Hypocrites which had premises south of Christ Church in an ancient half-timbered house chiefly given over to a bicycle shop. The club had rooms above the shop. It had a varied membership composed chiefly at this time of 'heavy-drinking, rather sombre Rugbeans and Wykehamists', according to Evelyn. The president of this grotesque rival to the Grid and the Canning was Lord Elmley, now Earl Beauchamp. One evening Terence Greenidge took Evelyn to the Hypocrites where a hilarious general meeting was in progress, one of the items on the agenda being the election of a new club secretary. Precisely how the resolution was arrived at is not remembered, but Greenidge assured me once that Evelyn having been greeted as an ideal Hypocrite was elected secretary before he had been elected member. He did not take his duties seriously, and soon after either resigned or was deposed (he confessed to uncertain memory about this), but he remained a member. Evelyn wrote of it: 'It was the stamping-ground of half my Oxford life and the source of friendships still warm today.'

Of these friendships some of the most important were gained through Lord Elmley. His father was head of the Lygon family, and in the next year Evelyn became close friends with Elmley's younger brother Hugh Lygon, and through 'Hughie' with the whole family. To some extent, a very limited one, Hughie (who died young in 1936) was Evelyn's model for Sebastian Flyte in *Brideshead Revisited*, a matter which will be discussed later. Hughie took him to the imposing family seat of Madresfield Court in Worcestershire, and this was the beginning of the 'vie de château' which he greatly enjoyed and for which taste he has been much criticized in a later age of inverted snobbery. This close friendship with the Lygons was the result of an important event in Oxford history which occurred after the Long Vacation of 1922 when Hughie came up.

In the Michaelmas term of 1922 Oxford underwent a revolution in the undergraduate world, and this was most immediately noticeable through the influence of new membership in the Hypocrites Club. In his autobiography Evelyn told how the club was invaded and occupied 'by a group of wanton Etonians who brought it to . . . dissolution. It then became notorious not only for drunkeness but for flamboyance of dress and manner which was in some cases patently homosexual. Elmley ordained that: "Gentlemen may prance but not dance", but his rule was not observed . . .' The dons in charge of undergraduate discipline looked with disapproval on this trend in Oxford life. Equally disapproving were the older generation of club members. Evelyn gave this description of their clash with the newcomers: 'The difference between the two antagonistic parties may be expressed in parody by saying that the older members were disposed to an archaic turn of phrase, calling: "Draw a stoop of ale, prithee", while the new members affected cockney, ordering "Just a nip of dry London, for me wind, dearie".' The last quotation may disguise the fact that this eruption was part of an attempt to revive in a wholly different and twentieth-century idiom the ideals of Walter Pater: from the autumn of 1922 may be dated the brief reign of the modern Oxford aesthetes.

The dominating figure among these reformers, soon to be the best known undergraduate of Oxford, was Harold Acton. He was quite clear in his mind about his objectives, it was his ambition to re-educate Oxford, no less, to carry Oxonian taste away from the Georgians, among whom it still lingered, away from the decaying *art nouveau* and to lead it towards the neglected fields of authentic contemporary literature and art. He set about his task of sweeping the stables clean by founding a new under-graduate magazine called *The Broom*, and by imposing his personality on his fellows by the exercise of a somewhat exotic personality (for his family home was in Florence) and even by carrying his aesthetic principles into his style of dress. This took the unexpected form of a new kind of Gothic Revival. Harold Acton's clothes reflected, besides their unusual modernities, an admiration for the past, and typically of the past then fashionably out of favour, that of the later nineteenth century. He wore a grey bowler hat, then as anachronistic in Oxford as Dr Routh's powdered bob-wig had been in the same city a century before. He wore black silk stocks and side-whiskers and other archaic elegancies, all somehow harmoniously combined with modern undergraduate styles, for he did not merely exhibit himself in fancy dress. With the two great advantages of a genuine poetic gift, and an essential seriousness of aim, the comedy which he played at Oxford was of real and in many ways of lasting influence.

Not only the members of the Hypocrites Club, but all sorts and kinds of contemporaries recognized in him the leading man among the under-graduates, and some a leader. Of those who banded with him in the furtherance of his mission, there were some who are now forgotten, some who only achieved notoriety, and a few who were to make considerable reputations.

Brian Howard came up to Oxford from Eton in the same term. He arrived with a little reputation for promise as a poet, but this had begun to fade before the end of his school days, and rapidly faded further during his inconclusive university career; thereafter his oblivion was swift except among those who knew him and found much amusement in his lifelong and shameless affectation. He was a spirited conversationalist and it could be said of him as Oscar Wilde said of himself that he put the best of his ability into his talk. Evelyn quoted Lady Caroline Lamb with reference to Howard. 'Mad, bad, and dangerous to know', he wrote. They were never friends.

Another of the aesthetes was Robert Byron. His whole life was informed by passionate antagonisms and furious enthusiasms. He made Harold's cause his own, and when various neo-aesthetic ventures failed due to official disapproval, notably a Victorian ballet in which Robert was to appear as the Queen and Harold to dance the part of Lytton Strachey, Robert responded with a maniac sense of persecution, a disposition which was never to leave him. With Evelyn he became close friends. The relationship was to be turbulent and ambivalent on both sides. How much or little it meant to Evelyn is hard to say.

In this same Michaelmas of young revolution, several other men with whom Evelyn made friends came up to the university. One was Peter Rodd (the second son of the ambassador Sir Rennell Rodd, later Lord Rennell), who was one of the most extraordinary products of the generation to which Evelyn belonged. He had intellectual abilities which can be compared with those of the greatest minds, and they gave him a breadth of learning which sometimes made him appear as a veritable *Stupor Mundi*. But these abilities were matched by an irresponsibility which would have been remarkable in a criminal. He had no ambition but instead a ceaseless thirst for adventure. He could have been a prominent academic, politician (revolutionary or otherwise), or a lawyer, a successful member, in fact, of any profession which depends on learning, but his whole life was spent in an apparently and perhaps genuinely conscious effort to avoid the achievement which was within his grasp. He was like a man who prefers to admire his talents as works of art, rather than to use them. He utterly fascinated Evelyn and was to have influence, of a kind not suspected then, on his life. Evelyn was always very sensitive on the subject of models for his fictional characters. He was easily irritated by assumptions of portraiture and caricature, but there were exceptions, some of which will be mentioned later. Peter Rodd was unquestionably the model for Basil Seal. Evelyn admitted it to his friends, and Peter acknowledged the fact. I was at a dinner with Evelyn at Cyril Connolly's house in London, shortly after Basil Seal had been launched in *Black Mischief*. The model and the caricature were discussed, no doubts being expressed on either side that Peter and Basil were mutual reflections. 'Haven't you had trouble with Peter?' asked Cyril. 'None at all,' replied Evelyn 'But don't you expect it?' went on Cyril. 'No,' said Evelyn. We all asked why. 'Because', said Evelyn magisterially, though less so than he would have done in later years, 'because you can draw any character as near to life as you want, and no offence will be taken provided you say that he is attractive to women.'

There was in this autumn of 1922 another friendship, one which grew from early Oxford acquaintance. It was with John Sutro, a scholar of Trinity. John had come up in the term before Evelyn, and had done good service to the university by reviving an undergraduate magazine called *The Cherwell*, formerly and now again a rival to *The Isis*. In this brief revolutionary period, *The Isis* and *The Cherwell* came into the respective positions of the organs of the Establishment and the Opposition. *The Cherwell* sided with the new tyrants, with the arts, with the aesthetes; *The Isis* more with the rowing men, the rugger teams, the cricket prospects and the Public School idea. As a Union member with early loyalties to *The Isis*, Evelyn continued as their Union reporter, but under the influence of his growing friendship with John Sutro he also became the reporter of the Union for *The Cherwell* too, in which Sutro had installed Christopher Hollis as editor. The Union was taken more seriously then than now, and its debates were recorded in *The Morning Post*.

Evelyn told how as a reporter of these debates his 'only scoop' was on one evening when John Sutro 'stood up to speak on the paper. It was evident that he had been drinking heavily and, as he spoke, the liquor worked strongly in him. After becoming increasingly incoherent, he received a note from the President: "Had you better not sit down?" He did so and remained for a few minutes stupefied on the committee bench under the bust of Gladstone, until he caught a laudatory, if ironic, mention of himself. This he applauded loudly, then rose and with difficulty made his way out of the debating hall to collapse in the garden. I recorded this event, as the *Morning Post* did not. It transpired that his parents were regular readers of the *Cherwell*. A special copy had to be printed for them with the passage deleted.'

Evelyn, with his increasing range of acquaintance, somewhat altered his way of life in the autumn of 1922. It became freer and wilder, but in one respect (because of the debts he had accumulated) it became more but not distinctly economical. He now did little entertaining in the form of lunch or dinner-parties, but instead evolved rowdy social occasions which could be run cheaply. He thus described what happened in his autobiography.

'When Parkes went down in my second year Terence and I formed the nucleus of a coterie which we used to call "the Hertford underworld". Tony Bushell, who later became a film actor, and my Lancing friend, P. F. Machin, were of us. We used, unless any of us was giving a luncheon party or going to one, to have our commons together in my rooms. This soon developed into my keeping open house for men from other colleges; sometimes as many as a dozen collected; Terence dubbed these assemblies "offal". We drank large quantities of beer and made a good deal of noise. Few of us could sing. We used to recite verse in unison.'

Among the aesthetes proper his closest friendship was with the leader, Harold Acton. The latter wrote in his *Memoirs of an Aesthete*: 'An almost inseparable boon companion at Oxford was a little faun called Evelyn Waugh. Though others assure me that he has changed past recognition, I still see him as a prancing faun, thinly disguised by conventional apparel. His wide-apart eyes, always ready to be startled under raised eyebrows, the curved sensual lips, the hyacinthine locks of hair, I had seen in marble and bronze at Naples, in the Vatican Museum, and on fountainheads all over Italy. The gentleness of his manner could not deceive me, nor could the neat black and white drawings, nor the taste for Eric Gill. Though his horns had been removed, he was capable of butting in other ways. So demure and yet so wild! A faun half-tamed by the Middle Ages, who would hide himself for months in some suburban retreat, and then burst upon the town with capricious caperings. His period of mediaeval tutelage drew him into a circle of Chestertonian friends, to Christopher Hollis and other robust wits already steering for Rome. They assembled in his rooms for what they called offal.'

Acton gave another and fuller account nearly twenty years after the appearance in 1948 of these memoirs.

'Spontaneous, ebullient, vivacious, then silent, sullen, staring at the world with critical distaste; barking at his tutorial bogie, swilling pints of ale, shouting nonsense rhymes in the street, then retiring like a monk into his cell to draw neat yet fanciful designs such as "The Tragical Death of Mr Will Huskisson" for Mr John Sutro, the president of the Oxford University Railway Club, or a new cover for "The Oxford Broom", Evelyn Waugh was an undergraduate of multiple moods and talents.

'Short, slim, alert, with wavy hair and wide-apart eyes that often sparkled with mischief, he seemed a faun (as I have said in my Memoirs), alternately wild and shy. He could be very wild with the smug politicians in embryo who struck solemn attitudes at the Oxford Union and he was quick to puncture their pomposity.

'His literary taste was practically formed: he preferred the prose of Bunyan to that of Pater, but I converted him from James Branch Cabell to Ronald Firbank and from the so-called Georgian poets to T. S. Eliot and the Sitwells. He had not yet decided whether to become a writer or a draughtsman, for he continued to design covers for novels under the influence of Eric Gill, whose woodcuts he admired. His appreciation of drawing was to serve him well as a writer and though he was unmusical he had a sharp ear for rhythm. His vision was strongly tinged with irony and he revelled in the absurdities of our acquaintances, the crankiness of certain dons. Neither he nor I affected gravity, "the joy of imbeciles", as Montesquieu defined it, but we took our pleasures seriously. I was nineteen and he was somewhat older when we met though I felt he was younger: he was decidedly insular with a suspicion of "foreign ways", and my early youth had been spent in Italy.

'Try as I might I could never acquire Evelyn's taste for beer, but because I delighted in his company I sipped it at his offal luncheons, where everybody talked at once, reciting Edith Sitwell's *Façade* and other poems, and expressing our *joie de vivre*. We were aesthetic hearties. There were no lilies and languors about us: on the whole we were pugnacious. Evelyn Waugh has evoked this period in "A Little Learning", but his own lovable qualities of heart and intelligence and physical charm could only be described by others. His apparent frivolity was the beginning of true wisdom.'

Many people believed when Harold Acton's memoirs came out that Evelyn was displeased at the description of him as a faun and that he would have preferred to have been the subject of a more imposing memory. I do not know what if any truth there may have been in these rumours as the only time Evelyn discussed the matter with me he was not in a serious mood. 'In his book,' said Evelyn to me one day when we were walking together in Gloucestershire, 'Harold Acton described me as a faun. What did he describe you as?'

'He didn't mention me in the book.'

'Oh?' said Evelyn on that high note which he would suddenly use. 'Why not? Didn't he think you were important enough?'

'Maybe. But you see the time at Oxford which Harold describes was before I went up. I could only have appeared as a digression.'

Evelyn looked grave. 'That's your alibi, is it?' he said.

'I regard it as unbreakable,' I answered.

We walked on in silence till Evelyn turned to me and said in a deep, grating voice: 'You're jealous of me because Harold Acton said I was like a faun, and no one has ever said that you are like a faun.'

The last remark was quite true.

A 'tutorial bogie' mentioned elsewhere by Harold indicates the History tutor of Hertford: C. R. M. F. Cruttwell. In his first two terms Evelyn was only the subject of Cruttwell's vague suspicion. In the autumn of 1922 this awkward relationship turned to passionate mutual hostility and Evelyn readily acknowledged in his autobiography that the chief fault lay with him and the 'fatuously haughty' airs with which he treated any advances from the older man. But it is most unlikely that even under the happiest circumstances they would have been easy together. Evelyn at this time and for some years to come was very generation-conscious. The twenties saw an intensification of the cult of 'the younger generation', but in university society at that time, at Oxford at any rate, the resulting conflict was less one between the old and the young as one between the untried young and their still young seniors; between those who, like Alec, had proved themselves in the ordeals of the Great War but were not, like Osbert Sitwell and Siegfried Sassoon, in revolt against militarism in every form: and those whose date of birth had fortuitously saved them from the ordeals. (In view of this it is a little strange that Alec and Evelyn remained mutually devoted.) In the Cruttwell-Evelyn relationship this conflict was epitomized. Cruttwell was no longer young by undergraduate standards, but he was not old; he was a middle-aged man, under forty, who had served throughout the war and through army experience had become a disciplinarian. 'As Dean of the college', wrote Evelyn, 'he seemed often to fancy himself in command of a recalcitrant platoon.' He was not going to stand any nonsense from 'Bolshies', and in his neglect of his work, and his rowdiness in college and outside, Evelyn was rapidly staging a revival of 'unlimited Bolshevism'. Cruttwell was not disposed to be tolerant of this.

Having passed his 'History Previous' at the end of the Trinity term, Evelyn was now set to work for his 'finals' which he would normally take two years later, at the end of the Trinity term of 1924. For this purpose Cruttwell now became his tutor. There were many who envied Evelyn his good fortune. Hertford men who remember Cruttwell say that he was an ideal tutor from whom his pupils could receive first-class education, but only if they were sympathetic to him. Evelyn was totally unsuited to be his pupil. With youthful anger, he only saw in him an embodiment of that military spirit against which he had first rebelled at Lancing, and the fact that Cruttwell was markedly eccentric and in un-military fashion wore his hair in a bob, as it was then called, did nothing to soften the other's antagonism; no more than did Cruttwell's occasional drinking excesses which might be thought to have appealed to the anarchist in Evelyn. On the other side the tutor took a violent dislike to his pupil. 'After a few sessions', Evelyn wrote, '[Cruttwell] fell into such frenzies of exasperation that for a time he refused to see me at all and I was left without tutoring of any kind.' As a Hertford friend of Cruttwell who knew both men at the time has remarked to me: 'Cruttwell was a man to be pitied, and young Evelyn Waugh, like all young men, was incapable of pity except for himself.'

It was long before Evelyn's hatred for this mentor was lost or even diminished. Throughout Evelyn's writing career, he borrowed his name in his fiction for ridiculous, contemptible or repellent minor characters. His only famous short story was originally entitled and published in a magazine as 'Mr Cruttwell's Little Holiday'. Only at the very end of his life did Evelyn make some restitution, probably moved by learning that in his last years Cruttwell, following several breakdowns, had all but lost his reason. In *A Little Learning* he wrote this memorable passage: '[Cruttwell] was, I now recognize, a wreck of the war in which he had served gallantly. No doubt a modern doctor would have named, even if he could not cure, his various neuroses. It was as though he had never cleaned himself of the muck of the trenches.'

Harold Acton refers also to the Railway Club. This needs some explanation. The club was founded by John Sutro and gave expression to that railway romanticism and railway scholarship which dates almost from the time of George Stephenson, and of which John Sutro was an enthusiastic and learned amateur. The cult appears to have declined with the recent disappearance of the fiery steam engine and the rise of the more efficient and restrained diesel locomotive. Except for an inaugural meeting in John Sutro's rooms, the sessions of the Railway Club were held on the railways. They occurred only three or four times a year. A private dining-car would he hired and attached to the Penzance–Aberdeen train. Dinner would be served to the club on the journey from Oxford to Leicester, where the members would disembark and after half an hour board a second private dining-car in which there were speeches over drinks as a north–south train carried them back to Oxford. The major speakers were usually Harold Acton and John Sutro, the latter, as a 'mimic of genius', rarely using his own voice. The first of these dinners took place on 28 November 1923, the last on the London–Brighton line in 1963. It was an undergraduate enterprise which survived the undergraduate days of the members. 'In later years,' wrote Evelyn, 'after we had gone down, our meetings became more elaborate and the membership wider so as to include friends of John's who had been at Cambridge or Sandhurst at the time of our formation. Chefs were then recruited from London restaurants and fine wines added to the fare. Silver cigarette boxes were presented to astonished engine-drivers and reception committees met us at our destinations.' The Railway Club was, with his friendship for John Sutro, Evelyn's happiest Oxford memory. The final 1963 meeting was entirely at his instigation. When writing his autobiography, Evelyn seems to have forgotten that John Sutro's example at Oxford was emulated at Cambridge and the members were eligible for both clubs.

Harold Acton's magazine *The Broom* played an important part in young Evelyn's life in the year of the Railway Club. Evelyn was still enjoying a misleading success as a draughtsman and was in much demand for *The Cherwell* and *The Broom*, O.U.D.S.* programmes, menus for dinners and the like. Inevitably his artistic ambitions seemed to him open to early realization. He attended the Ruskin School of Art in Oxford with another undergraduate, Peter Quennell, who was also to make a name in literature. On their studies together Evelyn makes this interesting comment: 'Peter, who had decorated his first book of verse, drew worse than I and realized the sooner where his talent lay. It was many years before I despaired of myself as a draughtsman. My meagre gift had been overpraised at home, at school and at Oxford. I never imagined myself a Titian or a Velasquez.

Oxford University Dramatic Society.

46

My ambition was to draw, decorate, design and illustrate. I worked with the brush and was entirely happy in my employment of it, as I was not when reading or writing.'

But Harold Acton, though enjoying Evelyn's work, saw that his friend was not an artist in the usual meaning of the term and persuaded him to cultivate instead his neglected literary ability. Harold's reputation, as the friend of the Sitwells and Gertrude Stein whom he brought down to astonish Oxford, and as the author of an acclaimed book of poems, *Aquarium*, was in the ascendant, and he thus easily influenced Evelyn. The result was Evelyn's first serious attempt at fiction. It was a macabre story of death entitled *Anthony, Who Sought Things That Were Lost*. It was set in a tyrannical grand dukedom of Italy in the year 1848. Harold published it in *The Broom* in June 1923. Fears aroused by the preciosity of the title are fully confirmed by reading.

Of this juvenile work Evelyn wrote that it 'betrays the unmistakeable influence of that preposterously spurious artefact, which quite captivated me at the age of nineteen, James Branch Cabell's *Jurgen*'. The severe self-judgement must stand, but it is to be noticed that Harold, according to his own account, had already begun to convert Evelyn from Cabell towards a worthier model, Ronald Firbank. Evelyn's story, gruesomely telling of an imprisoned pair of lovers, and the decay of their passion amid the horrors of the dungeon, and of how the love of 'the Lady Elizabeth' was transferred from 'Count Anthony' to the jailer, and of their murderous end, certainly shows the rubbishy influence of Cabell; but others are evident as well. There are weak echoes of Oscar Wilde's 'Happy Prince' stories, of Edgar Allan Poe, of Firbank. Oddly enough the strongest resemblance is to an author whom neither Evelyn nor Harold is likely to have read or even to have heard about then, Frederick Rolfe, 'Baron Corvo'. At that time he was completely forgotten. The story is not by any standards a good piece of writing, and only a person as perspicacious as Harold Acton could have seen promise of later fruition in it, but it made an impression on undergraduate opinion. Not a great impression, and Evelyn was not much encouraged so far as appears, but Harold Acton had nevertheless opened Evelyn's eyes a little. Evelyn was by no means convinced by this little success that his vocation was to writing, but he could not but be impressed by the fact that he was capable of enjoying literary success, even if of a very insignificant kind.

When Evelyn had mastered his craft he looked back on his early efforts with shame. I never heard him refer to 'Anthony', and after the appearance of Harold Acton's memoirs, in which I learned of it for the first time, I did not, to my regret, ask him about it because I knew how he disliked talking about his early work, including his early masterpieces. I doubt if he would have said anything of interest. He would probably have preferred to answer with the abrupt snub at which he was adept. He was right to forget 'Anthony'. It has never been republished, and small wonder.

It has been noticed earlier that the aesthetes, especially in the course of their invasion and occupation of the Hypocrites, had shown some homosexual character. They got the reputation of being a set of homosexuals. This was unjust. Some of them were, some of them were not, and their reputation for exclusive homosexuality was largely due to the exhibitionism of Brian Howard. But the disapproval of the authorities on this account was not entirely empty of reason. To those who disapproved of homosexuality their influence appeared certainly malign. Evelyn seemed an illustration of this. It must be said that at this period Evelyn entered an extreme homosexual phase. Names and details need not and should not be given, but, as Evelyn owned, not only to me but to many other of his friends, the phase, for the short time it lasted, was unrestrained, emotionally and physically. Of all persuasions none is so inclined to proselytism, and the exaggerated claims of proselytism, as homosexuality. Not long ago I read an article in a magazine written by and for homosexuals in which the suggestion was strongly conveyed that Evelyn remained inclined towards homosexuality throughout life. This is to misread him utterly, and in this case probably wilfully. Evelyn was never much shocked by homosexuality, even though later in life he became rather prudish in a capricious way about sexual matters. If he took one of his frequent dislikes to a man and found he was homosexual, then this would furnish him with ammunition. If he liked a man and found he was homosexual, he would treat the matter with indifference. He was indignant at some police persecutions of homosexuals. It is quite true that he was very interested in the subject, but he was interested in all things which shed light on human character. It is a main reason for his excellence as a novelist.

In one of his letters to Tom Driberg at Lancing Evelyn acted as the tempter to another weakness which, unlike that just discussed, had a permanent hold on Evelyn. 'Do let me', he wrote to his young friend, 'most seriously advise you to take to drink. There is nothing like the aesthetic pleasure of being drunk, and if you do it in the right way you can avoid being ill next day. That is the greatest thing Oxford has to teach.' The tempter failed and Tom Driberg never became an excessive drinker, but the tempter surrendered to his own blandishments. It can and must be said that Evelyn drank to excess from now on throughout his life. This raises a question which may as well be dealt with immediately, regardless of chronology.

Evelyn's diaries (taken up again in 1924) give the impression of a sot, of a man rarely sober and usually and offensively drunk. Contemporaries at Oxford allow that this horrible self-portrait is not baseless. Like many young men emancipated from the rigours of school, Evelyn not only drank too much but did so noisily. Unlike most young men he did not, after some months or a year, quieten down. He continued to make even slight excesses in drink the occasion for bawling and rowdiness. Cyril Connolly, who knew him only a little then, has an interesting memory of these years. He came across Evelyn making an abominable row outside the gate of Balliol College. 'Why do you have to make such a noise wherever you are?' angrily asked Cyril. 'I have to make a noise', came the astonishing reply, 'because I'm poor.' Cyril was impressed by this remark. 'It made sense,' as he said much later. He began to look on Evelyn as an interesting person.

Evelyn was always an interesting person, but for a long time rowdy drunken scenes, such as that outside Balliol, could hide the fact from all except a few intimates, and it says much for Cyril Connolly's perception that a chance remark revealed that here was something better than a bibulous ass. But most young men behave foolishly and there is nothing very remarkable in the case as recorded so far. What is more surprising is to find in the resumed diary a record of heavy drinking and drunkenness so persistently pursued that it reads like the autobiographical case-history of a total addict.

Evelyn's friends have defended the unpleasing character revealed in these diaries on the grounds that the document only shows Evelyn's proneness to exaggeration, affecting his description of himself and everything about him. They have also referred to his way of mixing fact and fiction in keeping with the novelist's instinct. The defence has been dismissed by those who credit themselves with detachment, as a good-natured but essentially untruthful apologia. In fact, the defence can be fairly proved by two considerations of fact.

While it is true that several eminent and rightly admired authors have been addicted to excessive drinking, it is also true that no such writer has gone so far as to become an alcoholic, in the medical sense, with the dubious and, if accepted, not very impressive exceptions in English letters of Edgar Allan Poe and Dylan Thomas. Now, if Evelyn's accounts of his drinking and frequent drunkenness were not exaggerated, then he must inevitably have become an alcoholic. Equally inevitably his mental faculties would have been influenced if not impaired and he could never have achieved literary excellence of the kind that he did. If he had left a collection of exciting but hysterical essays into the wildest romance, as the ever-drinking Edgar Allan Poe did, that would be one thing. But Evelyn's work in general, though intensely imaginative, gives an immediate impression of the concentration of intellect, of mental discipline, and his prose of precise and justified choice. None of this could conceivably be open to a man whose powers had been limited, and whose imagination had been inflamed in the manner he so fecklessly suggested. As evidence it should be remembered that if he undoubtedly drank excessively he was never a 'slave to alcohol'. As his companion in some of his later travels, I can testify that when cut off from drink by circumstances, the inconvenience never bothered him, and it is a fact, as all his acquaintances know, that in later years he regularly gave up strong drink throughout Lent, with difficulty it is true, but with success.

If the above is admitted, then, it may be rightly asked, why did he go on, long after his youth, in exaggerating, as men in youth often do, the extent of his drunken excesses? Why this persistent youthful silliness? Two answers can be given.

First he was a caricaturist. He conveyed his view of the truth through caricature, and as with all caricaturists he conveyed some untruth by the same means. Caricature and truth are compatible, but that does not mean that they are natural friends.

When he came to portray himself he thus inevitably presented a self-caricature. But he had an added incentive, a continuing and distressing psychological abnormality which took the form of a life-long tendency towards self-hatred. In later years he saw this as a 'sense of sin'. He was almost morbidly aware of his faults. Harold Acton hit a nail on the head when he said in his memoirs that Evelyn's 'lovable qualities . . . could only be described by others'. Evelyn, not only by ordinary modesty, but abnormally by his disposition, was quite incapable not only of that task but of any ordinary implication of good qualities. He needed to fight against so much self-reproach that he was constantly confronted by temptations to despair.

That, in my opinion, is the first explanation of this drawn-out and brutal self-misrepresentation; it is the self-portrait of a born caricaturist in continual danger of despair, continually subject to a death-wish.

But there is a second possible explanation wholly unrelated to the above. In a remarkable passage, Somerset Maugham noted that writers of fiction are usually somewhat 'ungrown up' in character. To invent stories and to listen to the inventions occupies a great part of childish activity. Most people in later years, when they put away childish things, retain the taste for listening to inventions (or no novels would sell well) but lose the taste for and ability to invent stories. But few people, except very dry and dreary ones, put away all their childish things. The novelist retains, among other things from his past, the wish and ability to invent stories, and this indicates that such a person has probably retained more childish things than most people do. If this idea, first put forward so far as I know by Somerset Maugham, is true, then it goes some way to explain an idiosyncrasy of Evelyn. All his friends, I believe, will admit that there was something child-like about him throughout life. His swift alternations between hilarious gaiety and dumb depression were very like the moods of highly-strung children. His affectation of archaic manners and the ways and tastes of the aged, though usually done in fun, seem to this observer at least in part a reaction against a Peter Pannish disposition. Let it not be thought that the story of Evelyn is the story of Peter Pan, but equally let it not be thought that he was free from the psychological dilemma that James Barrie so embarrassingly and so innocently and all too truthfully revealed to the world. Among the childish things that Evelyn did not put away there was the very young man's silly pleasure in trying to shock the world by extravagant self-accusations about drunkenness. Once more it must be noted that the diaries are suspect.

Evelyn was not one of those who in his third year tired of Oxford and longed to escape into the world without. To the end of his university days Oxford remained for him a 'Kingdom of Cockayne', but nevertheless he tried to shorten his Oxford career because he had become alarmed for himself. His debts were mounting and since he was doing almost no work he had before him the prospect of failure in the schools – and then what? Yet if his future looked inauspicious he still maintained hope. He still believed that he had sufficient ability to make a career as an artist. At the beginning of his third year, in the Michaelmas term of 1923, he asked his father to take him from Oxford and send him to Paris to study drawing and painting, but Arthur Waugh insisted that he must remain for his third year and sit for his degree at the end of the Trinity term of 1924. Evelyn grudgingly agreed. He felt consequently that 'as far as my schools went, I was in Oxford under protest. I perversely regarded it as the *laissez-passer* to a life of pure pleasure.'

As in the preceding year his main Oxford interest was in the cultivation of his friendships, the most important of which to him then was with a man a little older than himself called Alastair Graham. After Oxford their paths separated so widely that this friendship could not be fully maintained. All the others were continued in greater or lesser degree with few exceptions of which that with Robert Byron was a painful one. At this time Evelyn's friendship with Robert Byron remained very close and would have gone on so to the end of Robert's life if his hysterical anti-Catholicism had not later made continuation impossible. Many of Robert's friendships foundered on his ill-balanced temperament. This happened through the same cause with Robert's friendship with Lord Clonmore (now Earl of Wicklow) whom Evelyn had met through Robert. Of Clonmore Evelyn wrote that his 'extravagances were refined by a slightly antiquated habit of speech and infused by a Christian piety that was unique among us and lay hidden behind his stylish eccentricities'. Another friendship made through Robert was with David Talbot Rice who was later to become a distinguished Byzantinist. Evelyn described him as 'secretly studious'. Rice's friendship with Robert was never disturbed.

Some friendships that were far from close in those days became very important to him after, notably with Patrick Balfour (now Lord Kinross the distinguished historian of Kemal Ataturk and Turkey); with the brothers Alfred and Hubert Duggan, stepsons of Lord Curzon, the

Chancellor of the University, and Graham Greene whom Evelyn probably met through his cousin Claud Cockburn, then an undergraduate at Keble College. Evelyn recorded his impression that Graham Greene 'looked down on us . . . as childish and ostentatious'. He added: 'He certainly shared in none of our revelry.' In his last year Evelyn became distantly acquainted with Anthony Powell, whom, in later years, he was to admire perhaps more than any other contemporary English novelist, with the possible exception of Graham Greene.

All these friendships were recorded and commented on, for the most part with warm affection, in Evelyn's autobiography, but it seems possible from the style of his account that the scolding he received from Cyril Connolly outside Balliol left a wound disproportionate to the event. He seems also to have resented the fact that Maurice Bowra, then a young and recent and spectacular Fellow of Wadham College, paid little attention to him. Cyril and Maurice were friends, and of Cyril Evelyn wrote in his autobiography: 'He and Maurice Bowra were both acquaintances who became friends after I attracted some attention as a novelist.'

On the appearance of *A Little Learning* both were hurt, and Maurice was moved to protest to Evelyn against this implied accusation of 'tuft-hunting'. Evelyn replied that he had intended no such criticism and that he had merely stated a fact with due regard to chronology. No writer had or could have had a sharper appreciation of the value of words and phrases and of their implications, especially unkind ones. His apologia is not convincing. His relations with Maurice Bowra in later years were of the utmost ambivalence.

It may be that Evelyn resented, both in Maurice Bowra and Cyril Connolly, an aptitude, shared in all probability by other friends and acquaintances, to look on Evelyn as an eccentric worth some little cultivation because of the extent and amusement of his oddity. Some such predicament is suggested by another casual friendship made in his last year, one which later developed into a deep friendship. It was with Ralph Russell who at the time was studying theology and was later to become a Benedictine monk of the Downside Abbey community. Given Evelyn's entirely different type of character, the friendship seems improbable. Once, many years later, when asked about it, Evelyn said that the people with whom he was friends at Oxford tended for the most part to treat him as a 'freak'. Ralph Russell, on the other hand, had no such impulse: he treated him with the ordinary courtesy and respect that he would use to any other undergraduate of intelligence and interest. He made the other feel quite normal. Evelyn said that this was something he could never forget.

A glimpse of Evelyn in his last Oxford days. It is recorded by Harman Grisewood who in the Trinity term of 1924 went up from Ampleforth to sit for a scholarship examination: 'I can vividly remember my first meeting with him before I was an undergraduate. I was taken once or twice by David Talbot Rice to the Hypocrites Club. And there he was, very pink in the cheeks, small witty and fierce, quite alarming, but fascinating to a sixth form youth taking a scholarship exam. It was a very gloomy room if I remember rightly and Evelyn Waugh was like a bright spark from the fire.'

This was the end of the Academic Year, the period of exams. Harman Grisewood obtained a scholarship to Worcester College, and commenced scholar in the Michaelmas term of 1924. Evelyn sat for his finals, and as he knew he would, he did very poorly. The results, however, did not appear till the end of July after he had been examined *viva voce*. He did not completely fail for he obtained the feeble distinction of a Third Class degree. There was then some question at home and among the fellows of Hertford in consultation with his tutor as to whether he should stay up for another term, as he was entitled to do as a scholar and try again at the end of the Michaelmas term. His first and embittered tutor, Cruttwell, did not support the proposal. He wanted to be rid of this man. He had no word of consolation for the scholar who had failed to reap even the smallest harvest of honour for his college. He wrote: 'I cannot say that your Third does you anything but discredit: especially as it was not even a good one; and it is always at least foolish to allow oneself to be given an inappropriate intellectual label. I hope that you will soon settle in some sphere where you will give your intellect a better chance than in the History School.'

There is an odd and interesting note of prophecy about the letter. Cruttwell showed perception in judging that Evelyn was not well fitted to pursue historical studies, and though Evelyn was to write some interesting things in this field it was in spite of bias rather than because of natural aptitude. It seems an undeserved cruelty of Cruttwell's fate that when his former pupil did at length 'settle' into a congenial 'sphere' of activity according to his hope, Evelyn should have used it for purposes of revenge.

Evelyn left Hertford at the end of June 1924, but the bonds holding him to the city and university, unlike those holding him to Lancing, were never to be broken.

## Chapter 4

### 1924-1927

The episodes last considered may in one respect have been misleadingly described. Since Evelyn, from the nature of this book, was treated as the central character in the last chapter, an impression may have been caused that he was a leading personality of his undergraduate world, a rival if not in fame to Harold Acton, at least in notoriety to Brian Howard. Such an idea is false. He had a circle of friends, including Harold, John Sutro, Alastair Graham, Elmley, Hugh Lygon and David Plunket-Greene, all of whom gave him devoted friendship and who usually met at the Hypocrites Club. He also knew many O.U.D.S. men, notably Gyles Isham, their brightest star, whose performance as Hamlet in 1925 was to cause a theatrical sensation not only in Oxford but in London. But outside his varied group of friends Evelyn, in spite of wide acquaintance and a sustained reputation as a draughtsman, was little known in the university.

Let memory be called again in evidence. I went up to Oxford in 1926, two years after Evelyn had left. The name of Alec Waugh was well known to me, as it was to all our generation, as that of the author of an emancipatory experience in *The Loom of Youth*. During my Oxford days (regrettably few as I did even worse in the schools than Evelyn) I knew many of his friends. The reputations of Harold Acton and all the leading figures in the reign of the aesthetes became known to me early on, even before I met any of them. But I never heard from them or from anyone else at Oxford the name of Evelyn Waugh until the publication of *Decline and Fall* in 1928. Then everyone remembered him.

On one of his last days at Hertford he wrote a letter to Dudley Carew. It contained the following passage: 'Quite soon I am going to write a little book. It is going to be called "The Temple at Thatch" and will be about magic and madness.' The next paragraph begins: 'All the morning I have been drawing book plates to earn some money. I am, as always, fantastically destitute. Please get me any jobs which you think me capable of executing.' *The Temple at Thatch* continued for long to occupy him.

He was becoming increasingly aware of his vocation, but he had not yet heard its voice clearly.

Evelyn gave the last chapter of his autobiography a Thackerayish title: 'In Which Our Hero's Fortunes Fall Very Low'. They did, but not quite so low as he said. The opening of this dismal period was marked by a joyous event in the early autumn of 1924, the production of a film by Terence Greenidge (then studying at the Royal Academy of Dramatic Art), many sequences being shot in Arthur Waugh's house and garden. The principal actors were Terence, Evelyn, John Sutro, Elmley and, had they realized it, a great theatrical discovery, Elsa Lanchester. In those days she was little known as an actress, though Evelyn was inaccurate in saying that she had not yet become one, her first stage appearance having been in 1922. Her 'breakthrough' had precariously occurred in this year 1924 in her very brief appearance in Nigel Playfair's production of *The Way of the World*. Evelyn and his friends came to know her through their frequent attendance at a cabaret which she managed in Soho, and where she sometimes sang. It was called *The Cave of Harmony*.

The film was entitled *The Scarlet Woman*. The story was as simple as it was grotesque. The Pope (not identified) decided that the forcible conversion of England to the Roman obedience must be brought about instantly without regard to the claims of morality. The first move was to be the enforced reception into the Church of Rome of the Prince of Wales, from which the enforced reception of George V, the government and the country would follow without difficulty. For the accomplishment of his design the Pope picked on three main agents: the Catholic dean of Balliol (closely identified); an unscrupulous church dignitary, Cardinal Montefiasco, and a seductress who was to be set at the Prince of Wales. The popish plot misfired because a royal footman, acting as a double agent, transferred to the conspirators poison intended for the King and the Prince. Evelyn acted the part of the dean, F. F. Urquhart, always known in Oxford as 'Sligger', and also that of a minor character, a dissolute lord; John Sutro was the cardinal; Elmley the Lord Chamberlain, and Terence Greenidge took the part of an Anglican clergyman who with the Lord Chamberlain endeavoured to recall the seductress (Elsa Lanchester) to her better self, while falling for her charms. Alec took the part of the cardinal's debauched peasant mother. There was a pursuit sequence acted by Terence and Elsa Lanchester which was filmed in Kensington Gardens and manifestly based on an episode in that ancient classic *Way Down East*.

Arthur Waugh was delighted by this enterprise and willingly lent his house and garden. He enjoyed the results enormously and with a little persuasion would probably have taken a minor part himself. The hostility of the film against Sligger Urquhart, one of the mildest and best loved of Oxford dons, is perhaps due to the fact that at the end of Evelyn's last term Urquhart was believed, probably correctly, to have been urging the proctors to suppress the Hypocrites Club.

The film had a queer history. As is hardly necessary to state, it was never shown in public. It was shown several times privately at Oxford during the Michaelmas term, but only rarely after that, so it became a legend rather than an experience of Evelyn's later friends. Three copies were made. One was much later acquired by the National Film Archive, another was bought by the University of Texas, and the third remained the property of Terence Greenidge. Shortly before the war Evelyn was staying at Campion Hall, the Jesuit house at Oxford. The eminent Jesuit, Cyril Charles Martindale, was in residence at the time and he asked Evelyn about this film of which he had heard rumours. Evelyn told him and Father Martindale became so interested that he insisted that he must see it. Evelyn was embarrassed, but Father Martindale was not easily thwarted. So Evelyn got in touch with Terence Greenidge. The two of them were both nervous that the famous Jesuit might regret his permissive attitude and resent the irreverence bordering on blasphemy which informed the whole work, but he had insisted, so a showing was arranged. The fears of Terence and Evelyn were groundless. Not only did Father Martindale enjoy the film so much that he laughed till his tears flowed, but to add to the jest he took it upon himself to issue under his signature on the official form the *imprimatur* or official licence of the Roman Catholic Church that the work might be shown anywhere as it contained no matter pernicious or dangerous to the faithful, or likely to lead them into error. The completed form was duly photographed by a motion camera and added to the work. It follows that *The Scarlet Woman* must be the only film in the world that can boast this august permission or whose opening caption begins with the impressive words 'Nihil Obstat'.

This is to run ahead.

The part of Evelyn's life following his departure from Oxford in the summer of 1924 is very fully recorded in his diaries which were adumbrated in masterly fashion in his autobiography. To give a detailed account is unnecessary for two further reasons. First, that for the most part the diaries, the main source of information, are tedious as only a young man's boastful record of continual drunkenness can be. Second, that the record is especially suspect at this point. For example, allegations of homosexuality are abundant, often with reason, but in some cases with reference to people who only incurred censure for heterosexual excesses. There is a good deal of smart scandal-mongering for its own sake and without the excuse of a basis in truth. But what is interesting in the diaries at this moment is not the dubious chronicle but the ultimate impression of a young generation who felt hysterical and hopeless, an impression which was to serve Evelyn as what Henry James called 'convertible literary stuff' after circumstances had forced him to retire for a while from the rakish world and look at it from a distance. But all that still lay in the future.

After the delights of *The Scarlet Woman* he entered into the dismal period in earnest. His closest friend, Alastair Graham, left on 18 September 1924 for Africa where he had been offered openings which led to nothing. Evelyn celebrated the departure by buying and wearing a mourning ring.

He went with his friend to the boat, and his diary for that day contains a poignant record of how on returning to London he spent the day wandering about aimlessly to console himself for his loss. He makes it evident that he felt friendless and alone. On 22 September he commenced student at the Heatherley School of Fine Art.

The experience was disillusioning. He wrote in his diary: 'The whole place is full of girls – underbred houris, most of them – in gaudy overalls; they draw very badly and get much in the way of the youths who seem to be all of them bent on making commercial careers for themselves by illustrating Punch or advertising things. It does not seem to me likely that I shall find any pals among them.'

Nor did he. But he did not waste his time. He acquired yet more 'convertible literary stuff'. He acquired something yet more valuable: the knowledge that he was not a draughtsman, even if he was 'by no means the worst in the class'. He made his discovery through the fact that he suffered boredom. He wrote in his autobiography: 'I enjoyed making an agreeable arrangement of line and shadow on the paper, but was totally lacking in that obsession with solid form, the zeal for probing the structure of anatomy and for relating to one another the recessions of planes, which alone could make the long hours before the models exciting.'

It has been noted already that in this grim period our hero's fortunes did not sink quite so low as Evelyn later remembered. He says in his autobiography that his twenty-first birthday in October 1924 was not celebrated. The diaries tell a different story. His father cancelled his son's debt to him and made him a present of money. All his family gave him gifts. The 28th did not pass in cold-shouldering reproach. But Evelyn had by now made his self-discovery at the Art School and it was not one to make him happy. He was as miserable as he had ever been. After one term he left Heatherley's.

He found comfort in a rather surprising direction. He began to build fresh hopes on his old hobby and what he had learned from Francis Crease. He thought he saw his future as the designer of exquisite lettering for printing. He and Alastair Graham, before the latter's departure for Africa, 'had often projected a private printing press on which we hoped to produce books which I should decorate and sometimes write'. Such 'prestige' or 'quality' presses were far more common then than they are today. Evelyn went to exhibitions of printing and at one found what he took to be the work of a master.

He made contact with the master whose house and press were in Sussex, and on 19 December he went down to visit him as a prospective apprentice. He had been provisionally accepted, and Arthur Waugh had paid the master a deposit of £25. The visit was a disappointment to Evelyn. 'The cottage', he related in his autobiography, 'which gave the press its romantic name was a modern villa.' But worse than this the secret process whose results had so impressed him turned out to be a photographic one. A strong impression is allowed in *A Little Learning* that the master was a fraud through whom Evelyn saw without difficulty. Again the diaries tell a different story, and so does Evelyn's correspondence. In the first he merely indicates that the apprenticeship plan might be less pleasing in reality than it had appeared in prospect. But the correspondence shows that Evelyn continued to propose some sort of collaboration with the master and even to do some block-making for him till as late as March 1925.

Before meeting the master Evelyn had taken another initiative in search of employment. Through the Truman and Knightley Educational Trust he applied for an appointment as a schoolmaster in a preparatory school, a few days before his first meeting with the printer. This was not double dealing but due to the fact that, not having had an answer for a long time from the printer, he assumed that he was not interested in Evelyn's proposal, and Evelyn knew that an application for a teaching post, to be accepted quickly, had to be made before the end of the Christmas holidays. He was in great need of money because he had incurred new debts. On 12 November 1924 he had returned to Oxford at the invitation of John Sutro and had been feasted by his cronies. From this day in November, so he recorded in *A Little Learning*, 'I can date my decline accurately'. As a result he renewed his Oxford life.

Among Evelyn's closest friends were the Plunket-Greene family. He first met them through two brothers, Richard and David Plunket-Greene. The younger, David, had come up in Evelyn's last year, and their meeting-place was the usual one, the Hypocrites Club. Through them he met their mother, a daughter of Sir Hubert Parry, and their sister, Olivia Plunket-Greene. The mother, Gwen Greene, took to Evelyn and made him part of the family who consoled this period of disillusion and diminishing hope. But he found further perturbation of the spirit here too, for in December 1924 Evelyn fell deeply in love with Olivia Greene. This love persisted long and was never forgotten by Evelyn, but it was never returned. Evelyn discovered why: partly because her profound religious vein under her superficial appearance of reckless gaiety made her hate Evelyn's frivolous ideas about sex; partly because she found him physically repulsive. The relationship was a tortured one and even at the end, nearly thirty-three years later, it was not an easy one. Evelyn said in his auto-biography that he found it very difficult to describe her, and others who knew her well and loved her have found the same. He told of 'a peculiar fastidiousness, which did not prevent her from saying and doing out-rageous things, but preserved her essential delicacy quite intact'. He con-cluded: 'She nagged and bullied at times, she suffered from morbid self-consciousness, she was incapable of the ordinary arts and efforts of pleasing and was generally incapable of any kind of ostentation; a little crazy; truth-loving and in the end holy.'

Evelyn's application for a schoolmastership resulted in an encouraging reply from Denbighshire. He was requested to meet a headmaster who might employ him. The appointment was for 5 January 1925 at the Berners Hotel. It was a day of great surprises. Just as Evelyn was about to leave home for the hotel, Alastair Graham arrived unannounced from Africa, dishevelled and starving. He was invited to stay at Underhill, but Evelyn could not remain to welcome his friend. He went to the Berners Hotel where he was accepted by the schoolmaster. He recorded that evening: 'He is going to pay me £160 to teach little boys for him for a year. I think this will be bloody but most useful to a man as poor as I.'

The rest of that story is familiar from Evelyn's fiction and his own autobiographical account. Both are highly misleading as to the facts. There is one very odd and hardly explicable misrepresentation in the autobiography. The name of the headmaster is given as Vanhomrigh, and to persuade the reader that this was no invention Evelyn gave an added detail, that Mrs Vanhomrigh liked the name to be pronounced 'Vanummery'. But in fact the name was in no way extraordinary; it was quite unremarkable: Banks. It may be that Evelyn suppressed it so as to avoid needless embarrassment, as he suppressed the real name of 'Captain Grimes'. Both are in the diary and both were published in the extracts printed in *The Observer* in 1973. Perhaps Evelyn suppressed Banks's name with such care because he knew that he had done him an injustice.

Evelyn as a novelist and a self-portrait painter left a lasting impression that he was a complete failure as a schoolmaster, that he was hated by the boys, that the school was a fraudulent place of education, and that he was desperately unhappy. The last item is certainly true. The rest is almost certainly untrue. If we leave Evelyn's accounts aside and try to obtain a disinterested record of him as a pedagogue, a different picture emerges.

One of his pupils at Arnold House, Denbighshire, was the late Derek Verschoyle. I once asked him to give a brief talk on Evelyn the schoolmaster for a BBC radio programme in 1967. Here is what he said:

'Improbable though this may seem, I have a clear and detailed recollection, after forty-two years, of returning to my preparatory school for the spring term in January 1925.

'The school in question, Arnold House, which no longer exists, was an admirable institution in North Wales. The headmaster, Mr Banks, was a scholarly and elegant figure, who was notable among schoolmasters for keeping an excellent table – considerably better than the average Trust House of today. About fifty per cent of the boys came from Ireland, where preparatory schools have always been rather thin on the ground; the remainder came from Cheshire and Lancashire. The Irish boys greatly despised the English and took it out on them in the annual football match between the parties which enlivened St Patrick's day. Lancastrian parents redressed the balance by appearing in smart cars on visiting days, whereas Irish parents had to make do with decrepit taxis from the station.

'The reason why this particular *rentrée des classes* remains in my memory is that during the holidays my parents had received a letter from the headmaster indicating that for grave and familiar reasons three masters had been dismissed. As head of the school I had a particular interest in observing their replacements. Formal introductions to the three new ushers duly took place. Of two of them I retain no recollection whatsoever. The third was Evelyn Waugh.

'I should like to be able to record that my immediate impression was of being in the presence of a man of genius. But truth forces me to admit that what first struck me about him were his clothes, the like of which, coming as I had just done from a western extremity of Ireland, I had never seen before. He was wearing a tweed coat with leather buttons, very full plus fours, and a high-necked jumper over the top of which half an inch of checked shirt protruded. This was the uniform in which he appeared throughout the term from Monday to Friday inclusive. On Saturdays he varied his arrangements by wearing a pair of wide-bottomed flannel trousers. For attending church on Sundays and for dinner at the headmaster's table he wore a neat blue suit – except when there were parents of Irish boys to dine; on these occasions he had to put on a dinner-jacket. No such formality was thought necessary in the case of parents of Lancashire or Cheshire boys.

'Evelyn as a master was not an unpopular figure in this school. The masters who were disliked came from two categories – first those who nagged at their forms and made uncomplimentary reports to the headmaster about those of their charges who did not come up to their expectations And secondly those who were too keen by half about games. Evelyn did not offend against either of these principles. In the matter of academic studies he adopted a policy of live-and-let-live. It could not be said that he made any great formal effort to teach. On the other hand if any child showed curiosity on any specific point he attempted to satisfy it and sometimes succeeded. To those who were at the top of the senior form he extended a degree of tolerance which permitted the study of French novels not on any curriculum during what were in theory history lessons.

'I am happy to be able to record that I was able to extend to him a similar indulgence on a solitary occasion when he was told to give me a lesson on the organ, an instrument with which he was not familiar.

'In the matter of games he was in fact so undistinguished a performer that after a few humorous episodes it was thought better that he should not exercise with the senior boys. He was issued with a whistle and allowed to amble harmlessly around the football field with the ten-year-olds. In the summer term, still wearing his plus fours, he was a reluctant umpire at the cricket games of novices

'The school used to assemble every evening in a large apartment for an hour's preparation work, supervised by one of the junior masters. Most of them used to walk round the room snooping and occasionally proffering aid to those in trouble. When Evelyn was on duty he left the school to its own devices and scribbled busily away on work of his own. He was possibly occupied with his first never completed novel, *The Temple at Thatch*. To any boy impertinent enough to enquire what he was up to he would say that he was writing a History of the Eskimos.'

Verschoyle added that when Evelyn was in charge of communal walks there was much competition to be near him because he diverted the boys with his stories. This is in direct contradiction to Evelyn's own account.

Derek Verschoyle's guess that Evelyn's literary labours in the preparation hour were on *The Temple at Thatch* is unquestionably correct. It was never completed and the first chapters were only read by two people, the author and Harold Acton. Available knowledge of it is only a little less meagre than what we can find out about Shakespeare's *Love's Labour Won*. Harold Acton's impression will be given later, when it is related how he pronounced judgement. Evelyn's own description to Dudley Carew, that it was to be 'all about madness and magic', has been quoted already. When he came to write *A Little Learning* he had but this to say: 'I remember only that it was named *The Temple at Thatch* and concerned an undergraduate who inherited a property of which nothing was left except an eighteenth-century classical folly where he set up house and, I think, practised black magic.'

In March the term drew to an end and Evelyn had reason to feel that his position in the school was precarious. 'Mr Banks', he wrote in his diary, 'frequently expresses himself dissatisfied with the work I am doing – perhaps not without cause.' It also seems possible that he was beginning to lose confidence in *The Temple at Thatch* since, before its abandonment, his attention twice wandered from it to other subjects for a book. The first occasion was on 18 March when he noted: 'I have an idea for a book about Silenus which may or may not ever be written.' It never was.

On the last day of March 1925, or the day after, Evelyn took the train from Llandudno to London for the Easter holidays. He spent a few days quietly with a few friends and his family. On 6 April there occurs an ominous entry in the diary: 'This morning having retired to bed early after a pleasant and porty evening at the Savile with Alec I woke up at three and could not sleep. I wandered about the house in search of " Those Barren Leaves" and when I had found it I just lay awake and considered gravely how very little I have really enjoyed the last three days.'

This is the first mention by him in the diary or elsewhere of insomnia and the mental depression that accompanies it. The malady may have first afflicted him some time before. He was to suffer from it for the rest of his life; indeed, it shortened his life.

Among the friends whom he had rushed to see on his return to London were, of course, the Plunket-Greenes. He soon plunged back into the deep-drinking routine that he had left with sorrow three months before, and in his diary he records himself as almost incessantly drunk, though with intermissions. For example, he tells of going to a matinée with his mother and Olivia Greene to see Jack Buchanan and June in *Boodle* at the Empire, then a theatre. 'Fairly good. To bed early.' But two days later he was arrested with Matthew Ponsonby for drunkenness when in charge of a car and had to appear before a magistrate who fined him fifteen shillings and sixpence.

This adventure had an interesting sequel about which Evelyn heard some details from Billy Clonmore. As a Whig-turned-Socialist and as a suspected agent of the USSR, Matthew's father, Arthur Ponsonby was much disapproved in aristocratic society where he was scorned as a 'traitor to his class'. Matthew Ponsonby's improprieties escaped publicity but not gossip and rumour and as usual both were inaccurate. It was widely repeated in high society that the sedate and serious Arthur Ponsonby had been arrested and, according to Clonmore, his grandmother, the Duchess of Abercorn, was especially distressed to think of the plight of his poor children whose father was not only a shameless revolutionary but was now proved to be a drunkard as well.

The rest of April was spent by Evelyn first on Lundy Island with a party of the Plunket-Greenes and their friends, then with Alastair Graham and his mother, then for a few days at Oxford, and then in London. The record again becomes a tedious chronicle of heavy drinking and tales of bawdy. But during these holidays he found hopes of escape from Arnold House and from a profession which he found uncongenial. Alec learned that C. K. Scott-Moncrieff, whom Evelyn described in his diary as a 'homosexual translator living in Florence', was looking for a secretary, and when Alec told this to Evelyn the latter asked his brother to press his claims. Alec promised to do so but explained that this would take time and advised the other to make no immediate change in his situation. Evelyn knew that his love for Olivia Greene was hopeless, and so, with only remote prospects of rescue, he returned with a leaden heart to North Wales and Mr Banks's establishment. We must rejoice that his hopes were dashed, for otherwise he would never have met Captain Grimes.

Evelyn's fiction and his autobiography have given the world a lurid, detailed and convincing picture of Captain Grimes. One might reasonably expect that the diaries, not so far as is known intended for publication, would contain a truly horrific record of this scienceless pervert and his activities. In fact the diaries have little to tell. Evelyn recorded Grimes's arrival at Arnold House without comment, and then that he (Evelyn) tried to buy a revolver from him. On 14 May he recorded: 'The new usher is monotonously paederastic and talks only of the beauty of sleeping boys.'

On 3 July: 'Grimes and I went out and made ourselves drunk and he confessed all his previous career. He was expelled from Wellington, sent down
from Oxford and forced to resign his commission in the army. He has
left some schools precipitately, three in the middle of the term through his
being taken in Sodomy and one through his being drunk six nights in
succession. And yet he goes on getting better and better jobs without
difficulty. It was all very like Bruce & the spider.'

And that is all.

An entry: 'Yesterday there were the Sports' raises great hopes in a
reader, but nothing of interest follows. Of more significance is an entry:
'I am reading a book of essays by Bertrand Russell. In the meanwhile I
debate the simple paradoxes of suicide and achievement, work out the
scheme for a new book and negotiate with the man Grimes to buy a
revolver from him.' Presumably the revolver was intended for the suicide,
should he decide on it. It seems that the sale did not take place, or Evelyn
would probably have ended his life in Arnold House.

The remark about 'a new book' is of much interest. It marks the second
time that his attention wandered from *The Temple at Thatch* and refers to
an early work which did receive publication a year or so after. A few days
later at the end of May there is another entry on the subject: 'I have quite
suddenly received inspiration about my book. I am making the first
chapter a Cinema film and have been writing furiously ever since. I
honestly think that it is going to be rather good.' It was, in fact, rather
bad.

For a month Evelyn did not keep the diary. It reopens on 1 July 1925,
on a note of unaccustomed joy. Shortly before, he had heard from Alec
that Scott-Moncrieff wished to employ him as his secretary. With this
news he immediately went to Mr Banks and offered his resignation to take
effect at the end of the term. Banks accepted it. Evelyn then later took
Grimes and another master to the public house where they all became
'agreeably drunk'. For a day, so he recorded, he lived in ecstatic anticipation of an idyllic life in Florence. Nor was this his only source of mental
bliss.

He had sent the manuscript of the opening chapters of *The Temple at
Thatch* to Harold Acton, asking for criticism and confident of encouragement and praise.

His new-found bliss proved a mirage. In late June he heard from Harold
Acton who with his customary politeness, endeavouring, so far as he
could, to spare the other pain, told him that *The Temple at Thatch* was
rubbish. He expressed himself thus: 'Too English for my exotic taste. Too
much nid-nodding over port. It should be printed in a few elegant copies
for the friends who love you.' On relating this episode in *A Little Learning*,
Evelyn said: 'I did not then, nor do I now, dispute his judgement. I took
the exercise book in which the chapters were written and consigned it to

63

the furnace of the school boiler.' It was a hard blow and it may be significant that, though Evelyn kept all his letters from Harold Acton, this particular letter is missing from the collection.

Soon after came more bad news. On the last day of June he heard, probably from Alec, that Scott-Moncrieff had decided not to employ him. He believed that he could not withdraw his resignation as Mr Banks had seemed only too pleased to accept it. He was without resources.

Soon after this Evelyn attempted suicide. Having failed, presumably, to buy Grimes's pistol, he went down to the beach with the intention of drowning himself. In the autobiography he gave details of the dignified pathos with which he contrived to surround the tragedy, and of how he was surprised out of his plan by a jelly-fish. The reader of the diaries may be surprised to find no mention of this episode.


When Evelyn ended his autobiography with the scene on the shore, he concluded with these words: 'Then I climbed the sharp hill that led to all the years ahead.'

This suggests a break in his life. There was one, but as is frequent in any life, the transition from one phase to another was not sudden but came about gradually and untidily: he remained a schoolmaster for another year and a half while his fortunes sank lower.

On 27 July 1925 Evelyn left Arnold House for good. 'After some few valedictory discourtesies,' he recorded the day after, 'Mr Banks let me go early yesterday morning.' He must have thought, poor man, that he had seen and heard the last of Evelyn Waugh.

Arrived home in London, Evelyn, after making contact with his friends, set about finding himself new employment. He applied for work to directors of art galleries and editors of art magazines without success. His insomnia grew worse. Then there filtered through the gloom a ray of light.

Olivia Greene's eldest brother Richard was a junior master at a school at Aston Clinton in Buckinghamshire, and he told Evelyn that the headmaster was looking for another junior. To return to schoolmastering accorded ill with Evelyn's hopes, but to undergo the ordeal with a friend, and near London, seemed an immense improvement on what he had endured at Arnold House. So he applied. On 13 August he heard at Underhill that he had been accepted. The news came 'just before Richard and Elizabeth [Russell] and Olivia and Alastair came for dinner. It should have made the party a jolly one but somehow it did not – as far as I was concerned anyway. I was tired, and ill at ease, as I usually am with Olivia, and my father's jollity seemed more than usually distressing. The dinner at any rate was good.'

During August Evelyn finished the book about which he had 'quite suddenly received inspiration' in May. It did not, in fact, turn out to be a book but a 'long short story'. He gave it a title, *The Balance*, and arranged for it to be typed. 'It is odd,' he noted, 'but I think quite good.'

When it came back from the typist he sent it to Leonard Woolf on 18 September, hoping for publication by the Hogarth Press which specialized in very short books. Six days later on Thursday 24 September Evelyn drove with Richard Greene and his fiancée Elizabeth Russell to Aston Clinton, 'all three of us', recorded Evelyn, 'deeply depressed'. After a 'wretched dinner' in the school, 'Elizabeth drove back to London & left us to a house of echoing and ill lit passages & a frightful common room'. On the next day he listened to the headmaster's speech to the boys, delivered 'in a most unattractive & affected manner'. He was shown round the grounds by Richard Greene 'rather dismally'. The next day he 'began to be a little more at home in this frightful school'.

Aston Clinton was more of a 'crammer' establishment than an ordinary school. It specialized in teaching 'backward boys' incapable of passing the necessary examinations to the universities. Evelyn usually described his charges as 'the lunatics' or 'the mad boys'. A typical entry begins 'Taught lunatics. Played Rugby football. Drank at Bell [the local inn].' Except for his conviction that his charges were mentally deficient, this closely resembles the routine diary entries made at Arnold House, but the proximity of London and his Oxford friends soon made his life more eventful.

There are significant entries for 28 and 29 September 1925. His cousin Claud Cockburn sometimes visited him from Oxford, and sometimes from his family home at Tring. One result was one of the few literary entries for this time. 'Claud lent me a novel by Virginia Wolf [*sic*]', he wrote on the 28th, adding 'which I refuse to believe is good.' He was probably referring to *Mrs Dalloway* which came out in this year and was widely acclaimed at the time. By a remarkable irony he heard on the next day from Virginia Woolf's husband who returned the typescript of *The Balance*. Evelyn had sent a second copy to a literary agent. The latter likewise rejected and returned it and it too arrived back on the 29th. There is no evidence from the diaries that Evelyn was greatly distressed by this double blow. But it may possibly explain his return to the life of debauchery which was geographically available to him at Aston Clinton as it had not been at Arnold House.

The diary is very dreary reading during most of this autumn term. It is again a long monotonous record of drunkenness and drunken quarrels, of vomitings, hangovers and so on, only rarely enlivened by a touch of wit. There is one rather surprising passage where Evelyn records how in a public house he and his friends fell in with a young man who attached himself to their party, and how the young man bored them with his boastful accounts of his heavy drinking. Evelyn seemed quite unaware that in his diary he was depicting himself as precisely that kind of person. Then suddenly the diary becomes interesting.

On Saturday, 7 November the school dispersed for a long leave weekend and Evelyn went with Richard Greene and Elizabeth Russell to Oxford, the scene of most of the wild parties he went to. Early in the weekend he had a fall from a window in the Clarendon Hotel and sprained his ankle badly. He returned to London where he had to spend three days on a sofa in his father's 'frightful house'. There he began to think about the pre-Raphaelites. 'I want to write a book about them', he noted on Wednesday the 11th. On the 13th he returned to his duties at Aston Clinton, but was still obliged to lie all day on a sofa. He recorded on Saturday, 14 November:

'The Pre-Raphaelites still absorb me. I think I can say without affectation that during this last week I have lived with them night & day. Early in the morning with Holman Hunt – the only pre-Raphaelite – untiring, fearless, conscientious. Later in the day with Millais – never with *him* but with my biography of him – a modish Lytton Strachey biography. How he shines through Holman Hunt's local picture of him. Later when firelight & rum & loneliness have done their worst, with Rossetti, soaked in chloral & Philip Marston's "Why is he not some great exiled King, that we might give our lives in trying to restore him to his Kingdom?" '

Then the pre-Raphaelites were forgotten till the summer of the next year. In the meantime he returned to the life which the sprained ankle had interrupted. Again, for the most part, the diary has little interest except for those who enjoy the kind of boastful talk of drunkenness which so bored Evelyn in the case of the young man at the pub. But there are one or two gleams for those who know Evelyn's books. David Greene had become engaged to a young woman whose stepfather was a man of great wealth. The diary records how on 25 November she 'came down in a motor-car called a Phantom Rolls Royce . . . She lives in an opulent house in Grosvenor Square' . . . Why is there something familiar about this visit to a school by a rich beauty in a Rolls-Royce? The answer is Mrs Best-Chetwynde, better known as Lady Metroland.

In the Christmas holidays, in the last week of 1925, Evelyn with a new friend made his first visit to Paris. It seems to have been a dismal experience. It poured with rain the whole time. They ate and drank to excess. On their second evening they visited a homosexual brothel which specialized in 'petits enfants'. Evelyn and his friend proposed that one youth, dressed as an Egyptian girl, should be subjected to sodomy by a Negro, but the enterprise was abandoned as the fee demanded was beyond their means. Evelyn eventually left the brothel by himself. He noted: 'I took a taxi home & to bed in chastity. I think I do not regret it.' The next day was spent in more serious pursuits. Evelyn walked round the neighbourhood of St Sulpice and paid his first visit to the Louvre. He declared the

Winged Victory to be 'superb' but dismissed the Venus of Milo as 'very competent'. Among the paintings he 'soon got very tired of the Le Bruns & Le Soeurs et Cie and even a little glutted with Poussin', but he became an enthusiast for Philippe de Champaigne. The Mantegnas he pronounced 'excellent'. He had nothing to say about Leonardo da Vinci. After four days they returned.

'I hear', he wrote in his diary shortly after reaching home, 'that they are talking of starting a new year. I hope that it will be more of a success than the last.' 1926 cannot be said to have marked a high point of British success in the world, but it was eventful and it showed some development of Evelyn's career.

The Lent term of 1926 followed much the same pattern as the one before with visits to him from friends and visits by him to Oxford, the record as before filled with accounts of drunkenness. There was one big difference. Richard Greene who was now married had left for a better appointment as music teacher at Lancing where Evelyn visited them. Before leaving for Sussex, Richard Greene had given Evelyn a motor bicycle. Hereafter the diary has many accounts of mechanical breakdowns on his journeys.

On 14 March he was driven up to London by Richard Greene and his wife 'in their red car'. His aim was to see Olivia Greene again and he 'sat on her bed for some time trying to talk to her with my heart sinking & sinking'. The entry ends on a note which may excite curiosity: 'I returned by train more depressed than I have been for some weeks. On the way back I thought of a novel to write – but doubtless I shall do nothing of the sort.' Was this the origin of *Decline and Fall*?

If it was, his inventiveness may have been stimulated by two visits to him by an old acquaintance on 26 March and 1 April. His visitor was Captain Grimes. On the first occasion 'We lunched at The Bell and went to see the children at football', where Grimes fell in love with one of the younger boys. Of the second visit Evelyn recorded: 'Grimes of Denbighshire came down and was rather a bore – drunk all the time. He seduced a garage boy in the hedge.'

He spent the first part of the Easter holidays, which began on 12 April, in the demure society of his aunts at Midsomer Norton. He went down 'through rather lovely country' as soon as he was free. 'Since then', he recorded, 'I have read out-of-date novels in shabby easy chairs & listened to my aunts' condemnation of everything they know nothing about.' The spring of 1926 was the time of the General Strike.

When it eventually broke out in May, Alec was enrolled as a Special Constable, and Evelyn, after some days at Aston Clinton where, in the circumstances, only a few boys had arrived for the summer term, enrolled as a despatch rider, and then later as a reserve Special Constable. He seems to have spent most of his hours being called up for duty, and then told to go away and to report later, a routine with which he and many others became familiar when a greater conflict began thirteen years later.

In July Alastair Graham returned to England from a journey to Turkey, and he came down to Aston Clinton, staying a few days at the Bell. This visit led Evelyn to a further step on the still hidden path, as it was to him, towards the destined realization of his abilities. Graham had achieved the ambition that he had once shared with Evelyn: he now had a printing press. He wanted Evelyn to write something for him, and Evelyn suggested an essay on 'The Pre-Raphaelite Brotherhood'. They agreed, and under that title Evelyn wrote an essay which Alastair Graham printed. Evelyn could write the essay quickly as he had done his research in that period of intense study while convalescing. His father read the essay with much approval.

When the summer holidays came at the end of July 1926 he went with Alastair Graham and the latter's mother, a formidable lady who had doubts about Evelyn as a suitable person to be her son's closest friend, on a tour of Scotland. They spent most of their travels in visiting the country houses of Mrs Graham's friends. His diaries at this point have some nice touches, and internal evidence strongly suggests that the stuff of this experience of Scots country house life was converted into literary form twenty-eight years later when he came to write of the Isle of Mugg in *Officers and Gentlemen*. On the party's return to Barford, Mrs Graham turned on Evelyn and upbraided him for consistent rudeness during the trip. He recorded his innocence and bewilderment. Not usually but often he was surprised at having angered others by his behaviour.

The Scots journey was followed by a French one. Evelyn and Alastair Graham spent two days in Paris, then made the classic tour of the châteaux of the Loire. It was by now early September. These famous castles did not excite Evelyn's admiration. He had no word of praise for any of them, and a few expressive of boredom. The last they saw was Chambord, 'a monstrous building with what the book on Touraine calls " a dream city" on its roof'. More surprising than this is the entry a few days later on Chartres Cathedral. In later years Evelyn was to regard Chartres as the greatest work of architecture in the whole of Europe. In September 1926 all he had to say of his first impression was: 'The whole building crowded – people selling ginger bread pigs, little children pissing on the pillars, women asleep – gossiping and eating, and innumerable little processions with veils & candles and a good deal of money taking.' That is all.

Evelyn's schoolmastering at Aston Clinton during the autumn term involved no incident that illuminates his life or character. He suffered the misery attaching to debts, frequent drunkenness and frequent hangovers, but he was not as miserable as he allowed his friends to believe later.

There is positive evidence for this. A year or more after this time a recent Oxford friend, John Betjeman, was a junior master at a school in

Barnet, where according to a BBC recording he made for me, he 'was teaching the bottom form in football and cricket and divinity and things like that'. In the same recording John Betjeman told how Evelyn (no longer at Aston Clinton) used to visit him, and how the two of them had lunch together at a Barnet hotel where they drank 'a lot of very strong beer, and I was so drunk when I came back that I wasn't able to take the game of football, and the boys kindly took me up to my room and never said anything about it. That was the effect Evelyn had on my schoolmastering, the only one I remember. But he felt that just being a schoolmaster was rockingly funny, and I remember him telling me, when I was offered a job on *The Architectural Review*: "Don't take it. You'll never laugh as much as you do now." And he was quite right, of course.'

This evidence must be qualified by Evelyn's own account of the incident in *A Little Learning*: 'A young friend of mine, Mr John Betjeman, served his turn as a private schoolmaster. I visited him at his place of bondage and said, not entirely facetiously: "You will remember these schooldays as the happiest time of your life", but in my case there was no happiness; merely hilarity.'

Back to autumn 1926.

In October he received the proofs of his essay on 'The Pre-Raphaelite Brotherhood' and *The Balance* was published. The last event came about in the following way. Influenced by the example of Edward Marsh's publications of *Georgian Poetry* which had great effect on the taste of the time Arnold Lunn decided in 1921 to attempt something of the same kind in prose. The publishers were Chapman and Hall. After the first two numbers he lost interest in the venture, and the third number, of October 1926, was edited by Alec Waugh. He included *The Balance* which caused more comment than any other contribution, not, it may safely be asserted, on account of its merits or faults (which will be discussed later) but because it was the most *avant-garde*. Evelyn thus enjoyed some literary success from his first public appearance, and it says much for his judgement that he was not deceived by this heady experience. 'A very silly review', he wrote in his diary, 'in the Manchester Guardian this morning commends my contribution to Georgian Stories highly, but for the most futile reasons.'

At this time Kegan Paul were publishing a humorous series on the future, of which the most remarked was *Lars Porsena, or the Future of Swearing*, by Robert Graves. On the strength of his success with *The Balance*, Evelyn wrote to the publishers to suggest himself as the author of *Noah, or the Future of Intoxication*. The publishers welcomed the proposition but did not accept the finished article. No copy of it seems to have survived. At the time, Evelyn described it as 'mannered and literary'.

When the holidays came Evelyn did some more travelling. Alastair Graham had found employment as an honorary attaché to the British

Legation in Athens, the head of mission being Sir Percy Loraine in whose employment Graham was to spend some years. Evelyn left early on Christmas Eve, two days after Francis Crease arrived, at Mrs Waugh's invitation, to spend the holiday at Underhill.

He travelled by the swiftest route to Marseilles where he caught a boat to Brindisi, and thence to Athens where he stayed with Alastair Graham in the flat which he shared with another member of Sir Percy Loraine's legation, Leonard Bower. His visit seems to have been spent in dreary and drunken adventures in the Athenian underworld.

He mentioned that he went to the Acropolis but said nothing about it. The only sign of appreciation of the ancient glories of Athens to be found in the diaries is a reference to the 'very beautiful church of Daphne, full of mosaics'. This is the famous Byzantine church whose dome contains perhaps the finest mosaic picture in the world, representing Christ as the ruler of the Cosmos. The impression of a neglect of classical Greece in favour of an interest in the Byzantines probably reflects the influence of his Oxford friend Robert Byron who had preceded Evelyn to Greece shortly before. Robert's journey resulted in his first book, *Europe through the Looking Glass,* and the beginning of his lifelong devotion to Byzantine art and history which, typically of his pugnacity, involved a violent reaction against all Greek art of classical antiquity.

On the whole Evelyn got little pleasure from his journey to Athens. On 5 January he left intending to visit Delphi and Olympia, then to go to Brindisi and Rome before returning to England, but the boat did not follow its advertised course so Evelyn never saw Delphi, though he did go to Olympia, reaching it by train. On the way 'a Greek gave me his card & said he would write to me because he loved the English'. During the last part of this train journey 'a young man opposite me in a bow tie talked excellent French and advised me to go to the Hotel du Chemin de Fer. After a very long time I realized that he was a waiter – or else the son of the house – I have not yet discovered, and that he had been marketing & that the fowl, alive, under his arm, was for my dinner.' He followed the advice of the young man in the bow-tie and did not regret it. He found himself in a large hotel, such as was doubtless crowded in summer, as the sole guest.

Whether or not Robert Byron had tried to implant his own ridiculous antipathies in Evelyn's mind, they fell away in Olympia. 'After luncheon', he recorded, 'I went to see the Hermes of Praxiteles which is kept in a separate shed [from the Museum] in charge of the village idiot, embedded in concrete before a gray plush curtain. It is quite marvellous & well worth all the trouble I have taken to see it.'

On 8 January he left for the journey to Brindisi and Rome, reaching Italy on the 10th.

His reactions to Rome were traditional. He took a cab to St Peter's, and 'on the way every corner showed something beautiful. I gaped like any peasant at the size of St Peter's – how bad the frescoes are compared with those at Daphne. I climbed to the highest point of the dome. I lunched at a small restaurant opposite St Peter's. From there I took a cab to the Forum & enjoyed myself shamelessly marching about with a guide book identifying the various ruins.' He went to the principal monuments of Rome on a Cook's personally conducted tour and thus to the Vatican Museum. One may be reminded of Pugin on reading in the diary: 'The Sistine Chapel is disappointing. The roof is magnificent but the Last Judgement has lost all its colouring & has been repainted with a very weak blue. It does not seem to me as perfectly composed as I had expected. The great islands of figures seemed rather unsatisfactory.'

On 15 January he reached home 'very dirty and very hungry'. He spent a week resting, a rare thing with him then, and on the 24th he returned to Aston Clinton. He found a new colleague of whom he wrote: 'I at first conceived an intense dislike which has begun to soften a little. He is dull-looking with a small moustache, cheap and tidy clothes and – usually – boots.'

There was another new arrival, 'an admirable new matron who was at one time dame at Goodharts [a house in Lancing] & knew several of my friends there'. This admirable new matron was to be the cause of disaster to Evelyn.

As recorded in a previous chapter, Evelyn lost his religious faith at school but recognized that this was probably 'a phase'. Occasional remarks in the diary show that the loss was not absolute. On a few occasions he mentions going to Communion, the last time being in York Minster after the tour to Scotland. In the Lent term of 1927 at Aston Clinton he returned to his early wish to take Holy orders. He got in touch with a High Church clergyman. This coincided with other events whose juxtaposition was vividly conveyed by Evelyn. 'Next Thursday', to quote the diary for 26 February, 'I am to visit a Father Underhill about being a parson. Last night I was very drunk. How odd those two sentences seem together. About five minutes after I wrote the last sentence, while we [Evelyn and the new usher] were sitting over the fire laughing about our drunkenness of the night before, Crawford [the headmaster] suddenly arrived and sacked us both, me to leave immediately on the spot . . . Apparently that matron had been making trouble.'

Then and afterwards Evelyn was unclear in his mind as to what offence he had committed. Crawford accused him of assaulting the matron in French, which suggests either drunken rudeness or an attempt on her virtue. He did not defend himself. He left the next morning 'feeling rather like a housemaid who has been caught stealing gloves'. He went home 'and dined in a very sorrowful household'. The entry for the next day concludes with the words: 'It seems to me the time has arrived to set about being a man of letters.' Evelyn's serious career as a writer did in fact begin in 1927, but after some delay.

He had some encouragement. As a result of his success with *The Balance* he was invited by the editor of *The New Decameron* to contribute a story and so he 'spent two days writing a story about a Duke'. As it is never mentioned again it may be presumed that though it was accepted and paid for, it was not published. His desire to enter the Anglican priesthood received a decisive check. 'I went to tea with a person called Father Underhill who spoke respectfully of the Duke of Westminster & disrespectfully of my vocation to the Church.' A few days later he obtained another appointment as a schoolmaster.

On 7 March he wrote in his diary as follows: 'The School in Notting Hill is quite awful. All the masters drop their aitches & spit in the fire and scratch their genitals. The boys have close cropped heads & steel rimmed spectacles wound about with worsted. They pick their noses & scream at each other in a Cockney accent. For the first three days I had nothing to do but "invigilate" while one of the urchins did an exam. Since then I have been turned on to some coaching.'

He had the consolation of knowing that the term was more than half over and that he had only been engaged for that term. A little before the last quoted entry he had obtained an introduction to the editor of the *Daily Express* who agreed to employ him at £4 a week for a trial period of three weeks when the term ended. 'I don't know how much I shall like that,' he wrote in his diary, 'but it will be worth trying.'

Thus in April 1927 his career as a schoolmaster came to an end.

# Chapter 5

## 1927-1928

On 7 April 1927, when Evelyn was free to start afresh, he was not sure which way to go. 'I am in doubt', he wrote in his diary, 'whether to go on the Express or write a biography that Duckworth show some interest in.' Since its appearance at the end of 1926, the privately printed book on the pre-Raphaelite Brotherhood had come to the notice of Duckworth and they had been sufficiently impressed to propose to Evelyn a biography of Rossetti. This might have tempted him more had it not been for the fact that a month or so before, Sacheverell Sitwell, hearing that Evelyn was going to work on the *Express*, wrote to Beverley Baxter, then the managing editor, to commend Evelyn to his special care. It seemed that he would start with some unusual advantage.

Evelyn's career as a journalist in the employment of Lord Beaverbrook forms a blank and an enigma in his life. He said little about it at any time. There is no mention of it in any of his letters of 1927, and there is a gap in the diaries between 7 April and 23 May except for one short entry as follows:

'May the Ninth. I am just starting on my fifth week on "The Express".

'Duckworths commissioned the Rossetti biography and gave me £20 on the spot which I spent in a week. Since then I have made no money except the five pounds a week they pay me in Shoe Lane. I find the work most exhilarating tho' much of it is just sitting about in the office – noisy & at the present time very hot.

'A charming girl called Inez Holden works on the paper.'

Evidently he found his labours at the *Express* office so light that he felt confident that he could write the Rossetti biography in his spare time. Any doubts or anxiety he may have felt on that account were laid to rest on 23 May. His diary entry for that day began: 'I have got the sack from the Express and am looking forward to a holiday.' He wrote nothing, or nothing that was published under his name, for the paper. But his time had not been wasted in the office. Here without doubt was the origin of Lord Monomark and *The Daily Excess*, and though birth was distant Lord Copper had been conceived, with his immortal newspaper, *The Daily Beast*.

The entry on 7 April contains one passage of significance: 'I have met such a nice girl called Evelyn Gardiner [*sic*] & renewed friendship with Peter Quennell & Robert Byron.' Evelyn Gardner was the daughter of Lord Burghclere, a once prominent Liberal politician who had died about five years before. How Evelyn Waugh first met her is not recorded, nor does his correspondence and diary indicate how much he kept up the acquaintance during that summer. But the acquaintance was easily maintained as Evelyn Gardner was sharing a flat with Lady Pansy Pakenham, the sister of Lord Longford (elder brother of the present Lord Longford), with whom Evelyn Waugh had made friends at Oxford. Evelyn also met her with Dudley Carew who was now making some reputation as a novelist. On 23 May he noted: 'There have been some parties – rather a pleasing little one by Evelyn Gardner & Pansy Pakenham in Ebury Street.' A week later he took Evelyn Gardner to lunch at the new Green Park Hotel. This was in fact his last day as an employee of the *Daily Express*, and he was still available for service as a reporter. As such he was given an assignment by the editor after this lunch. He 'attended a fire in Soho where an Italian girl was supposed to have been brave but had actually done nothing at all'. (Was Evelyn a victim of that fundamental Press Law 'Unstory Unjob'?) The entry continues to relate that he 'then went off with Inez Holden' to a cinema and a round of drinks. If there was courtship by Evelyn Waugh of Evelyn Gardner, it was rudimentary and tepid at this stage. The diaries have more mention of Inez Holden.

There is a gap in the diary from 23 May till 21 July 1927, by which time he had 'finished about 12,000 words of the book on Rossetti without much difficulty. I think it will be fairly amusing. There are to be several other books about him next year unfortunately.' The next year was to mark the centenary of Rossetti's birth in 1828.

In the meantime he had taken a month's holiday in the South of France with his parents and Alec, whom he saw on to a boat at Marseilles setting out on one of his many journeys. When Evelyn returned he spent the last part of July and the beginning of August in the familiar round of London parties and there is a suggestion, in the wording rather than in any assertion, that he was beginning to sicken of these gaieties which he had first rapturously enjoyed in 'The Kingdom of Cockayne'. The Plunket-Greenes took a sudden enthusiastic interest in Negro dancers and musicians and Evelyn found himself living much of his time with the Plunket-Greenes in this world, listening perforce to loud Negro music which he enjoyed no more than any other kind. Alastair Graham came to London and Evelyn recorded a 'tedious and debauched night'.

On 13 August he fled from this debilitating life and took a room in the Abingdon Arms at Beckley near Oxford. He worked hard at his book and by the 23rd had written 40,000 words of it. He recorded that he felt easier in his mind about it. 'I think it is quite amusing in parts.'

74

He went into Oxford on most days and continued his researches into the pre-Raphaelites in the Union Library. The city and university were suffering from the emptiness of the Long Vacation, when the crowds of fellows, students and undergraduates are exchanged for crowds, much smaller then than now, of American and other tourists. But in the wilderness of Long Vac Oxford there are always a few stay-behinds from the great emigration. Evelyn found Billy Clonmore in residence 'studying to be a parson'.

It is evident from the diaries that Beckley had been the scene of many of Evelyn's outings in his undergraduate days. He mentions that 'the central figure nowadays seems to be a scorbutic baronet'. Of this person he noted: 'He keeps arriving in a rather smart car with hosts of disreputable men and stands drinks all round and makes jokes. He is just the sort of man whom Chris [Hollis] & I would have adored four years ago. I must say I find him rather a bore when I want to work. Besides I have lost the capacity for swilling down pint after pint of watery beer. How priggish all that looks.'

The road from Beckley to Oxford passes through Marston and Evelyn often called on his old master, Francis Crease. He found him 'particularly charming & witty in a way I had forgotten'. As a result of these meetings Evelyn found himself with an additional literary commitment. Francis Crease had decided to publish a selection of his decorative designs from a private printing press. Evelyn agreed to write a preface. In *A Little Learning* he says that he did this at Crease's request, and this may easily be correct, but Crease's few letters to Evelyn of 1927 suggest, perhaps inaccurately and artfully, that the initiative came not from him but from Evelyn. It may have come from both through discussion.

Evelyn wrote the preface at the beginning of October 1927 and it pleased Francis Crease. The folio was printed in the next year. Evelyn expressed himself, by his own admission, in terms of greater enthusiasm than he then felt. He led off with resounding praise: 'Only one man could have suitably undertaken to write a preface for this collection of temperate and exalted designs; that is John Ruskin.'

In the meantime Evelyn's life had become varied and precarious once more. He soon grew impatient of the tranquillity of Beckley, and when he heard that the scorbutic baronet was coming to stay at the Abingdon Arms he decided to forget his quarrel with Mrs Graham and go to Barford. 'I feel somehow', he noted at the end of August, 'that with those first three chapters my work at Beckley is over and I must go somewhere else'. He left for Barford and, so far as appears, did not return to Beckley till he went there for his honeymoon, nearly a year later. He strove on with his biography of Rossetti, at Barford and then at Underhill. There is no indication as to when he finished it but it would seem that he did so in November. On 9 September he had visited one of the last survivors among Rossetti's acquaintance, Sir Hall Caine. 'He received me in bed at the top of many flights of stairs. He wore a white woollen dressing gown & looked like a Carthusian Abbot. Enormously vain & theatrical, but more genial & humorous than I had expected. He told me a lot of really profitable things about Rossetti & Fanny Cornforth & Lizzie's suicide & C. A. Holme.' A month or so later Evelyn went to Kelmscott with Alastair Graham. He stated that one of the then inhabitants of this pre-Raphaelite shrine was a hermaphrodite. He was always liable to entertain, or pretend to entertain, odd suspicions regarding the sex of people he met. This visit to Kelmscott seems to have been his last piece of pre-Raphaelite research.

Early on in the period while he was finishing his book, Evelyn had had to face again the problem of finding employment and earning a competence. On 30 August he had noted: 'Saw a bloke about a job', but as there is no further reference to the matter, the bloke presumably decided against him. On 7 September he noted: 'I saw a woman at Golders Green about a singularly repulsive job which I think I shall have to take', but again there is no further reference. On Monday, 18 September, 'having got some money out of my father', he went to Aston Clinton and stayed at the Bell. 'They seem genuinely pleased to see me here', he wrote in his diary, 'and it is very comfortable and quiet. Before leaving I applied for a fantastic job about tooth brushes which I don't suppose will come to anything.' His guess was correct. Tooth brushes were to play no part in his professional life.

He was earning a little money by reviewing books for *The Bookman* (unconnected with the present *Books and Bookmen*), but he did not yet see himself as a writer, and this is odd at this point for the answer to his desperate quest for employment had for some weeks been staring him in the face. For all this time, undistracted by finishing Rossetti, by his insomnia (frequently referred to), by his continuing social life which included several heavy drinking parties a week, and while seeking employment, he was writing *Decline and Fall*. By the last week of September he had written 20,000 words of it. He gave little sign of his own feelings, either of confidence or the opposite, in what he wrote in his diary. It may be that he looked on it as no more than a *jeu d'esprit* never to be repeated. At all events he did not see himself as a novelist first and foremost by profession. He abandoned the search for employment and decided instead to equip himself thoroughly for a profession in which he would then excel, but the profession he chose was not a literary one. On 17 October he called at the Academy of Carpentry in Southampton Row. He was received by 'a very rude secretary and an amiable principal and arranged to go to a great many classes'. He was sure that he had found his true vocation. He started work at the Academy on the next day. He worked hard and with enjoyment.

The diary is not very informative for the next few weeks. He fell ill, but not seriously, towards the end of October when the following entry occurs: 'Sunday. Feeling a little less ill I went to church in Margaret Street where I was discomposed to observe Tom Driberg's satanic face in the congregation. He told me he was starving but would not come to luncheon. It is so like *Sinister Street*, meeting school friends at Mass. I gave him a penny.' Tom Driberg had come down from Oxford with a degree in the summer, and was now in the dire position that Evelyn knew well, of seeking without buoyant hopes for a new career. Not long after this Tom commenced journalist, with the help of the Sitwells, as in the case of Evelyn. He quickly achieved success.

The name of Evelyn Gardner appears with more frequency in the diary from September onwards, but never in a way to indicate the deep feelings that he undoubtedly had for her. He tells much more of his delight in carpentry. Consequently the following entries for 12 and 13 December come as a surprise to the reader.

'December 12th. Dined with Evelyn at the Ritz. Proposed marriage. inconclusive . . . rang up Pansy who advised in favour of marriage. Went to Sloane Square & discussed it. Went to Bowden Street & told Olivia. Home late & unable to sleep.

'December 13th. Evelyn rang up to say she had made up her mind to accept. Went to Southampton Row but was unable to work. Went to pub with Dudley & told him of engagement. Tea Evelyn.'

Thereafter occurs another gap in the diary, this time of nearly six months.

Evelyn's friends were as surprised and delighted at his engagement as Evelyn Gardner's mother was surprised and appalled. Harold Acton wrote to him on the first day of 1928: 'The news of your engagement has now reached me from two sources, so I hasten to tender my compliments and congratulations. I hear that you are very much in love and that your fiancée is a perfect darling. I do hope it will be my privilege to meet her in the nearest future, and that it will be all a real rollicking success. I feel for once it would be a good thing to leave the Greene milieu for a while if you can tear yourself away from such esurient narcotics – (except, of course, for Richard and his wife, whom I revere). But don't let David come forward with any of his advice, he is so nice and so foolish that I am sure his advice would be dangerous. How shall I address your letters in future: to Saint John, and to which: Evangelist or Baptist? It is a question to be pondered if you are engaged to an Evelyn. I am much excited, and am positively aching to hear the details. I hear she is very pretty and quite different from all the other girls in London – not that I would remind you of my opinions in regard to them. I allow myself to be thoroughly romantic about it, for it sounds so idyllic and you have it in you now to be so happy, and to make lasting your happiness. You must emerge, once

77

and for all, from the glooms, from what one should call the Dostoevski Period of your life . . . Yes, this news has cheered me. But what of the other news, that you have taken to carpentry? I am astonished and delighted by this, for there are such great things to be done in this direction, and the craftsman has long lain cold in the churchyard: I am sure you will make beautiful things.'

Evelyn kept none of the letters of congratulations which he received, except this one.

Evelyn Gardner was a refreshing change from most of the people whom Evelyn knew in London. She did not belong to the Wild-Party-Bright-Young-Things tribe. She was the same age as he was, twenty-four, but like Evelyn she was in many ways young for her age. She was without stability in those days. As sometimes happens in such cases, she became engaged to be married more frequently and on slighter grounds than is usual. She had betrothed herself to a highly unsuitable young man and been persuaded to break the engagement. Her mother then sent her to Australia to ease her emotional distress. During the voyage she fell in love with the purser on board the liner and accepted his proposal of marriage. This engagement was in turn broken, but was followed by another to a young man who appeared even less desirable than the original suitor. Again she was persuaded to break the engagement. A little later she met Evelyn with the consequence already narrated. A close friend of hers at the time of her engagement to Evelyn Waugh has written as follows to me: 'We became great friends, perhaps because of our contrasting natures. Evelyn Gardner had immense charm & a very generous nature, but she was essentially light, not sexy except in a superficial way. There will be no pre-marital scandals to conceal as far as she is concerned. I thought she would settle down once she was married.' As a girl she had the fashionable kind of prettiness associated with the late Edna Best.

The engagement was resisted to the end, a 'bitter end' to her mother, Lady Burghclere, and for that reason it was long. Because it was so long both the Evelyns felt sure of a successful marriage at the end.

To be just, why should Lady Burghclere have rejoiced at the prospect of a penniless carpenter, wholly unproven in his trade, as her son-in-law? It is true that Evelyn Waugh's eligibility improved slightly when his book on Rossetti was published in the spring of 1928. Writing is not so closely identified with want of social position as carpentry, but it is identifiable with pennilessness. It was so identified in the case of Evelyn Waugh's first book, *Rossetti His Life and Works*, dedicated to Evelyn Gardner.

*

With *Rossetti* he first appeared as a writer to be taken seriously; at home with his subject, confident in his command of language, certain of his object. This is a favourable moment briefly to recapitulate his literary development.

His earliest work had not only shown little promise but no firm indication of what sort of writer, if a writer at all, he was likely to become. The greatest literary critic imaginable would be unable to identify from the text alone the authorship of *Anthony Who Sought The Things That Were Lost* as that of Evelyn Waugh. The only characteristic of his later work to be found in that essay in preciosity is a certain boldness of approach, but this boldness is vitiated and almost cancelled by the evident vagueness of intention.

The most interesting of his early writings is *The Balance*, subtitled 'A Yarn of the Good Old Days of Broad Trousers and High Necked Jumpers'. Though it cannot be described as good, a literary detective might possibly discern its authorship from internal evidence. It contains dialogue, and though the most important single dialogue in the book is inept, some of it has a glimmer of Evelyn's later sparkle. It is difficult to say what the story is about as the narrative line is self-consciously complicated in the endeavour to be as modern as possible. It does emerge that there is a young man named Adam Dour, an art student, who is unhappily in love with a fashionable girl called Imogen Quest; that his frustrated suit drives him to attempt suicide by poison; that the attempt fails as he cannot prevent himself vomiting (closely described) thus expelling the lethal dose; that he then writes a farewell letter to Imogen and is about to drown himself but is dissuaded in the course of a conversation which he holds on a bridge, with his reflection in the water, and in which the two discuss 'the balance' between life and death. What makes the story especially difficult to follow is that most of it, following the 'inspiration' at Aston Clinton, takes the form of a film scenario which is represented as being watched by a large audience, some of whose comments are given. The people in the film spill over into the 'real life' story. It is easy to imagine James Joyce using a device of this kind. There are a few Joycean touches in the writing and it is possible that Evelyn had recently plunged into *Ulysses*. Joyce may have begotten this weak and misshapen child but he was not to be an influence on Evelyn. This was very fortunate. Like that of Wagner in the nineteenth century the influence of Joyce on his contemporaries in the twentieth was usually destructive and often fatal.

The failure of the story was inevitable from the fact that, as is apparent throughout, the author was attempting a picture of modern life without sufficient experience. The subject, almost against the writer's wish, so one may feel, gravitates back to Oxford. It begins as a parody of the debased drama of the cinema, but the story told by the fictitious film is concerned with the rakish life of Evelyn's undergraduate days, a subject wholly untypical of the cinema of the time. (Harold Lloyd's immortal *College Days* provides no exception.) As a result, the element of parody is entirely misdirected: it makes mock of a kind of film which no one had made or was likely to make. (*A Yank at Oxford* again provides no exception.) The climax of the story, the conversation between the hero and his reflection, is an abysmal mixture of sophistry and sentimentalism. In favour of *The Balance*, apart from some bright dialogue, can be claimed convincing descriptions of the squalor of debauchery. Evelyn wisely never had it reprinted, and I never heard him mention it. I was unaware of its existence until after his death.

The privately printed 'Pre-Raphaelite Brotherhood' was a competent and indeed brilliant essay of which no more need be remembered than that it served as a very useful trial run for the more ambitious and considered biography of Rossetti.

It will be remembered that when Evelyn lay as a convalescent on his father's sofa in 1926 he had planned to write a pre-Raphaelite biography in the manner of Lytton Strachey. At the time Evelyn came to write Rossetti, in 1927, Strachey's reputation was at its zenith and he was estimated, not only by his friends in Bloomsbury but by a large part of the reading public, as one of the great English writers and historians of all time. The rebels who decried this estimate were few, especially among the younger generation. (They included Robert Byron.) Evelyn had meanwhile joined them. He opened his first London-published book, *Rossetti His Life and Works*, with a caustic passage aimed at Strachey and his younger imitators. He remarks how the progress of literary fashion has resulted to a great extent 'in a new method; polite literature is the less polite for it'. He goes on:

'No doubt the old-fashioned biography will return, and, with the years, we shall once more learn to assist with our fathers' decorum at the lying-in-state of our great men; we shall see their catafalques heaped with the wreaths of august mourners, their limbs embalmed, robed, uniformed, and emblazoned with orders, their faces serenely composed and cleansed of all the stains of humanity. Meanwhile we must keep our tongue in our cheek, must we not, for fear it should loll out and reveal the idiot? We have discovered a jollier way of honouring our dead. The corpse has become the marionette. With bells on its fingers and wires on its toes it is jigged about to a "period dance" of our own piping; and who is not amused? Unfortunately, there is singularly little fun to be got out of Rossetti.'

If this seems to imply contempt of Strachey today, the implication was much stronger and more obvious then. But the most remarkable thing to note about this passage is the confident authority of the voice, such as had not been heard from Evelyn before and was to be a mark of his writing henceforward.

*Rossetti* is a sound, workmanlike account of the artist, his friends, and of the 'brotherhood' which formed around him. The research had been thorough and imaginative: the book has not been challenged as a contribution to art-history. It is commendably accurate and the presentation of fact is never subordinated to imaginative improvisation. The book gains considerable strength from the fact that not only had Evelyn made researches into the artistic activity, beliefs and practice of Rossetti, but that he had personal experience of painting.

The book is not only a biography. It was written with the idea of conveying a message, a message which today is so familiar as to be almost commonplace but was then, in a world of artistic appreciation dominated by Roger Fry, something of a novelty: that criticism and artistic achievement are separate activities; that while the former may help the latter, criticism must never dominate either the artist or those who seek to understand or enjoy his work. He put it thus in his first chapter:

'Criticism has narrowed and clarified from the time of Ruskin to the time of Mr Roger Fry; there is probably less nonsense talked about art than ever before, but it is impossible sometimes to suppress the suspicion that with it all there has been a good deal of impoverishment, and that only a part of the aesthetic problem has been solved . . .'

Evelyn was not yet the artistic conservative that he was to become. Later in the same paragraph he speaks of the 'pellucid excellencies of Picasso'.

When he returned to a final statement of his theme in the last chapter he included a defence of Rossetti's 'allusive or so-called "literary" appeal'. He put it thus: 'Why of the Arts should literature alone be expected to be "impure"? Why, because we are accustomed to expressing our daily wants in words, shall poetry not be allowed to traffick with other emotions besides the aesthetic emotion? If I may legitimately be frightened by *The Ancient Mariner*, why may I not also be by Wiertz? One day the critics will realize that by their rigid restriction of artistic scope they are making bores of all but the very greatest.'

The style shows a leap towards maturity, though he had not yet attained mastery. He was always to use occasionally the grand manner, the purple patch, but with more discipline than he showed in *Rossetti*. A year later he would not have written: 'Turner was seventy-one years old, sinking like one of his own tremendous sunsets in clouds of obscured glory', a sentence taken from his privately printed essay; nor would he have said of the Gothic revival: 'Romance threw up her frail machicolations against the inexorable advance of the industrial system.' But the sentiments behind these grandiose sentences were to remain unchanged. The humour, which is plentiful, is sometimes obviously derived. When he says of painting before Rossetti's time: 'It achieved a certain mellow harmony that went well with dining room mahogany and roast mutton', the reader hears an echo of Max Beerbohm's account of his visits to No. 2 The Pines; and when, recalling how Rossetti placed his sonnets in his wife's coffin, he added the comment 'Brown disapproved of the whole business', the reader is likely to remember Norman Douglas. There are moments of humour, however, which are in the true and inimitable Waugh manner, as when he wrote that the Victorian sculptor Woolner 'married one of the three handsome sisters called Waugh: Holman Hunt married both the others.' There is no explanatory comment.

There are numerous autobiographical touches: 'There is nothing like teaching to develop one's views', he wrote at one point. One passage shows unmistakably the strong influence of Robert Byron. Of Rossetti's most famous painting 'Beata Beatrix' he wrote: 'It is, perhaps, the most purely spiritual and devotional work of European Art since the fall of the Byzantine Empire.'

In just such exaggerated terms Robert Byron was apt to praise works of art for which he had a preference. Evelyn quickly lost this youthful habit of mind, Robert never completely.

The autobiographical element becomes strongest and also sadly prophetic in the many passages dealing with Rossetti's insomnia. Of Rossetti's over-indulgence in soporific drugs (in his case chloral) Evelyn wrote that 'from now onwards until about the end of his life [he] became increasingly dependent upon increasing doses, and the collapse which happened in June 1872 is directly attributable to the effects of this drug'. This is a fairly exact description of how Evelyn's life ended in 1966.

The book was well received by the critics, and was accorded the honour of a leading article in *The Times Literary Supplement* on 10 May 1928. But the honour was conferred with pompous condescension, a confusing parade of learning and learned jargon, and some carelessness. 'Miss Evelyn Waugh,' wrote the critic, 'Rossetti's latest biographer, is of the moment in dissatisfaction with the pure doctrine of Fry and her inability to free herself from it.' Later the critic descended to rudeness. 'Miss Waugh approaches the "squalid" Rossetti like some dainty miss of the 60s bringing the Italian organ-grinder a penny . . .'

The critic had written nonsense and Evelyn had him or her at his mercy. Boiling with rage, he wrote an effective answer which might have been more effective if it had been terser. It was published in the T.L.S. on 17 May.

'Sir, In this week's *Literary Supplement*, I notice, with gratitude, the prominence given to my life of Rossetti. Clearly it would be pretentious for a critic with pretentions even as modest as my own to genuine aesthetic standards to attempt to bandy opinions with a reviewer who considers that Rossetti's drawings "refine on" those of Ingres; but I hope you will allow me space in which to call attention to three points in which your article seems to misrepresent me.

'Your reviewer refers to me throughout as "Miss Waugh". My Christian name, I know, is occasionally regarded by people of limited social experience as belonging exclusively to one or other sex; but it is unnecessary to go further into my book than the paragraph charitably placed within the wrapper for the guidance of unleisured critics, to find my name with its correct prefix of "Mr." Surely some such investigation might in merest courtesy have been taken before your reviewer tumbled into print with such phrases as "a miss of the 6os". In the second place, she or he writes "the 'squalid' Rossetti", the inference of the inverted commas being that the phrase is my own; it is not. In the third place, there is nowhere in my book or in any other of my writings, any statement or suggestion that could possibly imply, to an intelligent reader, that I prefer "Morris's interminable flaccid 'grinds' to the best constructed narratives in English verse".

Your obedient servant,
Evelyn Arthur St John Waugh.'

This victory did little to assuage Evelyn's feelings. He wanted success with its rewards, and all he was getting from *Rossetti* was a *succès d'estime*, a major irritation of the literary life, especially when the writer is young, hoping to marry, and thus in need of money. It is not surprising to learn from Dudley Carew's account that under these circumstances Evelyn took to drink more violently than ever before.

In 1928 Evelyn's Oxford friend Patrick Balfour was working on a newspaper in Fleet Street as a contributor of paragraphs about London Society. As a loyal friend he gave Evelyn's book a flattering mention. 'Thank you so much for the advertisement,' Evelyn wrote on 20 February. 'As soon as I see any hope from my windows in the Slough of Despond I will let you know.

'As a matter of fact I think there will probably be an elopement quite soon.'

*Rossetti* had done nothing to soften the opposition by Lady Burghclere to the proposed marriage. So after a while the two Evelyns decided on defiance, conspiracy and elopement. But there was not an elopement as soon as Evelyn Waugh had led Patrick to believe. The plot was not carried out till June. Two entries in Evelyn Waugh's diary for 1928 tell the story.

'Friday June 23rd 1928. Evelyn and I began to go to Dulwich to see the pictures there but got bored waiting for the right bus so went instead to the Vicar General's office and bought a marriage licence. Lunched at Taglioni. Went to Warwick Square to see Harold and show him our licence. With him to Alec where we drank champagne.

'June 27th 1928. Evelyn and I were married at S. Pauls Portman Square at 12 oclock. A woman was typewriting on the altar. Harold best man. Robert Byron gave away the bride, Alec & Pansy the witnesses. Evelyn wore a new black & yellow jumper suit with scarf. Went to the 500 Club

83

& drank champagne cocktails under the suspicious eyes of Winifred Mackingtosh and Prince George of Russia. From there to luncheon at Boulestin. Very good luncheon. Then to Paddington on by train to Oxford & taxi to Beckley.'

They returned from their honeymoon at Beckley in the first week of July, and while looking for a house they stayed for a while at Underhill and then at Harold Acton's flat which he put at their disposal. It was only now that he announced his marriage to Lady Burghclere. In her reply to his letter she described herself as 'quite inexpressibly pained'. He went to visit her, but on this subject the diary only has the disappointing entry 'Saw Lady B in the morning'. In the meantime important events had happened in Evelyn's life, and to understand them the story must go back a short way.

By the time the two Evelyns were married he had finished *Decline and Fall*, which had been accepted and was being printed. This had come about in the following way. Evelyn had submitted his typescript to Duckworth, the publishers of his *Rossetti*, in May or early June. Duckworth were very shocked by the book and informed Evelyn that they could only publish the novel if he consented to make drastic alterations in the direction of strict decency. He quickly saw that the alterations they wanted would not only change but destroy the character of the book. He did not argue the matter at any length but took the typescript away and went straight to Chapman and Hall. He knew that his father would have scruples about publishing his son's novel, and moreover that this was not the kind of novel that his father was likely to enjoy or approve. But he also knew that his father was away for a few weeks, and he had faith in the *chargé d'affaires*, Ralph Strauss. His calculation was correct. The acting chairman read the book and spotted a winner, and (also aware of Arthur Waugh's scruples) Strauss not only accepted *Decline and Fall* as soon as he had had time to read it, but signed a contract with Evelyn before the chairman's return. The contract included a provision that Evelyn should draw line-illustrations for the book and a design for the wrapper, thus adding a little more to the author's profits. Evelyn had the galley proofs in the first part of July soon after his return from Beckley. Arthur Waugh acquiesced in the *coup d'état* and was probably glad that the decision had been forced upon him.

In September the Evelyns, who had been alternating between Harold Acton's flat and Underhill, at last found a house which they rented on a long lease. It was very small and was in Canonbury Square, Islington, where in those days housing was very cheap. They had so few belongings that they were able to economize by loading them on to a luggage push-cart and making the journey on foot. They were gay, happy and full of the reckless optimism of youth. Years after this Nancy Mitford said that they were like two little boys. Cyril Connolly said that their house was like a smart little bandbox. Here they were in Islington when in September *Decline and Fall* came out.

It would be wrong to say that Evelyn woke up to find himself famous, but it is correct to say that he woke up to find himself the talk of the town, meaning by 'town' those who knew something about public school and university life and fashionable society. He got some disapproving notices from critics who insisted that humour must be 'healthy' and it cannot be said that the subject of the novel is morally salubrious: it tells with relish of the triumph of the wicked. But the bad notices were greatly outnumbered by the good, and the latter included the praise of Arnold Bennett who, as the chief literary contributor to the *Evening Standard*, held a deserved position of influence as a critic which has not been equalled since. In the *New Statesman* the book received the unqualified praise of Cyril Connolly, then beginning to make a name as a critic of fiction. But this particular praise disquieted Evelyn. At the same time as *Decline and Fall* came out, so did a book by Harold Acton, to whom Evelyn had dedicated his own 'in Homage and Affection'. Harold appeared in public for the first time as a novelist, with Evelyn. His book, *Humdrum* (which Evelyn admired), was not in the same high class as Evelyn's, so at the expense of Harold Acton, Cyril Connolly had recourse to the reviewing technique whereby praise of one book is emphasized by blame on another. Harold Acton's distress clouded Evelyn's enjoyment of the welcome given to himself.

The sales of books are less affected by even the best criticism than they are by gossip and discussion, by readers pressing the book on their friends. I was in a nursing home when *Decline and Fall* came out, and Tom Driberg visited me and brought a copy. He began to read out some favourite passages and was literally unable to read them to the end because he and I were so overcome by laughter. This was one of hundreds of such scenes in London in September 1928, and that is how readership is built. John Betjeman has said: 'When I read the book it seemed to me so rockingly funny that nothing else would seem funny again.'

*Decline and Fall* remains one of the best known of Evelyn's books, and his biographer may therefore assume that the reader of Evelyn's biography has read it. There is no need here to outline the story. Only a few points of interest, which may have escaped general observation, need be mentioned.

In all Evelyn's fiction there is some element of the *roman à clef*, becoming ever smaller as he matured. In *Decline and Fall* it is often strong, though there seems to be no model for the heroine, Margot Beste-Chetwynde. Incidents from real life were often taken by Evelyn and then applied to a wholly different cast of players; this common novelist's practice was used by him in *Decline and Fall* as in much of his later work. It will be remembered that the hero Paul Pennyfeather makes the acquaintance of the

Beste-Chetwynde family by giving organ lessons to Peter, Margot's son. This is clearly borrowed from Evelyn's musical adventures with Derek Verschoyle, but there is no reason to associate Derek with Peter, Lord Pastmaster. Similarly he often borrowed existing names for his characters, both here and in later work, one reason, so he once told me, was that English names are so difficult to invent. 'What novelist', he said, 'could have invented the name Asquith?' He was warned by the bad examples in this respect of Dickens and Aldous Huxley. Of course he also liked to use names to tease the holders of them. In this novel there is allusion to a burglar who is called Cruttwell. Philbrick was the name of a fellow undergraduate of Balliol with whom he is said to have had bad relations. There had been a 'Miss Philbrick' in *The Balance*. Here the name is given to an irresistibly absurd swindler. There are doubtless other now forgotten examples of the same thing. Some usage of real names seems quite neutral. The headmaster, Dr Augustus Fagan, probably owed his surname to James Fagan, the distinguished founder of the Oxford Playhouse and a very prominent figure in the Oxford of the twenties, but there is no reason to suspect malice. It is otherwise with Evelyn's introduction into the story of a contemptibly ridiculous man of letters whom he called Jack Spire of *The London Hercules*. Through Dudley Carew, and probably through Alec as well, he had met Jack Squire of *The London Mercury* and taken a great dislike to him. David Lennox, the photographer, is a caricature of Cecil Beaton, which Evelyn made unmistakable by telling of a photograph of Mrs Beste-Chetwynde's head taken by Lennox from the back. (Cecil Beaton had taken a well-known photograph of Margot, Lady Oxford, from the same angle.) He had returned to his bullying ways with Cecil Beaton and he disguised the portrait only by adding repellent touches. In the first edition the name of Lennox's friend Miles Malpractice was very close to that of a living person. For fear of libel it was changed in the second edition. The close identification of Grimes was openly admitted by Evelyn in his autobiography. These are only a few of the clear identifications in the book. They gave malicious amusement to many of his friends but they gave no strength to his fiction. That he realized this may be deduced from his later performance.

The real powerful comic strength of the book lies in its perfect mingling of realism and fantasy.

The book was planned in a way that left it open to a fatal weakness. The main theme (one that Evelyn was often to use) was that of the natural victim exposed to forces with which he cannot contend. The victim as hero can defeat great talents, and in the end it was to cast a blemish on Evelyn's. But it cast none here.

Evelyn, as has been mentioned already, liked the purple patch. It was entirely out of place in this splendid farce, unless used farcically. Evelyn contrived to use it perfectly in a wonderful little parody of Walter Pater.

The occasion is the death of Grimes whom Pennyfeather meets again as a fellow convict and who escapes from gaol only to be drowned, it appears, in a quagmire. 'But Grimes, Paul at last realized, was of the immortals. He was a life force. Sentenced to death in Flanders, he popped up in Wales; drowned in Wales, he emerged in South America; engulfed in the dark mystery of Egdon Mire, he would rise again somewhere at some time, shaking from his limbs the musty integuments of the tomb. Surely he had followed in the Bacchic train of distant Arcady, and played on the reeds of myth by forgotten streams, and taught the childish satyrs the art of love? Had he not suffered unscathed the fearful dooms of all the offended gods of all the histories, fire, brimstone, and yawning earth-quakes, plague, and pestilence? Had he not stood, like the Pompeian sentry, while the Citadels of the Plain fell to ruin about his ears? Had he not, like some grease-caked Channel-swimmer, breasted the waves of the Deluge? Had he not moved unseen when the darkness covered the waters?'

The complete absence of obscene vocabulary in *Decline and Fall* might make it appear as only mild satire to some readers if it was published for the first time today, but on the other hand the colourful figure of Mr Sebastian Cholmondley, which amused even prudish readers in 1928, might now be looked upon with stern disapproval, especially by the Race Relations Board.

In later years Evelyn came to denigrate *Decline and Fall*. Of course he became weary and irritated by being told in print and by admirers that his first novel was his best, especially as it was not, but he came also to deny its virtues. The book was frequently and rightly praised for its originality, and it is probably true to say that it is the most original of all his books. He denied this. He insisted that it was excessively deri-vative. 'But from what?' I once asked him. 'Oh, a great many books, I'm afraid', he replied laughing, but he never particularized.

I suppose all works of fiction, good and bad, are derivative, and those that are wholly without ancestry, for example the later novels of Gertrude Stein, are unreadable for that very reason. In the case of Evelyn his pre-decessors are not easily discerned. Ronald Firbank is an obvious one. There is some resemblance of subject as they both wrote about the fashion-able world. Both had sharp ears for the fatuities of ordinary conversation. Both knew how to combine murderous satire with broad comedy, and both were fantasists. But when one has said that, one has said all. No one of any judgement could mistake one for the other. Evelyn greatly admired Firbank's contemporary Hector (Saki) Munro, and the chapter on the school sports in *Decline and Fall* has a subject after Saki's heart. Evelyn and Saki resemble each other also in their Englishry. But except in some of his dialogue, Saki's style and his approach to his subject are quite unlike Evelyn's. Saki's story, *The Unrest Cure*, is the closest of his writings to Evelyn's, but it is not very close. The resemblance to the early Aldous

Huxley novels, often remarked, is extremely superficial. There is one resemblance that I have not seen commented on. Mrs Beste-Chetwynde's situation, and her efficiency when selecting personnel for her chain of brothels, does strike me as a farcical version of *Mrs Warren's Profession*, but no sane person will assert that Evelyn Waugh as a writer is derivative from Bernard Shaw. There is a remote resemblance in *Decline and Fall* to the wit of Oscar Wilde, as shown in *The Importance of Being Earnest*, but it is as remote as the resemblance to Peacock. Evelyn had read, and often re-read, the novels of Dickens. The opening scene in *Decline and Fall* shows unmistakable Dickensian influence on the treatment of a subject which Dickens himself would never have used. All the names cited above are those of intensely original writers who resemble no one else closely, and whose imitators are forgotten because the originals are inimitable. That is true of Evelyn also.

Evelyn either bore long grudges, sometimes for obscure reasons, or surprisingly did not, when he might have been expected to. His friend at Duckworth was Tom Balston. The friendship continued undismayed despite Evelyn's recent unhappy experiences with the firm. When the novel came out he sent a copy to his friend and inscribed it: 'To Tom Balston – the stone that the Builder rejected.'

1928 was Evelyn's *annus mirabilis* and it closed in triumph. He now knew that he was a writer, but even now he was not quite sure, as will appear later, whether he should become a full-time, professional author, like his brother, or one who practises the craft of writing as a side-line.

# Chapter 6

## 1929-1930

A shadow of anxiety fell across this winter of content between 1928 and 1929. She-Evelyn, as their friends began to call young Mrs Waugh, fell ill in October. It appeared at first that she was suffering a bad attack of influenza, but later their doctor, whom He-Evelyn (as he came to be called) described as 'a cross between a butcher and a vet', diagnosed German measles. Whether or not he was right, she became extremely ill. A nurse had to be called in. Towards the end of the month she was able to get up for a few hours every day. She needed a fortnight's convalescence. Friends came to their help. The first few days of her convalescence were spent near Marlborough in the house which Alastair Graham shared with a friend. The rest of it was spent with Robert Byron who lived with his family, not far off, in their house in Savernake Forest. This phase of ill-health, which was only at its beginning in October and November of 1928, was possibly to be the cause of melancholy events.

The great success of *Decline and Fall* led to further opportunities: Evelyn was invited to review books in several newspapers, notably in *The Observer*, where he had attracted the notice of the literary editor, Viola Garvin. He got commissions in other papers and magazines. He was helped by the fact that the ablest literary agent in London, A. D. Peters, had invited Evelyn to become one of his clients. This happened in 1928, and Peters remained his agent and friend for the whole of Evelyn's subsequent career. The first piece of business Peters did for him was in late October 1928 when the *Evening Standard* wanted an article on the youth of England. Evelyn agreed. 'England has Youth. Make Use of It' was his title. He entered without shame into the Younger Generation cult of the time. Writing to A. D. Peters's partner, W. N. Roughead, on the subject of getting a firm footing in the Beaverbrook press, he said: 'It seems to me that it would be so nice if we could persuade them that I personify the English youth movement.' This was accomplished, but not easily. One difficulty was that though Evelyn was a first-rate journalist, editors did not always welcome contributions from this unconventional and explosive newcomer. One must remember again that he had not yet attained popular success. He had more rejections than acceptances from newspapers in the first year of his writing life, and without the persistent and strenuous efforts of Peters, he would have made a slow start in the journalist world. Another reason for his Fleet Street difficulties was that, though he found it profitable to write as the personification of the English Youth movement, he was too intelligent not to see through the absurdities of the cult, as silly then as it is now, and occasionally he did not disguise his contempt. This perplexed editors who like things to be set out in black and white.

One odd incident occurred in the course of Evelyn's slow conquest of Fleet Street. Early in 1929 the *Evening Standard* was running yet another series of articles on various aspects of the Youth of England question, and Evelyn proposed that he should write one on 'The Manners of the Younger Generation'. His neat handwriting was misread in Peters's office, with the result that the *Evening Standard* commissioned a contribution from the promising young novelist on 'The Mothers of the Younger Generation'. Evelyn wrote the article, undeterred by the total and accidental change of subject. He wrote to Peters: 'The misunderstanding about "Mothers" & "Manners" is unfortunate but not drastic.'

In the middle of January the Evelyns decided that in view of her recent illness they should, if possible, go abroad to find some sunshine. Their original plan was to sail round the Mediterranean as passengers in a cargo boat, but Peters was able to arrange more luxurious travel. He persuaded a shipping company to give them free passages for a Mediterranean cruise on a Norwegian ship, M.Y. *Stella Polaris*, in exchange for publicity. He got commissions for him to write travel articles for various magazines. A year later the articles with his notes were assembled and edited (with considerable alteration of fact) into Evelyn's first travel book, *Labels*. It will be considered later, but here it is useful to recall a striking passage which occurs early in the book and which suggests that even at this period he was not wholly decided whether to make authorship his profession.

. They went overland before joining the ship at Monte Carlo. Their first stop was in Paris where some American friends took them round the town. Late in their explorations they went to the then famous night-club *Le Grand Écart*. Here is Evelyn's account of what happened:

'A beautiful and splendidly dressed Englishwoman – who, as they say, shall be nameless – came to the next table. She was with a very nice-looking, enviable man who turned out later to be a Belgian baron. She knew someone in our party and there was an indistinct series of introductions. She said, "What did you say that boy's name was?"

'They said, "Evelyn Waugh."

'She said, "Who is he?"

'None of my friends knew. One of them suggested that she thought I was an English writer.

'She said, "I knew it. He is the one person in the world I have been longing to meet. . . . Please move up so that I can come and sit next to him."

'Then she came and talked to me.

'She said, "I should never have known from your photographs that you were a blond."

'I should not have known how to answer that, but fortunately there was no need as she went straight on. "Only last week I was reading an article by you in the *Evening Standard*. It was so beautiful that I cut it out and sent it to my mother."

'I said, "I got ten guineas for it."

'At this moment the Belgian baron asked her to dance. She said, "No, no. I am drinking in the genius of this wonderful young man." Then she said to me, "You know, I am psychic. The moment I came into this room to-night I *knew* that there was a *great personality* here, and I knew that I should find him before the evening was over."

'I suppose that real novelists get used to this kind of thing. It was new to me and very nice. I had only written two very dim books and still regarded myself less as a writer than an out-of-work private school-master.

'She said, "You know, there is only one other great genius in this age. Can you guess his name?"

'I suggested Einstein? No . . . Charlie Chaplin? No . . . James Joyce? No . . . Who?

'She said, "Maurice Dekobra. I must give him a little party at the Ritz for you to meet him. I should feel I had at least done something to justify my life if I had introduced you two great geniuses of the age. One must do something to justify one's life, don't you think, or don't you?"

'Everything went very harmoniously for a time. Then she said something that made me a little suspicious, "You know, I so love your books that I never travel without taking them all with me. I keep them in a row by my bed."

' "I suppose you aren't by any chance confusing me with my brother Alec? He has written many more books than I."

' "What did you say his name was?"

' "Alec."

' "Yes, of course. What's your name, then?"

' "Evelyn."

' "But . . . but they said you wrote."

' "Yes, I do a little. You see, I couldn't get any other sort of job."

'Her disappointment was as frank as her friendliness had been. "Well," she said, "how very unfortunate."

'Then she went to dance with her Belgian, and when she sat down she went to her former table. When we parted she said vaguely, "We're sure to run into one another again."

'I wonder. And I wonder whether she will add this book, and with it this anecdote, to her collection of my brother's works by the side of her bed.'

Their original plan was to sail on M.Y. *Stella Polaris* to Istanbul, then change ship for a cruise round the Black Sea, provided they succeeded in obtaining Russian visas. The attempt failed, fortunately as it turned out, so the journey was confined to the Mediterranean and one ship. Evelyn sent a brilliantly funny article about a visit to Naples. From there the ship sailed to Sicily and then eastwards to Haifa. By the time they reached Palestine Evelyn's wife had fallen ill again. She was too unwell to land and a nurse had to be recruited in Haifa to attend her personally. By the time the *Stella Polaris* reached Port Said she was suffering from severe pneumonia and had to be lowered ashore on a stretcher and taken to the British hospital. Her state was critical. On 29 March Evelyn wrote to Peters: 'Our trip so far has not been fun because Evelyn nearly died but I think it looks as if it will be all right now.'

When his wife was out of danger Evelyn went off for a few days to Cyprus to meet his old friend Alastair Graham who joined him from Athens. His behaviour in leaving his wife thus, though only for a few days, has been described as 'odd', with the implication that it was callous and may have led to future troubles. No such suggestion appears in any of the surviving documentation of the time. In fact, the situation was not very odd, as appears from a letter written by Evelyn to Harold Acton from Port Said. From this it is clear that both the Evelyns planned to go to Cyprus for a fortnight with Alastair Graham to help her recuperation. When the time came she was too weak to travel, so Evelyn went alone so as not to disappoint his old friend. There is no sign that his wife felt aggrieved then or after.

During all this time of travel, journalism and devastating anxiety, Evelyn was at work on a new novel. He was perhaps, and probably, among those who work most easily when work provides a distraction from present distress. Unlike the case of *Decline and Fall*, the subject of the new book came to him gradually after a short period of trial and error. Before leaving England he had proposed in a letter to Peters two novels, presumably to be written in the order given. After discussing various journalistic propositions for serials, he wrote: 'I would also write one humorous serial called "Gilded Young Man" dealing with the arrival in London of a young, handsome & incredibly wealthy marquess hitherto brought up in seclusion and the attempts made by various social, religious, political bodies & ambitious mothers to get hold of him.

'I would also write a detective serial about the murder of an author, rather Alec Waugh.

'I have both these stories fairly clear in my mind . . .'

The second proposition calls to mind the plot for a novel which he had worked out in the Christmas holidays from Lancing in 1920. Neither of these outlines bear any resemblance to his next book, or indeed to anything he wrote subsequently. How or precisely when his next subject came to him is nowhere recorded, but it was evidently on this journey which he once described to me as the Labeliad. By the time they were back at the end of May he had, according to correspondence with Peters, written 10,000 words of the new book and settled on its title: *Vile Bodies*.

By June 1929, after a slow sea-journey home, Evelyn's wife had recovered. Soon after return, their household was enlarged in the following way. One of She-Evelyn's closest friends was Nancy Mitford who at that time was growing impatient of family life. Her father, Lord Redesdale, had ancient ideas regarding the proper exercise of parental authority, and Nancy, who had not yet discovered her literary talent, found her pleasant London home in Rutland Gate a prison. She discussed her longing for freedom with her friend who immediately suggested that she could solve her problem by taking their spare room and living for the time being in Canonbury Square. The arrangement was particularly suitable, Nancy's friend insisted, because Evelyn was anxious to finish his book before the end of the summer and in time for autumn publication, so that he needed to be alone for much of the time during this period of intensive work. He planned to be away during most of the week in the country, at Beckley or at a hotel (which was to play a great part in his life) at Chagford in Devonshire; he would return to London for weekends unless joined by his wife in his retreat. It followed that she would be much alone so she welcomed the prospect of Nancy's companionship. Nancy accepted with joy. It was particularly easy for her to set up in her new address in Islington without any family disturbance, as her mother and father had gone to Canada and their London house was temporarily shut. The arrangement, under which *Vile Bodies* was brought near completion, worked happily for a while.

Suddenly the marriage was threatened with disaster. On 9 July Evelyn received a letter from his wife in which she told him that she had fallen in love with John Heygate, a friend of them both. For some reason, perhaps because he was stunned into inaction, Evelyn did not return to London till the 12th. When they were together again his wife confessed all, not only that she had fallen in love with this friend but that they had become lovers in the carnal sense. After a long discussion Evelyn said that he would forgive his wife and forget the whole business if she agreed to give up this man. She said she would do so. It seemed that a reconciliation had been contrived and Evelyn stayed on in London for a happy fortnight. On 26 July he left again to spend five days with some friends who lived in Cheshire and could give him the solitude he needed for his work. During his absence Evelyn's wife went to a party where her lover was one of the guests. Being a fashionable entertainment photographers were present, · and next morning she was horrified to see in a popular newspaper a picture of herself photographed with the lover she had promised to reject. She rushed to Nancy and poured out her fears. Nancy (who knew nothing about the quarrel or its being composed) told her she was making a fuss about nothing, and when her friend had explained that she had promised Evelyn never to see this man again, Nancy continued to treat the incident as trivial. She said, 'You can perfectly truthfully say that you met by accident, that the photograph wasn't your fault, and anyway that you love Evelyn.' Then the other said: 'I have never loved Evelyn.' Nancy was horrified, and the other explained that she had married Evelyn for the same reason, and only for the same reason, that Nancy had come to live with them in Islington: to escape parental tyranny. Nancy had grown to like and admire her friend's husband and as a consequence she was deeply shocked. She left immediately and the two women never met again.

On 1 August Evelyn returned home from Cheshire. He found the house, 'the smart little band-box', empty. There was no Nancy, no Evelyn, nothing. The two Evelyns had employed a 'daily woman' living close by, and Evelyn went to her to find out what had happened. She knew nothing. By the first post on the next day he received a letter from his wife saying that she had gone off with their friend and was living with him. By her the marriage was as lightly broken off as it had been entered into, but the effect on Evelyn was not light. He felt lost again in a world where he believed that, at last, after a painful struggle he had found safety. He fell into a state of absolute despair. Some of his friends even feared for his sanity.

During August his wife's friends persuaded him to agree not to petition for divorce, as he had decided, but to enter negotiations for a reconciliation. He agreed, but some time later, 'I subsequently realized', to quote his words, 'that I could not bring myself to do this.' He was not only bitter, but appalled and enraged. He filed a petition on 3 September 1929 with the professional aid of a solicitor who specialized in divorce cases, Mr E. S. P. Haynes. At Mr Haynes's office on 9 September Evelyn attended the gruesome formality at which the petition was served on his wife and on 'the Co-Respondent', and at which a professional informer identified the guilty parties. The case was undefended and after the 9th it went through with the long delays of such matters then. The two Evelyns never seem to have met again.

Evelyn's friends were shocked by the betrayal of which he had been the victim. This sense of outrage was so persistent among them that nearly forty years after, a clergyman, in the course of a sermon at a memorial service for Evelyn, felt obliged to dwell on the disloyalty to which he had been subjected. At the time, his friends wrote to him in furious sympathy, and in a spirit of denunciation of the young woman's heartlessness and duplicity. None of his friends seems to have remembered the wholly frivolous spirit in which the two Evelyns had decided to get married, least of all the clergyman who might have had most reason to lay stress on it. This is not the place to pronounce judgement, but one interpretation of the event, so it seems to me, should be noticed.

One of the most distressed of Evelyn's friends when this unexpected break-up occurred was Harold Acton, but he thought that he knew the answer to the riddle which the case presented. It was and remained his belief that the young woman's long period of illness, extending over some six months, had worked a change in her mind and feelings with the result that her love withered and vanished. Such a psychological experience is by no means rare. If the interpretation is correct, it would follow that what she told Nancy Mitford (that she had never loved Evelyn) was not a statement of fact but the expression of a delusion. Pansy Pakenham (now Lady Pansy Lamb) has agreed with Harold Acton's opinion.

The usual gloomy consequences followed. The little house in Canonbury Square was packed up and disposed of. (Details are not ascertainable for Evelyn kept few papers of this time.) He took a room for a while at the Savile Club to which he had been elected on the proposal of his father, for long an honoured member, and later he returned to live at Underhill after a visit to Ireland. In spite of the rally of his friends and the compassionate affection of his family, he felt degraded and gave way to an absurd fancy that he had become an object of mockery. On one occasion his ever-devoted friend John Sutro tried to cheer him by giving him dinner at the Savoy and, in spite of all John's assurances, Evelyn persisted in believing that the other diners were laughing at him. He had laughed mercilessly, and was to laugh mercilessly again, at others' misfortunes. He assumed that the cynic's disposition, which he had, was commonly shared.

A few biographical details emerge from this woeful episode. Twenty-seven years later Evelyn wrote an obituary article on Max Beerbohm for *The Sunday Times*. He had first met Beerbohm, 'an idol of my adolescence to whom every year deepened my devotion', through E. S. P. Haynes, and in the course of the article he said something about his professional dealings with the famous solicitor. He told how Haynes 'had acted for me . . . in a single disagreeable piece of legal business, but he gave me far more in oysters and hock during its transaction than he charged me in fees. He was the most remarkable of solicitors; a man who actually enjoyed the company of literary men of all ages and all reputations. A second Watts-Dunton, the reader will ask? Not a second Watts-Dunton. Haynes did not seek to restrain the pleasures of his clients; however extravagant he applauded and promoted them.'

On 23 August, while reconciliation was being urged upon him, Evelyn received a letter from the acting literary editor of the *Daily Mail*. Its contents must have caused him some surprise. 'Would you,' the acting editor asked, 'care to contribute an article to a series to be entitled rather vaguely "What I Think of Marriage"? I want to get as many points of view, preferably controversial, as possible . . .'

Perhaps even odder than the coincidence in time of this offer (which was not provoked by malice) is the fact that Evelyn had no hesitation in accepting it. He wrote to Peters: 'Could you please find out how long they want this article to be (the subject of which seems mildly cynical in my present circumstances) and what they will pay?' The *Daily Mail* offered £12 for 800 words from Evelyn on marriage, to be delivered as soon as possible. Then, true to form, the series was postponed. Early in October Evelyn was moved to write to Peters: 'I think that as the Daily Mail specially asked for the article in a hurry for immediate publication they ought to pay in advance don't you? Can you make them? Also perhaps they should be warned that if they delay too long, they will be printing my austere views on the sanctity of marriage in the same issue as the report of my divorce. Love and kisses to Roughead.'

The article appeared on 8 October. His title was 'Let the Marriage Ceremony Mean Something'. It is not memorable, and its main interest is in the ironical circumstances in which it was produced. But the article contains some good Waugh touches, as when he wrote: 'If the candidates find they cannot accept all the implications of churchmanship then let them forgo the pageantry of bridesmaids and bouquets and the wedding march and take a taxicab to the nearest register office.'

Before the appearance of the article Evelyn had received on 24 September a letter from John Heygate. 'Dear Evelyn,' it read, 'I have done you a great wrong. I am sorry. Will you forgive me?' That was all. The two men never met again, but they corresponded again as appears later.

A short but very important part of Evelyn's life was over. A vision of happiness had vanished as a mirage. Some of his friends saw, or believed they saw, a change in his character after August 1929; they saw a new hardness and bitterness and an utter disillusion which showed itself in cruelty. This is a matter on which I cannot have a grounded opinion. I first met him with Cyril Connolly some months after the episode was over. Certainly I had no impression of an angry, broken man. If I do have an opinion it is best expressed in a favourite expression of his own: 'He did not repine.' The evidence of his early life shows that he always had a tendency to cruelty; his every book, indeed almost every writing from his hand, shows a deep underlying bitterness; he had some illusions about the world, as appears much later, but they were fantastical; his serious thought was always free of illusion. There are descriptions of calamitous marriage in his fiction, and doubtless these were strongly influenced by his memories of 1929, but there are other descriptions, especially in his later writing, of stoical acceptance of destiny, and these also may have been strongly influenced by memories of that year. In so far as I allow myself an opinion, I believe that Evelyn, for all the anguish he endured, was not radically changed. But again I must insist that I have no memory of him earlier than 1930.

The disturbance in his life naturally delayed the completion of *Vile Bodies* so that he missed the autumn and Christmas market. His literary life, when he was not writing the novel, was occupied with journalism and largely unsuccessful attempts to obtain contracts for articles and stories in the press. In a world in which Barrie and A. A. Milne were still widely appreciated as humorists and wits (which they were), Evelyn Waugh's black humour was not commonly welcome to editors. Through Peters he offered to several papers two extracts from his new novel for serialization but only one of these, a condensed version of the hero's frustrated engagement, was accepted by only one paper for £30. The honour of this decision was to the credit of Miss Joyce Reynolds, the editor of *Harper's Bazaar*. (Evelyn referred to her in letters to Peters as 'a woman called Harper's Bazaar'.) His wide success as a journalist was still in the future, but some of the journalism he wrote at this time deserves to be remembered.

He had shown himself in *The Bookman* and *The Observer* as an able literary critic. In the first part of 1929 he wrote one of his best literary essays, one which well stands the test of time, on Ronald Firbank. He wrote it for *Life and Letters*, edited by his influential admirer Desmond MacCarthy. At this time the weekly magazine *The Sketch* ran a column called 'The Literary Lounger', and one week Evelyn was invited to review three novels. (One of them, *Sweet Charlatan*, was by his friend Inez Holden.) He devoted most of his space to a novel called *Living* by Henry Yorke, with whom he had made friends at Oxford. Henry Yorke (who wrote under the name of Henry Green) had already had one book, *Blindness*, published in 1926, when he was still an undergraduate. *Living* was his first mature work. It was manifestly based on his experiences as a factory hand in the works of the family business in Birmingham. It was written in a style which was then revolutionary, and has some affinity, though not very much, with that of Ivy Compton-Burnett: mercilessly economic, devoid of anything that could be described as decoration, closely confined to the closely observed. The critics gave *Living* a poor reception. Evelyn acclaimed this book as a 'triumph'. As a reviewer Evelyn did not often make 'discoveries', and some of his attempts to do so turned out to be fallacious, but in this case time proved his perspicacity.

One other and very odd literary venture should be noticed. It was Evelyn's Christmas card for 1929. He had sent satirical Christmas cards before this, but that for 1929 was the most memorable. I was with Patrick Balfour and Hugh Lygon in Patrick's house when it arrived. It was on a single page. On one side were printed in wild confusion headlines from the newspapers, including advertisements: 'Woman and Bones Mystery', 'Why have Indigestion?', '18 Atrocities this Year', 'Nearly Everyone can Write', 'Bunions Go!', 'Be a Successful Artist There is Joy and Profit in Creative Art', are a few of the offerings, some of which were printed upside down. On the other side were extracts from unfavourable reviews of *Decline and Fall*, one of the most condemnatory being by G. K. Chesterton.

Early in 1930 *Vile Bodies* came out. It was an immediate success and, unlike *Decline and Fall*, sold handsomely. He now became widely read and began to be famous.

The two novels are similar in that they both chiefly concern the fashionable world of Mayfair and the hysterical fooleries of the Bright Young Things. Both are anarchic in intention and effect. Both show a sustained brilliance of invention and both are uproariously funny. Inevitably they are linked together but they show interesting contrasts.

*Decline and Fall* is much more of a fantasy than *Vile Bodies*. There is no sense of doom in the earlier book; for all its succession of calamities its atmosphere is sunny and with something of the fairy-tale about it. *Vile Bodies* is dark and threatening in feeling, and it is not difficult to understand that the contrast is in large part due to the fact that whereas in *Decline and Fall* the author frequently has to rely on invention alone, in *Vile Bodies* there is the expression, even in some of the wildest of its farce, of experience. It is not surprising that many people have supposed that this dark element in the book reflects Evelyn's desolation at the breakdown of his marriage. It is an untenable view as the book was nearly finished when the breakdown occurred, and there is no change of mood from the beginning to the end.

The element of fantasy is, as hardly needs saying, by no means absent from *Vile Bodies*. He was still young and he still needed to rely on pure invention. As before he mixed fantasy and realism with exquisite skill. Two of his pure inventions stand out as masterly. At this time he had no experience whatsoever of the film industry, so that 'Wonderfilm's' mammoth production of *The Life of Wesley* is based on guesswork and rumour. As he was to discover later in life, his guesses were not so wide of the mark as he may have supposed at the time. The other pure invention in the book is Father Rothschild, S.J. Evelyn may have met one or two Catholic priests with Gwen Greene, but he had never met a Jesuit and had no friends among Catholic clergymen. Father Rothschild is a fine caricature of what Jesuits are supposed to be like in popular imagination, men wielding vast secret influence and sustained in their task by an incredible amassment of information. But this immensely enjoyable invention is flawed at one point. The scene is a magnificent reception at Anchorage House at which a conversation occurs between the Prime Minister, Mr Outrage, Lord Metroland and the Jesuit. The Prime Minister denounces the younger generation:

' "There's something wanton about these young people to-day. That stepson of yours, Metroland, and that girl of poor old Chasm's and young Throbbing's brother."

' "Don't you think," said Father Rothschild gently, "that perhaps it is all in some way historical? I don't think people ever *want* to lose their faith either in religion or anything else. I know very few young people, but it seems to me that they are all possessed with an almost fatal hunger for permanence. I think all these divorces show that. People aren't content just to muddle along nowadays ... And this word 'bogus' they all use ... They won't make the best of a bad job nowadays. My private school-master used to say, 'If a thing's worth doing at all, it's worth doing well.' My Church has taught that in different words for several centuries. But these young people have got hold of another end of the stick, and for all we know it may be the right one. They say, 'If a thing's not worth doing well, it's not worth doing at all.' It makes everything very difficult for them." '

This apologia for modern youth has sometimes been read with awe as showing Evelyn's essential and underlying seriousness. It has been taken as an expression of Evelyn's belief. I have never seen anything in it myself except sentimentalism and an artistic flaw which weakens the picture of Father Rothschild. This was Evelyn's own later view. We once had a conversation about the book and I told him I regretted this passage, the only thing I disliked in *Vile Bodies*. 'Yes,' he said, 'I regret it too. It's very silly.'

During the same conversation he told me of one of the technical devices he had used to give the book its dark character, a device so simple, and so often used by novelists, that I was surprised at my obtuseness in not having noticed it on my own before. The device consists of frequent allusion to the weather which in *Vile Bodies* is nearly always rainy. The device, which can be used as variously as weather is varied, was often used by Scott Fitzgerald, and this may be one reason why literary judges often saw in Fitzgerald a dominating influence on Evelyn's first books. In fact, Evelyn was immune from such influence, good and bad, as he had read none of Fitzgerald's books at the time, and did not do so for some years.

Those who in 1930 saw *Vile Bodies* as a continuation of *Decline and Fall* were pardonably misled not only by the reappearance of some characters but by the reappearance of the victim as hero. The opening chapters tell of the ruin of Adam Fenwick-Symes's hopes of literary fame by the action of puritanical excise and customs officers, an incident not unlike the sending down from the university of the innocent Paul Pennyfeather. But, perhaps in the course of composition, or however it was, Evelyn came to tire of victims, and by the time the story has got into its stride Adam has become something else. He is no Pennyfeather, but a trickster who can play up to the best of the crooked creatures who surround him, and the victim-character 'Ginger' (a rich relation of the later Atwater) becomes the clown of the piece.

The element of *roman à clef* was held to be strong in *Vile Bodies* at the time of its publication. In fact, it is notably weaker than in *Decline and Fall*. Only two total identifications can be made. 'Mrs Ape' is clearly contrived from Aimée Semphill MacPherson. The other identification is of the fictitious Lottie Crump of Shepheard's Hotel in Dover Street, with Mrs Lewis of the Cavendish Hotel in nearby Jermyn Street. Lottie's manner of speech and manner of running her hotel were identical with those of Rosa Lewis. The last-named was infuriated by the book. Someone must have informed on Evelyn, for it is hard to envisage her as a careful or critical reader. The circumstances are unknown, but, as I can testify personally, after the appearance of *Vile Bodies* she forbade Evelyn the house. She saw him as a purveyor of gossip, such as he had mocked in his novel in the characters of Lords Vanburgh and Balcairn. To add to the offence he had borrowed a name from the Cavendish Hotel staff. In the book the name of the social climbing vulgarian who does most of the entertaining is Archie Schwert. This was the name of her aged *maître d'hotel*. Rosa used to screech in rage: 'There are two bastards I'm not going to have in this house, one is that rotten little Donegall and the other is that little swine Evelyn Waugh.'

Some commentators have regarded the last chapter of the book, set in a scene of a Second World War (with antagonists unidentified), as another revelation of underlying seriousness, awful in its prophecy. I cannot regard it as other than a skilfully contrived finale. I think Evelyn regarded it as no graver than that. Thoughts of economic disaster and revolution were common then, but there was little fear of war in 1930.

Except for Father Rothschild's sudden descent into sentimentalism I have only expressed praise for *Vile Bodies*, but I will end with one adverse criticism. In common with many greatly gifted writers Evelyn often made mistakes in the choice of title. *Decline and Fall* is not on careful consideration a suitable title for the earlier book. It has often seemed to me that he originally intended to call it 'Fortune, a Much Maligned Lady', a phrase which recurs at crucial moments in the story, but there is no evidence of a change of title. This is only a guess. In his *Evelyn Waugh, Portrait of an Artist*, Frederick J. Stopp suggested that the second novel could more appropriately have been entitled 'Death at the Party'. There is no question of a change of title in this case because, as mentioned already, Evelyn's correspondence with Peters shows that he decided on 'Vile Bodies' early on in the writing. The phrase is mentioned once in the course of the book, but only in a bracketed parenthesis. Presumably he took it from the Authorized Version of St Paul's Epistle to the Philippians and from the Book of Common Prayer where, in the Burial Service, the same verse is quoted: '. . . The Lord Jesus Christ who shall change our vile body, that it may be likened unto his glorious body . . .' In both instances the reference is to the doctrine of the resurrection of the body, not a subject treated or mentioned in the book. I presume that he wanted a title to indicate that darkness of theme, the blackest of black humour, which informs the book, and remembering this horrific phrase he used it in the plural and thought no more about it.

The great success of *Vile Bodies* meant that Evelyn was immediately and increasingly 'lionized'. His acquaintance in fashionable society became greatly enlarged, and he accelerated the process of growth. He was taken up by the literary hostesses, notably Lady Colefax and Lady Cunard, through whom he came to know many members of the fashionable world. Among others he met and became friends with Lord Brownlow, the close companion of the Prince of Wales, and his wife Kitty. He used to go to stay with them at their famous house Belton (ascribed by some to Sir Christopher Wren) near Grantham, and he indulged his taste, already noted, for visiting at many fashionable country houses where he was welcome. His new acquaintances included many once well-known names, most now forgotten. But not all his new acquaintance was wholly frivolous. From around this time dates his friendship with Lord Berners, the musician and painter. Whether or not under the influence of his admiration for Evelyn's work, he himself attempted a little later the art of comic fiction. His novels are poor stuff, feeble echoes of Evelyn's, and they never reached beyond a circle of friends who could enjoy the private jokes on which these things were founded. They never strongly reflected the robust sense of farce which he genuinely shared with Evelyn. Outside literature, however, Berners was a man of deep and genuine talent, and the friendship which grew up between him and Evelyn was more authentic than some others that he formed in upper-class society.

Evelyn was far too cynical to be deceived by the protestations of admiration and affection which he received in the course of 'lionization'. He enjoyed the experience of being petted but saw through it. The subject will be considered again when the question of the appearance and reality of Evelyn's snobbery is looked into more closely than is appropriate here. It can be said, however, that at this time he did alienate some of his friends by assuming airs. He was not above the foolish practice of name-dropping, and using aristocratic nicknames in the course of conversation with such as could not possibly recognize whom he was talking about. If he saw through the follies of Vanity Fair, like Thackeray he indulged some unworthy respect for them too. What needs to be said immediately is that such respect was never a serious thing with him, but at this time he was not astute enough to avoid the manners of the new rich.

In May 1930, when he was again living at Underhill, Evelyn took up his diary once more. The first entries show that since the publication of *Vile Bodies* his luck in journalism had turned; now it was the editors who were wooing him. In telling of his journalist adventures the diary shows him to have been at once hard-headed in business, inclined to neglect his commitments for the sake of social fun, and to have had an astonishing capacity for hard concentrated work. He never lost his capacity for work till his last days. He never seems to have failed to deliver a promised article, though sometimes he did so a little late. He had an enviable gift: though gestation was sometimes gradual, he wrote quickly.

His diaries of 1930 not only reflect his way of life but contain interesting though wayward criticism.

'Monday 26th May. After dinner I went to the Savoy Theatre and said "I am Evelyn Waugh. Please give me a seat" so they did. I saw the last two acts of Robeson's Othello. Hopeless production but I like his great black booby face. It seemed to make all that silly stuff with the handkerchief quite convincing. After the theatre Frank Pakenham had a supper party at the Savoy.'

No reader would guess from this that Paul Robeson's magnificent performance of Othello was probably the finest of this century, though it is true that the production erred on the side of drabness.

On 10 June he has this comment: 'Dined Buck St went to Ruth Draper. Too human & philanthropic. A brilliant artist if she was satirical but always sentimental & sympathetic at heart. A brilliant sketch of an American wife. Supper Savoy Grill.' His social life was more restrained now than in Oxford days, but not radically different. He relates in one entry how he went home to sleep with a young woman 'but', he adds, 'both of us too drunk to enjoy ourselves'.

The new and abundant references to 'Buck St' (Buckingham Street) require explanation. This was the beautiful little house in Westminster of Bryan Guinness (now Lord Moyne) and his wife Diana (now Lady Mosley), Nancy Mitford's sister. Evelyn had met Bryan at Oxford in post-undergraduate days. They shared many friends and through Nancy Mitford they now shared more. With this young couple Evelyn came to be on close terms of friendship. It is not to play the presumptuous amateur of psychology to suggest that he was especially drawn to them because he saw in their felicity the image of what he had lost. For her he developed a romantic devotion. To say that he fell in love with her would be misleading. He was falling in love with another girl whom he hoped to marry; for Diana his feelings were close to love and troubadourish; his devotion was warmed by a sense of gratitude, for the Guinnesses had been wonderful friends to him in his unhappiness. He dedicated *Vile Bodies* to them. His affection for Diana was one of the deepest of his life.

In the summer he began to correct the proofs of his next book, the minor work called *Labels*. It was the first of the six travel books he was to write, and unique among them for its artful mixture of factual record and fiction.

The fiction entered the book in the following way. When he wrote the original articles and made notes for the book during his travels in the early part of 1929 he had been accompanied by his wife. When he came to write the book from the notes and articles he understandably did not wish to revive in himself memories of his married bliss. He therefore represented himself as a bachelor and invented two characters met on shipboard whom he called Geoffrey and Juliet, a young married couple with whom he strikes up a friendship. Juliet is lightly described but is clearly to be identified with his wife, if only because she is represented as going through the ordeal of severe illness which overtook her. Geoffrey is Evelyn's *alter ego* and his anxieties, which are movingly described, no doubt accurately reflect his own at that time.

The funniest passage in the book comes early on, when Evelyn records how he met an admirer of Alec Waugh; it has been quoted already. Wit is plentiful, but it is not a memorable travel book to be compared, for example, with Robert Byron's *Road to Oxiana*. It is a book of moments rather than a satisfying whole. It has much pleasing irreverence. Of the notorious Monte Carlo pigeon-shooting which he witnessed he wrote: 'The only convincing recommendation which I heard of this sport came from one of the visitors at the Bristol who remarked that it was not cricket.' In those days, and perhaps today too, it was cultural blasphemy to feel anything but reverence for ancient Minoan art. But in recording a stop at Crete, Evelyn has this to say:

'One cannot well judge the merits of Minoan painting, since only a few square inches of the vast area exposed to our consideration are earlier than the last twenty years, and their painters have tempered their zeal for reconstruction with a predilection for covers of *Vogue*.'

There is a fine anti-Romantic passage in the account of the return journey:

'I do not think I shall ever forget the sight of Etna at sunset; the mountain almost invisible in a blur of pastel grey, glowing on the top and then repeating its shape, as though reflected, in a wisp of grey smoke, with the whole horizon behind radiant with pink light, fading gently into a grey pastel sky. Nothing I have ever seen in Art or Nature was quite so revolting.'

*Labels* was well received but, quite rightly, as a minor effort. It kept his name before the public. It may be described as a pot-boiler, but strictures on such publications often ignore the qualities and contents of the pot, and the skill of the boiling.

# Chapter 7

## 1930-1932

Evelyn regarded September 1930 as marking the most important event of his life, his reception into the Roman Catholic Church. Little can be known beyond the main facts about this event. In days ahead, more than ten years later, he was to write much about the Catholic Church, to express strong opinions about its mission and subsequent changes in its liturgy, but he told little about the course of events which resulted in his own change of faith. What little he did tell indicates a rational approach to the faith, remarkable for lack of emotion. The opinion, still commonly maintained among Evelyn's acquaintance, that he became a Catholic to compensate himself for the emotional wound he had received on the break-up of his marriage, is supported by no evidence.

A more tenable opinion, at a superficial glance, is that Evelyn was drawn to Catholicism by his devotion to art and (for all his conventional obeisance to the 'pellucid excellencies of Picasso') especially to the art of the past; that he was attracted, in other words, by a sense of beauty. Until very recently, and to some small extent still, Catholic liturgy was surrounded by and expressed through symbolic art, all either of an extremely or mildly archaic kind. One of the fascinations of Catholic liturgy used to be the close-packed symbolism of even so short and simple a ceremony as a celebration of 'Low Mass', that is, the Mass shorn of all ornament and elaboration and confined to the essentials. It used to be one of the delights of being a Catholic to find that its ceremony involved an endless exploration. Many people have been drawn to the Catholic Church in the same way as they have been drawn to the worship of a great painter or composer, perceiving a glimpse of the sublime through great and effective art. This was in no way Evelyn's case, artist as he was.

As noted in preceding chapters, Evelyn's delight in ecclesiastical ceremony had formerly been very intense. He wrote in *A Little Learning*: 'That interest passed never to return. When, later, I became a Catholic it was not for the attraction of the ceremonies and I have never taken a special interest in their details.' This was written in 1963 or 1964. It is an accurate statement so far as it goes. It is quite true that Evelyn was without the 'special interest' he mentions and was easily bored by a long drawn-out celebration of High Mass. I once saw this comically illustrated by a little incident on which I teased him later and about which he did not defend himself. The occasion was High Mass at Farm Street one Sunday shortly after the war. As a treat we were given particularly beautiful singing (I forget the composer) but at somewhat greater length than usual. I saw Evelyn in the congregation, the picture of boredom and impatience. Presently a Jesuit father emerged from the sacristy to say a Low Mass in one of the side-chapels. Evelyn was within that side-chapel in a matter of seconds.

The large part that music plays in Catholic liturgy made it difficult for him, as a man with only the crudest appreciation of music, to enjoy or explore that liturgy's character. Gregorian chant was repulsive to him and even such overwhelming masterpieces as 'The Reproaches' (whose words are often ascribed to T. S. Eliot!), which since the sixteenth century have been sung on Good Friday to music by Palestrina, meant nothing to Evelyn at all. But when in the course of the post-war years, first the Holy Week Ceremonies and then all else were either abolished or reduced to pale-grey ordinariness; then Evelyn did find that his interest was not as dead as he had come to suppose. Out of loyalty to his Church he did not give expression to this regret in his autobiography. When it was taken away, though not before, Evelyn recognized the importance of liturgical art to his Catholic faith and practice.

Having now returned, unwillingly, to bachelor status, Evelyn in 1930 cultivated with renewed zest the companionship of his friends. He was a frequent visitor to the Lygons at Madresfield, saw much of his Oxford cronies, often saw Henry Yorke and his wife, Harold Acton, the Sitwells and Pansy Pakenham, now married to the painter Henry Lamb. From the Lambs Evelyn rented their house in Wiltshire for nearly a month in August 1930; but the people he saw most of at this time were his old friends the Plunket-Greenes.

Gwen and Olivia Greene were the only devout Catholics whom Evelyn knew well. If he had not known them his conversion would almost certainly have been a much more gradual and different process. From that it is easy to conclude that he was converted by Gwen Greene and her daughter. In a way he was but in a very indirect way. This part of his story has a strange irony.

A fact which has to be noticed, a fact which in large part explains Gwen Greene's conversion to Catholicism a few years before, is that she was a niece by marriage of Friedrich von Hügel. (Her mother, Lady Maud Parry, was the sister of Baroness von Hügel.) In the early twentieth century Hügel was one of the most influential theological scholars in Europe. A modernist and an uncomfortably acute biblical critic, he was at the same time admired as a reforming influence and deplored as a rebel against orthodoxy. Like Lord Acton he lived under the threat of excommunication, and like Acton he was, for all his 'modernism', a devout member of the Catholic Church. Among his convictions he disapproved of proselytism, and his suspicions were easily aroused when he heard of conversions which were due to personal influence. He believed that such decisions should come from deeper causes. He felt this so strongly that he himself conscientiously avoided any attempt to convert anyone to his beliefs. It was possibly to spare her uncle's feelings that Gwen Greene and her daughter did not become Roman Catholics until after Hügel's death in 1925.

Following her uncle's example, Gwen Greene made no attempt to convert Evelyn, but Evelyn did discuss religion with the mother and daughter from time to time. The manner of some of these discussions was unconventional. Olivia went to stay with Evelyn at the Lambs' house in Coombe Bissett, and there is this entry in his diary for 18 August: 'Olivia and I drove into Salisbury and bought some very good port from a slightly hostile wine merchant. That evening we got a little drunk and talked about religion.' Father Martin D'Arcy S.J. of the Farm Street Community has described the religious influence of the Greenes on Evelyn as follows:

'[Evelyn's] close friends Gwen Plunket-Greene and her daughter helped to make him act, but they did not make up his mind for him . . . Evelyn was never a borrower and had almost too set a mind to accept advice. No one could have made up that mind of his for him no more than anyone could have been co-author of his novels.' This statement needs to be qualified by one made by Evelyn himself. When Olivia Greene died he wrote of her to a friend: 'She bullied me into the Church.'

The entry in his diary for 27 August is significant. 'It rained all day. We did nothing. I wrote to Father D'Arcy.'

He had been introduced to Father Martin D'Arcy by Gwen Greene shortly before. It may be guessed that the letter of the 27th informed Father D'Arcy that Evelyn wished to place himself 'under instruction' with a view to being received into the Catholic Church. Father D'Arcy personally undertook the work of instruction. It was brief. Evelyn had informed himself about the main doctrines already. In a letter to me, Father D'Arcy thus described in outline his experience as the instructor of this catechumen.

'He was a man of very strong convictions and a clear mind. He had convinced himself very unsentimentally – with only an intellectual passion, of the truth of the Catholic faith, and that in it he must save his soul. Hence in his instructions or talks he always wanted to know exactly the meaning and content of the Catholic faith, and he would stop me, raise difficulties, – then immediately he was satisfied, he would ask me to go on. In this way he was one of the most satisfactory people to talk to about the faith, whom I have ever known. He was very different from one or two others I can think of, who kept on saying, "Yes, I think that corresponds with my experience".

'Evelyn would have nothing to do with that kind of talk. His prevailing desire was to learn what God revealed not what he felt. He was perhaps inclined to be too literal about the Last Things, and the message of the Gospel.

'What showed his sincerity was that, at the time, he thought that as a Catholic he would never be able to marry again and have children. His decision to seek admission into the Church therefore meant a considerable sacrifice.'

On 29 September Evelyn was formally received into the Catholic Church by Father D'Arcy, at the Church of the Immaculate Conception in Farm Street. His godparent was the charwoman then on duty, and used to this responsibility. He asked none of his friends, not even the Plunket-Greenes, to witness this solemn moment in his life, with one exception. This was his old school fellow of Lancing days, Tom Driberg, who was still and has remained a fervent Anglican. Tom was greatly surprised at being the only invited person, and remained surprised for many years. After Evelyn's death he and I were talking about him and it was then that Tom told me about the incident. Had Evelyn done it, he wondered, in the hopes of ensnaring his friend into the fold? That seemed an odd way to set about it, and unlikely. Pure affection? They had seen little of each other in the last two years. Suddenly, as we wrestled with the conundrum, Tom saw the explanation. At the time, he was working on the *Daily Express* in charge of a gossip column which he had founded under the name of William Hickey. Since Evelyn had not asked Tom to avoid any mention of the matter in his column, it stood to reason that he would mention it, since Evelyn was now 'news', and his conversion to the Catholic faith was almost in the class of a scoop. So Tom, of course, did mention it. Tom, in fact, had been used by his friend as part of an ingenious stratagem. If Evelyn's conversion was reported in the widest-selling newspaper in the country, then he would be spared the labour of writing numerous letters. So Tom argued it out.

It is not possible to prove the truth of Tom Driberg's hypothesis, but it is at the very least plausible. If it is a correct interpretation, as I think it is, then it forcibly illustrates the unemotional, almost prosy spirit in which Evelyn entered the Church.

His parents were greatly distressed at the step which he had taken, but there was no withdrawal of their abundant affection. His brother Alec was not distressed but puzzled. He has recorded that being without religious sense he found that for the first time there grew a lack of mutual understanding, and with it a lack of mutual sympathy between him and his brother. He has compared the situation with that of two persons who look at a stained-glass window, one from within the building where he sees images and colour, the other from without where he sees nothing but a dark blank. His own diary tells nothing of Evelyn's feelings. He made no entries after the beginning of September for more than a month. The entry for 27 August, quoted above, is the only diary reference to his conversion till 28 December.

In the meantime Evelyn, with the help of A. D. Peters, was planning the next phase of his literary career. No idea for another novel came to him and he turned once more to biography and travel. He told Peter (as his friends always called A. D. Peters and as Evelyn now began to do) that he wished to write a life of Swift. When Peter conveyed the proposition to Evelyn's American publishers they were enthusiastic and as a result, in July, Evelyn signed a contract for the book, with a small advance on royalties. But that is as far as the book ever went. Evelyn seems suddenly to have lost interest in this great subject, and no more is heard about it in the Peter-Evelyn correspondence, or elsewhere. He turned to travel.

In the autumn of 1930 the Negus Ras Tafari was to be proclaimed and crowned Emperor Haile Selassie of Ethiopia. Evelyn felt that the occasion might be interesting, and he asked Peter to get him an assignment as a special correspondent to Addis Ababa. Peter approached the *Daily News*, the *Daily Mail*, the *Daily Express*, the *Daily Telegraph* and *The Graphic* in England; the *Saturday Evening Post* and *Colliers* in the United States. They all refused the proposal except *The Graphic*, which commissioned a minimum of three articles at ten guineas each. It followed that if Evelyn was to attend the coronation he had to do so at his own expense. He decided to take the financial risk: to invest a large part of his earnings from *Vile Bodies* and his journalism (of which he did much at this time) in a travel book, and in hopes of a novel suggested by his experiences in distant lands.

The gamble was successful. He left London in early October and was in Addis Ababa in time for the coronation in November. He made two journeys in the interior of Ethiopia, and then travelled to Aden where the Resident and Commander-in-Chief was his cousin Stewart Symes, later to be Governor-General of the Sudan. From there he went back to Africa by way of Zanzibar. He went to Kenya, the Belgian Congo, and thence to Cape Town where he caught a boat to Southampton. He was back in March 1931. The whole of this journey cost him a little less than £500. It resulted in two books, *Remote People*, his second travel book, published in the summer of 1931, and his third novel, *Black Mischief*, published in 1932.

*Remote People* is in three parts: the first records his adventures in Ethiopia; the second his visit to the Aden Protectorate and Zanzibar; the third his adventures in British Africa and the Belgian Congo, and his return home. The book has claims to be considered the best of Evelyn's travel books, and of its three parts, the first is superior to the others, good as they are.

What chiefly gives this first part, whose main subject is Haile Selassie's coronation, an excellence above the others is the fact that early on in his visit to Addis Ababa Evelyn met a character after his own heart, a personage such as he might have invented in one of his novels. He was an eccentric American professor, of great learning and imagination, who was a mine of impressive misinformation. In an essay on Evelyn's travel books, Mr Eric Newby describes this person as a 'tiresome American professor' and as 'dreadful'. It is clear that Mr Newby had never known him and did not consult people who had.

He was Professor Thomas Whittemore, one of the leading authorities in his time on Byzantine art. He was largely responsible for the restoration of the mosaics in St Sophia. A Bostonian, a friend of Henry James, an emotional enthusiast of his subject, he had delightful and unusual conversational powers. I imagine that his dramatic style of talk, and his shameless use of the ultra-poetic phrase, reflected a style of cultivated conversation once admired and now entirely out of fashion. I heard him once describe Novgorod 'as though all the golden domes of Russia were plunged into the glittering and magic seas of Venice'. I told Evelyn about this once and he was much amused. Whittemore had used precisely the same phrase to him. His theatrical manner, and his deep tremulous voice contrasting oddly with his minute neat person, often allowed him to convey a rapid description in a way that conventional talk cannot. I once asked him what was the first and immediate impression that Henry James made on those who met him, and 'O-o-o-oh!' he moaned, almost literally cowering away, '*Heavy!*'

It appears that Whittemore's knowledge of Byzantine ceremony had given him a nodding acquaintance with Coptic liturgy which is in many respects related to it, and of which the Christian liturgy in Ethiopia is an offshoot. As happens to authorities, even the most eminent, Whittemore grew over-confident and while he began to look on himself as one who fully understood Ethiopian liturgy he wholly underestimated its divagations and its complexities. He was next to Evelyn during the enormously long coronation service and Mass. He undertook to explain the elaborate ceremonial. Anyone who knew Tom Whittemore can hear his voice in the section in which Evelyn tells how during the seemingly endless hours of the sacred celebration Whittemore would make occasional remarks.

' "They are beginning the Mass now", "That was the offertory", "No, I was wrong; it was the consecration", "No, I was wrong; I think it is the secret Gospel", "No, I think it must be the Epistle", "How very curious; I don't believe it was a Mass at all", "*Now* they *are* beginning the Mass . . ." and so on. Presently the bishops began to fumble among the bandboxes, and investiture began. At long intervals the Emperor was presented with robe, orb, spurs, spear, and finally with the crown. A salute of guns was fired, and the crowds outside, scattered all over the surrounding waste spaces, began to cheer; the imperial horses reared up, plunged on top of each other, kicked the gilding off the front of the coach, and broke their traces. The coachman sprang from the box and whipped them from a safe distance. Inside the pavilion there was a general sense of relief; it had all been very fine and impressive, now for a cigarette, a drink, and a change into less formal costume. Not a bit of it. The next thing was to crown the Empress and the heir apparent; another salvo of guns followed, during which an Abyssinian groom had two ribs broken in an attempt to unharness a pair of the imperial horses. Again we felt for our hats and gloves. But the Coptic choir still sang; the bishops then proceeded to take back the regalia with proper prayers, lections and canticles.

' "I have noticed some very curious variations in the Canon of the Mass," remarked the professor, "particularly with regard to the kiss of peace."

'Then the Mass began.'

With Whittemore Evelyn made his first interior journey in Ethiopia. Together they travelled to Debra Lebanos, north of Addis Ababa and a place of immense sanctity to Ethiopians. The adventures of that uncomfortable journey and Evelyn's gradually growing insight into his companion's character form a marvellous episode in *Remote People*. The monastery of Debra Lebanos was and is most famed for a sacred library of great antiquity. Evelyn saw in this sacred institution little but squalid and laughable barbarism; Whittemore looked upon it with veneration. The climax of the visit is exquisitely described.

'The professor then asked whether we might visit the library of which the world stood in awe. Why, certainly; there it was in the corner. The abuna produced a small key from his pocket and directed one of the priests to open the cupboard. They brought out five or six bundles wrapped in silk shawls, and, placing them with great care on the table, drew back the door-curtain to admit a shaft of light. The abuna lifted the corners of the shawl on the topmost bundle and revealed two pieces of board clumsily hinged together in the form of a diptych. Professor W. kissed them eagerly; they were then opened, revealing two coloured lithographs, apparently cut from a religious almanac printed in Germany some time towards the end of the last century, representing the Crucifixion and the Assumption, pasted on to the inner surfaces of the wood. The professor was clearly a little taken aback. "Dear, dear, how remarkably ugly they are," he remarked as he bent down to kiss them.'

This was by no means the first object that Whittemore had kissed in the course of the expedition. Among Evelyn's notes in his diary one reads: 'W kissed everything; knew nothing.' He was not much more merciful in the account he gave of the amazing 'W' in *Remote People*. But the story of Evelyn and Whittemore has an unexpected sequel. From this meeting Whittemore took a great liking to Evelyn, though I doubt if they met again; he became an enthusiastic reader of his books, would quote from them and conceived a special admiration for the picture of Ethiopia in *Remote People*. Did this show humourlessness or insensitiveness? Quite impossible. Did it show the vanity which is so extreme that it cannot recognize mockery? I never noticed vanity as a trait in Whittemore, and I believe that this extreme kind of vanity would have been obvious even in casual acquaintance. He had wit and an enormous sense of humour. I believe he enjoyed the picture of himself because it was so funny. I believe the explanation is as simple as that.

The second of Evelyn's journeys within Ethiopia was of some importance to historians of literature. Before leaving for Aden he visited Harar, where he met the French Catholic bishop, a man of great age called Monsignor Jerome. Here is Evelyn's account of his conversation with the bishop.

'I steered the conversation as delicately as I could from church expenses to Arthur Rimbaud. At first we were at cross purposes, because the bishop, being a little deaf, mistook my " poète" for " prêtre", and inflexibly maintained that no Father Rimbaud had ever, to his knowledge, ministered in Abyssinia. Later this difficulty was cleared up, and the bishop, turning the name over in his mind, remembered that he had, in fact, known Rimbaud quite well; a young man with a beard, who was in some trouble with his leg; a very serious man who did not go out much; he was always worried about business; not a good Catholic, though he had died at peace with the Church, the bishop understood, at Marseilles. He used to live with a native woman in a little house, now demolished, in the square; he had no children; probably the woman was still alive; she was not a native of Harar, and after Rimbaud's death she had gone back to her own people in Tigre . . . a very, very serious young man, the bishop repeated. He seemed to find this epithet the most satisfactory – very serious and sad.

'It was rather a disappointing interview. All the way to Harar I had nurtured the hope of finding something new about Rimbaud, perhaps even to encounter a half-caste son keeping a shop in some back street. The only significant thing I learned from the bishop was that, living in Harar, surrounded by so many radiant women, he should have chosen a mate from the stolid people of Tigre – a gross and perverse preference.'

In her biography of Rimbaud Enid Starkie indicated that Evelyn's talk with Monsignor Jerome established for the first time the location of Rimbaud's house in Harar during the final period of his life in Africa. This was probably the last conversation about him held by any European with someone who had known the poet in those days.

The rest of *Remote People* need not detain the reader. The second half is more like a conventional travel book than the earlier record of the coronation, and Professor W. and Aden, though, as with all Evelyn's travel books, it is crammed with arresting sketches of fellow travellers and other chance-met people, notably a more than usually grotesque missionary. Reference has been made to a diary entry of 28 December 1930. He was at Zanzibar on this date, and after a long interval received some mail. He recorded: 'Mostly letters of congratulation and vilification about my having become a Papist. Religious controversy seems the occupation of the lowest minds nowadays.' Not much to be gained there for an insight into his personal emotions about his conversion.

After his return in early March, the rest of 1931 was spent in hard work relieved by much social diversion. He worked up his diary into *Remote People* which was published in early November by Duckworth and later in the USA where it was called *They Were Still Dancing*, the opening words of the book. Again he chose, or was persuaded by his American publishers, into choosing a misleading title, in this case suggesting the wild and sacred capers of African tribes, rather than two Europeans foxtrotting through habit to the strains of a gramophone on board a second-rate French boat. He also worked on the novel which was to become famous as *Black Mischief*. Much of this work was done at the Easton Court Hotel at Chagford in Devonshire.

Evelyn had come to know this hotel through Alec who, some years back, had found it a welcome retreat for the labour of writing. The American proprietress, Mrs Cobb, was an admirable hostess. The whole feeling of the place under her regime was less that of a hotel than of a country house. Many writers of Evelyn's and Alec's time found it a delightful, indeed perfect, place in which to work. Cosy, humorous, withal discreet, Mrs Cobb respected writers for their profession and easily understood their needs. She could be quietly encouraging though she was never inquisitive. Many writers probably owed more to her than they did to the famous and publicized literary hostesses of London. Evelyn was very attached to her, but in writing to Hugh Lygon's sister about her, he allowed his fantasy to disguise very thoroughly the genuine respect he felt. He wrote some time in late 1931: 'I think I will tell you about this hotel. Well, it is very odd. Kept by a deserter from the Foreign Legion and an American lady called Mrs Postlethwaite Cobb who mixes menthol with her cigarettes. And we drink rye whisky in her bedroom and there are heaps of New York magazines & rather good, sophisticated food. I think it is a distributing centre for white slaves and cocaine or something like that. They never give one a bill.'

Except for letters written on serious occasions, such as the death of her brother, no letter of Evelyn to Mary Lygon was without fantasy. Another letter of late 1931 has a description of a weekend at Belton in the course of which Evelyn informed her: 'there was a pretty auburn-haired girl called Brendan Bracken, dressed up as a man.' He added that he was unable to resist sexual intercourse with this radiant beauty.

At this time the Lygon family had fallen on evil days. The circumstances should be recalled as they made a deep and manifest impression on Evelyn and strengthened his bonds of affection. The head of the family, Lord Beauchamp, had the misfortune to have homosexual tastes. His 'weaknesses', as his coevals used to term them, became widely known. His wife was a sister of the Duke of Westminster and the latter was consumed with indignant envy against his brother-in-law. The two men were in extreme contrast. Lord Beauchamp was the Warden of the Cinque Ports, the Lord-Lieutenant of Worcestershire, the Chancellor of London University, a Knight of the Order of the Garter, the Liberal leader in the House of Lords, a former Governor-General of Australia, and a former Minister of Cabinet rank. (It was he who had represented the Government at Buckingham Palace when George V signed the declaration of war in 1914.) In short, Beauchamp was a distinguished man, while his ducal brother-in-law was nothing but a fatuous, spoilt, ageing playboy. To add to the irritation of the Duke, Lord Beauchamp had three sons, while the other had no direct male heir. So the Duke decided to ruin his brother-in-law. He went to work with a will. He informed the King that as Sovereign he had inadvertently made a notorious homosexual a Knight of the Garter, and the King was deeply shocked. The Duke then informed his sister of her husband's irregularities, a difficult task as Lady Beauchamp had never heard of homosexuality before. The information led to a nervous collapse and endangered her sanity. He invited Beauchamp's four daughters to testify against their father. They enraged and bewildered their uncle by rejecting his proposition with contempt. Nevertheless the Duke did succeed in ruining Lord Beauchamp. The latter saw that he was defenceless. At the King's private request, he resigned all his official appointments. He decided to commit suicide but was argued out of it by Hughie. He went abroad. The result was disappointing to the Duke because, by overplaying his hand through informing the King, he denied himself the pleasure of a public scandal of more than Wildean dimensions. But he had not done too badly.

It is wonderful what a man can get away with if he is very rich indeed and also a duke. One might suppose that the squalid spectacle of a man, whose private life was unedifying, taking up the posture of a champion of moral rectitude and chastity through undisguised envy, and attempting a disgusting subornation of his victim's daughters; one might suppose that such an exhibition would revolt the coarsest taste. Not at all. The Duke of Westminster lost no friends through his endeavours, except the Lygon family. Lord Beauchamp lost all but a very few loyal friends, among whom was Stanley Baldwin. His children lost few friends, but they did lose some. The Duke felt that in refusing his entreaties the Lygons had let him down, and he made it clear that he did not like people who enjoyed his hospitality to maintain much friendship with them. To reject the luxuries he could offer was too much for his courtiers, so he kept his court intact. When he referred to the infinitely more gifted Beauchamp as 'my bugger-in-law', these hangers-on giggled with real or affected pleasure at what they declared to be his inimitable wit. Social climbers faced with a choice chose the Duke, and one or two homosexuals with social ambitions saw a new incentive to sycophancy. Lord Beauchamp's children met the crisis with a proud show of sceptical indifference, but under their assurance there could not but be bitter feelings. They could not be without resentment at the many friends who abandoned their father, and the few, including surprising ones, who abandoned themselves.

For Evelyn there was neither choice nor temptation to choice. The Duke had not taken him up, but even if he had, Evelyn's preference would have been clear. He had always loved the Lygons since he had come to know them through Elmley and Hughie in his second year at Oxford. As with the Plunket-Greenes, he 'fell in love with a family', though without the serious interest which came to inform his friendship with Gwen and Olivia Greene. The friendship was built on youth and hilarity, well epitomized by Mary Lygon one day when (about this time) she and Evelyn were sitting by a fountain in the garden of Madresfield, and on which was inscribed the motto 'The day is wasted on which we have not laughed'. Mary said to him: 'Well, we haven't wasted many days, have we?'

In Evelyn's 'first Madresfield period', Mary and her younger sister Dorothy were still 'in the schoolroom'. Evelyn was then a delight reserved to their two older brothers, Elmley and Hughie, and the elder sisters, Lady Lettice and Lady Sibell, as Lord Beauchamp always punctiliously described them when mentioning them to persons outside the family; but by 1930 Mary (always known as 'Maimie' and to Evelyn as 'Blondie') and Dorothy (sometimes for obscure reasons known as 'Coote' and sometimes as 'Poll') had emerged from the schoolroom. They became Evelyn's especial friends in the family. The relationship with these two, as with the rest of the family, took on more seriousness with the disasters of 1931, but it never lost its essential element of hilarity. The Lygons were (and are) among people who, even when confronted by catastrophe, never face life without a sense of humour. It is a rare spirit that shallower people regard as shallow.

The Lygons had been brought up to be proficient horsemen and horse-women. Madresfield is situated in first-class hunting country and the Lygons were prominent performers in the field. Under their persuasion Evelyn decided to take up hunting. He could ride but not with the mastery and skill needed to keep up with his friends in a run through 'big' country. So he decided to take tuition under a certain Captain Hance at his academy in Malvern. Evelyn could not have chosen a more exacting course of instruction or a more severe tutor than this former cavalryman. Most of the students at his academy were men with ambitions to excel in steeple-chasing and several of his former pupils triumphed at Aintree. Evelyn had not the right build for a horseman and so he never became proficient, but he pursued his studies with typical concentration, vigour and courage. He would often go out hunting with the Lygons from nearby Madresfield, and from the Easton Court Hotel he would follow the staghounds in Devonshire. He had frequent falls. This passion for hunting did not last above two years. Once after the war I asked him if he ever rode a horse now. 'No,' he said, 'I dislike it.' 'But', I said, 'I remember when you used to follow hounds with great boldness.' 'Only for social reasons,' he said.

I used occasionally to meet Captain Hance through my own friendship with the Lygons. He had a great devotion to the family. He was a genial man with much sense of fun, though not of a very subtle kind. I never thought of him as a subject of myth and fantasy, but that was how he appeared to Evelyn and as he soon appeared to the Lygons. Dorothy Lygon has well described the phenomena. 'Evelyn transposed the Captain and his family to an Olympian level . . . their least pronouncement was debated and scrutinized for omens and auguries.'

The myth-making was as much a Lygon habit as an Evelyn one, as indicated already by the Evelyn-Maimie correspondence. It was typical of the family that Maimie's ferocious one-eyed Pekinese was made a member of the Lord's Day Observance Society under the name of P. H. Grainger, the initials standing for Pretty Hound. Any one, human or otherwise, prominent or obscure, remarkable or ordinary, was likely to be the subject of a legend under Waugh-cum-Lygon treatment, so that the elevation of Captain Hance to Olympus is not surprising. What was less expectable was that Captain Hance became a cause and foundation of Evelyn's friendship with Lady Diana Duff Cooper, but that belongs to a slightly later time.

Evelyn was busy with journalism during the second half of 1931 and most of 1932. The majority of the short stories which later appeared in the collection *Mr Loveday's Little Outing* were written during these months for various magazines, including *Harper's* which, in the Lygon correspondence, became known as 'Lady Sibell's Bazaar', for the reason that she contributed an occasional article of fashionable gossip. He did little travel at this time, but he did go twice to France, once to Italy in 1932, and once in the same year to Spain. The last-mentioned journey was one of three which he was to make to that country. This first one bore no literary fruit; the second did. His residence at home was divided between Underhill and the Savile Club in London, and in the country was at the Easton Court Hotel, the Abingdon Arms at Beckley, occasionally at the

Spread Eagle Hotel at Thame, in frequent visits to Madresfield and a few to Belton.

In mid-August 1931 two important events occurred in Evelyn's literary life. He finished *Remote People* and began the writing of *Black Mischief*. By mid-September he had finished the first chapter which he sent to Peter in the hope of separate publication in a magazine. Eventually it was published separately for a small fee in Desmond MacCarthy's quarterly *Life and Letters*. Later many attempts were made by Peter to obtain serialization of the book, both in England and America, but the complexity of the story made it unmanageable for this purpose. The original title of the book was 'Accession', but Evelyn's American publishers complained that the term in American usage was lacking in force and even in meaning, and they suggested others from which Evelyn chose 'Black Mischief' Today that title would be rejected as excessively shocking.

Considering how quickly he wrote, once the gestation period was over, Evelyn took a long time, by his own standards, in the writing of *Black Mischief*, nearly a year. It was not ready for final submission to his publishers until the later part of June 1932. The reason for this was probably in part due to the elaborate involutions of the story, but probably also to the numerous distractions besetting him, and whose temptations he did little to repel since he had leaped to fame after the publication of *Vile Bodies*. Being an extravagant spender he also needed to make quick money and he often took on commissions without the time, or inclination, to carry them out completely. He took on tasks ill-adapted to his talents. One of these ventures was well described by the late John Paddy Carstairs.

He was the son of the famous comedian Nelson Keyes and had much of his father's farcical smartness of manner. In January 1932 Evelyn had been lent a flat by a friend in Albany. His affairs were in much disorder, and so for a short time in this 'Albany period' he engaged the services of Desmond MacCarthy's daughter Rachael (now Lady David Cecil) to act as his secretary. She did not remain long in this employment and Paddy Carstairs's account explains why, though it should be said that the mutual affection of Evelyn and Rachael was never impaired in the least. At this time, in January 1932, a film company, presided over by Basil Dean and named A.R.P. (Associated Radio Productions, later to be called Associated Talking Pictures Ltd), invited Evelyn to work for them, undeterred by the description of the film industry presented in *Vile Bodies*. He accepted. Here is Paddy Carstairs's account.

'I was teamed up to collaborate and more to guide Evelyn Waugh on a screen treatment of a Sapper book for Basil Dean. I was told to report to Albany, the smart Piccadilly flats where Waugh was then in residence.

'I found him delightful, urbane and of course with that dry, witty sense of humour which abounded in his novels of that time. Luckily (because I had heard he could be frosty) he seemed to like me. I think he had expected some profound and elderly collaborator, and it was a relief, I think, for him to find I was neither. I therefore found him warm and approachable. It was the time when he was much in the news and he was clearly enjoying his success.

'I used to arrive at his request "not too early, Paddy" about 10.30 and when inevitably Evelyn was still in bed. I would, at his suggestion, eat his breakfast while he dressed leisurely. By then it was approaching cocktail time for him, usually at the Ritz, and he would suggest we started work "after lunch, Paddy". After lunch meant three and usually Evelyn would appear about three-thirty and we would then have tea and a long talk about everything except our script. I would finally, tactfully, guide the conversation to the film but by then he would exclaim "Good heavens, is it nearly six? I must go to a cocktail party, so shall we start tomorrow?"

'And so it would be the next day and the next. Sometimes fascinating friends looked in, for example Patrick Balfour (now Lord Kinross) and the conversation was witty and the atmosphere genial and so, somehow, we didn't get on with the Treatment.

'I remember when he was off to the Ritz he was sartorially elegant and he would inevitably say "See you about three, then, Paddy?" and as he moved off he always winked at me as if to say, "It's great to be lionized, but don't for a moment think I am taking it seriously."

'Finally pressure was put on us so that we simply *had* to deliver a treatment and somehow Evelyn galvanized himself into activity. I remember there was a fire in a hotel in the story and with almost adolescent glee this was a sequence Evelyn enjoyed. He decided that one of the characters on hearing the fire alarm promptly groped for his false teeth in a glass near his bedside. Evelyn enacted this quite preposterously. It was odd to find, despite his very sophisticated comic books, he seemed to adore slapstick, the cornier the better. I found this very bizarre. Our completed treatment was never filmed and I don't think either of us was really surprised.'

In 1932 Evelyn made his only appearance as a man of the theatre. In the year before, a writer named Dennis Bradley had proposed to adapt *Vile Bodies* for theatrical purposes. After much argument about terms, he made a play out of the novel, and this was well received at private performances given at the Arts Theatre in July 1931. But the Lord Chamberlain of the time, Lord Cromer, refused to license the play for public performance, although he attended the Arts Theatre production and appeared to enjoy it. After Bradley had edited the dramatization and reduced the tone to a milder key, the Lord Chamberlain relented in March and the play was produced at the Vaudeville Theatre in April 1932, where it opened on the 15th and ran till the end of May. Evelyn did not like the much respectablized version of his novel, but on the whole he remained indifferent to the enterprise which brought him some money.

He was not a dramatist and after his schooldays never attempted to write a play.

His attention was elsewhere, on *Black Mischief*, which he finished in June and which was published at the end of September 1932.

It was his third novel and fully maintained and even enhanced the high position he had reached as a comic artist. It was the first of his novels with an exotic background. It was manifestly based on his experiences in Africa and Aden in 1930, in fact on the subject-matter of *Remote People*. Evelyn was at some pains, then and later, to disown any intention of caricaturing Ethiopia in his fictitious Empire of Azania, and he insisted that the land over which his Emperor Seth ruled had no more of detailed and identifiable realism than have Swift's Lilliput or Laputa. This was not a polite falsehood, but it was not the whole truth.

If Evelyn had only visited Zanzibar and Aden on his 1930 journey, then *Black Mischief* would be radically different from the book we have. Ethiopia is the backbone of this fiction, and there are details, such as the former Emperor Amurath's victory over European forces, and the survival of an imprisoned claimant to the throne, which were manifestly taken from recent Ethiopian history. Some of the less rational and less pleasing native customs of Azania were likewise modelled on those of Ethiopia as a reader of *Remote People* easily appreciates, but with his descriptions of Azanian life there are admixed many elements of 'darkest Africa', probably suggested by things he had seen or heard about in his journey through the Belgian Congo, and which are not reminiscent of Ethiopian ways. Azania is undoubtedly fictitious – up to a point, Lord Copper.

Evelyn was on sure ground, however, when he rejected as absurd the notion that the hero of the story, the Emperor Seth, was to be equated with the recently crowned Emperor of Ethiopia, Haile Selassie. Between the real man and the fictitious one there is no discernible point of resemblance. Whether Evelyn had any model in mind when he contrived this exquisite portrait of an African sovereign who had studied at Oxford and understood nothing which he had been taught, is very doubtful. Chance meetings with unnamed African Bachelors of Arts (Oxon.) are the most likely inspiration. The identification of the other hero of the story, Basil Seal, with Peter Rodd has been noted already. In only one respect is Peter Rodd disguised in the portrait of Seal. Rodd had very fair hair, platinum blond as it is called, and Basil Seal is described as dark-haired. This may not be merely an attempt at alibi on Evelyn's part. Basil Murray was dark-haired and, on Evelyn's own admission, he also contributed to the unforgettable picture of this ruthless young man whose heart is only touched, and then not deeply, when he finds that he has accidentally eaten his mistress at a cannibal feast.

As noted earlier, the element of *roman à clef* weakened with Evelyn's progress. It persisted more and more as a strictly private joke. Cruttwell appears again in *Black Mischief* but in a role which is nearer to neutrality than that of Toby the burglar. Here he is a tedious diner-out in fashionable London. A Mr Grainger makes a brief appearance, and the origin of his name is not far to seek. There is a very well drawn picture of an unsuccessful English businessman, and he is called Mr Jagger. The name was not lifted, as many readers probably suppose, from *Great Expectations*, but from a great friend of the Lygons who lived near Madresfield. (In Lygon parlance a valued friend was known as a 'jagger'.) It is said that the picture of the ludicrous British Minister in Azania was contrived in a revengeful spirit following a social snub to Evelyn from the British Legation in Addis Ababa. I find no confirmation of this and Evelyn's diary of 1930 suggests friendly relations with the Legation, with only occasional expressions of irritation at Legation inefficiency or 'panic'. There is one supposed identification which became almost famous. The preposterous Emperor's British Commander-in-Chief is called General Connolly, and his Negress wife, until raised to the Azanian peerage as a duchess, is called by him and everyone else 'Black Bitch'. The general's name was deliberately and unquestionably chosen by Evelyn in a spirit of fun from that of his friend Cyril Connolly. I remember well when I first heard of *Black Mischief*. I had been away in the country for some time, and Cyril and his first wife Jean had been in Paris. We had not met for a few months, so on coming to London in October I asked them to dinner. Cyril 'raved' as they say, he was 'in ecstasies' about *Black Mischief*. He said it was the best thing Evelyn had written. His wife told me about General Connolly and 'Black Bitch'. They both thought that the general was a great stroke. 'We don't mind,' laughed Cyril. Much later he expressed some offence about the book. Jean Connolly was dark, and by an inimical blond-preferrer could conceivably be hideously described as 'Black Bitch'. Doubtless, some affectionate friends pointed all this out. But the fact remains that Cyril Connolly took no offence at the time, only much later, and that any identification between him and the general is meaningless.

But the major identification of Azania with Ethiopia stands beyond dispute. I had never heard it disputed and, much later, the truth of the identification was brought home to me forcibly when I visited Ethiopia in 1956 while gathering information for a biography of Orde Wingate. I found among English people in the country a distinct impression that as one who intended to write on the subject of Ethiopia I was suspect. Did I know a writer called Evelyn Waugh, I was asked several times. When I replied that he was a close friend suspicion darkened into hostility. I was told that he had done more damage than any other Englishman to Anglo-Ethiopian relations and that the offence caused both by his travel book and his 'disgusting' novel would never be forgotten. It did seem to be forgotten, however, by Ethiopians. I met a considerable number of them, including some who had been educated at Oxford or Cambridge and might be presumed to have read the book, but they made no mention of it and seemed unmoved by the knowledge that I was proposing to write about their country. It may be, of course, that they were being polite.

There are other identifications to be made. One should be stated. Dame Mildred Porch and her colleague Miss Tin, valiant crusaders for humane treatment of animals and birth control, are almost certainly drawn from two ladies whom Evelyn met in Addis Ababa and who were crusading against vice and prostitution. His caricature of the ladies was to get him into trouble, but not with the ladies themselves.

The writing in *Black Mischief* shows advance on his style in the preceding two novels. From *Rossetti* onwards Evelyn's writing always showed the virtues of conciseness and economy, but in *Black Mischief* he brought to them a new mastery. Nowhere in this book as in the earlier ones can the reader find the odd unnecessary word. Adjectives are only used when needed and adverbs almost disappear. The structure of the book presented Evelyn with a new challenge. The setting is partly in Azania (which, geographically, can be described as an enlarged Zanzibar) and partly in the London of Lady Metroland (who seems to have lost Father Rothschild). This involves frequent changes of scenes and types of character, and in this respect the book may occasionally remind a reader of Aldous Huxley's *Point Counter Point*. The difference is that whereas Huxley's changes of subject and place are managed with all his accustomed clumsiness, so that one almost hears the scene-shifters setting up the props and bawling at each other behind the curtains, the changes in Evelyn's book flow with all the exquisite skill of a first-rate film whose cutting has been done by a master-craftsman. Both books were without doubt influenced by cinema technique. Evelyn showed himself an artist; Huxley a moralist trying in vain to use art for his purposes.

In a story largely set in an exotic scene, Evelyn could not resist indulging his taste for the purple patch. But he had learned the value of reticence again. Such patches occur very rarely in *Black Mischief*. They never interfere with the movement of the story; they never obtrude, in spite of the boldness and even unrestraint of their prose.

The last scene of the book is interesting. It illustrates how immensely political expectations have changed and been invalidated in forty years. After the horrors, brutalities and bloodshed of the war-torn Azania which Basil Seal served as a grotesque T. E. Lawrence (I think Lawrence was in Evelyn's mind), Seth's Empire is taken over by the League of Nations and placed under mandatory rule run by the French and British. In 1932 the Western world was still under the spell of the nineteenth-century vision and delusion of inevitable and humane progress. Evelyn's conclusion is in keeping with this accepted belief, though informed by despair. The drama and fury of Seth's reign and of its time of troubles is contrasted with the dull, flat and unprofitable world of tidy British administration. (The French are hardly mentioned in the finale.) Evelyn was an anarchist and he induced his readers in the last pages to look back with some longing to the good old world of Seth and General Connolly and the wilder Azanian tribes because, though their cannibalism might result in one accidentally eating one's sweetheart, this had been a world of colour while the other was pale-grey.

If the book had been only a little less well written this last chapter might have gone awry completely through the difficulty of its aim. It succeeds by the precision and subtlety of the contrasts which Evelyn evoked. As evening closes on the last scene a gramophone is heard from the fort, where much atrocity had been enacted in the old days, and among pieces from the works of Gilbert and Sullivan there come the strains of a trio which must embarrass their most devoted admirers:

> Three little maids from school are we
> Pert as a schoolgirl well can be . . .

The book was very well received though it could hardly fail to shock some readers and some reviewers in the popular press. The more educated, and what today would be called the more 'sophisticated' reviewers, had nothing but praise, with one severe and unexpected exception. *The Tablet*, the leading Catholic weekly, the only Catholic paper with claims to be considered as an intellectual equal of *The Spectator* and *The New Statesman*, gave the book a very bad notice. It was written as an editorial signed by the editor, a man called Oldmeadow. For long he had been a burden and a stifling element upon the younger Catholic intellectuals, including Evelyn's Oxford friend Douglas Woodruff. In those days in 1932, *The Tablet* was the personal property of the Catholic Primate of Great Britain, Cardinal Bourne, and though the Cardinal tended to liberal ideas and was insistent on the need for individual freedom, he approved Oldmeadow's puritanical and even obscurantist view of the danger of literature which did not adhere to conventional notions of decorum. *Black Mischief* was not written for such as Oldmeadow, and he took action. He described the book as atrocious and, carried away by his disgust, he entered the field of moral theology. He lamented that a Catholic should have had the audacity to write so hateful a book. He questioned whether the author of such a work could be described as a Catholic at all, and clearly indicated that he believed he could not be. He declared that the purpose of the book was immoral and that the opinions it put forward were heretical.

In the last-mentioned accusation Oldmeadow had in mind (to express a personal opinion) the account of Dame Mildred Porch and Miss Tin. It will be remembered that their propaganda for birth control was entirely misunderstood by the Azanian public who took their poster depicting a diseased, overcrowded African homestead swarming with undernourished children as a picture of the earthly paradise, while they saw in the contrasting cartoon depicting a rich, well-appointed, one-child home and family, a terrible warning against the temptations of the Evil One. The whole of this episode could be interpreted as a parody of Roman Catholic teaching on the much-questioned subject of birth control.

What was Evelyn to do? He decided to counterattack, but he did not do so in the usual way by writing to *The Tablet*. He wanted a victory over Oldmeadow which could be seen by the world. Once more (or for the first time if a former diagnosis is incorrect) he made use of Tom Driberg as one of the most widely read journalists in the country.

As a proficient columnist Tom had mentioned in the *Daily Express* the damning review of Evelyn's book (the talk of the town once more) by his co-religionist Oldmeadow. This suited Evelyn perfectly. He wrote to Tom and gave him permission to publish his letter. As a result the following paragraphs appeared under William Hickey's name on 11 September 1932:

'MAIL from EVELYN WAUGH, re "Tablet" attack (see this column yesterday):–

'Two aspects of "Tablet" article :–
(a) an unfavourable criticism,
(b) a moral lecture.

'The first is completely justifiable. A copy of my novel was sent to the "Tablet" for review, and the editor is therefore entitled to give his opinion of its literary quality in any terms he thinks suitable.

'In the second aspect he is in the position of a valet masquerading in his master's clothes. Long employment by a Prince of the Church has tempted him to ape his superiors, and, naturally enough, he gives an uncouth and impudent performance.'


This chapter may close by recording two events of the early thirties. They were both of much importance in Evelyn's life. Soon after his conversion to Catholicism Evelyn went to stay with Christopher Hollis and his wife who lived near Stonyhurst College where Christopher was teaching. Among the Jesuits resident there at the time was a genial American called Vincent Watson who had been concerned in the famous nullity case, allowed by the Vatican authorities, involving the Duke and Duchess of Marlborough. This had caused an outbreak of anti-Catholic hysteria in England, although the grounds on which the declaration of nullity were sought would have been acceptable to an Anglican ecclesiastical court, and probably to a British divorce court. But the hysteria would not be appeased and persists to this day. Allegations were widespread that the Duke bribed the Pope. It was about this case that Evelyn's later friend Ronald Knox remarked: 'Any old stick will do to beat the Church of Rome, and if it breaks, you've got two.'

Father Watson was an authority on Roman Church Law, and dining with the Hollises one evening, Evelyn asked him about the Marlborough case. He told Evelyn about it in detail and gave him some notion of the laws governing nullity cases, a subject which Evelyn had not hitherto studied. Later he discussed the circumstances of his own marriage and its break-up with Christopher Hollis who told him that, so far as he could see, the case of the two Evelyns was one in which a declaration of nullity would be allowed without difficulty. Evelyn considered this advice, but he did not act on it for nearly two years.

The other event was the beginning of one of Evelyn's most ardent friendships. He was easily attracted to beautiful women, and he was not chaste; but he was, as has been seen already, easily led into troubadourish devotions to women. His early devotion to Barbara Jacobs set a pattern which was to be repeated in his later life, that involving Diana Guinness being the most notable to date. In the summer of 1932 he met Lady Diana Duff Cooper.

A major theatrical 'sensation' of 1932 in London was the revival of Karl Volmöller's play *The Miracle* in which Tilly Losch played the part of the erring nun and Diana Cooper the part of the Blessed Virgin, the latter an exacting piece of acting as she was required to stand as a statue for long periods which seemed like hours. In her autobiography Diana described the ordeal, during which she used to pray to the Blessed Virgin for strength. One summer night in 1932 Lady Cunard gave a supper-party for her to which she invited Evelyn, and after the party Evelyn drove with Diana to the Café de Paris at Bray which was the final goal in a Bright Young Thing 'treasure hunt' with bright clues. But let Diana tell the story as she did to me for a BBC recording.

'*The Miracle* always brought me good things. And one night after the performance it brought me Evelyn Waugh. There was a bright young things' treasure hunt in full cry, and the kill was to be at an inn at Bray. When we arrived the hunt was up, but the merriment was still there, and I knew that night that I wanted to bind Evelyn to my heart with hoops of steel, should he let me.

'I supposed he'd been to the performance. I wondered if he approved of it. Many of his faith took a critical line though the morality pantomime had been overseen and regulated by the Fathers of Farm Street. He surely liked it or he would not have taken me to the Bray party.

'Already in the car, I wondered at him. He entranced me with his humour and led me through the mazes of a saga of which he seemed to be a part. It was called the Captain Hance saga. The Captain kept a riding academy near Madresfield, where Evelyn was learning advanced horse-manship. I knew by the end of the drive all the characters, their habits, their diets, their tempers, and before parting plans were made to continue the story in our next. Undoubtedly he approved of the play, for when I left for a long tour of acting in the provinces Evelyn came with me on and off for several weeks.

'It was during these most happy days that I learned to know and understand him and to form an attachment deep enough to last unplumbed and unclouded till his death.

'Evelyn was splendid with my mother, who came for the Edinburgh and Glasgow runs. She was very, very fond of him, and more fond when he had had a stiff whisky-and-soda. She approved only of the sober, yet never differentiated them from the tipsy.'

I remember the evening of their first meeting well. I was one of the treasure-hunting pack but gave up after a while and went to Bray where the girl I was with and myself shared a table with Evelyn and Diana (then a recent acquaintance). What I remember most vividly of the evening is not an account of the Hance saga, which as a subject may have been exhausted by then, but Evelyn's imitations of Lady Cunard which made us all laugh till it hurt and we wanted him to stop. He was one of Lady Cunard's lions at that time, but later he always refused her invitations. He regarded her as essentially silly and vulgar, which she was, and he even went so far at a later time as to assert that he felt shame at having accepted her hospitality in his years of struggle. This I regarded in turn as silly and vulgar.

His friendship with Diana inevitably brought him into friendship with her husband Alfred Duff Cooper. With the latter the relationship was from the first difficult and complex. On Evelyn's side it was foolish too. Duff Cooper had great admiration of Evelyn's writing and enjoyed his company. Evelyn, who at no time had shown jealousy of Alec as Barbara's husband or of Bryan Guinness as Diana's, conceived an odd jealousy of Duff Cooper as Diana's husband. He could never explain it except in terms of such vagueness and absurdity as suggested that it was inexplicable to himself. He used to hint that as a Freemason Duff Cooper was in the councils of assassins and communists, forgetful of the fact that if Duff Cooper had a political fault it was an occasional tendency towards excessive conservatism. The enmity must not be exaggerated, indeed enmity is too strong a term, but there was an antipathy on Evelyn's side which grew gradually. Duff's friendliness and Diana's love for Duff held it in check.

In the early stages of their acquaintance, before any antipathy was visible, there occurred an incident which always perplexed Duff. Evelyn had for long been an admirer of Hilaire Belloc, and his admiration increased after his conversion. Duff was a friend of Belloc whom he used to see regularly. One day, about this time, Evelyn asked Duff if he would introduce him to the great man. Nothing easier, replied Duff, as he and Belloc had an arrangement to lunch together once a month. He proposed that Evelyn should join them on the next occasion. When the appointed day came round, Evelyn arrived neatly dressed, in a state of perfect sobriety, and on his best behaviour. He was deferential to Belloc throughout the meal. He spoke very little, being clearly somewhat awed. He had explained that, owing to an appointment, he would be obliged to leave early after lunch. When he had left Duff asked Belloc what he thought of his brilliant young friend.

'He is possessed', replied Belloc.

How, Duff often asked afterwards, how, except by supernatural means, did Belloc know?

# Chapter 8

## 1932-1934

By the winter of 1932 Evelyn had not embarked on an ambitious journey for over two years and he felt a new stirring of wanderlust. He decided on South America, but there is no evidence in his published work or in any letter of that time to show any reason for the choice. He had no discernible objective such as Peter Fleming had when he went into the least known part of the Amazonian country, an exploit which resulted in his admirable book *Brazilian Adventure*. It has occurred to me that Evelyn's journey across Africa in 1931 had given him some notion of the experience of exploration, and that he wanted to test it at first hand in a country where every journey off the beaten track is of the nature of exploration. But if this was his secret reason, he kept it secret.

An acute critic of Evelyn Waugh's work has suggested to me a religious reason. He had seen something of Catholicism in the historic Mediterranean setting where Christianity first grew. He wanted to see it in remote places among remote people to whom the venerated names of Jerusalem and Rome could have little if any meaning at all. Some such impulse can be inferred from Evelyn's later writing, but again he gave no indication of such a purpose at the time.

If he did have a purpose it is as likely as not to have been the familiar one of escapism. He was in the awkward position of being involved in two affairs of the heart. In London he had fallen in love with a girl whom he hoped to marry if his former marriage were to be pronounced invalid. Inevitably, even if a plea of nullity succeeded (and he had as yet taken no steps towards it), he would have to wait a long time. Concurrently with this nerve-racking situation, he was being pursued by a married woman with whom he had enjoyed a liaison, and who had fallen deeply in love with him.

Through Peter he obtained commissions from a few newspapers and magazines for travel articles. He booked a passage to Georgetown, the capital city of British Guiana. He planned on arrival to travel on horseback, through the forest jungle tracks and the savannah of the colony, to Boa Vista, a frontier town situated forty miles within Brazil on the Rio Branco; from there to travel by rivercraft to Manaos, situated on the confluence of the Rio Negro and the Amazon. From Manaos he would find a boat bound for Europe.

In the last part of November 1932 Evelyn went to Scotland to attend Diana Cooper's appearance in *The Miracle* in Glasgow and Edinburgh. On the night of Friday, 25 November he left Edinburgh and went to Madresfield by a laborious cross-country railway journey by night, instead of speeding comfortably to London, whence comfortably to Worcester. He spent only one night with the Lygons but had an opportunity to greet his old tutor Captain Hance. On the 27th he went to London, and there he stayed for nearly a week, buying his kit and seeking the advice of men with South American experience, including Peter Fleming. On Friday, 2 December he embarked in the *Port of London* for Georgetown. On 4 December 1932 he once more began to keep a diary.

The diary starts off well with its description of life on this far from luxurious boat which, in moments of stress, rattled and 'squeaked like a pair of new boots', and in which he was attacked by a bedbug. It is strange, in fact, that in the resulting travel book Evelyn did not use some of the entries in the first part of the diary with their dialogues between Evelyn and the Guiana steward.

The boat arrived at the port of Georgetown on 22 December, and on 3 January 1933 Evelyn left it thankfully for his journey to Boa Vista which, after three long halts on the way, he reached on 4 February. His plans to continue south by river to Manaos went awry so he returned by the way he had come to Georgetown where he arrived in the first week of April and whence he sailed home on the 5th, the ninety-second day since he had started out on 3 January.

The diary which Evelyn kept during this adventure is of very little interest. It consists of notes to serve as a rough guide to dates, places, names, incidents. There is little of amusing or perspicacious description. When he came to write his travel book *Ninety Two Days* he relied more on his memory than on his notes. Some of the most striking incidents in the book are not recognizable in the diary at all. *Ninety Two Days* suffered nothing from this, but, as will be mentioned later, because it was written at a time of some overwork, it is a lesser travel book than *Remote People*; it is a book of moments rather than of strong narrative. Nevertheless it contains some of Evelyn's best travel writing and description of scenery.

As in his experiences in Africa he was fortunate in meeting people of the kind he liked to describe. His companion and guide in the first half of his journey to Boa Vista was the district commissioner of the Kurupukari district, about 160 miles south of Georgetown. He was a man of mixed race called Mr Haynes who appears in the book as 'Mr Bain'. The first part of the journey was done by paddle-steamer from New Amsterdam, east of Georgetown, up the River Berbice. Evelyn and the district commissioner planned to travel thus for only a short way (for twelve hours) to a stopping place where they would meet their horses and servants. On the boat a rancher, a friend of 'Mr Bain', joined them and Evelyn found what he overheard from their talk together rather disturbing:

'Conversation was all between Mr Bain and the rancher, and mostly about horses. Quite different standards of quality seemed to be observed here from those I used to learn from Captain Hance.

' "I tell you, Mr Bain, that buckskin of mine was the finest mare in this district. You didn't have to use no spur or whip to her. Why, before you was on her back, almost, she was off like the wind and *nothing* would stop her. And if she didn't want to go any particular way *nothing* would make her. Why I've been carried six miles out of my course many a time, pulling at her with all my strength. *And* how she could rear."

' "Yes, she *could* rear," said Mr Bain in wistful admiration, "it was lovely to see her."

' "And if she got you down she'd roll on you. She wouldn't get up till she'd broken every bone in your body. She killed one of my boys that way."

' "But what about my Tiger?"

' "Ah, he was a good horse. You could see by the way he rolled his eyes."

' "Did you ever see him *buck*? Why, he'd buck all over the corral. And he was wicked too. He struck out at you if he got a chance."

' "That was a *good* horse, Tiger. What became of him?"

' "Broke his back. He bolted over some rocks into a creek with one of the boys riding him."

' "Still, you know I think for *bucking* my Shark . . ."

'And so it went on. Presently I asked in some apprehension, "And the horse I am to ride to-morrow. Is he a *good* horse too?"

' "One of the strongest in the country," said Mr Bain. "It will be just like the English Grand National for you." '

When he came face to face with the ordeal of mastering these 'good' horses, Evelyn found opposite reasons for disquiet.

'We mounted and made to start off. My pony would not move.

' "Loosen de reins," they said.

'I loosened the reins and kicked him and hit. He took a few steps backwards.

' "Loosen de reins," they said.

'Then I saw how they were riding, with the reins hanging quite loose, their hands folded on the front of the saddle. That is the style all over this part of the world.'

There are many fine aphorisms of Mr Bain given in the book, notably 'The black man got a very inferior complex', but perhaps his greatest moment was when they were riding through the jungle and Evelyn was listening to the sundown outbreak of animal voices all about him.

'There was one insect which buzzed in a particular manner. "Listen," said Mr Bain one day, "that is most interesting. It is what we call the 'six o'clock beetle', because he always makes that noise at exactly six o'clock."

' "But it's now a quarter past four."

' "Yes, that is what is so interesting."

'At one time and another in the country I heard the "six o'clock beetle" at every hour of the day and night.

'But experienced "bush men" say that they can tell the time as accurately by the sounds of the bush, as a mariner can by the sun.'

The two most interesting episodes recorded both in the diary and the book are Evelyn's meeting with a half-caste rancher called Mr Christie, and his dismal visit to and escape from Boa Vista. In the diary the Christie episode is briefly noted; in the book it is memorably recorded; but it came into its own a year later when Mr Christie, transformed into 'Mr Todd', is the chief protagonist of the penultimate episode of *A Handful of Dust*. Evelyn's record in the book of his visit to Boa Vista where he stayed at the Benedictine monastery contains a wonderful evocation of depressed spirits in a depressing place.

If Evelyn had temptations to lush writing and purple patches about the majestic jungle scenery through which he rode, he resisted them. Only once did he allow himself a purple patch, and his subject was not the jungle.

He records how through the ordeals of travel his vision of Boa Vista became gradually enhanced because it was a real genuine, authentic town, a city, a human centre made with the hands of civilized men. He longed for it. He heard dismaying details from the few people he met, who knew the place, but the vision persisted until at last he reached this run-down hopeless wreck of a place. Thus he recorded his reaction:

'Already, in the few hours of my sojourn there the Boa Vista of my imagination had come to grief. Gone; engulfed in an earthquake, uprooted by a tornado and tossed sky-high like chaff in the wind, scorched up with brimstone like Gomorrah, toppled over with trumpets like Jericho, ploughed like Carthage, bought, demolished and transported brick by brick to another continent as though it had taken the fancy of Mr Hearst; tall Troy was down.'

The account in the book of Evelyn's escape from Boa Vista is fine comedy. He had outstayed his welcome at the monastery and he was longing to go, but there was no prospect of a boat to Manaos for weeks. So he decided to return to Georgetown. He made all the arrangements, but no arrangements could stand up to the apathetic incompetence of the degenerate people he had to rely on. He made his formal adieux, then found he had to stay after all and thus had to return to his far from welcoming hosts. This happened more than once. In all he made three departures, the last one without any adieux, shamefacedly, in secret. It was the sort of painfully comic incident in describing which Evelyn excelled.

There are two interesting entries in his diary during his 'days of degrading boredom' in Boa Vista. On 12 February he noted: 'Wrote a bad article yesterday but thought plot for short story.' On the 14th he noted: 'Finished short story.' The short story was called 'The Man Who Liked Dickens'. This was the origin of *A Handful of Dust*.

Evelyn was back from South America in the first days of May 1933. After a few days in London at his father's house he went to Bath where he took rooms at the Grand Pump Room Hotel. It may be that an attraction to Bath was allied to an attraction to the nearby Benedictine monastery of Downside where his old Oxford acquaintance Ralph Russell was an ordained monk. This was the beginning of Evelyn's long connection with Downside.

He had large arrears of work to make good, as the primitive almost non-existent postal services in Guiana and northern Brazil had not allowed him while on his journey to send back articles to the papers which had commissioned them. The success of *Black Mischief* resulted in offers, in addition to the articles he owed, from several other newspapers and magazines. At the same time he had to work up the raw material of his diaries into a travel book. He found himself in the awkward literary predicament of having to write journalism and a book simultaneously on the same theme. It is not surprising that both suffered. The Peter–Evelyn correspondence of this time contains a large and sad proportion of letters from editors who 'while admiring the exceptional quality and interest of Mr Waugh's article' (or story) felt 'very reluctantly compelled' to reject it for publication in the paper concerned. Some were franker and said that the articles or stories were not up to Evelyn's standard.

Evelyn's situation must not be exaggerated. More articles were accepted than rejected, and Evelyn's state of debt was redeemed as a result of his work during the later part of 1933. Amid some failure, some deserved, he enjoyed one resounding success. This was his short story, 'The Man Who Liked Dickens.' Editors took it in England and the United States, and Peter had no difficulty in obtaining maximum fees for it. It was first published in England in *Nash's Magazine* and concurrently in the United States in *The Cosmopolitan* in September. Evelyn did not normally excel in the short story, but this particular one is worthy of Maupassant or Somerset Maugham at their best. If it had not been incorporated into the novel which it originated, then there can be little doubt that this would be by far the best known of his short stories.

Evelyn's private life entered a critical stage in the second half of 1933. He remained deeply in love and longed to marry again. 'Unspiritual' as

Evelyn was, little as he had reformed his way of life after his conversion in 1930, his loyalty to the Catholic Church was absolute. For connubial happiness he would not sacrifice his religion, and indeed he had little choice in the matter as the girl whom he loved was herself a Catholic *pratiquante et croyante* who would have rejected such a sacrifice as wrong. Since his talks with Christopher Hollis and Father Vincent Watson in 1930, he had consulted other Catholic friends, notably Douglas Woodruff, and possibly a clergyman with whom he had become friends, the Dominican preacher Father Bede Jarrett, the 'Provincial' or head of his order in Great Britain. After hearing the circumstances which would form the basis of the case for a declaration of nullity, everyone consulted agreed that this case was simple and that a nullity declaration would be given after the usual proceedings. Their advice was in no way at fault but obstacles which no one could have expected were placed in Evelyn's way.

By the rules governing the procedure of the Roman Catholic matrimonial courts before their revision following the Second Vatican Council, procedure which was in complete contrast to that of divorce courts in most countries, Evelyn, as one of the parties closely involved in the case, did not have the right to appear as plaintiff. Instead, the case needed to be laid before the court at the instance of an ecclesiastical official charged with the duty of deciding whether or not a hearing was in the public interest. This official was described as 'The Promoter of Justice', and his role, though differing in many ways, was comparable to that of the Director of Public Prosecutions in England. If the Promoter was satisfied that a case existed, he referred it to the local diocesan tribunal which was empowered to hear evidence and pronounce judgement. In a nullity case, however, if the judgement was in favour of a declaration of nullity, the case had to pass through yet another phase before it was terminated. Each diocesan tribunal included an official who was described as 'The Defender of the Marriage Bond', and after a judgement that a marriage was null this official had the duty of appealing against it or, to be more exact, of requesting a review of the case in a second court. He had the option of submitting the appeal to the next tribunal in seniority above it (if the diocese was suffragan, for example), to another diocesan tribunal of which every diocese had one appointed for the purpose by Rome, or directly to the competent court in Rome. For the moment what needs to be remembered is that Evelyn put his case to the ecclesiastical authorities; the Promoter was satisfied that a case for a declaration of nullity of marriage existed, and it was duly referred to the diocesan tribunal of the Archbishopric of Westminster. The tribunal heard evidence from Evelyn and his former wife and from close friends of both who had been in their confidence at the time of their marriage. This hearing of evidence occupied five sessions during October and November 1933. The law's delay, usually longer in ecclesiastical than in civil courts, meant that the judgement, in favour of a declaration of nullity, was not given till 28 June 1935. By now the appeal stage had been reached and the Defender of the Marriage Bond decided to refer the case to Rome. All this lay in the future.

The details of the case need not detain the reader beyond a brief summary of the facts. The case was founded on a simple proposition. It was that the two Evelyns had entered marriage in an unserious spirit since they had mutually agreed on two conditions: first that whenever one or the other found the union irksome they would divorce; second that by employing methods of birth control they would have no children in the foreseeable future. Both reservations invalidated the marriage according to Catholic theology and teaching. The difficulty was to prove that these thoughts and decisions, these 'acts of will', to employ theological language, were fully present in the minds both of the man and his wife when they married. Documentary evidence is rare in such matters.


On 30 January 1933 Hitler became German Chancellor. It was Germany's and Europe's black day. The Nazi regime was to dominate European affairs for a little over twelve years, always malignly. Evelyn, in common with most of his generation, took little if any interest in politics. His performance as a true-blue Tory at the Oxford Union had been no more than a performance. If ultra-Toryism had been the fashion he might well have appeared as a red revolutionary, without the slightest faith in the cause. But his religious sense, the one unifying factor in his discordant life, made him conscious of the power of evil. His consciousness of that power was so intense that it could at moments lead him into grotesque ideas, but he was never tempted, as most of the polite and erudite western world was, to believe that there was no such thing as evil. He used to say, as most of his friends remember, that there was so much evil in himself that to deny the existence of evil would be, for him at least, an impossible act, contrary to his experience and common sense.

Whether or not he instinctively and immediately saw the evil of Nazism I cannot say. Someone who saw him more often than I did in early 1933 might have the answer. He always got enjoyment from taking up un-acceptable views: he appeared as a revolutionary to entrenched diehard conservatives, and as a rigid conservative to Left-Wing friends and acquaintance; or, more effectually maddening, he would accuse either of fatuous timidity because of the illogical moderation of their views. It is not surprising that when the Nazis came to power and showed the world what stuff they were made of; when even their most duped well-wishers outside Germany began to have doubts, and the Nazis were generally dis-liked in England; it is not surprising that Evelyn ran true to form and waspishly for a while posed as an apologist for Hitler. He never did so with any seriousness, and he wrote no article in the press in defence of Nazism or its leader. He could easily have done so had he wished. He confined himself to farcical championship signalized by the frequent adornment of his letters to Maimie Lygon with swastikas and slogans, notably 'Heill [sic] Hitler'. A superficial observer might well conclude that he was indifferent to the rise of Nazism, and that if he had a preference, he had one (as an anti-Communist) in its favour.

A personal memory interferes with this simple picture. I was a close friend of the girl he wanted to marry and of her mother. It so happened that the girl's mother, who was a fashionable hostess in London, had taken up a German who was of the Führer's intimate circle. He was the notorious Putzi Hanfstaengel who had sheltered Hitler after the unsuccessful Nazi putsch in Munich in 1923. It seems to have been Nazi policy at the time to send this man to England in the hope, long entertained by Nazis, that to obtain friends in the fashionable society of London was to bring great influence to bear on the British Government. At all events there Putzi was making a great impression on hostesses who have since preferred to forget their favourable reception of him. He also succeeded in making a good impression in certain intellectual circles, for he was more talented than most Nazi representatives. He was a gifted amateur pianist who could play Schubert, Schumann and Chopin with a violence exceeding what is appropriate even to Wagner at his stormiest. One evening the mother of Evelyn's girl gave a party in her London house and I was one of the guests. The lion of the evening was Putzi. At an appropriate moment, when all the guests had arrived and settled down, our hostess asked Putzi if he would play. He duly consented, and having murdered various major composers for the piano in his own inimitable way, his hostess beseeched him to sing a certain song which had taken her fancy. He consented again. He was not a singer but he was a master of the *disant* technique, half-speech half-singing. The title of the piece I forget, and indeed its subject, but it was clearly anti-clerical and anti-Jewish. I only remember the last of the refrain: '*Die Juden und die Jesuiten.*' These words Putzi spat out with the venom the song required. Few of his audience knew German (and Evelyn none at all) and the song was received with restrained and polite giggles. But Evelyn took action. '*Die Juden und die Jesuiten*' was not difficult to interpret. After the first verse of the song, Evelyn got up from his chair and ostentatiously escorted his girl, the daughter of the house, from the room. It may be plausibly said, and probably will be said, that Evelyn only did this out of loyalty to the Jesuits by whose community he had been received into the Catholic Church, and that the incident tells nothing about his possible anti-Nazism. I can only say this: that Evelyn's action made me, who stayed on after to enjoy the party, feel rather a worm, and I did wish afterwards that I had had the guts to follow his example.

I remember meeting him the next day. I laughed with him about his ostentatious departure. He was but little troubled by the fact that he had hardly understood a word of the offending song. 'But I think I did the right thing – didn't I?' he asked, without any apparent lack of confidence. 'Absolutely right', I said

At the end of the summer of 1933 Evelyn embarked on another journey, this time not in the spirit of exploration but partly in that of pleasure-seeking and partly of philanthropy. It was to prove fateful.

Here I may introduce an important activity of Evelyn's life. Since Oxford he had maintained his friendship with Alfred Duggan who had become an extreme, and as most of his friends thought, a hopeless case of alcoholism. He had been born a Catholic but had abandoned his religion. Evelyn believed that Alfred Duggan was essentially a man of fine character and great talent, both of which would flower if he could be reclaimed from the drunken stupor in which he passed most of his time, and further he believed that this could only be brought about if Alfred could be induced to resume his religious faith. He worked hard on this self-imposed mission for many years, organizing medical cures, taking him to the Benedictine monastery of Ampleforth for religious retreats, enduring many and maddening setbacks, until at length, long after this time, he saw the success of his efforts manifested by Alfred's happy private life and public literary success.

In the late summer of this year Evelyn had the idea of accompanying Alfred on one of Arnold Lunn's Hellenic cruises. This particular one set out from Venice at the end of August. Among the passengers were several people whom both Alfred and Evelyn knew: Robert Byron, Father D'Arcy and Peter Acton, a member of a family with whom Evelyn was to have much to do. Among those whom he had not met before was Miss Gabriel Herbert. Her family had a villa called Altachiara at Portofino where the boat called in late September, in the closing stages of the tour. Gabriel invited Evelyn, Alfred Duggan and Peter Acton to stay for a few days at Altachiara. Her mother and her two sisters, Bridget and Laura, were 'in residence' with a large party. Mrs Herbert was 'interested and pleased' to meet Evelyn, of whom she was given a favourable account by Father Ronald Knox who was one of the house guests at the villa. All seemed set for a pleasant visit, but in the event things did not run with perfect smoothness. Tension was supplied, as it so often is, by the subject of Ireland to which land Mrs Herbert, as a Vesey, had the passionate and possessive devotion of the 'Protestant Ascendancy' families. The story is best told in the words of Gabriel (now Mrs Alick Dru). I quote from a letter:

'The storm broke during lunch, after they had been there two or three days: Mother decided, intuitively, that E and Peter were making jokes about Ireland – always a dicey subject – and mocking her. It was fortunate (?) that a basket full of hard Italian buns had been placed beside her; she threw them, overarm, with good aim, at our guests. These buns are quasi-indestructible; but they broke. She got up and left, with composure, saying "See they are gone by tea time". Bridget and I decided it would be best if they were out of sight for a time; she undertook to restore calm at Altachiara, while I took them for a drive "to see the countryside". We "saw the countryside" for six hours; at intervals I telephoned to Bridget, saying "they are getting very tired and we have stopped and had drinks and food quite a lot". The answer remained discouraging "Give them more spaghetti". It was after 9 when we were allowed to creep back into the house. The following morning the sirocco, actual and symbolic, had blown over. Everyone met on good terms; E. and Peter stayed on two or three days; the incident was never, never referred to.'

Gabriel Dru makes no mention of a further disturbing element in the visit which, luckily, resulted in no storm. During the night there could be heard at intervals the patter of two pairs of bare feet, following one another. They were those of Alfred Duggan in search of strong drink and those of his protecting genius Evelyn determined on rescue. Mrs Herbert was a sound sleeper and did not hear.

This visit to Portofino was the occasion of Evelyn's first meeting with Laura Herbert.

Evelyn's correspondence with Peter shows that he spent the last part of 1933 and the first part of 1934 in writing at the Easton Court Hotel, varied with visits to London where he usually stayed at the Savile Club, and visits to Madresfield, Belton and other country houses. In Mrs Cobb's cosy establishment (whose telegram code was very appropriately 'Nannie, Chagford') Evelyn finished *Ninety Two Days*, but too late for the autumn and Christmas market, so it came out in the spring of 1934. He also completed the stories later collected under the title *Mr Loveday's Little Outing*, all of which were accepted for publication by English or American magazines, sometimes after haggling. The best known by far of these stories had quite a rough passage. As mentioned earlier it first appeared under a different title: 'Mr Cruttwell's Little Holiday'. In England it was first offered to *Harper's Bazaar*, but the timing was perhaps tactless: Evelyn wrote to Roughead at Peters as follows:

'Dear Roughie,

I'm sorry Miss Reynolds finds my story lacking in Yuletyde cheere. If it was anyone else I'd tell her to go to hell, but she is an old customer and has proved herself a girl of honour on more than one occasion, so I think the best thing will be to offer her the story about a dog which I wrote for that cad - - - -. It is a poor story, but she may think it preferable. Then - - - - - - can have the looney bin one. If he doesn't like it he can go without anything and the Strand can see it. If they don't like it, it can go back to Miss Reynolds for a later issue. It has the best opening sentence I have seen for years.'

The 'story about a dog' is called 'On Guard'. It is an undisguised portrait of Maimie Lygon and Grainger. It is a very minor work. The opening sentence of the 'looney bin' story runs as follows: ' "You will find your father greatly changed," ' remarked Lady Moping, as the car turned into the gates of the County Asylum'.

Evelyn was occupied by various other journalist commissions during the winter of 1933–4 and at one point he was asked by the BBC to write a programme and replied, via Peter, that he would accept if the payment was acceptable. The discussion ended with a postcard to Peter which read: 'B.B.C.L.S.D.N.B.G.E.W.' His relations with the BBC were rarely happy.


During all this time his main concern was with a new novel, *A Handful of Dust*, which was published in early September 1934. In an article which he wrote for the American *Life* magazine, twelve years later, he described the novel's genesis, the only occasion, so far as I know, when he willingly gave away the secrets of the workshop. The origin of the story, as mentioned previously, was in his short story 'The Man Who Liked Dickens', and the origin of that was in a brief rest he enjoyed, two days before reaching Boa Vista, at the ranch of Mr Christie, already mentioned. Christie was a religious enthusiast, manifestly half-mad. He claimed that he possessed the gift of precognition and that he had been given a prophetic vision of Evelyn's arrival, in which Evelyn appeared to the other as 'a sweetly toned harmonium', a misleading description. In his story Evelyn had stripped Mr Christie of his religious ecstasy and substituted a mania for the work of Charles Dickens. He had made him illiterate, a frequent condition in South America then (perhaps now) so that to enjoy the works of the great novelist this enthusiast needed an educated and captive reader. It has been suggested by Frederick J. Stopp in his illuminating book that the story was influenced by thoughts of the mysterious disappearance of Colonel Fawcett. This is a long shot but not merely fantastical, for we know that Evelyn consulted Peter Fleming before setting out for Guiana, and no one was more apt to frame a story from a casual remark. Whatever was the doom of Fawcett, it is unlikely to have been anything but horrible. Evelyn made the doom of his hero, Tony Last, horrible in the extreme.

Here is Evelyn's account of how he came to write *A Handful of Dust*.

'I had just written a short story about a man trapped in the jungle, ending his days reading Dickens aloud. The idea came quite naturally from the experience of visiting a lonely settler of that kind and reflecting how easily he could hold me prisoner. Then, after the short story was written and published, the idea kept working in my mind. I wanted to discover how the prisoner got there, and eventually the thing grew into a study of other sorts of savages at home and the civilized man's helpless plight among them.'

The novel was at first called 'A Handful of Ashes'. (This has always seemed to me the right title.) Then, when there had been some dispute with his American publishers, he inclined to a new title 'Fourth Decade'. In the book the hero is a little over thirty. Finally, either from his own initiative or that of Peter, he settled for 'A Handful of Dust'. The reference to T. S. Eliot's *Waste Land*, stressed by a four-line quotation from the poem, may have given the book a certain extra selling value, but the title was not apposite.

*A Handful of Dust* marks a new development in Evelyn's writing, one that he was not to follow consistently, but which brought with it a striking contrast between his 'early' and 'late' manner. Many of his readers were dismayed at the change. This was not only due to prejudice and silly conservatism, but to the way in which the book was first presented to the public. In England it first came out in the form of instalments of a serial in *Vogue*. This was a great mistake which neither Evelyn nor Peter recognized. (If they had it would probably have made no difference for Evelyn needed the money.) The mistake lay in the forcing on Evelyn of an alien form. He had the inestimable literary gifts of directness, of concise expression, of perfect economy. All these should, in theory, have gone to the making of a great writer of short stories. They did not. As mentioned already, he only wrote two really remarkable and outstanding short stories, 'Mr Loveday's Little Outing' and 'The Man Who Liked Dickens'. All the rest add nothing to his reputation and if anything lessen it.

By cutting the novel up into a series of episodes, or short stories, little of its strength was visible. The first instalments gave the impression that Evelyn had abandoned his fierce satire and was now writing a conventional novel about upper-class country life, only poking the very gentlest fun at its occasional absurdities. I remember finding Cyril Connolly in a state of alarm and dismay after reading the opening instalment. 'I don't know what's happened to Evelyn!' he cried. 'His new novel is all about a happy county family, and a dear little boy – it's dreadful! I see what Madresfield and Belton and all this snobbery have done to him. They've destroyed him as a writer.' As early as 1934 the idea was growing in fashionable literary circles that the gentry and their life, especially in the country, were not decent subjects for fiction unless treated in a spirit of revolutionary anger. The new Puritanism was slowly getting into its stride. I do not blame Cyril, however. Taken out of context, the description of Tony Last and Lady Brenda, his captivating wife, and their naughty little boy, and the country house 'Hetton' to which the hero gives a traditional and extravagant affection, does read like Galsworthy at his worst. Taken out of context, that is, not otherwise.

The essential story of *A Handful of Dust* goes back to Evelyn's recurrent theme, the victim as hero, though with a difference, as always. In *A Handful of Dust* there is also a moral theme, implied never stated: 'a study of . . . savages . . . and the civilized man's helpless plight among them'. If this theme had been indicated before, it had been so in a spirit of laughing indifference. In this book Evelyn manifestly took up graver attitudes and followed serious convictions. He had long been aware of the important and usually well-hidden fact that civilization is a frail structure, of the nature of durable but not thick ice under which lies chaos and its evil. These grave thoughts never interfere with the speed and skill of the narration. Evelyn's wise decision to confine their expressions to implication not only eliminated all moralizing (this we would expect) but eliminated any oppressive consciousness on the reader's side that this is, as it is unmistakably, a book with a message. Here, as it were, is the book's secret, and Evelyn's scrupulous care not to give the secret away makes it the more telling when the secret comes to light, as it must to any discerning reader. By his skilful disguise of his message as comedy of manners, he achieved the very difficult feat of making the victim as hero a person to be taken seriously.

To what extent this novel, whose main theme is the break-up of an apparently happy marriage, is autobiographical or not is very hard to say. The family circumstances of Tony Last bear no resemblance to those of Evelyn in 1929, but the description of the wife Lady Brenda does undoubtedly correspond to something in Evelyn's life. She is 'ash-blonde' and is described as a nereid, so that her entrancing attitudes in bed are likened to those of a mythological water-nymph disporting her beauty in the sea. Lady Brenda's was a type that always captivated Evelyn. Miss Edna Best has already been cited as a perfect example of the kind of beauty he most enjoyed. His first wife was another; so was the girl whom he hoped to marry at this time. I remember that nearly twenty years after this I was with Evelyn in Tel Aviv and in our hotel there was staying an attractive young woman, the wife of a British diplomat, precisely of the type. I said to myself, 'Evelyn will fall for that girl.' In those days Tel Aviv was an uncomfortable place with the saving merit of much genuine communal life, so that one inevitably met one's fellow guests in any hotel. I thus made the young woman's acquaintance and soon after introduced her to Evelyn. He fell for her immediately.

The penultimate chapter of the book ('The Man Who Liked Dickens') is so horribly macabre that the American magazine which published a serialization asked for a happy ending. The remuneration was tempting and on Peter's advice Evelyn supplied one. He performed the difficult feat with characteristic competence. He did not droop to so far beneath the original as had Nahum Tate in the case of *King Lear* but as Raymond Mortimer rightly estimated, when this alternative ending was published with his short stories, if it had been the original ending of *A Handful of Dust*, then the novel would not rank as a major achievement of the author.

When the book came out in 1934 the general opinion of Evelyn's public and critics was that he had written his best book to date. It was praised as a feat beyond those of his first three novels. The verdict has held, and at the time of writing many reputable judges would go so far as to say that *A Handful of Dust* is the best of all his novels. Certainly it is the least open to critical reproach: the construction is flawless and the incorporation of 'The Man Who Liked Dickens' into a very different subject is an astonishing feat of literary skill and sense. He may have owed something to his acquired skill as a carpenter.

The book had and still has some critics. The faults of which it is accused are mostly matters of pernickety taste, but some are not easily dismissed. It has been objected that the episode of the death in a hunting accident of the little boy shows Evelyn grossly surrendering to his sentimental inclinations. In other books he incurs this charge, but not here, in my opinion. There is an identical incident in Thackeray's very sentimental *Barry Lyndon*. Comparison of the two treatments are entirely in Evelyn's favour. In his there is not one maudlin sentence or word to act as an indefensible 'tear-jerker'. The death of a child invariably jerks tears, as it should, but it is not an outlandish subject. 'It is common.' Furthermore, the final scene of the episode, in which the Horatio of the story, Jock Grant-Menzies, breaks the news of the boy's death to his mother, is worthy of the greatest English novelists. This is a harrowing scene, but again it depends on no word or even nuance that can be described as 'sentimental' in the usual meaning.

There was one critic who did not receive the book with acclaim. Oldmeadow had not forgotten his discomfiture at the hands of Evelyn in the year of *Black Mischief*. He gave this book a bad review in *The Tablet*. His main line of attack was ridiculous; he maintained that the terrible end of the novel, with its grisly humour, manifested a morbid spirit which could not be reconciled with the faith or conduct of a Catholic. But his second line of criticism had some substance to it. He objected to the persistence in this more serious book of the farce of his earlier ones. At moments in the book there occur awkward because unintended discords as the grotesque world of Lady Metroland impinges on the unfarcical world of the hero which is grotesque in an entirely different way, and is drawn with realism, not caricature. Evelyn would have done better to have forgotten Lady Metroland and her world altogether. What was a masterstroke in the first three books became a blemish on the fourth.

One can see how Evelyn had been led into this mistake. He had attempted the same mixture of farce and comedy, that most difficult of conjunctions, in the London scenes of *Black Mischief,* where Lady Seal and Sir Joseph Mannering and their like mingle with perfect credibility with Lady Metroland, Lord Monomark and kindred clowns. But then *Black Mischief* was at heart a gigantic farce, and the everydayness of Sir Joseph neatly stressed the outlandish character of the English and African worlds into which the story takes the reader. In *A Handful of Dust* the world within which the story moves is not outlandish or farcical. It follows inevitably that the recurrence of the Metroland world does read like a hangover from Evelyn's 'earlier manner' bringing, as is the way of hangovers, no enrichment.

There are other blemishes, such as the needless length of the drunk scenes between the hero and his Horatio (reflections of the odd taste for dwelling on drunkenness shown in the diaries), but they are all relatively unimportant. No amount of 'imperfectionism' could seriously endanger this masterly structure. There are only five or six novels of this century which can seriously challenge it.

There is one interesting hangover in the book. Cruttwell is there again, less innocuously than in *Black Mischief,* for there are hints that the osteopath of this name is an unscrupulous fraud. It was not to be the last appearance of Cruttwell's name in Evelyn's fiction.

Though not all Oldmeadow's objections were totally invalid, his main contention that no respectable Catholic should ever write on any subject capable of disturbing the reader was so manifestly idiotic that the opposition to him in the Catholic circles which influenced *The Tablet* grew apace, and his patron Cardinal Bourne was reported to have expressed doubt of the man's wisdom in pursuing a policy of such unrestrained Puritanism. In the correspondence columns of the paper Evelyn was strongly supported, and among his defenders there figured as signatory with others to a letter of protest Father Bede Jarret, one of the most influential clergymen of the time. This was the beginning of Oldmeadow's downfall.

Evelyn's private correspondence of this time contains many letters of praise for *A Handful of Dust,* and the writers of many of them were those whose esteem an author must crave. Desmond MacCarthy wrote to Evelyn at a moment of grief, a week after the death of his friend Roger Fry. For some days, he told Evelyn, he could not read the book, 'But last night,' he continued, 'in one of those empty painless hours for which one does not know whether to be grateful or resentful, I took up your book & read it through. That I could do *that* shows I think that there is something besides the wit and point which are delightful – that it has humanity in it as well as brilliance & vivacity. Don't think that I do not know that its excellent & skilful vivacity did not play an important part in the hold it maintained over me – of course I owe my hours of complete forgetfulness also to that. But if your story itself had been only a "handful of dust", however sparkling, I don't think I shd have read it through – this week. No: it would have been impossible . . .' Hilaire Belloc wrote to him, 'I can read hardly anything nowadays: and when a friend gave me The Handful of Dust to read because I had nothing for the train journey back to town I was sure I shouldn't get beyond 3 pages. I never do. It's a curse on me. But I could not let it go & I took it with me in cabs, foodplaces, busses [*sic*] & everywhere till I had finished it at a go. It is really a remarkable thing . . .' He received the unstinted praise of Rebecca West, Lord David Cecil, and of Maurice Baring who had just published *The Lonely Lady of Dulwich*, a fact which prompted him to say with impish competitiveness, 'I don't think it is as sad a book as mine.'

He received among his letters two adverse judgements. One was from Henry Yorke who disliked the end of the book: the journey of Tony Last to South America and his ghastly and presumably lifelong imprisonment by 'the man who liked Dickens'. Henry started his letter boldly. 'The book was entirely spoilt for me by the end.' He admitted to a prejudice against exotic backgrounds (certainly one cannot imagine Henry Yorke as Henry Green using one) but then went carefully into his objection:

'Most seriously though I dont think the Demerara trip is real at all, or rather I feel the end is so fantastic that it throws the rest out of proportion. Arent you mixing two things together? The first part of the book is convincing, a real picture of people one has met and may at any moment meet again. Then comes the perfectly possible, very moving, & beautifully written death of that horrible little boy after which the family breaks up. Then the father goes abroad with that very well drawn horror Messinger. That too is splendid & I've no complaints. But then to let Tony be detained by some madman introduces an entirely fresh note & we are with phantasy with a ph at once. I was terrified towards the end by thinking you would let him die of fever which to my mind would have been false but what you did do to him was far far worse. It seemed manufactured & not real.'

I believe that most reputable critics will reject Henry Yorke's criticism as prejudiced. I have sometimes thought that in 1936 Evelyn published the tame ending he contrived for American serialization in order to prove to Henry that he was wrong. But the guess is rash as the collection in which it appeared was manifestly a piece of 'book-making'. The pages needed filling and this piece was not without considerable talent.

The second piece of adverse criticism was less technical and concerned with moral as much as literary questions. It came from J. B. Priestley whom Evelyn knew superficially through Alec and Peter. He wrote as follows:

'Many thanks for sending me a copy of your new book. I read it – skipping nothing – at one sitting, mostly in the small hours, for I do not happen to be sleeping very well just now. I do not think it a better book than the others, though I can imagine why you should think so, and, indeed, there is in it a bitter force beyond anything that appeared in the others. The end, too, is a glorious example of the funny-grotesque-horrible.

'My one adverse criticism – and I should not make it if it had not some bearing on your future work – is that all the people in the book are altogether too light weight. It did not matter to me what happened to Tony and Brenda and Mr Beaver. My own opinion is that you should leave this world of society light weights now. You have got everything out of them that it is possible to get. Let your imitators feed on the remains.'

In this letter J. B. Priestley anticipated much criticism of Evelyn which was to come from believers in Left-Wing policies and 'life-style'. It does not stand up well to scrutiny. It was, in effect, a non-religious version of Oldmeadow's objections to *Black Mischief* (rather than to *A Handful of Dust*): that a good author should concern himself with edifying or at least 'socially significant' subjects. Through the mental habits of Puritanism they had both come to forget the essential truth that a writer can only give of his best when writing on a subject that interests him.

As mentioned already, *A Handful of Dust* came out in September 1934. The story must go back a little to the summer of that year when Evelyn did another journey to a remote part of the world, this time to Spitzbergen. It was as though he wished to experience in travel the extremest contrast to what he had endured in the jungle and savannah of Guiana and Brazil; he had faced the ordeal of heat, he would now face the ordeal of arctic cold. This is to suggest that he had a purpose, but none is recorded, or even hinted at, either in the short essay on the adventure which he wrote after, or in the diary which he kept in the first part of July and in which he told how he came to join the expedition. The most probable explanation, in fact, is that, having finished his novel he felt at a loose end and joined the expedition for want of anything else to do, and in the hope of a stimulating experience.

It happened thus. He went to see Gerald Berners one evening at the end of June at his house in Halkin Street. 'After tea', he recorded, 'I did not know where to go so I walked across Belgrave Square to see if anyone was at home at Halkin House.' The last-mentioned place was Lord Beauchamp's town house and still used by his children. There Evelyn found Hughie 'in the library drinking gin'. Hughie was not often in London in those days. He was usually in the country, farming without the least success.

Poor Hughie in his post-Oxford days had no successes: he was failure-prone in a strange abnormal way. He believed, rightly as it turned out, that his incapacity was due to physical ill-health, but instead of consulting a good doctor he made strenuous efforts to make himself 'physically fit' by following employments which made demands on his physical energy. He worked for some time in a racing stable, took up boxing and went for long training walks and runs, and then worked hard at farming, but all to no avail. Alec Waugh mistakenly refers to him (or seems to refer to him) as one who 'drank himself to an early death'. This is the reverse of the fact. At Oxford and in his immediate post-Oxford years he indulged in much debauchery, just as Evelyn had done, but he took a sudden revulsion against this kind of life and at this time drank very moderately and had a genuine horror of drunkenness. Evelyn's description of him 'in the library drinking gin' suggests a degraded soak. Evelyn more probably found him mixing himself a moderate cocktail.

On this evening at Halkin House on 5 July Hughie told Evelyn that he was going with a friend 'Sandy' (now Sir Alexander) Glen on an Arctic expedition: a reconnaissance trek in Spitzbergen for the Oxford University Arctic Expedition of 1935–6. Glen had already been on University Arctic expeditions in 1932 and 1933. When Hughie asked him, Evelyn immediately agreed to come too. They left London two days later. On 8 July they left England for Norway on a Norwegian boat which landed them after several calls at the northernmost port on the Norwegian coast on the 14th. Here they changed boats and began the journey across the Barents Sea to Spitzbergen, which they sighted on the 17th, and where they landed on the 18th, at a coalmining station. This was then the only inhabited place in that grim country. By seal-trapping craft they went along the coast as far north as they could to an area of west Spitzbergen which they intended to reconnoitre. Everything went wrong, mainly due to an unexpected thaw. They were lucky to get back to the coalmining station from where they made two more small reconnaissances. On 15 August they left and reached Norway on the 17th. A week later, on the 24th, they were back in England.

# Chapter 9

## 1934-1936

Evelyn kept no diary from the early days of the Arctic enterprise in 1934 to the summer of 1936. Nor did he keep many letters of that time. It is therefore not possible to say with any certainty precisely when he decided to give all his energies to writing the life of the great Jesuit saint and martyr, Edmund Campion. Very typically he liked to shock people by asserting preposterous reasons for temporarily abandoning fiction for biography. He used to declare as a fact that to write a book edifying to Catholics would speed matters in the Roman courts regarding the declaration of nullity, still pending in 1935. I heard this from Evelyn himself at the time. There is no reason to believe, it should be said in passing, that the court in Rome was in the event influenced in the smallest way by Evelyn's new-won status as a 'Catholic writer'. Roman courts are no more influenced by such considerations than British ones. The idea that Catholic matrimonial cases are conducted in a corrupt way is so deep-seated in English minds, however, that it is necessary to state this easily ascertainable fact.

Evelyn was as reticent about his virtues as he was flaunting of his vices. But in the case of his biography of Campion, he did not hide his merit under a bushel. There can be no doubt of the sincerity of his main and published explanation of this temporary redirection of his talents. 'In 1934', he wrote in his preface, 'when Campion Hall, Oxford, was being rebuilt on a site and in a manner more worthy of its distinction than its old home in St Giles's, I wished to do something to mark my joy in the occasion and my gratitude to the then Master, to whom, under God, I owe my faith.' The 'then Master' was Father Martin D'Arcy. Evelyn nowhere made public the fact that all the author's profits from the book were made over by contract to Campion Hall.

When the book was republished in 1961 he added some pertinent reflections. 'We are nearer Campion than when I wrote of him. We have seen the Church drawn underground in country after country. In fragments and whispers we get news of other saints in the prison camps of Eastern and South-Eastern Europe, of cruelty and degradation more savage than anything in Tudor England, of the same, pure light shining in darkness, uncomprehended. The haunted, trapped, murdered priest is our contemporary and Campion's voice sounds to us across the centuries as though he were walking at our elbow.'

The words remain as true at the time of writing as they were nearly fifteen years ago.

Evelyn's *Edmund Campion* is probably the least read book of his maturity. To a great part of his readership he had no business with Tudor history: raging farce in the style of *Decline and Fall* was his 'thing'. Let him stick to his last. Let him keep a violin as did Monsieur Ingres, but let him not attempt a concert appearance. Above all, let him not, as one who could not be impartial, attempt a history of the conflict of Catholicism and Protestantism in the crucial years of Queen Elizabeth.

Evelyn was not insensitive to these charges. That he was incapable of writing anything but farcical novels was a proposition that he rejected, but that he was not equipped to be a historian he humbly admitted. In 1935 the latest full biographical work on Edmund Campion was that by the convert Anglican parson and scholar Richard Simpson (1820–70), whose book was published in 1867. After nearly seventy years Simpson's book had inevitably become out of date and thus inaccurate in part. With commendable modesty Evelyn wrote in his preface: 'There is great need for a complete, scholar's work on the subject. This is not it. All I have done is select the incidents which struck a novelist as important, and relate them in a single narrative.'

'A novelist's impression' is a minimizing description but not entirely at fault. It indicates some of the merit of the book, for in Good Queen Bess Evelyn found a character perfectly suited to his descriptive powers. Few things even in his fiction can compare in excellence with the account, with which the book opens, of Queen Elizabeth in her last days:

'She sat on the floor, propped up with cushions, sleepless and silent, her eyes constantly open, fixed on the ground, oblivious to the coming and going of her councillors and attendants. She had done nothing to recognize her successor; she had made no provision for the disposal of her personal property, of the vast, heterogeneous accumulation of a lifetime, in which presents had come to her daily from all parts of the world; closets and cupboards stacked high with jewellery, coin, bric-à-brac; the wardrobe of two thousand outmoded dresses. There was always company in the little withdrawing room waiting for her to speak, but she sighed and sipped and kept her silence. She had round her neck a piece of gold the size of an angel, engraved with characters; it had been left to her lately by a wise woman who had died in Wales at the age of a hundred and twenty. Sir John Stanhope had assured her that as long as she wore this talisman she could not die. There was no need yet for doctors or lawyers or statesmen or clergy.'

There is another brief description of the Queen in 1581, twenty-two years before her death. The occasion was after Campion's arrest when he was taken from the Tower to Leicester House to be interrogated by Lord Leicester and the Queen in person.

'We cannot know what hopes may have stirred in Campion's heart as he recognized the home of his old friend and patron; as the guard led him through the familiar, frequented anterooms to the Earl's apartment. The doors were thrown open; the soldiers at his side stiffened; they were in the presence of the Queen. Beside her chair stood Leicester, Bedford and two Secretaries of State. The guards stood back and Campion advanced to make his salutations.

'It was a singular meeting.

'The grime of the dungeon was still on Campion; his limbs as he knelt were stiff from his imprisonment.

'The vast red wig nodded acknowledgement; the jewels and braid and gold lace glittered and the sunken, painted face smiled in recognition. They received him courteously, almost affectionately.'

In contrast is the portrait of Pius V and Evelyn's apologia for his fateful and perhaps fatal action in 1570 when he excommunicated the Queen and released her subjects from their obedience. Few readers are likely to be in sympathy with the writer at this point.

'His contemporaries and the vast majority of subsequent historians regarded the Pope's action as ill-judged. It has been represented as a gesture of medievalism, futile in an age of new, vigorous nationalism, and its author as an ineffectual and deluded champion, stumbling through the mists, in the ill-fitting, antiquated armour of Gregory and Innocent; a disastrous figure, provoking instead of a few buffets for Sancho Panza the bloody ruin of English Catholicism. That is the verdict of sober criticism, both Catholic and Protestant, and yet, as one studies that odd and compelling face which peers obliquely from Zucchero's portrait at Stonyhurst, emaciated, with its lofty and narrow forehead, the great, beaked nose, the eyes prominent in their deep sockets, and, above all else, the serene and secret curve of the lips, a doubt rises, and a hope; had he, perhaps, in those withdrawn, exalted hours before his crucifix, learned something that was hidden from the statesmen of his time and the succeeding generations of historians; seen through and beyond the present and the immediate future; understood that there was to be no easy way of reconciliation, but that it was only through blood and hatred and derision that the faith was one day to return to England?'

This is to evade by recourse to rhetoric the fact that Pius V was a persecutor who went to extremes considered intolerable even by the murderous standards of his time, and that he never seems to have scrupled to support his principles by the use of atrocity. If Pius V is to be venerated as a model of sanctity and wisdom, then the case against Campion's persecutors is sensibly weakened. Far more effective though historically dubious is the passage, much on the same subject, in which Evelyn contrasts the state of mind of the rulers of England with that of the martyr. In the following quotation the first word 'They' refers to the Queen and her principal ministers: 'The Family of Love' was an unorthodox Puritan sect of the time.

'They had no desire to kill the virtuous and gifted man who had once been their friend, a man moreover, who could still be of good service to them. From earliest youth, among those nearest them, they had been used to the spectacle of men who would risk their lives for power, but to die deliberately, without hope of release, for an idea, was something beyond their comprehension. They knew that it happened; they had seen it in the preceding reign, but not among people of their own acquaintance; humble, eccentric men had gone to the stake; argumentative men had gone into exile in Germany and Geneva, but Elizabeth and Cecil and Dudley had quietly conformed to the prevailing fashion; they had told their beads and eaten fish on Fridays, confessed and taken communion. Faith – as something concrete and indestructible, of such transcendent value that, once it was held, all other possessions became a mere encumbrance – was unknown to them; in rare, pensive moments shadows loomed and flickered across their minds, sentiment, conscience, fear of the unknown; some years Leicester patronized the Catholics, at others "the Family of Love"; Elizabeth looked now on the crucifix, now on a talisman; Bible and Demonology lay together beside her bed. What correspondence, even in their charity, could they have with Campion?'

This passage may give some notion of how masterly is the main portrait, that of Edmund Campion, even if Evelyn's contention that the rulers of Elizabethan England were strangers to religious idealism is fanciful.

He wrote the book at Belton, Newton Ferrers and Mells. His friends the Brownlows at Belton, and his friends the Abdys at Newton Ferrers (not far from Mrs Cobb's hotel), both gave him the kind of hospitality he needed, a well-appointed workroom, as much solitude as he wanted, and as much entertaining and fooling as he wanted. At Newton Ferrers he could indulge his old and persistent taste for fine printing and supremely beautiful book-production in Sir Robert Abdy's library, and his other persistent interest in carpentry in Sir Robert's small and fastidiously chosen collection of French furniture of the eighteenth century. (It has been said that Sir Robert Abdy at that time dismissed all furniture as valueless except what had been made in France during two years of the reign of Louis XV and a few months of the reign of Louis XVI.) Evelyn certainly spent a good deal of this time at the Easton Court Hotel, but probably most of it at Mells where his friend Christopher Hollis had a house. Evelyn would take rooms in the village, in the house of a certain Mrs Long, a former Belgian governess and refugee, and at this time the wife of the Mells estate carpenter. Mells was a scene of tradition, piety and tragedy. Since the sixteenth century it had belonged to the Horner

Lady Diana Duff Cooper arriving on the *Homeric*, with her mother, the Duchess of Rutland, after leaving the cast of *The Miracle* to help her husband in his election campaign at Oldham

Evelyn and Laura Waugh on their wedding day

family, but the heir to the property had been killed in the First World War, as had Raymond Asquith, the husband of his sister and heiress Katherine. Yet despite so much devastation Mells in the 1930s breathed optimism. Katherine Asquith had found more than consolation, but as well encouragement and inspiration in the Roman Catholic faith. Mells, that most Protestant of English places, became a fervent centre of Catholic belief and practice. The Asquith family from dedicated Protestantism became standard bearers of the old faith. What more congenial atmosphere in which to write about Campion?

A frequent visitor to Mells was Ronald Knox who would stay here and at nearby Downside. Evelyn had first met him at Oxford where he was University Catholic chaplain from 1926 to 1939, and then, as related already, he had met him again at Portofino in 1933. Yet the intimate friendship that grew between them is not much evidenced before 1945. At this time they were still casual acquaintances, not meeting often. It is very likely that with his more wide-ranging historical knowledge and his Anglican scholarship Knox helped Evelyn occasionally in the composition of *Edmund Campion*. What is certain is that the two men were mutually attracted from the first though the friendship was rather slow in growing.

Not far from Mells is Pixton, the home of the Herbert family. Evelyn often visited them. His previously mentioned love-affair had come to an end in the previous year and he was now falling in love with Laura who in 1935 was nineteen years old. She has been described by her sister Gabriel at the time of Evelyn's first meeting with her at Portofino in 1933 as having 'a quality of self containedness and irony' and as one who 'steered a determined course of non-involvement'. She maintained these characteristics in later years. She was not detached from the events of her life but she was never overwhelmed by them.

She and her brother and two sisters were the children of Aubrey Herbert, a half-brother of the explorer Lord Carnarvon who financed and took part in the enterprise in Upper Egypt which resulted in the discovery by Howard Carter of the funerary treasure of Tutankhamen. Aubrey Herbert himself was a remarkable man, a considerable Orientalist, eccentric like most of that fraternity, a Conservative Member of Parliament who was the despair of the Whips' Office, especially in the First World War when he embarrassed the Government by making pro-Turkish speeches both in and out of the House of Commons; a man who was loved by everyone who knew him and who has been shamefully forgotten, not even having been given the entry which his life entitled him to in the Dictionary of National Biography.

He died in 1923. In his last years he had contemplated conversion to the Roman Catholic faith. After his death his widow took this step. Later her daughters followed her example. (Their brother Auberon was only a year old when Aubrey Herbert died so he was brought up as a Catholic.) The family had become dedicated Catholics, for all Mrs Herbert's Protestant Ascendancy background.

Evelyn's letters to Laura during 1935 are full of devotion and tell in his simple, bold and direct way how he came to feel about her: that she was indispensable to him, that without her to share his experiences any joy was halved. Not long before her death in 1973, Laura gave me these letters, but she asked me to be very sparing in quotation of intensely personal matter. It is therefore after self-questioning and doubt that I quote part of the letter in which he proposed marriage to her. I have been eased in my decision by considering the fact that there is probably no letter of Evelyn which contains such candid self-analysis and which illustrates his character so sharply by implication and idiosyncrasy. The letter is undated but the reference to 'wop priests' indicates that it was written after the verdict had been given by the diocesan tribunal, while his case was, as he supposed, under scrutiny in Rome, and before his leaving England in August 1935, therefore probably in July of that year. Here is the extract. ('Grant' refers to Eddie Grant who was engaged to Laura's sister Bridget.)

'Tell you what you might do while you are alone at Pixton. You might think about me a bit & whether, if those wop priests ever come to a decent decision, you could bear the idea of marrying me. Of course you haven't got to decide, but think about it. I can't advise you in my favour because I think it would be beastly for you, but think how nice it would be for me. I am restless & moody & misanthropic & lazy & have no money except what I earn and if I got ill you would starve. In fact its a lousy proposition. On the other hand I think I could do a Grant and reform & become quite strict about not getting drunk and I am pretty sure I shall be faithful. Also there is always a fair chance that there will be another bigger economic crash in which case if you have married a nobleman with a great house you might find yourself starving, while I am very clever and could probably earn a living of some sort somewhere. Also though you would be taking on an elderly buffer, I am one without fixed habits. You wouldn't find yourself confined to any particular place or group. Also I have practically no living relatives except one brother whom I scarcely know. You would not find yourself involved in a large family & all their rows & you would not be patronized & interfered with by odious sisters-in-law & aunts as often happens. All these are very small advantages compared with the awfulness of my character. I have always tried to be nice to you & you may have got it into your head that I am nice really, but that is all rot. It is only to you & for you. I am jealous & impatient – but there is no point in going into a whole list of my vices. You are a critical girl and Ive no doubt that you know them all and a great many I dont know myself. But the point I wanted to make is that if you marry most people, you are marrying a great number of objects & other people as well, well if you marry me there is nothing else involved, and that is an advantage as well as a disadvantage. My only tie of any kind is my work. That means that for several months each year we should have to separate or you would have to share some very lonely place with me. But apart from that we could do what we liked – go where we liked – and if you married a soldier or stockbroker or member of parliament or master of hounds you would be more tied. When I tell my friends that I am in love with a girl of 19 they look shocked and say "wretched child" but I dont look on you as very young even in your beauty and I dont think there is any sense in the line that you cannot possibly commit yourself to a decision that affects your whole life for years yet. But anyway there is no point in your deciding or even answering. I may never get free of your cousin Evelyn. Above all things, darling, dont fret at all. But just turn the matter over in your dear head.'

The last reference may be obscure. It concerns the fact that Lady Burghclere had been a sister of Aubrey Herbert's half-brother Lord Carnarvon, and therefore Laura and She-Evelyn were first cousins, a strange irony which later was not to go unremarked in the Herbert family when Evelyn's engagement had been announced. 'I thought we'd heard the last of that young man', said one of Laura's elderly female relatives. Laura's answer to Evelyn's letter quoted above seems not to have been preserved.

To return to Evelyn's writing.

*Edmund Campion* was finished in May 1935 and published later in that year. Evelyn had become fascinated by the knowledge of Tudor England, much of it new, which he had gained in the course of his researches, and it became (as I well remember from talks with him at the time) something of a besetting preoccupation. Like others who have entered the historian's arena, lightly armed, with but a limited objective, he was aware that he was treading spacious and dangerous ground, but he wanted to explore further the intriguing question as to why there was in England, in Queen Elizabeth's day, this terrifying religious situation in the midst of which Campion was martyred. Was it merely part of the reaction from the bloody proceedings of Queen Mary I's policy? At all events, after finishing *Campion*, Evelyn was seized with an ambition to follow his book with a life of Elizabeth's predecessor.

Max Beerbohm wrote an entrancing essay about famous or remarkable books which had never in fact been written. He confined himself to the world of fiction and his leading subject is *Walter Lorraine* by Arthur Pendennis. Writing at a later time than he did, he could have added Evelyn Waugh's *Life of Jonathan Swift* and his *Life of Queen Mary I*, its proper title I feel, though in the brief surviving correspondence about it with Peter the book is referred to as *Bloody Mary*. In fact, *Rossetti* and *Edmund Campion* are Evelyn's only adventures into English history.

A year after *Edmund Campion*'s appearance the book earned for Evelyn the Hawthornden prize. The recommendation to the responsible committee had been made by David Cecil, a proof, if proof were needed, of his selflessness in judging literary matters. Evelyn had treated the Cecil family in a hostile spirit in his book, and to drive home his dislike of their political origins he had grossly exaggerated the lowliness of their pre-Elizabethan social position, a libel which might endear them to a modern readership but appealed to only a minority of the contemporary one. The Hawthornden prize was the first of the relatively few public recognitions (which included no official one) which Evelyn was to receive. It is rather odd that it celebrated his least read book, the only one in which his humour though not absent (that would have been impossible) is kept severely in the background. Henry Yorke expressed the feeling of many of Evelyn's friends and admirers in the letter he wrote to him on this occasion.

'I saw Patrick [Balfour] last night who told me you had been given the Hawthornden prize for Campion. I would congratulate you on it if it was not for the fact that you are the outstanding writer of our generation & that recognition of this kind has been due to you for a long time. It may sound ungracious to put it in the way I have just done but I do feel hotly that there is not one book you have published which is not very far beyond the books they have given the prize for up till now. It takes time for outstanding work to get through their thick skulls.'

In June 1935 judgement was at last given by the diocesan tribunal on the case for a declaration of nullity of Evelyn's marriage. The case was upheld. It now remained for the Defender of the Marriage Bond to make the obligatory appeal. As mentioned earlier, it had been decided to make the appeal to Rome. After judgement, the definitive declaration from Rome could be expected in three months or so. Evelyn felt that his main difficulties were over.

In the same summer of 1935 Peter came to an agreement with Chapman and Hall and with his American agents that Evelyn's next book, instead of being a biography of Mary I, should be a collection of his short stories to be published in the next year. This was the origin of Evelyn's only book of short stories. The name of Cruttwell was dropped from the main story, perhaps because it came into prominence in 1935 when he stood for the parliamentary constituency of Oxford University and was defeated by A. P. Herbert. In the meantime, Evelyn's literary activity was again diverted from novel writing, this time into journalism. Peter, after several setbacks from editors, obtained for Evelyn a contract with the *Daily Mail* to act as their special correspondent in Abyssinia. War with Italy was expected there soon. Evelyn described the Fleet Street situation perfectly:

'Abyssinia was News. Everyone with any claims to African experience was cashing in. Travel books whose first editions had long since been remaindered were being reissued in startling wrappers. Literary agents were busy peddling the second serial rights of long-forgotten articles. Files were being searched for photographs of any inhospitable-looking people – Patagonian Indians, Borneo head-hunters, Australian aborigines – which could be reproduced to illustrate Abyssinian culture. In the circumstances anyone who had actually spent a few weeks in Abyssinia itself, and had read the dozen or so books which constituted the entire English bibliography of the subject, might claim to be an expert, and in this unfamiliar but not uncongenial disguise I secured employment with the only London newspaper which seemed to be taking a sane view of the situation, as a "war correspondent".'

Before setting out by ship from Liverpool on 7 August Evelyn had an encounter which was to have odd results. He met a well-known diplomat and his wife: Victor (later Sir Victor) and Peggy Mallet. At that time Victor Mallet was Counsellor at the British Legation in Tehran, and he suggested that, if he found time, Evelyn should make a detour on his way home and visit them in Persia. It was not difficult. There was an admirable air service from Palestine via Baghdad. Evelyn thanked them and said that he would not forget their kind invitation. Nor did he.

Evelyn was a very good journalist but he was not a successful war correspondent in 1935. Partly this was the fault of a prodigiously incompetent sub-editor in London who not only falsified his despatches but suppressed the most important one, thus missing a notable scoop sent by Evelyn. Partly this was because the war of 1935-6 was not one in which any correspondent was likely to be successful. In addition there was some personal prejudice against Evelyn dating from his former visit and because of his scepticism regarding the British interpretation of events in 'gallant little Abyssinia' which editors, with an eye on sales, liked to see reflected in messages from the front; for all that the *Daily Mail* did not share the extremist view of most of the Press. On 24 August Evelyn wrote to Laura soon after his arrival in Addis Ababa.

'I am universally regarded as an Italian spy. In fact my name is mud all round – with the Legation because of a novel I wrote which they think was about them (it wasnt) with the Ethiopians because of the "Mail's" policy, with the other journalists because I am not really a journalist and it is black leg labour. Fortunately an old chum name of Balfour is here and that makes all the difference in the world.

'Nothing could be less romantic than my circumstances at present. There are something like 50 press people in the town, photographers etc. all told. There is no news and no possibility of getting any; and my idiot editor keeps cabling me to know exactly what arrangements I am making for cabling news in the event of the destruction of all means of communication. There is a pleasant enough mob of cosmopolitan, polyglot adventurers, spies, armament touts, soldiers of fortune etc. The only people who are not at all disturbed in the routine of their lives are the Abyssinians themselves who are absolutely self satisfied and confident of victory, not only for maintaining their independence but driving the Italians to the sea & conquering the Red Sea coast.'

The 'old chum name of Balfour' was Patrick Balfour who was acting as special correspondent for the *Evening Standard*.

September 1935 may be described, so far as Evelyn was concerned, as the month of the bungled scoops.

The Abyssinian war, greeted with such excitement and such anticipation of profit by editors of the Western World, proved a disappointment in its opening, its course and its result. The opening was particularly exasperating. It seemed to be perpetually delayed. Ethiopian mobilization and Italian aggression were frequently reported by correspondents but always just without that genuine touch of authority which would have made it safe for editors to print without the risk of any subsequent obligation 'to regret to inform their readers, etc.' Evelyn was wisely reticent during this time when spokesmen, invariably described as 'in touch with reliable circles', were making their piles and packets out of rumours. He made what he thought was a scoop when, in Harar, he and Patrick Balfour uncovered an odd episode, the arrest and imprisonment by Abyssinian officials on charges of espionage of a French count and his wife who were living nearby. Unfortunately this scoop was nullified by another one by other correspondents in Addis Ababa, a genuine scoop for once, news of the so-called Rickett Anglo-American oil concession.* The editors for whom Evelyn and Patrick were working showed irritation at their having missed this opportunity for 'hard news' about the Rickett affair through their absence in Harar from Addis Ababa. And then, on returning to the capital, Evelyn got a real scoop, all to himself.

He had made friends with the Italian Minister accredited to the Emperor. (Italian–Abyssinian relations were still technically normal.) The Italian was called Count Vinci. Since Evelyn had made no secret of his disgust at Abyssinian barbarism or of where his sympathies lay, Count Vinci treated him as a person deserving of more confidence than he reposed in other journalists. On 7 September 1935 Vinci asked the Ethiopian Foreign

* Mr F. W. Rickett, vividly described in *Waugh in Abyssinia*, was the English negotiator for certain American oil interests for a large concession for mineral mine-working in Abyssinia. The concession was granted but proved abortive and, according to Evelyn Waugh, fraudulent. News of the transaction was particularly embarrassing to the British Government, especially as the oil interest was wrongly described as 'Anglo-American', because at the time Mr Baldwin's administration was busy propagating the notion that Britain was the stainless champion of Abyssinia against the military aggression and economic greed of Italy.

Minister to issue permission for the five Italian consuls in Abyssinia, and one Italian commercial agent, to leave the country. The Foreign Minister prevaricated until Vinci informed him on 18 September that, unless he received the permission at once, he would instruct his subordinates to leave without it, adding that the responsibility for any consequent 'incidents' would lie with the Emperor's Government. This threat scared the Foreign Minister into giving the permission, but only after four days' delay, on the 22nd. Before this, however, Vinci had told Evelyn, and him alone of the correspondents, about his action. Evelyn immediately saw the importance of what he had learned. It meant that the Italians planned to open the campaign within a matter of two weeks from the 18th. He composed a despatch for the *Daily Mail*. But knowing well that the Post Office officials had a way of selling the text of the more interesting telegrams of one correspondent to others he wrote the despatch in Latin. Unfortunately the sub-editor who handled the message in London was without education and he had not the wit to seek someone who could do this simple piece of translation for him. The despatch was not printed and Evelyn received sharp instructions not to waste the newspaper's money on foolish jokes. The news, which might have been 'exclusive', only appeared in the *Daily Mail* when the story was common property.

If possibly self-interested, it was self-controlled and considerate of Evelyn not to mention the name of the sub-editor, nor even the episode, in his subsequent book *Waugh in Abyssinia*.

Evelyn's calculation was correct and soon after there followed what may be called the Affair of the Nurse of Adowa. In the first days of October the Italian assault began by a bombing raid on that town. It was officially asserted that the raid was concentrated on the hospital, resulting in the deaths of many women and children. Let the rest of the story be told in Evelyn's words:

'When we began to look for details, our doubts were aroused whether there had ever been a hospital there at all. No such thing existed as a native hospital; no Red Cross units had yet appeared in the field; the medical work of the country was entirely in mission hands. The headquarters of these organizations knew nothing about a hospital at Adowa, nor did the Consulates know of any of their nationals engaged there. . .

'The most circumstantial story came from an American negro who was employed as aviator by the Ethiopian government. I met him at his tailor's on the Saturday morning, ordering a fine new uniform. He had been at Adowa, he claimed, at the time of the bombardment. More than this, he had been drinking cocoa with the nurse five minutes before her death. She was a handsome lady, thirty-two years old, five foot five in height. . .

'Cables were soon arriving from London and New York: "Require earliest name life story photograph American nurse upblown Adowa."

We replied "Nurse unupblown", and after a few days she disappeared from the news.'

Patrick has assured me that the fine telegraphese message 'Nurse unupblown' was drafted by Evelyn.

*In humanitate est odisse quem laesisse.* The *Daily Mail* having injured Evelyn's reputation as a journalist by ignoring his scoop told him that he was not giving them satisfaction. The editorial staff was not giving Evelyn satisfaction in return so he joyfully took the opportunity to resign his appointment and, as he hoped, to leave for home. But he found obstacles in his way which he described in a letter to Laura. The letter is undated as usual but probably belongs to November. It was written in typewriting, a craft which he had not yet mastered, and so far as I know never did.

'IT is not proving so easy to leave the mail as they have made themselves so unpopular by abusing the abyssinians that they cant get a visa for another chap to come in. They sent a chap but he is stuckat Djiboutiand that is no place to be stuck in it is about the worst place in theworld next to london and this particular chap has gone bats on account of the heat and thinks he is a lepper. So i cant very well leave them flat without anyone here at all and it looks as if i shall die in harness as they say. I am sure you will sympathise because you are lazy too.

so there was a very sad banquet at the palace the night before last & the lights failed 5 times & we all talked on as if nothing had happened except p balfour who laughed & all the americans thought in vry vr very bad taste but he was laughing because a SPANiard said to him I wish you were a girl then I could pinch you So I read in the paper that Bridget is to marry Capt grant. I have bought a picture of the battle of Adowa it is rather disgusting so i will give it to d abdy n ot you.'

d abdy is Lady Diana Abdy who has been referred to already. It should also be explained that at this time Laura's sister Bridget became officially engaged to Eddie Grant.

There is a more self-revealing passage in another typewritten letter to Laura of about this time: 'Things have settled down again just as before except that there is no news and if there were we should not be allowed to sen it by the censor whom I have tild tou about The telepone to the north is cut and the only news we get comes on the wireless from europe via eritrea. No one is allowed to leave Addis so all those adventures i came for will not happen. Sad. Still all this wil make a funny novel so it isnt wasted. The only trouble is there is no chance of making a serious war book as i hoped . . .'

The funny novel was realized but the 'war book' was not very serious. Nevertheless a war book did appear.

In December the *Daily Mail* succeeded in getting a visa for their man in Djibouti. Evelyn made over his assignment to him, and hearing again from the *Daily Mail* that they no longer wished to retain him in their employment, he was able to resign definitively. He hesitated whether to return or whether to stay on independently. He hesitated only for a short time. 'The prospect', he wrote, 'seemed unendurably dismal. I had long wanted to spend Christmas at Bethlehem. This was the opportunity.' So he left with relief.

While he was in Palestine Evelyn remembered the invitation he had received from Victor and Peggy Mallet. Unfortunately he had not made a careful note of the details, and as a result his clear, precise, but often fallacious memory caught him out; he had a clear and precise memory that Victor Mallet was the British Ambassador in Iraq, and so precise was the memory that he did not trouble to check it. He found that there were frequent air services from Lydda to Iraq, as Mallet had, he clearly remembered, told him. So he sent a telegram to the British Ambassador, Baghdad: 'Would I be welcome if I came to you for weekend Evelyn Waugh.' Next day the answer came. 'Fairly. Ambassador.'

After the friendliness which the Mallets had shown him in London, this answer seemed cold, almost offensive. What had he – what could he have done to annoy them? Probably, he consoled himself by believing, the text had been distorted. 'Fairly' was probably a misinterpretation of 'lovely' or something of the kind. 'Verify your references' was the last advice to a friend of the venerable and learned Doctor Routh of Magdalen in his hundredth year. Evelyn felt above such advice, so great was the precision and clarity of his memory. A little later in life, having been often caught out by it, he would have followed the warning; had he done so now he would have found that in December 1935 Victor Mallet was Counsellor and Chargé d'Affaires at the British Legation in Tehran, whereas our Ambassador in Iraq was Sir Archibald Clark-Kerr. Unaware of his miscalculations, Evelyn telegraphed his time of arrival and sailed happily 'air-wise' to Baghdad.

Archie Clark-Kerr who had previously been Minister in China, and was subsequently to be Ambassador to Russia and then to the United States, was at this time a man of fifty-four though he looked younger. He was a reader and admirer of Evelyn's books. His wife, usually known as 'Tita' was a Chilean lady of great beauty and at least thirty years his junior, and looking younger. Neither of them had met Evelyn. They were both pleased to do so, but this abrupt proposal without even an introduction struck them both as 'cool'. Archie Kerr was the last person to take a determined stand on protocol, so he was not moved to any sort of indignation, rather to puzzlement.

Evelyn arrived at Baghdad airport and found an Embassy car to meet him. He was driven to the Ambassador's residence. He was ushered within. After a minute or two he was greeted by a small and lovely blonde, for it should be remarked that Tita was what is called 'petite' whereas Peggy Mallet, like her sisters, is tall and has been since youth of somewhat imposing presence. 'How do you do', said the little blonde. 'Are you Mr Waugh?' 'Yes, I am. I'm glad my telegram arrived all right', answered Evelyn. She asked the usual polite things, whether he had had a smooth flight, if the customs had not made excessive trouble, if the Embassy car had been there to receive him, and so on. Evelyn gave the right replies and at length said, 'Well, perhaps you ought to take me to the Ambassadress.' 'I am the Ambassadress,' replied Tita. Evelyn laughed. 'I'm sorry,' he said, 'but I know the Ambassadress', and he laughed again, supposing that he was the victim of some youthful attempt at ragging. Tita insisted on her rightful position. Evelyn asserted that the Ambassadress, Mrs Mallet, bore no resemblance to the girl before him. There was no Mrs Mallet in the whole place, Tita told him. Slowly and awfully the enormity of his mistake was made plain and dawned upon him. But happily Archie Kerr saw the whole confusion as a glorious joke, and he and Evelyn became friends.

Evelyn returned to England in January 1936, travelling by way of Rome. There he boldly applied through the Embassy for an interview with the Duce. The Italian army was in difficulties in Abyssinia owing to the terrain, and the Duce wished to hear about the country, as seen from the Abyssinian side, from someone with recent experience. So, on condition that Evelyn did not publish any account of the meeting (which is why it is unmentioned in his book), he was given an appointment at the Palazzo Venezia. Evelyn, whom I saw soon after his return, told me that he gave the Duce a very gloomy account of the difficulties facing his army, but that probably his account had been dismissed as British propaganda. He also told me that he had found the Duce's personality very impressive. Like many others, he said, he had been faced with the ordeal of walking the length of Mussolini's enormous room in the Palazzo up to his writing-table where the great man of destiny was waiting to receive his guest. It was, he told me, a theatrically designed setting in which most people would look ridiculous, and in which (all the more so through his satirical eyes) he expected the Duce so to appear. But on the contrary, he said, he did not seem ridiculous at all. He could carry it off with ease.

The next year was to show how much biased in his favour Evelyn was. He returned to London with joy, but to many anxieties.

# Chapter 10

## 1936-1937

On his return to England in January 1936 Evelyn quickly settled down to a routine of hard work. His aim was to turn to profit the abundance of experience he had amassed in 1935, though it was some time before he converted that experience into its most remunerative and rewarding literary form. The novel had to wait until he was free of his immediate commitments. The most important of these was a contract with Tom Burns, then working for Longmans Green, for a full-length travel book relating his adventures as a war correspondent in Abyssinia. It was expected that this would take him three months or so. In the event it took him much longer. He treated the assignment with seriousness, for he was not content to write an adventure story, especially after the beginning of May 1936 when events in Abyssinia took a dramatic turn. Faced by treachery within and overwhelming force without, Haile Selassie fled, whereupon the Empire of Abyssinia, whose inauguration Evelyn had witnessed with Tom Whittemore in 1930, disintegrated, and Italian victory was swift. In face of what appeared as a decisive event, Evelyn wished to record what he took to be 'the end of the story', and on 29 July he went to Abyssinia for a little over a month so that his book might include an account of the establishment of the new Roman Empire in Africa. As a result it was not finished till the autumn and did not come out till the end of October.

In addition to this commitment to write a book, Evelyn sought, through Peter, to secure a platform in the British press from which he might give a weekly commentary on affairs in Abyssinia and put forward his own pro-Italian and thus unpopular views. Peter approached *The Sunday Times* and *The Observer* in vain. He then approached *The Spectator* whose literary editor in 1936 was Evelyn's old pupil Derek Verschoyle, but again in vain. Abyssinia by early 1936 was not only no longer 'newsworthy' in the eyes of the British Press but was decidedly unmarketable. People preferred not to hear about the affair, as often happens in the case of sudden passions which prove disappointing when consummated. But this search for journalistic employment was not without result. From this time dates Evelyn's more frequent appearances in *The Spectator*, the work of Derek Verschoyle, it seems, rather than of Wilson Harris, the editor.

For most of the time during the first months of 1936 Evelyn was living at the Easton Court Hotel under the aegis of Nannie Cobb, toiling at his book, writing the occasional commissioned article and the occasional letter to the press, one to *The Times* in May summing up the Abyssinian situation after the Emperor's flight in terms which he capriciously made unacceptable by implying praise of the Hoare-Laval Agreement, and another to *The Listener* in answer to and castigating the arch-Protestant Dr Kensit for his ill-informed strictures on *Campion*. On his visits to London he occasionally stayed at Underhill, more often at the Savile Club and sometimes at a club he had recently joined, the St James's in Piccadilly. He often went for weekend visits to Madresfield and Belton. He pursued his love for Laura Herbert, but with some inhibition because he remained unsure of his situation.

The reason for this was a very odd episode in his life, one which has been much misreported and which should be briefly described here. When he returned to England in early 1936, he was in hope that his plea for a declaration of nullity, accepted by the diocesan tribunal, would have been confirmed in Rome. To his appalled amazement he found, on ringing up the Secretariat of the tribunal, that nothing on the subject had been heard from Rome, and that the case was still 'pending'. He was alarmed; he suspected that the Court of Appeal had discovered some insuperable objection and that the plea had been finally disallowed. He consulted Catholic friends and they, or it may have been one, advised him to invite the Bishop-President to lunch for an intimate talk and then – well, the Bishop might be sufficiently broad-minded or indiscreet (depending on how one looked at it) to tell him the facts . . . It was worth trying.

Evelyn acted on the advice. He invited the Bishop to lunch at the Ritz hotel. He was an attentive host. He was always punctilious about asking clergymen to say grace before and after meals and he may have manœuvred the Bishop into blessing this ill-starred table. When the waiter came up for his orders Evelyn said to the Bishop: 'Well, what would you like to begin with? Oysters, smoked salmon, caviare?' The Bishop replied, 'Yes, that sounds very nice', and ate all three delicacies.

Mr Douglas Woodruff has ingeniously argued that the Bishop's expensive response denotes not his gluttony but his unworldliness. I think this explanation is sophisticated. Not even the most ascetic Bishop, whose duties must occasionally take him to public functions in the world, could be quite as unworldly as this explanation requires, and in fact the Bishop in question went into fashionable society quite often. I prefer a simpler solution. It is known that the Bishop was afflicted with a stammer and he may have replied with some circumlocution or oddity of phrase to avoid an awkward word, as stammerers often do. This could easily have given Evelyn an idea, for on such slender grounds he often built enormous fabrics of legend. I believe that as a historical record of events this tale of the Bishop feasting on a mixed plate of oysters, salmon and caviare should not be taken with any more seriousness than attaches to Evelyn's continual libels and the sagas with which he surrounded the name of Captain Hance.

However that was, Evelyn came away from his meeting with the Bishop with an assurance that all was well and he only needed to wait patiently. Again it has been urged by apologists for the man that the Bishop's stammer may have led to a misunderstanding. (This seems rather a strained argument, especially as Evelyn was not the only person to have been misinformed by the Bishop.) What is certain is that after the meeting Evelyn still felt that something was wrong, and so he got in touch with the Notary of the tribunal, that is, the official charged with its management. He asked him to call on him at the Savile Club. They had met before. To Evelyn's anxious questioning the young clergyman explained that the situation was as follows: the papers relating to his case were still in the Bishop-President's office whence they had never been forwarded to Rome. The reason why there was no affirmation from Rome on the plea for nullity was that it had not so far been brought to the attention of any Roman Court. It was as simple as that.

Evelyn was deeply shocked. He concluded that the Bishop had deliberately lied to him. Mr Christopher Hollis has told me that from this time onwards Evelyn conceived a suspicion of clergy, a belief that they were prone to dishonesty, and that as a result, for all his devotion to the Church he became, like Belloc, something of an anti-clerical. I think myself there was very little anti-clericalism in Evelyn, far less than in the case of Belloc (who had it as a French Republican) but that, like Belloc, he had an ideal of clergymen as pastors of flocks, an ideal that he set so high that any divagation from it, even a trivial one, could shock him easily. This serious divagation appalled him.

In small part the times were to blame. The dishonourable incapacity shown by the Bishop in this case was chiefly his own heavy responsibility, but under efficient administration such incapacity would have been checked. There was no such administration in the years when this happened. Since 1934 the English Roman Catholic Primate, Cardinal Bourne, had been gravely ill and he had not delegated authority sufficiently to prevent consequent administrative disarray. From this it followed that the Bishop-President not only gave in to his natural tendency towards indolence and inaction, but also allowed himself to become overburdened with work. Hence his blundering complicity (to put the matter mildly) in an act of injustice. But in 1936 the remedy lay to hand.

On 1 January Cardinal Bourne died. Within two months, after the usual consultations, the Pope unofficially nominated Arthur Hinsley as his successor. The appointment surprised many people as Hinsley was over seventy and the times seemed to call for a younger man, but the new archbishop's vigour and capacity were remarkable and unimpaired by age; his name is rightly honoured as that of one of the great English church- men. During his days as unofficial Archbishop-elect, days which he spent in Rome as a Canon of St Peter's, Hinsley was told by several English fellow-Catholics about the scandalous circumstances surrounding Evelyn's plea for a declaration of nullity. In March, when he was officially ap- pointed to Westminster, he was visited by the Notary who gave him full details. Hinsley did what little he could to influence the courts to accelerate their procedure in this artificially delayed case, while giving orders for the immediate despatch of the papers to Rome. One of his first acts on reaching Westminster was to accept the resignation of the Bishop- President, and it is suspected that he encouraged the resignation before he received it. After that proceedings were slow, as they usually are in all matters of law, but long before the year was out the declaration of nullity was ratified in the Roman courts.

What were Evelyn's reactions to this drawn-out ordeal? It is not easy to say. It was a matter he rarely discussed. In an escapist spirit he preferred to treat it farcically, and with myth-making. One probable myth has just been given in some detail. He told me himself the other myth that he had written *Campion* so as to impress favourably the judging ecclesiastics. Evelyn gave a third myth wide currency among his friends. This was to the effect that after his wife's second marriage had broken down, John Heygate wrote to Evelyn and told him that, conscious that he had wronged him, he was prepared to persuade Evelyn's lawful wife to return to him, adding that he was confident of success. Evelyn, so the story continues, was placed in a very awkward position by this honourable attempt to make amends. If Heygate's generous action became known then it made nonsense of Evelyn's case for a declaration of nullity. Somehow, it is alleged, Evelyn got out of the predicament. This story is still widely believed.

The truth is very different and simpler and can be given on the authority of John Heygate himself. In 1936, having made a second marriage and having become a devout Anglican, John Heygate became a frequent attendant at the services in his local church. One day the rector asked him why he never partook of Communion. Heygate replied that he believed himself to be unworthy, having been the guilty co-respondent in the divorce case of 1929. The rector referred the question to his bishop who was the famous Dr Bell of Chichester. On learning the facts, Dr Bell conveyed to Heygate that he might consider himself eligible to take Communion, provided he obtained the forgiveness of the man he had wronged. So Heygate wrote to Evelyn explaining the circumstances.

Evelyn answered with a postcard: 'O.K.E.W.' This was shown to Dr Bell, 'who seemed rather surprised, but was satisfied'. Those were the facts on which Evelyn, with his sleepless instinct for story-telling, built an entertaining fabric of farce.

I only once heard Evelyn speak gravely of this matter. It was about twelve years after 1936. I forget how the subject cropped up, but it came into the conversation naturally and I asked him about his 'famous annulment'. 'Well,' he said, 'it nearly drove me mad, but I can never feel any bitterness about it. I regard it as manifestly the work of the Holy Ghost and God's care of even the worst of his servants. If things had gone as I wanted, I would never have married Laura and I would have been deprived of the joy I have from my children.' There were tears in his eyes which he hastily mastered by immediately making some grotesque comment which provoked laughter in the worst of taste. I remembered the incident because his family life was an area in which he rarely disclosed his real feelings to others. One who saw him frequently during this time was Father Martin D'Arcy. To him he showed the deeper springs of his feelings, his reasoned faith and his tenacity in it. 'Evelyn', Father D'Arcy has written, 'had been so assured of the nullity that he was looking forward to marrying again and I was naturally worried at what might be the effect of all this [the Bishop-President's deception] on his new-found faith. He realized my fears and wrote me a letter, which seems to have been lost, to the effect that I need not worry about his faith as no amount of bungling or knavery in Church circles would weaken it.'

In the middle of June Chapman and Hall published *Mr Loveday's Little Outing and Other Sad Stories*. The contents have been mentioned in part and in passing already; the book is not an important feature of Evelyn's literary life, so it need not detain the reader beyond a couple of paragraphs.

The excellence of the eponymous story is in no doubt. It may have been based on the report of some atrocity of the kind in the newspapers; it was widely remembered some twenty years later when an almost identical disaster occurred as a result of misguided progressivism in the treatment of criminal lunatics, a grim subject which Evelyn had already effectively guyed in *Decline and Fall*. Under the title 'By Special Request', the mild ending to *A Handful of Dust* contrived for the American serialization was reprinted. It has been discussed already. The third piece, 'Cruise', was an excursion into a style of glossy-magazine gossip-writing story which has happily disappeared. In 'Cruise' Evelyn fell, probably unawares, under the influence of A. P. Herbert's once much lauded *The Trials of Topsy*. The story which followed it, 'Period Piece', was a skilful variation on the theme of *Plus ça change plus c'est la même chose* and was as fully worthy of Evelyn as 'On Guard' (already considered) was not.

'Incident in Azania' should have become better known than it did. The scene of the story was life in an outpost of the British Empire and was set in the Protectorate regime of Azania following the events related in *Black Mischief*. The kind of incident and the kind of life depicted had been both more thoroughly dealt with by Somerset Maugham, but the 'truth to nature' of Evelyn's picture of that now vanished world will strike any witness of it as authentic. By 1936 Somerset Maugham had made the subject over-familiar, a fact which may account for the neglect of 'Incident in Azania'. The stories which followed it showed Evelyn indulging his taste for fantasy conjoined with realism. 'Out of Depth' is a not wholly successful little outing on the Time-Machine; the debt to H. G. Wells (against whom Evelyn was unashamedly prejudiced) is too obvious. The succeeding story, 'Excursion in Reality', is one of Evelyn's few ventures into the obscene unreality of the film-world. Here a reader may strongly feel that, for all its many excellencies, the story is a display of raw material for a fine piece of fiction rather than the thing itself. 'Love in the Slump' is based on the over-worked material of his early novels; it reads like a parody of his writing. (Strange that no other writer has parodied his intensely idiosyncratic style.) The last two stories are both flawed. 'Bella Fleace Gave a Party' is supposed to be based on an incident which did actually happen: an ambitious hostess, it was related, gave a party but the invitations were not posted. The legend or fact was very well known in those days and by 1936 had grown 'something musty'. Many readers must have known the end of the story from the beginning. The same fatal weakness was in the last story, 'Winner Takes All'. It is designed to have a surprise ending, but, as Raymond Mortimer noticed in a review, the title gave the show away early on.

The book enjoyed success in England and later on in the United States where it was published in October. It kept Evelyn's reputation in the public eye, but, except possibly for the title-story, added little to the reputation. Even his most fervent admirers could not but notice that the quality of the stories was very uneven.

In July 1936 Evelyn started to keep a diary again. He was in Ireland at the beginning of the month and the first entry runs as follows: 'Tuesday July 7th Holyhead midnight. Sleeper & sandwich. Euston 5.30 daylight. Drove through empty streets to St James's where I found telegram. "Decision favourable. Godfrey." Bath. Shaved. Lay down but did not sleep. At 8 rang up Bruton Street [the Herbert town house] & was told that Laura had gone to Church. Dressed and went to Farm Street. Laura and Mary [Herbert] there. Knelt behind them & told Laura news in porch.' The 'Godfrey' mentioned in the above extract was the Catholic Archbishop of that name, and it was he who had presided in Rome over the Court which ratified the decision of the Westminster diocesan tribunal allowing a plea for a declaration of nullity in the case of Evelyn's marriage.

Evelyn Waugh photographed in front of Piers Court with
Picture Post journalist Tim Raison, now a Tory M.P.

Relaxing in an armchair,
a gift from Ian Fleming

Randolph Churchill:
Evelyn wrote to his friend,
Mrs Ian Fleming, to say that
he and Randolph Churchill
broke off relations for ever
approximately once a year
and they always made it up

Being free now to marry, Evelyn became involved in house-hunting. From the beginning he and Laura, on the evidence of the diaries, agreed that they wished to live in the country, far outside 'Greater London'. Evelyn went occasionally on these visits of inspection with Diana Cooper who held decided views on where and how people she knew should live. But what the diaries chiefly tell is of constant meetings of Laura and Evelyn. When he said in a quoted letter that he could only half-enjoy what he enjoyed without her he was speaking the truth literally.

His friends were puzzled by Laura. One needed to meet her often before getting to know her. She presented, in most superficial ways, a strong contrast to Evelyn in character. He was always very talkative and she said little. Contrasted with his garrulity, as it often was, especially in his cups, her reserve seemed like silence. To superficial observers they seemed an ill-assorted couple; in fact they were the reverse, but the reason why this was so lay far below surface appearances, and the writer, who knew both well, would not hazard a plunge into those depths.

On 29 July Evelyn set off on his visit to Abyssinia. He travelled by train to Rome, intending to sail on the *Leonardo da Vinci* from Naples. He was seen off at Victoria Station by Tom Burns who had made this journey possible by persuading Longmans Green to agree to an advance which, with a large advance from Chapman and Hall on his forthcoming novel, covered most of the expenses. (His efforts to obtain newspaper commissions in England and America had uniformly failed.) Before his departure Tom Burns had decided on the title of the book. Evelyn wanted to call it *A Disappointing War* but Tom, as a professional publisher, knew that a title that suggested disappointment would unquestionably result in disappointing sales. People don't rush to buy books with names such as *A Dreary Anticlimax*; what was wanted was something crisp and intriguing so Tom insisted on *Waugh in Abyssinia* and forced his decision on Evelyn. The latter accepted it reluctantly, a fact he made plain when parts of the book were republished ten years later. People do not as a rule enjoy puns on their names.

He spent a week in Rome, occupied mostly in wearisome manœuvres in the Foreign Ministry, in a department which appears as 'Stampa' in the diaries, to obtain his visa for Italian-occupied Abyssinia. As the first non-Italian journalist to go to Abyssinia since the war he was closely scrutinized, but at length he was granted the promised visa in time for him to leave Naples on the *Leonardo da Vinci* on 7 August. 'My cabin appalling', he noted in his diary, 'but everyone extremely agreeable. All Italians except one Belgian.'

His adventures thereafter are recorded in *Waugh in Abyssinia*. He wrote few letters during this excursion and the only newspaper article he wrote was not on the subject of Abyssinia. It was a review of Aldous Huxley's last long novel, *Eyeless in Gaza*, and is worth remembering. Of all that imperfect writer's ambitious productions, this novel had the least merit; it was his worst book, by far. Its appearance brought to an end Huxley's claim to be one of the great writers in the tradition of the English novel, and the fact was mercilessly emphasized a little later by Cyril Connolly's parody, *Told in Gath*, a masterpiece in itself of destructive criticism. At the time when Evelyn wrote his devastating review in 1936, Aldous Huxley held so great a position in the world of the intelligentsia that his feeblest productions were received by the critics with deference. Evelyn struck out boldly and fiercely against Huxley's ill-conceived work of didactic fiction at a time when its author seemed almost unassailable. His attack on this political novel made little impression, however, because Evelyn himself was already gaining the reputation of being a political eccentric. His eccentricity ran to the Right and did not follow the flock to the Left; he did not baa with Victor Gollancz and his Left Book Club crowd which included among its prophets a thoughtful but ludicrous critic of Evelyn, in John Strachey; all this was a relief to many at a time of crowd-judgement disguised as something better, but Evelyn very soon showed, especially in *Waugh in Abyssinia*, that he went with the pendulum beyond its allowed sweep.

Rose Macaulay described the book as 'a Fascist tract'. She was an emotional person who, like Evelyn, sometimes (not often) imagined moral turpitude in any opinion which was in extreme disagreement with her own. As a devoted Liberal, in keeping with her august family traditions, Rose saw a beacon of hope in the League of Nations and believed, not quite wrongly, that this light had been wantonly extinguished by the brutal and antiquated imperialism of Mussolini. Evelyn's view was in direct opposition. He believed, not quite wrongly, that Italy had been ill-used by a succession of Abyssinian regimes. He believed also, not quite wrongly, that the resulting conflict was one between civilization (Which, under Belloc's influence, he exclusively associated with Europe) and barbarism, of which in Abyssinia he had seen all he needed to see. Evelyn's view was thus as thoroughly uncongenial as possible to Rose Macaulay. In this case the 'unerring sentence of Time' is in Rose Macaulay's favour.

His book opened with one of the best chapters to be found in any of his travel pieces. It is called 'The Intelligent Woman's Guide to the Ethiopian Question'. Persons learned in the history of Abyssinia have assured me that as a short generalizing appreciation of the complexities of its subject, addressed to the 'common reader', it is without rival. I have heard it described as an equivalent in its different sphere, of Evelyn's friend Robert Byron's short and masterly *An Essay on India* which had been published, though with little notice, in 1931. The next four chapters of Evelyn's book, entitled in order 'Addis Ababa During the Last Days', 'Harar and Jijiga', 'Waiting for the War' and 'Anticlimax', gave an account, entertaining as Evelyn alone knew how to make it, of his adventures in Abyssinia as a war correspondent. Some of it has been quoted above. Then came the two chapters which moved Rose Macaulay to describe the book as 'a Fascist tract'. The sixth chapter was called 'Addis Ababa During the First Days of the Italian Empire'. The seventh and last 'The Road'.

In these last two chapters Evelyn made his sympathies quite plain. In his description of Addis Ababa under the Italian regime he implies throughout and sometimes states an opinion that under intensely difficult circumstances the Italians were doing fine work in the cause of civilized progress. He was particularly impressed by the Viceroy, Marshal Graziani, who received him with the personal charm that made him a hero to his troops even in the coming days of shameful and total defeat. Evelyn wished to travel northwards and Graziani immediately issued the necessary permit. He left the Marshal's presence, he wrote, 'with the impression of one of the most amiable and sensible men I had met for a long time'. Evelyn was not to be blamed for not foreseeing the revolting severity of Graziani's later rule which, more than anything else, was responsible for reviving loyalty to the Emperor, but he can be blamed for his blindness to the fact that the Italian enterprise was a crime, bound to have terrible consequences.

It must not be supposed that these last two chapters are devoid of Evelyn's special brand of humour. In his journey to the north he went to Asmara, Graziani having recommended him by telegram to the good offices of the garrison commander. Evelyn relates the unfortunate sequel: 'Like many others before him, [the commanding officer] was deluded by my Christian name and for two days flitted between airport and railway station, meeting every possible conveyance, in a high state of amorous excitement. His friends declared that he had, with great difficulty, pro-cured a bouquet of crimson roses. The trousered and unshaven figure which finally greeted him must have been a hideous blow.'

The foregoing quotation has been taken from the last chapter, 'The Road'. The contents, like the title, seem to show the influence of Belloc who saw in Mussolini a Napoleon, and in both only benevolent power and greatness. Italian policy in Abyssinia was concentrated on building a great trunk road northwards from the capital to the Red Sea coast, with a network of subsidiaries, and a further road-system to the south and east to the Somali coast. It was a great enterprise which, like Hitler's *auto-bahns*, was successfully carried through. It seized on Evelyn's uncritical admiration, as the autobahns did on many British dupes in Germany. 'A main road in England', he wrote, 'is a foul and destructive thing, carrying the ravages of barbarism into a civilized land – noise, smell, abominable architecture and inglorious dangers. Here in Africa it brings order and fertility.'

Evelyn carried this facile and naïve admiration farther in the con-cluding words of the book: '. . . along the roads will pass the eagles of ancient Rome, as they came to our savage ancestors in France and Britain and Germany, bringing some rubbish and some mischief: a good deal of vulgar talk and some sharp misfortunes for individual opponents: but above and beyond and entirely predominating, the inestimable gifts of fine workmanship and clear judgement – the two determining qualities of the human spirit, by which alone, under God, man grows and flourishes.'

There is an echo of Kipling here too. Although proposals were made by Italian publishing houses, I can find no evidence that the book was translated into Italian, in which form it would have found an ardent public. I do not know if Evelyn later repented his short-sighted homage: if so, I think retraction would have been partial and conditional. He never lost his Bellocian conviction that Mussolini was a very great man indeed. But in 1946, *When the Going Was Good* was published by Duckworth; it contained, in Evelyn's words, 'all that I wish to preserve of the four travel books I wrote between the years 1929 and 1935'. The selection from *Waugh in Abyssinia* contained no extract from the last two chapters. Perhaps there was a little repentance.

During this summer further misfortune had fallen upon the Lygon family and from it Evelyn suffered the loss of a great friend. The circumstances should be remembered as they manifestly influenced Evelyn later.

On 28 July, the day before Evelyn left England on his journey, Lady Beauchamp died suddenly. At the time Lord Beauchamp was in Venice. As soon as he heard the news he made contact with a young English lawyer of his acquaintance, Richard Elwes, who was on holiday there with his wife (who is my sister). Beauchamp told him that he was determined to return to England, if it were conceivably possible, for his wife's funeral. Elwes hurried back to London and went to see Norman Birkett whom he knew well, and who at that time held a senior position in the office of the Attorney-General. The case was complicated by the fact that at the instance of the Duke of Westminster a warrant for Beauchamp's arrest on homosexual charges had been issued by the Home Office, and since the warrant only applied in the United Kingdom, Beauchamp became officially not voluntarily an exile. The Attorney-General's office were in sympathy with the proposition that the warrant should be regarded as non-operative during a visit by Beauchamp to attend the funeral. But the ultimate decision lay with the Home Secretary, at that time Sir John Simon, a man of agile mind but somewhat defective in more amiable human excellences. Furthermore, the Attorney-General had been anticipated by the Duke, who appealed against any provision that Beauchamp should be allowed to desecrate by his odious presence the interment of 'his beloved sister', for whom he cared only so far as a man can care for a useful instrument. Sir John Simon found it hard to make up his mind but on the whole seemed to incline to the view that the law should be allowed to run its full course, no matter how inhuman that course might be. As a result of all this, when Lord Beauchamp accompanied by one of his daughters arrived at Dover on a cross-Channel steamer, Richard Elwes went aboard and urged him to stay on the boat and return with it to the Continent, as it was far from certain that on arrival he would not be immediately arrested. With a heavy heart Beauchamp agreed and went back to Venice.

Less than a month after this, on 19 August, he had to undergo another and worse bereavement. Hughie had been increasingly unwell for several months. His failures had multiplied. He had got entangled in debt which resulted in bankruptcy (soon redeemed); the violent physical exertions by which he thought he could restore his health failed utterly; he still refused to consult a reliable doctor. In August 1936 he went for a motoring tour in Germany with a friend. On the 19th they spent a long hot day driving in an open car. It has been suggested that Hughie was afflicted by sunstroke. At the end of the day he got out of the car to ask directions from a passer-by, fell, and in falling fractured his skull. He never recovered full consciousness and died the same night.

The effect on Lord Beauchamp was as terrible as might be expected. He remembered how Hughie had dissuaded him from suicide, how he had not prevented his son's bankruptcy, and he was filled with grief made more extreme by something like remorse. Once again he sought out Richard Elwes, who was now his legal adviser. He told him that he was returning to Madresfield for Hughie's funeral and that he would risk arrest. He refused to be deterred. Elwes put the case with its new implications to Norman Birkett and the latter and his colleagues renewed their request to the Home Secretary. Even Sir John Simon felt moved to mercy. It was felt that Lord Beauchamp had suffered as much as a man can be asked to and, to the great indignation of the Duke of Westminster and his admirers and courtiers, the warrant was suspended and later annulled. Lord Beauchamp was allowed to attend unmolested his beloved son's funeral, and in the course of the next year he returned to Madresfield. Gone were the meretricious splendours of old. He was happy nonetheless to be back but, having acquired the habit, he continued to spend much time abroad. For long periods during the short remainder of his life he returned to Madresfield and dwelt once more as the squire in the home of his ancestors.

The episode, which has been given in some fullness of outline, may seem a digression to some readers. It is not that, for although Evelyn played no part in it and was away while most of these things were happening, this was the foundation of an ambitious book which some believe to be his masterpiece, others believe to be a magnificent failure, and others believe indicated the decay of a talent which in its glorious spring had promised more than it ultimately gave. Such judgements are for later consideration. What should be said now is that the impression made on Evelyn by this episode was deep and productive, but the gestation of it into 'convertible literary stuff' very slow, as was often the case with him.

Not long after Evelyn's return in September he was at work on the comic novel which, he had assured Laura Herbert a little less than a year before, was to prove that his ordeals in Abyssinia were 'not a waste of time'. He began the book at Mells in his rooms in Mrs Long's house on 15 October 1936. He recorded the event in his diary. 'On Thursday 15th made very good start with the first pages of a novel, describing Diana's early morning.' The reader who knows the book will recognize the opening scene in which Mrs Stitch, the wife of Algernon Stitch the Cabinet Minister, is shown beginning and organizing her day. None of his friends doubted, or could doubt, that Mrs Stitch was a caricaturist's impression of Diana Cooper and, to leave no possibility of doubt, the very lightly drawn background figure of Algernon Stitch bears a decided resemblance to her husband Alfred Duff Cooper. The case was exceptional in other ways too. Not only did Diana Cooper recognize her image in the distorting mirror but she rejoiced at it; she was indeed positively irritated by well-meaning people who affected to see no resemblance between herself and this extraordinary figure of fiction. When Mrs Stitch re-emerged in Evelyn's last work, Diana was as delighted as though some signal honour had been conferred on her.

The writing of the book took Evelyn a long time by his standards, sixteen months. This was not because he found his subject-matter difficult to master, though he did feel compelled to undertake a massive revision at the end, but because he was subject to so many other calls on his time. The most important of these was his marriage to Laura Herbert in April 1937.

Marriage, in Evelyn's case as in most, involved a long and fatiguing process of house-hunting. They both wished for a house in the West Country with which they both had family associations. They nearly bought the vicarage at Whatley, near Frome, and very nearly indeed a house at Nunney, within the precincts of the half-ruined castle, but finally settled, in January 1937, for a house called Piers Court, not far from Dursley and Stroud in Gloucestershire. Inspection tours of the above-mentioned and numerous other houses which may be forgotten delayed the act of 'creation', so Evelyn's novel moved slowly. In need of money, as an engaged man, he was in negotiation, through Peter, for journalistic commissions yielding quick returns. Peter obtained a sizeable number for him, but it is astonishing to the researcher to find how many offers for serialization of the first chapters of the new novel were turned down (usually with expressions of admiration) by editors. *Waugh in Abyssinia* was a failure, from a financial point of view, both in England and America so Evelyn was forced to devote as much of his time as he could not only to journalism but pursuits of a semi-literary nature, all this when arrangements for his forthcoming marriage were in any case hindering him from concentration on his new book. One may be surprised, looking at the distractions, that the book did not take him longer than sixteen months.

One of these distractions was of its very nature doomed to failure but brought him a large financial reward. It dated from November 1936 when Peter conveyed to Evelyn a proposition from Alexander Korda, then at the height of his enormous and unmerited reputation as a film director of genius, inviting him to compose a script for a film which Korda had as yet but vaguely envisaged in general terms. The film was to be on the subject of cabaret girls and was at first to be known as *Lovelies from America*, a title which Korda, after wrestling with his artistic soul, eventually changed to *Lovelies over London*. Through Peter's negotiating skill Evelyn made £750 out of the proposition. Like most of the famous impresario's widely publicized film ventures, this one cost his backers a good deal of money, enriched a few, wasted the time and talents of everyone concerned, inexplicably added to Korda's huge hollow reputation, and came to absolutely nothing, vanishing through the horn gate of dreams, and leaving not a rack behind.

Evelyn spent the Christmas of 1936 at Pixton, and his diary for 26 December contains the last record of him as a hunting man. He wrote: 'Hunted and galloped into 2 gate posts.' Frost set in shortly after, hunting temporarily ceased, and Evelyn bade a final and not reluctant farewell to the sport. Thereafter he went to London where he seems from his diary to have spent most of his time seeing old friends, of whom the name of Hubert Duggan is more often mentioned than before. He bought Laura an engagement ring, and the 'forthcoming' wedding was announced in *The Times* on 13 January. A typical diary entry occurs a day or two later: 'Dined with Olivia one evening. Very depressing. Stark crazy & roaring drunk. Went to see my parents. Yorkes lunched with me at St James' Sunday. Saw Korda who accepted film.' The last word is a misnomer for 'treatment', a word which in film jargon indicates the practical outline (not the detailed script) of a hitherto only imagined cinema-drama. That is the last mention of *Lovelies over London*.

Easter came early in 1937, at the end of March. Evelyn spent Holy Week at the Benedictine monastery of Ampleforth in Yorkshire. He records that it was an uneventful stay and described himself as 'entertaining dumb little boys and monks'.

Two points may be made in connection with this visit to Ampleforth. Evelyn notes in his diary that in the course of it he visited Castle Howard, then occupied by Geoffrey Howard and his family, the property having been left away from the heads of the family who built it, the Earls of Carlisle. Memories of Lord Beauchamp's return to a very different and more reasonably-sized country house, Madresfield, were fresh in Evelyn's mind. Admittedly the influence of these different and conjoined impressions can only be guess-work, but the significance of the juxtaposition can be defended. The other point is that Evelyn attended several Holy Week retreats at Ampleforth, and on one or several of them (but clearly not this one) he took Alfred Duggan with him in pursuit of his doubly dedicated work of reclamation. On one occasion, about which Evelyn told me, Alfred was not only sober but in a state of exalted gratitude for his rescue from the horrors of alcoholism. All seemed to go well until one day he vanished. He was discovered in Scarborough in the throes of an intense drinking bout.

Evelyn took his mother to Gloucestershire to show her Piers Court and arranged to rent 21 Mulberry Walk, Chelsea, as his first married home with Laura. Here they were to live until Piers Court was ready for them. 'Wedding invitations went out', he noted in his diary, '& have been almost universally refused. Presents have come in, mostly of poor quality, except from the Asquiths who have given us a superb candelabra, sconces and table.' He noted later that he had also received two handsome carpets, one from the Abdys and one from Gerald Berners. I do not remember what my wife and I gave Evelyn as a wedding present, but knowing his extravagant and intolerant standards I fear it must have impressed him as of 'poor quality'.

Until three days before his marriage Evelyn stayed at Underhill with his parents. On 14 April 1937 he noted in his diary 'Left Highgate for good'. He took a room at the St James's Club. On the 16th, his last day as a bachelor, he dined with the Yorkes. On Saturday the 17th he was married. He left this record in his diary: 'Early Mass, d'Arcy, with Laura & Herberts & Woodruffs. Breakfast St James, Douglas [Woodruff] and [Francis] Howard [now Lord Howard of Penrith]. Henry [Yorke] came later. Changed & pick-me-up at Parkins [the Piccadilly chemist] and to Church where got married to Laura.' Father D'Arcy officiated at the ceremony which took place at Farm Street. The honeymoon was spent at Altachiara. On 18 April Evelyn wrote in his diary: 'Lovely day, lovely house, lovely wife, great happiness.'

One of the happinesses of this honeymoon, which was not unmarred by storms (what association with Evelyn was not?); one happiness was certainly deeply satisfying. At last he could concentrate his mind and writing on the new novel. 'Working fairly hard and fairly well', he wrote in his diary in early May, though this evidence must be qualified by an entry on the 17th, 'Wrote novel very badly all week'.

They returned from their honeymoon at the end of May and stayed first at Flemings Hotel and then at Pixton before settling into their *nachtasyl* in 21 Mulberry Walk. Evelyn's diary stops at this point. His further movements are best followed in his correspondence with Peter, a correspondence which shows that his journalistic prospects were not brightening in spite of some alleviations. The magazines were putting up a continued resistance (always accompanied by congratulations on Evelyn's literary brilliance) to extracts from, or serializations of the new novel which by now had received its title from the author: *Scoop*. At length in August Peter was able to overcome the opposition of *The Strand Magazine*. It agreed to take the first section of *Scoop*, under the title of *Mrs Stitch Fails for the First Time*, duly edited by the author into the form of a 'long short story'.

This slender triumph was followed by others. The idea seems to have spread to editors that there might be money in Evelyn, and there were other offers for extracts and adaptations from magazines in England and America, most of which Evelyn accepted. To offset his transient journalistic success there occurred a setback in September 1937, the month he and Laura moved to Piers Court in the village of Stinchcombe, the lovely house which he hereafter usually referred to as 'Stinkers'; there occurred at this time the final collapse of *Nash's Magazine*, one of the first of many magazines on both sides of the Atlantic to fail before the onset of grosser tastes, and a consistent patron of Evelyn as journalist.

One tempting offer, more tempting even than those of the grotesque Korda, came to nothing, and the student of Evelyn's life can only render thanks that this was so.

In 1934 the well-known author H. V. Morton had written a best-seller, *In the Steps of the Master*, a popular and well-considered account of the archaeological discoveries and theories about the Holy Land and Jerusalem as it was in the time of Jesus Christ. (The book remains influential on popular preachers and parish priests to this day.) After an interval he followed his book about Jesus Christ with a second similar success in 1936, *In the Steps of St Paul*. Thereafter 'Steps' became the rage among publishers, and some of them remembered Evelyn. In 1937 there followed discussion between publishers, Evelyn and Peter on whether Evelyn should record the 'Steps' of St Peter, St Francis Xavier, or St Patrick. Evelyn's own preference was of a profane kind. He wanted to write a book called *In the Steps of Caesar*. He shared the French idea, of which Belloc was a strong propagandist, that unless a country had undergone the ferocities of Roman conquest, it could never be accounted civilized. It was an idea that excited the imagination of many people interested in history, but of no serious historian. One must rejoice that Evelyn's talents were not wasted on this barren proposition.

I remember Evelyn and Laura very well in their brief sojourn at 21 Mulberry Walk. One occasion stands out in my memory: a cocktail-party they gave in the summer of 1937, a sort of 'coming out party' for themselves on their return from their honeymoon, a party at which the guests presented every sort of contrast: frivolous young Lord and Lady Brownlow rubbing shoulders with growling, saturnine Belloc. One of the first people I saw was Alfred Duggan, and then Laura rushed up to me exclaiming, 'You must see Evelyn immediately, He's raving about your book. He's been sent it to review.' 'Oh, God', I said, remembering Evelyn's murderous severity as a critic.

The circumstances were unusual and I believe such as had an influence on one of Evelyn's friendships. Let me relate them. Two years before this Robert Byron and I had travelled together in Persia and Afghanistan. Robert was researching for Athur Upham Pope's monumental *Survey of Persian Art* and for a book of his own about Islamic architecture in Middle Asia, and myself for a book about the leading German agent in Persia during World War I, Wilhelm Wassmuss. The literary consequences were in my case, a now rightly forgotten book called *Wassmuss*; in Robert's case *The Road to Oxiana* which is still remembered because it was his best book by far, and because it opened a window into the stuffy chamber of European studies of Islamic architecture. Our adventures also gave me the idea of a book of travel stories. I called my book *Stranger Wonders* remembering John Gay's lines about the travel-writer who 'with various wonders feasts his sight – What stranger wonders does he write!'

Evelyn was generous with his congratulations. 'For the first time,' he said, 'I have read a book by a friend without embarrassment.' I was delighted by this hyperbole, especially when Evelyn added, 'I am going to go to town on it in my review.' A few miniutes later Alfred Duggan was carried out unconscious. 'It's a useful tip,' murmured Evelyn to me, 'if you ask an old soak, to ask more than one, as those on their feet know how to cope with the casualties.'

My book *Stranger Wonders* is not one of which I am ashamed. The stories in it are based on experience and observation and are quite amusingly told. It is a very light production, makes no pretensions to be anything else, but I fear was enormously overestimated by Evelyn. This was very pleasant for me at the time, and I think has consequences on Evelyn's writing. In a later book, *Work Suspended*, I find one incident which very distinctly echoes an incident in my last story *Invention*.

Robert Byron's book, artfully disguised as a collection of diary jottings of no special significance, was in my opinion a minor masterpiece, an opinion I find shared by scholars and lovers of literature. It put forward ideas on the origins of the high achievement of Islamic building which specialized scholarship has since confirmed. It was written in an easy and attractive diarist manner, informed by sensibility and humour. All Robert's many literary faults seemed to fall away from him, except one.

The book is marred by his uncontrolled aggressiveness. This aggressiveness, often taking the form of a proud parade of such hobby-horses as his belief that there was only one art and one civilization, the Byzantine; this combative insistence was, like all aggression, occasionally fatal to his truthfulness. Like Evelyn, Robert indulged crazy apprehensions about what are best described as 'world-enemies'. Evelyn saw them in Freemasons, an apprehension that was part of the mental furniture he unwisely borrowed from Belloc. Robert, in insular style, saw these enemies in Roman Catholics and lived in as great a dread of a Vatican conspiracy as any dupe of Titus Oates. Robert foolishly introduced this anti-Catholic mania into his book, and he did it in a way that Evelyn recognized as fraudulent. Robert was a very poor linguist. All the non-English conversations recorded in his book are invented. Among them is a supposed talk with a Greek priest in the Church of the Holy Sepulchre in Jerusalem. The Greek priest is represented as expressing his utter contempt of Roman Catholic pilgrims. Evelyn spotted that this was Robert up to his old tricks, as it was. I was there and can positively affirm that even if the nice-mannered young priest had descended to vulgar abuse, Robert would have missed it through ignorance of Greek.

At that time Evelyn was given travel books to review in *The Spectator*, *Time and Tide*, and a delightful but shortlived weekly magazine *Night and Day*. By an unhappy chance which often falls to the lot of a reviewer, and which the more mercenary welcome, Evelyn was sometimes given more than one book to review in one article, thus obliging him to perceive or fancy a relationship between the books in order to make a coherent article. In this case he was given Robert's book and mine. As reviewers of two books often do, he used one with which to beat the other, and on this occasion, annoyed by Robert's manifest lie about Jerusalem, he used me as a stick with which to beat Robert. He called the review 'Civilization and Culture' and put forward the proposition that whereas I could attain to civilization Robert could only rise to culture. I have no hesitation in declaring the judgement totally fallacious, depending on an overestimate of one book and an underestimate of another. I believe that Robert never forgave Evelyn for this, and I would not be surprised to learn that he thought Evelyn and I had been squared by Farm Street. Happily this unfortunate incident occasioned no break in my friendship with Robert.

I think Evelyn would not have written as he did or erred so deplorably in his judgement if an element of bitter personal hostility had not come to poison the relations of the two friends, a matter in which Robert was entirely to blame. Robert's narrow sympathies made him indignant at all conversions to the Catholic Church, so Evelyn had already become a potential enemy. Further shocked in his typical insular fashion, that Evelyn had been allowed his nullity plea, and presuming the worst,

Robert had become more violently and hysterically anti-Catholic than before. Whenever they met, Robert lost no opportunity of exasperating Evelyn by anti-Catholic tirades in which he often descended to the grossest blasphemy. After a while Evelyn, like their friend Billy Clonmore and others, found it impossible to take this mixture of prejudice, ignorance, loutishness and sheer silliness with good humour. The friendship slowly terminated.

Evelyn had not yet totally emancipated himself from the thraldom of Korda who was a possessive man anxious, as he later told Cecil Beaton, to 'buy' promising people, and, having bought one as he supposed he had in Evelyn, he did not like to part with such a one, even if he could only use him as the dog did the manger. Evelyn, having done his distracting work on *Lovelies over London*, was still faced with a contracted obligation, for which he had received a small advance, to provide a film 'treatment' for a play by Henri Bernstein. What the play was, or just how it also vanished through the horn gate of dreams, does not appear from the Peter–Evelyn correspondence.

What does appear is that by the autumn of 1937 there was no further association of Evelyn with the talent-wasting Korda. It also appears that by November he had at long last finished *Scoop*, the first of his books to be finished at Piers Court. Reading it through, Evelyn found it in a thoroughly untidy shape. The reason for this has been indicated. He needed money and therefore he had set not only the beginning but several sets of chapters in a short-story form so as to make them acceptable for serialization, for which Peter had finally achieved contracts. It followed inevitably that the book was very badly constructed. Evelyn was first and foremost a craftsman, and he wanted this book, as he wanted all his books, to be a model of design and joinery. I have never seen the 'November version' of *Scoop*, if it exists, but the Peter–Evelyn correspondence does show that the work of revision took Evelyn from some unspecified time in November till the middle of February 1938, a period of at least three months, the time sometimes taken by him in writing a whole book. He probably enjoyed these three months. He said to me once: 'I like tinkering. Craftsmen do.'

*Scoop* was finished at last. It came out at the end of May among the 'Spring Books' of 1938. In the meantime Laura had given birth to their first child on 9 March, a girl whom they named at the christening a week later, Maria Teresa, and who was known after as Teresa or Tessa.

*Scoop* was justly acclaimed, and those who declared it to be one of Evelyn's best books which would be long remembered were wholly justified. It is as alive today as when it came out, though it has inevitably become somewhat 'dated'. The 'dating', however, in the pejorative sense, remains a matter of detail. The scene is Abyssinia again, and Abyssinia had even by 1938 become dated in the sense that it had ceased to be a major preoccupation of the Great Powers. Another piece of 'dating' is more damaging. There is a sinister leading character with purple-dyed hair who is represented as a person of indeterminate nationality, superhuman ability and grotesque dishonesty. He is given the name 'Mr Baldwin'. At the end of May 1938 Stanley Baldwin was still presiding over his fourth administration and most of the British public saw in him a rugged personification of British respectability. To see Mr Baldwin as a leading figure in this farce, personifying all the cosmopolitan unrespectabilities, was irresistibly funny at the time, and though the joke may not have quite vanished for a reader of today, it will have faded.

Scoop was Evelyn's fourth book and second novel about Abyssinia. There must have been some danger, and Evelyn must have been aware of it, that here was over-cultivated ground. What could there be to add to what he had written in *Remote People, Black Mischief* and *Waugh in Abyssinia*? The answer was: journalism, and if he felt any anxiety about exhausted themes he overcame it boldly, by piling comedy upon comedy, by the erection of a wild Nonesuch Palace of Foolery before which criticism had to be silent or itself appear ridiculous. *Scoop* is as farcical as *Decline and Fall*.

He subtitled the book 'A Novel about Journalists' and it is just that; by the time he came to write it he had some ten years' varied experience of his subject. He could write on it with great assurance. Towering over the journalists who throng the story is the newspaper magnate Lord Copper, an imaginary portrait (by Evelyn's own admission) of Lord Beaverbrook whom Evelyn had met, served under spasmodically, but never came to know. The word 'portrait' may be too exact, for Lord Copper's megalomania bordering on insanity is more reminiscent of Lord Northcliffe than any other Press-Baron. But, like Beaverbrook and Northcliffe, Lord Copper feels he is a 'big man' and self-consciously acts the part. His outsize positiveness is beautifully emphasized by the contrast presented by his hesitant Foreign Editor, Mr Salter. He it is who, out of respect for and fear of his master, sets a fashion in the office of *The Daily Beast* whereby the words 'Yes' and 'No' are avoided. The affirmative is expressed by the phrase 'Definitely, Lord Copper', the negative by 'Up to a point, Lord Copper'. The potentials of this fine invention were not wasted by Evelyn in the dialogue.

The story is as complicated as the plot of the most sophisticated French or English eighteenth-century farce. Even to outline it would waste space and weary the reader. A few facts about the book should alone be mentioned.

Evelyn stuck to a theme which had served him well already: the victim as hero. But here he uses the theme with a big difference. The victim, again selected as in *Decline and Fall* as a result of mistaken identity, is not condemned by a malevolent world to persecution and maltreatment, but rather is he exalted by Lord Copper to a high and precarious position, in the manner of the sacrificial Kings of Ancient Mexico, and accorded success, honours and rewards in every lavish conceivable excess. The victim escapes the doom which the reader feels is preparing as he refuses his stupendous elevation; as it were, he abdicates before the priests can get at him.

Of Mrs Stitch and the courageous and instinctive humour with which the model accepted the caricature something has been said.

Possibly the most remarkable and certainly the most memorable thing in the book is the picture of the journalist's life, sometimes lightly sketched, sometimes painted with bold brush-strokes on a large canvas, both feats achieved with the success of a master hand. One of Evelyn's most horrific portraits is of the victim-hero's main journalist colleague whose full name is never given. (The victim-hero is called 'William Boot'; the colleague is referred to throughout as 'Corker'.) The last-named is the quintessential vulturous foreign correspondent, and in the picture of this folk-hero of the twentieth century a reader may feel that Evelyn poured all the dislike he had felt for most of his colleagues of the Italo–Abyssinian war. In a few words he gives an unforgettable picture of the cheerful free-masonry which binds such men the world over and which Evelyn observed without sympathy. Corker arrives at his assignment and meets three fellow-reporters. 'Shumble, Whelper, and Pigge knew Corker; they had loitered together of old on many a doorstep and forced an entry into many a stricken home. "Thought you'd be on this train," said Shumble.'

With equal precision Evelyn drew a picture of the correspondent's dilemma which he had witnessed in Ethiopia. On arrival the bewildered William Boot asks what the situation is:

' "Lousy," said Pigge.

"I've been told to go to the front."

"That's what we all want to do. But in the first place there isn't any front, and in the second place we couldn't go to it if there was. You can't move outside the town without a permit, and you can't get a permit."

"Then what are you sending?" asked Corker.

"Colour stuff," said Pigge, with great disgust.'

Anyone who has worked for a newspaper in a far country, especially at some moment of newsworthy crisis, will recognize the fidelity of that miniature.

But the finest picture of the life of journalism is in the last section of the novel, entitled 'Banquet'. Readers may remember that as a result of William Boot's accidental scoop the victim-hero is accorded a banquet by Lord Copper who has already made him famous as 'Boot of *The Beast*'. The opening paragraph of the last section is a fine, perhaps one should say a supreme example of Evelyn's comedic prose. It may appropriately be given in full:

'Lord Copper quite often gave banquets; it would be an understatement to say that no one enjoyed them more than the host, for no one else enjoyed them at all, while Lord Copper positively exulted in every minute. For him they satisfied every requirement of a happy evening's entertainment; like everything that was to Lord Copper's taste, they were a little over life-size, unduly large and unduly long; they took place in restaurants which existed solely for such purposes, amid decorations which reminded Lord Copper of his execrable country seat at East Finchley; the provisions were copious, very bad and very expensive; the guests were assembled for no other reason than that Lord Copper had ordered it; they did not want to see each other; they had no reason to rejoice on the occasions which Lord Copper celebrated; they were there either because it was part of their job or because they were glad of a free dinner. Many were already on Lord Copper's pay roll and they thus found their working day prolonged by some three hours without recompense – with the forfeit, indeed, of the considerable expenses of dressing up, coming out at night, and missing the last train home; those who were normally the slaves of other masters were, Lord Copper felt, his for the evening. He had brought them and bound them, hand and foot, with consommé and cream of chicken, turbot and saddle, duck and pêche melba; and afterwards, when the cigars had been furtively pocketed and the brandy glasses filled with the horrible brown compound for which Lord Copper was paying two pounds a bottle, there came the golden hour when he rose to speak at whatever length he liked and on whatever subject, without fear of rivalry or interruption.'

Before leaving *Scoop*, one idiosyncrasy of the book must be mentioned. It is the only book by Evelyn in which the direct influence of P. G. Wodehouse is clearly acknowledged. Readers may remember that the victim-hero, William Boot, has two uncles permanently resident at the ancestral home of Boot Magna Hall, Uncle Roderick and Uncle Theodore. These are manifest kith and kin of Galahad Threepwood of Blandings Castle, and Uncle Fred who caused such anxiety to his nephew in the Drones Club. Uncle Theodore, by a characteristic piece of Wodehouse sleight-of-hand, is the guest of honour at the Boot Banquet, instead of the victim-hero (who has already run away), and at one point Evelyn reveals his debt: 'Uncle Theodore, after touching infelicitously on a variety of topics, had found common ground with the distinguished guest on his right; they had both, in another age, known a man named Bertie Wodehouse-Bonner.'

Other singularities of the book may be mentioned. It has been stated earlier that Evelyn did not include nursery servants among those he ridiculed. In the uppermost rooms of Boot Magna there are three retired ex-nannies. They are all quite ridiculous. But the fun poked at them is mild and affectionate; Evelyn wrote nothing likely to have distressed

Lucy of Chilcompton, should she, by some improbable chance, have come to read the book.

In *Scoop* Cruttwell made his last appearance, as an adviser on tropical equipment to what looks like the Army and Navy Stores.

*Scoop* was the last novel that Evelyn wrote before the outbreak of war in 1939.

# Chapter 11

## 1937-1939

In November 1937 Evelyn became somewhat alarmed (how seriously would be hard to say) by the vagaries of his memory. On the 12th he wrote: 'I have been surprised lately by blanks and blurs in my memory, being reminded by Laura of quite recent events which delighted me & which I have now completely forgotten. I have therefore decided to try once more to keep a daily journal.' He kept it only for two months, after which he did not resume it for eighteen months.

During this winter and the first months of 1938 Evelyn's life was not eventful. He became greatly preoccupied with the garden of Piers Court, which he planned and organized very well. A typical entry in the diary runs: 'Mass in Dursley Y.M.C.A. Garden planning. Mary [Herbert] left soon after luncheon and I fell asleep exhausted by hospitality. Dug a little, read Sunday papers, chess.' The country gentleman's life. There are remarks scattered here and there in the record which provoke more curiosity: 'Started work again on new novel'; 'More work on novel which is taking some shape'. This novel, like many admirable enterprises of that time, was not completed. But it marked an important step in Evelyn's literary career nonetheless, and it will be considered later.

He began for the moment to forget the delights of London, but he never took a deep pleasure in country life, even though he was experiencing it under ideal conditions: with a wife with whom he was passionately in love and in a charming and elegant country house in a lovely countryside. He admired and wished to belong to the world of Tony Last, but I think he felt more at home in Lady Metroland's.

Suddenly in May 1938 Evelyn's life was forced into a new direction; the new novel had to be abandoned for other claims on his literary abilities; he needed to take a long journey once more though not in the explorer spirit and style. This is what happened. Clive Pearson, a younger son of the first Lord Cowdray, acting as a representative of the extensive Pearson commercial interests in Central America, asked Evelyn if he was prepared to go to Mexico in order to write a book about that country. The reason for this approach was that the Mexican Government which had come to power in 1934 under General Lazaro Cardenas had brought to a climax a long legislative process of Marxist tendency and had expropriated, confiscated and nationalized foreign holdings, which represented most of the major industries of the country. The Pearson interests in oil and railways were considerable and had been among the first victims of this socialist policy of a government acting as the agent of communist-dominated trades unions. British opinion was ignorant about what had happened, but in so far as it was with information it got it from the Left-Wing press which instinctively hailed Cardenas as a great progressive reformer, applauded his grandiose plans for public welfare regardless of whether they were being carried out or not, and averted its attention from the injustice, intolerance and persecutions of the regime. Kingsley Martin, as was to be expected, became a vociferous champion of this exotic tyranny. Clive Pearson wanted the truth to become known and he had the idea that a widely read book by a popular author would achieve this result and effectively undo Mexican Government and British Socialist propaganda which was not unsuccessfully depicting the first Lord Cowdray and his successors as ruthless exploiters and enemies of the people and the Mexican State.

In the absence of a diary it is not clear how Clive Pearson made this approach, and the remaining Peter–Evelyn correspondence on the subject dates from after the beginning of negotiations. Evelyn wrote to Peter on 24 May: 'A very rich chap wants me to write a book about Mexico. I gather he is willing to subsidize it. I am seeing him on Wednesday & will turn him onto you for thumb-screwing.' By this time Peter was already in correspondence with Clive Pearson.

The negotiation was held up till the middle of June while Evelyn and Laura went on a journey to Hungary. Again, in the absence of a diary, nothing is known about that journey beyond the fact that they went to Budapest; but whether or not they were pleased or interested or impressed or dismayed is nowhere evidenced. I do not remember hearing Evelyn mention Hungary.

The Pearsons proved to be munificent patrons. All expenses were paid for Evelyn and Laura to sail to New York and from there to Vera Cruz; to spend two months in Mexico and to return. They also paid for a comprehensive insurance policy which was to prove a great boon as, on returning to England, Laura was found to be suffering from appendicitis and the terms of the policy were held to cover the expenses of the operation. The fruit of this princely generosity was a book by Evelyn which he first entitled *Pickpocket Government* and sub-titled 'The Mexican Object Lesson'. Later, at Clive Pearson's suggestion, he changed the main title to *Robbery Under Law*. It occupied Evelyn throughout the winter of 1938–9 and into the spring. It appeared in the summer of 1939.

Without the guidance of a diary the movements of Evelyn and Laura at this time are not easy to follow, being only recorded in the Peter–Evelyn correspondence and (very vaguely as to dates) in the book.

They left England on the S.S. *Bremen* (against the advice of Peter who thought one should not support Nazi commerce at this time) on 27 July 1938. Early in August they arrived in Mexico City. After a little less than two months in the country they returned by train to New York whence they sailed home, arriving back in England on 12 October 1938.

It is a point of some interest that this journey gave Evelyn his first experience – briefly and insignificantly – of the United States. Such, no matter how brief and without significance, is always a memorable experience in the life of a European. Whatever impression it made on Evelyn is not reflected in his book, unless it may be discovered in his rather pleased insistence on the forgotten fact that, until relatively recent times, Mexico, and not the English colonies or their successor, the United States, was the centre of civilization in the American continent.

This is among several fallacies which Evelyn exposes with all his accustomed relish of the pain he may have caused opinionated people, the principal fallacy being the sheepish belief of what Evelyn's friend John Sutro used to call 'The Kingsley Martin Youth Brigade' that General Cardenas's regime (which bore a far from accidental resemblance to that of Adolf Hitler) was a great step forward to the earthly paradise. It is convenient to consider the book now.

It appeared at a very bad moment, in the summer of 1939, during which Adolf Hitler was manœuvring for a resumption of the Great War and facilitating his chances of victory by wearing down the nerves of his enemies by a succession of scares. During this season of recurrent and ominous crises, people had little time to spare for the disasters and breaches of trust proceeding in distant Mexico, so Evelyn's book failed. Many of his admirers do not know, even today, that Evelyn wrote a book about the Mexico of Cardenas. It is significant that in her comprehensive account of Evelyn's writings (which included the rare *Pre-Raphaelite Brotherhood*) Rose Macaulay, in her 1946 essay on Evelyn, made no mention of this book. It could have added reinforcement to the hostile sections. The evidence is that she did not know of it.

I do not know whether the book's inevitable failure in the bookshops, and its consequent failure to achieve Clive Pearson's purpose, influenced Evelyn, but he seemed afterwards to have regarded it with displeasure and even shame, and it is the only one of his pre-war travel books to be unrepresented in the extracts which made up *When the Going Was Good* in 1946. I think Evelyn was mistaken, as all writers sometimes are about their own work. If he looked on the book as a piece of hack-work, then this was true only in the sense that the subject, hurriedly studied, was not one of his choice, but wholly untrue in any sense, no matter how slight, that he had been bought by Clive Pearson for propaganda purposes. Evelyn was never up for sale, though Alexander Korda had thought he was. Clive Pearson was too well versed in the ways of the world to have made the mistake. Evelyn dismissed the book from the canon of his works in the preface to *When the Going Was Good* as follows: 'There was a fifth [travel] book, *Robbery Under Law*, about Mexico, which I am content to leave in oblivion, for it dealt little with travel and much with political questions.'

Had I been Evelyn's literary adviser at the time, a functionary he never dreamed up or employed, I would have urged him to include extracts from this book by citing the identical arguments which persuaded him to exclude it. Because it dealt with 'political questions' it is of great autobiographical though not perhaps much wider importance. Nowhere in his writings did he state with greater clarity his political convictions and preferences, and he expressed both within the context of his faith and his view of human destiny. In this respect the book was in keeping with the literary fashion of the time. The Spanish Civil War had attracted an enormous number of writers to visit its carnage in the role of reporters, and the ideological character of the struggle incited most of them in their subsequent reports to proclaim their deepest beliefs. Every week new books appeared, usually from Left-Wing sympathizers, usually affirming adherence to Marxist faith, under cover of describing the Spanish War. In a sense *Robbery Under Law* was Evelyn's Spanish War book, for, as he said, Mexico had a like attraction for the Left because it appeared to its simplifying visionaries as a country in which the same war had been fought and from which the Left had emerged with total victory. Evelyn, however, was among the few who rightly or wrongly viewed the struggle both in Spain and Mexico from the angle of Right-Wing sympathies, and of sharp antipathy to the New Idealism. He makes this quite plain in his first chapter.

Describing the different types of tourists he met, he has this to say: 'Besides the holidaymakers and the sentimentalists there is a third rapidly increasing group of foreign visitors to Mexico. These are the ideologues; first in Moscow, then in Barcelona, now in Mexico these credulous pilgrims pursue their quest for the promised land; constantly disappointed, never disillusioned, ever thirsty for the phrases in which they find refreshment. They have flocked to Mexico in the last few months for the present rulers have picked up a Marxist vocabulary so that, from being proverbial for misgovernment, the republic, now at its nadir of internal happiness and external importance, greatly to the surprise of its citizens, has achieved the oddest of reputations – that of "contemporary significance".'

He concludes the chapter with a passage inspired by contempt of Victor Gollancz's 'Left Book Club': 'Readers, bored with the privilege of a free press, have lately imposed on themselves a voluntary censorship; they have banded themselves into Book Clubs so that they may be perfectly confident that whatever they read will be written with the intention of confirming their existing opinions.

'Let me, then, warn the reader that I was a Conservative when I went to Mexico and that everything I saw there strengthened my opinions. I believe that man is, by nature, an exile and will never be self-sufficient or complete on this earth; that his chances of happiness and virtue, here, remain more or less constant through the centuries and, generally speaking, are not much affected by the political and economic conditions in which he lives; that the balance of good and ill tends to revert to a norm; that sudden changes of physical condition are usually ill, and are advocated by the wrong people for the wrong reasons; that the intellectual communists of today have personal, irrelevant grounds for their antagonism to society, which they are trying to exploit. I believe in government; that men cannot live together without rules but that these should be kept at the bare minimum of safety; that there is no form of government ordained from God as being better than any other; that the anarchic elements in society are so strong that it is a whole time task to keep the peace. I believe that inequalities of wealth and position are inevitable and that it is therefore meaningless to discuss the advantages of their elimination; that men naturally arrange themselves in a system of classes; that such a system is necessary for any form of co-operative work, more particularly the work of keeping a nation together. I believe in nationality; not in terms of race or of divine commissions for world conquest, but simply this: mankind inevitably organizes itself into communities according to its geographical distribution; these communities by sharing a common history develop common characteristics and inspire a local loyalty; the individual family develops most happily and fully when it accepts these natural limits. I do not think that British prosperity must necessarily be inimical to anyone else, but if, on occasions, it is, I want Britain to prosper and not her rivals. I believe that war and conquest are inevitable; that is how history has been made and that is how it will develop. I believe that Art is a natural function of man; it so happens that most of the greatest art has appeared under systems of political tyranny, but I do not think it has a connection with any particular system, least of all with representative government, as nowadays in England, America and France it seems popular to believe; artists have always spent some of their spare time in flattering the governments under whom they live, so it is natural that, at the moment, English, American and French artists should be volubly democratic.

'Having read this brief summary of the political opinions I took with me to Mexico, the reader who finds it unsympathetic may send the book back to her library and apply for something more soothing. Heaven knows, she will find plenty there.'

Gollancz, Kingsley Martin and his Brigade, evidently became something of an obsession with Evelyn. In his central chapter, on the subject of the Oil Industry, he gave them another bloody nose. He records how all conversations of Englishmen with Mexicans invariabiy came round to the confiscations. He was asked many times – What did the British people feel about it? He does not give his reply to his interlocutors but he answers thus to himself: 'As for the feelings of the British public, these are only aroused when they see politics in simple terms of underdog and oppressor. They have not yet got used to thinking of British Companies as underdogs. Moreover the confiscations had been accompanied by a number of potent phrases about democracy. If the Japanese, or Nationalist-Spaniards, or Germans or Italians had taken our oil, then there would have been a series of meetings in the Albert Hall; but the Mexicans had a Left Book Club vocabulary. It so happened that the Mexican regime showed features which elsewhere would be damning: the government was autocratic; the autocrat was a General; there was only one political party; educational appointments were political and the teaching purely state-propagandist; history books were being edited on the lines of nationalist self-assertion ... Some of the British public knew these things, some did not; but to the politically minded, vocal minority, one thing was of paramount importance: when the Mexicans saluted their bosses they raised the arm with a clenched fist, not with extended fingers. So they were all right; they were democrats, like ourselves and the French.

'It is true that the majority of Englishmen do not think in quite such simple terms, but it is the minority who edit the weeklies and hold meetings in Trafalgar Square.'

Enough has been quoted, I hope, to show that, whether or not the opinions put forward command assent, the book is not the despicable thing that Evelyn treated it as being later. Like all his travel books this one contains moments of high farce, the most memorable in *Robbery Under Law* being the account of the Six Year Plan Exhibition at which Evelyn found that all the exhibits with few exceptions were imported goods. There is also what could have been an unforgettable piece of farce if he had chosen to expand on it only a little more. Evelyn was in Mexico when the European world went through its most dangerous political crisis since 1914, that of Czechoslovakia in September 1938. None the less painfully for his remoteness, he watched it at a safe distance. He records how one day in Mexico City the newspapers all carried the headlines *Guerra Inevitabile* but the next day were filled with news that led to the conclusion that peace (of a kind) was inevitable. Of course Evelyn and Laura wanted to know what was happening, so they set themselves to decipher the Spanish texts. What the newspapers did with one accord make clear was that the rescue of humanity from the horrors of a second world war was exclusively the work of General Cardenas.

People who have made a close study of the Mexico of that time do not regard *Robbery Under Law* as a very valuable contribution to its subject. They will allow that Evelyn exposed some facts that needed telling and which fatuous Leftist optimism was hiding, but they will insist that in spite of his manifest efforts to be fair he presented a one-sided picture. Evelyn named the leading authorities who had expressed views contrary to his own, and he advised his readers not to reach conclusions on his testimony alone. He was scrupulous in asserting the paucity of his credentials. All this gave him a strong case against those who accused him of writing an anti-Leftist tract. But it is one thing to state conditions of fairness and another to practise fairness. Authorities deserving of respect assert that there is much more to be said on the side of the Mexican governmental supporters of that time than any reader of Evelyn's book would suspect. Evelyn wrote at a disadvantage; he had abundantly the gift of describing, albeit as a caricaturist, the times in which he lived, but, for all his intelligent respect for the past, he could never be a historian except of a peripheral kind. His successful 'Intelligent Woman's Guide to the Ethiopian Question' may be regarded as a 'lucky break', made possible by the fact that so little is known about so much of the Ethiopian past that a learned authority on the subject is almost a contradiction in terms. It has for centuries been otherwise with Mexico. Evelyn makes uncompromising generalizations about the country, its remote and its recent past, which require considerable evidence in support, and which he does not give. His attribution of a dominant and sinister force in modern Mexican affairs to Freemasonry is presented as a self-evident fact, and the reader is not invited to question this hazardous and Bellocian conclusion. Whether it is a *jeu de préjugé* or not I leave to more learned opinion than mine (or Evelyn's). As an admirer of Spanish Colonial administration in Central America, a position as bold as it was unfashionable, he dismissed not only the claims made for the Aztec non-Christian civilization but also those made for the Mexican calendar, preserved on a carved stone, as something with which 'ingenious, cross-word minds have played . . . for 150 years and devised various explanations flattering to its Aztec carvers'. There is no hint, or reason for a general reader to guess that most scientific opinion, then and now, accepts the claim for the accuracy of this calendar, an accuracy greater than any European calculations can show. An authority of wide experience, Sir Robert Marett, sums up the value of *Robbery Under Law* as follows: 'I do not see how the book can be regarded as a serious contribution to the vast literature on the Mexican Revolution (both pro and con) which is now available to the student of Mexican affairs. For example, in my view Waugh's book does not begin to compare in importance with Graham Greene's splendid novel *The Power and the Glory* which, while equally hostile to the Cardenas Government, provides a profound and moving picture of Mexico during the time of the religious persecution. Waugh merely provides a political thesis of a very debatable kind.'

The last point made by Sir Robert Marett refers to a coincidence of great interest. In 1938 Evelyn's fellow-writer Graham Greene also visited Mexico. The literary consequences were a travel book, *Lawless Roads*, published shortly before *Robbery Under Law* in 1939 (and reviewed in *The Spectator* by Evelyn, not too kindly), and one of the great novels of modern times, *The Power and the Glory*. Graham Greene turned his Mexican adventures to better account. He stuck to his last. He did not attempt a political thesis or history, but triumphantly attempted the interpretation, through the eyes of an artist, of an unhappy place at a miserable time.

Back to the end of 1938.

Evelyn and Laura returned to Piers Court for their last peace-time Christmas together, shortly after which Laura fell ill with appendicitis for the second time. Their doctor now declared that the operation, formerly pronounced as a matter for choice, was necessary and urgent. It was performed in Bristol early in January 1939, and the expenses of both it and the nursing home charges were met by the insurance policy which formed part of the contract which Evelyn had signed with the Pearson interests. As a mark of his gratitude to the insurance company concerned, for their generous interpretation of terms, Evelyn thereafter insured his family with them.

Evelyn's life during the first part of 1939 was not very active. This was a common fate then. Doctor Johnson remarked that 'when a man knows he is to be hanged in a fortnight, it concentrates his mind wonderfully', and his statement is usually taken to be true. But no one, I think, would assert that the powers of concentration are intensified by a man's knowledge that in a fortnight he may be hanged, depending on circumstances, his chances being about fifty-fifty. This was the emotional situation of Europeans, except for the select number organizing the outbreak of war, from 19 March to September 1939. Most of the time most people felt distracted and doomed.

Evelyn continued with his journalism, appearing with most regularity in *The Spectator*. Tom Burns brought him an offer from Longmans Green to write a history of the Jesuits, to appear in time for the celebration of the fourth centenary, in September 1940, of Paul III's recognition of the Society. Evelyn was greatly tempted by this project and so, rather unexpectedly, were his American publishers, Little, Brown and Company, but A. D. Peters gave it a cooler welcome. In the event, in spite of Tom Burns's enthusiasm and offer of good terms, nothing came of the plan. This was, unquestionably I think, something to be grateful for as it meant that Evelyn's main literary energies were forced into ways where they could stimulate his gifts into fresh flowering. But at the time he regretted the failure of Tom Burns's project, partly perhaps, leaving aside his devotion to the Society of Jesus, because the mechanical toil of research lends itself to escapism in a way that the ceaseless imaginative effort of inventive writing cannot. He returned to the novel which he had set aside in 1938. His diary, which he resumed later in the year, shows that he worked slowly and with the utmost difficulty. He sought escapism more effectively in gardening.

I used to see him from time to time in those days and before he went to Mexico. We generally met in the house of Cyril and Jean Connolly in the Kings Road, Chelsea. Evelyn and Cyril were on less easy terms than they had been before the outbreak of the Spanish Civil War: Cyril was an enthusiastic and hardly critical supporter of the Republican Coalition side, Evelyn as enthusiastically and even less critically a supporter of the Nationalists under General Franco. It was a time of some fanaticism, and those, like George Orwell, who could support one side and retain their faculties for precise appraisal were rare. Evelyn, essentially more emotional than intellectual at any time, too prone to rush into battle against real or surmised enemies, saw the struggle in straight terms as solely and simply a stand by men of goodwill against the encroachments of Russian Communism and the tyranny of Josef Stalin, and the fact that the last-mentioned was at that time highly esteemed on the Left made Evelyn's simplifications all the more plausible.

There are two points that should be made. Unlike some other British sympathizers with the Nationalist cause, Evelyn did not become a hero-worshipper of General Franco. If he was asked to read (as I have no doubt he was) some of the propaganda biographies of the General then being put about in England, he must have laughed them to scorn. Afterwards he never saw the Franco Regime as an earthly Paradise. The second point is that though he looked with perhaps culpable mildness on the fact that the Nationalists won through allying themselves with the most ignoble political forces in Europe, and though in common with many intelligent Englishmen (including Harold Nicolson, oddly enough) he never shook off the Napoleonic spell cast by Mussolini, he never deviated from that contempt of Nazism which he had shown when Herr Hanfstaengel sang his anti-Jewish song. The emotional commitments occasioned by the Spanish Civil War excited some of his co-religionists in England, including friends of his, to look with new admiration on Hitler and the Nazi movement. Evelyn was never a party to this. He regarded him and it to the end with detestation.

Though the difference between him and Cyril Connolly was strong and taken seriously by both, I never witnessed one of those violent altercations in which Evelyn delighted. But when the two of them were together at this time one could feel that each had a pistol in his pocket, and conversation tended to be appropriately over-guarded.

One memory of the immediate prewar years is purely concerned with personality. Often at Cyril Connolly's house the young and then little known but highly controversial poet Dylan Thomas would be present.

In those days, and indeed to the end of his life, Thomas bore a striking resemblance to Evelyn. They were both short, though Thomas was markedly the smaller of the two. Like Evelyn, Dylan Thomas had glaring eyes and one knew that he was observing everything. Like Evelyn, the young poet had vulgar taste in clothes with a preference for checked suits, but of louder and more appalling checks than Evelyn would have worn. His voice was like Evelyn's, deep and musical, and like Evelyn's his conversation was largely made up of fantasy and parody. Like Evelyn, he drank to excess, but unlike Evelyn he always showed signs of drunkenness. I do not think that I ever saw him sober. Dylan Thomas was a caricature of Evelyn and Evelyn knew it. He asked Cyril, after one meeting, not to ask him to the house when the poet was to be there. He told me that he looked with horror on the young man. 'He's exactly what I would have been if I had not become a Catholic', he said. He may have been right.

In June 1939 *Robbery Under Law* was published with the little success that has been mentioned. It was politely reviewed, but one critic made the commonest of all reviewing mistakes: he did not read the book thoroughly but satisfied himself with the customary flip-through. He collected spicy material on which to build his article but had not worked hard enough to grasp the author's intention or point of view. In his resumed diary Evelyn recorded for 30 June: 'Review in Daily Mail, very well intentioned, saying that my book is full of repulsive stories about the immorality of priests and nuns.'

This was the beginning of a battle with the *Daily Mail* which lasted nearly six weeks. Evelyn wrote a letter of protest. The newspaper refused to publish it. 'Fair comment,' they said. 'Misrepresentation', said Evelyn with more truth. He consulted a lawyer and after much wearisome discussion the *Daily Mail* capitulated; on 9 August Evelyn could record in his diary: 'The "Daily Mail" are publishing an apology in my words and paying my legal expenses – a very satisfactory conclusion.' He was to have further conflicts with the Press.

He toiled without elation at his novel. On 27 July he recorded: 'I have rewritten the first chapter of the novel about six times and at last got it into tolerable shape.' As the war crisis grew more menacing, so it continued. 'Russia and Germany have agreed to neutrality pact so there seems no reason why war should be delayed. As in September of last year it is difficult to concentrate on work at the moment . . . I spent a restless day but am maintaining our record of being the only English family to eschew the radio throughout the crisis.' This was written on the 22nd and 23rd of August. Then as the final feeble hopes flickered out and the worst became certain, Evelyn threw off some of the lethargy that goes with misery and took on new energy. On the 25th he wrote: 'The news shows no prospect of peace. The Pope's appeal was in terms so general & trite that it passes unnoticed here where no one doubts that peace is preferable to war. Perhaps it may have some meaning in Italy where they have not heard the same sentiments every day of their lives. I have written to Basil Dufferin to ask if he can put me in touch with M.I. I presume they are feverish in London. Worked well at novel.' On the next day, the 26th, he noted: 'Worked well at novel. I have introduced the character who came here to beg, saying he was on The New Statesman and an authority on ballistics, as the driver who killed the father. I suspect he will assume a prominent place in the story.' Thus Evelyn announced the birth of Atwater, one of his major inventions. One would like to know the identity of 'the character who came here to beg' but, since he is mentioned nowhere else in the diaries and his dubious credentials offer no line of promising enquiry, he must be classed as lost without trace.

Evelyn's friend, the delightful and gifted Lord Dufferin (referred to above), was at that time Colonial Undersecretary, and in answer to Evelyn's plea, he put him 'in touch' with the Military Intelligence Services, but without effect, as appears from an entry in the diary dated 1st September: 'My offer of service rejected by M.I. Have written, to please Laura, rather than from any hope of result, to Sir Robert Vansittart . . .' He had no success there either, and like many men over the age of thirty he found himself out of employment for what seemed a long time after the outbreak of war. He was forced to devote his energies to his novel.

The most revealing entry in his diary for 1939 was made a little before the last-quoted entry, on 27 August. He gave what might be called his personal war-aims. 'My inclinations are to join the army as a private. Laura is better placed than most wives and if I can let the house for the duration very well placed financially. I have to consider 30 years of novel-writing ahead of me. Nothing would be more likely than work in a Government office to finish me as a writer, nothing more likely to stimulate me than a complete change of habit. There is a symbolic difference between fighting as a soldier and serving as a civilian, even if the civilian is more valuable.'

This is perhaps the most perspicacious entry in his diary made at any time. As he foresaw, the Ministry of Information, his most obvious destination from an official point of view, sucked dry the talents of many promising writers who, at best, were left thereafter maimed by an incurable tendency to cliché-writing and a falsified sense of their audience. Life in the services gave rise to much short-lived and overrated authorship, but I can call to mind no case of it wearing out or in any way damaging the authentic talent of a made writer, provided that he survived. Evelyn never served as a private, in which capacity he might have irretrievably damaged his unit by a deep undermining operation. Instead he was to serve as an officer, never rising above the rank of Captain, the despair of all his seniors, some of his fellow-officers, and most of his juniors. His greatest enemies were the men he commanded. He was genuinely patriotic, but that did not mean that the rebel who had almost disrupted the Officers' Training Corps at Lancing, and who had mocked the Two Minutes' Silence in 1919, did not live on in the anarchic novelist of the 1920s and '30s, least of all when, forced by circumstances, he became a soldier.

# Chapter 12

## 1939

On the first Sunday of September 1939 Evelyn abandoned his resolve not to follow the crisis of Western civilization through the BBC news service. His diary entry for the 3rd reads as follows: 'Mass, Communion. After breakfast the Prime Minister broadcast that war had begun. He did it very well.'

Later, when Neville Chamberlain's political mistakes were more apparent, and later still when certain dishonourable tergiversations in his conduct of affairs were made public, many people who had listened to that broadcast announcement with emotion remembered or seemed to remember how indignant they had felt because it introduced a personal note. Among those who persisted in admiration of the short speech was George Orwell: he admired it precisely because it was personal, and he pointed out that this was right since war primarily engages personal feelings. These may have been Evelyn's reactions too.

On the same day evacuees began to arrive in Dursley and Stinchcombe from the neighbouring great towns. Evelyn took note of the event and observed its consequences closely. He was to find use for his observations before very long.

He was still without employment. His letter to Vansittart had suggested that in view of his wide experience as a traveller and journalist he was qualified to act as a liaison officer between Government departments and foreign war correspondents. Vansittart had returned a 'civil answer' (a favourite expression of Lord Beauchamp who had died in 1938) and referred his application to Lord Perth who for a brief period was in charge of the nascent Ministry of Information until the inept appointment of its first official head, Lord MacMillan. Peter had already been recruited to the new organization, so Evelyn wrote to him and to Perth urging his qualifications. This move seems to have had some result but of a kind that threatened to condemn Evelyn to that kind of service which he most wanted to avoid. He wrote in his diary on 5 September: 'There seems no demand for cannon fodder at the moment. I got a letter from Ministry of Information saying I was on their list and must not apply for other national service until I heard from them.' His spirits sank, as did those of most people in England at that time.

His diary entry for 18 September shows Evelyn indulging a fashionable pastime of that heavy hour, prognosticating the course of the war. Most prophecies of the time, as the contemporary Press shows, erred on the side of wistful optimism; Evelyn went to the other extreme but with more of accuracy than most. 'The war seems likely to develop into an attack on Great Britain by an alliance of Russia, Germany, Japan & perhaps Italy, with France bought out and U.S.A. a sympathetic onlooker.' It is terrifying to remember that it was in Hitler's power to bring about that invincible alliance.

Evelyn calmed his spirits by working in his garden, filled with envy of Alec who had been posted to the British Army in France. Much later in the war Alec was seconded to the Middle East Command and served in Baghdad where I met him once or twice. He never had difficulty in finding employment; for Evelyn it was always a struggle while the war lasted. In 1939 that and the ruinous prospect of having Piers Court on his hands gave him continual temptation to despair. Then hope sprung up regarding Piers Court. A Dominican nun inspected the house and grounds and considered £600 a year a reasonable rent for a small school which she needed to evacuate to the country.

In the end the Dominican nun did solve the pressing question of Piers Court. The school, run by her order, did take over the house for the duration of the war She came at the end of a long line of applicants, some fraudulent, and of whom most of the more genuine were hoping for comfortable quarters at a minute rent. Their number included the 'keeper of an idiot school' and a female religious enthusiast from America who wanted to convert Evelyn to an obscure theological system described by her as 'mutation'. The Dominican nun seems to have been the first acceptable or commonsensical client they had.

The solution of the Piers Court problem involved all the domestic turmoil which was expected. While the nuns and their charges moved in, Laura and Evelyn moved out on 29 September, their first refuge being Pixton. They went there after visiting Mells where they stayed with Lady Horner. They saw much of Christopher Hollis who had taken a teaching appointment at Downside School so as to make a local Roxburgh available for war service. (He taught at Downside for the Michaelmas term. After that, in 1940, he served in the Home Guard and then in the RAF.) The Dominican solution of Evelyn's house problem made no difference, as hardly needs saying, to his immediate personal anxiety: how to find employment in what was eventually to be called 'the war effort'.

Before leaving Piers Court Evelyn had heard from the author Ian Hay (John Hay Beith in real life) who at that time was Director of Public Relations at the War Office, to tell him that he might hope for the kind of liaison appointment he had asked for. But this hope was soon to prove a mirage.

On 2 October Laura's brother-in-law Eddie Grant received a summons to the War Office where he was accorded the liaison post on which Beith had tempted Evelyn to build his hopes.

So Evelyn had to pursue his search for employment from the beginning again. There were rumours that the Brigade of Guards were very short of officers and that the Naval Intelligence departments were looking for recruits, so Evelyn wrote to the commanding officer of the Welsh Guards and to an acquaintance at the Admiralty. On 16 October he received a letter from the Admiralty requesting him to call at his convenience. He went up to London the same day. He stayed with his parents at Underhill. 'My father', Evelyn noted in his diary, 'is taking the 6th form at Highgate grammar school in a course of Victorian poetry – unpaid but apparently welcome work to him.'

His visit to the Admiralty the next day was fruitless. His acquaintance there was Ian Fleming, Peter Fleming's brother, and Ian, to quote the diary, 'told me that there was no immediate chance for employment, but that my name was "on the list". From there to the War Office.' How reminiscent of the time these entries are! Especially to men of Evelyn's generation then. Not old enough, as many of them thought, to retire from the exertions and dangers of active service, not young enough to be wanted in a modern army, navy or air force. Like out-of-work actors in the age of Mr Crummles we slouched from theatre to theatre, willing to take the feeblest walking-on part.

He returned to Pixton and to more dashed hopes. He recorded on 21 October: 'By the second post a letter from Welsh guards unaccountably telling me that their list has been revised and that they had no room for me. My first feeling was that there must be someone at the War Office blocking my chances; my second that Col. [illegible name] had become notorious for his generosity in giving commissions and has been rebuked. Whatever the reason, I was thrown into despair. I now had no irons in the fire. That night I tried a new sleeping draught made by the local doctor. He admitted later that it was what he used to give mothers in travail. I slept well but woke feeling on the verge of melancholy mania.'

The indications are that when Evelyn had received this refusal from the Brigade of Guards he applied, possibly through Ian Fleming, for a commission in the Royal Marines, and that he wrote to his old acquaintance of Belton, Brendan Bracken, for help. But there is no surviving documentation in evidence of this supposition. It must be guess-work.

Evelyn's earlier remark that there must be someone 'blocking my chances' is of interest. There may have been. Spy-mania was less in World War II than in its predecessor, but ever since the Spanish Nationalist commanders had boasted of a 'Fifth Column' in besieged Madrid, there existed in official circles a widespread fear and suspicion that the enemy might have dangerous agents and sympathizers living unsuspected within the walls. Suspicion extended to the politically unorthodox. Certainly Robert Byron who was vainly seeking for employment at the same time, was discriminated against as a result of his noisy tirades against Neville Chamberlain, in spite of the fact that these had been a private activity. Although we were at peace with Italy and Spain, Evelyn's publicly expressed admiration of Fascism in *Waugh in Abyssinia*, and contempt of Western Liberal democracy and sympathy with General Franco in *Robbery Under Law*, may have aroused suspicion as to his political reliability. The suspicions were not groundless. He was to show that he was not politically reliable in the sense of being politically subservient in all things.

Added to the anxieties of Evelyn and Laura was the fact, in which they took joy, that she was pregnant and the local doctor at Pixton accurately forecast the birth for the middle of November. Though joyful this was nevertheless an added cause for anxiety. Evelyn looked round for escape from the despairing mood which accompanies unemployment. He took the most sensible course. On 23 October he left Pixton for Chagford and the tender care of Mrs Cobb and resumed work on his neglected novel.

Immediately the prospect brightened. He found that he could write with zest and on the 24th he could note in his diary: 'Wrote all the morning. The second chapter taking shape and, more important, ideas springing.' On the 26th: 'Working well. Over 4,000 words done since I arrived. A letter from Humbert Wolfe very kindly volunteering to push my fortunes with the War Office . . . A letter from Brendan Bracken saying that Winston Churchill [then First Lord of the Admiralty] had strongly supported my claim to a commission in the Marines.' There is nothing surprising in Winston Churchill giving Evelyn support as he had been an admirer of his books since the publication of *Decline and Fall*. The support probably hastened his being commissioned, a fact one may regret.

For the moment Evelyn was relatively happy, relative that is to say to the unhappiness of the time and to his own limited capacity for happiness. He was working hard and well on his novel, hindered occasionally from concentration by the fatigue brought on by his increasing insomnia, but for the most part enjoying the unique pleasure reserved to a writer who is performing at the top of his capacity, and who knows that he is. He wrote to Roughead in the course of a letter: 'Re novel. About 15,000 words were done & jolly well done before the war. Its fate depends on mine. If no one wants my patriotic services at once I think I may retire to the Faro Islands & finish it.' Would that he had done so! On 1 November he wrote in his diary: 'I take the MS of my novel up to my bedroom for fear it should be burned in the night. It has in fact got to interest me so much that for the first time since the war begun I have ceased to fret about not being on active service. Perhaps that means that I shall shortly get a commission.' Unfortunately it did.

Evelyn had no delusions about what the war was likely to mean. As has been said already, while most people's prognostications erred on the side of optimism, his reflected his pessimism. It is generally forgotten today that the 'Phoney War' was a time not of agonized anticipation, as most people who lived through it affect to remember it now, but of the empty happiness that goes with presumptuous hope, of cloud-cuckoo-land proclamations of 'war aims', of lunatic dreams of a future perfect order to be achieved by this most imperfect of means, of an uninhibited building of castles in the air. All this irritated Evelyn with his logical and sometimes overprecise mind. He had no use for cloud-cuckoo war aims: the only war aim was to win by killing great numbers of the enemy's population and preventing them killing great numbers of one's own; as for the utopias and air-castles, they seemed to him not only silly but malign.

During this time, when he seems to have reconciled himself to the un-likelihood of any service appointment, Evelyn 'opened negotiations with Chapman & Hall, Osbert Sitwell and David Cecil with the idea of starting a monthly magazine under the title of "Duration".' The fate of this short-lived enterprise becomes clear later.

At about midday on 17 November Evelyn was rung up at Chagford from Pixton to be told that Laura was in labour. Immediately he drove over and shortly before midnight his eldest son, later christened Auberon, was born. Evelyn was as overjoyed as the delivered mother. His desire for a son and heir could not have been stronger if he had been a reigning prince. On 18 November he noted in his diary: 'Laura happier than she is likely to be again', and three days later: 'The last few days have been delightful for Laura. She is drowsy & contented. I am living at a boarding house in the village where the women believe I was tipsy on Friday night.'

It is necessary to go back a little to get an idea of how the next great change in his life came about. His friends working in ministries were pressing his claims. On 3 November he recorded: 'A note from Bracken speaking well of his own efforts on my behalf with the marines . . .' On the 21st, immediately following the entry quoted in the preceding para-graph, he wrote: 'The Marines have sent me a long questionnaire asking among other things if I am a chronic bedwetter. It seems probable that I am going to get a commission there.' On the next day he received a sum-mons from London to undergo a medical test and an interview at the headquarters of the Royal Marine Forces. On 23 November he went to London and then to Underhill where he dined and spent the night, 'finding my parents', he recorded, 'markedly unsympathetic to my project of joining the war'. They might have been yet more unsympathetic if they had known that his 'project' meant abandoning for ever what if com-pleted would almost certainly have been a great novel, possibly his best.

Evelyn's diary entry for 24 November is memorable: 'Went straight to the Medical board which was a flat in St James's. Doctors in shabby white coats strolled in and out smoking cigarettes. I went first to have my eyes tested and did deplorably. When asked to read at a distance with one eye I could not distinguish lines, let alone letters. I managed to cheat a little by peering over the top. Then I went into the next room where the doctor said, "Let's see your birthday suit. Ah, middle-aged spread. Do you wear dentures?" He tapped me with a hammer in various organs. Then I was free to dress. I was given a sealed envelope to take to the Admiralty. In the taxi I unsealed it and found a chit to say that I had been examined and found unfit for service. It seemed scarcely worthwhile going for the interview.

'A colonel(?) in khaki greeted me in the most affable way, apologized for keeping me waiting and gradually it dawned on me that I was being accepted. He said, "The doctors do not think much of your eyesight. Can you read that?" – pointing to a large advertisement across the street. I could. "Anyway most of your work will be in the dark." Then he gave me a choice between Marine Infantry, a force being raised for raiding parties, and Artillery, an anti-aircraft unit for work in the Shetlands. I chose the former and left in good humour.'

Evelyn was now an officer, in fact if not yet in theory. He went from his interview to the St James's Club. He recorded: 'Peters lunched with me at my club. Spoke grimly of the Ministry of Information.' Did Peters guess that he was supplying him with 'convertible literary stuff'? Probably.

It was a varied day. Having visited Hubert Duggan and Phyllis de Janzé with whom Hubert was then living, and having found them 'obsessed with war news & both a little gloomier than when I last saw them', he returned to write letters at his club when he found a message 'that the editor of the American magazine "Life" was at the Savoy and wanted to see me. I nearly did not go, but finally went and found a lugubrious kind of Baboon who commissioned two articles at the startling price of $1,000 apiece, a sum which if it materializes, will go a long way to settling my immediate debts.'

Evelyn celebrated his entry into the army by a reversion to his bachelor 'life-style'. Enriched by his interview with the lugubrious baboon, he felt elated, and 'drank a lot of champagne with various people sitting about in the club & took a magnum to dinner at Patrick Balfour's. He told me that my idea for a magazine had already been anticipated by the rump of the Left wing under Connolly.' Thus did *Duration* expire through lack of interest, while *Horizon* was born through Cyril Connolly's courageous gamble. The diary goes on: 'I went to the Slip in and drank two bottles of champagne & a bottle of rum with Kathleen Meyrick. I was sick at about 5. Nov. 25th. The subsequent hangover removed all illusions of heroism. I went to confession at Farm Street . . .' Evelyn had instinctively wandered back into the world of *Vile Bodies*. He did not stay there, but throughout the war he did not drop this renewed acquaintance.

For admirers of Evelyn's prologue chapter to *Brideshead Revisited* and of the first volume of the War Trilogy, in both of which the Marines seen from an elderly subaltern's point of view are wonderfully well described; for such readers only Evelyn's diary for December 1939 and for most of 1940 has a special interest as a display of raw material. His sleepless observation was at work, receiving impressions later to be transmuted into fiction.

Unless the particular case concerns in a vital manner important historical events, detailed accounts of individual wartime service in an army are, with few exceptions, wearisome reading. Except for one incident at the very end in which he became personally involved in great issues, Evelyn's military career is not among the exceptions, and the 'convertible literary stuff' has been admirably converted by himself in his fiction, and by two of his companions in arms: by Lord Birkenhead, in David Pryce Jones's compilation, and by Mr John St John, in his book *To the War with Waugh*.

Rather than relate at second-hand what has perhaps rather too often been related at first-hand, that is to say, the experience with its ordeals, griefs and joys of the humbly placed soldier, I intend to outline briefly Evelyn's wartime career, and then to revert in detail to points of interest.

As related already, he obtained a commission in the Royal Marines without the necessity of going through the appalling drudgery of an Officers' Training Unit, known as an OCTU in those early days of abbreviational Newspeak. (I forget what the C stood for.) For this there were two reasons: first, that faced with immediate expansion the Force was very short of officers, and second, that Evelyn enjoyed the formidable privilege of the First Lord's personal support. In the light of later events his second advantage appears somewhat ironical.

Evelyn served in three different units and in three extra-regimental appointments. In the case of an officer who reaches high rank such a number of transfers would not be remarkable, but in the case of Evelyn, who never rose above junior rank, it was most unusual. Anyone with army experience knows how any commanding officer will fight, if not to the death to the last ditch, to retain his juniors of whom he is invariably short. With Evelyn it was otherwise, and the reason, which he recognized clearly enough, was obvious. Commanding officers, from generals to battalion commanders, were only too pleased to see him transferred from their jurisdiction. They found him critical and disruptive. The prestige he had justly accumulated as a writer of shining talent made him welcome, but the discovery that the anarchy of his wit was the expression of a deep-rooted and searching and destructive scepticism, applied indiscriminately to small things as well as great, made commanders from company to divisional level doubt if the retention of this officer was profitable in the circumstances of war. He made few friends in the army, except through former friends, and commanders among the new friends were glad to see him go.

In the fiction which he wrote on the prompting of his wartime experiences, he asserts, or rather seems to assert (for the relation of fiction to real experience must always be guess-work), that he had a great love for the army. The fictitious 'I' of *Brideshead Revisited* talks of a 'love-affair' with the army which Charles Ryder had felt. Most of Evelyn's readers have very naturally taken this as an expression of his personal feelings. I find myself left doubting. I think it more likely that the fiction is only indirectly representational, and reflects a hope and an ideal rather than an emotional involvement which Evelyn went through. He admired the tradition of the officer and gentleman, but then he admired the tradition of the country squire living as a benevolent sovereign on his acres, but found in practice that the life was rather boring. So, I think, he felt about army life. Once more it was a case of disillusion with the world of Tony Last, for all his preference for it over the world of Basil Seal and Margot Metroland.

To concentrate on the outline. Evelyn remained an officer in the Royal Marines for approximately a year, from December 1939 to November 1940. He served first in Chatham, then in Deal, then in the neighbourhood of Bisley in Hampshire. In August 1940 his battalion embarked as part of a mixed force for an undisclosed destination and military operation which turned out to be the attempted engagement at Dakar. He was back in England with his unit at the end of October. Before leaving England he had heard through Brendan Bracken of a new raiding force then being raised, later to be known as the Commandos and placed under a new organization later known as Combined Operations. He was officially seconded to the new force in November 1940, and later in order to ease the transfer he was, at the request of his immediate chief, Colonel Robert Laycock, also seconded from the Royal Marines to the Royal Horse Guards. The secondment was not officially accomplished till 1942.

In 1941 he went with Colonel Laycock's unit, known as No. 8 Commando, to Egypt, and to the Middle East Command. There he took part in various small operations, but most notably, and showing exemplary courage, in the battle for Crete. Throughout the battle he was Colonel Laycock's Personal Assistant.

By the end of 1941 No. 8 Commando were back in England and their Battalion Headquarters were at Sherborne in Dorset. There Evelyn remained with them during most of 1942, with several special assignments to Combined Operations Headquarters in London as an Intelligence Officer. In July 1943 Colonel Laycock was ordered to take No. 8 Commando to Italy. Evelyn, to his lasting embitterment, was not included by Laycock among the officers selected for this operational mission. He endeavoured to obtain a reversal of the decision in vain. However, in the course of the subsequent dispute with Lord Lovat, who was acting as Laycock's representative at Combined Operations Headquarters, a friend, Lord Lovat's cousin Colonel William Stirling, invited him to become one of his officers in a new unit which, with the support of Winston Churchill, he was in the process of raising: the 2nd Special Air Service Regiment. The nucleus of the unit had been raised and was serving in North Africa. Evelyn was officially transferred to Bill Stirling's command in October 1943 and (with myself) he was under instructions to join the S.A.S. in North Africa in November, but the orders were cancelled owing to the happily changed situation of the Allied Forces.

In the meantime an unusual interruption had occurred in Evelyn's military career. Brendan Bracken was now the Minister of Information, the first successful holder of that post since its establishment in 1939. He was the first such Minister to know Fleet Street and its workings at first-hand, and the first to have (from journalism and from his conversations with Winston Churchill) some dim notion of literary invention and the literary career. To him Evelyn appealed in September 1943, having been posted to the regimental headquarters of the Royal Horse Guards at Windsor, for his official support in a request to the War Office that Evelyn should be granted indefinite leave to enable him to write a book. Bracken did as he was asked. The Military Secretary and his Department were not unnaturally taken aback. Eventually Evelyn was granted the leave conditionally in January 1944. He went to Chagford where he began to write *Brideshead Revisited*. In February he was recalled to duty by a perplexed War Office to fill two successive appointments as aide-de-camp to Generals Thomas and Graham. The role of ADC was ill-suited to Evelyn's character and abilities and the appointments were unsuccessful, and of brief duration. He returned to Chagford.

In the meantime the 2nd S.A.S. Regiment to which Evelyn now officially belonged returned under Bill Stirling from North Africa and went into camp in Scotland where Stirling began a regimental reorganization. Evelyn's position, as the foregoing makes plain, was anomalous. At a time of reorganization and when the whole situation of the S.A.S. regiments was under dispute at the War Office, Bill Stirling was not anxious for the disruptive presence of Evelyn. It so happened that Evelyn had severely injured his knee during parachute training in December 1943. Bill Stirling took the occasion to grant Evelyn sick-leave and to renew the 'literary leave' reluctantly agreed and capriciously though only spasmodically cancelled by the War Office. In May Bill Stirling, as a result of disagreements with his immediate seniors, was forced to relinquish his command. He was succeeded by Colonel Brian Franks, a former fellow-officer of Evelyn in No. 8 Commando. Colonel Franks felt the undesirability of Evelyn as a regimental officer even more strongly than his predecessor had done. By now *Brideshead Revisited* was finished; the injured knee was restored; early in June Evelyn reported for duty to Colonel Franks at regimental headquarters in Scotland. The dilemma of Colonel Franks was resolved at the end of the month by an unexpected request for his services: Acting under the instructions of his chief, Brigadier Fitzroy Maclean, Randolph Churchill asked for Evelyn to be seconded to 37th Military Mission in Jugoslavia, of which Churchill was in charge of a subsidiary section in Croatia. The transfer was agreed and, after being delayed in an air-crash in which Evelyn nearly lost his life, he reached Croatia in September 1944. The rest of his war service except for short intervals in Italy was spent in Jugoslavia from where he returned to England in March 1945, a little less than two months before the end of the war in Europe.

Such in outline was Evelyn's career as a soldier. It left him deeply disillusioned, a fact which tended to increase his disposition towards melancholy, but he had the satisfaction of knowing that the direction he had taken in 1939 was the rewarding one from the point of view of his literary ability (even though it probably meant the loss of his best book). He summed up his situation thus on 7 May 1945. To understand the passage the reader should realize that he had begun to write a life of St Helena, the mother of the Emperor Constantine.

'All day there was expectation of VE day and finally at 9 [p.m.] it was announced for tomorrow. Carolyn [Cobb] resentful that she does not feel elated. It is pleasant to end the war in plain clothes, writing. I remember at the start of it all writing to Frank Pakenham that its value for us would be to show us finally that we are not "men of action". I took longer than him to learn it. I regard the greatest danger I went through that of becoming one of Churchill's young men, of getting a medal & standing for Parliament; if things had gone, as then seemed right, in the first two years, that is what I should be now. I thank God to find myself still a writer & at work on something as "uncontemporary" as I am.'

# Chapter 13

## 1939-1941

And now for highlights and some details.

During World War II an addendum to King's Regulations laid down that no one serving in His Majesty's forces was to keep a private diary. The rule was ignored by everyone from the Chief of the General Staff to the humblest soldier or sailor who felt some urge to record his thoughts and adventures at so stirring a time, and I know of no official prosecution against those who were guilty of this act of disobedience and 'insecurity'. Evelyn continued to keep his diary from his reception into the Royal Marines to the last month of 1940. There then occurs a gap in the record which is made good, however, by retrospective passages. The day-to-day record remains spasmodic, though including a full diary of his experiences in the battle for Crete in 1941, until March 1943. From this date on it is maintained daily till the end of the war and after. There are revelations that one may miss with regret, for example some description of the genesis of his writing in those years, but the record is fairly easily put together with the help of his business letters (usually undated and recklessly candid) to A. D. Peters. Peter, as mentioned already, served for a while in the Ministry of Information and was later seconded to the Ministry of Food where the difficult propaganda proposition to make food restriction popular was brilliantly achieved under the direction of Lord Woolton.

To consider first what immediately happened under the stress of the times to Evelyn's writing career. Evelyn continued haltingly with his novel after joining the Marines and did not give up the contest until February 1940 when the work was suspended after two chapters, never to be resumed. He had difficulty in getting this fragment published, not because editors or publishers doubted its quality, but because its shape, two long chapters, made it awkward to fit into the conventional dimensions of a book or a magazine: too short for one, too long for the other. In the end, and after wearisome arguments with various interested and hesitant parties, the first chapter was published in shortened form by Cyril Connolly in *Horizon* in late 1941 and in full, as a short book, by Chapman and Hall in December 1942, by which time our hero's fortunes had sunk very low. *Work Suspended*, as it was finally entitled, was the last of Evelyn's books to be published in his father's lifetime. It will be considered later.

In the meantime Evelyn had by the end of 1941 conceived and executed in full another novel, *Put Out More Flags*. Whereas the genesis and progress of *Work Suspended* is fully documented in Evelyn's diary and correspondence with Peter and Roughead, there is no mention of the second novel in either until it had been completed. The whole of 'POMF', as Evelyn used to call it (as opposed to 'Suspenders'), was written while he was an officer of the Royal Marines, and probably finished while he was under Colonel Laycock in the Commandos. It was ready to be submitted to Chapman and Hall by the end of the summer of 1941, and was published in 1942. Before considering its character and qualities some account of his life as a Marine Officer may be given.

The record may be brief, for the reasons stated already. There is little in the experiences noted in the diary which he kept while serving in the Royal Marines, which is not closely mirrored in the fiction which it prompted. The Force itself is perfectly described in his invention much later of 'The Halberdiers', and the reader of the diaries who knows Evelyn's last ambitious work, the War Trilogy, and 'Pomf', will often recognize the origin of some event or comment or even minute detail. We meet Brigadier Ritchie-Hook early in 1941; we learn that the model 'looks like something expelled from Sing-Sing & talks like a boy in the Fourth Form at School – teeth like a stoat, ears like a faun, eyes alight like a child playing pirates "We have to biff them, gentlemen".' What the diaries do not reveal will come as a surprise to most readers, and a disappointment to some. Evelyn seems to have had no fellow-officer in the Marines (or elsewhere in the war for that matter) who remotely resembled Apthorpe.

But the Ur-Ritchie Hook became an object of close study. The poor man probably had little notion that he was under the merciless scrutiny of his subaltern when he asked the latter to lunch at his family home near Bisley. Evelyn records: 'He took me to a depraved villa of stock broker's Tudor. I asked if he had built it himself. "Built it? It's four or five hundred years old." '

When the spring and summer of 1940 came, and with them the German invasions of Belgium and Holland, followed by the rapid Nazi victory over France in May and June, Evelyn's battalion met these shattering events, according to his diary, with a mixture of inherited British indifference to 'foreign affairs' and excitement at the prospect of action. On 22 May he wrote in his diary: 'I lectured to the Coy. upon the international situation & depressed myself so much that I could barely continue speaking.'

During this time, before the ultimate catastrophe in France of June 1940, he took short leave on 25 May for what he described as 'an idyllic weekend with Laura at Alton in the Sun Hotel . . .' In the same entry he wrote: 'Read P. G. Wodehouse (who has been lost along with the channel ports).' The P. G. Wodehouse affair was to concern Evelyn Waugh and myself closely some twenty years later.

At Bisley on 27 June 1940 he found an official summons to report 'soonest' at the Ministry of Information. He went up to London on the 28th. 'Arriving there', he recorded, 'I found the news of Belgian surrender on the streets together with women selling flags for "Animal Day". Had hair cut & bought pants. Went to M of I where Graham Greene propounded a scheme for official writers to the forces & himself wanted to become a marine; also Burns. I said I thought the official writer racket might be convenient if we found ourselves permanently in a defensive rôle in the Far East, or if I were incapacitated & set to training. [A common fate of the wounded.]'

In the event Graham Greene never became any sort of 'official writer', except for presumably never to be published works composed in West Africa for M.I.6. Tom Burns was later seconded to the British Embassy in Madrid. The Official Writer Scheme (characteristic of the empty-headed idealism of the 'Phoney War' and already out of date by May 1940) did not die. Eighteen months later it enjoyed a minor revival in which Evelyn played a hilarious part.

After the evacuation of Dunkirk and the French surrender, most men in the services and most units faced the prospect of a long period of static defence and the boredom of a besieged citadel. Evelyn's battalion provided no exception until early June when the battalion was assigned to the Anglo-French operation on Dakar in French West Africa.

From the beginning the operation was what is known in common military parlance as a 'balls-up'. The authorities seemed at that hour of destiny uncertain whether to use these relatively well-equipped though at the best half-trained troops in coastal defence against the expected invasion attempt, or to use them to strengthen the Dakar operational force. Official uncertainty was translated into cumbersome and ludicrous fact. The battalion was sent to Wales to embark, then embarked at Bristol, then, after sailing and returning, disembarked and sent to Cornwall to man the Southern Coastal defences. From here Evelyn took forty-eight hours' leave which he used in order to find out more about the new Commando force from Brendan Bracken, now installed in Downing Street as the Prime Minister's right-hand man, though officially still only his Parliamentary Private Secretary. Bracken advised him to write to Colonel Robert Laycock, whom he knew. Eventually Evelyn's battalion sailed at the end of August 1940 to Dakar by way of the Azores and Freetown which they reached on 17 September. On 22 September there occurred the attempted operation and its fiasco. Evelyn's battalion did not land but retreated in their commandeered vessel to Freetown which they reached on the 27th or 28th. They reached Gibraltar on the 15th and Scotland on the 27th of October.

The diaries are not very enjoyable reading for the most part of this period, but there are amazing flashes, such as this interesting Anglo-African description of an air-raid: 'Steam chicken topside drop plenty no good shit'; and an even odder example of English usage in a dialogue between a British soldier and a Negro singing in his canoe. 'Fuck off, you black bastard.' 'Oh officer, sah, you have not taken your Eno's.'

Evelyn found wartime Gibraltar relaxing and agreeable, though he noted the tensions of the place. He received his first mail since August and his first personal news about the Battle of Britain. 'All letters from home are about air raids . . . Henry Yorke no doubt fighting fires day & night. The armed forces cut a small figure. We are like wives reading letters from the trenches.'

He also received some professional news of interest. Bob Laycock had answered his letter to say that he would have room for him in his new assignment in Combined Operations and asked him to call on him when next in London. Evelyn decided to get seconded from his battalion as soon as he officially could in order to join his fortunes to those of Bob Laycock, one of the very few men for whom he conceived some degree of hero-worship. Less than ten days after leaving Gibraltar the battalion was back in Scotland.

During those weeks from August to October on a troopship Evelyn began the first draft of *Put Out More Flags*. By the end of the next year, 1941, the completed book was given to Chapman and Hall. They published it in 1942. In the next year they published *Work Suspended*. Though 'Suspenders' was written and finished long before 'Pomf' was begun, the earlier publication of 'Pomf' suggests to me that it is best considered first.

The title is a bit of a conundrum. Evelyn made no mystery of it. He drew it from the works of a Chinese sage, perhaps brought to his attention by his old friend Harold Acton who had returned to England from Florence in 1939 and was at this time serving in the RAF. 'A man getting drunk at a farewell party', so runs the sage's counsel, 'should strike a musical tone, in order to strengthen his spirit . . . and a drunk military man should order gallons and put out more flags in order to increase his military splendour.' This is followed on the title page by a second quotation from the wisdom of ancient China: 'A little injustice in the heart can be drowned by wine; but a great injustice in the world can be drowned only by the sword.'

Precisely how these two quotations apply to the book is not easy to decide. The first one indicates plainly enough the splendid farce in which

Basil Seal, Lady Metroland and the Bacchic train are with us again; the second the dark thread, darker than in any of the previous farces, which runs through the story. Otherwise they seem to have no relevance whatever. But *Put Out More Flags* is a good catchy title, and I doubt if Evelyn accorded it more significance.

The book is constructed on odd but firm lines. It has two heroes, Ambrose Silk, who occupies the front of the stage during the first half of the novel, and Basil Seal, never a back-stage figure, who usurps the principal role in the second half. Both can be described as victim-as-hero, though only up to a point, Lord Copper. Ambrose Silk is a comic Hamlet; Basil Seal a farcical Iago. Neither can appeal to the reader's sympathy for a second. Neither are supposed to.

The origin of the story, apart from an obvious source in Evelyn's rakish premarital days, lay in the memory of the arrival of the evacuees in Stinchcombe. From the very slight acquaintance with them reflected in the diaries, Evelyn, as was his way, seems to have dreamed up monstrous fictions. The Connolly children are a masterly caricature of urban waifs, wholly fashioned, I think, out of his imagination. The story of how Basil Seal contrived to make a fortune out of these three unwanted bastards by fraudulent billeting orders shows Evelyn's invention at its most active as well as its most ingenious. Equally skilful as a piece of craftsmanship is the exquisitely manipulated intrigue whereby Basil Seal, to obtain a captaincy, acts as *agent provocateur* to Ambrose Silk who is skilfully manoeuvred into the posture of a Fascist agent. Silk meets his doom by way of the Ministry of Information which Evelyn had so dreaded in August 1939 and of which he had received much rewarding information since.

Basil Seal remains as he was, compounded of Peter Rodd and Basil Murray in the main, and if possible slightly less honest than when last met in Azania. But the dark thread in the story touches even him. There is pathos of a kind when Basil Seal is moved to protection of his discarded mistress Angela Lyne who has taken to solitary drinking bouts.

Ambrose Silk is a fine invention. He is closely modelled on Brian Howard. He is represented as half-Jewish, as a flashy amateur of modernism in all forms, including fashionable Left-Wing political opinions, and as a homosexual with a special preference for young Germans; all of which was true of Brian Howard in real life. Evelyn drew Brian's features and weaknesses with a care that might be called loving, were it not for the known fact that Evelyn despised and disliked this model intensely. Only in one respect did Evelyn radically depart from the original; Evelyn drew Silk as a Left-Wing writer who enjoyed a wide reputation and much esteem, whereas, in fact, Brian Howard's literary reputation, never very high and confined to his cronies, had virtually terminated. Since leaving Oxford he had published but one slim volume of verse called *God Save the*

*King*. It was intended to shock but succeeded in causing not even a mild ripple of interest in the literary world of which he believed he should be acknowledged as an ornament and a leader. Compared to Brian, Enoch Soames was a prodigy of creative energy.

Beautifully drawn, and far less exaggerated than a later generation of readers may be prepared to believe, is the picture of the self-conscious advanced Youth (of which Evelyn had once been a member in the Youth-crazed '20s and '30s) which by 1939 had become Communist, and in which Silk, rejected as old and out of date, tries to act as a jazzed-up Socrates, and where Basil Seal finds a very temporary mistress in Poppet Green. Basil, after a night of pleasure, is with Poppet in her studio on the fateful Sunday morning of the declaration of war when the air-raid alert sirens (mistakenly) first sounded. The following dialogue gives the spirit of this part of the novel, a literally true picture of a section of the younger generation.

' "Oh God," she said. "You've done it. They've come."

' "Faultless timing," said Basil cheerfully. "That's always been Hitler's strong point."

'Poppet began to dress in an ineffectual fever of reproach . . .

' "I wish I'd never met you. I wish I'd been to church. I was brought up in a convent. I wanted to be a nun once. I wish I was a nun. I'm going to be killed. Oh, I wish I was a nun. Where's my gas-mask? I shall go mad if I don't find my gas-mask!"

There are some singularities of the novel which should be noticed before leaving it. One is the appearance of Sir Alaistair Digby-Vane-Trumping-ton in a transformed shape. It may be remembered that Trumpington was one of the young Oxford bloods who in a drunken rag brought about the expulsion of Paul Pennyfeather from Scone College, Oxford. He reappeared with his wife Sonia in *Black Mischief* as a friend of Basil Seal. In neither book was he presented as a pleasing character. In *Put Out More Flags* he appears as a very estimable man, serving as a private soldier and endeavouring in this way to repay his debt to a society which, he felt, had given him far more than he had earned. An allusion in the book makes it clear, I think, that Evelyn was prompted here by the thought of T. E. Lawrence serving in the ranks of the RAF. I am not sure whether this bold innovation, so alien to Evelyn's previous fiction, is successful or not. There is a suspicion of awkward sentimentality about it. But then time of war is also time of sentimentality.

The second singularity is unquestionably successful. This is the picture of Barbara Sothill, Basil Seal's sister. In this Evelyn drew with a sure hand the picture of an attractive and virtuous woman. With the exception of Mrs Stitch (who is too fantastic to be taken with any seriousness) all his attractive women had been bitches or idiots or both, sometimes, as with Brenda Last, not far off criminality. In Barbara Sothill Evelyn showed that he was not the prisoner of this monstrous regiment of women. Perhaps in *Put Out More Flags* he achieved this rare feat, which most critics thought beyond him, because he had already attempted it successfully in the as yet unpublished *Work Suspended*.

The book has a lesser singularity which merits remark. Evelyn was still, in common with most British people, a fervent admirer of Winston Churchill. He dedicated the book to 'Major Randolph Churchill, Fourth Hussars, Member of Parliament'. In his dedicatory letter he apologizes for taking as his theme 'a race of ghosts', and he concludes, 'Here they are in that odd, dead period before the Churchillian renaissance.' But Evelyn was never perfectly at home with a widely shared enthusiasm. The final episode in the book takes place in the summer of 1940, when that renaissance began. Sir Joseph Mainwaring is talking to Lady Seal: 'There's a new spirit abroad,' he said. 'I see it on every side.'

'And, poor booby, he was bang right.' "

The book was well received by the critics. The general feeling of them and of Evelyn's readers was chiefly one of thankfulness and relief that the war and its sobering and indeed depressing effect on a majority of men had not darkened Evelyn's bright and fantastic gifts. He was the subject of a gratifying chorus of praise. The great jester was back at his jesting. In one small department of life, if nowhere else, this was a case of 'business as usual'.

Within this chorus there sounded one or two notes that were not in simple harmony; not discordantly, but not wholeheartedly joining in the voice of praise. In *The New Statesman* the book was reviewed by Alan Pryce-Jones. His article included this passage: 'The more discriminating, while they laugh, make a minor reservation, however. Aren't the great, ramshackle houses now too finely observed? Don't the casual details ring too carefully true? One cannot imagine any of these young men, shameless as they are in the conduct of life, doing up the bottom button of their waistcoat; and is not each overtone of adultery – in not somewhere obvious like Berkeley Square but a knowing by-street, say Montpelier Walk – recorded with rather too modish an air?'

It was the complaint of Oldmeadow and J. B. Priestley in a new and fashionable and less solemn guise. Evelyn was wasting his talents on unworthy material, lacking in 'social significance' and the reverse of edifying. He was to hear a good deal more of this kind of criticism in the next three years.

On arriving back from the fiasco in Africa in October 1940, Evelyn had set about making contact with Bob Laycock in order to establish his transfer to and position in the new command. He succeeded and on the 13th reported for duty to No. 8 Commando at Largs, near Glasgow. At the Marine Hotel in that seaside town he found many of his fellow-officers, several of whom he knew already: Philip Dunne (of the family of the poet John Donne), Toby Milbanke (whose sister-in-law was to play a part in Evelyn's life), Randolph Churchill (the Prime Minister's son), Harry Stavordale (Lord Ilchester's son and heir), Dermot Daly (well known as an amateur steeplechase rider), Peter Milton (Lord Fitzwilliam's son and heir), and Robin Campbell (the son of the Ambassador Sir Ronald Campbell). There was no vacant post for Evelyn. For anyone who served as an officer in the army in the war, it became quite a familiar experience to receive an appointment, to hurry to it, sometimes at the urgent request of the commanding officer, to be informed on arrival that there was no vacancy and never had been. 'Well, now, what would you like to do?' was how the senior frequently greeted his newly arrived and expectant junior. It strikes me as odd that Evelyn, who had suffered it, never introduced this particular military inconvenience into his fiction about the army.

Unavoidably Harry Stavordale, Peter Milton and the others named above formed something of a 'smart set' of whom Evelyn recorded: 'The smart set drink a very great deal, play cards for high figures, dine nightly in Glasgow & telephone to their trainers endlessly.' There was no antag-onism between them and the others. The reason was that since the army has a stronger class-consciousness than the civilian world, but a quite different and unrelated one, it followed that with amiability (and all the above-named were very amiable), the smart set, in Evelyn's words, 'got along very nicely with the more serious soldiers'. These good relations were disturbed by the arrival of several wives of the smart set, for they included one who, in Evelyn's words, 'had never been with dandies before'. According to Evelyn she was 'matey, noisy and mischievous'. She tried to make up lost ground by the familiar device of giggling tale-bearing. She feigned friendship with one of the unsmart serious soldiers 'and one evening drew him out' on the subject of the smart set 'to such an extent that he called them "scum", a verdict which she promptly repeated with unhappy results'. She hoped that her prank would earn the applause of the dandies, but its effect was the opposite. This shallow but grim little comedy, which Evelyn never forgot, and which was very much the kind of raw material he used, was never reflected in what he wrote. In the end the term 'scum' attached itself as a nickname to Philip Dunne alone. It was used by Evelyn and one or two others to differentiate him from Philip Dunn, the son of Sir James Dunn, the Canadian businessman. The two men had a great number of friends in common. I would say, 'I saw Philip Dunne this morning.' Evelyn would answer, 'Which one do you mean? Scum Dunne or Rich Dunn?'

At the end of November 1940 misfortune overtook Evelyn and Laura. She was living in a cottage near her mother's house, Pixton, pregnant and expecting her delivery at any moment. A diary entry for 4 December reads as follows: 'On Saturday night, Nov 30th, Mary [Herbert] telephoned to say that Laura had begun her labour. The child, a girl, was born at midday on Sunday and died 24 hours later. It was an easy birth, very sudden at the end, and Laura is in good health. I travelled on Sunday night and Monday morning, arriving at Taunton junction at 10.30. The baby died shortly after my arrival. I saw her when she was dead – a blue, slatey colour. Poor little girl, she was not wanted. Mary had had her christened Mary the day before. The funeral was this morning in Brushford church-yard. I spent the night at Pixton so as to be in time for the mass. The rest of the time I have spent by Laura's side, talking, doing crosswords etc.'

When No. 8 Commando was finally established soon after Evelyn's arrival it consisted of ten troops, each of fifty men, a troop being commanded by a captain with two subalterns under him. Bob Laycock commanded the unit, of the size of an enlarged battalion or small brigade. He held the rank of Lieutenant-Colonel and was promoted to full Colonel when the unit went overseas. Evelyn's ambition was to be a troop commander. He never succeeded, for which he recklessly blamed Bob Laycock for un-fairly discriminating against him. Bob, with good reason, blamed Evelyn's total incapacity for establishing any sort of human relations with his men. The latter were working-class people and Evelyn had (I regret to have to say) an instinctive distaste for the working classes.

After some exercises of doubtful value, according to Evelyn's depressing account in his diary, No. 8 Commando embarked for Egypt in February 1941. They sailed by the Cape and on 8 March arrived at Suez, then crowded with military and other shipping and in much confusion.

It was on Evelyn's troopship that a widely renowned comic incident occurred. One must remember that in March, when they arrived at Suez, Winston Churchill's immortal tribute to the RAF was fresh in men's minds. Evelyn recorded the little incident thus in his diary: 'The feelings of the Bde were well summed up by an inscription found on the troop decks of Glengyle. "Never in the history of human endeavour have so few been so buggered about by so many." '

No. 8 Commando went into camp at Sidi Bish near Alexandria. Evelyn, as the intellectual of the party, was appointed intelligence officer. He grew a beard and would sit in his tent with a sun-helmet on his head regardless of the weather. So Brian Franks remembered him on first reporting to the Commando. When Philip Dunne told him that the men called him 'the red-bearded dwarf' Evelyn removed the beard (which according to

Brian Franks did not grow elegantly) but retained the moustache which he kept to the end of the war.

His diary for this time includes some exquisite pen-portraits of his fellow-officers. One of these I met through a colleague in the department of GHQ Cairo where I worked. The two men belonged to the same regiment and as my department, among other ill-defined duties, was involved in some of the propaganda work of the Middle East Command, Evelyn's fellow-officer appealed repeatedly to my colleague to obtain him a propagandist appointment. A man less adapted to the arts of persuasion, especially addressed to a Levantine audience, would be hard to imagine. I had met him two or three times at Mrs Marriott's house and he had caused 'quite a thrill in society' at a dinner-party when in a loud voice he asked the Commander-in-Chief's Personal Assistant for details of Middle East strategy, tactical intentions and state of equipment. I was always puzzled by his seeking my colleague's help in furthering his passionate desire to organize propaganda, until Evelyn's diaries solved the problem for me many years later. Evelyn recorded that he 'looked like a Hollywood hanger-on and in fact had been one . . . When I met him at Largs he was a fire-eater talking of shooting Germans like rats. As "Workshop" [a code name for an operation] became likely he became restless saying with perfect frankness, "You know, old boy, I don't like this idea of a spot being 'forever England'." When he saw Evetts [the Divisional Commander] whom he called "Death and Destruction", and heard his speech about a "bellyful of fighting" he immediately applied for special leave to Cairo . . . He wished to make himself propaganda chief in charge of the morale of Middle East Forces.'

Evelyn made no literary use of the exquisitely malicious picture just quoted.

He made very literal use of one member of his Commanding Officer's immediate staff. This unfortunate officer, who later suffered a total nervous collapse in Crete, an incident on which Evelyn looked with a merciless lack of compassion, figures in the War Trilogy as 'Major Hound'. In camp, and out of a battle zone, he was a stern disciplinarian and he thought, not without reason, that Evelyn and his section of three Intelligence clerks were not as fully prepared for action as others. He represented to Bob Laycock that they should undergo basic training, beginning with some 'square-bashing'. Bob was in agreement and as a result put it to Evelyn with his accustomed suavity. He said, at the end: 'I think, Evelyn, you must do something about training your Intelligence section.' Evelyn took offence. He considered that he had mastered the art of officering, with zeal and satisfactory result. So he contrived a revenge.

My authority for relating this incident is Brian Franks. He told it to me as follows: 'The Colonel had had a late night in Alexandria and had returned in the early hours of the morning, no doubt all in the course of duty, but Evelyn chose this particular moment, as dawn broke, to drill his Intelligence section of three men within a few yards of the Commander's hut. One was a very long piece of asparagus with thick spectacles. Number two was fairly square, and very stupid. Number three was a midget. And there they were, out to be drilled. And I remember that Evelyn's first command was: "Form fours!" So it continued until the Commander put his head out of the window and said: "That's enough, I won't ask you to train your section again".' In spite of this and other absurdities at the expense of authority, Bob Laycock continued to feel that Evelyn had a special contribution to give, and kept him near him in the ordeals ahead.

I have mentioned the name of Mrs Marriott. She was a daughter of the famous American businessman Otto Kahn and the wife of Colonel (later Major-General Sir John) Marriott, at that time commanding the second battalion of the Scots Guards in what we all called then 'The Western Desert'. John Marriott was usually away from Cairo with his regiment while his wife Maude, always known as Mo-mo, and her mother, the redoubtable Mrs Kahn, lived in a fashionable suburb. Mo-mo had a great taste for fashionable life and her house in Gesirah, even amid the anxieties and deprivations of the years of defeat, gave back an echo of pre-war Mayfair in the London season. The 'smart set' of No. 8 Commando gravitated thither instinctively, like needles to a magnet. It was in this house that I again met some old friends, among them notably Harry Stavordale and Philip Dunne, and where I heard the indeterminate fire-eater make his searching enquiries of the Commander-in-Chief's intentions, strategy and military preparedness. It was here that I met Evelyn again for the first time in the war.

I remember that he took up with enthusiasm a term invented by Mrs Marriott and myself to describe such beings as the indeterminate fire-eater, 'the whisky wolves', and I was rather surprised afterwards, and perhaps disappointed, to find that Evelyn never used it in his fiction. He was enormous fun, however dour he may have been at Sidi Bish, and to hear him rattling away on the absurdities of his regimental life was a joy and relief after the confined and humourless world of GHQ in which I spent all but a little of my days; he was, in his perverse way, a breath of fresh air.

He was the first friend I met in Egypt who could give me an eye-witness account of the *Blitzkrieg* on London, a subject of anxiety to everyone overseas with a family at home. I remember a lunch we had alone together when he told me with the utmost frankness the facts of the case as he saw them. 'The Germans have done some very fine demolition work', he said in his precise and abrupt way, then listed some nineteenth-century monstrosities which had vanished. 'They nearly gave us Buckingham Palace as it was in William IV's time, but the booby in charge miscalculated, so we are left with the Webb front. That was just bad luck. No use crying over spilt milk.'

'But the food shortages', I asked. 'Do people have enough?'

'Depends what they want,' he answered. 'I tried eating outside Claridge's once, but I didn't try twice. Oh no. But in Claridges you have nothing to complain of at all. I believe the Ritz is all right too.'

'But my wife and son are in the country. Is it – '

'I spend as little time there as I can. The butcher at Pixton died of undernourishment the other day. And by the way,' he asked, changing the subject, 'why are you sometimes in uniform and sometimes not? Does your commanding officer cashier you from time to time and then apply for your reinstatement? I want to know because I feel that something like that is liable to happen with Bob and me.'

'In the department I work for we have to meet a great number of Cairenes and Alexandrians, most of them technically enemy nationals. I need to meet them in totally unofficial circumstances, and that is easier done in civilian clothes.'

'I don't think you make the best use of your opportunities. If I was in your position I would wear a grey morning suit, a thing I've always wanted to have, and a grey top-hat which I think very becoming. I would have no difficulty in explaining that I could not possibly do my work efficiently if I was dressed otherwise.'

What joy it was to hold such mad conversation when most of my daily companions were long-faced bores! I owe a debt which I can never repay to Mrs Marriott because with her wholly estimable regard for flippancy and its place in life, she always assembled around her what was gay and charming and provoked merriment. She was much disapproved by the long-faced, and at a time when the ludicrous myth was being established that we were not fighting the war to defeat Hitler and Nazism, so much as to promote Socialism, Mrs Marriott, with her predilection for fashion-able society, was said by the long-faced, who saw in her an obstacle to a golden future, to be an iniquitous and deciding influence on appointments and promotions. If that highly improbable situation had existed, then Evelyn would have received a Divisional Command at least. Unfortunately the case was otherwise. He had been promoted to acting Temporary Captain in the Royal Marines, had reverted to Lieutenant on joining No. 8 Commando, was restored to a temporary Captaincy on becoming Bob Laycock's officer in charge of Intelligence. Later he was confirmed in his captaincy. In spite of Mrs Marriott and the rumours of the credulous long-faced, he never rose higher.

I have other Evelyn memories of that time, and of other crazy conversations. Not all the memories are happy. A great friend of mine in Cairo at that time was Adrian Bishop, a man, I thought, very much after Evelyn's taste. I brought them together at a dinner-party at a Cairo house, but the meeting was a failure. Both were wits, and while the meeting of great wits may be as fortunate as that between Dr Johnson and John Wilkes, it may be as unfortunate as that between Congreve and Voltaire. This one belonged to the last-mentioned category. They did not get on, as I could see, and later I heard that after dinner, at Shepheard's Hotel, they had almost quarrelled. 'Dreadful friend you have', said Evelyn; 'I don't know that I liked Evelyn Waugh', said Adrian afterwards.

Evelyn took part in one or two minor operations off the coast, but they were ineffectual and need not detain the reader. His main adventure was when he went to Crete as Bob Laycock's Intelligence Officer and personal assistant. Though it may seem to some readers that I am evading a climax, I intend to give no space to Evelyn's deeds in that terrible defeat. The reason is simple: that he related the whole grisly story himself in the second volume of his War Trilogy *Officers and Gentlemen*. In this case he followed his experience in his fiction closely, as a reader of his diary and the trilogy can easily appreciate. To vindicate how and to what extent the two diverge is to deal in minutiae and can be safely left to scholars. He seems to have embarked on 20 or 21 May at Alexandria and to have returned with Bob in the first week of June 1941.

I remember Evelyn after his return very well. He came to my office in GHQ with our friend Bill Stirling, who was later to be Evelyn's commander. He showed little if any sign of the frightful ordeal he had been through. He sat, highly amused at the unlikely succession of people who called on me, but his mood changed when I asked him about Crete. He was full of anger. He said that he had never seen anything so degrading as the cowardice that infected the spirit of the army. He declared that Crete had been surrendered without need; that both the officers and men were hypnotized into defeatism by the continuous dive-bombing which with a little courage one could stand up to; that the fighting spirit of the British armed services was so meagre that we had not the slightest hope of defeating the Germans; that he had taken part in a military disgrace, a fact that he would remember with shame for the rest of his life. As Evelyn was a pertinacious talker, and in moments of indignation such as this spoke with a loud voice, I felt some anxiety, as Italians and Germans (all devoted to the cause of freedom in a way that sometimes shamed their British colleagues, but enemy nationals nonetheless) were frequently passing in and out of the room. I felt anxiety because this was a time of suspicion and there were only too many people around, notably among the sillier officers in my department, who sought to earn promotion by delation. I was aware of prying eyes and keyhole ears and of the elementary needs of prudence, which virtue we had learned to call 'security'. Having argued in vain with Evelyn, I turned to Bill Stirling: 'Do stop him, Bill', I said. Bill shrugged his shoulders and laughed, 'I've given up trying to stop Evelyn years ago', he answered. 'It can't be done.'

What he said was true, and I think the fact cost Evelyn dear. He spoke in this furious and extreme way of what he had seen in Crete to many people, including people he met for the first time, and I dare say that reports of his defeatism got back to the ears of authority, and that this accounts in part for the difficulties he encountered soon afterwards. It made him unpopular among many of the officers and men of No. 8 Commando.

Whether Evelyn was justified in his indignation is a question which military historians must decide. The classic defence of British involvement in Greece and Crete is that this, with the Jugoslav anti-German rising, delayed Hitler's attack on Russia, and that, as events show, postponement of the invasion was fatal to the chances of German victory. Therefore, it is argued, though it imperilled our position in Egypt, the enterprise was strategically valuable. On the particular matter of Crete, Winston Churchill eloquently maintained in the third volume of his *History of the Second World War* that though the Germans undoubtedly succeeded in their attack on the island, they only achieved a Pyrrhic victory, and that the price they had to pay was their incapacity, through loss of aircraft and men, to implement their grand design of a seizure of power in Syria, Iraq and Persia. These ideas have been disputed and are doubtless open to qualification, but what can be said for certain is that German reports of the battle of Crete make it quite clear that Evelyn's despondency about what he took to be the lack of fighting spirit in the British forces in Crete was, to say the least, exaggerated.

The battle of Crete was Evelyn's first experience of military action. Bob Laycock was impressed by the cool courage which he showed throughout the action. The comments on the battle in the diaries are curiously impersonal. In one place he describes the dive-bombing which more than anything else succeeded in shattering the morale of the troops as 'monotonous' and in another he says that 'it was overdone, like everything German'. While they were crossing back to Alexandria in a crammed vessel, Bob asked him what his impressions were of his first battle. 'Like German opera,' replied Evelyn, 'too long and too loud.'

After the disaster of Crete there was an inevitable reorganization of the Middle East forces. In these circumstances no role was found for No. 8 Commando, so the unit was partially and temporarily disbanded, and Bob Laycock was eventually ordered to return with the nucleus to England. Evelyn returned to duty with the Royal Marines, and as a Marine officer he sailed from Suez in the first week of July, and after a long journey by the Cape, across the Atlantic, and then by Iceland he landed at Liverpool on 3 September 1941. It was probably during this journey that he completed *Put Out More Flags*. He was not to serve overseas again for nearly three years.

## Chapter 14

### 1941-1944

After experiencing at close quarters the terrible crisis of the summer of 1941, Evelyn entered a blank period of his life so far as military action was concerned, and this persisted till the summer of 1944. His diary from September 1941 to the end of October 1942 occupies only eleven pages of a notebook. It then ceases for nearly five months. During most of this time a more interesting source of information is to be found in his business correspondence. Although A. D. Peters was now working at the Board of Trade, it was to him that most of Evelyn's letters were addressed. His friend Roughead was serving in the Royal Navy.

On arrival on 3 September 1941 he took a weekend leave at Pixton and reported on the Monday to Royal Marine Headquarters barracks in Plymouth. He was given fourteen days' leave which he presumably spent with Laura and the children in their cottage at Pixton. On reporting back to Plymouth on about 20 September he was posted, by the roundabout process common to all the services, to the 12th Battalion, then stationed on Hayling Island, on the eastern side of Portsmouth harbour. 'It was with this Bn', he noted in his diary, 'that I first realized the quality of the new troops & officers they have trained during the last year. With [one] exception . . . there was no officer who would have been worth making a corporal. One had been a sergeant but had deteriorated by promotion. The chief topic of conversation in mess was complaints of rates of pay.' Oh, Hooper, as Carlyle might have been moved to exclaim, dost thou cast thy shadow before thee into this gossiping Marine-mess?

Evelyn was not happy in the 12th Battalion. He yearned for Bob Laycock and Harry Stavordale and Phil Dunne and Robin Campbell, though not perhaps for the chief Whisky Wolf of No. 8 Commando. Rescue was not very far off.

On 5 January 1942 Evelyn went on a course for Company Commanders held for four weeks at Colinton, Edinburgh. By a remarkable coincidence the course was held in the house of his great-great-grandfather, Lord Cockburn. Laura joined him and they settled in the Caledonia Hotel in Edinburgh till 7 February. Evelyn seems to have got on well with the teaching staff and his fellow-students. 'The chief oddity', he noted in his diary, 'was the psycho-analysts, the army have become alarmed at the poor type of officers coming from the O.C.T.Us, a large proportion of whom, after passing out, are sent away from their regiments as unsuitable. So, like Romans consulting Sybilline books they decided in despair to call in psychologists. As these unhappy men had never met an officer in their lives and had no conception what they were expected to look for, they were set loose on us with the idea that we are presumably more or less satisfactory types. I think they found us very puzzlng. I was interviewed by a neurotic creature dressed as a major who tried to impute unhappiness and frustration to me at all stages of adolescence . . .

'We had a series of intelligence tests . . . Most of us made a mockery of this.'

Having passed out well from the course, Evelyn expected to be made a Company Commander, and in March there occurred a reorganization in which this promotion could be expected. But Evelyn was not promoted. At the same time another future was preparing for him.

Bob Laycock (who had been reported missing on a Commando raid in December 1941) was back in England and had been promoted to the command of the Special Services Brigade, the official title of what was still popularly known as 'the Commandos'. Though as conscious of Evelyn's military faults as any of Evelyn's past and present colonels and brigadiers, Bob wanted him. The results of this preference belong to the summer of 1942 and may be left for the moment.

Before turning to 1942 it is worth recalling Evelyn's own account of an occasion when he came into much public notice. The occasion was in the first week of April. Evelyn's fame as a writer had recently been enhanced by the publication of *Put Out More Flags* in mid-March. He was obviously desirable prey for radio.

Television was in a rudimentary state and was to remain so for most of ten years. Radio was then at the zenith of its influence. It is hard for subsequent generations to realize that up to 1950 or thereabouts radio programmes could make the headlines, while television ones never did. It seemed that radio was displacing the newspaper industry, and in England the BBC with its monopoly seemed likely to take over the entire communications business. These were common opinions in 1942, and they seemed strengthened and almost proved by the great influence then exerted by discussion programmes and the 'radio personalities' who took part in them. Some of the latter were people of distinction and intelligence, such as Rose Macaulay and Julian Huxley; others were solely 'personalities' as may be the case with a mentally subnormal theatrical star; others were charlatans getting into the act. Pre-eminent in the last category was Professor, formerly known as Doctor, Cyril Joad whose right to an academic title was frequently and damagingly disputed. He was the star-turn of the most entertaining and noticed of these discussion programmes, *The Brains Trust*, as it was entitled with some lack of humility. It is difficult to believe today that this vain, third-rate political journalist was a great formative influence on public opinion, the subject of questions in Parliament and leading articles, but so it was, thanks to the power of unchallenged radio in an age when entertainment was necessarily limited.

After the course, and his failure to obtain a Company command, Evelyn was granted ten days' leave which he spent in London with Laura. On 2 April, after a morning 'that I was obliged to waste . . . going from Admiralty to War Office to R.M. Office to get permission to broadcast', he performed with the Brains Trust in the afternoon.

He described the experience thus: 'The other guests were Sir William Beveridge, don-civil servant [Beveridge, whose report had not yet been published, was not then popularly famous], and an inconsiderable clergyman, the Dean of St Paul's. The professionals were [Commander] Campbell [a highly esteemed personality], vulgar, insincere, conceited, and Joad, goat-like, libidinous, garrulous. I was delighted to observe the derision in which he was held by all the BBC staff . . . The questions were too general to allow of proper discussion within our limits. "Does knowledge lead to happiness", "How should you answer your child's question 'Who is God?' " Joad bounced in his chair with eagerness to speak. I missed the chance to crush him over the question of compulsory church parades.

'One question we had was on the subject of equal pay for soldiers and civilians. Beveridge and Campbell smugly supported it, so I suggested that if they felt like that about it they had better make a start by accepting one third for their afternoon's work . . . When the machine was switched off, I raised the question again and asked whether we were all agreed to give our £20 to a war fund. The savants were aghast. Beveridge said: "It would be a gesture." "No, simply a test of sincerity." Campbell: "Well of course I'm ready to do what the others will but I think it would be impossible from the point of view of BBC administration." BBC official: "No, not at all. Perfectly easy." Joad whined, "I never gave an opinion on that question." "Does that mean you refuse to come in?" "No, I will agree if the others do." So I left them, saying, "I am sorry you have had such an unprofitable afternoon." But I knew they meant to go back on their word, and they did.'

In mid-April Evelyn learned that Bob Laycock had applied for his services with the result that, probably through jealousy, always a strong factor in inter-service affairs, especially in wartime, the Royal Marine Commando, then being raised, also asked for him. Evelyn's long-suffering Company Commander 'was greatly puzzled at this sudden demand for me'. Bob won but insisted that Evelyn should be seconded from the Royal Marines to the army. Through Bob's influence this was done. On 9 May 1942 Evelyn was transferred to Bob's regiment, the Royal Horse Guards, with the rank of temporary Acting Captain. On the 11th he rejoined his old companions in arms of No. 8 Commando at Ardrossan in Ayrshire.

In the night of 10 June 1942 Laura gave birth to a daughter who was christened Margaret. Evelyn was given leave and went to Pixton for a few days.

It has been mentioned already that in the preceding winter the first part of *Work Suspended* had appeared in *Horizon*. Soon after this, *Put Out More Flags* was published by Chapman and Hall on 16 March, and was very well received.

For the moment, Evelyn was in a strong position in the world of contemporary literature; one might almost say an impregnable position. But this was of no help to him then.

As a corollary to the above, I may mention the very odd fact that in the next year, in March 1943, Evelyn was requested by Combined Operations Headquarters to write a 'personality handout', intended for American readers, on the subject of Hilary Saunders, the kind of writer who was esteemed by the authorities then. He was the author of *The Battle of Britain, Pioneers O Pioneers, Per Ardua, The Green Beret* and *The Red Beret*, and other such stuff. It was a time when a first-rate writer might easily find himself pushed into a position where he was required to boost a second- or third-rate one who was far more needed by the authorities. But Evelyn was not quite wasted as a writer by authority.

Officially he was a member of Bob Laycock's Brigade Headquarters Staff, with vaguely defined duties, conveniently described as those of an Intelligence Officer. As usually happens in modern administration, centralization increased and, as Evelyn rightly noted, there was little for Brigade Headquarters to do, since most of their duties were carried out by Combined Operations Headquarters under Vice-Admiral Lord Louis Mountbatten. Evelyn reckoned, again rightly, that Bob was retaining his Headquarters as a cadre against the day when he would be the Force Commander. In the circumstances of 1942 Evelyn was often 'loaned' to Lord Louis's Headquarters, usually to help in drafting reports destined for important circulation. Brian Franks has told me how admirable Evelyn's drafts were; how he was able in a few hours to condense complex and overelaborated material into a concise shape, without any loss of essential material and with a great access of readability.

An absurd incident of Evelyn's work at Combined Operations Headquarters deserves to be remembered. To understand the incident, it must be remembered that the commandant of the Commando Training School at Achnacarry, in the west coast Highlands of Scotland, was a certain Colonel Vaughan, an amiable and efficient officer, but like all school commandants given to correctitude. One day Colonel Vaughan was required to report to Lord Louis's Headquarters in Richmond Terrace. Evelyn was on one of his assignments there on the same day. Officers of the Household Cavalry, when without their armour and panaches, are granted in compensation the privilege of wearing red hatbands with their khaki uniforms. The most junior officer was thus liable to be mistaken for one of very senior rank. On the day in question Colonel Vaughan went up to the house in Richmond Terrace, outside the main door of which he saw an officer smoking a cigar. Deluded by the red hatband, Colonel Vaughan gave a smart salute, to be acknowledged by an arrogantly casual raising of his riding whip by Acting Temporary Captain Waugh. About a year after this, I was training under Colonel Vaughan, and he still spoke of the incident with voluble indignation. It seems that on this day in 1942 he had quickly understood his mistake and said something uncomplimentary to Captain Waugh. Evelyn later responded by spreading extraordinary but happily rarely believed stories about Colonel Vaughan's licentious private life. He insisted that the mistaken salute was Colonel Vaughan's way of conveying a criminal invitation. When I challenged Evelyn later about these stories, he admitted that they were all inventions. 'It was Bob's fault,' he said with typical unfairness, 'he drove me mad by his ill-treatment.'

Evelyn, somewhat vaguely employed, as indicated above, accompanied Bob Laycock on his wide-ranging inspections of units of the Special Service Brigade both in England and Scotland, the Brigade Headquarters remaining at Ardrossan in Ayrshire. The details are to be found in his diaries, often with interesting, and very often with scandalous, comment. One entry made in September 1942 is interesting. He tells how in the course of one tour of duty they came to stay for a night with the Duff Coopers at Bognor where Diana had taken a house. Evelyn chronicles the 'usual' disagreeable scene with Duff Cooper because the latter had spread rumours in Evelyn's beloved White's Club, to which he had been elected on Bob's proposal in 1941, that he was a 'Nazi agent'. This allegation was prompted by a remark which he had made to Duff: namely, that Hitler's New Order was not different in character from 'Vergil's idea of the Roman Empire'.

In October 1942 Bob Laycock decided to move his Brigade Headquarters from Scotland to the area of Southern Command in England, and he chose Sherborne in Dorset as his Headquarters site. Early in October, while Bob was away in London, the advance party which included Evelyn and Philip Dunne went to Sherborne to arrange camp-sites and billets. By this time Evelyn had conceived the idea that Bob Laycock had lost confidence in him.

Evelyn was half-right, half-wrong. In fact, Bob was and remained Evelyn's devoted friend. At the same time, Bob was a very efficient professional soldier who was not willing to fall into that worst and common military error of sacrificing unit-effectiveness for personal preference. Bob knew that Evelyn could never fit into any military structure. He hoped that he was wrong and, as events in the next year showed, he needed to be persuaded that he was right, even though he knew it all the time.

On 28 October Evelyn wrote in his diary: 'My 39th birthday. A good year. I have begotten a fine daughter, published a successful book, drunk about 300 bottles of wine and smoked 300 or more Havana cigars. I have got back to soldiering among friends. This time last year I was on my way to Howick to join 5 [battalion] R.M. I got steadily worse as a soldier with the passage of time but more patient & humble – as far as soldiering is concerned. I have about £900 in hand and no grave debts except to the government; health excellent except when impaired by wine; a wife I love, agreeable work in surroundings of great beauty. Well, that is as much as one can hope for.'

He did not mention his numerous business interests at the time. One of these was a proposal for a film of *Put Out More Flags,* and the negotiations should be remembered. Evelyn emerges from it with credit. The proposal came from Alexander Korda. It had little chance of being translated into reality, not merely because it came from a source notorious for unrealization, but because the mood of 1942 was growing unreceptive of any frivolous treatment of the war. But before this consideration had moved Korda and his advisers not to venture the necessary funds and to abandon the 'Pomf' film project, Evelyn had been paid £1500, nominally as a retaining fee. Evelyn was under no obligation of any kind to refund this payment when the project was abandoned. But he did refund it. The reason was that the negotiator had been his old friend John Sutro, and Evelyn felt that if he did not refund the money the financial loss to the company might reflect badly on Sutro's professional career.

At this time Evelyn was in dispute with A. D. Peters and Chapman and Hall (though not with his father who had virtually retired) about the publication of *Work Suspended.* Evelyn wanted the fragment published as it was. Peter, with Chapman and Hall, resisted him, arguing rightly that so excellent a piece of writing could 'keep' safely until it could be combined into a book filled out with other occasional pieces, the form in which it has later appeared in paperback. But Evelyn was against this, and in my opinion rightly so. It was the best thing he had written, and he was determined that it should stand on its own, even at financial loss which he could ill-afford.

In the end, after much argument, the book was published in a limited edition of five hundred copies on 21 December 1942.

The book shows a considerable change in Evelyn's writing. It has three salient features which had never appeared in his fiction before this. It is written in the first person, and successfully so; the 'I' of the story, called

John Plant, is a careful self-portrait and not the usual colourless narrator of most first-person fiction. John Plant is a successful writer, but not of the same kind as Evelyn: he makes a good living out of writing detective stories. There is another writer in the story, Roger Simmonds, who by no stretch of the imagination can be ascribed to self-portraiture. But what little the reader is told about Simmonds's work might pass as a description of Evelyn's. He is a successful humorist and at the time of the story he is changing his style and subject-matter (as Evelyn was doing) to the dismay of his publisher Mr Benwell. John Plant simultaneously wishes to abandon a profitable line in favour of something more adventurous. I like to think that Evelyn may have been a little influenced by my story *Invention* where a similar situation had been described (not, alas, with Evelyn's skill). I am led to this boastful supposition because when Evelyn and I talked about writing, he several times urged me to specialize in the short story which he believed to be my vocational field, and he mentioned this story *Invention* which he said showed more promise than anything else I had written hitherto.

The second feature which sets this apart from all his previous fiction is the virtual absence of plot. Critics and admirers who believed, on abundant evidence, that Evelyn, like many writers, good and bad, was utterly dependent on plot, were shown that this was as false a judgement in his case as it had been in that of Maupassant.

The story is in two parts: 'A Death' and 'A Birth', and their subject can be summarized in a few lines. The first part (published in *Horizon* in February as *My Father's House*) relates how, while abroad, John Plant learns of the death of his father, a half-conventional half-eccentric Royal Academician. He returns, visits his father's house, now his inheritance, in St John's Wood, and relates his memories and emotions. The second part is less eventful. In his efforts to reorganize his life, altered by his paternal loss and inheritance, he falls in with his friend and fellow-writer Roger Simmonds, who has become a Communist and married an heiress at the same time. Plant falls in love, ardently and chastely, with Simmonds's wife who, delightedly and chastely, returns his affection. But when her child is born her interest wanders from the *ami de la maison*, John Plant, to her son and first-born. And that is all.

The two parts are not as disparate as a summary may suggest, indeed the strength of this invention is in the strength of a connecting link, a far stronger one than Roger Simmonds. The link is supplied by one of the most successful and amazing of all Evelyn's imagined characters, Arthur Atwater, the down-at-heel lost soul of the aspirant lower middle class, lower public school, lower intelligentsia, lower human being, one might be tempted to say, physically nauseating and mentally magazine-educated. He appears quite surprisingly in both chapters, but not as a *deus ex machina*, for surprise is of the very nature of the man, a trait which Evelyn indicates with masterly subtlety.

In writing of a book in which one not only finds much to admire but, quite literally, nothing to fault, it is easy to imagine virtues. Evelyn's apparent emancipation from the plot may be a delusion brought on by the simple fact that the novel was not finished. I ought to be able to say with certainty. Evelyn told Philip Dunne in detail how the story would develop, and when Philip and I were fellow-officers at a later period in the war, he told me in the course of a train journey we made together. Unhappily I made no note at the time, and I have now forgotten everything he told me. With Philip's death in 1965 I fear that the secret is beyond recall.

The third surprising feature of the book is the most unexpected and, looking back on his whole work, the least welcome to many minds. It is to be found in a change of style. For the first time since *Decline and Fall* Evelyn allowed himself to luxuriate in emotional prose. He threw off the inhibitions which, with great effort, he had imposed on his prose after his early biography of Rossetti. Not since those now distant days had he allowed himself to write such things as this:

'To write of someone loved, of oneself loving, above all of oneself being loved – how can these things be done with propriety? How can they be done at all? . . . Love, which has its own life, its hours of sleep and waking, its health and sickness, growth, death and immortality, its ignorance and knowledge, experiment and mastery – how can one relate this hooded stranger to the men and women with whom he keeps pace? It is a problem beyond the proper scope of letters.'

A harsh critic may protest that this (and many similar passages) brings the writer into peril of sentimentality. One can say the same of much emotional prose, including that of the greatest masters. The question is (as David Cecil rightly insisted in the case of Dickens's very vulnerable prose on the death of Tom Pinch) does it work?

The answer which I give in complete confidence is the same as his. Yes. It not only 'works' at this point in the book where Evelyn is dealing with a subject that has defeated many writers: description of a passionate love devoid of erotic intent, but it 'works' in the numerous emotional passages in which he describes his sudden grief, for example, at the abandonment through necessity of his father's tasteless but nonetheless loved house and the narrator's own subsequent homelessness.

The uncompleted novel had an origin in his experience. On this occasion he acknowledged it frankly. It came from his lonely days after the breakdown of his first marriage, when, as related already, he spent most of his time with Bryan and Diana Guinness whom he had met through Diana's sister, Nancy Mitford. At the time when the book appeared many of Evelyn's friends who remembered him in 1929 and 1930 assumed that

Roger and Lucy Simmonds in the story were intended as portraits of Bryan and Diana Guinness. I have known Bryan Guinness (now Lord Moyne) since we were at Oxford together in 1926, and Diana since the time of her first marriage. Though I knew nothing about Evelyn's life in 1929 and 1930, I would quickly have detected a resemblance to my two friends in this fiction informed by Evelyn's merciless observation. In fact I saw, and still see, a distinct resemblance in Roger Simmonds, with his half-witted *New Statesman* doctrinaire Communism, to a man who is a friend of mine. I taxed Evelyn with the cruelty of his picture. He was bewildered. In fact my friend, who became a friend of Evelyn after the war, had never met him. As for any identification of Lucy Simmonds with Diana (now Lady Mosley) this is absurd if only on the grounds that Diana is and was a strongly definite character whereas, if *Work Suspended* has a fault, it is that Lucy Simmonds is too vague in outline to allow the reader to join the narrator in his chaste love.

The vagueness of the drawing of Lucy Simmonds may be a consequence of delicacy of feeling (not a very likely explanation), or it may be that he knew that he was treading fresh and perilous ground. He later attempted with success in 'Pomf' a convincing picture of a virtuous woman, but here he went further and attempted to depict the experience of love with such a woman. The picture of Lucy is not as effective as that of Barbara Sothill, but it must not be thought to be a blot on the book. I have given my opinion of this book as among the best things Evelyn wrote, and I see it as a book without blots. I do not see how it could have been made better. The only thing I regret about *Work Suspended* is not within the fiction: it is the dedicatory letter to Alexander Woolcott. He says that he abandoned the book on the outbreak of war because he felt that in the sterner times ahead the kind of people he wrote about would cease to be of interest and that the kind of people who read his novels would soon cease to exist. Some years later I challenged Evelyn on this opinion which I believed and still believe to be nonsense. He made no defence and admitted that he had been completely wrong. 'Great mistake to foretell the future', he said.

He remained extremely sensitive to the charge that he had used his friendship for Bryan and Diana as raw material for *Work Suspended*, as though he had disregarded the fact that this might cause pain. What made him sensitive was the fact that when the little book came out Diana, with her husband Sir Oswald Mosley, had been jailed without trial as a vigorous member of the Fascist party. Evelyn had sent her a copy of the book, and the thought that his gesture might be interpreted as hostile and unkind to Diana in her misfortune tormented him. The full facts of the case came out in two letters in a correspondence which he had with her at the very end of his life. The first letter is dated 9 March 1966, and was evidently written under a misapprehension. The text is self-explanatory.

'It was a delight to get a letter from you & to hear that you sometimes think of me.

'It is not clear whether you have completed your memoirs & published them & that I somehow missed them or whether you are still working on them. I long to read them. My "Little Learning" dealt with adolescence, before I knew you. It is truthful in the sense of stating nothing false but, of course, it omits a good deal. My brother's memoirs were embarrassingly revealing. I am now at work in a desultory way on a second volume which presents graver problems because I must mention several living people.

'You ask why our friendship petered out. The explanation is discreditable to me at a time when I greatly needed kindness, after my desertion by my first wife. I was infatuated with you. Not of course that I aspired to your bed but I wanted you to myself as special confidant or comrade. After Jonathan's birth you began to enlarge your circle. I felt lower in your affections than Harold Acton & Robert Byron and I couldn't compete or take a humbler place. Politics had not then raised their ugly head.'

The second was written three weeks later, after Diana had written jokingly to Evelyn to say that he had had the last word with his 'cruel portrait'.

'Beware of writing to me. I always answer. It is part of my great boringness, never going out or telephoning. An inherited weakness. My father spent the last 20 years of his life writing letters. If someone thanked him for a wedding present he thanked them for thanking him & there was no end to the exchange but death. Nancy pretended she was going blind to choke me off.

'But I must not leave you with the delusion that *Work Suspended* was a cruel portrait of you. It was perhaps to some extent a portrait of me in love with you, but there is not a single point in common between you and the heroine except pregnancy. Yours was the first pregnancy I observed.

'I sent you a copy when you were in jug. Surely you remember me well enough to know I should not have done such a thing at such a time if I thought it a "cruel portrait"?' The rest of the letter is on other subjects.

Diana has explained to me that this moving letter, one of the very last he wrote, was in fact unnecessary as she had never seriously suspected Evelyn of attempting a picture of her in Lucy. She had thought that he would take her joking accusation with laughter.


During the winter of 1942/3 Evelyn remained at Sherborne. Laura joined him there, where they seem to have lived in lodgings. Brigade Headquarters were housed in a nearby rectory at Colesworth with the incumbent 'and his bearded wife'. Evelyn describes them as 'an enchanting couple'. The Rector confided to him his fear and conviction that the Germans would land by parachute in his meadow, and asked for ammunition against that event, but his wife preferred an extra ration of petrol. 'They think the world of that,' remarked the Rector. 'They' was 'a professor of London'. (Doubtless some expert on petrol storage in the Ministry of Economic Warfare.)

At the end of the year he made a significant entry in his diary. 'I wrote a review of Graham Greene [British Dramatists] for the Spectator and meditate starting a novel.' The meditations were to turn to action a year later.

In this autumn of 1942 Jakie, the fourth and youngest son of Lord Astor, arrived at Sherborne in command of a unit of the 'Phantom' organization, a communications unit with special skills and training suited to organizations such as the Special Service Brigade and similar bodies. I once asked Jakie whether he and Evelyn became friends at Sherborne. No, he said, no, he found it impossible. It was, he explained, not because of personal antipathy; it was because of Evelyn's utter unfitness to be an officer. He told me that he hated to see Evelyn drilling the men or even assuming any position of command over them, even the most trivial. 'He never hesitated to take advantage of the fact that while he was a highly educated man, most of them were barely literate. He bullied them in a way they were unused to. He bewildered them, purposely. I found it embarrassing.'

Jakie in no way exaggerated. I have been told on reliable and quite unprejudiced authority that so extreme was the dislike of the men that, unknown to Evelyn, Bob Laycock set a special guard on Evelyn's sleeping quarters. In Crete an officer of No. 8 Commando had been killed in action, but the circumstances were odd and it was widely suspected that this intensely unpopular man had in fact been murdered by one of his subordinates. (Certainly this was Evelyn's opinion.) Bob was taking no chances.

In the later part of March 1943 there was much reorganization in the Brigade, and with it inevitably much promotion. Many officers gained in rank and responsibility, but not Evelyn. He was passed over as before. He felt this 'blow to his professional pride' keenly. Bob felt that he owed him an explanation, but he did not mince his words, rather did he have recourse to whatever is the opposite operation. He told Evelyn that he had become 'so unpopular as to be unemployable'. Evelyn's first comment on this painful episode was typical and terse. 'My future very uncertain.'

In the first part of 1943 our hero's fortunes sank very low indeed. As in the anxious and miserable days of September 1939, he found himself not wanted. The full depth of the anticlimax was struck in the summer of 1943. The Brigade was assigned a role with the Allied forces in North

Africa, then rapidly approaching the consummation of their victory. From North Africa they expected (correctly) to be involved in the invasion of Italy. Their role was known as 'Operation Husky'. Bob wished to take Evelyn with him, and unfortunately told him so. Many of Evelyn's fellow-officers felt with reason that this was unwise. Their objections were conveyed to Bob by Brian Franks, an ironical circumstance as it turned out. Brian Franks has told me how the interview went. 'You will regret it, Brigadier,' he said. 'Evelyn's appointment will only introduce discord and weaken the Brigade as a coherent fighting force. None of us can see that you will get anything from it at all. And apart from everything else, Evelyn will probably get shot.' 'That's a chance we all have to take.' 'Oh, I don't mean by the enemy.'

Bob was persuaded, but, most unwisely and through friendship, he compromised, so as to soften Evelyn's distress, by giving him a written assurance that he and his batman were to be included in his first reinforcements. The Brigade moved overseas in June 1943. In the same month Arthur Waugh died. The impact on Evelyn of these events is best described in his own words taken from his diary.

'On June 24 my father died & Brigade HQ. left London for operation "Husky". It was an unfortunate coincidence as I was distracted from one by the other. I was angry with Bob for leaving me behind so easily. My father died with disconcerting suddenness. I spent most of the next few days at Highgate. The funeral was on the 27th at Hampstead. I spent some weary hours going through my father's papers & destroying letters. He kept up a large correspondence with very dull people. My mother's mind seems clouded by the business. Laura & I had Bron brought up to interest her.'

Evelyn was under orders to report to the Brigade Depot and Training Centre at Achnacarry in Inverness. He appealed against these orders on the grounds that he had a duty to be with his aged mother in her trouble and that until Alec (for whom compassionate leave had been officially requested) could arrive in England from Baghdad, the unhappy old lady would have no family member near her. The appeal was accepted; partly perhaps because the Achnacarry Commandant Colonel Vaughan had no wish to take Evelyn on to his staff. But Evelyn's ultimate destiny was a question that would have to be decided soon, and the Deputy Brigade Commander, Lord Lovat, shared all the misgivings of Evelyn's fellow-officers and none of Bob Laycock's predilection. He was determined that Evelyn should not be posted to Operation Husky. Evelyn conceived the idea that he was the object of gross discrimination. He believed that he was the object of unreasoning prejudice on the part not only of Lord Lovat but more so of the Vice-Chief of Combined Operations, Brigadier (later Major-General) Charles Haydon. He even went so far as to appeal to Lord Louis in person against Haydon's supposed unfairness. He tried hard to

obtain Bob Laycock's personal intervention, but Bob remained profession-
ally aloof, howsoever strong his personal preferences and sympathy
might be. For this Evelyn found it impossible to forgive Bob for a long
time. He had clearly given in to a temptation to persecution mania, that
sovereign device for self-exculpation. He saw himself as the victim of a
plot. It never seemed to occur to him in those days that his own temperament, his difficulty in establishing tolerable relations with his colleagues
and subordinates, his delight in causing offence, his childish and ostentatious indiscipline, had anything to do with it at all.

As a result of the situation, as it formed, Evelyn was urged by Haydon
to offer his resignation 'for the Brigade's good' (not perhaps a tactful way
of putting it). Evelyn did so on 17 July 1943. Thereafter he was with the
Royal Horse Guards, who found little employment for him.

Sir Fitzroy Maclean, who was to be Evelyn's chief in 1944, has given a
misleading account of these events (which in detail would occupy many
tedious pages) in Mr David Pryce-Jones's compilation. He says in his brief
contribution: 'Shimi Lovat [Randolph Churchill] explained, had at once
got rid of Evelyn. This abrupt liquidation, arising from some obscure
Roman Catholic vendetta, struck him as grossly unfair.' Both authorities,
Churchill and Maclean, were entirely at fault. There was no vendetta
and the fact that Lord Lovat, Charles Haydon and Evelyn were all Roman
Catholics had no influence whatsoever on what happened. If all three
had been dedicated atheists the outcome would have been no different.
There was no vendetta outside Randolph Churchill's imagination; there
was no plot outside Evelyn's; he was not 'liquidated' in the sense of being
dismissed from the Special Service Brigade; he tendered his resignation,
under some pressure it is true. The resignation was accepted. The only
correct item in Sir Fitzroy's account is that Evelyn regarded his treatment,
especially by Charles Haydon, as having been grossly unfair.

After 17 July Evelyn was truly back to Square One. He reported to the
Royal Horse Guards Depot at Windsor where he found as his companions
'middle-aged, embittered subalterns'.

I remember Evelyn about this time describing his residence at Windsor.
'Good pictures,' he said, 'poor conversation.' But at long last, from late
August onwards, he had hopes of rescue from this time-wasting lull in
his life. After his brother David's capture in North Africa, William Stirling
had returned to England in the hopes of reconstituting David's unit, the
Special Air Service battalion, and expanding it to the dimensions of a small
brigade. In this he was strongly opposed by the orthodox soldiery who did
not wish to see yet another 'special' unit established, but Stirling enjoyed
the advantage of the personal support of the Prime Minister to whom
commando-type organizations were always welcome, and to whom
Stirling was frequently allowed access. He had another advantage in the
fact that this was another time of reorganization. On 25 August the

British and American Chiefs of Staff, at the suggestion of the President and Mr Churchill, set up the South East Asia Command under the supreme direction of Lord Louis Mountbatten. He was to leave England for his new post in September. Bob Laycock, while remaining till the finish of Operation Husky as Brigade Commander, was promoted Major-General and appointed to succeed Lord Louis as Chief of Combined Operations, under which command Bill Stirling's unit would operate when and if established. This time Evelyn obtained some advantage from the re-shuffling of the pack. Bill Stirling's paramount need was to get his case across for an enlarged Special Air Service, and for this he needed to have his arguments well marshalled on paper. He got Evelyn to do this for him. He promised to give Evelyn an appointment in the S.A.S. as soon as his plans were accepted, but he could promise nothing more definite, as his plans were the object of much resistance, making his whole position very precarious. Evelyn was able to give Bill all his time because his Commanding Officer in Windsor had nothing for him to do, and when Evelyn asked him in September for indefinite leave until he obtained a posting to an active unit, the Colonel immediately agreed and hastened to regularize the matter with the War Office. In the end Bill got what he wanted, and Evelyn's prose was no small contributory factor.

In October Bill was able to give Evelyn a definite though not officially confirmed posting in the S.A.S. Regiment as it was now called. The unit was being formed on brigade dimensions. It consisted of two British battalions, of which Bill Stirling commanded one, and two French battalions, under Bill's command. The French battalions were recruited from men who preferred to serve under British rather than Gaullist command, disgusted with political differences which flourished under the administration of the heroic general. (In the same month Bill rescued me from Achnacarry.)

So, in an untidy sort of way, Evelyn had got what he wanted; a posting to a fighting unit. The Special Air Service was stationed in North Africa and Evelyn and I were under orders to join them in mid-November 1943. But by then the Allied victory over the Germans in the South Mediterranean was virtually complete. The Army Command did not wish to see their forces accumulating in that theatre, and S.A.S. received orders to return to Britain after accomplishing some subsidiary tasks in invaded Italy. As a result Evelyn and I found ourselves figuring in a large list of unwanted persons. We were informed at the last moment. I well remember Evelyn ringing me up early on the morning scheduled for our departure to announce our 'cancellation'. He sounded in the depths of gloom. I had reason to believe from what I had learned from Bill Stirling himself, and in the world of semi-informed military gossip in which we both moved, that the return of the S.A.S. to Britain had already been decided. I said to Evelyn something of this kind: 'Well, it's not so bad. I have spent half the war in unnecessary journeys, and it is such a fag having to travel miles to somewhere only to be ordered back on arrival. Lunch with me at White's.' Like a funeral bell, Evelyn answered: 'It means *return to unit* for us both. Windsor for me. Achnacarry for you. Yes, I'll lunch at White's.' He was, as I soon discovered, only too correct about the *return to unit* question; very soon we both fell victim to an administrative officer who specialized in organizing unnecessary journeys. Every effort was made to send Evelyn back to Windsor where he was unwelcome; every effort was made to get me to Achnacarry where Colonel Vaughan was faced with a serious overcrowding problem resulting from a recent fire which had destroyed much of the interior of the Cameron Scotch Baronial Castle.

I had been instructed by my Commanding Officer, Bill Stirling, typically without anything in writing and at the bar of White's Club, to 'arrange parachute training for his officers'. The names, which included mine and Evelyn's, would be given to Combined Operations Headquarters. Arrangements were to be made with the Special Operations Executive, S.O.E., the most famous and the least respectable of the many 'special' organizations which rose up in the course of World War II.

Bill returned to Africa, I proceeded with my task, and accomplished it, despite the absence of written instructions, through a stroke of luck. Bob was back in England for some days. He gave me the signed manuscript I needed, and was soon to be helpful in other ways. There was that specialist in unnecessary journeys, a major whom Evelyn described to me as 'a Jew with his hair dyed purple', a description which I took to be fanciful until I met the man, in Hobart House. This man, I presume a member of a personnel department, had bawled Evelyn out of his room the day before with orders to return to his unit at Windsor. He was obviously a man who had never exercised command of any sort with the result that his new responsibilities had gone to his head. On my entrance he positively screamed at me that I must instantly leave for Achnacarry. He held forth on the subject and at the mildest interruption roared out: 'Will you let me speak? Will you allow me a word?' But my luck held. That evening I met Bob Laycock. I told him of my 'awkwardness'. 'But', he exclaimed, 'you can't go to Achnacarry. It's been burnt down.' Next day the purple-haired major screamed to me as I entered his room, 'Why aren't you at Achnacarry?' 'Because it's been burned down,' I answered. His rage heightened but for once I retained my presence of mind and told him, not quite truthfully, that I was under orders, in case of doubt, to invite him to refer the matter to General Laycock – if he knew whom I meant – Of course I do!' he exploded. That hurdle was over. For the next one I had 'recourse to ignominious arts which I had learned in the profession of staff officer and diplomat. I played on his vanity. I said I had something to say that was of top, superfine 'security'; perhaps he would like to be with me alone. He glanced at his subordinate, a young officer plainly embarrassed by his chief's vulgar behaviour, hesitated for a second, then said I might speak out. I told him of my negotiations, via Combined Operations, with S.O.E. I exaggerated the necessary secrecy; I stressed my intimacy with Bob. I said that only to such as himself could I confide so great a matter. This pleased him. Having severely told me that I ought to have said this before, he gave in. We were reprieved. 'Odd you dislike that man so much', said Antony Head to me later. 'I always find him so charming.' 'You and Evelyn obviously rub him up the wrong way', said Bob. 'He's always perfectly delightful to me.'

We went on parachute training in December. Our exercises were held in Tatton Park, near Manchester, where, through making a faulty landing, Evelyn severely damaged a knee. Before telling of that episode, the story must leave the military sphere and concentrate on Evelyn's private life which was, at this time, of more lasting significance than the public career to which he was always ill-fitted.

The story must go back to mid-August before he had begun work for Bill Stirling; the period when sincerely and with little reason he believed himself to be an ill-used man and was eating out his heart with boredom among the good paintings and unrewarding conversation of Windsor. He saw no future for himself as a combatant in the war. He was approached by the Allied Military Government of Italy (AMGOT) and by the Political Warfare Executive (PWE), both of whom wished to make use of his intellectual abilities, and though nothing came of their attempts, he did not resist their overtures as firmly as he had those of the Ministry of Information in 1939. On 17 August he made the following very interesting entry into his diary:

'I do not want any more experiences of life. I have quite enough bottled and carefully laid in the cellar, some still ripening, most ready for drinking, a little beginning to lose its body . . . I don't want to influence opinions, events, or expose humbug or anything of that kind. I don't want to be of service to anyone or anything. I simply want to do my work as an artist.'

It was over two years since Evelyn had practised the art in which he excelled and he was filled with the impatience of frustration. He had said in the passage quoted above: 'I do not want any more experiences of life.' He was thinking in the short term. Ironically enough he was shortly after to meet an experience which was to have an enormous effect on him and was to contribute to a major episode of his next novel.

His friend Hubert Duggan was critically ill at the end of September 1943. Like his brother Alfred he had been born a Catholic but had not practised his religion for many years. He lived in a little house in Chapel Street which for some years he had shared with his mistress, Phyllis de

Janzé. She had died earlier in the year. On 12 October Evelyn recorded in his diary that he found 'Hubert very much worse. This morning for the first time he began to talk of religion and of returning to the Church but has no stréngth for reasoned argument and needs the presence of someone holy. I suggested a nun though nothing seems to come of it much, though Lady Curzon [Hubert's mother] seems sympathetic. It seems in Hubert's mind that it would be a betrayal of Phyllis to profess repentance of his life with her.'

On the 13th Hubert had manifestly reached the end of his life, and Evelyn took action to bring a priest to him to administer absolution and the sacrament of Extreme Unction, sometimes known as the Last Rites. Evelyn's account occurs in two sections in his diary. The 'Marcella' referred to is Hubert's sister Mrs Rice, the 'Fr Devasse' is Father Devas, an uncle of the artist Anthony Devas, and then the Rector of the Farm Street Community.

'I went to see Fr Dempsey who is the Catholic Chaplain for the West London District to consult him about Hubert. He was a big fat peasant who said: "I know a priest who is a fine gentleman. Would it not be better to get him? I should put my foot in it." He telephoned some Irish nuns. "It's a great work of charity you would be doing, Mother . . ." to have a sister available in case she was needed. He gave me a medal. "Just hide it somewhere in the room. I have known most wonderful cases of Grace brought about in just that way." When I got to Chapel Street Lady Curzon told me that it was not expected Hubert would live through the day. As Dempsey had gone out I went to Farm Street & brought back Fr Devasse. Marcella did not want him to come in. She & Ellen were sitting by him supporting him in a chair saying, "You are getting well. You have nothing on your conscience." I brought Fr Devasse in and he gave Hubert absolution. Hubert said "Thank you father" which was taken as his assent.'

This all occurred in the morning. The diary reverts to the subject in recording the afternoon.

'I went back to Chapel Street. Numerous doctors – one particularly unattractive one from Canada – Marcella more than ever hostile. Fr Devasse very quiet & simple & humble trying to make sense of all the confusion, knowing just what he wanted – to anoint Hubert – & patiently explaining "Look all I shall do is to put oil on his forehead and say a prayer. Look the oil is in this little box. It is nothing to be frightened of." And so by knowing what he wanted & sticking to that, when I was all for arguing it out from first principles, he got what he wanted & Hubert crossed himself and later called me up and said "When I became a Catholic it was not from fear," so he knew what happened and accepted it. So we spent the day watching for a spark of gratitude for the love of God and saw the spark.'

The whole of this incident, altered in detail to suit the story, and omitting the grotesque episode of the medal, was eight months later to be described in what is probably the most famous scene in *Brideshead Revisited*.

In December Evelyn and I went with Philip Dunne, who had also joined Bill Stirling's unit, and with three young officers of the S.A.S. to be trained in parachuting at the S.O.E. school at Manchester, making our descents into Tatton Park. I will tell a little about that later. After this adventure I was sent to Scotland as an instructor on a general training course arranged for Bill's two French battalions, while Evelyn went in the opposite direction, first to London for treatment of his injured knee, and finally ending up in January in Devonshire in the Easton Court Hotel at Chagford where he set himself to the writing of *Brideshead Revisited*.

To understand how this came about the story must momentarily go back some years, to Evelyn's meeting with Graham Greene and Tom Burns at the Ministry of Information in May 1941, when Graham 'propounded a scheme for official writers'.

No more was heard of this ludicrous idea till October 1941 when a manifesto was published in *Horizon* signed by Arthur Calder-Marshall, Cyril Connolly, Bonamy Dobrée, Tom Harrisson, Arthur Koestler, Alun Lewis, George Orwell and Stephen Spender. Their main proposition was 'the formation of an official group of war writers'. The manifesto was not felicitously worded. It was stated that 'when war broke out, many writers were hesitant . . . With the invasion of Russia, feeling has crystallized. It is no longer possible for anyone to stand back and call the war an imperialist war.' Evelyn set himself the not very difficult task of answering this rubbish and his letter appeared in December 1941. 'What a picture of fun it makes of English writers!' he wrote. 'First, while Europe was overrun, they were "hesitant". Then one enemy fell out, over the division of the spoils, with his larger and wealthier partner. This welcome but not unforeseen diversion "crystallized" our writers' "feelings".'

Evelyn made no reference to this episode later in his diary. But the subject may have lingered in a recess of his mind. This can only be guesswork, but it may be remembered that when Graham Greene had first put the suggestion to him, Evelyn had, while rejecting it, mentioned that 'the official writer racket might be convenient' in certain circumstances. In January 1944 Evelyn found that such a 'racket' would suit him well. He wanted to have at least three months' leave to write a novel which he had in his head.

It is not quite clear why the indefinite leave, until posting, which had been granted to him in September 1943, did not cover his requirements. There seems to be some episode unrecorded in the diary and his correspondence. At all events he needed some more definite release from duty for three months, if he was to write his book.

He played boldly and followed an artful strategy. He knew that it would be useless to appeal unsupported to the War Office. He knew that the first really efficient Minister of Information, Brendan Bracken, fancied himself as a man of wide education and culture and that he was one of the Prime Minister's intimate friends. He may have known also that in spite of War Office distrust of the Ministry of Information, Brendan Bracken had achieved the apparently impossible feat of obtaining an admiring following in the War Office as a result of the excellent advice he had given to General Montgomery regarding publicity.

In January 1944 Evelyn wrote to Brendan Bracken requesting his support for an application to the War Office for three months' leave. He made no claim that his purpose could be of immediate advantage to the work of the Ministry. He put his cards on the table. The relevant passages are in the last three paragraphs.

'This novel will have no direct dealing with the war and it is not pretended that it will have any immediate propaganda value. On the other hand it is hoped that it may cause innocent amusement and relaxation to a number of readers and it is understood that entertainment is now regarded as a legitimate contribution to the war effort.

'It is a peculiarity of the literary profession that, once an idea becomes fully formed in the author's mind, it cannot be left unexploited without deterioration. If, in fact, the book is not written now it will never be written.

'On the completion of the writing I shall be able to return to duty with my mind unencumbered either by other preoccupations or by the financial uncertainty caused by the necessity of supporting a large family on the pay of a lieutenant. I shall be able to offer myself in the hope that some opportunity will then have arisen in which I can serve my regiment.

> 'I have the honour, Sir, to be
> Your obedient servant
> (signed) Evelyn Waugh
> Lieutenant, Royal Horse Guards.'

(It should be explained that Evelyn retained the acting and temporary rank of Captain, but while not on active duty he reverted to Lieutenant's pay.)

There then followed a long game of cat-and-mouse between Evelyn and the War Office, with the Ministry of Information occasionally joining in as an extra though hardly carnivorous cat, leaving the mouse time to write between pounces.

Brendan Bracken supported Evelyn's application in principle, and it seemed to Evelyn at the end of January that he had what he wanted. He thought his troubles were over. They were not.

On 29 January he left London and after a weekend at Pixton he moved to Chagford on the 31st. 'I still have a cold', he noted in his diary, 'and am low in spirits but I feel full of literary power which only this evening gives place to qualms of impotence.' On 1 February he began to write *Brideshead Revisited*. 'I found my mind stiff and my diction stilted but by dinner time I had finished 1300 words all of which were written twice and many three times before I got the time sequence and the transitions satisfactory, but I think it is now all right.' He continued working steadily, achieving 1500-2000 words a day. Then on 8 February came the first pounce. 'A disgusting note from M of I suggesting that my leave is far from certain.' Questions were evidently being asked in the War Office about this unique case. It may have been depression at receiving this news that led him to make an entry in his diary, typical of his bitter late war mood. 'It is hard to be fighting against Rome. We bombed Castel Gandolfo [the Pope's country villa]. The Russians now propose a partition of East Prussia. It is a fact that the Germans now represent Europe against the world. Thank God Japan is not on our side too.' For the moment nothing followed the warning from the Ministry of Information. On the evening of 14 February he wrote 3000 words in three hours, and next day 'treated myself as a kind of invalid as a result'. From Friday the 18th to Ash Wednesday the 23rd February, Laura, who was pregnant, came to stay at the hotel. Three days later the foreshadowed blow fell. On 26 February his Commanding Officer in Windsor rang him up to say that the War Office had turned down his application for leave and he was to report for duty as an ADC to a General.

The General in question was the commander of the 43rd Division, Major-General Ivor (later Sir Ivor) Thomas. The appointment failed, and how it failed has been the subject of myth, much of it invented by Evelyn himself. His own account in his diary is less hilarious and more credible than later ones, and was written within a day or two of the event. At lunch at the Apéritif Restaurant Evelyn warned General Thomas that he was not cut out to be an ideal aide-de-camp. The General seems to have taken a liking to Evelyn nevertheless and wished him to take the appointment temporarily 'on approval'. Evelyn wrote in his diary on 2 March: 'On Tuesday I went to his head quarters for a week's trial – today returned unaccepted. This is a great relief. The primary lack of sympathy seemed to come from my being slightly drunk in his mess on the first evening. I told him I could not change the habits of a life time for a whim of his.'

The War Office having rejected his plea for leave, his alternative to the staff appointment was idleness at Windsor. 'My sole interest now is in my novel', he wrote in a sadly telling sentence.

But he was spared Windsor. 'No sooner was I quit of one General', he recorded on 9 March, 'than a second was produced for me like a rabbit from a hat.' The new prospective employer was Major-General Miles (now Sir Miles) Graham who had become well known as General Montgomery's Chief Administrative Officer in Egypt and North Africa. Evelyn described him as 'on the surface a more human fellow than Tomkins'. Miles Graham told him that if he accepted an appointment as his Personal Assistant he might not need him for six weeks. Evelyn accepted the appointment and was duly given six weeks' leave. In ecstasy he went back to Chagford with Laura, but hardly had he settled down to work again than he received an official letter cancelling the leave given by Miles Graham. It looks as though someone in the War Office, possibly our friend the purple-haired major, had made it his dedicated aim to prevent Captain Waugh receiving so much leave for a grossly unmilitary purpose. Evelyn found himself 'stunned' and inhibited from work. 'One day', he wrote in his diary, 'believing it to be the first of a long period of work, is worth a week of odd days on which I expect the summons to move.'

While in London he had written again to Brendan Bracken, and though he had no answer it is possible that Brendan worked privately on his behalf, as the summons to move never came. Soon Evelyn was writing as fast as ever, and on 21 March he sent off another 13,000 words to be typed and had his 'teeth into a new chapter'. He noted that 'English writers, at forty, either set about prophesying or acquiring a style. Thank God I think I am beginning to acquire a style.' He added: 'No news from the War Office. It is just that having so often suffered so sharply from their dilatoriness, I should at length profit by it.' He was, in fact, never summoned by Miles Graham who had made other and more suitable arrangements regarding a Personal Assistant, but on 1 April, after Laura's last visit to Chagford before the soon expected birth of their next child he received a telegram from Windsor telling him to report to a Colonel Tufton of the War Office Public Relations Departent. Evelyn noted: 'It is not quite as disastrous as it might be for I have come to a suitable halting stage.'

He went up to London and spent two weeks 'waiting for an appointment to conduct journalists round the second front'. On 29 April he was informed by the public relations office that they had no employment for him. At this, the cat-and-mouse torment to which he was subjected suddenly proved unendurable. This utter waste of time 'inflamed my persecution mania to the extent that I wrote to Bob, who was on leave, asking for his help in getting me six clear weeks to finish my book'. There was little or nothing that Bob could do. He could not be expected to quarrel with a War Office ruling involving an officer who was no longer under his command. But Evelyn could not see it this way. He was right to speak of persecution mania. He could not rid his mind of the idea that Bob had been guilty of treachery and false dealing in not taking him on Operation Husky and that he was continuing his ill-treatment. He used to call him 'chucker'. Quite falsely he saw him as being in sinister alliance with the obstructors.

On 3 May he returned to Chagford, risking official displeasure. He wrote on 4 May: 'Today I painfully picked up the threads of a very difficult chapter of love-making on a liner.'

Hardly had he recommenced his task than the cat pounced again. In the afternoon of the 5th a telegram from Windsor arrived. It 'ordered me to report to a room in Hobart House on the afternoon of the 11th'. The next day he received a letter from Windsor 'making it clear that the telegram was not their doing'. This aroused hopes in Evelyn 'that it may be Bob at work to get my release'. In this supposition he was mistaken, but rescue was at hand and Bob was to be instrumental in making it effective.

On 9 May he confessed in his diary to some doubts about *Brideshead Revisited*, a thing he had not done since his first day at work on 1 February. He had just finished that crucial chapter in the book in which the narrator becomes the heroine's lover on board a transatlantic liner.

On 11 May he reported, as ordered, to Hobart House. But before this latest pounce of the War Office cat, the mouse had grown confident of his means of baffling the savage animal. On the 9th he had received a telegram from Bob saying that he had urged his case on Bill Stirling. Evelyn could reflect that Bill had already given him a posting which only needed official endorsement, and that thanks to Bill's pertinacity things were now going his way.

The interview at Hobart House, as reported in Evelyn's diary, was worthy of his wildest fiction. 'I found the room at Hobart House full of scourings of the army, patriotic old men longing for a job, obvious young blackguards. We were seen in turn by a weary but quite civil Lt.Col. and a major. The Col said: "We've two jobs for you. I don't know which will appeal to you more. You can be a welfare officer in a transit camp in India." I said that was not one I should choose. "Or you can be an assistant registrar at a hospital." I said if I had to have one or the other I would have the latter. Then he said: "By the way are you educated? Were you at a University?"

' "Yes, Oxford."

' "Well they are very much in need of an educated officer at the War Office, G.3. Chemical Warfare."

' "My education was classical & historical."

' "Oh that doesn't matter. All they want is *education*."

'As soon as I left them', the diary continues, 'I beetled round to Bob at COHQ and said "Get me out of this quick!" ' Bob immediately telephoned to Hobart House and told the authorities there that Evelyn was not available as Colonel Stirling needed him. On the next day Evelyn saw Bill who was now in a position to confirm officially the posting to S.A.S. On the excuse of extended sick-leave, for Evelyn's knee was not quite healed, Bill also granted him six weeks' leave to finish his book.

Bill should be remembered and honoured as an enlightened patron of letters. Evelyn went to Chagford the same day, and on the next day, 13 May, Laura gave birth to a daughter who was christened Harriet May.

The cat made one last pounce, not lethal in intention, merely time-wasting. On 30 May he received a summons to Windsor. He went there on the 31st 'in order to be told the address of 2 SAS Rgt to which I had written daily for weeks, which the Life Guard adjutant said was too secret for the post'. On the same day he saw a fellow-officer of the S.A.S. with whom he had become close friends, Basil Bennet. The latter had grave news for him. Bill had had serious differences both with his Brigadier and his Divisional Commander; as a result he had been asked to resign his command, and had done so. His place had been taken by Brian Franks who was now Evelyn's Commanding Officer. By a fortunate coincidence Evelyn met Brian in London on his way back from Windsor. The new Colonel, for reasons not hard to guess, hastened to confirm Bill's arrangements with Evelyn and told him that he might remain unmolested at Chagford until he had finished his book.

His diary entry for 6 June is revealing: 'This morning at breakfast the waiter told me the second front had opened. I sat down early to work and wrote a fine passage on Lord Marchmain's death agonies. Carolyn [Cobb] came to tell me that the popular front was open. I sent for the priest to give Lord Marchmain the last sacraments. I worked through till 4 o'clock & finished the last chapter – the last dialogue poor – took it to the post . . . There only remains now the epilogue which is easy meat. My only fear is lest the invasion upsets my typist at St Leonards, or the posts to him with my manuscript.' Not perhaps quite typical of the spirit of the Blues on D-Day.

The whole book was finished, typed, corrected and delivered to Peter by 16 June. Evelyn had second thoughts about it much later, but at the time he was in no doubt that it was his finest achievement. It marked a change in his writing more radical than any he had shown hitherto. It is a large subject and I intend to discuss it in a separate chapter.

Evelyn reported to Brian Franks that he had finished his novel, which he described to him as 'a masterpiece'. He said that his knee was quite mended and having no further reason to be on leave he wished to return to active service. What were the Colonel's orders? I was with Brian Franks when he received the letter at his headquarters at Ardchullery Lodge, a property of Bill Stirling in Perthshire. Brian was dismayed. 'What on earth shall I do with him?' he groaned. 'I can't very well tell him to take another three months' leave and write another book, which is what I would like to do.' We all bent our minds to the problem which was not an easy one, for Brian had set an absolute condition on any solution. 'I'm not going to allow him near the men', he had asserted. 'Get him up here and see what he wants to do', I suggested. 'I know exactly what he wants to do', said Brian. 'He wants to mess up the men, and the regiment, and the brigade, and Airborne Corps if possible.' I was described at the time as the Operational Intelligence Officer and I suggested that with the second front opened and voluminous enemy documentation becoming available, Evelyn might be useful as an addition to the Intelligence staff. The Chief Intelligence Officer, Major Barkworth, turned pale at this suggestion but admitted that paper work was likely to grow beyond the capacity of the present staff. Nothing was decided, but Brian Franks sent a telegram to Evelyn ordering him to report to Ardchullery at his earliest convenience. He arrived with Basil Bennet on 23 June.

Evelyn did me the honour of describing me as a 'companion in arms' when he published his book *Men at Arms* in 1952. We had done a great deal of what is often called 'Whitehall soldiering' together in the difficult days when Bill Stirling was striving to organize the S.A.S. Regiment, and I have related one shared experience in the case of the purple-haired major. But the only times in which we were in a more honourable sense companions in arms were in December 1943 when we were both parachuted over Tatton Park and at Ardchullery where the S.A.S. Regiment was conducting final exercises before being sent to the invasion front. On both occasions Evelyn was the most delightful of companions. It is true that on our parachute course he took a perverse delight in bewildering the other officers on training, most of whom were very young men. Having ordered a bottle of wine for himself at dinner in mess, he would hold forth on campaigns he had served in, notably the Zulu War. 'It was Mr Gladstone who let us down as usual,' he would say in his deep gruff tone, 'not that I was ever partial to that Jewish feller, Mr Disraeli. Mr Canning was the man for me.' I wish I had been appointed censor of the young men's letters!

I was complacent in the face of my Colonel's anxiety, because, not having been with him at Sherborne, I had never known the darker side of Captain Waugh on service. But I had had a tiny glimpse of it. One day stands out in my memory as the most negatively doleful of all days. We were taken to an aerodrome for our first jump into Tatton Park. A wind got up and jumping was considered too dangerous. But the weather forecasters assured the aerodrome that a lull was on the way. For five hours we waited for the lull in a Nissen hut. No one had thought to bring a book to read. It was like solitary confinement *en masse*. Even the oldest and worst newspaper would have been something; there was not even that. Late in the afternoon the officer in charge of parachuting that afternoon appeared in the hut. The lull had arrived, but it was short and only two aeroplanes would go up. They would take a few from the various units represented. S.A.S. was only allotted two men. He went down the list picking candidates at random. When he came to S.A.S. he picked from the hand-raisers

Philip Dunne and me. Feeling rather like a prisoner being ordered to the guillotine in the French Revolution, I followed Philip to our well-upholstered tumbril. As we were about to start I caught a glimpse of Evelyn's face through a window of the Nissen hut. Never have I seen envy, hate and rage so effortlessly conjoined in a human face, every emotion concentrated in his glaring eyes. But his ill-humour had passed by the time we got back from our 'drop'. (Going down through the hole was rather like being hanged.)

At Ardchullery he was in a charming and relaxed mood as befitted a man who had just achieved an ambitious enterprise. When not taking part in a military exercise it was important to retain one's physical fitness by long and strenuous walks, so Evelyn, myself, and whom he used to call 'my great new friend', Basil Bennet, used to set out together for a walk along the rough lanes going through the woods of the lovely Perth countryside. Evelyn did not relish this cult of physical perfection. After three miles or so Basil or I would say: 'Do you think we can decently go back now?' Without a word Evelyn would about turn and start walking swiftly in the homeward direction. This was a daily phenomenon. In the mess Basil and I and Barkworth delighted in his conversation, but there were others with whom he did not get on. One was a deplorable young officer whom we used to call Captain Foulenough. He was the incarnation of the young military cad, both in appearance with his low forehead and old-fashioned moustache, and in his mind which was crammed with an enormous and hideous collection of smutty stories. There was also a young Frenchman who would have been a very agreeable companion but for a habit of loudly smacking his lips in an agitated manner in moments of silence. I shared irritation at this with Evelyn, but Evelyn made no effort to disguise his emotion.

These were lesser shadows in a pleasant time. A larger one, a more dreadful tension, brooded over us. Evelyn put it mildly. 'Brian', he wrote in his diary, 'was so shy of having me under his command as to be almost hostile.' Evelyn did not mention that Brian Franks had told him privately that on no account was he going to allow him near the men. The first phrase following the last quoted sentence has a familiar ring: 'I was in some doubt as to my future . . .'

Though I delighted in Evelyn's companionship my sympathies were entirely with my Colonel. To fit Evelyn into the humblest military organization was an impossible task. I think dreadful disarray might have fallen on that proposed transit camp in India, and on that threatened hospital. Quite suddenly the tension lifted. I took a prominent part in the process.

As an Intelligence Officer I was often used as a liaison officer in matters which could be more easily thrashed out in conversation than in lengthy correspondence. I was used thus in the frequent negotiations between

Airborne Corps, Combined Operations Headquarters and Bill Stirling's invention, the little brigade within the S.A.S. Brigade, now commanded by Brian. I remember being seen off from Glasgow on the night train to Euston by Evelyn and Basil one evening in the last days of June. I forget on what mission I was sent on that occasion. It was a hectic time for us, as the S.A.S. role changed daily with the general military situation. At all events on 28 June I spent a busy morning at Combined Operations Headquarters, and at the end of it went to White's Club for refreshment and relaxation. I had not been there many minutes before I heard the loud and unmistakable voice of Randolph Churchill at the bar, saying: 'Where the hell is Evelyn Waugh? I've tried everywhere! No one can tell me! I need him immediately!'

I went quickly to the bar. I said, 'Randolph, did you say you want Evelyn? I think I can help you. What's it for?'

'I've spent the morning with my father,' he explained, 'and it's now all fixed; I've been commissioned to undertake a subordinate mission under Fitzroy Maclean in Jugoslavia; I'll be in Croatia actually. I told Fitz before I left that I must have officers I can talk to and he agreed with me that Evelyn was just the chap for me. It's all very secret,' he added, his voice rising in volume, 'so don't tell anyone. But where the hell *is* Evelyn? How can I get him? I've asked Bob. I've asked the Blues. I've asked everyone I can bloody well think of. No one seems to know.'

I said, 'Randolph, if you just stay where you are, I think I can get him for you. Don't go for five minutes. Where are you staying?' He told me he was at the Dorchester Hotel.

I put through a 'priority call', as it was known then, to Ardchullery. I told Brian the bare fact that Randolph wished to see Evelyn in London, the next day if possible, regarding a likely and important appointment. The note of relief excited by my words was fully audible over the telephone. I rushed back to the bar and told Randolph that Evelyn would be with him at the Dorchester Hotel the following morning. In gratitude he gave me a drink which I had certainly earned. Later in the day Brian received enquiries from Bob Laycock and Windsor. Evelyn came down on the night train. I did not see him again until after his return from Croatia.

# Chapter 15

*Brideshead Revisited, The Sacred and Profane Memories of Captain Charles Ryder,* was Evelyn's most ambitious work since his first appearance as a novelist. No longer was he content to be the author of brilliant short fiction. He intended, as he seems to have intended in *Work Suspended* judging by the length of its first two chapters, to emulate the example of Thackeray by writing a book of the ample dimensions of *Vanity Fair* or *Pendennis.*

While the greater Dickens has almost always proved a disastrous model, the influence of Thackeray on succeeding writers has often been beneficial. Evelyn had a wide and deep knowledge of his writings, in fact I think that he had read everything he wrote. The influence is most evident here in the plot which could easily be that of a Thackeray novel; indeed if Evelyn had a literary model it was most likely to have been *The History of Henry Esmond.* The scene in *Brideshead Revisited* when Lord Marchmain returns after long absence to his ancestral home can hardly not recall a similar scene in *Esmond.* There is no copying of Thackeray in the book, but there is Thackeray's breadth and sometimes recklessness of description, and sometimes his sentimentality though in a very different idiom. The people in the story are of the type and class that Thackeray described to perfection. There is everywhere Thackeray's power of 'creating character'. This is generally admitted. The hostile critics of the book assert that there is everywhere Thackeray's snobbery as well.

Thackeray has for long not only been accused of being a snob, but has been almost excommunicated from English literature for the fault by some esteemed critics of today. Was he guilty? Well, he wrote *The Book of Snobs* originally entitled *The Snobs of England by One of Themselves,* and the majority of its readers agree that it is so good because Thackeray *was* of their number and wrote with professional knowledge. As most people know, the word 'snob' meant something very different in Thackeray's time: it was then of wide, vague meaning and usually more equivalent to the modern terms 'vulgarian' or 'bore'. Originally it meant a cobbler, thence a plebeian or mobsman. But it was Thackeray more than anyone else who gave it its present and enduring meaning of a 'person with exaggerated respect for social position'. Does not that fact tell us something? I do not think that anyone who was not a snob in our sense of the term could have written *A Little Dinner at Timmins*.

The fact that Thackeray poked fun at aristocratic society is beside the point. This aspect of the question, and the whole question of the treatment of aristocracy in novels, was perfectly summarized by Max Beerbohm in his great book *Seven Men*. 'Aristocrats . . . may be as beautiful as all that, but, for fear of thinking ourselves snobbish, we won't believe it. We do believe it, however, and revel in it, when the novelist saves his face and ours by a pervading irony . . . Disraeli's great ladies and lords won't do for his irony is but latent in his homage, and thus the reader feels himself called on to worship and in duty bound to scoff. All's well, though, when the homage is latent in the irony. Thackeray, inviting us to laugh and frown over the follies of Mayfair, enables us to reel with him in a secret orgy of veneration for those fools.'

Is the last sentence of that paragraph applicable to Evelyn? He faced the accusation that Max implied against Thackeray. Was he also guilty?

If one answers 'Up to a point', the phrase must not be taken as evasive. I will return to this later.

Few people are quite devoid of snobbishness, and a good deal of everyday snobbishness is no worse than rather silly. To enjoy being seen in conversation with a duke or a very famous man is not a crime, and those who treat it as such are usually victims of their own morbid class-consciousness. The vice, as opposed to the harmless silliness, in snobbishness has never been more astutely indicated than in an essay on the subject by Desmond MacCarthy. 'It is not', he wrote, 'the foolishly looking-up that offends me, but the foolishly looking-down; not the belief in the existence of the "right" kind of people, but the belief that there are "wrong" kinds of people.' How does Evelyn come out of what one might call the MacCarthy test?

Not very well, I regret to have to say. To particularize: his belief in the existence of the 'right' kind of people was very much weaker than his belief that there are 'wrong' kinds. His 'foolishly looking-up' was little if anything more than a natural consequence of that attraction to panache to which he admitted in his autobiography; the looking-up lacked the persistence of the dedicated snob and lord-worshipper. He never sought the society of dull people howsoever ornamented with titles they might be. I well remember the case of a certain lord of ancient lineage and impressive appearance, the owner of an imposing family seat, who at the time was the very pinnacle of fashion. I was sitting with Evelyn in White's one day when this majestic being strode through the club. I asked Evelyn if he knew him. 'Yes', he sighed, 'I used to meet him with the Lygons.' I asked him if he liked him. He shook his head. 'He's dull', he groaned, 'so dull – so dull. Oh he's so dull! And you can imagine how much I *wanted* to like him.' True looking-up snobbishness does not speak like that nor give in so readily. It is of sterner stuff.

The more distressing side of Evelyn's snobbishness, the 'foolishly looking-down' also needs some qualification. It has been stated by several people, most recently in 1974 in an article by Mr Beverley Nichols, that Evelyn was ignominiously ashamed of his origins and early years; that he wanted to forget Hampstead, Highgate, Lancing and Hertford, and wanted his friends to forget about his connection with them too; that he wanted people to suppose that he came from a home more like Chatsworth than Underhill and that his education was obtained at Eton and Christ Church or their great equivalents. This is all totally mistaken. In Arthur Waugh's time he frequently took his young friends of the fashionable world to Underhill. I had many conversations with him about Lancing and Hertford. He never gave the slightest hint of being ashamed of these places and, while I do not know his views about other famous schools, he had no liking for Eton, chiefly on account of what he believed to be its irreligious type of education.

The incident of the lord whom Evelyn wanted to like can alone dispose of the more interesting, though in my opinion equally fallacious view, put forward by Sir Cecil Beaton in his published diaries. He wrote: 'Evelyn and I now moved in more exalted spheres than when we lived in Hampstead and Highgate. In our own way we were both snobs . . . My particular snobbery was more in the nature of wanting to become part of the " *culturi*". [Italian slang, presumably, perhaps meaning 'cultured ones'] . . . Evelyn was attracted by the foibles of those who lived in large, aristocratic houses.' This subtle self-praise is based on a misreading of Evelyn's life and character.

The misreading, shared by many, was prompted by Evelyn's deplorable proneness to 'foolishly looking-down'.

With him this usually took the hateful form of clever bullying. He was horribly adept at putting people he met ill at ease as regards their social manners and position. He enjoyed doing it to those who were unsure of themselves and in unfamiliar surroundings. He could be chivalrously kind to people down on their luck, but to the naturally weak he was as merciless as he had been in his bullying school days. I witnessed the spectacle many times and it always utterly disgusted me. It was useless to remonstrate as I sometimes did because he was always ready with a witty and plausibly logical defence. This form of bullying was a perversion, and a grossly unworthy one, of his aggressive spirit which rejoiced in conflict. With an opponent who stood up to him, no one could show himself more of a 'bonny fighter', either verbally or in writing, but Evelyn seemed quite insensitive to the ignobility attending the transformation of 'the erect, the manly foe' into the mean-spirited persecutor. He was never much influenced by the common desire to be liked.

## 1944 et seq.

*Brideshead Revisited* was published in a limited edition in December 1944 and, after a revision, it came out in a public edition in May 1945. It was again and more drastically revised in 1959. The revisions were the result of the criticisms which he received after the first edition which was limited to presentation copies. (Peter raised no objections to this extravagance because he knew that he and the publishers were on to a winner). Most of them were matters of detail. Nancy Mitford corrected points concerning female dress in the twenties, all of which he followed, but the most important correction of detail came from Ronald Knox. It concerned the scene, indirectly reported in the book, in which the parish priest closes the Catholic private chapel of Brideshead. Evelyn had never witnessed such an event and he imagined how it would occur. Ronald Knox gave him the facts, which are more prosaic than would appear from Evelyn's original description. He shortened the passage which remains nonetheless one of the most memorable in the book. In all, however, the revisions, in spite of Evelyn's care and labour, made little if any difference to the character of the novel.

*Brideshead Revisited* is one of the most widely read of all Evelyn's books and without being overbold I think I may presume that the great majority of present readers, even all of them, know the subject and the story. There is one persistent mistake, however, to which the book gives rise and which comes from forgetfulness of the story, and this I should correct. Brideshead is the name of an imagined and magnificent country house built in the eighteenth century by the family of Lord Marchmain whose surname is Flyte. They are Catholics at the time of the story, and this is the origin of an idea that Evelyn was endeavouring to portray the life of one of the old Catholic English families, such as the Langdales, the Howards or the Arundells. In fact a reading of the novel shows that the Flytes were an Anglican family, recently and almost accidentally made Catholic by Lord Marchmain's marriage into one of these traditional Catholic families and his (not very sincere) conversion to the Old Faith for the sake of his wife whom he has long deserted, with his religion, at the time when the book opens. The book is not on such a theme as Hugh Benson might have relished, the persistence of the Old Faith in a family despite persecution and other vicissitudes of time and history; it rather has the theme of the continual renascence of the faith, under the most unlikely and even unworthy circumstances.

In his own experience, Evelyn did not have much acquaintance with the old Catholics, as they used to be called, but this misconception about *Brideshead Revisited* gave rise to a second one, more common in the United States and the English-speaking world overseas than in Britain, that Evelyn's Catholicism was closely connected with his social ambitions. He was not wholly innocent of 'foolishly looking-up', but he did not look that way.

The reception of the book on the issue of the first edition was so enthusiastic that one can almost use the word ecstatic with precision. It came mostly from friends, it is true, but these friends contained a considerable proportion of people with claims to high and inalienable critical standards, Henry Yorke, Graham Greene, Desmond MacCarthy, Osbert Sitwell and John Betjeman. This opening chorus of praise was almost inevitable, though it largely reflected idiosyncratic qualities of the book. Winter 1944 was a grim time in spite of the success of what Mrs Cobb had called 'the popular front' and the certainty of victory over Nazism. It was, despite all that, an age of disillusion, of shortening rations, increasing discomfort and more and more an all-pervading shabbiness. Into this drab world there flashed for the happy few this immense entertainment, with its colour, its appeal to nostalgia stronger then than at most times, its wit, its unconcern with the 'pressing' problems of the hour and showing the slightest sociological interest; abounding with what the world was most short of, fun. Further to the book's advantage, the fun was not confined to surface and frivolity; through it there sounded a grave note attuned to the seriousness of the preoccupations of a dreadful hour. The essential subject of the book was not youthful irresponsibility, youthful and mature love, the pageant of fashion, the splendour of aristocratic society, but certain Last Things: how to face death, the Christian Truths, the world-wide claims of the Catholic Church.

The book could hardly fail to delight at any time in the nineteen forties. Even those who were disturbed at the change in Evelyn's style and approach to his subject matter were entranced at the brilliance of the dialogue, of the characterization, of the ingenious invention. As a recipient of the first edition I can testify to the excitement and admiration that I felt and shared with many others on first reading *Brideshead Revisited*. I regret none of this thirty years later as I still believe, and I believe balanced opinion will continue to believe, that, for all its blemishes, this was a very considerable work.

The book had a boldness and originality of theme less easy to discern now than when it first came out. Not since the time of Robert Hugh Benson and his brother Arthur Benson, over thirty years before, had novelists of high ambition taken Christian religion as the main subject of a fiction to be treated without scepticism. There had grown up a literary convention whereby religious faith was only referred to in a novel, if at all, as a detail of the background or of character-sketching, or as the object of ridicule or attack, but never treated with implied or explicit respect. (Maurice Baring was an exception.) To write seriously, as a believer, in a novel, was felt to be, in the slang of the period, 'shy-making'. Graham Greene's use of a Roman Catholic theme in *Brighton Rock* was acceptable because the story, being about criminals, implied an equation of religion with psychological abnormality, and added to the horror of the tale. The same author's use of a central religious theme in his great book *The Power and the Glory* (published in 1940) was again acceptable to the prevailing convention, because the story was set in an exotic scene. But Evelyn was doing something which seemed in England to have gone out of fashion for ever; he was making religion the central point of a story about contemporary English life, and approaching his theme with respect and awe. If Evelyn had been a French writer he could have written a French equivalent of *Brideshead Revisited* within a living tradition. As an English novelist he was exploring neglected territory, and if he sometimes went astray in his handling of his main theme, it was chiefly for that reason.

Since 1944 several writers including Graham Greene have attempted serious unsceptical treatment of orthodox Christian religion in novels, notably Iris Murdoch among Anglicans in *The Bell*. I think they all owe rather more to the example of Evelyn's novel than is commonly recognized.

But even to those who rejected Evelyn's right to construct a novel on a Christian religious theme, and to the many smart critics who were thrown into a state of indignation by his use of aristocratic characters in place of the fashionable workers, the book was irresistible for the dialogue and the narration. Above all for the abundant delineation of character. It has been said that a master of fiction will always limit the number of characters that he depicts 'in the round'. Otherwise the balance comes into peril. The possibly true story of how our supreme poet felt obliged for this reason to kill Mercutio early on in the play is something musty. A more striking illustration, to my mind, is that many people regard the title 'The Merchant of Venice' as referring to *mercator pessimus* Shylock rather than to the conventionally portrayed Antonio who is the hero. Evelyn with utterly reckless abandon took no thought about such dangers. He fairly crowded his stage with living beings, from his Marine Commanding officer whose moustache was composed of 'porcine bristles' to the German expatriate in Morocco with his sinister lisp; the most lightly sketched of his characters has the vitality of a leading figure. When he recorded in his diary that he felt 'full of literary power' he was not guilty of idle boasting.

But amid the chorus of praise that greeted the first presentation edition, there were some dissident voices. Several of the critics who received the book read it with disapproval, mostly for conventional, prejudiced reasons, but also for more defensible ones. They were dismayed by the lushness and sentimentality of much of the writing. It is quite true that in the prose of *Brideshead Revisited* Evelyn relied, to an extent that he had never done before, on metaphor, and metaphor, when used to excess, can lead, like a will-o'-the-wisp, into the swamps and perils of slush. The sentimentality is undoubtedly there, the charge is not false, but some discrimination can be made in Evelyn's favour. The sentimental passages in the long Oxford sequence at the beginning can be strongly defended on the grounds that Evelyn is here showing life as seen through an undergraduate's eyes, and that, though no undergraduate likes to admit to such a thing, the period of late adolescence is one of intense sentimentality. (Most student movements are based on it.)

Where the sentimentality spoils the book is not here but in the ill-managed love-scenes between the narrator, Charles Ryder, and the heroine, Julia Flyte. This was the only criticism I had of the book when it first appeared. I found these scenes embarrassing, 'shy-making', or as Mary Lygon used to say: they made one hum. I was bold enough to say so to Evelyn in conversation one day (after I had written him a letter of congratulation which I think he liked because he kept it) but he was unmoved. My point of objection, to which I still hold, is that he spoilt the first love-scenes on the liner by dragging in a solemn reference to a ludicrous film of the 'twenties about the French Revolution, a melodramatic affair called *Orphans of the Storm*. This interpretation of the event by Arthur Griffiths was far less respectable than the absurdities of Baroness Orczy. I put all this to him.

Evelyn did not give way an inch. 'Why didn't you like the film?' he asked with blazing eyes, carefully shifting the ground.

'I liked it enormously. But I was very young at the time. And ignorant too'.

'So was I. My object was to renew your enjoyment. You ought to have more gratitude.'

To show how little he accepted such criticism, when the revised version came out in 1945, one of the chapter headings contrived for it was 'Orphans of the Storm'. I think this incident was indicative of more than obstinacy. He was in love with the book.

The most unworthy and ridiculous of the hostile criticism which met the book from the first, came from professional literary critics, and was based on wholly insincere protestations of class preference. To admit in print to friendship with the family of a marquess, to admire his traditions and to find pleasure in the beauty and luxury of his family seat – and without a word of sociological criticism of such things – this, they declared, hurt their sensibilities.

Had they but known it, their role was the same as that of Dickens's critics who attacked him, on the appearance of *Oliver Twist*, for showing an unwholesome interest in the criminal underworld. Dickens (who felt constrained to write an apologia) was accused of being indefensibly 'low'; Evelyn was accused of being indefensibly 'high'. That the act of climbing on to the Left-going band-waggon was also vulgar and not very edifying never occurred to these 'critics of life'. Evelyn described their performance in crude terms; he called it 'sucking up to the lower classes'.

This view, what might be called the Beveridge-conditioned view, received wide and public expression when the book came out in 1945, but with a difference. The great mass of this later hostile criticism centred on Evelyn's depiction of a character who is only referred to once in the main novel, but is to the fore in the prologue and epilogue. He is a sub-altern of lower middle class origin, called Hooper. Not long before Evelyn began to write the novel in the February of 1944 the Vice-President of the United States, Henry Wallace, had declared that 'this is the century of the Common Man'. In a brief lecture, Max Beerbohm had made inimitable fun of this idiotic assertion of faith, but though many people mocked Henry Wallace's words and joined in praising Max's wisdom when the lecture was published, the great overriding sense of public opinion was on Wallace's side, and on Hooper's side. Frightened intellectuals hurried to get on the popular side and Hooper became a symbol of an injured class of men, the now deified Common Man, and a proof of Evelyn's wrong values.

To return to the dissident voices in the first chorus of praise. One came from Henry Yorke but was manifestly prejudiced and concerned with his personal faith which was that of a convinced and anti-Popish Protestant. The theme, he told Evelyn, 'was not easy for me. As you can imagine my heart was in my mouth all through the death bed scene, hoping against hope that the old man would not give way, that is take the course he eventually did. But I don't know when you have written more power-fully & with such command as you have done here. The suspense is superb'.

Amid the praise a very telling adverse criticism, to the effect that Evelyn had overdrawn the aristocratic glamour of the Flyte world, was given to him by Pansy Lamb. She wrote in the course of a long letter '. . . you cannot make me nostalgic about the world I knew in the 1920s. And yet it was the same world as you describe, or at any rate impinged on it. I was a debutante in 1922, & though neither smart nor rich went to three dances in historic houses, Norfolk House, Dorchester House, Grosvenor House & may have seen Julia Flyte. Yet, even in retrospect it all seems very dull. Most of the girls were drab & dowdy & the men even more so. The only glamorous girl I remember was Daphne Vivian now Weymouth [now the writer Mrs Fielding] . . . it was somehow dim & dispersed. No-body was brilliant, beautiful, rich & owner of a wonderful home though some were one or the other. Most were respectable, well-to-do, narrow minded with ideals no way differing from Hooper's except that their basic ration was larger. Hooperism is only the transcription in cheaper terms of the upper class outlook of 1920 & like most mass-reproductions is not flattering to its originators . . .' This anticipated much of the hostile

251

criticism which was to appear in the summer of 1945, but unlike the writings of the professionals was based not on prejudice but on knowledge. I think Pansy Lamb gave a true criticism. Evelyn had been caught'looking-up' a bit too much.

Something may be said about the origins of the story and the characters. Evelyn in this book was drawing more directly than he had done before from his experience and there was consequently less of his fantasy and more of his observation. The family situation of the Flyte family was unquestionably taken from that of the Lygon family in the early 1930s, though the circumstances of Lord Marchmain's exile bear no relation to those of Lord Beauchamp's. The great house, Brideshead, has no resemblance to Madresfield, with the exception, as Dorothy Lygon has pointed out, of the *art nouveau* chapel. The original of Brideshead can doubtfully be traced to many great houses which Evelyn knew, but I fancy that a strong contribution was made by Castle Howard. The surmounting and majestic lantern of Castle Howard may well have suggested the dome of Brideshead, and the fountain facing its south front is of the proportions and magnificence of the fountain described in the book. The details of the latter fountain, however, were taken from the great fountain in the Piazza Navona in Rome, as Evelyn told me. The origin of the characters has been much disputed, but that of the most interesting one, Sebastian Flyte, is not in doubt. His circumstances and something of his appearance was taken in part from Hugh Lygon, as can be stated on Evelyn's own testimony, but a stronger contribution was made by memories of his Oxford friendship with Alastair Graham. This assertion again relies on Evelyn's own testimony and is supported by the curious fact that in the manuscript the name Alastair sometimes occurs in the place of Sebastian. The rest of the Flyte family seem to be invented and no distinct model for any of them has been traced with any confidence. I met Lady Marchmain just before the appearance of the book, but found, rather to my disappointment, that Evelyn did not know the lady.

The narrator's father is a very fine invention and, like the father in *Work Suspended*, drawn from Arthur Waugh, though again the original is much disguised. This is Arthur Waugh as he might have been if he had been selfish, without affection, and markedly unpleasant.

One of the most interesting characters in the book is Julia Flyte's husband, Rex Mottram. He is closely modelled on Brendan Bracken. Evelyn frequently denied this, but I once cornered him, telling him that he had rather spoilt the portrait by giving Mottram black hair instead of Brendan's red hair, and that if he thought this was not a picture of Brendan he was most unobservant. He capitulated and admitted that Mottram was indeed Bracken. I fancy I was one of very few to have received this admission. His denials were prompted by some feelings of guilt, I believe. Without Brendan Bracken's support he would never have been able to write *Brideshead Revisited* and this cruel portrait was an act of blatant ingratitude. The case for the defence is plain. Evelyn was before all things an artist and craftsman. He would have been no more capable of spoiling a novel by including a flattering portrait for interested reasons than of impoverishing a novel by cutting out a cruel portrait from a sense of obligation. This is to follow a 'hard saying', but the artist or writer who does not follow it dooms himself to second-rateness.

As it was Evelyn, for all that he owed him a great debt, drew the portrait with zest. He detested Brendan Bracken and everything he stood for, the coarseness of Fleet Street and big business with their worship of success and money-making artfully disguised as selfless patriotism. He hated the man's fraudulency especially as it was practised in regions which he regarded as sacred, the world of art and literature. Brendan Bracken was an extraordinary phenomenon. He was spiritual kin of the dervishes of Persia who (to quote James Morier) live on the principle 'that you can achieve anything by impudence'. Bracken posed as a man of enormous knowledge of architecture, painting and letters, especially architecture, and he forced this conception of himself on others by the boldest means. He once gave me a learned lecture on my family's house in Yorkshire which I had of course known intimately from my earliest childhood, a fact which he knew, and not one word of what he said was even vaguely close to the reality of the case. He knew that too but it did not put him off. I once introduced him to a son of the famous Irish physician, statesman and writer, St John Gogarty. He immediately gave my friend a detailed account of the distinguished and versatile career of his illustrious parent. I feel sure that, when, as a minister, he had audiences of the king, he loaded George VI with quantities of information on the history and beauties of Windsor Castle and Buckingham Palace, and any other royal property that came to his mind. Had he met T. S. Eliot, as he may have done, he must have told him about developments in twentieth-century poetry. He encouraged the baseless rumour that he was an illegitimate son of Winston Churchill. It remains extraordinary that the Bracken performance, in spite of its transparent charlatanism, did not make him a figure of fun but deeply impressed his acquaintance in the business, journalist and political worlds. He was quoted as an authority and even looked up to as a sage. Among his associates, he was never recognized as the hoax he was, except by Randolph Churchill. It is related, on apparently good authority, that after having met President Roosevelt for the first time, shortly before the war, Brendan Bracken held forth to a dining club in London in terms laudatory of the President such as went beyond those of his most enthusiastic supporters. Randolph was among the diners, and, when Bracken paused to take breath, exclaimed: 'Are you going to claim *him* as your father *too*?'

How could Evelyn resist such a target? He did not resist it, as we know, but he had the decency to recognize his ingratitude in his many and insincere denials.

Another and more minor character of great interest is Mr Samgrass of All Souls College, Oxford. Here there is no problem regarding the identity of the model; indeed, contrary to his usual custom, Evelyn was annoyed when his friends did not recognize the material whence he contrived the portrait. Samgrass is Maurice Bowra, who was Warden of Wadham College, Oxford. With him Evelyn's relations were always ambivalent. Whenever he went to Oxford Evelyn went to see him. They corresponded frequently. Maurice used to stay with Evelyn and Laura in the country. Yet Evelyn always spoke against Maurice, and Maurice frequently mocked Evelyn, though both were polite and affectionate in their meetings. When *Brideshead Revisited* came out Maurice was a recipient of the first edition. No letter of congratulation has been preserved. He was a much more vulnerable and sensitive man than he liked to appear and he could hardly have been pleased by this unmistakable portrait in which he was quite unfairly represented as a toady and a crook. But, while Maurice liked to giggle with the denigrators, he was too clever to identify himself with them, or to show any trace of hurt feelings. 'Brilliant! Brilliant!' he used to chortle, 'perhaps too brilliant! Perhaps too much of the wedding cake style about it, but a remarkable achievement for all that. I hope', he would add, darting his eyes towards whomever he was addressing, 'you spotted *me*. What a piece of artistry that is – best thing in the whole book.' When Maurice's words were repeated to Evelyn, the latter was not pleased.

Much controversy has been expended on the origin of the most entertaining of the minor characters, Anthony Blanche. On the book's appearance Evelyn's friends unanimously identified Blanche with Harold Acton, and since Evelyn gave his character a cosmopolitan background, an Eton education and made him an undergraduate of Christ Church, all of which was literally true of Harold Acton, and as he furthermore put into Blanche's mouth some genuine sayings of Harold Acton, made Blanche the central figure of some authentic Acton incidents, and portrayed him as the ruling aesthete of Oxford in the 1920s, the identification was inevitable. Harold Acton was understandably hurt by this caricature drawn by one of his oldest and closest friends, though he made no mention of this in the letter he sent on the book's publication. Evelyn tried to make amends by insisting that the character, apart from its large component of pure invention, was based on Brian Howard. If one looks at the portrait closely one may see that many characteristics of Howard are reproduced. Blanche is of partly Jewish origin which was true of Howard and is not true of Acton. The reiterated 'my dear' of Blanche's conversation was typical of Brian Howard's, not of Harold Acton's way of talking. Anthony Blanche's appearance is described in terms more suited to Howard than Acton.

Other details linking this amazing portrait with Brian Howard could be mentioned, but they are all unimportant. The alibi fails. Anthony Blanche is shown as influencing young Oxford, just as Harold Acton did. Brian Howard never influenced anyone except possibly some waif whom he picked up. Anthony Blanche is shown as a man of authentic culture and strong intellect. His best moment in the book is when he gives the narrator a talking-to about the danger to an artist of the English cult of charm. Harold Acton can be imagined as saying the same things. Brian Howard lacked the necessary intelligence and perspicacity. He was, unlike Harold Acton and Anthony Blanche, a shallow trifler in the fashions of art and literature, no more. He was not a big enough mind and personality to fill the role allotted to Anthony Blanche in the book. Harold Acton is. But the final test, to my mind, is to remember an undoubted portrait of Howard, Ambrose Silk. That the two characters, Silk and Blanche, were drawn from the same model is quite untenable.

The most remarkable invention in the book is without doubt Sebastian. Evelyn here achieved the very difficult feat of conveying the glamour of youth and privileged position without any recourse to romanticizing; the whole portrait is instinct with reality. The 'unerring sentence of time' may well be that, of all Evelyn's many invented characters, Sebastian is the most successful, and indeed a perfect piece of drawing and painting. For that reason the description of Sebastian's decay is intensely moving.

Another masterpiece is Sebastian's mother, Lady Marchmain. I can think of no writer, learned in Freudian and other psychological doctrine, who has presented so convincing a picture of the kindly mother-figure and *Ewige Frau* who, with the best and kindest intentions, exerts a lethal stranglehold on all around her. As I have said, I met the model but Evelyn did not till much later. Cordelia, Sebastian's youngest sister, is a marvel of characterization too. She is so wonderfully well achieved that Nancy Mitford was moved to the mistaken opinion that the narrator was in love with Cordelia secretly, and not with her older sister, but hid this fact!

Of the minor characters I have discussed the most interesting. Rex Mottram and Anthony Blanche tower over them, and I think Mottram's original was too vain to recognize himself in this only faintly distorting mirror. There was no trouble at all events. Lord Marchmain obviously gave Evelyn many tempting openings, but he did not explore them. He is faintly drawn and only comes to life on his death-bed. But he has one very interesting characteristic which appears a little before then, when he gives a truly snobbish and boastful description of his ancestors. This passage, the delirious wanderings in the clouded mind of a dying man, was mistaken by the Hooperists to be an expression of Evelyn's own snobbishness. If there was a grain of truth in this idea, it was one of microscopic dimensions. To believe it fully, and with resentment, as the arch-denigrator Rose Macaulay did ('Catholic tract' she used to hiss) was to credit Evelyn with no sense of humour at all. In fact what he was doing, and I discussed the episode with him several times, was to indicate, with some romantic overtone, an interesting fact which he had noted in his *vie de château*, namely that 'exaggerated respect for social position' is a much more common weakness among the nobility than among the lesser gentry or the middle classes. If you want to see snobbishness at work full steam, go among those at whom it is aimed. Thackeray knew this. Evelyn knew this. Most of his critics did not.

Then the blemishes. I have mentioned a tendency to overuse of metaphor resulting in sentimentality. The major blemishes are more serious. I see them as two: one partial, one total and beyond redemption by any process of revision.

Let me deal with the partial blemish first.

The novel has two main themes: the Roman Catholic religion and its power over unlikely subjects of its discipline; and the love of the narrator, Charles Ryder, for Sebastian's sister Lady Julia Flyte.

As a Roman Catholic since birth, I have no difficulty in following Evelyn's religious theme, or the emotion which prompted it, or the belief of which it is an expression. But, re-reading the book, I have often wondered what I would make of it if I was not a Catholic, especially if I had Henry Yorke's antipathy to Catholicism? I think I would be led to regard the Catholic Church as institutionalized fantasy, The book which is notable for its breadth of observation and sympathy is, in this respect, solely addressed to believing Catholics and admirers of the Catholic Church. The general reader is rather left in the cold.

To consider the worst blemish.

The theme of Charles Ryder, the narrator, and his love for Julia fails throughout. Reference has been made to Thackeray's *History of Henry Esmond*, and it will be remembered that one of the major strengths of that great book is the captivating figure of Beatrix. Every reader falls in love with her, or at least has no difficulty at all in imagining how a man would do so. Julia is the Beatrix of Brideshead. She never comes to life. From her first appearance as a smart débutante to her last as a disillusioned divorced woman she remains dead as mutton. Evelyn brought every device he could think of to make her vital and irresistible. He made her not only of outstanding beauty, of overwhelming glamour, and radiantly dressed; he made her impulsive, petulant, with the cruelty that has at its command the kindliness that can soothe. But to no avail. The result is a carefully modelled wax mannequin. One may admire the beauty, the glamour and the modelling, but she remains a wax-work. Perhaps Evelyn tried too hard. Perhaps he failed with this central character because he was not drawing in the life-class; no one has yet discerned or suggested a model for Julia.

Julia fails especially because she stands throughout the later part of the novel in contrast, intended to heighten her attraction, to Charles's odious wife Celia. For Celia he had a model, a fact which he confided to me under a vow of secrecy which I will not break. Celia is everything Evelyn hated; shallow, 'smartistic' (a term coined by Cyril Connolly), sophisticated, sham through and through. So, quite unintentionally, is Julia. But Celia is alive and Julia is not. That is the real contrast. Julia's sudden repentance is expressed in a long monologue which Desmond MacCarthy, an enthusiastic admirer of the book, strongly disapproved as he told Evelyn in a letter of June 1945. There can be no doubt that MacCarthy was right and that this recklessly emotional passage is quite unconvincing. In fact Julia adds seriously to the partial blemish of Evelyn's unavailing effort to depict the Catholic faith as a true one deserving of unconditional loyalty. She contributes to that theme an ugly note of religiosity. She makes it ludicrous. It will be remembered that on completion of the main novel, Evelyn wrote in his diary that the last dialogue was 'poor'. It is between Charles Ryder and Julia. Of course it was poor, because all the dialogues between these two are poor.

And what about Hooper? Is not the 'looking-down' upon Hooper a blemish? I think not, for these reasons: it is to return to Puritan censorship of the most damaging kind if it is to be insisted that writers must manifest an edifying moral attitude towards their subjects. Evelyn in the character of the far from lovable Charles Ryder (a possible blemish because 'I' should catch the sympathy of the audience) does look down on Hooper, for explained reasons, but he makes no bones about it. I agree with every critic that looking down is sinful. But – and it is a big but – in the delineation of Hooper the artist's hand is firm, and Hooper gains by that. Readers remember Hooper. They tend to forget Julia. I think it significant that in the numerous letters Evelyn received after the presentation edition the only person to mention Julia was Pansy Lamb, and then in somewhat discouraging terms. Common little Hooper had a colossal advantage over glittering, aristocratic Lady Julia. He was alive.

Anything else? There is one singularity of the book which may be mentioned. This is the only one by Evelyn in which he made use, and good use too, of his adventures in the Arctic Circle. As said already his prose in *Brideshead Revisited* relied much on metaphor. In the last part of the story the master-metaphor is of the arctic trapper or explorer in his hut threatened by the accumulating snow and the inevitable avalanche. Memories of Hugh Lygon may have influenced him.

Unlike nearly all other occasions of publication of his books, this time

Evelyn was much impressed by the criticism of *Brideshead Revisited*. It prompted him to those revisions which, in my opinion, were a waste of time. They did not alter and hardly modified what he had written already. He gave a considered but not his definitive opinion of the book in a preface written after the second revision in 1959, fifteen years after he had completed the book. Some extracts are given here:

'This novel, which is here re-issued with many small additions and some substantial cuts, lost me such esteem as I once enjoyed among my contemporaries and led me into an unfamiliar world of fan-mail and press photographers. Its theme – the operation of divine grace on a group of diverse but closely connected characters – was perhaps presumptuously large, but I make no apology for it. I am less happy about its form, whose more glaring defects may be blamed on the circumstances in which it was written.'

'I wrote with a zest that was quite strange to me and also with impatience to get back to the war. It was a bleak period of present privation and threatening disaster – the period of soya beans and Basic English – and in consequence the book is infused with a kind of gluttony, for food and wine, for the splendours of the recent past, and for rhetorical and ornamental language, which now with a full stomach I find distasteful. I have modified the grosser passages but have not obliterated them because they are an essential part of the book.'

To fall from high to low esteem is always extremely painful, and, contemptuous as Evelyn affected to be of the opinion of the intelligentsia, especially in 1945 when it was hypocritically professing ardent Socialism and the New Puritanism, I think he greatly minded what he called the loss of 'such esteem as I once enjoyed among my contemporaries'.

What distress he felt was effectively but never permanently soothed by an unexpected and unexpectable tribute which he received two years after the book came out. The circumstances were these. In the later years of the war, and for three years after, Max Beerbohm and his first wife Florence lived in a house near Stroud, lent to them by Stephen Crane. He thus lived only eight or nine miles from Stinchcombe. Evelyn had not met Max since the far-off days when he used to dine at the house of E. S. P. Haynes. He doubted if Max would remember him, and he longed to renew the acquaintance. He told me this and I offered to act as go-between, so my wife and I went to stay at Stinchcombe and arranged to take Evelyn and Laura to tea with the Beerbohms. Max was in splendid form and the meeting was a success. Some days after, Evelyn wrote to Max enclosing a copy of *Brideshead Revisited*. On 22 May 1947 Max replied as follows:

'Dear Evelyn Waugh,

'You are wrong about the "high privilege". It was *mine*, in that the Christophers brought the Evelyns to see me. And you are wrong about "homage" too; for you are a more gifted man than ever I was. And again you are wrong in supposing that I had not read "Brideshead Revisited": I had done so at the time when it was first published, and I remember well the great outward brilliance of it and the inward strength and depth. I shall now read it again, for I am one of "those who have the leisure to read a book for the interest of the writer's use of language". And you are a master of language when you write for print: it is only when you write a letter or inscribe a book that you go astray!

'With best regards to Mrs Evelyn,
'Yours sincerely Max Beerbohm.'

# Chapter 16

## 1944-1945

The story must return to the fateful 28 June 1944. Evelyn left Scotland that night and on the morning of the 29th reported to his old acquaintance Randolph Churchill, whom he described as 'preposterous and lovable', at the Dorchester Hotel, London. In his diary he briefly told what happened. Randolph, he related 'asked me to go with him to Croatia in the belief that I should be able to heal the Great Schism between the Catholic and Orthodox churches – something with which he has just become acquainted and finds a hindrance to his war policy'. They left London in the evening of 4 July. They reached Gibraltar on the morning of the 5th, flying on to their first destination, Algiers, which they reached on the afternoon of the same day. In January Duff Cooper had been appointed British representative to General de Gaulle's Committee of National Liberation, in effect, since the 'turn of the tide', the provisional Government of France. Duff set up what had become in effect an embassy in a large villa in Algiers, and thither Randolph and Evelyn went to stay at the end of the first stage of their journey.

They stayed for three days. Diana was overjoyed to see them, but she soon found that Evelyn was remarkably difficult to entertain. As he grew older he became more and more subject to those fits of devastating gloom which all his friends remember with pain. Diana became disturbed. She asked Evelyn what was wrong. Nothing, he said, why did she ask? 'Because you look so utterly miserable', she answered, 'and I wondered if something had happened to make you seriously unhappy.'

'Nothing at all', he said. 'I have been assigned to a very interesting mission with Randolph who is an old friend. My private life is one of the greatest felicity: I have a wife and children whom I love deeply. My professional life is at the moment all that I could wish. I have just finished a book with which I am very pleased, and think is the best I have written. I can say that I have every cause for happiness.'

'Well,' Diana could only say, with a sigh and a laugh, 'I wish you would *show* it a bit more.' But he remained immovably glum till the end of the visit. On 7 July he and Randolph received a movement order to 'proceed' on the next day by RAF plane to Catania in Sicily, from where they would be flown to Jugoslavia later in the day.

They left Algiers on the 8th, but at Catania they were told that weather conditions had delayed their onward flight, so it was not till 10 July that Randolph and Evelyn flew from Catania to Vis, an off-shore island of German-occupied Jugoslavia. Here Tito was in temporary retreat, having been forced from the Dalmatian mainland by a German offensive; here with him was Evelyn's overall chief, the head of 37th British Military Mission, Brigadier Fitzroy Maclean, whom he now met for the first time. Evelyn recorded his impression of the Jugoslav leader: 'Tito like Lesbian.' Thereafter he invariably referred to Tito as 'she' and frequently insisted in his talk that in fact Tito was a woman. This was very rash. Evelyn should have known from his previous experience of the Balkans that he was surrounded by informers. A day or two later Tito joined Fitzroy Maclean's party for a bathe. Fitzroy has related what happened when he introduced Evelyn to the Partisan leader. ' "Captain Waugh", I said, producing Evelyn, "of the Royal Horse Guards." Tito shook him by the hand, looking at him through clear, steady, light-blue eyes. "Ask Captain Waugh", he said, "why he thinks I am a woman".' Fitzroy has told me that this was the only occasion in his experience when Evelyn was at a loss for a reply.

On the next day, or the day after, Evelyn and Randolph flew to Bari. It must be remembered that, on the island of Vis, Evelyn had not wasted his time by indulging exclusively in the pleasures of banqueting and bathing and libelling Tito. He had read Maclean's reports and had looked about him. He wrote in his diary: 'Too early to give any opinion but I have as yet seen nothing that justifies Randolph's assertion to the pope that "the whole trend" was against communism.'

The reference to the Pope needs some explanation. In June while on his way back to England from Jugoslavia, Randolph had stopped for a few days in Rome and thereby been involved in a notable comedy. He had sought a private audience with Pius XII and this was willingly accorded to him as the son of his father. His initiative was a wise move on Randolph's part as 37th Mission was accredited to the Communist leader Tito, support of whom by the British Government was causing anxiety in the Vatican, and Randolph's future part in the mission was to be concerned with mainly Catholic Croatia. The Pope received the son of the British Prime Minister in a friendly way, while Randolph endeavoured, without any apparent success, to allay the Pope's fears about Tito. Then, when the conversation showed signs of reaching its natural end, Randolph, in order to keep it going, told the Pope that he hoped to recruit Evelyn Waugh to his staff. The words seem to convey no meaning. Randolph asked whether His Holiness knew him. Waugh? Waugh? No, the Pope did not know the gentleman's name. But, persisted Randolph, had his Holiness not read Captain Waugh's books? So he wrote books? No, the Pope regretted that he had not read any books by a Captain Waugh. Unperturbed,

Randolph explained his enquiry: 'I thought Captain Waugh's reputation might be known to your Holiness, because *he's* a Catholic too.'

Having been told variations of this story, I once asked Randolph if there was any truth in it, whereupon he gave me the account which I have repeated above. With his ceaseless and vigorous bluster he seemed bewildered by any suggestion that his words had been ill-chosen.

During three days in Bari Randolph and Evelyn collected their supplies, established a parachute-supply system with the RAF and arranged their own flight to Croatia. Their destination was Topusko, about forty miles south of Zagreb. They left on the evening of 16 July, and it is a matter for wonder that any of them survived. What happened is best told in the words of Evelyn's diary:

'As soon as we flew out to sea the lights were put out and we flew in darkness. After some hours I was conscious by my ears that we were descending and circling the airfield. Then we suddenly shot upwards and the next thing I knew was that I was walking in a cornfield by the light of the burning aeroplane talking to a strange British officer about the progress of the war in a detached fashion and that he was saying, " You'd better sit down for a bit, Skipper".'

Randolph and Evelyn were back in Bari by the 18th, in the British military hospital there. They were given leave for convalescence and on about 10 September 1944 Randolph and Evelyn set out again for Croatia, leaving Rome by RAF aircraft for Topusko, the Partisan Headquarters.


The political and military situations in Jugoslavia were complicated beyond all possibilities of simple outline description. Especially is this true in writing for the English-speaking reader. There is no episode either in his experience or 'folk-memory' which is likely to provoke thoughts of a parallel, unless it is the situation, whose unravelment defies all but specialist historians, of Scotland in the early years of the Puritan Commonwealth, the situation terminated only by Cromwell's crushing military victories and the flight of Charles II.

To have recourse to crude generalizations: here in Jugoslavia in 1944, as in Scotland in the mid seventeenth century, there was a war-situation between the native population and exterior enemies, masked by a fraudulent peace. This war situation in turn masked a civil war situation, both situations involving exterior interests which became more and more closely involved. Great Britain held a foremost place among these exterior nterests in Jugoslavia, and interpreted the situation in oversimplified terms. In foreign policy, it is difficult to make allowance in time of war, when decisions must be made within the hour, for the 'particoloured mind'. Jugoslavia was full of such minds in 1944, for which none of the outside Powers attempted to make allowance.

After the German-Italian conquest of Jugoslavia in 1941, the country had been divided into Independent Croatia (called N.D.H. in newspeak) under the rule of Anton Pavelich, and five occupied zones under the authorities of Germany, Italy, Hungary, Bulgaria and Albania. All areas were the scenes of resistance which were not co-ordinated. The situation has been well summarized, so far as summary is possible, by Stevan K. Pavlowitch: 'So different were the conditions in partitioned Yugoslavia, that in one year there had been three different mass risings, in three different regions, for three different reasons, against three different enemies. In the N.D.H. the Serbs had risen in self-defence against extermination by Croatian pro-Axis extremists. In Serbia they had risen against the Germans in an upsurge of patriotic pro-Allied optimism. In Montenegro, they had risen against an Italian formal attempt to put the clock back [by reviving the defunct Montenegrin Kingdom]. Soon divided into Communists and anti-Communists, the insurgents were thereafter to fight a civil war between themselves which, more often than not, took first place over the original aims of their respective risings.'

Immediately after the conquest, many officers of the defeated royal army had taken to the mountains with their weapons, leading armed bands of their soldiers, determined to fight on. To quote from Elizabeth Wiskemann's *Europe of The Dictators*: 'The best known of them was Draza Mihailovich who with a mixed following established himself ... in western Serbia on 11 May 1941. Mihailovich was the old style of Serb officer, loyal to the Karageorgevich dynasty, disdainful or indifferent towards other Yugoslavs, conservative, Orthodox . . . In keeping with British war-policy to give encouragement to any and all resistance movements in Nazi-dominated Europe, the Government of Winston Churchill gave all the help they could afford to Mihailovich who was recognized as the Jugoslav commander in the field by the Jugoslav King and Government in exile.'

The British Government showed enormous inconsistency in their dealings with resistance movements. Insurgents in France, in far more frequent communication with London and much better if not lavishly supplied from England, were continually being held back from premature action by the Government departments responsible for contact with them. In distant Jugoslavia the resistance, first headed by Mihailovich, followed the same waiting policy but thus became the cause of British impatience. After a publicity-honeymoon during which, with BBC aid, Mihailovich was presented to the British and American radio-listenership as the supreme hero of freedom, Winston Churchill and his advisers demanded quicker results than were forthcoming. On his side Mihailovich insisted that he and his followers must bide their time, till an Allied landing in force was imminent or had been achieved. This was precisely the policy which the British Government imposed, often with difficulty, on the French Resistance, but when it was spontaneously carried out by the Jugoslav Resistance, it was censured as showing a half-hearted attitude. Mihailovich was accused, and in fact was guilty of clandestine and local accommodations with the Germans and Italians. He did this through necessity in common with all Resistance movements. In the case of the French these actions were understood in London; in the case of Mihailovich they came to be regarded as double-dealing.

The great discrepancy between British treatment of the French and Jugoslav resistances may possibly be explained by the fact that though it went against Winston Churchill's own strategical preference, the pressure for a vast-scale offensive, a 'second front', in northern France and not in the Balkans, was too strong to be resisted. If the French Resistance bided its time it would enjoy its logical military reward when the second front opened, as it had done by the time that concerns us. But a Jugoslav biding of time was likely to receive the meagrest military reward because no second front was likely to open there while the outcome of the war was in any doubt at all. Yet to abandon all aid to the Jugoslav Resistance was to give the Germans a temporary but real advantage and to heighten Russian suspicion of the West, already extreme enough. The British felt themselves tied to an ineffective and doubtfully loyal resistance.

In 1944 a heaven-sent solution appeared to British policy-makers in the person of the Communist leader Josip Broz who has already appeared in this story under his *nom de guerre* Tito. He was far more interested in the civil war than in the world war and he saw his enemy primarily in the figure of Mihailovich, as Mihailovich saw his main enemy in Tito. As leader of 'the Partisans' as his followers were called (while the followers of Mihailovich were usually called 'Chetniks') Tito enjoyed one great advantage over his rival and enemy. He could 'sell himself'; he could put himself across. Mihailovich could not. If ever the telegraphic correspondence between Winston Churchill and Mihailovich is published, blame for the Prime Minister's apparent disloyalty to Mihailovich is likely to be weakened by praise for his patience. Mihailovich was averse to a plain answer to a plain question and enjoyed long-winded circumlocutions involving a great deal of theological matter. Tito replied to over-simplified questions with over-simplified answers. This was much more to official taste. He appeared moreover to see his main enemy in the Germans and made it seem that he was only prevented from successful campaigns against them by the hostility of Mihailovich. How much if any truth there was in this remains a matter for debate.

The British first made contact with Tito in 1943 through S.O.E. and in the person of William Deakin, a young Fellow of Wadham College,

Oxford. Later in the year, a further mission to Tito, with wider authority to negotiate, was headed by the former diplomat Fitzroy Maclean. This was the mission (37th) to which Evelyn was later accredited. The major result of the reports received by the Prime Minister from Deakin and Maclean was that British material aid and political support were switched from Mihailovich to Tito.

The long-term merit of the new course depended on whether 'satisfactory relations' could in fact be established with the Communists of Jugoslavia. Like most such enterprises in the thirties and forties this act of appeasement failed in the political sphere. It soothed neither the Russians nor the Jugoslav Left, neither Stalin nor Tito. Elizabeth Wiskemann ably summed up the results of the British new course:

'It was a curious situation. The Russians had given publicity to Tito because it suited them to do so, but they proved unreliable allies of the Yugoslav Partisans from the beginning, since Stalin did not like nations to free themselves even when their liberators were Communists. Tito, on the other hand, was so good a Communist that he suspected the British of "imperialistic" motives, although they proved to be his most serious and reliable allies, ignoring ideology and judging only by results.'

Such in crude terms was the extraordinary situation to which Randolph and Evelyn flew in September 1944. If this outline is found easy to follow, this is probably an indication of its inadequacy. Every statement made above is open to much qualification, and the situation contained many elements not mentioned in this crude guide: racial, religious, historical, economic and ideological. It is doubtful if any member of 37th Military Mission completely mastered the problem.

Evelyn had been chosen officially for membership of 37th Military Mission because it was thought that as a Catholic he would be well placed to help in negotiations with Croatian leaders who were his co-religionists. There can be little doubt that Evelyn, as a Catholic, was able to discover from Catholic clergymen a great deal that would otherwise have remained unknown about the religious situation in Jugoslavia, discoveries which were not welcome to his superiors as will shortly appear. But as a member of a mission formally accredited to Marshal Tito he was not conveniently placed. His detestation of Communism was in no way abated, and as pro-Russian hysteria increased among Englishmen, and as the Kingsley Martin Youth Brigade became more and more the mouthpiece of current political opinion, so did his tendency to reaction deepen.

Admirable as his reaction may appear in retrospect, he suffered from the myopia which afflicts most writers, and artists of any kind, when they mix in or are forced into politics. Like all reactionaries, he was incapable of a positive proposition. He saw through Tito in 1944 as surely as Elizabeth Wiskemann did, writing twenty-two years later; but he had no alternative British policy to suggest in the place of the ruthless pragmatic solution implicit in the reports of Deakin and Maclean. Unlike most opponents of the new British course, however, he never became an admirer of the unfortunate Mihailovich.

During their first month together at Topusko, Randolph and Evelyn had little to do beyond making acquaintances. They grew increasingly aware of the suspicion by which they were surrounded. Evelyn recorded in his diary on 24 September: 'The [Partisan] staff have shown anxiety about our activities, primarily, I think, Randolph's drunken political conversations. Time passes slowly.' As always in Slavonic countries the routine was enlivened by the occasional banquet, at one of which Evelyn noted that there were: 'Rousing choruses in Russian, Yugoslav, and a language said to be English; a propaganda play from the Russian about a boy getting a medal from the State school; a dialogue between Hitler and Reaction, played by a kind of witch; and a play about a cowardly soldier who becomes brave through shooting a German. My Communist neighbour said, "You see, in spite of war we have the arts".'

Early in October they witnessed action near by. Evelyn did not state whether the enemy were Chetniks, collaborationist Croats, or Germans, but, whatever the facts of the case, he was not impressed. A day or two after there occurred an incident typical of Communist society. A peasant party leader came from Zagreb to visit Randolph and to discuss an alliance with Communists. As he left the house he was carried off by the secret police. Evelyn recorded: 'Randolph, half drunk, rushed off to see Hebrang, the Communist boss, and has been typing endless signals ever since.' What happened to the unfortunate party leader was not discovered. For the 13 October there is a diary entry which most readers of the diary may have anticipated: 'Randolph and I at dinner – I wondering how long I could bear his company, and he I think faintly conscious of strain.' But rescue, in the form of additional company, was immediately at hand.

When Randolph went to London in June he was not only in search of Evelyn as a companion, but of his friend and exact contemporary Lord Birkenhead. While in the case of Evelyn the commanding officer concerned was only too anxious to expedite the secondment, it was otherwise with Freddy Birkenhead. He was working in the Political Warfare Executive (P.W.E.) and his superiors, landed with a certain proportion of throw-outs and crooks, were loth to part with this gifted man who, unlike Evelyn, was easy to get on with and made friends wherever he went. So the secondment took a long time. It took so long, in fact, that when Freddy arrived, Randolph and Evelyn seem to have literally forgotten that he was expected. Witty, highly educated, the best of companions, Freddy's arrival came as a great joy in a period of great gloom.

Not long after Freddy's arrival Belgrade fell. The German defeat was everywhere visible, even, according to some eye-witness records, in the bomb-shelter of the demented Führer himself. Yet there were still seven months of war to endure. Evelyn was to see no more battle action except for one minor occasion which occurred on 22 October 1944. It would appear likely that an informer had told the Germans that at Topusko there was a British mission headed by no less a person than Winston Churchill's son, Randolph. It would seem likely that the Germans, always liable to be over-influenced by famous names and personalities, and probably believing that Randolph, through his august parentage, was an enormously influential member of the House of Commons, supposed that the annihilation of the sub-mission would be a catastrophic blow to the Allies. They therefore mounted (this is still guesswork) a bombing raid on Topusko. But the days had gone by when the Germans possessed air power sufficient to annihilate localities, least of all in a minor theatre of war. Even the ill-informed Germans did not believe Randolph to be a target worth the full offensive power of their hard-pressed Air Force. So on the 22nd a minor air raid was made on Topusko in the hope of a lucky hit. I follow an account of what happened given to me by Randolph.

On hearing the alert, Randolph summoned the household together and ordered them to the fields where they took refuge in a ditch. Evelyn followed them, the last out of the house, and the weather being cold he put on a sheepskin coat of local make, bright white in colour. While the rest of them were accommodating themselves in the ditch, Evelyn remained outside in the field watching the oncoming German aircraft which soon began the dropping of bombs and machine-gunning. Randolph screamed to him to get into the ditch, but he did not move. Then in furious rage Randolph ordered him to take off his coat at least. This last order he obeyed but in no helpful manner, throwing the white coat on the ground where it provided as fine and perhaps more conspicuous target for the airmen as it had done on his back. The raid did not last long; little damage was done, and none to Randolph's headquarters. When it was over, with no following parachute descent, the party returned to the house and sat down to breakfast. Randolph wished to smooth down the acrimony of the preceding hour. He told Evelyn he was sorry if he had been offensively rude to him. Evelyn replied, according to Randolph: 'It was not your rudeness that offended me, but your cowardice.' (According to Freddy Birkenhead's account in Mr Pryce-Jones's book, this exchange occured at least a day later. He differs from Randolph's account in many particulars.)

Randolph related that after this incident it was clear to him that they must part. 'Now Evelyn,' he said, 'you can't expect me to stand for this.

We must go different ways.' Evelyn agreed. 'Can't you find me' he asked, 'some nice little mission in some other part of the country?'

That was the difficulty: 'some other part of the country'. In spite of their manifest defeat the Germans and their Jugoslav collaborators were still too thick on the ground to allow any but the most restricted movement. So Evelyn and Randolph remained doomed to propinquity.

Evelyn's affection for Randolph was never wholly extinguished, but burned low at frequent moments of which this was one. He wrote at the time: 'The facts are that he is a bore – with no intellectual invention or agility – has a child-like retentive memory and repetition takes the place of thought. He has set himself very low aims and has not the self-control to pursue them steadfastly. He has no independence of character and his engaging affection comes from this. He is not a good companion for a long period, but the conclusion is always the same – that no one else would have chosen me nor would anyone else have accepted him. We are both at the end of our tether as far as war work is concerned and must make what we can of it.'

November passed very much along the same lines as October had. Randolph's mission was involved in no action of war. The three men got more on each other's nerves. Three incidents may be recalled from the diaries. The first is political. According to an entry made on 3 November, the local Communist boss, Matija Hebrang came to dine with the mission. He 'was quite explicit about Communist aims here, contrasting the movement here with that in Greece where they had attempted to seize power first and then beat the Germans; here they fought the Germans first and were now prepared to seize power. 'The time has come when we can begin to ask those who have fought with us what their aims are after the war.' 'Randolph', the entry concludes, 'was too drunk and too eager to speak himself to appreciate what was said.' The last sentence can be taken with some reserve since Evelyn, as mentioned already, was apt to exaggerate other people's excesses in drink as much as he did his own. But of Randolph's garrulousness exaggeration is hardly possible. It was this that led to the second incident, a personal one. Driven mad by Randolph's ceaseless torrent of speech, Evelyn and Freddy invested money in a scheme to confine him to silence. They each bet him £10 that he could not read the Holy Bible through in a stated number of days. Randolph immediately agreed. The endeavour to maintain Randolph in silence failed from the beginning as, in spite of the advantages of an Eton and Oxford education, he remained to the end of his days almost incredibly ill-read. (Once when challeged by Cyril Connolly to say who Sainte-Beuve was, he replied that she was an abbess celebrated for her sanctity in medieval France.) He could not refrain from commentary. The Bible came to him as something new. 'I say', he cried on one occasion, 'did you know this came in the Bible, "Bring my grey hairs with sorrow to the grave?"' He was as thrilled at this new discovery as he had been earlier by that of the Great Schism. But Randolph's most frequent commentary on the great revelation seems to have been: 'God! Isn't God a shit!'

The third incident, also personal, is simply stated. An entry of 20 November 1944 tells that the proofs (presumably, by this time, the page-proofs) of *Brideshead Revisited* arrived. Evelyn corrected them in his room in Randolph's little headquarter house. He stated in his diary that he suffered much anxiety as to whether the precious document would ever reach England. It did, by good luck.

In pursuit of his very reasonable wish to find employment for Evelyn elsewhere than in Topusko Randolph had not been idle. He had intrigued for a transfer. In November his desire was fulfilled but in over-abundant measure. Towards the end of the month, Freddy was ordered to report to Bari, when and how he could, his secondment having been terminated by P.W.E. So Randolph lost his only boon companion. On the last day of the month a signal arrived at Topusko ordering Evelyn to report for duty at Dubrovnik, the southernmost port of Dalmatia. The road was sometimes open, sometimes in the hands of enemy troops. As soon as he could make the journey by jeep, Evelyn set off for his new assignment which he reached after much hazard in the first week of December. Randolph's submission under Fitzroy Maclean, so unexpectedly revealed to me in White's Club in June, was coming to an end.

After Topusko Evelyn saw no more service in a battle zone. His career as a front-line soldier was at an end. But he still had a role to play in the events of World War II, a political not a military role, and in some ways of greater general interest than any other he played from 1939 to 1945. He reached the coastal town of Split on the evening of 4 December, and on the next day met his predecessor from whom he was to take over in Dubrovnik. He received orders to go to Bari for consultation and in the afternoon of the 5th he embarked on a troopship for Brindisi which he reached in the early morning of the 6th. On the 7th he drove to Bari. Uncomfortable as life was at that time in Italy, it was preferable to the privations and tensions of Topusko, especially as in Bari Evelyn found no lack of friends, among them Freddy Birkenhead, William Deakin, Constant Lambert, an Oxford friend Charlie Brocklehurst, and not very far off at San Severo, Dorothy Lygon. In the liberated part of Italy where he was, he could enjoy the unaccustomed pleasure of going about freely.

On 9 December he made the following important entry in his diary: 'Busy and rather weary. Sent a signal to Fitzroy Maclean seeking authority to make an enquiry and a report on the religious situation.' Fitzroy gave the authority and thus began Evelyn's last notable activity in the war.

There was relatively little religious persecution at Topusko while Evelyn, Randolph and Freddy had lived there under the ever suspicious eyes of Partisan headquarters, but Evelyn had sensed an enmity to Christianity in Tito's following. Unlike Randolph he had listened to Hebrang's indiscretions and had drawn the irresistible conclusions: Jugoslavia was being converted, as rapidly as possible, to anti-religious Communism.

On 18 December Evelyn sailed from Bari to Dubrovnik to take charge of his 'nice little mission' which proved to be the reverse of nice, though perhaps it was nicer than Topusko. He stayed in Dubrovnik for a little over two months. His main preoccupation was his self-imposed duty of enquiring into the state of religious toleration and its opposite in the emerging Jugoslavia of Dictator Tito. He also found himself involved in the affairs of a family named Mustapic who claimed British national status. He found their situation perplexing and strongly suspected that Mrs Mustapic and her 'daughters' constituted a house of ill fame.

On 6 January 1945, the feast of the Epiphany, Evelyn made a very interesting note in his diary: 'Communion at the Franciscan church. I had never before realized how specially Epiphany is the feast of artists – twelve days late after St Joseph & the angels and the shepherds & even the ox and the ass the exotic caravan arrives with its black pages and ostrich plumes, brought there by book-learning and speculation; they have had a long journey across the desert, the splendid gifts are travel-worn & not nearly so splendid as they looked when they were being packed up in Babylon, they have made the most disastrous mistakes – they even asked the way of Herod & provoked the massacre of the innocents – but they got to Bethlehem in the end & their gifts are accepted, prophetic gifts that find their way into the language of the church in a number of places. It is a very complete allegory.' Here was the germ of the finest piece of poetic prose Evelyn was to write, in St Helena's prayer at Bethlehem which occurs in his only historical novel. The Epiphany remained his favourite Church feast.

On 7 January he received from Nancy Mitford first news about the reception of *Brideshead Revisited*. She declared the book a classic. Soon letters of congratulation began to arrive thick and fast and Evelyn enjoyed the first fruits of his great literary success in Dubrovnik, amid people who knew nothing about it, and among British colleagues who for the most part were unaware that he was a writer by profession, and would not have been favourably impressed if they had known.

Early in the new year Evelyn made friends in Dubrovnik with a sculptor named Paravicini from whom he commissioned a portrait bust of himself for £50. He told the artist that he wished the bust to be executed in the style of Roubiliac. According to Evelyn's account he said: '*J'ai le gout de*

*Prince Paul. Faites-moi comme un oeuvre de Roubiliac'*, to which Paravicini replied: '*Mais mon capitaine, vous manquez le personnage.*'

When completed the bust presented a competent likeness of Evelyn. In time he got it back to England where it was given a place on the sideboard in the dining-room, first at Piers Court and then at his last home, Combe Florey near Taunton. It was always crowned by his Royal Horse Guards cap, and still is *in ejus memoriam* at the time of writing.

As may be imagined Evelyn's investigations did not endear him to the Partisan authorities who were quick to notice his dislike of Communism. They endeavoured to frustrate him by every sort of administrative obstruction, their principal aim being to manoeuvre him out of Dubrovnik and his dangerous association with clergymen. He asked for his recall. The desired instructions came, and on 20 February he sailed from Dubrovnik to Bari. He never returned to Jugoslavia.

His immediate superior in Bari was Major John Clarke with whom Evelyn enjoyed pleasant relations. He immediately approved of Evelyn's plans for himself. These were to go to Rome with the object of obtaining a private audience of the Pope; to write a full report on the religious situation in Jugoslavia; then to return to England where he would submit the report to the Foreign Office (who had expressed their great interest) for transmission by them to Fitzroy Maclean. While at Bari he heard a piece of news which provoked him to extend his plans. The Foreign Office along with most other ministries were suffering in 1945, as they had done in 1918, from a shortage of personnel after several years in which there had been no intake of young men. In these circumstances the Civil Service was prepared to offer appointments on a regular footing to men and women who, through the chance of war, had acquired rare and valuable experience. Those responsible for Foreign Office appointments had let 37th Military Mission know that mission members would have favourable consideration if they applied for consular posts in Jugoslavia. Determined to do everything he could to make the authorities aware of Communist religious persecution, and if possible to mitigate it, Evelyn sent in his name as an applicant. He was encouraged in this by Deakin ('sympathetic to my consular ambition') who was evidently beginning to have second thoughts about Tito. The Foreign Office has had some odd consuls in its time. (Sir Richard Burton was one.) But it did not take on Consul Waugh. He would not have been happy in his post, wherever it might have been.

On 24 February he left Bari for Rome. He was well supplied with introductions. One of them was from myself to John de Salis who had a wide Vatican acquaintance. They were all of a kind to help him in his aim of being received by the Pope in private audience. He met Sir Francis D'Arcy Osborne, the British Minister to the Holy See, who reminded him of Lord Beauchamp. He met Cardinals Tardini and Montini, the men closest to the Pope, and President Roosevelt's special envoy Myron C. Taylor 'elderly, handsome, obtuse'. A great joy to him was the arrival in Rome of his friends Douglas and Mia Woodruff.

On 2 March his purpose was attained. Evelyn's diary record of his audience with Pius XII is the only one there is. It is unhappily meagre, but he never enlarged on it so it must do: 'Private audience at 9.30. Just time to step into St Peter's and pray for guidance. Then into Cortile Damasos [Cortile di San Damaso] up the lift to the second floor – through a series of dazzling ante-rooms full of men who looked like the general staff of King Bomba, then without waiting at all into the presence. A white figure at a table in a general background of splendour but I was unable to look about. Genuflected three times & sat by his side. I was warned that his English was parrot talk so loudly asked to speak French. Embarked at once on Jugo Slav Church affairs, gave him brief résumé, mentioned Ritoig. He took it all in, said " Ca n'est pas la liberté," then gave his English parrot talk of how many children had I and that he saw the naval review at Portsmouth. Gave me rosaries for my children and a "special" blessing. But I left him convinced that he had understood what I came for. That was all I asked.' It should be explained that Mgr. Ritoig was the dean of St Mark's Cathedral in Zagreb, one of the very few Catholic Church dignitaries to have fully associated himself with Tito's national movement. As he had been associated first with the royalists and then with the Italians before his latest conversion, he was looked on by most people as a peculiarly evil kind of Vicar of Bray, but Evelyn, surprisingly enough, took a favourable view of him.

Later in the day on 2 March Evelyn had a further interview with Cardinal Tardini who conveyed to him the good impression that he had made on Pius XII. The cardinal said that the Pope admired the work Evelyn was doing 'for the church & civilization,' and (unconsciously quoting Napoleon III) added his own encouragement by saying: 'Continuez.'

Evelyn continued the good work but it was nearly brought to nothing by a disaster. On 4 March, Evelyn returned to Bari. There he started preparatory work on his report. On the 9th occurred the disaster. He changed his lodgings, leaving his hotel in Bari for the villa nearby where the Mission had its local headquarters. His baggage was stolen in the course of the move. It contained not only his most necessary personal belongings but all the documents containing the evidence on which he proposed to base the report. He was in despair until the next day, the 10th, when the military police reported the recovery of the baggage. On the next day Evelyn sat down to complete the report. He worked hard and by 13 March he had written half of it. On the same day he heard that Fitzroy Maclean was shortly coming out of Jugoslavia, and Evelyn decided that it would be politic for him to go to London as soon as possible. If he did this, the completed report could be given to Maclean on the spot with himself available to join in discussion of it. On 15 March he 'flew straight & smooth over the cloud which opened at 12.20 to reveal Versailles below us.' That night he was in London. He stayed at the Hyde Park Hotel in Basil Bennet's personal suite and dined with his old comrade of No. 8 Commando, Peter Beatty, at White's, the place where, in a sense, his Jugoslavia adventure had begun.

Evelyn's main occupation on his return was the report which will be considered later. This was varied by entertaining the friends from whom he had long been separated; his male friends usually at White's, his women friends usually at Wilton's for whose manager Mr Marks he had a special affection, and whom he introduced, quite unrecognizably, into his histori-cal novel. The toil of writing the report was also varied by visits to the Foreign Office where he often met Mr (later Sir Edwin) Chapman Andrews. They had known each other in Ethiopia, a country in whose destiny 'Chappie' had played a significant part in 1940, and from whom Evelyn received hope and encouragement in his 'consular ambitions'.

At the end of March Evelyn presented his report. On that occasion he had an interview with Mr Douglas Howard 'who', he related in his diary, 'could not give an answer to my request to circulate my Croatian report among Catholic MPs, Bishops & editors. "Please don't think I am being obstructive". How often I have heard that; how often I shall hear it again.'

The report should now be briefly considered.

As mentioned earlier Tito and his Communist Partisan following had appeared to the British Government as a deliverance from an apparently insoluble politico-military problem. Though Tito had not disguised the fact that he was suspicious of his British allies, the latter had in no way changed their minds about him. In the Foreign Office and the War Office he was the centre of hope and admiration. The enthusiasm for the USSR was not at the feverish pitch which it had reached in 1942 but it was still strong in 1945 and from it the Communist Jugoslav leader enjoyed much reflected warmth and esteem. It is not surprising that such a climate of opinion was not favourable to Evelyn's report which was entitled *Church and State in Liberated Croatia* and which opened, after a synopsis, with the following introductory paragraphs:

'Whatever changes may have taken place recently in the heart of Russia, the Communists of Yugoslavia still profess a pure Marxist faith.

'There is a fundamental, irreconcilable difference (which it is not the purpose of this report to examine in detail) between communism and Christianity in their conceptions of the nature and purpose of man . . .

'In the Orthodox Church a long tradition of subservience to temporal rulers, Emperors, and Sultans, has reduced the legacy of the apostles to, at the best, an oriental mysticism remote from human obligations or, at the worst, to the mere observance of a rite unconnected with moral and social duty and, accordingly, amenable to absorption in the civil government.

'Hitherto communism has mainly dealt with Orthodox Christians; now it is advancing West raising an unsolved (and perhaps insoluble) problem in the relations of Church and State.

'Croatia, where, as the Germans retreat, a predominantly Catholic country is falling under a predominantly Communist rule, provides an example of this problem, though local peculiarities, examined below, both of Church and State, complicate and confuse the essential issue.

'The help given to the National Liberation movement by Great Britain has been extensive and, in the opinion of many observers, decisive. Some responsibility therefore rests with Great Britain for the consequence of its success.'

This line of thought was not in accord with that prevailing in Whitehall. Nor was the tone of the second section, entitled *The Party*, which opened thus:

'The Yugoslav Army of National Liberation, popularly called "Partisans", is an organized revolutionary army whose main characteristics are extreme youth, ignorance, hardiness, pride in the immediate past, confidence in the immediate future, intolerance of dissent, xenophobia, comradeship, sobriety, chastity.

'The régime which they impose in the rear of the retreating Germans has, to the superficial observer, most of the signs of nazism . . .'

As mentioned earlier Evelyn, unlike Randolph, listened when Hebrang was perhaps telling more than he was supposed to. Evelyn now conveyed this information.

'Power resides only in the party working through the commissars in the army, through O.Z.N.A. (the secret police), and through the party members in the committees . . . The party has learned the lesson of Spain that heresy hunts must not be indulged in war-time and that a social revolution against private property and the Church must not be attempted until complete power is attained.'

The quotations given so far may suggest a certain bias in the report. The impression is not a false one but unless one reads the whole report it is easily exaggerated. What bias there is, and it is not slight, is greatly corrected in the fifth chapter of the report entitled 'The Church and the Ustase'. This body of men (more correctly called the Ustashas, meaning 'The Upright') played a role in Pavelich Croatia analogous to that of the Communist Party in the USSR, the Sturm Abteilungen in Nazi Germany, the Falangists in Nationalist Spain. They were the activists of the Croatian new order, and like their protectors and models in Fascist Italy, they did not stop short of murder. It was they who had assassinated King

Alexander in Marseilles in 1934 with Fascist connivance and after Fascist training.

When these dubiously upright men came into power under Pavelich after the Allied defeat in 1941, they instituted a regime of revenge in the newly independent state, mostly directed against the Serbs, a large majority in the country as a whole but a minority in Croatia. This nationalist quarrel immediately turned into a religious one: between the Catholic Croats and the Orthodox Serbs. There ensued in late June 1941 scenes of persecution such as had not been witnessed in that part of the world for more than three hundred years. To add to the crimes of the new regime, Pavelich sought to obtain German goodwill by a persecution of the Jews of Croatia, a minority too small to have influence or to excite anti-Semitism. The Catholic clergy of Croatia (whom Evelyn would like to have defended) did not, with few exceptions of which the Archbishop of Zagreb seems to have been the finest, give an edifying or inspiring example. The Franciscans were prominent among the persecutors.

The penultimate chapter was entitled 'The Church and the Partisans.' It is almost as long as all the preceding parts of the report, too long for any representative quotation. Evelyn begins by restating the irreconcilable and mutual opposition of the Catholic Church and Communism. He indicates, what is not likely to be seriously questioned today, that the Tito regime was determined to emerge triumphantly from an absolutely inevitable struggle with the Churches, especially the Catholic Church.

This long, chilling, carefully evidenced chapter is followed by a short and interesting one entitled 'Partisans and the Orthodox Church.' Evelyn pointed out that Titoist policy towards the Orthodox Church was far less brutal because in this case Tito was dealing with an overall national majority, because he needed to conform with Russian policy which had been forced into a less intolerant attitude towards the Orthodox Church than its usual one by the stress of war, and because, if Tito had any ambition to become an overlord of the Balkans, he needed Orthodox Church support. Whether Tito entertained the last-named ambition is still open to debate. If he did, it was quelled by his later quarrel with Stalin and the Russian Communist leaders, a quarrel of which there was then no sign.

The report ends with a paragraph that is likely to strike one on a first reading as unremarkable. It was to lead to important consequences, not as regards policy, as Evelyn certainly hoped, but as regards himself personally.

'Conclusion.

'Great Britain has given great assistance to the establishment of a régime which threatens to destroy the Catholic Faith in a region where there are now some 5,000,000 Catholics. There is no hope for them from inside their country. Marshal Tito has paid lip-service to many liberal principles, including that of freedom of worship. He may still be amenable to advice from his powerful Allies. If he were informed that the position of the Church under his rule is causing alarm, that it is not the policy of the Allies to destroy one illiberal régime in Europe in order to substitute another, that a Government which violates one of the principles of the Atlantic Charter cannot be regarded as acceptable, he might be induced to modify his policy far enough to give the Church a chance of life.'

The report was submitted to Fitzroy Maclean through the Foreign Office, in the last part of March 1945. By that time Fitzroy was no longer Evelyn's chief as 37th Military Mission had been disbanded. Though the report was addressed to him, under the new circumstances it was treated as a report to the Foreign Office. It was referred to the Secretary of State, Anthony Eden, by whose authority a copy was sent for comment to the newly appointed British Ambassador in Belgrade, Ralph Stevenson. His comments were received early in May.

By that time the report had already aroused feeling in the Foreign Office. This was inevitable, because if what it said was to be taken as authoritative in the full sense, both as regards the recorded facts and its conclusion, then British foreign policy stood accused of an irrevocable and profound misjudgement. By no conceivable political twist could the error be rectified, if error it was. To repudiate Tito unless he conformed to conditions which in the nature of things were wholly unacceptable to him, to withdraw the recklessly given friendship so late in the day, was to jeopardize not only British prestige in the Balkans, then being exerted to its full in the hope of a satisfactory termination to the state of civil war in Greece, but it was to exacerbate, perhaps to a fatal degree, the worsening relations of Great Britain and all western Europe with the Russia of Stalin.

From the Foreign Office point of view the hope of a solution to this problem lay in two possibilities: to be able to discredit the report, or to discredit its author. Ralph Stevenson's reply was impatiently awaited.

In the meantime the Foreign Office view was lucidly stated by the Permanent Undersecretary, Sir Orme Sargent. He had been informed of Evelyn's wish to be allowed to distribute the document among leading Catholics. Immediately after reading it on 29 March Sargent wrote as follows:

'I would like Brig. Maclean's views on this report as well as those of Mr Stevenson. This is an official report written by a military officer while on duty; and I see no reason why we should agree that the author should use it as propaganda against the Government's policy. Not only must it not be published, but he should be told that if he shows it to persons outside the F.O. & W.O. he does so without consent & at his own risk.'

Until Stevenson's report arrived the Foreign Office was without the necessary ammunition to counter-attack on the policy front so it followed that before the ammunition train arrived from Belgrade the question was debated whether or not to have resort to disciplinary action in the hope of discrediting Evelyn.

It was known that in Rome Evelyn had seen several leading Churchmen, Cardinals Montini and Tardini among them, and that he had been received in private audience by the Pope. Those in the Foreign Office who were concerned in the affair suspected that Evelyn had had no scruples about conveying 'information gathered in the course of duty to outside persons'. Their suspicions were justified, as is perfectly clear from Evelyn's diary. The question arose as to whether, if the suspicions could be grounded on evidence, Evelyn should not be court martialled, at the request of the Foreign Office, for calculated indiscretions 'not in the interest of His Majesty's Government'. Had a decision in that sense been taken, the court martial would probably have been held *in camera*, for security reasons, but there was always the Press, restive after five and a half years irksome censorship, and Evelyn was a first-rate journalist. A Press explosion was the likely result – and how Evelyn would have enjoyed it! These possibilities were foreseen in the Foreign Office, and the effort to discredit the author of the report by these means was abandoned in favour of the effort to discredit the report itself. A key role in the abandonment of the proposition to have Evelyn court martialled was taken by Fitzroy Maclean when, in response to Orme Sargent's request, he gave his views by word of mouth to one of Sargent's colleagues at the beginning of April. When he came to the question of the proposed court martial Fitzroy wisely avoided all suggestion of acting through loyalty (though I have no doubt he did) by basing his argument on strictly technical considerations. 'Brigadier Maclean suggested that there might be some difficulty in catching Captain Waugh under the Official Secrets Acts. The Report was written in London and was communicated to Brigadier Maclean after he had ceased to be the head of No 37 Military Mission. This was not known when previous minutes were written.'

Then on 17 May 1945, the ammunition at last arrived from Belgrade.

Ralph Stevenson's despatch to Anthony Eden was just what the Foreign Office wanted. Couched in that anodyne style of which the diplomatic service is master, and plentifully stocked with the more impressive kind of cliché, it suavely diminished the pretensions to gravity of Evelyn's report. It stressed that this was essentially a prejudiced document. 'The issue', the ambassador wrote, 'cannot be treated with true impartiality either by Catholics or non-Catholics and Captain Waugh is no exception to this rule.' In the next paragraph he followed this up with a harder thrust. 'In the atmosphere of intense prejudice and narrow hatred of Balkan civil war and in view of the lack of control which the central authority has often had, and still seems to have, over the more violent members of the movement who, many of them, appear now to be concentrated in O.Z.N.A., it is perhaps surprising that the instances of persecution produced by Captain Waugh should be so few.'

The bulk of the despatch is occupied with showing that the record of the Catholic Church in Jugoslavia was one of much fuller commitment to the common Fascist and Nazi cause than appeared in the report. The ambassador furnished supporting evidence, all strengthening the underlying theme that Evelyn's apparent lack of bias was not genuine but merely contrived. Towards the end occurs this damning passage. 'The Catholic clergy of Dubrovnik provide the source of a large part of the information contained in Captain Waugh's report. The evidence produced by them was translated for Captain Waugh by Mr Carey, the assistant press secretary at this embassy, who points out that significant passages of their evidence have been omitted.' Stevenson supplied enough of the missing information to make the comment all the more deadly. Evelyn seems foolishly to have given way to the temptation to doctor his evidence.

No comment was made by the ambassador on Evelyn's insistence that Great Britain, as Tito's only vigorous supporter in his years of frustration and struggle, had a special responsibility for the type of regime imposed by circumstances on the Jugoslav peoples. His last paragraph contains a comment very characteristic of the period: 'The measure of oppression of the Catholic Church in this country in future will doubtless be the measure of communist influence in the régime.' British official opinion, and British opinion in general, hesitated to accept the unwelcome fact that Tito's regime was not one with Communist influence in it, but *was* a Communist regime. Barrington Ward, as editor of *The Times*, was to persist for several years yet in trying to persuade his readers that Tito was not so illiberal as he appeared. His attitude to Tito (and to Stalin) was not unlike that of his predecessor, Geoffrey Dawson to Hitler and his party. Tyrannical acts and atrocities were played down; worthless concessions and fraudulent elections were played up. Ward and his like, and the 'establishment' of Whitehall were indulging once more in wishful thinking. Evelyn showed political realism.

For all that, Evelyn, with his inexperience of official life, was no match for Ralph Stevenson and Orme Sargent when it came to challenging policy, especially when challenging a policy which could not be altered, and he suffered defeat in the Foreign Office. His disclosures were treated as of no importance.

But he did not give up the struggle. He prepared for a renewed assault. In the middle of May, a new personage makes a brief entry into the story: the formidable French churchman, Cardinal Eugène Tisserant, Secretary of the Congregation of the Eastern Church. This man of honoured memory conveyed to the British Minister to the Holy See a memorandum on Titoist persecution of the Catholic Church. Several members of the concerned departments in the Foreign Office saw in the Tisserant memorandum, which Sir Francis D'Arcy Osborne sent home with a despatch, proof positive that the Cardinal had been shown Evelyn's report. The grounds for the supposition were first that the main contention, namely that British support of Tito gave the British Government a heavy and special responsibility for the character of Tito's regime, was identical with the main contention and conclusion of Evelyn's report, and secondly it was noted that the details of persecution and massacre were similar in both reports. A point to notice is that Evelyn's assertion about Britain's special responsibility for the regime in Jugoslavia was not a subtle one, it was an obvious one, and the coincidence of it being pressed in two independent reports was not remarkable. The similarity in both reports of the details of persecution and murder are probably to be ascribed to nothing more unusual than the fact that in both cases the facts reported are true. (The two accounts are not similar in style.)

The Southern Department of the Foreign Office now concentrated on discrediting Tisserant's memorandum. Advantage was taken of a remark made by Tisserant to D'Arcy Osborne and reported in the latter's despatch: 'Even if certain Catholic ecclesiastics did play a political role during the war', the cardinal had said, 'this is not sufficient reason for slaughtering the whole lot.' The last phrase is clearly a figure of speech and to take it as a precise description of the situation is to turn it into nonsense. This the concerned parties in the Foreign Office hastened to do. Two minutes, of the 28th and 29 May, are revealing:

'The details reported may in many cases be true, but the attitude of the writer, & of Cardinal Tisserant as expressed in his comment, is of course biassed. R8555 puts the question in the right perspective, as Mr Addis minuted. Copy Belgrade.

'There is no reason whatever to suppose that the Partisans are "slaughtering the whole lot", & wild assertions of this kind show how little reliance can be placed on His Eminence's other statements.'

The Chancery of the British Embassy in Belgrade poured a further douche of cold water on Cardinal Tisserant's memorandum. It was finally ignored, not even remembered in England till mentioned, by Mr Anthony Rhodes in his masterly book *The Vatican in The Age of The Dictators 1922–1945.*

That was the end of the Tisserant episode. Had it occurred earlier it would almost certainly have had a deep effect on 'our hero's fortunes'. As it was, he may even have been unaware of it. Sometime between 23 April and 1 May he heard with relief that the Foreign Office (possibly influenced by the events just described) had wisely declined to appoint him to a consular post. He recorded, 'I have the news that my application to go back to Jugo-Slavia has been refused and I am much content. Honour is satisfied. I am glad to have done all I could to go back & glad not to be going.'

Evelyn did not mention that he had in the meanwhile engaged the interest of a fellow Catholic who was a member of Parliament, Captain (later Sir John) McEwen. The latter was one of the relatively few politicians who were alarmed at the surrender of principle in the pursuit of victory.

On 30 May 1945, one of the last days on which the House of Commons sat under the first premiership of Winston Churchill, the following exchange occurred at Question Time.

'*Captain McEwen* asked the Secretary of State for Foreign Affairs what action His Majesty's Government propose to take to alleviate the sufferings of the Catholic population of Croatia under Marshal Tito's regime, in view of the responsibility incurred by Great Britain through the assistance rendered by us to the National Liberation Movement.

'*Mr Eden:* My hon. and gallant Friend will understand that I cannot accept the implication that the assistance rendered by us to the National Liberation Movement of Yugoslavia in the struggle against Germany makes His Majesty's Government responsible for the internal administration of the Yugoslav State. This must remain the responsibility of the Yugoslav Government.

'*Captain McEwen:* Would it not be as well, in any case, to make it clear to Marshal Tito that it is not the policy of the Allied Powers, having got rid of one illiberal Power in Europe, to encourage the substitution of another.'

Anthony Eden was spared the embarrassment of answering Jock McEwen's supplementary by the intervention of the Communist member, William Gallacher, who put up an irrelevant supplementary question of his own. So ended, in a second defeat, Evelyn's battle. Except for debunking articles in the British Press about Tito, Evelyn took no further part in Jugoslavian affairs. His war service was over.

1945, the year of final victory over Hitler and the Nazis, was not Britain's finest hour. The gross needs of war, notably the alliance with Russia, had corroded those British principles which had grown from necessity and idealism and in defence of which the nation had taken up arms. That protest against persecution and massacre should be dismissed with irritation and condemned as bias within the walls of a British ministry would have surprised and pained an earlier generation. That Evelyn was biased is hardly to be denied. Was it just therefore, as the Foreign Office of the time concluded, to ignore Evelyn as a deceptive guide to the situation?

Let the last word be with Anthony Rhodes, writing nearly thirty years after these events, in 1973.

'The whole episode is proof of the strong support given to Marshal Tito by the British Government, disinclined to hear a word against him and his Communist regime, because it was resisting Hitler. Yet events in the Communist "satellite" countries since 1945 – the arrests and persecution of priests, still not abated today – would seem to confirm that Captain Evelyn Waugh's diagnosis of Communist persecution of the Church in the new "satellite" states was broadly correct.'

## Chapter 17

### 1945-1946

The end of the war found Evelyn in the Easton Court Hotel at Chagford. His reflections on his own situation at that historic moment have been quoted already. Some explanation is needed for his reference to a life of St Helena.

When the presentation edition of *Brideshead Revisited* came out, he naturally sent one to Katherine Asquith. In her letter of appreciation she said that she regretted that with his great and proved literary ability he confined himself to fiction and did not write 'a real book'. Unexpectedly he was influenced by this criticism. He may also have believed (I am remembering things he said to me about this time) that he had worked himself out as a novelist, a predicament that all novelists dread. Certainly a long period was to elapse before he again attempted a novel on the scale of *Brideshead Revisited*. Instinct probably told him to lie fallow.

How Evelyn was first drawn to the subject of St Helena is nowhere evidenced, nor how he proposed to write a serious work of history centred on the biography of a person so shadowy. Nothing is known for certain about St Helena beyond that she was the pious mother of the Emperor Constantine, and that in her old age she travelled to the Holy Land where she built churches. Even her famous discovery of the True Cross is suspiciously unmentioned by people writing in or close to her time and in her part of the world. The difficulties of his chosen task were obviously very great, but the attraction of the subject for Evelyn was powerful and remained with him.

He began the writing of this never-to-be-finished work on 7 May, the day before VE day, at Chagford. He persisted (with breakdowns) till well into 1946. He needed to make himself familiar with the fourth-century world, and he read widely and consulted scholars. He recorded in his diary a scene, which I well remember, for 21 February 1946. 'Hurried luncheon with Christopher Sykes, Simon Elwes etc. then to Golders Green to see Prof. Marmostein, a jewish authority on 4th century, venerable, guttural, vague. He tried to convince me that a legend of a sword falling from heaven at a peasant's feet & being used for his decapitation was identical with the story of the Empress digging a bit of wood out of the ground & taking it to Rome.' He was to have some hard things to say of sophisticated men of learning, and some of them may have had an origin in Golders Green. What I chiefly remember of that February occasion was that Evelyn was full of his subject and could hardly speak of anything else.

Yet Evelyn clearly recognized that he had chosen so hazardous a subject that he might fail. Hence frequent abandonment of the book. About four months before the visit to Golders Green last mentioned, in early October 1945, there is this surprising entry in the diary: 'I have begun a novel of school life in 1919 – as untopical a theme as could be found.' How far he progressed and for how long is unknown. No manuscript has survived. Nor has any fragment of the life of St Helena. The first has vanished without trace, the second has vanished leaving a large trace in Evelyn's historical novel.

Evelyn remained some time at Chagford. Piers Court was still occupied by his Dominican tenants who were planning, too slowly for Evelyn's taste, their emigration to permanent quarters. The family were still at Pixton, Laura frequently visiting Chagford or accompanying Evelyn to London.

There is one very sad entry in Evelyn's diary following a visit to Pixton in late April 1945. He saw his old hero Belloc again, now in his last years and losing his reason. 'Poor Mr Belloc', he wrote, '[looks] as though the grave were the only place for him. He has grown a splendid white beard and in his cloak, which with his hat he wears indoors & always, he seemed an archimandrite. He lost & stole whatever went into his pockets; toast, cigarettes, books never appeared like the reverse of a conjuror's hat. He talked incessantly, producing with great clarity the grievances of 40 years ago, that the English worshipped the Germans & respected only wealth in one another, that the rich enslaved the poor by lying to them, that the dons at Oxford are paid by the rich to lie. Perhaps in 40 years time I shall make myself tedious denouncing communism in this way. "The Bank of England would not let Napoleon found an empire." "The French are a Catholic people." At times he was coaxed by the women to sing and then with face alight with simple joy & many lapses of memory, he quavered out the French marching songs and snatches from the music halls of his youth. He is conscious of being decrepit & forgetful but not of being a bore.'

Evelyn met Belloc at least once more after this, at his home in Sussex, but the old man seemed vague as to his visitor's identity.

Evelyn returned to the literary life under happy circumstances. He was enjoying enormous success from *Brideshead Revisited*. The first public edition, published by Chapman and Hall in May 1945, sold out with gratifying financial rewards for the author and needed to be reprinted. In the United States it was even more successful. It was nominated 'Book of the Month' which represented profits worth about $20,000.

Evelyn was conscious that there were flies in the amber. He regretted that his success was marred by coarseness: for every discerning reader of the class of Desmond MacCarthy there were a dozen silly giggling girls who liked reading about lords. He was depressed by gossip on the subject which he heard on a visit to Oxford made with his old friends Frank Pakenham and John Betjeman. 'Sat in Maurice's garden and heard black reports on Brideshead "Cecil Beaton's favourite book." "Connolly does a funny imitation of Marchmain's death bed." "I didn't know you had been in love with Auberon." ' (Evidently some ill-informed person identified Sebastian with Auberon Herbert.)

In common with most writers he affected to be unmoved by bad reviews. A large proportion of them were very silly and were more concerned with manifesting sympathy with the new cult of the common man than with serious literary preoccupations. But he received one or two deadly thrusts. The most deadly, and the one that he most consistently tried to laugh off, came from the formidable American critic, Edmund Wilson.

Evelyn maintained, not quite fallaciously, that Wilson was prejudiced against him on personal grounds; as an anti-Catholic; as an Anglophobe who fanatically resented the very mention of British class-differences; as a man who disliked the author of *Brideshead Revisited*. There was a case of sorts to build on all these premises. But if the last, personal antagonism, was founded in experience, the fault was entirely Evelyn's.

In 1945 the two men had not met. Evelyn only knew Wilson as the author of one of the most remarkable books of criticism written in this century, *Axel's Castle*. Evelyn admired it, as well he might, and the acquaintance might have been of the happiest sort if it had not been for a literary dinner party given by Cyril Connolly, at which the two met in April 1945. Among the guests Evelyn mentioned 'an insignificant Yank named Edmund Wilson', not a precise or telling description.

Towards the end of dinner Edmund Wilson left the room for a while, and one of the young women guests, who was very much up in the literary gossip of London, said to the others: 'Oh this gives me an opportunity to say that no one on any account must ask him about his novel. It's just been refused by his English publisher on the grounds that it's pornographic and he's terribly upset.'

The novel in question was *Memoirs of Hecate County*.

As soon as Edmund Wilson returned to the room Evelyn started a conversation with him. According to Stephen Spender who was present and recalled the occasion after nearly thirty years, it went somewhat as follows:

Evelyn Waugh: Mr Wilson, are we to have the pleasure of reading some new work from your pen?

Edmund Wilson: I have a new book but it's not going to be published in this country.

Evelyn Waugh: Is that your decision or your publisher's?

Edmund Wilson: My publisher.

Evelyn Waugh: Mr Wilson, you must understand that there's a grave paper shortage in this country –

Edmund Wilson: This has nothing to do with the paper shortage.

Evelyn Waugh: But my dear Mr Wilson, what other reason for witholding your book from your English admirers can there possibly be?

Edmund Wilson: There is a different reason.

Evelyn Waugh: Mr. Wilson, I have always hoped that one day we would have the privilege of reading a novel by you.

Edmund Wilson: The book I've referred to is a novel.

Evelyn Waugh: Then what possible reason can there be for your publisher not letting us read it?

Edmund Wilson: They say that it would be banned under the laws relating to pornography.

At this there was a long pause broken by Evelyn saying: 'Mr Wilson, in cases like yours, I always advise publication in Cairo.'

At the time Edmund Wilson was writing *Europe Without Baedeker* and it is Stephen Spender's view that the anti-British animus in that book owed something to this unhappy meeting.

In January 1946 Edmund Wilson had the task of reviewing *Brideshead Revisited* in the United States. His review, like all Edmund Wilson's criticism, was intelligent and sensitive, and this gave all the more edge to his hostility. He approached the subject with some unaccustomed affectation, of writing more in sorrow than in anger. 'The new novel by Evelyn Waugh', he opened, 'has been a bitter blow to this critic.' This did not lead him to underestimate the merits of the comic chapters, but it did lead him to exaggerate the faults of the others. Like many of his inferiors he pressed the accusation of snobbery to excess, and of the famous death scene he descended to this cheap witticism: 'The reader has an uncomfortable feeling that what has caused Mr Waugh's hero to plump on his knees is not, perhaps, the sign of the cross but the prestige, in the person of Lord Marchmain, of one of the oldest families in England.'

There were awkward comparisons with Galsworthy and a last cruel stab when he predicted an immense success for the book, not on account of its merits but on account of its conformity with the qualities required of best-selling trash.

It is impossible to imagine Edmund Wilson as an admirer of *Brideshead Revisited* without the reservations he made. He became increasingly and sometimes hastily impatient of Evelyn's conservatism. He was the most eminent of those who believed that Evelyn reached his zenith in *A Handful of Dust*, then maintained the standard in a lesser book *Put Out More Flags*, and thereafter declined.

The evidence is that Evelyn Waugh was hurt by the disparagement which Edmund Wilson was to repeat in denigrating criticism of his next two books. Many years after this Evelyn was to be interviewed for the *Paris Review* by Belloc's grandson Julian Jebb. Part of the latter's report reads as follows:

Interviewer: Have you found any professional criticism of your work illuminating or helpful? Edmund Wilson, for example?

Waugh: Is he an American?

Interviewer: Yes.

Waugh: I don't think what they have to say is of much interest, do you?

One reason why Evelyn may have resented Edmund Wilson's criticism, and why, apart from his frequent impulse to cruelty, he had behaved so badly to him at the dinner party, was that shortly before the *Brideshead Revisited* article Wilson had accorded the highest praise to Cyril Connolly's book *The Unquiet Grave*. Its contents had first appeared anonymously in Cyril Connolly's monthly magazine *Horizon*, then been published as a book under the pseudonym *Palinurus* in 1944, with an enthusiastic encomium of the 'unknown' author written by the editor of *Horizon*! The book largely consists of nostalgic recollections of and reflections on France, French life, and French culture. At the end of the war in England, when siege conditions had made this island more insular than usual, when emotions of nostalgia were stronger than usual, when those who loved France watched her humiliation with love and grief and passionately admired the heroic defiance of General de Gaulle and the Free French Movement; at this time, when home-produced culture was at a low ebb, Cyril's book with its melancholy, in pleasing contrast to the official optimism of propaganda, was received by a limited though varied public with extravagant acclaim.

Singularly free from literary envy, Evelyn was irritated by this success. He was always irritated by overpraise (as I was to find to my cost a year later), and in this case he especially disliked the insincere anonymity and the fraudulent puff by the real author. He disliked the shape of the book: aphorisms, quotations, brief essays, thrown together under what he took to be a fictitious general design, aided by what he took to be a meaningless reference to classical mythology in the pseudonym Palinurus. He put all this in a review of the book published in *The Tablet* in November 1945. With malign skill he maintained, as he had a strict though far from perfect right to do, that the anonymity of the authorship allowed him complete freedom in guessing what manner of man had written the book. He made merciless fun of the fact that the book was much admired by Lady Cunard (who after the success of *Brideshead Revisited* had unsuccessfully pursued Evelyn with invitations) and the second Lady Rothermere (later to be a very close friend). Evelyn referred to them and their hangers-on as 'the literary ladies of the Dorchester Hotel' and indicated that they had led the success of the book. Cyril refused to read the review for fear it would destroy his friendship with Evelyn, but was eventually persuaded to do so by a friend of both who told Cyril, with doubtful sincerity, that, if read with care, the review was flattering rather than denigratory. He referred to the fact that Evelyn had accorded praise to Cyril's fine mastery of prose; just as Edmund Wilson had to the matchless comedy within *Brideshead Revisited*.

So ended what one may call 'The Edmund Wilson Affair' and its companion picture 'The Palinurus Affair'.

The wider-ranging 'Brideshead Affair', of which these were parts, had still a long way to go, through many episodes, few of which are as worthy of detail as the foregoing. Throughout it all one may note on Evelyn's side an anti-American impetus that was new to him. It may be (and if the surmise is correct it is not to his credit) that it was thus that he expressed his dismay at becoming a best-seller along with many purveyors of rubbish. Sometimes his dismay took the merely brutal form of insulting behaviour. Mary Lygon has told me of an unhappy occasion when she invited him to a dinner party to meet some admirers who included a well-known American theatrical producer and his wife. The last-mentioned addressed him thus: 'Oh Mr Waugh, I have just been reading your new book *Brideshead Revisited*, and I think it's one of the best books I have ever read.' To which Evelyn replied: 'I thought it was good myself, but now that I know that a vulgar, common American woman like yourself admires it, I am not so sure.' After that, as Maimie has said, the dinner party became 'sticky'.

Wit appears, however, in a correspondence at the end of January 1946 between the representative of *Time* and *Life* magazines in London, and Evelyn. The proposition from *Time* and *Life* was put to Evelyn in a letter of which the main subject is in this extract.

'Dear Mr Waugh,

'Some of our New York editors, numbered among your many American admirers, have suggested that we should publish in LIFE a photographic feature dramatizing characters and scenes from your novels. This they wish us to produce as quickly as possible in England, since "Brideshead Revisited" is Book of the Month for January . . .

'LIFE now wishes our staff photographer, David Scherman, to undertake the story in photographs only, and we face a monumental job, combining difficulties of obtaining suitable models, backgrounds, clothes and props . . .'

His co-operation was again asked for, and the hurry and urgency of the enterprise were again stressed. 'Without consulting you', it was conceded, 'the project will be like blind flying.'

Evelyn replied as follows:

'Dear Madam,

'I read your letter of yesterday with curiosity & reread it with compassion. I am afraid you are unfamiliar with the laws of my country. The situation is not that my co-operation is desirable but that my permission is necessary before you publish a series of photographs illustrating my novels. I have been unable to find any phrase in your letter that can be construed as seeking this permission.

'You say: "Without consulting you the project will be like blind flying." I assure you it will be far more hazardous. I will send a big blue incorruptible policeman to lock you up and the only "monumental" work Mr Scherman is likely to do is to break stones on Dartmoor.'

That was the end of that, but it foreshadowed further strife in Hollywood.

After *Brideshead Revisited* Evelyn did little writing, as noted already, and his literary output was for a while confined to occasional pieces. The most famous of them, and not quite forgotten now, was an article for the American magazine *Life*. It was entitled 'Fanfare' and took the form of a reply to the thousands of fan-letters he had received from American women and (so he asserted) one man in response to the American publication of *Brideshead Revisited*. In the main it consisted of a spirited and successful defence of his novel. He gored his critics of whom only Edmund Wilson was mentioned by name. It was published in April 1946. A less remarked occasional piece, written in the first part of the same year, was an introduction to a new edition of Hector (Saki) Munro's novel *The Unbearable Bassington*. He wrote it in March at the request of Graham Greene, then a director of Eyre and Spottiswoode who brought out the new edition. It ranks high in the large mass of Evelyn's literary criticism.

But the most singular and perhaps the most interesting feature of Evelyn's literary activity in the immediate post-Brideshead period is to be found in the considerable amount of work he did for other writers. He was responsible for many of the more felicitous details in Nancy Mitford's novel *The Pursuit of Love* which came out in September 1945. Evelyn's friendship with her had remained constant since the distant days of Canonbury Square. She had made a slight reputation for herself as a novelist before the war. Her books were amusing but could not be taken with any seriousness because the matter was too thin and the imitation of Evelyn's farce too self-evident. With *The Pursuit of Love* Nancy showed a sudden and rich fulfilment of the mild promise of her early fiction. This was a remarkable autobiographical novel, brimming with a comedy that only occasionally overflowed into discordant farce and then with such irresistible appeal to the sense of humour that to frown became prudish. Whenever he was in London in 1944 and 1945 Evelyn had read Nancy's typescript and proofs and made many suggestions almost all of which, so she told me, she followed. I wish I could remember more of what she said about this. Evelyn was a precise if not scholarly grammarian, while Nancy freely admitted that she had no grammar at all. Of all successful writers I have known, she was, if possible more than

Evelyn, the least pretentious. She had no hesitation in owning to her literary debts. If the grammar of her successful novel was nowhere offensive, she put this mainly to the credit of Evelyn. (Throughout her writing life she had grammatical advisers whom she followed.) To Evelyn she cheerfully gave the credit of the dignified yet catchy title. To Evelyn also was due, on Nancy's authority, what has seemed to many careful readers the most remarkable passage in *The Pursuit of Love*. It is that in which the entrance hall of 'Uncle Matthew's' country house is described, with its walls decorated with sporting trophies and weapons of war, ancient and modern, and from which, the narrator concludes, the overriding theme of the great room was death. I once told Nancy how much I admired the passage and she immediately answered: 'That was Evelyn.'

To polish, perhaps to do more and to give distinction to Nancy Mitford's book was, for Evelyn, the labour we delight in. She was the most enchanting of women, gay, full of raillery, beautiful, high-spirited, withal affectionate; she made Heywood Hill's bookshop where she worked the scene of a perpetual gathering of friends. Evelyn used to call there almost every morning when he was in London. She was the devoted wife of Peter Rodd, under increasing difficulties, and so remained till 1958 when the marriage finally broke up, as any marriage with Basil Seal was bound to do. When she left London early in 1946 and settled in Paris permanently no small thing went out of Evelyn's life.

To help Nancy to achieve literary distinction was among the joys of his life then, but a similar and sombre task awaited him in the case of another writer with whom he was only slightly acquainted, and who was also in need of help. The man was Moray MacLaren. He was a writer of ability rather than brilliance or eminence, but very much more genuinely talented than most critics' pets about whose later fate, as Logan Pearsall Smith cruelly put it, one may as well enquire as about what happened to last year's snow. He had fallen on evil days through giving way to temptations to despair. His spiritual and emotional predicament was very close to that of Evelyn. Having knowledge of Poland and the Polish language, he was employed in the war, to quote his self-record in *Who's Who*, as 'attached to Foreign Office as Head of Polish Region Political Intelligence Dept., 1940–1945.'

Like Evelyn he had found himself forced to watch and to act as an agent in what he took to be the betrayal of principles, and the betrayal of people who had received solemn British promises of support. At the end of the war he believed that he had taken part in a crime. He suffered something of the nature of a nervous breakdown. Like Evelyn he was a Roman Catholic, but unlike Evelyn he abandoned his religion at this moment of spiritual crisis. He was overtaken by utter loss of faith in everything and everyone. He found himself unable to work and sought consolation in heavy drinking.

Evelyn probably heard about Moray's plight from A. D. Peters, or some other member of Moray's club, the Savile. Evelyn immediately took action. Soon after his return from Jugoslavia he wrote to Moray MacLaren and went to visit him, either in Scotland or elsewhere. His immediate object was to recall him to his religion, the only possible form of rescue, he insisted, from the deadly sin of despair. By force of personality, as in the case of Hubert Duggan, he recalled Moray MacLaren to his religion.

Evelyn had learned about Moray's monetary situation. It was not desperate, but it was not good. Evelyn, then enjoying the windfall of *Brideshead Revisited*, hastened to send Moray a handsome cheque. He also urged Moray to take up his writing again and enquired what he planned. Moray told him that he wished to write a novel. Evelyn in his reply said that if the other wanted an opinion or suggestions he would gladly read his typescript. The book in question was *Escape and Return*.

It is one thing for an author of repute to give needed and effective encouragement to a less successful writer. It is another to get the less successful writer's work accepted by a publisher. 'Yes, well I've done what I can, but I'm afraid – ' is an utterance that must have been frequently heard in this connection. Not so from Evelyn in the case of Moray MacLaren. He had been made a director of Chapman and Hall on de-mobilization and was able and willing to exert influence. He did so and obtained acceptance of the book at a board meeting in February 1946. Evelyn was the only member to have read Moray MacLaren's typescript, so that the acceptance was his special responsibility. He had nothing to fear. The book was a success. Thereafter Moray MacLaren enjoyed a modest but highly reputable literary career. He threw off the self-destructive mood of despair and shortly after married happily.

A similar story can be told about Evelyn and one who for long had been a close friend, Alfred Duggan. During the war Alfred had found employ-ment as a school teacher and then had moved to dairy work on the land. He had also put himself under the care of a certain Doctor Dent who had achieved a great reputation for his success in dealing with apparently incurable cases of alcoholism. He succeeded completely in the case of Alfred Duggan. By 1948 Alfred was working near Cambridge, under a government scheme for ex-Service men, to be trained as a dairyman, and in this employment he was happy. But his mother Lady Curzon's doctor, possibly on the advice of Dent, warned her that it was dangerous for such a man to live alone, and at her entreaty he moved to Robertsbridge in Sussex near which he lived with her in her modest dwelling (very modest after the splendours of Curzon's day) called Bodiam Manor. He asked Evelyn's help in finding some employment and he said that he would prefer some such occupation as a shop-assistant or a railway porter but that in view of his mother's prejudices he knew that he would have to take a more intellectual task. Evelyn finally encouraged him to write.

He helped him with introductions to editors, some of which proved effective; but he insisted that what he should do was to write a book on a historical subject. He persuaded him and in 1946 Alfred began to write.

At the time when Evelyn and Alfred had been young men together at Oxford, the historical novel appeared to be the dodo among literary forms, a monster that had survived almost to within living memory and was now as extinct as the great lizards. In common opinion its last serious flights had been taken in the late nineteenth century, notably under the influence of Walter Pater and Robert Louis Stevenson. Historical novels were still being written, to be sure, but they were not written by respected authors for a respectable readership; though many of them sold well they were puny creatures, crocodiles, at best, not to be compared with the tremendous saurians of old. All this was changed in the late nineteen twenties and the nineteen thirties when there was a wholly unexpected revival of this decayed form. It seems to have started in the German-speaking world with the novels of Leon Feuchtwanger. In England it was associated primarily with the names of Rose Macaulay and Mr Robert Graves.

Encouraged by Evelyn's unflagging belief that his friend had it in him to be a literary artist, Alfred decided to attempt a work of historical fiction, to enter the field whose soil had seemed to be exhausted through over-exploitation and had, to the amazement of readers, been successfully recultivated in English. The result was Alfred Duggan's first novel *Knight with Armour* written in 1946. He had the usual difficulties of one who sets out late, with no literary reputation. The book was not accepted till 1948 and not published by Faber until 1950.

The story, told with a skill superior to that of most craftsmen who have practised the art since youth, was set in the period of the First Crusade. He told Evelyn: 'I dodged most of the tricky parts by choosing a period that is not too well documented and characters who did not talk any form of English, archaic or not. But describing any world later than Chaucer must be very difficult indeed.'

This is in part conventional self-disparagement, but is also sound criticism. Alfred Duggan knew that he was too old to begin to acquire the massive classical learning of Robert Graves (he was forty-five in 1946), and he had found a way of avoiding the tushery that many even of the greatest practitioners of the historical novel have found themselves forced to use, when describing an English-speaking 'world later than Chaucer'.

Alfred Duggan lived till 1964 and from this time to its close his life was serene. He remained a fervent believer in his religion. In January 1953 he got married in defiance of prudent counsels. Evelyn was not among the prudent counsellors; to an appeal to him from Lady Curzon in 1952 to 'reason' with Alfred, and persuade him not to marry he replied negatively.

Finding that their union was barren, Alfred and his wife decided to adopt a son in 1955. Evelyn gave what help in this that he could, and later in arrangements for their adopted son's education.

Alfred continued to write historical novels which received remunerative though never spectacular sales. They were little noticed by the leading critics. The field reopened by Rose Macaulay and Robert Graves in England, and by other people in Germany and France, certainly yielded good immediate harvest, but could anyone be certain that this was sound fictional culture? Most critics are frightened of appearing foolish if they back a winner before it has won. Without absurdly claiming that he was a 'great writer', it can be asserted that Alfred Duggan was among those who proved that the historical novel was not only capable of revival but is still in its vigour and a difficult but essential part of our literary heritage.

So far as Alfred Duggan was concerned, none of this would have come about had it not been for Evelyn's persistent intervention in his affairs.

Evelyn had grave faults, some of them most unpleasing. Let those who read with disgust his repellent and childish reiteration of drunken and vomitous and offensive scenes from his life; let those above all who feel from his own ugly self-portrait that they are better than he was, remember the names of Moray MacLaren and Alfred Duggan. Let them also remember, to which I can testify on personal knowledge, that there were other similar cases, concerning persons whose names would mean nothing except to a very few. Evelyn was a scrupulous churchgoer and sometimes ludicrously pedantic in his observance of certain church rules, but unlike many admired persons *'parmi les dévots'* he lived his religion.

During most of this time, what may be called the early postwar period, Evelyn continued in virtual literary idleness. His preface to *The Unbearable Bassington* has been mentioned. The first book to appear under his name after the war was a selection of pieces drawn from his prewar travel books and entitled *When the Going Was Good*. It was published by Duckworth in 1946. As mentioned earlier all his travel books were represented in it except *Robbery Under Law*.

In his preface he recalled the passion for travel to remote places which was shared by most of the young men of his generation. He wrote as follows: 'These were the years when Mr Peter Fleming went to the Gobi Desert, Mr Graham Greene to the Liberian hinterland; Robert Byron – vital today, as of old, in our memories; all his exuberant zest in the opportunities of our time now, alas! tragically and untimely quenched – to the ruins of Persia.'

Sincerity was second nature to Evelyn, and he found it hard to abandon, even in the slightest way, for the sake of good manners or good taste. But these words of homage to Robert Byron were without any sincerity whatsoever.

Why? I can only guess. Evelyn continued to resent, and resented to the end of his life, Robert's hysterical and uninformed anti-Catholicism and his habit of blasphemy. He also resented the great reputation that Robert was acquiring at the end of his life, because, in Evelyn's opinion, it was fraudulent: Robert was treated as a learned man and the distinguished author of learned books, whereas he often showed astonishing ignorance. In common with many of his fellow-writers Evelyn regarded Robert as lacking in natural literary talent, as a clumsy manipulator of our language, who confused seriousness with pomposity, and protest or disagreement with cheap abuse; as for his politics Evelyn regarded them as no more than a violent expression of the fashionable Leftist silliness of Kingsley Martin's *New Statesman*. In short Evelyn saw in Robert a phenomenon which invariably roused his ire, a thoroughly overrated man. Professor Lindemann shared his view, as did a few others, but it remained a rare one. But there was something else about Robert which, I believe, led Evelyn to this unfelt reverence. The homage was, I believe, not directed to Robert but to Oxford. Robert was the only man among Evelyn's close friends of his Oxford days who lost his life through enemy action in the war. He was drowned when the ship on which he was travelling was torpedoed in February 1941. He reiterated this homage at the end of 1946 when he reviewed a book by myself called *Four Studies in Loyalty* which included a biographical essay on Robert. Again, he did not mean a word of it.

Evelyn's private life went through much the same vicissitudes, disappointments, unexpected turns of fate and frustrations as most people endured during the uncomfortable period of convalescence following the removal of the disease of Nazism and the Allied victory of 1945. It so happened that Evelyn was staying with Randolph Churchill at his house at Ickleford near Hitchin in July when the results of the 1945 General Election were belatedly declared with the news of the overwhelming Labour victory and the defeat of Winston Churchill and the Conservatives. Evelyn described Randolph as 'dazed by adversity'.

His experiences in Jugoslavia had terminated his former admiration for Winston Churchill, and so, unlike most of his friends, he did not see the surprising fall of Churchill from office as a tragic event, but he did see as calamitous the rise to power of the Labour Party, with its egalitarian goals, its elevation of the deadly sin of envy to the status of a social virtue, or, in the hideous jargon of the time, of something necessary to social engineering; with its official, pitiful trust in the friendliness and upright intentions of Josef Stalin – 'Left can speak to Left' it was frequently said; all this he saw as matter for the utmost alarm and disgust. Evelyn entered into that period of intense conservatism which lasted the rest of his life. It affected not only his ideas but his manner and dress.

An interesting comparison has been drawn by Mr Malcolm Muggeridge of Evelyn with George Orwell. Mr Muggeridge pointed out that both had strong tendencies to 'bovarism', to the desire to appear as different from the reality. Both came from similar social backgrounds, but whereas Orwell disguised himself elaborately, both in his manner of life and dress, as a member of the working classes to which he never belonged and never could belong, Evelyn in his increasing conservatism disguised himself as a member of an ancient landed family. Neither succeeded in their painstaking deceptions. The similarity is acutely observed, but the difference is missed. George Orwell believed ardently in his imposture, indeed with a sincerity which absolves it of blame. Evelyn no more believed in his own imposture than he was impressed by unrewarding aristocracy. Orwell's performance, which can remind one of T. E. Lawrence, was informed by a deep seriousness, and a concern for the poor, Evelyn's by a sleepless sense of farce. Evelyn's attempts to dress himself up as the fine old English squire, like Orwell's attempts in an opposite direction, were completely unsuccessful. Orwell in his poverty-stricken clothes was quite obviously a well educated and distinguished gentleman. Evelyn could never be mistaken for a modern Sir Roger de Coverley. He could easily be mistaken for a bookmaker. I was unwittingly responsible for part of his habitual and monstrous turn-out.

When the war was over and one ceased to wear uniform, there was a widely shared impulse to turn with unwonted eagerness towards one's civilian clothes. The smell of moth-balls became familiar. One day, looking through my half-forgotten wardrobe I came across a rather dandyish piece, a grey bowler hat. With a dark grey suit I found this rather becoming, and thus clad I went to White's. Sitting on the leather-seated fender, glaring at every member who came in, was Evelyn. He leapt to his feet on my entrance, his eyes blazing and haggard with that concentrated look of jealousy that I remembered from Tatton Park. 'Give me that hat!' he cried.

I refused, saying it was a hat I valued and loved.

'Where did you get it?'

I told him that it came from Lock's in St James's Street. The same day Evelyn went to Lock's shop who in due time sent him from their stores 'one white Coke hat'. This he wore frequently from then on, not only in summer for which such hats are designed, but at all seasons.

A grey bowler hat worn with the right sort of clothes can have dignity, but not when worn with the sort of suit Evelyn ordered shortly after. There is a cloth exclusively woven for officers of the Household Cavalry, used in the making of travelling and sporting overcoats and now usually for country caps. Never in history had this cloth been used for the making of a suit. On a light reddish-brown background it has a bright red check about three inches square. Evelyn made tailoring history by ordering a suit in this cloth. The result surpassed the wildest extravagances of an old-fashioned music-hall comedian. A weird touch of obscenity was added, as the tailor cut the cloth in such a way that a bright red line from the checks ran down the fly buttons. The ensemble of this suit and one white Coke hat sensibly diminished any resemblance Evelyn might have had to the Old English Squire. He enjoyed the farce of all this, especially as it increased the sourness of his critics.

In March 1946 Evelyn was officially invited with many other writers and professional men to attend the trials of Nazis being held at Nuremberg. He went at the very end of March staying in Paris on the way with Duff and Diana Cooper. At that time travel outside Britain was forbidden unless proof of the official necessity of a journey abroad could be furnished. Government, in Great Britain and even more in France, having acquired a novel extension of power through the necessities of war was loth to relinquish it, as happens. Many people found themselves acquiring new skills in the composition of dubiously honest letters of request and invitation. While an official invitation to Nuremberg excused Evelyn's journey to Germany, a formal invitation to the British Embassy was needed for his passage through France. Evelyn wrote to Diana to ask for this. She had not learned the new trickery and replied on a postcard: 'Oh yes please Stitch.' The authorities in charge of visas questioned the evidence. They only allowed him a two day visa to cover passage. He made a longer stay in Paris on the way home as an American general gave him a movement order which covered a delay in France.

One might expect Evelyn to have been moved to strong feeling by the Nuremberg trials. He expressed none. His brief description of the scene in his diary is less memorable than many others.

Among the British lawyers assembled there he found a great desire to bring P. G. Wodehouse to trial. This made an impression on Evelyn which was lasting and resulted in action fifteen years later. He had an admiration for Wodehouse and from now on he began to study this odd case.

In the summer of 1946 Evelyn received an invitation to take part in that increasing phenomenon of modern life, an international festival and conference held in some famous city in honour and on the subject of something or other. With Robert Byron I had attended an early manifestation of this new institution in 1935 as a 'delegate' (though who had delegated us was never clear) to a conference on Persian art held for no particular reason in Leningrad. It followed what became the usual routine: there was no need for those attending the conference to know anything about the subject, or even to have heard of it; a good time was had by all until – with a chilling cessation of official welcome and of lavish banqueting the delegate was smoothly moved from the position of honoured guest to that of suspect foreigner.

In Evelyn's case the scene of the conference and festival was Spain, the subject the little known one of the Spanish Dominican clergyman, Francisco de Vittoria. I doubt if Evelyn had heard of him before. The friar, who lived in the sixteenth century, was in fact one of the pioneers of international law, whose fame has been eclipsed, (according to Spanish ideas through Protestant prejudice), by that of the later Grotius. 1946 was the fourth centenary year of Vittoria's birth and a congress with junketings was called under government auspices. The time was unpropitious. The war had ended but a year before and the victorious Allies were not feeling friendly towards Spain whose Head of State was now the sole remaining sample of a Fascist or at least quasi-Fascist Dictator. It was remembered that not very long before he had sent a 'Blue Division' to fight in Russia with the German army. As a result of these circumstances, acceptances of the many invitations sent out were fewer than had been hoped. There was a marked shortage of lawyers among the expected guests. To quote Douglas Woodruff: 'It was indicated that one did not have to be a professor of Law to be very welcome at these celebrations, and Evelyn gladly accepted an invitation for the chance of a new experience.'

He and Douglas Woodruff set off for Madrid on 15 June. Things went wrong from the start. While Professor Brierley of All Souls College, Oxford, a genuine student of international law and thus of Vittoria, was met at Madrid by 'some suave lawyers' and conducted to the best hotel, Evelyn and Douglas were given rooms in one of the worst. The Congress was not quite so bogus, not so totally unconnected with its subject (like my Congress in the USSR) as they had been led to believe. The authorities had arranged a sightseeing tour of Castile to entertain the international jurists during the days of postponement. Evelyn and Douglas forced themselves, not altogether with welcome, on to this jaunt which was not enjoyable but was preferable to idleness in a hot city. One diary entry can stand for several: 'At banquet I sat next monoglot, deaf octogenarian.'

There were many banquets and *vins d'honneur*. The sight-seeing activities were either agonizingly long or unsatisfyingly short. Evelyn throughout harboured a feeling that he and Douglas were looked on as gate-crashers. To allay suspicion he presented one of the 'suave lawyers', whom he described as a 'weary old queen', with a copy of *Brideshead*, and another with a copy of the Spanish edition of *A Handful of Dust* which he had either brought with him or found in a shop. That Evelyn's suspicions were justified is suggested by the fact that when the Congress, of whose sessions Douglas and Evelyn had attended but a few at the beginning out of politeness rather than eagerness to learn of the achievements of Vittoria; when these centenary celebrations came to an end and the harsh relations of irritable government and unwanted foreigner had been re-established, arrangements for air passages had been made for all the other delegates, but not for Evelyn and his friend.

Evelyn was both in and out of luck. In their endeavour to placate

Russian sensibilities the British Government were considering breaking off diplomatic relations with Spain, but in June 1946 had not yet recalled their Ambassador. At that time the British Ambassador to Spain was Victor Mallet who has entered Evelyn's story already. He was away in late June, probably trying vainly to dissuade the British Government from their act of appeasement, but his vivacious and brilliant wife Peggy Mallet was in Madrid and gave Evelyn much good company. But he and Douglas equally needed some official help and according to Evelyn they failed to obtain it from the Embassy. In the end Douglas persuaded the Foreign Minister to put two officials off an aeroplane to England for the two stranded visitors.

He arrived back in London on 2 July. During his absence his youngest son, christened Septimus, had been born.


This visit to Spain was Evelyn's first peace-time journey, excluding the quasi-official visit to Nuremberg via Paris. It was a needed stimulant and it led to a worthy literary result. I can find no evidence that Evelyn wrote an article, long or short, for any paper or magazine, reporting this visit to Spain. He kept his experience for a short book published in 1947 *Scott-King's Modern Europe*.

It is less a novel than a 'long short story', that shining light of the age of Henry James, now as little acceptable as a collection of triolets. Its unfashionable length possibly explains why the book has been underrated. It is beautifully thought out and constructed and those who enjoy Evelyn as a clown can find here all the farce they can want. The serious undertone is left to make its own effect deep down, with little help from the instrumentalist.

The story is simple and clearly suggested by his Spanish experiences. Scott-King is the Classics master at an ancient but not famous public school. He is not unlike 'Mr Chips', a description Evelyn would have resented as he hated the kind of sentimentality about schools indulged by James Hilton. (He liked to propagate the myth that James Hilton and Jack Hylton the band-leader were identical.) This Chips-like Scott-King is one of very few authorities in Europe on an imaginary seventeenth-century Latinist poet Bellorius whose centenary is being celebrated in the country of his origin, a country cautiously described as 'Neutralia'.

In the invented person of Scott-King, he projected a person in some ways the opposite of himself: one who rejoiced in obscurity, who liked to be the little known translator of the least famous of poets, taking a certain pride 'unknown in the New World' in the fact that his fame could not conceivably move beyond certain severely circumscribed limits, well outside the range of newspapers and radio. As a distinguished Bellorius scholar Mr Scott-King receives an invitation to the Neutralian celebrations, and in a dare-devil moment he accepts. He finds himself in a motley throng among whom he is in a very small minority of people who have the vaguest notion who Bellorius was. (This is a deliberate reversal of the situation of Douglas and Evelyn in Spain.) Scott-King also finds that the Bellorius celebration is but one of a number taking place at the same time. (This was the situation of the Vittoria celebrants in Madrid in June 1946.) Scott-King experiences the sudden change from fulsome acclaim to undisguised unwelcome that Evelyn and Douglas and Robert and I endured when official festivities terminated. (In the novel the transition is made more dramatic by the simultaneous occurrence of a ministerial reshuffle such as did not occur in Spain at the time.) By a well-managed exaggeration of the difficulties Evelyn and Douglas went through in escaping from the scene of hospitality back to their homeland, Scott-King finds himself at one point disguised as a nun, at another mixed up in clandestine Zionist immigration to Palestine, and only after a Mediterranean tour of indescribable discomfort, back amid the modest comforts of the masters' common room at his school. The last episode is an interview between Scott-King and the headmaster. The latter wishes to terminate the classical syllabus and division of which the other is in charge.

The book ends with the following exchange between the two men:

' "What are we to do? Parents are not interested in producing the 'complete man' any more. They want to qualify their boys for jobs in the modern world. You can hardly blame them, can you?"

' "Oh yes", said Scott-King. "I can and do." . . .

' "Has it ever occurred to you that a time may come when there will be no more classical boys at all?"

' "Oh yes. Often."

' "What I was going to suggest was – I wonder if you will consider taking some other subject as well as the classics? History, for example, preferably economic history?"

' "No, head master."

' "But, you know, there may be something of a crisis ahead."

' "Yes, head master."

' "Then what do you intend to do?"

' "If you approve, head master, I will stay as I am here as long as any boy wants to read the classics. I think it would be very wicked indeed to do anything to fit a boy for the modern world."

' "It's a short-sighted view, Scott-King."

' "There, head master, with all respect, I differ from you profoundly. I think it the most long-sighted view it is possible to take".'

All critics and all readers, excepting the initiated, took Neutralia for a picture not of Spain but of Jugoslavia. Though nothing like the adventures of Scott-King had happened to Evelyn in Jugoslavia, I think they were right. He was obviously working on experience, and one can usually tell this, though of course there are many doubtful cases. Unless one has experienced an 'international conference' on something or other, one cannot write of the successive scenes of mismanagement with the mastery Evelyn shows here. It is true that there are many details given which apply easily to Spain and not at all to Jugoslavia, but most of the details are Jugoslavian. The description of Neutralia as a 'former Hapsburg dominion' certainly applies more easily to Croatia than to Spain, but it is consciously vague, and careless readers think more readily of the Spanish Bourbons than the Spanish Hapsburgs. The head of the Neutralian State is referred to as 'the Marshal', a title eagerly seized on from the USSR by Marshal Tito and never assumed by General Franco. The regime under which Scott-King suffered his ordeals is clearly Left-Wing, an accusation of which General Franco's regime was innocent. Evelyn seems to have said to himself at some point in the adventure: 'Now suppose all this was happening in Belgrade and Jugoslavia . . .'

At all events the result was happy. In 1947 Evelyn appeared as the writer of a novel for the first time for three years; not as the writer of a masterpiece, but of a masterly minor work.

# Chapter 18

## 1946-1948

What may be called the Brideshead Boom went on and reached its climax in 1947. This was not followed in the classical style by a Brideshead Slump or Crash; people who liked *Brideshead Revisited* at the time of its publication continue to like it; the Boom, in fact, goes on, while the Brideshead Slump had opened simultaneously with the Boom. Those who found it insufferable in 1944 persist in their sentiment thirty years later. You paid your money and you took your choice.

In the age of Dickens and Thackeray the success of *Brideshead Revisited* would have made its author rich enough to be relieved for life of all financial anxiety. It was otherwise in an age which expressed its belief in economic justice by penal taxation applied indiscriminately to earned or unearned wealth. Evelyn needed to make yet more money out of his success if he was to enjoy more than fleeting prosperity. The way to do that was to exploit the immense resources of the film industry, and A. D. Peters made it his business to grasp this opportunity. Peter was as skilful at negotiation with film companies as with publishers. With both he knew how far he could go without arousing a damaging opposition, and with American film companies he could go very far indeed. He was however inhibited in this case by the author's conscience. As an artist, Evelyn was fearful that Hollywood magnoperators (to borrow a useful term coined by Max Beerbohm) would make a hideous vulgarization of his most ambitious work.

I remember talking to him on the subject when negotiations had only just begun. I advised him to give Peter a free hand and 'to go in and collect'. He said that in return for any number of pieces of silver he would not betray his standards and commit artistic suicide. 'But it wouldn't be artistic suicide', I insisted. 'It would be more like Peter's pence.'

Evelyn would have none of my argument. 'You are in some ways embarrassingly naïve', he said. 'You have no notion of what these people might want to do to my book.'

'I have every notion', I replied. 'I have seen many films in my lifetime and I have read Beachcomber's account of Sol Hogwasch's film entitled "The Life of Bach".'

'He was a musician, wasn't he?'

'Even you know that.'

'Well, I'm not musical. I can only judge by what they do to novels.'

'So can I. I've seen at least three bad films based on *Vanity Fair*. Does that make any difference to Thackeray's position? I saw a frightful film of *Nicholas Nickleby* and another called *Wuthering Heights* but no one feels differently about Dickens or Emily Brontë as a result. You have just seen a very bad film of *Hamlet*. You told me so yourself. Does that film make the slightest difference to Shakespeare's reputation or your reverence for him? If he'd made his reputation as a film script-writer and director and so on, of course it would. But he didn't and nor have you.'

Evelyn was in an obstinate mood. 'I'm not Shakespeare,' he said, 'or Thackeray or Emily Brontë. They lived out of the age of films. They are immune from the contagion. I am not.'

I remain convinced that my point of view was a more reasonable one than Evelyn's, though I have always found his feelings in the matter easy to understand, and I respect the contrary view. It was the contrary view which prevailed in the end. It showed the strength of Evelyn's dedication as an artist. As indicated already, for its sake he was prepared ruthlessly to ignore the interests of others, and now he showed that for its sake he was prepared to ignore his own. But this is to anticipate.

In the last part of 1946 Evelyn's main preoccupation lay in finding a new house. He and Laura had good reason to believe that Piers Court and the little village of Stinchcombe would soon be engulfed by the town of Dursley under the latest town-planning scheme. They first contemplated a move westwards to Somerset, but then became convinced that a farther move, to Ireland, was the real solution. Evelyn set down his own thoughts on the matter in November 1946.

'Throughout the day constantly recurring thoughts of Ireland. Not so much of what I should find there as what I should shake off here.'

In early December Evelyn and Laura went to Ireland to inspect houses on offer, including Gormanston, reputedly the scene of much ghostly manifestation. They were so taken with it that they authorized their house agent to bid at the sale, but on the way back Evelyn read in an evening paper that a part of the Gormanston grounds had been bought for a Butlin's holiday camp, so he immediately cancelled his offer by telegram.

The rest of the story of Evelyn's contemplated migration to Ireland may as well be told now, regardless of the demands of strict chronology. Not till the summer of 1947 did he make up his mind, after two more visits to Ireland to inspect houses. His second visit was from 30 April to 7 May 1947. None of the houses he and Laura saw tempted them and Evelyn did not much fancy 'the English refugees' whom he met. He told me on his return that at one house the mother of the owner said: 'My daughter is unfortunately unable to show you round the house and grounds as she has lost all interest in life.' His third and last visit was made early in June. They only saw one house, in very Irish circumstances: 'The agent gave us luncheon & tried to induce us not to purchase the place. Laura liked it & so did I.'

In August 1947 *The Daily Telegraph* asked him to visit Norway, Sweden and Denmark and commissioned articles by him on those countries. He accepted and the result was two brilliant articles published in November. On this venture he was away from 17 August to 2 September. He met many young members of the intelligentsia in Stockholm and Oslo, and later in Copenhagen. He seems from the diary to have been very bored most of the time. He took a great dislike to Oslo where one evening he dined with the publisher who was bringing him out in Norway. The other guest was an authoress. 'She never spoke except to ask me if I had read "Julie Nortch" (Juliana of Norwich, it transpired) drank a lot & looked like a malevolent boarding house proprietress.' He was happy in Copenhagen which he left on 2 September 'with regret'. He flew back to London, having reached an important decision which he described thus in his diary.

'During my tour I decided to abandon the idea of settling in Ireland. Reasons. 1. Noble. The Church in England needs me. 2. Ignoble. It would be bad for my reputation as a writer. 3. Indifferent. There is no reason to suppose life in Ireland will be more tolerable than here. My children must be English. I should become an anachronism. The socialists are piling up repressive measures now. It would seem I was flying from them. If I am to be a national figure I must stay at home. The Americans will lose interest in an emigrant & the Irish would not be interested.'

That was the end of the Ireland proposition. By September 1947 much had happened and Evelyn had finished a new book. The story must return to November 1946.

On the 14th Evelyn received a cable from A. D. Peters who was in America, conveying Metro Goldwin Mayer's terms for a film of *Brideshead Revisited*. They had already taken up the option on the film rights for £3000 free of tax. They now offered Evelyn and Laura a trip to Hollywood and a month's stay there, with all expenses paid, to enable him to discuss the film treatment with the directors. If Evelyn accepted the proposed film treatment he would be paid a further 40,000 dollars less the money paid on MGM taking up the option. Evelyn accepted these princely terms. He and Laura decided to leave for the United States in late January.

The reason for so late a departure was that Evelyn decided to undergo an operation to relieve him of what used in the glorious prose of the old Bromo boxes to be described as 'that distressing and almost universal complaint THE PILES'. (Evelyn so admired the grandiloquent English of that advertisement that he tried to the end of his life, and in vain, to acquire one of the old boxes.) At all events, early in the New Year he obtained a private room in St John and St Elizabeth's hospital and underwent the operation.

Evelyn arranged for numerous visits from his friends, including myself. I remember that meeting very well. In the month before, my book *Four Studies in Loyalty* had come out. It had been overpraised and Evelyn had given it a very flattering review in *The Tablet*. He now made good his lapse. Glaring at me from his bed, he said, after we had been talking a a while: "Your essay on Robert is utterly misleading. He couldn't write and his ideas about art were as ludicrous as his politics. He was a modern version of Roger Fry, without Fry's occasional instinct for a good painting. Besides your essay was squeamish. You said nothing about his perpetual buggery.'

'You may find it hard to believe,' I replied, 'but until I was told so after my book came out, I never knew he was homosexual.'

'You ought to research harder.'

'I should have done. I made some gross historical errors in the portrait of my great-uncle.'

'I liked that part very much. But I didn't like the story about the Persian man. Again it was too squeamish. It ought to have been more like Ackerley's book "Hindoo Holiday". That's the way to deal with Oriental subjects.'

'I know Ackerley's book well and admire it. But it's about Indian life. My story is about Persian life which is entirely different. I know little about Indians, but Persians are very genteel and ultra-refined in their manners. If they offend against sexual morality they do it *sub rosa*. To have written in the style of Ackerley would have been to misrepresent the whole picture. You make the common English mistake of believing that Indians and Persians are much of a muchness. It's you who need to do some research there.'

He accepted defeat with a grunt and then with a renewed glare said: 'The last bit about the French Resistance was no good at all. Better to have thrown it away. You took an epic theme and wrote a clever article on it. Deplorable.'

It was not unlike the scene between Anthony Blanch and Charles Ryder after the exhibition in *Brideshead Revisited*. I reminded him that he had described the book in other terms in *The Tablet*. He replied:

'I was overcome by affection.'

'Balls.'

Before going I asked about his illness and recovery. He told me that the operation had caused him much pain and that the consequent treatment was such as he could not bring himself to describe. I said I supposed that he was now relieved of much chronic pain and must be thankful it was over.

'No,' he said, 'the operation was not necessary, but might conceivably have become so later on.'

'Not necessary? Then why did you have it done?'

'Perfectionism.'

On 25 January 1947 Evelyn and Laura embarked on *The America* and sailed for New York which they reached on the 31st. They were met by one whom Evelyn described as 'a feeble young man sent to meet us by MGM', but who proved too feeble to achieve the encounter until they 'had got through customs and the battle was over'. They went to rooms booked for them by MGM at the Waldorf Astoria Hotel.

This was virtually Evelyn's first visit to New York or the United States, his previous visit after the Mexican journey having been very hurried and without any literary result. Now he fastened his eye on this new strange country. His goal and his place of longest visitation, and of most fruitful result, was Los Angeles, but his diary entries for New York are far more interesting than those he wrote in California.

Evelyn went by appointment to see the editor of *Good Housekeeping*, then said to be the most widely circulated magazine in the United States. The following odd converation took place on the subject of an illustration for one of Evelyn's stories.

'This illustration is by the very best artist in the country.'

'What did you pay for it?'

'2,500 dollars.'

'But you could have got a real picture for that.'

The editor then said, 'What's more, this illustration is about the story. Often they have nothing to do with it.'

'Why?'

'Artists as important as —— are so busy they don't get around to reading what they illustrate. Maybe they have a secretary make them a synopsis. Then maybe they get mixed. We can't control artists as important as ——.' (The name is suppressed in the original, probably because Evelyn did not catch it.)

In the first week of February they left New York for California. The golden age of American railway luxury, soon to be terminated by the rise of air travel, was still persisting. They travelled west on the famous train *the 20th Century*. After changing trains in Chicago they reached Los Angeles on 6 February 1947.

He was visited in his hotel, the Bel Air, by the two prospective directors of the film. They were called Gordon and MacGuinness, and on the 7th, so he related: 'We went to what was called a "conference" which consisted of McGuinness coming for 10 minutes and talking balls.'

It will be remembered that in the immortal Sol Hogwasch's film *The Life of Bach*, one of the great director's problems was to find a musician to compose suitable music. In the case of the proposed film of *Brideshead*

*Revisited* the director needed to find a writer. He had succeeded in his search and had chosen Mr Keith Winter whom Evelyn had already met with Somerset Maugham. Mr Winter was the author of an ingenious and well-written novel *Other Man's Saucer* which had brought him some acclaim in the early thirties. He turned to play-writing after writing other novels of merit; then he had been absorbed into the film industry some years before. From the tone of his diary entries one has the impression that Evelyn was not in the completest sympathy with Keith Winter. 'He has been,' he noted, 'in Hollywood for years and sees "Brideshead" purely as a love story. None of them see the theological implication, though McGuinness says that "a religious approach puts an American audience on your side". There was something a little luxurious in talking in great detail about every implication of a book which the others are paid to know thoroughly.'

To intrude a personal opinion which has already been touched on, I am not sure that Mr Winter and his colleagues were not right, in the sense that the theological implications were not deftly made a part of the original book, in fact rather than implications the religious element became a crudely overstated theme, damaging to the book as a whole. I fear that the central love story was only too much in Hollywood taste. Was it at this moment that Evelyn began to react against his own ambitious invention?

American life, all of which was new to him, was distasteful to Evelyn at this first encounter, and he made notes on it which, if published at the time, would have resulted in an uproar to equal the historic Dickens row.

At the time he affected to dislike Americans, 'Goodness, how I don't like them', he wrote to Mary Lygon; yet in later years I often heard him speak in praise of Americans in general, comparing them favourably with English people. When his deepest convictions were not involved, Evelyn could be surprisingly inconsistent, swinging from one opinion to its opposite.

When the Californian adventure was over Evelyn recorded: 'Our lives in Hollywood changed greatly with the arrival of the Elweses.' This refers to the painter Simon Elwes and his wife Gloria, a sister of Peter Rodd. Simon and Gloria were staying with a friend, Mrs Cowdin, and Evelyn related in his diary that from the arrival of Simon and Gloria, Andrea Cowdin became in effect the hostess of Evelyn and Laura, though they continued to have rooms and to sleep in their hotel. Staying with Andrea Cowdin at the same time was the then very well-known English playwright Freddie Lonsdale. The latter was a delightful man whom I knew well, but not well enough to suspect the harrowing sense of insecurity underneath a gay manner. His daughter has related in two books that Lonsdale was painfully aware of his defective education, and avoided encounters with people of erudite wit, such as Evelyn had. He was terrified of Evelyn and avoided meeting him although virtually living in the same house. He never appeared at meals so long as Evelyn was around.

There was another compatriot who was on a brief visit to Los Angeles, coinciding with Evelyn's. The compatriot was Lady Milbanke, later, after Sir John Milbanke's death, to become Princess Dimitri of Russia. Of Australian origin, Sheila Milbanke was one who shone in the fashionable London world of the twenties and thirties, and was among Evelyn's friends. She was a most amusing and amiable woman and held to be one of taste. On one of their meetings, presumably at Mrs Cowdin's house, Sheila told Evelyn that she had been shown a graveyard, just outside Los Angeles, which for sheer exquisite sensitive beauty surpassed anything she had seen of that kind. In its power of faith and consolation it was unique. It was religion and art brought to their highest possible association.

Evelyn was naturally stimulated by these tidings. He went with Sheila to Forest Lawn. He was as intrigued by this institution as she was, but in a very different way. He was puzzled as to the organization and administration behind this famous and elaborate burial place. He obtained as much of the available advertising literature on it as he could. He obtained also technical pamphlets on the correct treatment of corpses. Whether or not he visited the laboratories where the corpses were prepared for the 'slumber rooms' and sometimes mummified I do not know, but I fancy he obtained considerable allowance of entry. I do not see how otherwise he could have collected the mass of literature, evidently written for those under training in the mortuary, which he brought home with him. After his initial visit with Sheila he went to Forest Lawn almost every day during the remainder of his visit. He made a thorough investigation of the place.

In the meantime the proposal for a film of *Brideshead Revisited* languished and died. To quote his diary: 'MGM slipped more and more from the scene. Gordon, I think, lost heart as soon as I explained to him what "Brideshead" was about, until in the end when the censor made some difficulties he accepted them as an easy excuse for abandoning the whole project. I was equally relieved. Winter remained in a kind of trance throughout. MGM were consistently munificent and we left as we had come in effortless luxury.' According to Douglas Woodruff the 'censor' mentioned in this entry was, possibly, the Catholic Legion of Decency who objected to the references to adultery.

He and Laura sailed back on the *Queen Elizabeth* arriving home early in April. Soon after, Holy Week came round and he went to spend a religious retreat at Downside.

I remember going to Piers Court soon after the return of Evelyn and Laura from the United States. I enjoyed the visit as I enjoyed all visits to Piers Court in spite of the hazards, but on this occasion I found myself rather short of sleep. Evelyn liked talking to a late hour, and as a result of his insomnia he was a habitual early riser. If the visitor was an old friend he would come into his bedroom and urge him to get up, sometimes long before inclination. Hours of sleep were rarely very long when staying with him, but on this occasion on going to bed I was given a great mass of reading matter from Forest Lawn, and was expected to have mastered it by the morning. Till the early hours I found myself studying the techniques required to remove the ghastly expression often left on the faces of strangulated suicides. It was during this weekend that my wife and I introduced Evelyn and Laura to Max Beerbohm.

He wrote several articles on 'Californian burial customs', for various papers and magazines both in England and the United States, but these efforts were not enough to assuage the haunting inspiration of Forest Lawn. His predicament was expressed in that of his repellent hero (Dennis) in the resultant novel:

'On this last evening in Los Angeles Dennis knew he was a favourite of Fortune. Others, better men than he, had foundered here and perished. The strand was littered with their bones. He was leaving it not only unravished but enriched. He was adding his bit to the wreckage; something that had long irked him, his young heart, and was carrying back instead the artist's load, a great, shapeless chunk of experience; bearing it home to his ancient and comfortless shore; to work on it hard and long...'

Evelyn worked on his 'chunk of experience' throughout the summer of 1947 and he seems to have finished the first draft of *The Loved One* by the time he set out for Scandinavia in August. By November 1947 he could send a completed typescript to Cyril Connolly who had offered to devote a whole number of *Horizon* to this long short story. (It was about the same length as *Scott-King's Modern Europe*.) *Horizon* published *The Loved One* in February 1948. This was followed shortly after by a large paper edition of 250 copies signed by the author and the illustrator Stuart Boyle. He sent me one of these with the inscription: 'For the Loved One Christopher Sykes in the hope of his joyful resurrection from Evelyn Waugh.'

At the time of writing *The Loved One* (mortician's jargon for a corpse) Evelyn was still a fairly young man as years are counted today but he felt the weight of age already. For 28 October 1947 he made this sombre and revealing entry in his diary: 'My 44th birthday I am a very much older man than this time last year, physically infirm & lethargic. Mentally I have reached a stage of non-attachment which if combined with a high state of prayer – as it is not – would be edifying. I have kept none of the resolutions made this day a year ago. I have vast reasons for gratitude but am seldom conscious of them. I have written two good stories "Scott-King's Modern Europe" and "The Loved One" in the course of the year & have decided to remain in England. I have added a number of beautiful books to my collection & a few valueless pictures. I have given large sums to Church funds & have been drunk less often. I have been more comfortable than most Englishmen.'

I may add a note on the 'valueless pictures'. I had lunch with him at White's one day in 1947 and afterwards he took me to a picture gallery nearby in Jermyn Street where he was due to meet Diana Cooper. We met at the appointed time. Evelyn had asked the picture dealer to reserve two 'subject paintings' for him painted, as I learned from Mr Pryce-Jones's book, by Robert Musgrave Joy in 1851. They were entitled 'The Pleasures of Travel 1751', and the same for 1851. In the first a highwayman holds a pistol at the travellers who (all in unconvincing costume of the period) faint, surrender, or put up ineffectual resistance. In the second a ticket collector appears courteously in the place of the highwayman, and the travellers (in authentic mid-Victorian costume) are seen courteously producing their tickets from purses and pockets. Evelyn wanted to know Diana's opinion. She was in no doubt at all and urged him to buy the pictures at the price which was asked. They both spoke about them as they might of works of Rembrandt, while I was doing all I could to suppress my giggles. I think Evelyn paid about £300 for the two. Today they must be worth thousands. Later he had a third picture painted by Richard Eurich following a similar construction, to illustrate the theme applied to 1951, showing the interior of an aeroplane when the crash is inevitable. Every possible detail contributing to horror and irony was included at Evelyn's insistence. Admiring Eurich's work in his house one day I said: 'Many people must be shocked, aren't they?' Evelyn replied, 'I hope so.' It is a picture worthy of the taste shown by the author of *The Loved One* to which I must now return.

Anyone who supposed that the possibly excessive nostalgia manifested in *Brideshead Revisited*, or the sentimental passages which he allowed himself in that great if imperfect achievement; anyone who supposed that Evelyn had lost his talent or capacity for black humour (though there had been plenty of that in *Scott-King's Modern Europe*) was shown to be gravely mistaken. No other book by Evelyn has blacker humour, none other a clearer invitation to despair.

The opening of the book is among Evelyn's best, and it is worth extended quotation:

'All day the heat had been barely supportable but at evening a breeze arose in the west, blowing from the heart of the setting sun and from the ocean, which lay unseen, unheard behind the scrubby foothills. It shook the rusty fingers of palm-leaf and swelled the dry sounds of summer, the frog-voices, the grating cicadas, and the ever present pulse of music from the neighbouring native huts.

'In that kindly light the stained and blistered paint of the bungalow and the plot of weeds between the veranda and the dry water-hole lost their extreme shabbiness, and the two Englishmen, each in his rocking-chair, each with his whisky and soda and his outdated magazine, the counterparts of numberless fellow-countrymen exiled in the barbarous regions of the world, shared in the brief illusory rehabilitation.

' "Ambrose Abercrombie will be here shortly", said the elder. "I don't know why. He left a message he would come. Find another glass, Dennis, if you can." Then he added more petulantly: "Kierkegaard, Kafka, Connolly, Compton Burnett, Sartre, 'Scottie' Wilson. Who are they? What do they want?"

' "I've heard of some of them. They were being talked about in London at the time I left."

' "They talked of 'Scottie' Wilson?"

' "No. I don't think so. Not of him."

' "That's 'Scottie' Wilson. Those drawings there. Do they make any sense to you?"

' "No".

' "No".

'Sir Francis Hinsley's momentary animation subsided. He let fall his copy of *Horizon* and gazed towards the patch of deepening shadow which had once been a pool. His was a sensitive, intelligent face, blurred somewhat by soft living and long boredom. "It was Hopkins once," he said; "Joyce and Freud and Gertrude Stein. I couldn't make any sense of *them* either. I never was much good at anything new. 'Arnold Bennett's debt to Zola'; 'Flecker's debt to Henley.' That was the nearest I went to the moderns..." '

(Scottie Wilson was an artist recently taken up by *Horizon*.)

It is not till page 4 that the reader is given to understand definitely that the scene is not some remote British colony in Africa or Asia but Los Angeles. The first section of the book is occupied with an evocation of the hideous life of the film industry in Hollywood and the extravagantly self-conscious Englishry of the British community there, all conveyed with exquisite irony made all the more deadly by its economy. In his diary Evelyn related that he was not on easy terms with the Hollywood British. I dare say there is a small element of revenge in the opening section. Sir Aubrey Smith was said to look with special suspicion on Evelyn, and I dare say that he is the original (with much variation) of the immensely successful Sir Ambrose Abercrombie. Contrasted with him is the 'has-been' Sir Francis Hinsley. We watch the latter's fall to total failure and this leads to his suicide which in turn leads the loathsome hero Dennis to Whispering Glades the supreme burial ground of Los Angeles. There he meets the pathetic heroine, Aimée Thanatogenos, a cosmetician in the service of the corpses.

Sensitive as he was about ascriptions to models in real life which were often, and usually wrongly, deduced from his work, Evelyn never denied that Whispering Glades is carefully drawn, as realistically as possible, from Forest Lawn. Indeed he had no alternative. Whispering Glades is a photograph of Forest Lawn. When I went there in 1969 I felt that I had been there before. 'The Dreamer's' greeting message inscribed on an open marble book was there almost word for word. As in Evelyn's novel the air was overloaded with lush piped music, and piped recordings of 'the murmur of innumerable bees'. (Real bees sting.) Where Evelyn had 'The Wee Kirk o' Auld Lang Syne', I found 'The Wee Kirk o' the Heather'. To mention all the parallels would become wearisome.

*The Loved One* has excited several writers to make psychological excursions in the hope of discovering a deeper impulse than appears in this odd novel centred on death and the undertaker's profession. I think like most excursions of the kind this particular one is a waste of time. I prefer Evelyn's own explanation: 'The ideas I had in mind were 1. Quite predominantly, over-excitement with the scene. 2. The Anglo-American impasse – "never the twain shall meet". 3. There is no such thing as an "American". They are all exiles uprooted, transplanted and doomed to sterility. The ancestral gods they have abjured get them in the end. 4. The European raiders who come for the spoils and if they are lucky make for home with them. 5. *Mememto mori.*'

Reason 3 was possibly suggested by a remark made to him by a dining car attendant on his way from Chicago to the Pacific Coast. It is recorded in his diary. Explaining some unfamiliar preference in food or drink Evelyn explained: 'I am a foreigner', at which the attendant replied: 'In this country we are all foreigners.'

I do not see that there is any advantage in adventuring further into Evelyn's intentions than those given in the brief account quoted above, which he wrote for Cyril Connolly. I cannot add much more, although before he began to write the book I had many talks with him about Forest Lawn. He frequently reverted to one thought. It was this: that if the ancient Egyptians had not been morbidly obsessed with funerary celebration we should know little about them. Suppose that our age became best known to the remote future through our burial customs and monuments to the dead, would distant posterity perhaps have the clue to the kind of mind that prevails in the twentieth century, as we believe we have the clue to the prevailing beliefs of the ancient Egyptians?

In his articles Evelyn developed this idea but not extensively. It is barely implied in the book.

The black humour of *The Loved One* finds a gruesome climax at the end. The hero Dennis has a secret, that he also, like the heroine, is a mortician, though not at such a place as Whispering Glades but at a cemetery for pet animals known as The Happier Hunting Ground. He keeps this from Aimée Thanatogenos whom he successfully woos by sending her, as his own compositions, master works which he takes from the Oxford Book of English Verse. He thus proves a successful rival to

Aimée's superior, Mr Joyboy the chief mortician of Whispering Glades. Distracted by divided allegiance she seeks solace and guidance from a guru who runs an advice column in the press. Finally, when she knows the worst about Dennis, Aimée commits suicide in Mr Joyboy's laboratory. Joyboy appeals to Dennis for help, for the suicide if discovered could mean the finish of a great career. In return for an exorbitant reward Dennis cremates Aimée as a pet dog at The Happier Hunting Ground and leaves America. So ends the story.

When published *The Loved One* was acclaimed as a masterpiece by most readers and critics, though many readers and a few critics were shocked at its heartlessness. Lady Colefax, an early and faithful admirer, declared that she would never see Evelyn again after such a disgusting exhibition. (Of course she did in fact.) The harshest critic was again Edmund Wilson. He was not shocked but contemptuous. He wrote: 'To the non-religious reader the patrons and proprietors of Whispering Glades seem more sensible than the priest-guided Evelyn Waugh. What the former are trying to do is, after all, to gloss over physical death with smooth lawns and soothing rites; but, for the Catholic, the fact of death is not to be feared at all; he is solaced with the fantasy of another world in which everyone who has died in the flesh is somehow supposed to be still alive, and in which it is supposed to be possible to help souls advance themselves by buying candles to burn in churches.' Like many people who dash into religious controversy in a spirit of blind rage, he had not studied his subject or his antagonist's beliefs.

Edmund Wilson also accused Evelyn of lack of originality, of using jokes about American life which are possibly fresh in England but are stale in the United States. He did not particularize. He may have been referring to a case at law which occurred during the war in which a well-known figure was shown to have captured a young woman's affections by addressing to her some of Shakespeare's sonnets (presumably edited for the purpose) as his own work. This may have given Evelyn the idea of Dennis sending Aimée extracts from the *Oxford Book of English Verse*. There is a distinct possibility of plagiarism in the episode of the wise Brahmin guru. In the story, the guru's column is written by two down-at-heel, hard-drinking and wholly cynical journalists. The subject is closely similar to that of Nathanal West's short novel *Miss Lonelyhearts*, a fine work of black humour which Evelyn must have known. But even if both these borrowings can be proved, I do not see that they lessen the book's stature. Its master impression is of powerful and horrifying originality. If the American usage is sometimes stale to Americans, the English reader certainly does not notice any such fault.

The appearance of *The Loved One* occasioned a notable comedy. Chapman and Hall's legal adviser was given the typescript and became worried about Evelyn's position in the event of a libel action. Enquiries confirmed that Whispering Glades was very easily identified as a picture of an existing cemetery. The publishers thereupon told A. D. Peters that they were reluctant to publish the book as it stood, as a libel action brought by the proprietors of Forest Lawn would undoubtedly succeed. To rewrite the book in such a way as to remove the resemblance between the fictional and the authentic cemeteries was to impose an impossible task on Evelyn. The situation seemed hopeless, but Evelyn found a solution.

He found it in a friend, Lord Stanley of Alderley, a younger contemporary of Evelyn, a man of uproariously high spirits, a close friend and admirer. In him Evelyn now saw a saviour. He and Ed Stanley entered a conspiracy. Evelyn in pursuance of a clandestine agreement gave the other a typescript of the book. After reading the typescript, Ed wrote to his lawyers to inform them that he proposed to add a codicil to his will stating that on his death he wished his body to be transported to Los Angeles for burial in Forest Lawn, as he understood that this cemetery bore some resemblance to the beautiful one so movingly described by his friend Mr Evelyn Waugh.

A. D. Peters showed the documents to the publishers, saying that they would form the basis of the defence in the event of a libel action. If necessary Lord Stanley would open negotiations for a Forest Lawn plot. The legal adviser agreed that while some danger remained, the knowledge that *The Loved One* had persuaded a member of the British House of Lords to seek his last resting place in Forest Lawn would probably deter the cemetery from suing the author and publishers. The codicil remained as part of Ed's will for over ten years; then when the danger seemed to have passed, he revoked it because he considered it would unfairly involve his heir in great expenses.

The book was published in America at the same time as its appearance in England in 1948. It did not cause the offence which Evelyn expected. Many Americans resented the way that undertaking was becoming big business; that undertakers' firms were trying to bring pressure on legislatures to force bereaved people into needless expenses, ruinous to the poor; that the whole of this 'racket' should be conducted with so much and such nauseating sentimentality. For details of the racket one should read Jessica Mitford's book *The American Way of Death*. Evelyn gained more American admirers than enemies by *The Loved One*.

My own visit to Forest Lawn was made in 1969. I went in a big transparent bus with a company consisting mostly of middle-aged American women. We were subjected to a crushing torrent of propaganda. I noticed that all the companions to whom I talked in the course of this visitation were inclined to take a sceptical view of the Dreamer's vision. I dare say that some of the credit for that should go to Evelyn.

# Chapter 19

## 1948-1950

Between finishing *The Loved One* and starting his next Evelyn allowed himself some rest. It was now that his friendship with Ronald Knox, whom he usually met at Mells, became close. During the war years Ronald had completed his translation of the New Testament and it was published in 1945. Evelyn was carried away by admiration, though much later he had second thoughts about it. At this time he publicly proclaimed his belief that his friend had proved himself to be among the three or four most remarkable English writers of the century. He was influenced towards this opinion not only by the translation but by a remarkable and wrongly forgotten pamphlet, one of the best things Knox wrote, called *God and the Atom*. Evelyn tried hard by frequent public references to the pamphlet to draw attention to it and excite interest, but he failed.

In 1948 Ronald Knox had two daunting tasks in hand. One was to translate the Old Testament single handed; the other a scholarly work which was to be entitled *Enthusiasm*, using that word in its original meaning, namely 'that very horrid thing' the claim to a personal revelation of the will of God. He was much moved by Evelyn's admiration and his efforts on his behalf. He dedicated *Enthusiasm* to him. It was published in 1950.

Ronald, one of the most delightful of men, became a frequent visitor to Piers Court. The great charm of Ronald's personality, invisible to some because of his shyness, was clearly one cause of this strong friendship, but they had, apart from their religious preoccupations and the common bond of conversion, a deep 'profane' interest: the English language. I never shared Evelyn's enormous admiration of our friend's writing. In his younger days Knox's gifts as a parodist and controversialist had seemed to me second to none, but the prose of his later years, even in his best things, seemed to me lifeless, and his translations of the Bible distressingly genteel and completely lacking in that poetry which is the essence of such passages as St Paul's utterance on Charity or the opening chapter of St John's Gospel. But Ronald Knox, for all his imperfections as a writer, had a scholar's grasp of the meaning and right use of language. The lax usage which was an inevitable result of the shrinkage of Scott-King's field of activity, the daily abominations to be found in books, magazines (highbrow and lowbrow) and the newspapers, were a subject literally of pain to Ronald Knox. He rejoiced in usage, such as Evelyn's, which never had in it a word of which the writer had not a full grasp of its meaning and derivation. Like Sir Walter Scott, Evelyn had a sleepless curiosity about words, and as with good Sir Walter, the taste did not lead him to pedantry.

Like Sir Walter Scott, a writer to whom he bore not the faintest resemblance otherwise, Evelyn was genuinely grateful to anyone who gave him a fresh insight into a word. He bought me a bottle of claret because I had revealed to him the derivation of the word 'gas' from the Greek 'chaos'. Thereafter 'chaos' was always used by us for 'gas' in our conversation. He put me in his debt once more by revealing to me the real meaning of the word 'effete', which I had hitherto supposed to be a term of opprobrium.

Evelyn was always prepared to learn from other people, unlike conceited writers of less assured talent, and I never knew him to show envy of other writers' achievements or success. When he conducted a vendetta against a writer, as he undoubtedly did against Cyril Connolly, he acted as he did because he thought that there was something essentially wrong about the achievement, never out of simple jealousy.

There was little jealousy in Evelyn, but there was some, and it came out in queer ways. His devotion to Diana was, as I have said, always a little tinged with jealousy. I think that this was the root cause of his hostility to Duff Cooper. When the latter retired from the British Embassy in Paris in 1948, some of his friends clubbed together to give a dinner to Diana and him at the Ritz. Duff was consulted as to the guests and who should propose his and Diana's health. He seemed delighted at the whole proposition. I was among those responsible for making arrangements. Evelyn was not. (For rather obvious reasons.) He was infuriated. He did what he could to wreck the party; first by muddling up the names on the guests' places at the table just before they went in, then by jeering comments while the festival was proceeding, then by writing to his friends afterwards that the party had been a disaster which had greatly annoyed Duff and Diana, especially Diana. I lunched with Duff and Diana the next day. Unless they can be described as the most polished hypocrites I have met or am likely to meet, Evelyn's denunciations were absolute nonsense. It was an odd episode, to be attributed, I feel sure, to the jealousy that he felt with regard to this beloved friend who put up with more from Evelyn than from any other of her friends, and she had several difficult ones. He tended to be possessive as regards her. He liked people to make friends with Diana through him and to maintain the friendship, but with him. Totally independent actions of friendship to Diana roused his resentment. But jealousy was not a constant temptation to him, as despair was, and he could usually resist it with ease. When it appeared in him it was invariably in an odd form.

This recalls to me another experience of Evelyn's worser side. He was jealous of my close friendship with T. S. Eliot. He was clearly displeased that my wife and I never asked him to our house when Eliot was a guest. He dropped hints that he would like to meet Eliot. I dropped hints to Eliot, who was an admirer of Evelyn's writing, that Evelyn would like to meet him. Nothing came of it. Eliot hated rows and he knew, I think, that a meeting between two such uncompromising characters as himself and Evelyn could lead to an unhappy result.

But Evelyn was indefatigable in his pursuit of the great poet. He said to me one day: 'This close companion of yours, Eliot, a poet almost as famous as Stephen Spender I believe:' (He always pronounced the name Spender in Germanic style, though he always pronounced the names of German nationals in English style: Goering became Gorring and Hegel, Heegle), 'this famous poet, Tom they call him, lives with a cripple called Hayward whom I used to know. Since you won't introduce me to the poet, will you do the next best thing and re-introduce me to the cripple?'

I said I would and did. Rarely have I regretted a fulfilled promise more. John Hayward, T. S. Eliot's companion since 1946, and through whom I came to know the poet, was a severely disabled man. As with many cripples, the effect of his infirmity on his character was not wholly agreeable. If he was one of the most courageous men I have ever known, John Hayward was also one of the most treacherous and mischief-making. Hardly had I introduced Evelyn and John than a rather uncannily well-placed remark by John excited Evelyn to an explosive outpouring of religious polemics, wholly unsuited to the occasion and grossly insulting to the memory of my father. It was all deeply embarrassing, especially as there were other people present. I regret that I did not have the wit to go away and leave Evelyn to muddle out the results of his own loathsome behaviour. But the two sequels are in my opinion the most instructive part of the episode.

At the time I was acting as second-in-command to Harman Grisewood in the management of the Third Programme of the BBC. The morning after this displeasing encounter I was rung up in my office from the BBC switchboard to say that there was a courier from a shop with a parcel addressed to me. I asked the operator to give orders for it to be left at the reception desk. It was too large, he or she said, besides which the courier had instructions to deliver the parcel personally to my office. All right, I said, tell him to bring it up whatever it was. Presently the courier, aided by a BBC porter, tapped at my door. There entered two figures staggering and puffing under the weight of an enormous, a gigantic flower decoration, a wrought basket of orchids, and other expensive flowers. To this stupendous tribute was attached a note 'With love from Evelyn'. To cart this offering home in a taxi, quite apart from the embarrassment of manoeuvring the object downstairs amid the mockery of colleagues, and in the street amid the mockery of the mob, presented additional problems. It was difficult to maintain my indignation at a high temperature after this however.

The other sequel was distressing to Evelyn. He began a correspondence with John Hayward and his letters always contained amusing references to Eliot. They were intended to be shown to him, as they were, but they failed of result. Eliot had certainly heard from the gossip-prone Hayward an account of the disgusting scene which Evelyn had made on his visit, (an account, I feel sure, in which everyone concerned was painted in the blackest colours), and his determination not to meet Evelyn became fixed. So Evelyn never met the great poet from whose works (inappropriately I think) he had taken the title of what was perhaps his best novel.

Having given a picture of Evelyn at his most atrocious in social intercourse, let me remember an incident of the time, in 1949, which shows him at his most pleasing, though perhaps his most pleasing might not have been to everyone's taste. At the time I was literary editor of *the New English Review* then under the chairmanship of Sir Charles Petrie. Like all literary editors I was on a perpetual hunt for contributors, and the name of Evelyn was ever before me. One day searching amid the mass of twaddle that encumbers a literary editor's office I found just the thing for Evelyn with whom I was lunching that day. It was a book about Logan Pearsall Smith by his friend Robert Gathorne-Hardy. I believed Evelyn had known and admired Pearsall Smith, and if he had not – what a subject for him! I put the book in my pocket and went off to join Laura and Evelyn at Wilton's Oyster Bar and Restaurant. In those days they were housed in much smaller premises than the present ones, and it was no place for conversation not intended to be overheard.

Evelyn was in exuberant mood. People who knew him will remember that he had an extraordinary passion for watches. The purchase of watches is a frequent subject in the diaries, from the early ones written when he was poor to the later ones when he was rich. Hardly had we sat down than an argument about watches began between Laura and Evelyn. Laura had settled an account with a watch-mender. The watch was now in her bag and she asked Evelyn to put it in one of his waistcoat pockets. He refused. She protested. 'It's such a bore in my bag', she said. Evelyn would not give way. Laura appealed in vain. 'All your pockets are empty', she said. 'By no means *all*', replied Evelyn with a glare. Laura appealed to me. I adopted a conciliatory tone. 'Why don't you put the watch in your pocket?' I pleaded.

Evelyn put on a judicial air. With glaring eyes, and in a serious manner, he explained the situation. 'Because,' he said in a voice of thunder, 'if I were to put the watch in my pocket, and if later someone were to pick me up by the heels and shake me, then *two* watches would fall out of my pockets and I would thus be made to look ridiculous.'

It was the gravity with which he gave this summing up which made it so wonderful. He had the great comedian's ability to follow up one *coup* immediately with another. When we had recovered our breath I asked him if being held upside down and shaken was a thing that often happened to him. 'Not much outside the St James's Club,' he said with the same gravity, 'but it is sinful presumption, unless I have read my theology wrong, to expect that God has made any man capable of predicting what may or may not happen to him, or immune from possible calamities.'

We had eaten our oysters and other delicacies supplied by Mr Marks, and our luncheon (long before Nancy Mitford Evelyn rejected the word 'lunch' as plebeian, though it has a respectable ancestry) was drawing to an end when I introduced the subject of the book. He knew that I was literary editor of *the New English Review*, and also that the remuneration was meagre.

'Evelyn, will you review a book for me?' I asked.

'No.'

'What a pity. The subject is one after your own heart.'

'What is the subject?'

'Logan Pearsall Smith.'

'Is it a reissue of his writings?'

'No. It's a portrait of him by his jagger, Robert Gathorne-Hardy. It looks a bit catty and unfair, but he knew him well.'

'How soon do you want my article?'

'Within a fortnight. But since you've refused, don't bother. I'll do it myself.'

'No you don't. I'm going to do it.'

'But I want to do it.'

'But you just asked *me* to do it.'

'And you just said you wouldn't.'

'Well I will. Give me the book.'

'All right. I'll send it to you tomorrow.'

'Why tomorrow not today?'

'Because I want to read the book myself. You'll have it tomorrow.'

At this Evelyn began to cry. When I say he cried, I mean that he began to yell in the manner of a two-year-old child, gurgling between ear-splitting ululations 'I-want-the-book-now.' In the confined space of the little restaurant the noise caused much sensation. I hastily gave him the book and his howls of agony instantly stopped. He wrote a very interesting article on the subject of Logan Pearsall Smith.

From 1945 he had been preparing himself for his next book. Recognizing that St Helena was too shadowy a figure to be the subject of a precise work of history, perhaps encouraged by his own encouragement of Alfred Duggan, he decided on a bold step: to make an attempt on the recently reopened field of the historical novel. Early in 1946 he had abandoned the notion of a history of the age of Constantine centred on her. Instead he would imagine her, imagine the Emperor Constantine and the Flavians, imagine Rome and Constantinople and the Empire in decay in the fourth century, and do what he would with them. Among the many unreliable accounts of St Helena's origin, one of the most dubious is that she was a British princess, a daughter of the possibly historic King Cole after whom Colchester is said to be named. Evelyn decided that she should be a daughter of this British King.

He worked long on this book. It was not finished till the end of 1949 but the first fragment of it to be published appeared as early as January 1947.

I lunched with Evelyn one day in the winter of 1949–50. He told me he had just finished his book which was now with the printers.

'Any good?' I asked with our customary lack of ceremony.

'It's *very* good', said Evelyn. 'It's very good *indeed*. It's as good as anything written by that Chelsea friend of yours.'

'I have many friends in Chelsea. Which one?'

'Not that crippled man. The other one. Tom Something.'

'Tom Eliot.'

'I think you mean T. S. Eliot. It's just as good as anything he can do. In prose I mean. You've never written anything so good. I don't think Graham Greene has or Tony Powell. It's far the best book I have ever written or ever will write. It's almost as good as Quennell.'

'When does it come out? I must get it.'

'Don't bother. A copy will be on its way to you soon.'

There was much farce in all this, of course, but it was not complete farce. Evelyn, to the end of his life, believed *Helena* to be his best book, combining good construction, permissible invention, grasp of the period dealt with and the authorities upon it, in a satisfying work of fiction.

Few readers of Evelyn's books agree with this judgement. Many regard it as a calamitous aberration of his talent. Others regard it as a magnificent failure. Few would rank it with *A Handful of Dust*.

I find *Helena* a very difficult book to judge. All Evelyn's merits are present in it, his wit, his broad humour, his irony; in addition it contains some of the best pieces of evocative writing that he achieved at any time. The 'purple patches', the attempts at 'fine writing' which sometimes failed in *Brideshead Revisited*, eminently succeeded here. Why then is not the book obviously the masterpiece that Evelyn supposed it to be?

Unevenness is not a mortal blemish. Many great books by the greatest of writers contain deplorable passages. Supreme masters have set their names to some drivel in the midst of their best things. Homer is not the only great poet who nods. Certainly *Helena* is an uneven book, containing passages utterly unworthy of its author. The most flagrant of these is found in a conversation between Helena (who has a pet monkey) and 'the Christian Cicero' Lactantius. 'Suppose,' says Lactantius, 'suppose that in years to come, when the Church's troubles seem to be over, there should come an apostate of my own trade, a false historian, with the mind of Cicero or Tacitus and the soul of an animal,' and he nodded towards the gibbon who fretted his golden chain and chattered for fruit . . .' The pun, a miserably obvious one, fails to come off, and certainly fails to carry the reader to the side of Lactantius. *C'est plus qu'un crime, c'est une faute.*

The other most evident literary mistake in the book is the introduction in the later part of the character of the Wandering Jew who reveals to the Empress Helena in a dream the location of the buried cross on which Jesus Christ suffered. The Wandering Jew speaks in the accents of a London East End go-getting Yid, the kind that Jewish comedians for years portrayed on the music-hall stage till Zionism and the Jewish tragedies of our time caused Jews to frown on such self-mockery. It is all competently managed by Evelyn, but it never rises above the music-hall original which he, like myself, must have often seen in his young days. It was not a type of comedy in which he was equipped to compete with the old hands. But there is another and deeper-founded objection to the introduction of the Wandering Jew into the story.

More simply and more uncompromisingly than in any other of Evelyn's fictions, this one has a message. There is no question, as there was in *Brideshead Revisited*, of 'theological implications'; this book contains a theological statement. Its message is this: that whereas other great religions refer their origins to strange cosmic confrontations, unidentifiable in space and time, and are thus not prepared to enter into argument as opposed to mystical speculation on the subject, the Christian religion, uniquely before the age of Islam, depended on definite historical facts, far more so than the Jewish Revelation, which depended on events ascribed to a dim and distant period easily described as in part mythological. These facts were briefly that a man born in the time of Augustus, in the East Mediterranean provinces, and after manifestations and utterances which revealed him to those who knew him best as the Son of God, had been, during the reign of Tiberius, *crucifixus etiam pro nobis sub Pontio Pilato.* Since all this had happened not very long ago, (not farther away, as Evelyn said in his introduction, 'than between ourselves and King Charles I') it was essential, so the convert Helena saw it, to make people realize that these things really happened, here on this earth, literally, under exactly the same polity, and amid circumstances roughly the same as were familiar to her and her contemporaries. While Christian sophists argued about Homoiousion and Homoousion the down-to-earth reality of Christ's life was being forgotten. Evelyn put these words into Helena's mouth: 'Just at this moment when everyone is forgetting it and chattering about the hypostatic union, there's a solid chunk of wood waiting for them to have their silly heads knocked against. I'm going off to find it.'

In the words just quoted he expressed the dominant theme of the book: the literal reality of the Cross. But the intrusion of the Wandering Jew seriously weakens the dominance of this admirable theme. The story becomes one of miraculous dreams, and legends in which no serious person believes. The book becomes discordant, without clear intention, and ends lamely, almost in a pietist spirit.

I think the book's weakness throughout lies in expression of a false estimate. Unlike Islam, another down-to-earth religion, Christianity does not depend on relics. They are regarded, and even in decadent times have always been regarded as 'aids to devotion', nothing more than that. Jerusalem is a holy city to Christians, but its total destruction would not disturb Christianity as the total destruction of Mecca and the Ka'aba would disturb Islam.

I have mentioned the faults which seem to me to damage the book. It is one that I know better than any other by Evelyn because, at his suggestion, I turned the last chapters of it into a radio play for the Third Programme, and studying it closely I came to recognize to what heights he had risen as a master of English. The characterization, notably of Constantine, is exquisite, and the use of irony equally so. In the detailed but economic description of Constantine's murder of the Empress Fausta all the horror of ancient Rome comes alive. There are few evocations of Rome and its changing character to equal the one which Evelyn wrote marking Helena's first impression of the city.

One of the most delectable touches of irony in this book so rich in irony concerns the almost certainly fraudulent 'donation of Constantine'. It was said, possibly with truth, that the Emperor relinquished Rome to Pope Sylvester on moving the capital to Constantinople. A document known as the *Constitutum Constantini* was forged in the eighth century to supply the unhappily missing evidence. Evelyn deals with the original incident in a brief scene between Constantine and Sylvester. Constantine speaks first:

' "You can have your old Rome, Holy Father, with its Peter and Paul and its tunnels full of martyrs. *We* start with no unpleasant associations; in innocence with Divine Wisdom and Peace. I shall set up my Labarum there . . . where it will be appreciated. As for the old Rome, it's yours."

' "To quote the judicious Gaius, 'a ruinous legacy'," remarked one domestic prelate to another.

' "But I rather wish we had it in writing all the same."

' "We will, monsignore. We will." '

The most famous and, in my opinion, the finest passage in the book is Helena's prayer to the Three Magi. Evelyn's Dubrovnik diary leaves no question as to the origin of the passage:

'Like me, you were late in coming. The shepherds were here long before; even the cattle. They had joined the chorus of angels before you were on your way. For you the primordial discipline of the heavens was relaxed and a new defiant light blazed amid the disconcerted stars.

'How laboriously you came, taking sights and calculating, where the shepherds had run barefoot! How odd you looked on the road, attended by what outlandish liveries, laden with such preposterous gifts!

'You came at length to the final stage of your pilgrimage and the great star stood still above you. What did you do? You stopped to call on King Herod. Deadly exchange of compliments in which there began that unended war of mobs and magistrates against the innocent!

'Yet you came, and were not turned away. You too found room before the manger. Your gifts were not needed, but they were accepted and put carefully by, for they were brought with love. In that new order of charity that had just come to life, there was room for you, too. You were not lower in the eyes of the holy family than the ox or the ass.

'You are my especial patrons, and patrons of all latecomers, of all who have a tedious journey to make to the truth, of all who are confused with knowledge and speculation, of all who through politeness make themselves partners in guilt, of all who stand in danger by reason of their talents.

'Dear cousins, pray for me, and for my poor overloaded son. May he, too, before the end find kneeling-space in the straw. Pray for the great, lest they perish utterly. And pray for Lactantius and Marcias and the young poets of Trèves and for the souls of my wild, blind ancestors; for their sly foe Odysseus and for the great Longinus.

'For His sake who did not reject your curious gifts, pray always for all the learned, the oblique, the delicate. Let them not be quite forgotten at the Throne of God when the simple come into their kingdom.'

When this was recited by Dame Flora Robson in the dramatization which I produced for the Third Programme, the emotional effect was overpowering. She sought permission later on to repeat it at an Epiphany Service in her local church, a permission that Evelyn gladly gave. The whole of this production, with a fine impersonation by Sir John Gielgud of the Emperor Constantine, gave me the idea that the novel ought to have been written in the form of a play. It was astounding how the little noticed characters leaped to life, not only through the skill of the actors but through the force of Evelyn's language. Vast themes can be more easily contained within little space in the drama than in a novel. A short novel on the stupendous theme of The Decline and Fall of the Roman

Empire and the triumph of Christianity is an impossibility, but not so necessarily a play.

Evelyn had never written a play after his school days, and he was too old to learn a new and difficult craft, perhaps the most difficult of all the literary crafts. The reader should remember that he always regarded himself, first and foremost, as a craftsman.

# Chapter 20

## 1948-1951

The story has to go back a little way to the late nineteen forties when two friendships were revived. Easter fell on 28 March in 1948 and on the 24th Evelyn went to Downside for the Holy Week retreat and to attend the incomparably beautiful Holy Week Services in one of the last years when they were performed in all their majesty and poetry. I joined Evelyn there on Good Friday evening. He reproached me with laxity in arriving so late when most of the services were over. I told him I always attended the first part of Holy Week in London so as to hear the singing of the choir at Tenebrae on Wednesday and Thursday evenings, and of Palestrina's 'Reproaches' at the Good Friday Mass of the Presanctified, at Westminster Cathedral. To tone-deaf Evelyn this explanation was incomprehensible and not to be believed. 'Many people dislike going to Church,' he said pompously, 'but on Good Friday you ought to make the effort, even though it is not compulsory.'

Evelyn spent most of his time with his old friend Dom Ralph Russell, but he did not stay in the monastery, but in a house belonging to a cousin, Agnes Holmes. Evelyn introduced me to her in his own manner. 'This is my cousin Agnes, Miss Holmes. I'm staying here because she keeps a common lodging house.' Miss Holmes, to whom I took an instant liking, was not the kind to be daunted by Evelyn's ostentatious bad taste. She ragged him as effectively as he tried to rag her.

The diary contains one entry of great interest. Downside is but two miles or so from Chilcompton. He called on Lucy, 'now old & a grandmother – sick & not much elated by my visit'. This is the only mention of Lucy in the diaries.

On Easter Sunday he went home, and spent the following weekend with Lord and Lady Bath in their house near Longleat, the great family seat of Lord Bath's family. Among the house party was one of Evelyn's former fellow officers of No. 8 Commando, also the fellow officer's girl-friend whom he intended to marry when her divorce was through. Of his former companion in arms Evelyn recorded that the other had become 'fat, vain, opinionated, off-hand & generally spoilt'.

The facts warrant a less favourable impression of himself. He does not indicate that his growing conservatism carried with it a growing Puritanism (quite unsuited to his anarchical character and his own past) which made him extremely intolerant about divorce and to people involved in it. The fact is that he behaved to his friend and to the woman in the case with studied rudeness. No reader would guess from his account that his friend had been gravely mutilated in the war and had lost a limb. As often happens, a psychological consequence of his mutilation was an irrational but harrowing sense of inferiority which he had resisted and overcome with difficulty. When the party was over he asked Daphne Bath (now the writer Mrs Fielding) never to ask him with Evelyn again as he had found that, as a result of the treatment he had endured from his former friend, he was faced with all his psychological difficulties again. Though far from coarse-grained, Evelyn could be astonishingly insensitive. But I do not think he was unaware of what he was doing. He retained his streak of cruelty.

During this weekend visit he was taken by his hosts to a house on the Longleat estate where lived Gwen Plunket-Greene and her daughter, and thus Evelyn again met his old love Olivia Greene. Neither the diaries nor Evelyn's letters give any reason to suppose that in the last dozen years or so they had had any communication or even seen each other. Since the days of their close friendship, Olivia had entered an extreme phase of religious enthusiasm, believing herself to be not only in some kind of special personal relationship with God, while remaining an orthodox Catholic and subservient to the authority of Rome, but, in pursuit of the teaching of Christ, to have a special mission to help in the spreading of Communism in the world. On this renewal of a once dominant affection, Evelyn described her thus:

'Olivia 1/3 drunk 1/3 insane 1/3 genius. I have been involved since in a long correspondence with her in which she claims to be guided by God to give Gwen's money to the communists.'

The correspondence was not long in time (though it was not wholly abandoned till her death in 1955) but very long measured by the size of her letters. Here is a quotation from one which was written in answer to a letter which has not survived.

'Darling Evelyn,

'Balls to *you*.

'Of *course* capitalism is a crime. I would have no objection to inheritance if everybody could inherit. It's not remotely like Terence [Greenidge] on Lundy Island. Paul Robeson is a *highly* intelligent man & *yet* he holds *my* point of view. *And* he is not an invalid maiden lady living in a remote forest. He has spent years of his life in Russia & all over the continent & I think his son was brought up in Russia.

'I *fully* realize my false position in that I live entirely by the ill gotten gains of capital. In sending the labour papers money I do not consider I am giving them a gift but merely returning a minute trifle of my robbery.

'It was kind of my robber ancestors to leave me my inheritance & *I appreciate* it but I cannot uphold their point of view as an IDEAL. Unfortunately having been brought up under the system of systematic robbery I was not brought up to earn my own living & am an invalid anyhow. I don't think God wants me to kill myself & I still feel there may be some *mental* effort I could do to help both the Catholic church *and* Communism...'

And so on for eight pages, further complicated by almost idolatrous praises of Rimbaud. It must be remembered that, exasperating as she was, Olivia Greene lost no friends. Though it is quite invisible in her letters, it was the one-third genius that counted with those who knew her.

The second friendship was more of a beginning than a revival; it was with the writer whom Evelyn considered the most distinguished of his contemporaries, Graham Greene. They had known each other but slightly in their Oxford days. The first letters of their later correspondence which have been preserved belong to 1937 when Evelyn wrote a weekly article of literary criticism for *Night and Day*, the brilliant magazine in which Graham was a moving spirit. The letters are strictly businesslike in tone and suggest only a distant acquaintance. No wartime letters survive, but the next letters written in 1946 show that friendship had been established. They correspond throughout 1947; Graham came to stay at Piers Court in the autumn, and sent him signed copies of two of his earlier books, *Stamboul Train* (1932) and *England Made Me* (1935). They saw each other frequently in London. By 1948 they were firm friends and Evelyn revealed the depth of his affection, a thing he very rarely did, in the course of a letter written in October (the month of his birthday) of 1952. He wrote: 'I am just completing my 49th year. You are just beginning yours. It is the grand climacteric which sets the course of the rest of one's life, I am told. It has been a year of lost friends for me. Not by death but wear and tear. Our friendship started rather late. Pray God it lasts ...' It did, till the very end of Evelyn's life.

To return to 1948. In the summer an event occurred to bring discord to this relatively new friendship, and might well have done so in the case of a man less large-minded than Graham Greene, or of a man less eager to relish the farce of life than Evelyn.

In the early summer of this year there was published *The Heart of the Matter* by Graham Greene. Like *Brideshead Revisited* its central theme was devotion to the Catholic faith, treated here without melodrama and in a profoundly interesting way. Like *Brideshead Revisited* it shocked and angered readers, numerous in the intelligentsia, who, remaining stuck in the conventions of the time, could not discriminate between religion and religiosity, and who saw a potentially great author sliding with others into sentimentalism. Like *Brideshead Revisited*, and in part perhaps for the same reasons as aroused intelligentsia opposition, it enjoyed an enormous popular success, both in Great Britain and the United States. It was sent to Evelyn to review for *The Tablet*.

To follow what then happened the reader needs to be reminded of the basic elements of the story. It is set in West Africa, which Graham knew well from his war service as an Intelligence Officer. The central character is called Scobie, a senior police official, married to an exasperating woman (Louise) who loves him possessively and whom he has ceased to love. She hates the life of West Africa and wants to escape. Scobie and his wife are devoted Catholics. He is rigidly honest but finds himself involved in shady proceedings through borrowing money from a Syrian merchant to allow his wife to sail to South Africa for a respite from the odious life of West Africa. He is moved to do this by pity, and it is thus by pity that he is dragged down into venality. Pity causes him to help a pathetic very young widow who has survived a month in an open boat after a torpedo attack in which her husband was drowned. He falls in love with her in the way ageing men fall in love with very young women. She becomes his mistress. He thinks no one knows, but a few do. A Welfare worker warns his wife who returns. He pretends love for her and innocence. To maintain the pretence he needs to partake of Holy Communion with her, though his unrepentable adultery has placed him in a state of mortal sin. He offers his damnation as a sacrifice on behalf of the two women in his life. Driven on always by pity, he obtains sleeping tablets with which, in his final sin, he commits suicide.

Such an outline gives but the feeblest idea of the quality and power of this book. Graham Greene prefaced it with a quotation from the writings of the great religious poet Charles Péguy: '*Le pécheur est au coeur même de chrétienté . . . Nul n'est aussi compétent que le pécheur en matière de chrétienté. Nul, si ce n'est le saint.*'

Evelyn's review appeared in *The Tablet* on 5 June 1948. It was a long article, one of his best from a strictly literary point of view, devoted to two subjects: Graham Greene as a writer, and secondly the purpose and moral of this book. On both subjects, in my opinion, Evelyn made some serious errors.

On the first Evelyn wrote: '. . . the style of writing is grim. It is not specifically literary style at all.' This strongly suggests an excessively dry writer, a suggestion which is unquestionably false as Graham Greene is a master of description and evocation, in whose writing every word tells, and typically so in this great book. Its harshest critic could not describe it as dry, in any pejorative sense. The major point that Evelyn made is that Graham Greene was a writer equipped to take as his subject the gravest questions that face the destiny of a man, and to write about them convincingly. That was his main and sustained theme in the first part of the review.

Evelyn's second subject, the moral significance of the book, aroused controversy. In the penultimate paragraph he expressed it thus: 'We are told that [Scobie] is actuated throughout by love of God. A love, it is true, that falls short of trust, but a love, we must suppose, which sanctifies his sins. That is the heart of the matter. Is such a sacrifice feasible? To me the idea is totally unintelligible, but it is not unfamiliar. Did the Quietists not speak in something like these terms? . . . To me the idea of willing my own damnation for the love of God is either a very loose poetical expression or a mad blasphemy . . .'

The editor, Douglas Woodruff, added a postscript to this review, written by a certain Canon Joseph Cartmell. The Canon gave strong approval to Evelyn's opinions and conclusions. 'Mr Evelyn Waugh's comments', he wrote, 'on the theology of this book are, in my view, unimpeachable.'

A fortnight later a controversy broke out and lasted for a month in the correspondence columns of *The Tablet*. In the course of it Graham Greene and the right of literary freedom were vigorously defended by Abbot Butler of Downside (now Bishop Butler) and Father Martindale among others. The other side was supported by people unknown outside Roman Catholic society.

Evelyn found himself in an invidious position, one moreover likely to draw ridicule on him. Here was the begetter of Basil Seal scolding a fellow writer for describing offences which were not recognizable as such, except by those versed in religious matters. He found himself in Oldmeadow's shoes and, like Oldmeadow, he found the attack he made on a book in the cause of propriety met not by a defence mounted by libertines, but by pious and distinguished clergymen. It would not have been remarkable if it had caused a coolness between the two novelists.

Nothing of the sort happened. After the controversy had opened in *The Tablet* Graham wrote as follows:

'Dear Evelyn, You've made me very conceited. Thank you very very much. There's no other living writer whom I would rather receive praise (& criticism) from. A small point – I did not regard Scobie as a saint, & his offering his damnation up was intended to show how muddled a mind full of good will could become when once "off the rails."

'I'm on the way to N.Y. to draw up a contract! Thank you so much for your advice . . . Can I visit you some time in July? My time is going to be freer. I'll write to propose myself.

'I thought the Canon rather complacent. Can't one write books about moral cowardice?'

Evelyn answered as follows:

'Dear Graham, I am delighted that you did not take the review amiss. My admiration for the book was great – as I hope I made plain.

'It was your putting that quotation from Péguy at the beginning which led me astray. I think it will lead others astray. Indeed I saw a review by

Raymond Mortimer in which he states without the hesitation I expressed, that you thought Scobie a saint.

'I think you will have a great deal of troublesome controversy in U.S.A. The Bishops there are waiting to jump on decadent European Catholicism – or so it seemed to me – and I just escaped delation by sending everyone to heaven . . .' (The last reference is to *The Loved One*).

In the last issue of *The Tablet* which featured the controversy, the news was given that *The Heart of The Matter* had been banned in Eire. When contemplating migration, Evelyn seems to have overlooked the difficulties he was likely to encounter from the Irish censorship.

Evelyn and Graham met often in the course of 1948. On one date-fixing postcard Evelyn wrote some self-revealing words: 'Yes, let us lunch on Tuesday but not in a restaurant. I fall into ungovernable rages with waiters and am sorry afterwards, too late. So let it be your flat or my club whichever suits you best.'

In August of this year he was invited by Tom Burns to edit a book published in America under the title *The Seven Storeyed Mountain*. It was by Father Thomas Merton, an American Cistercian monk, and was a spiritual autobiography. Evelyn's task was to cut the book and polish Merton's English usage. It was published in England later under the title *Elected Silence*. Evelyn's admiration for Thomas Merton's thought (to a lesser extent his writing) was great. I could never share in it fully. I found myself antagonized by the fact that in *Elected Silence* the author declares that a potent force in his conversion was the sermon on Hell recorded in James Joyce's novel *Portrait of the Artist as a Young Man*. If true, I thought and still think this was evidence of an ill-conditioned and certainly ill-judging mind; if untrue this was an unworthy prank, playing to the gallery with meretricious paradox. I was given the book to review for some paper and said as much. Evelyn was not pleased. Like Ronald Knox he was a fundamentalist, or perhaps it would be more accurate to say there was a strong element of fundamentalism in his religion. Like Ronald Knox (who was not called Knox for nothing) he saw no objection or difficulty in the doctrine of Hell and everlasting punishment. I told him once that I believed that Hell was his favourite dogma. 'If', he replied, 'we were allowed "favourite dogmas" it might be. If you mean I see nothing to doubt in it, and no cause in it for "modernist" squeamish revulsion, you are quite right.'

The friendship of Evelyn and Graham Greene was largely founded on their shared religion, though this did not mean that they were in full agreement on it. Graham Greene was a Socialist and resented the conservatism of Catholic custom and fashion at the time; Evelyn regarded

Socialism as the root cause of most modern heresy, and rejoiced in any sign that the ruling episcopal hierarchy regarded Catholicism and progress, in the superficial sense usually given to the latter word, as irreconcilable. Evelyn's attitude was that of William ('Ideal') Ward: let the bounds of the Pope's infallibility be set wider and wider; let Pius IX's *Syllabus Errorum* be declared central and inalienable doctrine. Graham's attitude was very different from this. But, like Evelyn, like Thomas Merton, like Ronald Knox, he found no temptation to doubt the doctrine of Hell.

Evelyn enjoyed another close friendship which was largely founded on religious preoccupations, with John and Penelope Betjeman, who were at that time living in Wantage. It reached a climax in 1948. He had known John since the nineteen twenties and Penelope (through her brother Roger Chetwode) for almost as long. He yearned for John to be converted from Anglo-Catholicism to the Roman Catholic Church, and urged this step upon him in the course of a long correspondence which increased in intensity during these immediate post-war years. Evelyn was not a born missionary. In his efforts to disprove to John the claims of the Anglican Church he could not resist farcical and sometimes obscene invective which could only have stiffened the other's resistance. When he was in the hospital of St John and St Elizabeth, however, in January 1947, Evelyn wrote several letters to John on the same theme in a more serious spirit.

The last of these letters ended thus:

'Almost anyone who becomes a Catholic makes sacrifices. Some very large ones. Yours I think would be greater than most for you have built your life & learning & art round the Church of England. I can well understand your reluctance to start a new life in middle-age with any literary & aesthetic predilection the other way. It is easy to say "Well I'll just wait until an Archangel is sent to make the announcement to me personally in God's good time. Meanwhile I'll believe in the Incarnation on two days a week and continue my catalogue of Anglican Churches."

'Finally, do consider my first letter. 1. We may both be wrong. 2. We can't both be right. 3. You cannot be right and I wrong. 4. If I am right you are wrong. Which of these statements do you deny? A real protestant could deny 3. But your Wantage waifs [Anglo-Catholic clergymen] don't and can't.

'But there is a year's painful transition ahead for you if you decide to follow your mind instead of your emotions. You may shirk it.'

These exhortations were fruitless, but Penelope, quite independently, after long and varied study, and under no persuasion from anyone else, was received into the Roman Catholic Church in March 1948. The only religious correspondence between her and Evelyn was after her conversion, and concerned superficial topics such as Catholic custom in the matter of Christmas and Easter offerings, the tipping of sacristans, etc. A large part of their correspondence before this had been on horses and harness.

It will be remembered by readers that in her young days in Britain St Helena, according to Evelyn, had had a passion for horses, riding and hunting, and that she first met her husband Constantius Chlorus in one of King Còle's harness rooms. All the information which Evelyn needed for these scenes, apart from that stored in his memory from the old days of Captain Hance, was supplied by Penelope. She was and still is a passionate horsewoman. In his description of harness in the fourth century he only made one mistake in the book, by referring to spurs. It seems they were not known in Europe till the sixth century.

When the book was published in 1950, Evelyn kept a promise made to Penelope in 1947, and dedicated it to her. He told me and other friends that the character of Helena was modelled on her. I do not disbelieve this, but apart from the taste for horses the resemblance is not easy to detect.

In the autumn of 1948 Evelyn accepted an invitation from *Life* magazine to return to the United States and give some lectures sponsored by the Luce organization. He also received invitations to lecture at Catholic Universities, foundations and societies in America, most of which he accepted. On 28 October he noted in his diary: 'My 45th birthday. An unproductive and unhealthy year. The start pray God of a better.' On the 31st he sailed to New York, returned in mid-December for Christmas with his children and then returned to America to complete his engagements in January 1949. One of his lecture subjects was Graham Greene and he owned to his friend later that he had thereby been responsible for spreading the notion of Graham Greene as a 'Catholic author', a piece of critical pigeon-holing that afflicted both Evelyn and Graham and was resented by both.

The year 1949 was not an eventful one in Evelyn's literary life. Thomas Merton's *Elected Silence*, mentioned already, came out edited and with an introduction by Evelyn. It did not cause such excitement in England as it had done in the United States. Outside Catholic circles it was little noticed. Soon after Evelyn's return from America in April there came out another book on which he had done his own share in the year before: *The Sermons of Monsignor Ronald Knox*, chosen and introduced by Evelyn. He continued to write articles and reviews, the most noticed of which was 'The American Epoch in the Catholic Church', illustrating the special American contribution to Roman Catholic devotion and customs. It appeared in *Life* magazine in the United States and in Catholic intellectual magazines in his home country. As with *Elected Silence* and the Knox sermons, it was little noticed in Great Britain outside Catholic circles though it was the cause of interest and criticism in America.

After his return, his private life was not unusually eventful for the good reason that throughout the rest of this year he was toiling at *Helena*. There is however one incident in his private life in 1949 which is worth recalling because it shows Evelyn in conjunction with other eminent personalities of the time.

One day Evelyn asked me if I would accompany him on a short visit to Paris, as he wished to see Nancy Mitford and Diana Cooper who with her husband was then living in a house at Chantilly which Duff had been given by the French Government on his retirement as Ambassador at the end of 1947. Reluctantly I had to tell Evelyn that I could not afford to accompany him. Evelyn thereupon asked whether I would come as his secretary and *homme d'affaires*, or as Diana Cooper later described it, his 'understrapper', my salary to be paid in the form of the expenses of the journey. I agreed.

I made all arrangements for the forthcoming visit with a travel agency, with Diana Cooper, with Nancy Mitford and to my surprise with the family of the great French poet Paul Claudel. I am connected by marriage with Claudel's daughter-in-law and it so happened that she and her husband Henri Claudel were in London at the time. I mentioned to them that I was shortly going to Paris for a few days whereupon, on hearing the circumstances, they said that I *must* bring Evelyn to visit *Monsieur l'Ambassadeur*, as the great man was addressed and referred to by his family. Claudel it seemed was a passionate admirer of Evelyn's novels and had been talking about him enthusiastically recently after reading *The Loved One*. (Though he spoke English with difficulty, Claudel read it widely and with ease.) We made a tentative date for a luncheon at the poet's house, confirmed in Paris. I obtained temporary membership for Evelyn and myself of the Travellers' Club in Paris. I think I proved myself rather an efficient secretary.

Evelyn was much surprised at the invitation to meet Claudel. He was also rather nervous, so much so that before driving to the Claudel apartment he insisted on us both praying for success in the *Madeleine*. Our petitions were but partially granted. Evelyn was so shy of speaking French to a French master and so fearful of not understanding what was said to him that he feigned total ignorance of the language and throughout lunch conversed with his host through the interpretation of Henri and Christine Claudel. The host was in high spirits and questioned Evelyn closely and with overflowing mirth about the burial customs of Forest Lawn. 'They really do that? It is not a pardonable invention? But the clergy in Los Angeles – what do they make of all this?' And so on. Among other things, he said that he had been told that Evelyn was accused of snobbery. He said that Evelyn should accept such accusations as a compliment; delight in excellence was easily confused with snobbery by ignorant people.

At the end of this formidable and excellent repast, we moved into the main room of the apartment. There then occurred an incident of which Evelyn gave many accounts which vary essentially from what I remember.

Claudel kept a book of press-cuttings. In it he had collected a great number of press-photographs in which, either by the photographer's incompetence or malice, eminent people were made to look ridiculous. They were very funny and Claudel kept up a continuous and witty commentary while displaying these treasures. According to Evelyn, Claudel turned a page on which there was a grotesque photograph funnier than any hitherto. Evelyn roared with redoubled laughter upon which Claudel shut the book, rose and stiffly said goodbye. The photograph that had aroused Evelyn's special mirth was of Claudel. I was sitting on the sofa with Evelyn and Claudel and witnessed no such *faux pas*. I remember the session going on for a long time, for Claudel was showing off his favourite toy, and Madame Claudel evidently wishing to retire to her afternoon rest. Her daughter-in-law came over and whispered something to *Monsieur l'Ambassadeur*, whereupon he closed the book, we all rose and Evelyn and I took our leave. The dramatic story of Evelyn's gaffe was first told by him when he described the meeting next day to Diana Cooper. I was as surprised as she. He stuck to it after that and came to believe it sincerely. I feel fairly sure that it was his novelist's instinct at work again, and what set it going was, I hazard, the fact that he somehow detected that Claudel for all his geniality did not like him. Later Claudel told a friend of mine that he had been very interested to meet Evelyn Waugh '*mais*' he added, '*il lui manque l'allure du vrai gentleman.*'

The next day Evelyn and I lunched with Nancy Mitford for Evelyn to meet the celebrated Dominican, Père Couturier. The latter was at that time a very well known clergyman in Paris, an extreme modernist, an enthusiast for Catholic reform, a close friend of Picasso for whose cause he was a spirited apologist. He stood in fact for everything that Evelyn most loathed, yet Evelyn was eager to meet this controversial figure. The meeting was not a success. Nancy drew out the famous Dominican who began a eulogy of his famous friend. 'In the whole world' I remember him saying, 'there can be no more intensely creative force', and 'imagine the tragic situation of such a man. Picasso once said to me " You do not know what it is to say something over and over again to a world that is *stone deaf*!"' It was all expressed with exquisite French refinement and skill, but I remember having an uneasy feeling (though not sharing Evelyn's hostility to modern French painting) that the performance was more than a little phoney.

For Evelyn it was a challenge which he picked up joyfully. Since the middle of the war his hearing had rapidly worsened. He had been placed at the table at an angle from the Dominican which made it hard for him to hear everything Père Couturier said. Nancy offered to change places with Evelyn so that he could hear easily. 'I have not heard everything the reverend gentleman has said,' replied Evelyn, 'but I have heard enough of it not to want to hear more.' The Dominican had enough English to follow this. He and Evelyn then engaged, with the help of Nancy who was sitting between them, in a battle of wits in which the Dominican, versed in the arts of apologetics, triumphed easily. The party ended on a note of awkward good humour.

After lunch Evelyn and Nancy and I drove to the Duff Cooper house at Chantilly. We were to spend the night there and return in the morning. That encounter also ended in something like disaster. It may have been Evelyn's defeat at the hands of Père Couturier; it may have been his sly detection of Paul Claudel's distaste; whatever it was, he was in that recurrent mood when his overriding wish was to let loose some anarchy.

All went well till after dinner. Then came chaos. Duff Cooper maintained in France the English custom of 'sitting over the port' with the male guests. Evelyn took this opportunity to needle Duff, using all his deadly efficiency in carrying out the operation. Duff launched temporarily into a pet theme: the iniquity of the 'men of Munich', whose follies had made certain a perpetual Left-Wing Government of Great Britain. Evelyn mildly contested this opinion: appeasement was undeniably the cause of British commitment to perpetual Left-Wingism, yes, but not only the appeasement policies of Chamberlain and his friends, surely? Was not the Ministry of Information in the war equally to blame? What with its 'Arms for Russia' weeks in factories, its untiring and mendacious propaganda about the heaven-on-earth realized in the USSR of Stalin, all in support of Churchill's policy designed to appease the appetite of that blood-stained tyrant? Was not *that* a deeper cause of British bewildered preference for the Left?

Evelyn had not forgotten, as Duff well knew, that he, Duff, had been Minister of Information at the time in June 1941 when Great Britain and Russia were forced by Hitler into alliance. The main impetus for the pro-Russian hysteria in Britain came not from Duff but from his successor Brendan Bracken, but it was Duff, helpless before circumstances, who had set the avalanche moving. It was not an incident of his public life on which he looked back with satisfaction. Evelyn knew that too. His quiet insistence swiftly and surely produced a storm.

Suddenly Duff lost his temper. He went red in the face, he shook, his voice rose higher and higher till it was a shriek. He did not attempt an argued reply to Evelyn (and rightly perhaps because, unhappily for Duff, everything Evelyn had said was true); he took to random abuse of the wildest, coarsest kind. 'It's rotten little rats like you', he yelled, 'who have brought about the downfall of the country.' He went on to accuse Evelyn of cynicism, of hatred of decency, homosexualism, cowardice, pacifism, and other enormities. The sudden storm was short. As though nothing had happened Duff turned to me and invited me to help myself to port and pass the decanter on. Evelyn showed no sign of offence. Later on in the evening he told me that scenes of this kind were more or less routine when he was with Duff. I found and still find this difficult to believe.

As to what happened after I am still not clear. Duff was particularly charming and attentive as a host for the rest of the evening. In the morning we had to leave at about 10 o'clock because our hired chauffeur and car had to keep another appointment in Paris at midday. It was said afterwards that arrangements had been made for us to visit the Château of Chantilly under specially privileged conditions, but these were not mentioned at the time. Certainly Diana was displeased by the way things had turned out, but she had not been present at the odious scene after dinner, in which Duff had behaved worse than Evelyn. At all events Nancy and Evelyn and I left Chantilly and returned to Paris under a cloud. None of us was ever quite clear as to why.

The next day Evelyn and I returned to London. It is by that jaunt to Paris that I best remember Evelyn in 1949.

Evelyn did some travelling in 1950. He went to Italy in the spring, travelling by way of Paris, judging by Nancy Mitford's letters. He went to Rome and visited his old friend Harold Acton in Florence. In the absence of any diary kept at this time, dates must remain uncertain. So must incidents. It may have been during this journey that there occurred an incident of which I was told later by Nancy Mitford. Undeterred by the failure of the encounter with Père Couturier, she asked Evelyn to dine with a young French intellectual who was anxious to meet him. He spoke English fluently. (His identity is unknown to me.) The dinner was a disaster. Evelyn met all the young man's advances with sarcasm and rudeness and in fact behaved with such atrocious incivility and unkindness that the admirer was reduced to tears. When the ordeal was over Nancy angrily asked Evelyn why he had behaved so outrageously; how he could show such gratuitous cruelty while at the same time proclaiming himself a believing Christian and a practising Catholic. Evelyn offered no defence but gave an explanation of his behaviour which became familiar to many of his friends. 'You have no idea', he said, 'how much nastier I would be if I was not a Catholic. Without supernatural aid I would hardly be a human being.'

In July there came a new proposal for a film of *Brideshead Revisited*. Evelyn had by now completely fallen out of love with the book. In March he had written to Graham Greene in the postscript to a letter: 'Talking of rereading, I reread "Brideshead" and was appalled. I can find many excuses – that it was the product, *Consule Braken*, of Spam, Nissen huts, black-out – but it won't do for peace-time. The plot seemed to me excellent. I am going to spend the summer rewriting it.' (As I have said already this rewriting was a waste of time. The only profitable rewriting would have been to remove Julia.)

Evelyn may have seen in the new film proposal a chance to set right errors made *Consule Bracken*. The proposed film was unconnected with the MGM proposition of four years before but came from a group who had sought out Graham Greene as the scriptwriter. (It should be mentioned that shortly before this a brilliant film *The Third Man* based on Graham Greene's fiction and scripted by him had been produced by Carol Reed.) Evelyn was overjoyed at the proposal, for Graham Greene, he knew, would not show Hollywood insensitiveness to the theological implications of the novel. 'Please don't try to get out of "Brideshead",' he wrote to Graham on 26 July, 'I am sure you can make a fine film of it. Don't think I shall be cantankerous. I am cantankerous but not about that sort of thing – about cooking and theology and clothes and grammar and dogs.' I do not think there was any insincerity in this. I believe he would have proved an uncantankerous colleague of Graham Greene. I often saw them together and, due doubtless to the formidable personality of the other, as formidable as his own, I never saw Evelyn misbehave in his presence.

As the reader does not need to be told, nothing came of this later *Brideshead Revisited* proposal. The film company concerned ran out of money, and the project disappeared, a familiar sequence of events.

In the middle of October 1950 Evelyn and Laura went again to the United States where they stayed for about a month, so they were away when *Helena* came out. Evelyn had lecture engagements, mostly in Catholic foundations. Alec Waugh was living in New York at the time and the two brothers saw much of each other again. Their happiest meeting was a dinner party arranged by Alec Waugh from which they went to the new musical *Kiss Me Kate*. Evelyn was entranced by this ingenious and admirable entertainment in which a conventional musical comedy was with great skill conjoined with a performance of *The Taming of the Shrew*. When it came to London in 1951 Evelyn went to it at least half a dozen times. It prompted the only occasion that I recall when Evelyn sought spiritual guidance from me.

He was concerned as to whether he ought to confess to falsehood and dishonesty. He told me that he thought he was guilty of sinful deception, but was not sure. Anticipating the role of his confessor I asked him to tell me all about it. He told me that his eldest daughter, Teresa, was being educated at a convent and that on a recent visit to London he had asked for her to be given leave to lunch and spend the afternoon with her father. The nuns had refused saying that Tessa had already had her allotted ration of such leave during the current term, and that extension of the privilege was only granted for pressing family reasons or for strictly educational purposes. Evelyn replied that for the good of her education he wished to take his daughter to a Shakespeare matinée. At this the nuns relented. The matinée was *Kiss Me Kate*. Ought he to confess this ingenious duping .

of the nuns? 'You boast about your theological insight,' he said, 'use it now.'

I replied in some such words as these: 'Compared to most of your crimes, this seems to me a very mild offence. But you have been guilty of that kind of equivocation which Jesuits are accused of and which is tellingly denounced by the Porter in the Murder Scene in *Macbeth*.'

'You never listen to anyone but yourself. I told you this was not a matinée performance of *Macbeth* but of *Kiss Me Kate*, and what I want to know is: was I guilty of deception in describing it to the nuns as a Shakespeare matinée?'

'Of course you were.'

'I see. But technically my words were not a lie.'

'That is true of all the best deceptions.'

'Then I should confess this.'

'Yes.'

This dialogue referred back to conversations which Evelyn and I had had earlier on theological questions. The Roman Catholic Church was in some disarray, little compared to the disarray which was to follow. The policy of the Pope during the war, which was based on a reliance on diplomacy, had failed completely, largely because Pius XII was an inept diplomatist. Lost ground needed to be recovered throughout Europe and the first attempt took the form of renewed and exaggerated devotionalism. The supposed visions and miracles of Fatima in Portugal were given an approval hitherto reserved only for Lourdes; the strong and traditional devotion to the Mother of Christ in the Catholic Church was given renewed prominence by the proposal by Pius XII to give the notion of the Assumption, hitherto accepted as a pious legend or an allegory, to be believed or otherwise according to taste, the force and status of a defined doctrine.

It was on this last-mentioned subject that Evelyn and I had had many arguments. I saw the Pope's move as bringing the Catholic Church into ridicule and trivializing essential belief. In this I was not alone among my co-religionists. Evelyn took the opposite view. As a fundamentalist he liked the proposed doctrine because it defied rationalism, and he was delighted later, when the doctrine was defined by the Pope in 1950, that the declaration was accompanied by an encyclical letter which eschewed all thought of compromise, and implicitly stressed that the definition was a summons to faith irrespective of the claims of reason. He was delighted that the letter, by the literalism of its interpretation, put to flight many Catholic clergymen who, often relying on the arguments of the eminent Anglican theologian C. S. Lewis, had consoled worried parishioners with assurances that the terms of the definition would not put any insufferable burden on the mind. In the course of our discussions Evelyn frequently accused me of crypto-Protestantism, atheism, of being under Communist influence, and, in the revived language of nineteenth century theology, of being a weak-kneed, cowardly 'minimiser'. But we never quarrelled.

In October 1950 *Helena* was published. The indifferent reception given to what Evelyn believed to be by far his best book was the greatest disappointment of his whole literary life, as he told me and other friends.

The only whole-hearted praise he received was offered in private, while in public, compared to *The Loved One*, it was a flop. He told me that the extent of the flop was brought home to him most forcibly by one incident. *The Loved One* had moved the Queen (now Queen Elizabeth the Queen Mother) to write him a letter of appreciation in her own hand. His son Auberon has told me that Evelyn received this letter 'ecstatically'. So he presented his next book to the Queen. But there was no royal hand-written response to *Helena*, only formal thanks and acknowledgement.

For all its failure with the critics and the general public, *Helena* moved Henry Luce and the directors of *Life Magazine* (his faithful patrons despite his earlier threat of legal prosecution) to invite Evelyn to contribute some articles on the Near East: on Israel and Jordan as the scene of sacred history visited by St Helena, and on Syria, Lebanon and Turkey as the scene of the Constantinian Empire which he had described. Evelyn asked me to accompany him. Again I was forced to say that I could not afford to do so. This time he did not ask me to be his secretary but instead offered to procure me a contract with *Life* similar to his own. He was as good as his word. *Life* furnished me with expense money on the same generous scale as they allowed Evelyn. He was to write an article on Palestine, Jordan and Syria, concentrating on the theme of the Holy Places; I was to turn in an article on Turkey Today, the latter being a topic of interest then as Turkey wished to become a member of NATO (though hardly described as an Atlantic power). Thus Evelyn and I divided his empire between us in the style of the successors of Constantine, but, I delight to record, without the usual discords of such divisions.

I had a house in London then, so I made the arrangements. 1951 was a time when bureaucracy (still enjoying unaccustomed war-time powers) was trying to keep citizens under its eye by raising numerous obstacles to foreign travel. To obtain travellers' cheques from our dollars I needed to attend at a bank to fill up numerous forms. On this matter Evelyn showed at his silliest and most tiresome. His signature was required on some of these forms. The courteous and capable bank official who took me through all this tedious routine told me that he had rung up Evelyn (who was in London at the St James's Club) asking him to come to the bank to sign, and Evelyn had replied that he refused to go to the bank as it was the bank's business to wait on him, not his to wait on the bank. The bank official, who seemed not without considerable sense of humour, suggested a way out. I could sign instead but only if Evelyn first signed a witnessed

337

paper giving me authority to do so for twenty-four hours. Later in the day I found Evelyn who signed the paper which the bank official (a reader of Evelyn's books I suspect) had drafted. The witness was Ed Stanley. Thus I got the travellers' cheques but only after needless trouble, delay and journeys to the city, through Evelyn's ludicrous and self-important behaviour. I saw tumults ahead, but, as mentioned already, none occurred on this pilgrimage to the Holy Sepulchre or in Syria and Turkey.

On about 20 January 1951 we went by train to Rome and thence by air to Israel. We stayed at Tel Aviv before moving to Jerusalem. It was in Tel Aviv that Evelyn and I met, at our very uncomfortable hotel, the young English woman, whom I have mentioned earlier in this book, who bore a distinct resemblance both to his first wife and the girl whom he later wanted to marry. I have recorded my instinctive feeling that Evelyn would fall for her, as he did. I knew her family who come from the same part of Yorkshire as does mine. Her name was Mrs Wilson, the daughter-in-law of the famous physician Lord Moran. Evelyn's slight and brief acquaintance with her was to have formidable results later, if one is to believe all Evelyn's accounts of a confused episode in his life.

From Jerusalem we went to Nazareth and ultimately to Damascus and later Beirut. From the Lebanon we flew to Turkey via Cyprus, staying first in Ankara and then in Istanbul. We returned by air to Rome by way of Athens, and thence by train home, by way of Paris. From this journey came Evelyn's *Life* articles on the Holy Places, later made into a short book which does not call for any detailed consideration here. It is a good imaginative account, not overloaded with minutiae or pietism. My article was not printed. It must be one of the most expensive unpublished works on Turkey in the history of letters.

I do not intend to give anything resembling a day by day or week by week account of this journey. We suffered many of the exasperations which are the lot of every traveller in those embattled and bureaucracy-ridden regions. In Jordan and Syria we were under continual threat of arrest as agents of subversion. In Jerusalem I actually was arrested by a policeman one afternoon. When an English-speaking officer was eventually produced he told me that I was being held because I was not wearing Arab head-dress, and he politely asked for an explanation. I said that as I cannot talk Arabic I would feel very foolish if I walked about dressed as an Arab. Someone might wish to talk to me! The officer gravely released me with a warning that if I wore a hat I was liable to be mistaken for an Israeli spy. Suchlike absurdities beset our path all the way from Israel to Turkey.

This was the only occasion when I saw Evelyn at work on research for a piece of writing. 'I never plan an article much ahead,' he said, 'I just loaf around till the story breaks in my head.' We went round the Christian shrines in Jerusalem, especially round the Church of the Holy Sepulchre in much detail. This church, shared by some six denominations of which the Greek, Roman Catholic, and Armenian are the principals, has been the scene of much scandalous sectarian strife, but not so much as horror-struck travellers relate on returning home. After our daily visits, in which we often availed ourselves of the ministrations of the guides (mostly Arab Christians), it became clear where most of the terrible stories (alas not all) have their origin. Here, and in the deeply moving shrine known as the Church of 'Ecce Homo', Evelyn set about his work with intense application but, I saw with surprise, hardly ever writing down a note. 'Once I started I'd never have time to look', he said.

There is only one way to find out about the life of the Church of the Holy Sepulchre, an extraordinary life to which some clergymen of all the main denominations give their lives, as some laymen do to chess, and that way is to stay on the premises as a guest of one of the communities. Only at Easter and on one or two other major festivals are there large scale religious services by day (with most unedifying disorder), but normally all the services of the three great Christian sects take place at night after the doors have been ceremonially closed and the key handed over, according to ancient tradition, to the clergy within by representatives of the two Moslem families who are reliably believed to be directly descended from the guardians appointed by the Caliph Omar. (The Caliph built a minaret near the church in honour of Jesus Christ, and the daily muezzin utters the call to prayer from a modern structure on the same site, the only minaret built as an adjunct to a Christian Church.)

Evelyn and I stayed with the Franciscan Community attached to the church, and witnessed the night-long services, including the Greek and Roman Catholic Masses, and the dramatic moment, when, with the prosiness of what is done daily, a priest hands back the key to the Moslem guardians. I have a vivid memory of Evelyn during that fascinating though exhausting experience. He knew all the guide-spread stories of sectarian strife, but unlike most Christians of most denominations he found relish in them, and would have been glad of proof that they were all true. I think he hoped to witness some scandalous incident. In the seventeenth century he would never have incurred the then often fatal accusation of 'tolerationism.'

At our early supper, at about five in the afternoon, Evelyn asked the Franciscan brother, a young American who acted as our host, to tell us the routine followed in the services. The brother explained it lucidly. First, he said, at about half past eleven one of the brothers of the Greek or Armenian communities goes round the church with clappers to awaken the Greek and Armenian clergy whose offices are the first to begin. (The Roman Catholics have their own morning call arrangements.) 'I see,' said Evelyn who was taking notes for once, '11.30 p.m. Heretics and Schismatics woken up. Then what?' 'Oh Mr Waugh!' said the American brother, 'we look upon them rather as our brethren in Christ.' Evelyn answered with a grunt expressive of disapproval. The Franciscan outlined the rest of the routine and at six we went to bed.

At about a quarter past eleven Evelyn and I stole into the church and made ourselves comfortable on the empty divan occupied in the day-time by the Moslem guardians. Sure enough, at half past the man with the clappers came round, and soon after the Greek matins began. Not long after that the Armenian matins began. At about half past one in the morning the Gregorian chant of the Catholic matins joined in to form the full discordant chorus of the church. (The guides inform their customers that the sects aim to shout each other down.) I found this polyphony strangely moving, the Latin 'saecula saeculorum Amen' mingling with the reiterated Armenian 'Divornia' and the Greek 'Kyrie Eleison'. We walked round the church and I remember the presiding Greek ecclesiastic catching sight of us and politely raising his biretta in salutation. We returned to the divan for a nap before the Greek Mass but the singing was too much for sleep, especially as a new choir broke in from one of the upstairs chapels. 'Noisy buggers, aren't they?' was Evelyn's only comment on this part of the celebrations.

After the Greek Mass, at which the tomb is the altar, there follows the Armenian Mass celebrated likewise at the tomb. Then occurs the handing back of the key to the Moslem guardians at about four o'clock. The doors are opened. After the Latin Mass (also said on the tomb) it was around five o'clock when Evelyn and I left the church. There were signs of dawn and we heard the muezzin's cry: 'Allahu Akbar.' It was an unforgettable and deeply moving experience.

The reader will not be surprised to learn that in the tense political Arab-Jewish situation of that time, Evelyn's sympathies were with the Arabs and his feelings towards the Zionists of Israel were extremely hostile. Circumstances made it difficult for him to maintain a consistent attitude. In Israel, where he looked with distaste on the life around him, everyone he met had read at least one of his books and some had read them all. Wherever we went we met people eager to meet the author, and able to talk to him intelligently about his work. Moreover he found it hard to maintain hostility in the presence of such a civilized and engaging man as the late Professor Leo Kohn, at that time a political adviser to the Ministry for Foreign Affairs, and whom we met frequently in Tel Aviv. We met a few Zionist fanatics who fortified Evelyn's prejudice, but they were outnumbered by courteous and intelligent men and women pleased at the opportunity of discussing the Israeli situation with a person of formidable intellect. For all his Belloc-conditioned and Chesterton-conditioned ideas Evelyn could not but admire the constructive determination in the spirit of Israel. He was much edified by a visit to a rigorously orthodox kibbutz south of Tel Aviv, where we were entertained to luncheon in orthodox style.

His situation was quite different in Jordan. None of the Jordanians we met had heard of him. For them he and I were two more pressmen and the fact that we came to old Jerusalem from Israel made us objects of grave official suspicion, for it was the belief of Arabs and their supporters then that Israel was controlled by Moscow. When Evelyn called on the Minister of Culture, then in Jerusalem, His Excellency told him to go away because he could not be bothered with reporters. Later the Minister seems to have been informed that Evelyn was of some eminence, for at a party one evening at the British Consulate he met him again and made a very full apology, too full in fact to carry conviction. His Excellency was not instructed in the merits of 'Occam's Razor'. He said that his behaviour was not only to be explained by the fact that he had not caught Evelyn's name, but was due also to the fact that he was very ill that day, that he had been wearing new boots which did not fit, and that he was drunk at the time; he had given orders that Evelyn might go wherever he wished and had ordered two of his most senior officials to wait on him next day. Evelyn graciously accepted this apology, which I think was even more extended than I have indicated. When in due course the officials called on us, they did not ease matters. They spent their whole time describing in detail the horrors of Israel and its Russian-dominated character. They were not interested in seeking information about Israel but of imparting it to us. Evelyn found himself manoeuvred into acting as an apologist for the object of his aversion. He suggested that they might be exaggerating the Communist character of Israel and Zionism. His remark was met by a patronizing laugh from the younger of the two. He could give proof, he said, of Muscovite domination of Israel. A friend of his had visited a frontier post and listened to the Israeli soldiers talking, and they were talking – in Russian! At this the older and more talkative official said, as though to put the discussion on a very serious basis, that to an earnest enquirer there could be no doubt about it: Hitler himself had stated that this was so on more than one occasion, and furthermore it was fully admitted on the Jewish side in The Protocols of the Elders of Zion. Evelyn was not used to being talked down to as an ignoramus, and though he was visibly irritated, he was also visibly enjoying the sheer farce of this scene. There was no explosion but his sympathy with the Arab cause was put under severe strain. He did not change sides. Of his many comments on the situation the one that probably expressed his feelings most accurately, and which I enjoyed most, was made one day as we were walking through the thronged streets of Jerusalem. Gazing on the picturesque scene around us Evelyn said: 'They dress better on this side, but conversation is less rewarding. Dressy but dull, you might call them.' 'Like the late Lord Lonsdale', I suggested. 'Precisely.'

We were subjected to almost as many frustrations as had beset Mr Scott-King in Neutralia. Under these circumstances Evelyn behaved very

well, very well indeed by his standards, but there was one occasion when
the eternal anarchist in him took over. I did not come out of it very well.
It was not an occasion of frustration; there was no excuse for the episode.
It happened as follows. A junior official of the British Embassy in Beirut
who had been detailed to give us any help we needed, and whom I knew
slightly, invited us to come after dinner to meet some of his relations.
Evelyn had done himself rather well at dinner (we were in what he called
'the caviare belt') and by the time the young official arrived in his car to
pick us up, Evelyn was not quite sober. The relations turned out to be a
family of missionaries, and far more like missionaries as represented on
the old-fashioned music-hall stage than such people usually are. They
regaled us with cocoa. Evelyn was in aggressive mood and turned to
political discussion. How did they manage, he asked in a menacing tone
and with glaring eyes, now that the blessings of French rule had been
withdrawn? Evelyn was informed that they enjoyed good relations with
the Lebanese Government. How was that possible, he asked, or did they
have ample supplies of arms and ammunition? No, they had no arms.
But, Evelyn went on, when the natives rise who shoots them now that
there is no longer a French army in the country? At this point, when
consternation was on every face, the telephone rang. We were expecting
news from the hotel about the time of our flight in the morning and the
young official had mercifully left the number of this house with the hotel
porter. Evelyn took the call. In his absence I feebly tried to explain away
my friend's behaviour as the result of a very trying day, but I think the
family were not so simple that they had not discerned the real reason.
My feeble performance was chiefly due to the fact that though I disapproved of the sort of things Evelyn was saying, and was indeed very
shocked, especially as I knew that his grotesque opinions were 'not altogether fool', I could not help finding the whole scene monstrously,
disgracefully, wrongly but irresistibly funny. Evelyn came back into the
room to say that our flight left very early so we ought to be going. I
gave an exaggerated account of the amount of packing I needed to do and
the evening thus drew to an end. I wished I had stood up to Evelyn and
at least tried to call him to order, if for no nobler reason than that my
supine behaviour must have suggested to these decent prim people that I
also was of Evelyn's mind.

I did remonstrate with him later when he tried to throw the whole
blame on to the young official. 'It was a disgraceful thing to do,' he said,
'to ask two elderly and very distinguished men to drink cocoa.'

This was Evelyn's only serious misdemeanour on these travels.

We went to Turkey where, after a brief stay in Ankara, our paths
separated. Evelyn, still in search of Holy Places, went to Izmir, formerly
Smyrna, near which is to be found one of the numerous tombs of the
Virgin Mary, in the area of Ephesus. I continued my profane study of

Turkey by staying on a few days longer in Ankara and then visiting Eskisehir. We met in Bursa and from there caught a boat at the nearest port for Istanbul.

When studying for my essay on Robert Byron, I had made myself familiar in a very rough-and-ready way with Byzantine art and architecture. I had done this chiefly through Robert's books. I had not seen Santa Sophia since a youthful journey in 1927, and I was longing to see it again with more informed eyes. We arrived at night and I could hardly wait for the morning. Evelyn did not share my excitement.

It was during these Istanbul days that I was first aware of the extent of Evelyn's deep and embittered dislike of Robert Byron. He took it out on the splendours of ancient Constantinople. He came with me to Santa Sophia, not only on our first day but on all days, and did what he could to make it impossible for me to enjoy and admire that defaced but splendid cathedral. He kept up a continual commentary of denigration. 'It was just a fad of Robert,' he used to say, 'he hadn't done his work and was sent down without a degree so he turned against the classics, and proclaimed post-classical Greek art as the ideal. He was so embarrassingly ignorant that he thought he'd discovered it.' This was typical of his performance within the building. Outside he was no less scoffing. 'It sits there like a great toad,' he would say, 'imagine it a small building and its nothing, whereas a small baroque church can have all the beauty of the Gesú in Rome and more. It's impressive because it's big, like a great big toad.' Once as we were walking towards Santa Sophia, I asked him if he had ever given Robert his views about the supreme Byzantine masterpiece. 'I hated him!' he cried passionately, 'I hated him! I hated him!'

In the first half of March we returned. It was a lovely early spring day when we arrived in Paris. As we drove from the station over the Seine, Notre Dame shone in the light of the rising sun, a heavenly vision. 'Look at that,' said Evelyn, 'and then think of all that Byzantine muck we've been seeing.'

That was the last journey I did with Evelyn. It remains a happy memory. I was very relieved when researching for this book to find that Evelyn kept no diary during this time.

# Chapter 21

## 1951-1953

On 18 August 1951 Evelyn wrote in the course of a letter to Graham Greene: 'I am writing an interminable novel about army life, obsessed by memories of military dialogue.' This is the first mention by Evelyn, so far as I know, of his work on the War Trilogy which was to be his last large-scale work of fiction. It was to occupy him on and off till 1961. The letter was one of thanks for a copy of Graham's novel *The End of the Affair* which had just been published and which Evelyn admired. On account of this book Evelyn again deprived me of sleep at Piers Court when I went to stay there for a night soon afterwards.

In Graham Greene's novel the principal male character is a writer called Bendrix, and commenting on him Evelyn, in the letter quoted above, made one of his rare remarks about his own writing routine: 'I was greatly encouraged, by the way, to read that Bendrix thinks 1000 words a good day's work. I used to write 3000 & can still sometimes do 1200. But I suspect Bendrix writes better than I.' He also offered Graham a subject: 'In America when a man is ordained priest he gets a proposal from an insurance company that he shall take out a policy against being unfrocked. This apparently is true. Ronnie Knox suggests it as a plot for you – a priest of such charity that he simulates sin in order to help the destitute.' Graham did not act on the suggestion.

I saw a great deal of Evelyn during the rest of 1951 after our return from the Levant in March. The main reason for that was my production of a radio version of the second part of *Helena*. Evelyn hoped to make good, by means of a radio broadcast, the failure of the novel in the book market, and I was eager to help him. It seemed to me an ideal subject for the Third Programme, then directed by Harman Grisewood, a friend and admirer of Evelyn. But though the Third Programme, and indeed the whole BBC, was always on the look-out for contributions from distinguished writers, Harman and I had to battle hard for *Helena*. I had not realized before this the extent to which Evelyn was disliked in the BBC. The reason was not far to seek. Though the Corporation had several distinguished writers and poets working for it, a larger proportion of those responsible for the literary part of its output were men of talent who had not fulfilled earlier promise. They were naturally envious of one whose gifts, in their own estimation, were in no way above their own, but who, nevertheless, had hit the jackpot. Most of such people were extremely class-conscious and thus repelled by his extreme conservatism, and his openly expressed contempt for the age of the common man. They represented that host of readers who had resented Evelyn's unsympathetic portrayal of Hooper in *Brideshead Revisited*. When Evelyn offered the BBC *Helena*, the novel by him that they most despised, these people instinctively obstructed its chance of success.

Evelyn had never been at pains to be on good terms with the BBC. Not very long before this, the mutual relations had worsened when the Corporation had put a large proposition to him. It was the custom then for the Home Service (now Radio 4) to introduce the Sovereign's Christmas broadcast by an hour's 'world round-up' programme. It had been decided to approach Evelyn in the hope that he would take on the task of introducing the programme. It was felt at Broadcasting House that the Corporation should send as their ambassador a literary man. An appointment was made at the Hyde Park Hotel. With singular maladroitness the emissary chosen was a disappointed novelist, a deeply class-conscious man whose self-esteem bordered on mania, and who regarded Evelyn's work as decidedly inferior to his own. Being a man who looked on good manners as servility unworthy of genius, he did not attempt to win Evelyn's agreement by any exercise of charm, wisely perhaps as he had little to exercise. He preferred an attempt at impressing the other.

Evelyn was angered by the incident which he long remembered. He said to me once, 'Why does your Corporation send people like Kurkweiler to me and expect to get anything out of me?' In fact the BBC emissary bore a sturdy English name, but Evelyn always insisted that this man (who later displayed some sympathy with Nazism) was a German Jewish refugee whose real name was Kurkweiler. The proposition came to nothing.

This had happened six years before, but the memory lingered on, and 'Kurkweiler', accepted by his employers at his own enormous valuation, was of weight in Third Programme counsels. The opinion was circulated, propagated, encouraged, and almost turned into a decision that *Helena* was not worth any considerable expense and need not involve first-rate actors. I wanted something very much more ambitious, and in the end obtained it. Evelyn had made the offer in January 1951 and from March the battle of *Helena* occupied most of the year till I recorded the production, before the December broadcast, in October.

This low BBC estimate of Evelyn was not typical of any literary opinion then, but it was not a rarity. He was regarded as an outstanding writer. Yet he was never accorded any official recognition, either by the universities or the Sovereign. He minded this much more than I expected. 'But Evelyn,' I remonstrated with him once, 'you can't really want to be a knight when you see the mediocrities who do get knighted.' 'I would go on my knees', said Evelyn, 'to Mr Attlee; I would lick his boots if he wanted; I would lie in the mud outside Downing Street, if he promised in return to advise the King to make me a knight.' As with other of Evelyn's extravaganzas this was 'not altogether fool'.

In the New Year Honours for 1951 Maurice Bowra was given a knighthood. All Evelyn's ambivalence towards Maurice caused him to look on the honour with unconcealable envy and open indignation. 'They've made Maurice a knight,' he said in one letter, 'for translating poetry out of languages he doesn't know.' (It is quite true that like many scholarly linguists Maurice was an inept speaker of foreign languages and found them hard to understand when spoken.) 'It is really very odd,' Evelyn wrote to Nancy Mitford, 'as he has done nothing to deserve it except be head of the College at Oxford and publish a few books no one has ever read.' Quelling his feelings Evelyn nevertheless wrote a polite letter of congratulation to Maurice. The latter's reply added to the other's exasperation. 'It was very good of you', said Maurice, 'to write. A Knighthood is the only respectable honour left – far better than the O.M. or C.H. or D.B.E.' A doubtful opinion, which Evelyn derisively quoted in letters.

Evelyn felt he must do something about it. In the event, he did two things. Before leaving with me on our 'trip to Jerusalem', he wrote to Penelope Betjeman suggesting a rag on Maurice, namely that as a member of the equestrian order he should be supplied with a charger and spurs. Penelope entered thoroughly into the spirit of the rag and wrote to Evelyn as follows soon after:

'I have to-day sent Sir Maurice my very favourite pair of spurs with delicately sharp rowels. I think your idea of a charger an excellent one and am writing by this post to bold Baron Moyne asking him to send one over at his earliest convenience in a horse box. He breeds a very fiery strain of Arab war horse.'

The 'bold Baron Moyne' is Evelyn's old friend Bryan Guinness. On second thoughts, however, the plan to despatch a horse to Wadham College was abandoned.

Evelyn's second act of revenge was subtle and occurred shortly after our return from Turkey. He offered, at my insistence, to give a broadcast talk for the BBC on the 'Hundred Best Books' exhibition organized by the National Book League. The organizers insisted that the title by which the exhibition was popularly known was fallacious: the exhibition really aimed, they said, at showing the hundred 'most representative' books in English by Englishmen, written during the first half of the twentieth century. For all that 'the hundred best books' was what the exhibition was taken to be. It was not well-organized. Too much fashionable twaddle found its way in and reputable authors were almost invariably represented by their first success, by a book therefore showing immaturity. Freya Stark was represented by *The Valley of the Assassins*, Evelyn, to his intense annoyance by *Decline and Fall*. Maurice Bowra was also represented, by a book called *The Heritage of Symbolism* which came out in culture-starved England during the war, and for that reason was much over-praised. But Maurice was represented. Evelyn saw his chance.

His offer to give a broadcast talk on the exhibition was accepted by the BBC. The talk was not one of Evelyn's best efforts. He gave rein to his prejudices too freely and he erred, as he rarely did, on the side of over-complication and sophisticated argument. A member of the Talks Department in the BBC pointed out the weaknesses of the essay in what Evelyn took to be patronizing terms. 'I don't want to take a course in "creative writing" from this nonentity', he said to me. He did make a few alterations nonetheless, but he did not change his reference to Maurice Bowra. Since the exhibition claimed to be 'representative', so he argued, *The Heritage of Symbolism* could be taken as typical of the kind of book knights write.

This tiff with the BBC did not improve his relations with the Corporation or lessen my difficulties in the battle for *Helena*.

During all this year Evelyn was toiling away at the first book of his War Trilogy. Judging by a letter from Chapman and Hall, he finished the book by December. He took the very greatest pains to get army details correct as a result of which his correspondence for this year contains a large assortment of letters to and from men with whom he had served in the war, notably Bob Laycock. These are the most interesting. They show that Evelyn originally planned to make his hero, Guy Crouchback, become an officer in the Brigade of Guards in World War II. A letter from Bob of 1 September 1951 setting forth the extraordinary anomalies and complications in the structure and administration of the Household Troops decided Evelyn to settle for a fictitious regiment 'The Halberdiers', akin to the Brigade of Guards and to the Royal Marines.

All Evelyn's bitterness about his supposed ill-treatment at the hands of 'Chucker' had evaporated and the friendship was fully renewed.

The main part of Evelyn's correspondence, and one of his main delights, was his frequent exchange of letters with Nancy Mitford who was now living in a beautiful groundfloor apartment in Paris in the rue Monsieur. Her removal from London left a gap in Evelyn's life in England that he never ceased to lament. This deep friendship was in large part a case of the mutual attraction of opposites. Not only was she a stranger to Evelyn's tendency to morbid unhappiness, but on the contrary she was one of the most joyous of beings, and disaster public and private could not quell her infectious delight in life; when I last saw her, when she was dying of an agonizing disease, the old joyousness was still there. In Paris she was radiantly happy. She wrote to Evelyn in one letter: 'I only ask the '50s to be as heavenly as the '40s – for me. I suppose you will blow up. But everybody must see the world out of his own little window & *I* enjoyed every moment of the 1940s. What is so nice & *so* unexpected about life is the way it improves as it goes along. I think you should impress this fact on your children because I think young people have an awful feeling that life is slipping past them & they must do something – catch something – they don't quite know what, whereas they've only got to wait & it *all* comes.' And in a letter written at the end of 1951 she wrote this to Evelyn: 'A terrible article by Mauriac about death beds saying there is no such thing as a happy one because either you believe & are facing possible hell or you don't believe & it is le néant. I always feel that as everything in life is so heavenly probably death is too (I don't mean dying but actual death).'

Among the things they enjoyed in common, love of literature being the most serious, there was enjoyment of gossip. On Evelyn's side the gossip was often malicious, on Nancy's rarely. Her gossip was valuable to him as with his growing conservatism there went a growing insularity. Nancy acted as a check on this tendency.

No friendship with Evelyn was perpetually tranquil, not even this one which was perhaps the happiest and most serene he enjoyed in the course of his life. A brief clouding-over occurred in September 1951. It was occasioned by Evelyn's religious bigotry. At this time Nancy used to write for *The Sunday Times* a weekly column of light-hearted news and comment from Paris and in one of these she made an inaccurate reference to a forgotten scandal in the Roman Catholic Church concerning two 'modernists' in the days of Pius X, the French Abbé Brémond and the English Father Tyrell. She had obtained her misinformation from a godson of Brémond. After making enquiries from his friends among the Farm Street clergy, Evelyn corrected her in a letter which did not open with the usual endearments.

'My dear Nancy, Brémond left the Jesuits by his own wish & with the consent of his superiors some time before Tyrell's death . . .' He then gave an elucidation of the facts. The letter ended offensively: 'There is no reason why you should know all this, but if you don't know, would it not be better to avoid the subject.

'Would it not be best always to avoid any reference to the Church or to your Creator. Your intrusions into this strange world are always fatuous. With love E.'

Nancy called him to order. Her reply is without the usual opening: 'Don't start My dear Nancy I don't like it. I can't agree that I must be debarred from ever mentioning anything to do with your Creator. Try & remember that he also created me.' She then entered into details, and ended: 'I don't defend my inaccuracies but it's your TONE that nettles me. Love from Nancy.'

The cloud passed. No storm broke. Before leaving the Nancy-Evelyn letters for the moment two of Evelyn's letters may be quoted, as of exceptional interest. In the autumn of 1951 Nancy's publisher, Hamish Hamilton, had proposed a new edition of her pre-war novels, and under the influence of Jamie Hamilton's charm on a visit to Paris, she had agreed. On rereading the books she was appalled at their inferior quality. The best of them, she considered, was *Wigs on the Green*, but she hated the idea of it appearing in 1951. Readers may remember that it was a satirical novel making fun of the British Union of Fascists and of Fascism and Nazism in general. Written in 1934, when the full horror of these movements was not widely understood, and toned down so as not to give too much offence to her sister Diana and her brother-in-law Sir Oswald Mosley the British Fascist leader, it treated with gentle mirth a subject that seventeen years later could only be contemplated with indignation and disgust. Nevertheless it was undoubtedly her best early novel. She wanted to withdraw her agreement, but felt this was unfair to her publisher and friend. She asked Evelyn's advice. He gave very good advice (which was not followed) in a reply written in November or December 1951.

'You could write a most amusing and interesting and popular work in this way: Describe yourself in 1951 taking up "Wigs on the Green" & rereading it for the first time since its publication. Print 2/3 or half of the original text with constant interruptions from your 1951 self asking: "Why did I say that?" or saying "This still seems funny. Why?" So in the easiest & most informal way possible you could write your reminiscences & the history of the deteriorating world and the improving authoress.

'It would be fun to write & huge fun to read. Do do it that way.

'You could produce a magnum opus with minimum of labour and all the critics would acclaim it as a great "DOCUMENT".'

The other letter is undated as to the year and probably belongs to July 1952. The circumstances of writing were these. In the autumn of 1951 Hamish Hamilton had published *The Blessing* by Nancy. Evelyn had read the typescript, corrected the grammar and punctuation and made a few suggestions some of which she had followed. Its fate was not unlike that of *The Loved One*. It became a best-seller, but both publisher and author were nervous of the American reaction because (as Nancy's readers will remember) one of the protagonists is an American bore beautifully named Hector Dexter. He and his friends were described with ruthless wit and observation in a manner likely to offend American feelings. Inevitably some American readers were offended, but a much larger proportion took delight in this caricature and the book enjoyed a prodigious sale in the United States. Inevitably, and for the first time it seems, she received an enormous fan-mail. She asked Evelyn's advice on how to cope with this mass of letters. He replied as follows:

'I am not greatly troubled by fans nowadays. Less than one a day on the average. No sour grapes when I say they were an infernal nuisance.

'I divide them into:

(a) Humble expressions of admiration. To them a post-card saying: "I am delighted to learn that you enjoyed my book. E.W."

(b) Impudent criticism. No answer.

(c) Bores who wish to tell me about themselves. Post-card saying. "Thank you for interesting letter. E.W.".

(d) Technical criticism. eg. One has made a character go to Salisbury from Paddington. Post-card "Many thanks for your valuable suggestion. E.W."

(e) Humble aspirations of would-be writers. If attractive a letter of discouragement. If unattractive a post-card.

(f) Requests from University Clubs for a lecture. Printed refusal.

(g) Requests from Catholic Clubs for lecture. Acceptance.

(h) American students of "Creative Writing" who are writing theses about one or want one, virtually, to write their theses for them. Printed refusal.

(i) Tourists who invite themselves to one's house. Printed refusal.

(j) Manuscripts sent for advice. Return without comment. I also have some post-cards with my photograph on them which I send to nuns.

'In cases of any impudent letters from married women I write to the husband warning him that his wife is attempting to enter into correspondence with strange men.

'Oh and of course

(k) Autograph collectors: no answer.

(l) Indians & Germans asking for free copies of one's books: no answer.

(m) Very rich Americans: polite letter. They are capable of buying 100 copies for Christmas presents.

'I think that more or less covers the field.'

Early in October 1951 Evelyn became involved in an unlikely adventure which need not detain the reader for more than a paragraph because it ended as a non-event. He was approached by a group of students of Edinburgh University to stand as a candidate for the Rectorship. The election was due in November. He accepted. He told me about it one day in White's. 'I must have been mad, mustn't I?' he said. I agreed, but I thought later that the ferocious scenes which accompany the installation might have been to his anarchic taste. His chances were slight because he had more enemies than supporters among the Scottish students. His supporters widely exhibited a poster consisting of an enormously enlarged photograph of an atomic explosion conveying the legend 'Waugh is Declared'. In the event he had not a hope as at the last moment Sir Alexander Fleming put himself forward as a candidate and a great majority voted for this august opponent.

In the meantime Evelyn had become engaged in another controversy in *The Tablet*, one which he ridiculously mishandled. On 27 October 1951 there appeared an article, offensive to Evelyn, by a Dominican clergyman Father Gerard Meath. It was a review of a book by Dorothy Sayers on the subject of St Helena. The article put forward the foolish and untenable proposition that whereas Dorothy Sayers respected St Helena for her piety and spiritual insight, Evelyn mainly respected her out of snobbish reverence for her high social position as Roman Empress. It was an ignorant accusation and Evelyn was justified in his indignation. If he had stuck to it he would have won a resounding literary victory over the Dominican. But very foolishly he laid equal if not more stress on the fact that Father Meath had referred throughout his article to 'Miss Sayers' and to the other as 'Evelyn Waugh' omitting the 'Mr'. In his reply to *The Tablet* he referred to the reverend author as 'Meath'.

Evelyn was so incensed by the article that he threatened legal proceedings for libel and consulted his solicitors, but happily they persuaded him not to move against *The Tablet* and his old friend Douglas Woodruff, noting that he had weakened his case by taking his stand on the Mr business.

It is odd that Evelyn should have wantonly risked heavy legal expenses at this time as he was in financial difficulties which were causing him the utmost alarm. The circumstances are best described in his own words in a letter to Nancy Mitford.

'For some time I have been aware that I seemed to be in easier circumstances than most of my friends & accounted for it with saws like "solvency is a matter of temperament" and by thinking of all the nuns who are praying for me, bringing me in pounds when I give them shillings, and so on.

'Well last week I said to Laura "are you sure you arent overdrawn at the bank?" "No, I don't think so. I'm sure they'd tell me if I were?" "Well do ask." So she did and, my dear, she had an overdraft of £6,420 which had been quietly mounting up for years. There is no possible way to pay it off, as her capital is in trust and for me to earn that much more, I should have to earn about 150,000. Well its a sad prospect isn't it. I shall have to go to prison but that is hell nowadays with wireless & lectures & psychiatry. Oh for the Marshalsea.'

This was written in 1950 but he continued to worry about his finances throughout 1951 and after that, not that it ever seemed to prevent him doing what he wanted.

In December 1951 the radio version of *Helena*, drafted by myself and revised by Evelyn, was broadcast by the BBC. I asked Evelyn not to attend the rehearsals. I had learned by bitter experience that an author attending rehearsals cannot help interfering with the actors, resulting in divided counsels and uncertain performances. Tyrone Guthrie once said that if by some miracle Shakespeare walked into his rehearsals of *Hamlet*, he would ask him to leave. Bernard Shaw's plays always had to be re-rehearsed after he had gone from the theatre. Few authors understand this and I expected Evelyn like most of them to take offence. I was prepared for a row but happily the craftsman in him took over. He grasped the point and submitted. He did however come to the studio to meet the cast who included John Gielgud, Flora Robson, Isabel Jeans, Patience Collier and James MacKechnie, then the topmost performer as a narrator. After the broadcast Evelyn expressed his great joy at the performance to several people, even going so far as to say that it was better than the book, certainly an exaggeration. To me, however, he sent only harsh criticism, finding fault with all the main actors except Isabel Jeans and Flora Robson. Unfortunately I have not kept his letter, in which he accused me of acting under the direction of Father Meath.

Early in 1952, having completed his novel *Men at Arms*, Evelyn felt the longing to travel again, although he had told Nancy Mitford that after his Eastern travels with me he was never going abroad again, 'Never, never, never, never, never, NEVER.' But his Pitt-like resolve was broken within a few weeks. Until his last years this resolve and its breach became almost a routine. On this occasion he wanted to go to Sicily and again he asked me to accompany him. Again he offered to pay my expenses or to get me a rewarding journalistic contract. I refused. I was very busy with my own work at the time, but that was not the only or chief reason for my refusal. I had noticed a change coming over Evelyn lately, and not a change for the better. He was becoming more arrogant, more quarrelsome, and indulged his horrible delight in needling on sensitive spots more freely than usual. I preferred to retain happy memories of former journeys and my abiding affection intact.

The outcome proved that in this instance my decision was wise. Seeking for an even-tempered companion, a 'jagger' in Lygon parlance, he obtained the agreement of Harold Acton to go with him to Sicily. Harold told me and John Sutro that what he had looked forward to as an amusing adventure turned out to be a nightmarish ordeal. Evelyn was consistently rude, offensive, sulky, and the needling went on non-stop. He made a row in every hotel and in every restaurant. Every chance acquaintance was insulted. The culmination, though not violent, was extremely painful to his companion.

One evening he and Harold were invited to drinks with a man whom Harold knew, the British Consul in Palermo. Evelyn behaved as badly as he had done when he and I visited the missionaries of Beirut, but in a different way. After they had been talking pleasantly enough for a while the Consul said something of this kind: 'Mr Waugh, some of the English residents here run a little literary society. The members would be delighted to meet you. I wonder if I could persuade you to give them a brief talk?'

'No' said Evelyn.

'I wish I could persuade you', went on the Consul. 'News of your arrival has spread and they will be very disappointed. I promised to ask you.'

'If', said Evelyn, 'you want me to lecture to this society of yours, then you must write to my agent A. D. Peters in London and he will negotiate terms.' Harold Acton, with his unfailing tact, deftly turned the conversation. In the more harmonious atmosphere thus brought about he mentioned that a year ago Evelyn had travelled in Turkey, a country of which the Consul had some experience.

'Would you', asked the Consul, 'like to see some rather interesting photographs which I took in eastern Anatolia?'

'No,' said Evelyn.

Once again Harold guided the conversation on to more neutral ground. Once again a harmonious atmosphere seemed to be established, until Evelyn turned to the Consul and said: 'You mentioned a minute ago that you had some photographs of eastern Anatolia?'

'Yes', said the Consul.

'And you asked me if I would like to look at them?'

'Yes', said the Consul.

'Why did you think I wanted to look at your photographs of eastern Anatolia? Why should I want to look at any photographs of any part of Anatolia?'

Harold rose and said that they should be getting back to their hotel.

In the same year Evelyn caused a scene at one of his favourite clubs The Beefsteak, which can be described as a 'general conversation club'. The members lunch and dine at one table and introductions are traditionally not made (a custom which has resulted in some interesting mishaps). Evelyn had made himself some enemies at this club by needling fellow-members against whom he harboured prejudice, notably Derek Curtis Bennett and Sir Malcolm Sargent. Many members, including me, shared these two prejudices. But no one had sympathy with Evelyn when he was so intolerably rude to the club porter that the latter lost his head and not only responded in kind but made a scene of protest in the street. A committee meeting debated whether to request Evelyn's resignation. In view of the fact that both parties to the quarrel had behaved wrongly the request was not made, but Evelyn never went to The Beefsteak again. In his letter to John Sutro describing the misadventures in Sicily Harold Acton had expressed serious alarm that Evelyn was becoming mentally unbalanced. He was right. Mr Pinfold was on the way.

Later in the year *Men at Arms* was published. Evelyn did not rate it highly. He wrote to Nancy Mitford: 'I have finished that novel – slogging, inelegant, boring – and what little point it has will only be revealed in the fourth volume at least four years hence. Still there were some dunderheads who didn't appreciate *Helena*. Perhaps they will like it.' He wrote to Graham Greene: 'I finished that book I was writing. *Not* good. Of course all writers write some bad books but it seems a pity at this particular time. It has some excellent farce, but only for a few pages. The rest very dull. Well, the war was like that.'

When it was published in the summer, it had what is called a 'mixed reception'. This was inevitable for one reason: its main theme being army life it is very much a 'men only' book, drawing heavily and with photographic detail on regimental life in the period of the 'Phoney War', on the defeat of 1940 as seen from England, and on the Dakar fiasco in which Evelyn had taken part. In some respects it was a repetition of *Put Out More Flags* seen from a different, military and less farcical angle. Its admirers were chiefly attracted by the character Apthorpe who threatened to become the protagonist of the story. Evelyn told Nancy that Apthorpe had taken 'the bit between his teeth'. Those who were disappointed were in independent agreement with Evelyn's opinions quoted above. Diana Cooper was among the disappointed and as usual was outspoken on the subject. 'I thought', she told Evelyn, 'that you were going to give us a modern *War and Peace*, but it's much more like *Mrs Dale's Diary*.'

The partial failure of the book was due to a familiar error of which Evelyn judging by his letter to Nancy Mitford, seems to have been partly aware: his writing was never amenable to publication by instalments. This book was the first of three instalments, a large instalment of a very long book but an instalment nonetheless. Though Evelyn did me the singular honour of dedicating it to me, I have never greatly cared for this book. I found myself reluctantly in agreement with Diana Cooper. I will return to the subject when I consider the trilogy *Sword of Honour* as a whole.

When the book had been published Evelyn made another journey in the autumn. He found part of the expenses in journalist contracts. He went alone, to Goa, for the celebrations of the four hundredth anniversary of the death of St Francis Xavier, a patron saint of Indian Christianity. He could have gone direct by sea but, by his own account, preferred to enter overland from Belgaum, to the north-east of Goa, though how he reached that landlocked district and city he did not tell. It must be remembered that in 1952 Goa was still administered by Portugal and was a last remaining relic of the Portuguese Empire founded in the fifteenth and sixteenth centuries. Evelyn saw it in the last days before it experienced the privilege and ordeal of modern liberation. He may have looked with an over-indulgent eye on this land which is the only largely Catholic part of India. In what he wrote he found again an opportunity to tilt against fashionable progressivist ideas, in pursuit of his perennial crusade. He wrote in a wholeheartedly pro-Portuguese spirit, but he conceded to the anti-imperialists that 'Portuguese rule was violent in its early days, neglectful later; only in the present generation has it begun to redeem its past.'

He wrote to Nancy Mitford on 10 February 1953: 'Yes, home from India some time now. Goa was heaven. I wrote a few words about it for your great new friends, Picture Post, but what with the Portuguese telegraphist & Mr Hulton's sub-editor, they got sadly buggered. Now I have written a most instructive article which no one will print.' The 'instructive article' was ultimately published in *The Month*, the Jesuit periodical edited by his friend Father Philip Caraman.

In the spring of 1953 Chapman and Hall produced a new book by Evelyn, *Love Among the Ruins*. It is a fantasy of the future, a short nightmare on the subject of the perfected Socialist state, with the Euthanasia centre as the main scene of the story. It has had its admirers, but they are only to be found among the uncritically dedicated or those who see a depth of meaning in all Evelyn's writings. I see it as the least book of Evelyn's maturity. Of course there are some of his inimitable touches, but there are not more than touches. It lacks originality, a very rare fault with Evelyn. It is manifestly based in part on Max Beerbohm's parody of H. G. Wells in *A Christmas Garland*, in part on his friend George Orwell's *1984*, and (if one can plagiarize oneself) in part on *The Loved One*. The central joke is that the heroine has a 'long, silken, corn-gold beard', and it cannot be maintained that bearded women are an unused subject for jesting. The poet Parsnip (vaguely identifiable as W. H. Auden) reappears from *Put Out More Flags*. Evelyn derived from this book none of the artist's satisfaction in accomplishment. '*Love Among the Ruins*', he wrote to Graham Greene, 'was a bit of nonsense begun 3 years ago & hastily finished & injudiciously published. But I don't think it quite as bad as most reviewers do.' The reviewer pack was out and baying for the blood of Evelyn who seemed for once to be cornered. But if the book was not quite as bad as the reviewers said, it was nearly.

I saw little of Evelyn during the last part of 1952 and the first part of 1953, for the reasons I have already given. I preferred to keep our acquaintance to occasional exchanges of letters which were always friendly. He expressed himself, not only to me, as distressed by my avoidance but when we did meet by chance he was invariably unpleasant. If I had known the reason for his increasingly odd behaviour I would have accepted his invitations to meet, and have refused to be offended by the needling, but it would not have been easy.

A small incident in the first part of 1953 was to have a disproportionate effect on Evelyn's state of mind. The BBC were running a series of inter-

view programmes then, called 'Frankly Speaking', in which some celebrated person was interviewed on his or her opinions and tastes. Evelyn
was chosen as a victim, was invited and surprisingly he accepted. A
recording van went down to Piers Court from Bristol with two interviewers. Evelyn did not give them a very friendly reception. Before they
started the recording Evelyn said to them: 'Please understand that you
address me as *Mr* Waugh. My surname is pronounced that way.' 'Of
course,' said one of the interviewers, 'we know that.' 'Do you?' said
Evelyn, 'I distinctly heard one of you say Wuff.' They laughed till they
saw to their amazement that Evelyn was serious.

The interviewers had made a familiar mistake. They presumed that
Evelyn was less intelligent than they and that this crusted conservative
would be easy game, easily flustered and put on the defensive. They thought
they could easily needle this lethally skilful needler. As I listened to the
subsequent broadcast I almost began to feel sorry for them. It was like
watching inexperienced toreadors taking on a bull who knew all the
tricks of the ring. They were gravely horned.

'You have not much sympathy with the man in the street, have you,
Mr Waugh?' So I remember an early question. 'You must understand', I
seem to remember Evelyn replying, 'that the man in the street does not
exist. He is a modern myth. There are individual men and women, each
one of whom has an individual and immortal soul, and such beings need
to use streets from time to time.'

Presently, with renewed confidence, they moved to the ever-popular
topic of capital punishment. Evelyn declared himself emphatically in
favour of it in the case of certain crimes, notably murder.

'But supposing, Mr Waugh,' said one of the interviewers, 'that you were
ordered to carry out the hanging yourself. What would you say then?'

'I would say', replied Evelyn calmly, 'that there was something very odd
about Home Office administration, if novelists were called on to perform
an operation which I believe requires training and considerable technical
skill.'

'But if, for the sake of argument, you *were* ordered to do it. Would you?'

'Yes,' replied Evelyn on that high note he sometimes used, 'yes . . .
Yes . . .'

I remember no more of the interview, except that Evelyn scored throughout. It was a triumph for him. Yet the evidence is that he looked on the
occasion as an ugly humiliation. There is no doubt that he expressed his
personal feelings when he wrote later that the chief interviewer 'seemed
to believe that anyone sufficiently eminent to be interviewed by him must
have something to hide, must be an impostor whom it was his business to
trap and expose . . . There was the hint of the under-dog's snarl . . . they
left an unpleasant memory which grew sharper in the weeks before the
record was broadcast.'

The North Front of Castle Howard: A house visited from Ampleforth
by Evelyn in pre-war years and possibly a model for Brideshead

Evelyn and his biographer in front of the Parthenon

A study in amiability

Some time later Lord Kinross (formerly as Patrick Balfour Evelyn's colleague in Abyssinia) told me that Evelyn was in a very unhappy state of mind and that my studied avoidance of him hurt him greatly. The fact is that Evelyn was falling into a state of persecution-mania, and quite small and sometimes quite irrelevant occurrences, such as the BBC interview in which he rather than the interviewers had acted as persecutor, increased a delusion of conspiracy against him. I was touched by what Patrick told me and by a postcard from Evelyn which began 'Why do you hate me so?', though the pathetic note was not maintained as he then went on to refer in typical Evelyn fashion to the studies in Zionism which I was then pursuing. He suggested that my Jewish masters had ordered me to abandon my Christian acquaintance. At all events I decided that the estrangement should end so when Evelyn invited me to dine with him at the St James's Club I accepted.

The reconciliation failed totally, but not through Evelyn's or my fault. We were joined at our table by one of the most colossal bores of London, and as his ponderous and humorously worldly-wise anecdotes followed each other in a line that stretched to the crack of doom, Evelyn's good humour diminished and evaporated. When the bore left us Evelyn was in that offensive mood which had brought about our breach and we parted on bad terms. But this part of the story ended happily. A few days later we met again by chance and lunched together. There was no bore present to cast an evil spell, and we found ourselves again on the old terms. After that we usually met whenever we were both in London.

I remember one meeting which belongs to the autumn of 1953. There were several friends of Evelyn having a drink with him one evening in White's. Among them was Graham Greene who was in a state of great indignation. These were the days when under the tolerance of a supine President Senator Joe McCarthy was pursuing his anti-Communist campaign and adding a new dimension to the truth of Doctor Johnson's great aphorism that 'Patriotism is the last refuge of a scoundrel.' The Senator's progress had struck Graham Greene who was planning to go to the United States. McCarthy's delators had discovered that when Graham was an undergraduate at Oxford he had for a short time belonged to a Communist club. As a result he was refused a visa by the American Embassy. Graham fulminated against this injustice, characteristic of that evil American epoch, ending up by saying 'Anyway it's given me an idea for a political novel. It will be fun to write about politics for a change, and not always about God.'

Evelyn was usually very sensitive to even the mildest hint of blasphemy, but on this occasion he was unperturbed. 'Oh?' he responded on his high note, 'I wouldn't give up writing about God at this stage if I was you. It would be like P. G. Wodehouse dropping Jeeves half-way through the Wooster series.' It was said in such a way that no offence could possibly be taken and Graham was the first to laugh at Evelyn's ingenious comparison. (The result of Graham's change of direction was *The Quiet American*.)

I did not see Evelyn again from that autumn till the Holy Week retreat at Downside at Easter 1954. By that time he had been through an ordeal which he made famous.

# Chapter 22

Evelyn freely admitted that *The Ordeal of Gilbert Pinfold* was closely autobiographical. He could hardly do otherwise as he had described his experiences in detail to several of his friends. The events occurred between late January and early March 1954. It is significant that in his diaries he refers to the book as his 'novel', in inverted commas.

Before he set out on his journey to Ceylon in order to escape the worst of the English winter, Evelyn had grown absurdly alarmed by certain bizarre phenomena, and by certain events which troubled him about the state of his mind. The West Country is a favourite habitat of faith-healers and those who seek occult knowledge by ghostly means, the most famous and newest among the last-named being 'The Box'. This last is part of a strange healing practice whereby a physical part of the patient, human or animal, a few hairs or preferably a sample of blood, is sent to the practitioner who puts it into a box whence waves are supposedly transmitted in hopes of effecting a cure. A large proportion, perhaps a majority of the faith-healers and box-manipulators are charlatans, but there are exceptions. Few scientists have troubled to investigate the box seriously but it has attracted the attention of some students of RADAR and of the implications of RADAR theory.

Living in the West Country Evelyn inevitably heard about the box. His friend Lady Diana Abdy, who lived in Cornwall, had sought help of the box as a cure for migraine. A relative of his friend Patrick Kinross had been unexpectedly cured of severe pain following a slipped disc, by desperate recourse to a box-manipulator in the West. Evelyn seems to have interpreted everything he heard about the box as showing it to be suspect and probably diabolical. More strangely he connected it with the BBC interview from which he had emerged victorious, but which he continued to regard as a sinister humiliation. He was possibly right in connecting the possible efficacy of the box with electro-magnetic wave activity, but his suspicion that the BBC interviewing team were intent on some malign conspiracy against him was a manifest case of persecution-mania.

Small events added to this state of mind, my avoidance of him being one.

But what made him anxious about the state of his mind was a very ordinary mishap. As happens to men as they approach old age (in 1953 Evelyn was only fifty but steady drinking and the use of ever stronger drugs against his insomnia made him seem older) his memory became impaired. He rarely forgot anything of any significance, but he tended more strongly to remember wrongly yet with precision. At Christmas 1953 John Betjeman gave him an elaborately ornamental washstand, the work of the Victorian craftsman William Burges with panels painted by Sir Edward Poynton. When it arrived at Piers Court Evelyn found it different to what he remembered when John had presented it to him at Patrick Kinross's house. On its arrival he thought he detected that a finely wrought bronze tap was missing. He made extensive enquiries of the carriers, of John, and Patrick. It emerged that there had never been such a tap. Evelyn was worried, a fact reflected in the fullness with which he recorded the incident in his diary, and the prominence which he gave to it in *The Ordeal of Gilbert Pinfold*. He began to fear that his mind was giving way.

The diary entry on this by no means singular mishap is the more surprising because on the same day he received news which would normally have excited him to interesting and perhaps lengthy comment. On 1 January 1954 Duff Cooper had died aboard ship in the first stage of a voyage to Jamaica. In his diary Evelyn merely noted: 'News of Duff's sudden death in Vigo bay. My last words to Diana when she telephoned to say goodbye, were sharp. Clocks barely moving. Has half an hour past? no five minutes.'

After a visit to London with Laura and the children, and a visit to Piers Court by Ronald Knox, Evelyn sailed for Ceylon on a small ship, and into the Pinfold experience, in the second half of January 1954.

He kept no diary after 12 January, and since he was unaccompanied the only documentary evidence is in the novel. The book provides reliable evidence of the shape and general character of the experience, but not of the events in detail. His accounts to his friends varied widely. He gave one to Diana Cooper which was very different in detail from the one which he gave me. Except for one letter in which Evelyn merely stated that the defective piping in the ship was making it possible for him to overhear the talk in other cabins, and was causing him annoyance, (not a disturbing letter in itself) Laura seems, understandably enough, to have destroyed the letters which alarmed her and roused her to action. He seems to have written nothing about the experience to Nancy Mitford until it was safely over, but he gave her no details. The varying detailed accounts seem all to have been given by word of mouth.

The variations on the theme were never radical. It is possible that they were all true and that the reason he never gave precisely the same account to two people was the simple one that under the stress of a great mental disturbance, his memory was confused.

I will mention one variation he gave to me, as I have never seen or heard it referred to elsewhere. Soon after the boat had begun her voyage and Evelyn had begun to fancy the hearing of voices; soon after he had begun to suspect that he might be the victim of some practical joke, he was sitting on deck when he noticed a very pretty young woman taking her morning exercise. When she passed him the second time he felt sure that he had met her somewhere, and by the time she appeared on her third round he had remembered exactly, so he thought. This was Mrs Wilson. He rose and greeted her. 'Mrs Wilson, I haven't seen you since you and your husband were in Tel Aviv', he said. She looked bewildered. 'Surely you remember', he said. 'Three years ago. My name is Evelyn Waugh, and I came out with Christopher Sykes whom you knew before. We attended the christening of your child in Jerusalem.' She still looked bewildered. 'I'm sorry', she said at length, 'I'm afraid you've made a mistake. I am not called Mrs Wilson. I've never been to Tel Aviv or Jerusalem. I know no one called Christopher Sykes, and I don't remember ever having met you, Mr Waugh.' Instead of withdrawing gracefully from his mistake Evelyn persisted in trying to remind the young woman of their former meetings. In the end she cut the conversation short. 'I'm sorry, you've made a mistake', she said, and walked quickly away. At this, Evelyn told me, all his lingering doubts were removed, and he was certain that what he had first taken for a joke was in fact a well-organized plot against him. Thereafter I was frequently referred to by the voices (I appear in the fiction under the name of Roger Stillingfleet) and the delusion grew and persisted as described in the novel. All Evelyn's verbal accounts that I know of related how he believed he had overheard one night the sounds of the burial of a murdered man at sea, and at dinner had rallied the captain on the subject, to the captain's great bewilderment, and how he had complained to the captain that his radiograms were not sent off but distributed to the other passengers by the wireless signals officer – a complaint that was proved to be baseless. It seems that these things were undoubtedly part of the hallucination.

The boat presumably sailed by the Bay of Biscay and Gibraltar to Suez. At all ports of call Evelyn sent letters to Laura, and one or two to Diana Cooper. Diana was made uneasy by them, and telephoned to Laura. By so doing she confirmed the other's growing fears. Laura decided that Evelyn must be got back.

The next part of the story has been vividly told in Lady Donaldson's book *Portrait of a Country Neighbour*. Jack and Frankie Donaldson had gone to live near Piers Court in 1947 and in the following year they became friends of Evelyn and Laura. Soon after Evelyn had left in January 1954 Laura drove over to their house, and, to quote the book:

'She told us she was horribly worried about him. She asked for our word that what she was about to say would go no further, and then for Jack's

EVELYN WAUGH

help. She said that Evelyn had seemed very ill and melancholy when he
left, but that, since with every day he spent at home he became worse, she
had let him go, believing that nothing but the change would cure him.
She then read to us selected parts of several letters she had received from
him. In these letters he said that travelling on the ship with him there
was a party of "existentialists" who had perfected a form of long-range
telepathy. For some reason of which he was not aware, he had incurred
their hostility and they were using their unusual gift to persecute him.
It had begun by his being plagued by the sound of his name in the air,
and, at night when he went to bed, by half-heard conversations in which
his name constantly occurred and which seemed at first to come from the
next door cabin. Soon he was allowed no respite from these voices by day
or night and he was quite unable to sleep. The last of the letters was
written from a hotel in Cairo and said that he had left the ship and intended to continue his journey over land in order to escape from his
enemies. It was this letter which brought Laura to see us. Evelyn said
that he had had twenty-four hours peace in the hotel in Cairo but on the
second day the voices had mockingly resumed their continuous conversation and their extraordinary power seemed in no way diminished
through separation by miles of ocean. He referred to a neighbour who
believed in the ministration of "the Box" – a matter which had earned his
amusement and scorn – and said that he now believed he had been wrong
in dismissing so easily the possibility of this kind of long-distance control.
Then he apologized for the incoherence of his expression. It was not very
easy, he said, to write coherently when every sentence you wrote was
immediately repeated by a bodiless voice.

'This is all I remember of his letters, and I think it was all that at that
time he said. But it was enough. Not merely the matter but the manner
of these letters was so totally unlike Evelyn – the sadly apologetic air, the
defeated spirit . . . Only the handwriting convinced one they were written
by him.

'Laura said she felt someone must go and fetch him back. She had
thought it over and believed it must be a man, partly in case Evelyn was
getting into trouble, but chiefly because – in spite of the dispirited letters –
he might be belligerently unwilling to accept this kind of interference.
She asked Jack if he would go.

'It was immediately arranged that she should give him a cheque for a
sufficient sum of money and that he would take the first aeroplane. But
when he came to make the arrangements he found that he could not enter
Colombo without a certificate of inoculation against typhoid – a paper
which takes ten days to obtain. We considered whether he should nevertheless go and either bribe or force his way in, a thing Laura said Evelyn
had often done in the past in other countries. Finally it was decided that
both he and Laura should have the first of the injections and go together

362

before the second only if it seemed absolutely necessary. Before the period was up Evelyn solved the difficulty by announcing by cable that he was on his way home.

'When Laura asked Jack to go she warned us that she thought it possible that, when Evelyn recovered his mind, he might be so angry that she had confided in us that it would spoil our friendship for ever. Consequently, when she went to London to meet him we did not expect to hear, unless privately from her, any news of either of them for several weeks. When she discussed with me what she was going to say and do when she met him, I felt very much frightened, because she proposed to behave as one would to a person who is sane, whereas it seemed to me that Evelyn was quite clearly insane. I thought her approach should be more tentative and more subtle. However, she was immovable in her opinion.'

What happened then was told to Jack and Frankie by Evelyn and Laura together at Piers Court soon after. Frankie repeated the story in her book.

'As Laura walked up the stairs of the Hyde Park Hotel she heard a voice ask in a high, unrecognizable squeak whether she had yet arrived. She looked up and to her surprise saw Evelyn. She said that his voice was distorted by disuse, because for weeks he had spoken to no one. I have no idea whether this is a likely effect.

'As soon as they reached their bedroom Evelyn began to tell Laura what had happened to him. He said that on board ship there had been a family named Black. The father of this family was someone they knew. He was the man who had interrogated him in a broadcast interview he had recently given. This man had a wife, a son and a daughter and the whole family used the infernal powers he had told her about to persecute him. Only the daughter showed any mercy, and she at times seemed to pity him. This girl he told Laura they also knew. She was engaged to a young man – he mentioned the name – who lived in Wotton-under-Edge and who had brought her to luncheon at Piers Court.

' "But Evelyn," Laura objected, "that girl's name wasn't Black, it was So-and-So, and she had nothing to do with the BBC man."

'Laura said that when she said this Evelyn saw almost at once it was true. He reacted to this startling piece of information in the manner of the sane. They discussed the details for some time and Laura tried to persuade him that he had been ill and must see a doctor. Very well, he replied, but before doing so they would test other links in his story. He took command of the situation, devised a plan and told Laura how to carry it out. On his instructions she telephoned to the BBC and asked to speak to Mr Black. To her horror the answering voice said that Mr Black was at present away. She asked where he was and when he was expected to return, and then she was told that he had been in hospital for some weeks, and although he was recovering from his illness, it was not yet known when he would return.

'So much for Mr and Miss Black. Yet Evelyn could still hear their voices. They decided at this point to ask Father Caraman to come round and advise them.'

The story can here be taken up by Father Philip Caraman.

'I met Evelyn on his return from Ceylon in March 1954 · · ·

'On the evening of Evelyn's arrival in London Laura rang me up at Farm St and asked me to come to dinner at the Hyde Park Hotel at 8 p.m.; only she and Evelyn would be there. This was about 5.30; about three-quarters of an hour later Laura rang again and asked me to make it 7.30: she gave no reason for the sudden invitation or for the change of time.

'I knew nothing of Evelyn's condition and I had not seen him or had occasion to write to him for many months. When I arrived at the Hyde Park I was surprised to be hustled straight into the dining-room without any preliminary conversation or drink. Almost immediately after sitting down Evelyn who was opposite me at a square table, leaned across and asked me abruptly to exorcise him: this (he explained) was the reason why I had been invited to dinner. He said he was being tormented by devils; then he repeated aloud to me what his voices had just told him about myself: nothing insulting but (as far as I recollect) simply that I was a priest who had power to put his tormentors to flight. My first reaction was to suppose that Evelyn was acting the madman. Only when he persisted and became pressing in his demand for an exorcism did I begin to fear he might be in earnest.

'Fortunately, as it turned out, Evelyn left the table half way through dinner to go to the lavatory. While he was out of the room I asked Laura to tell me whether Evelyn was serious. In retrospect it was the most foolish question I have asked anyone in my life. Laura was white with anxiety. Then she told me hurriedly about the letters Evelyn had been sending her from India.

'When Evelyn returned I made it clear to him that there could be no exorcism until he had seen a doctor. Then I excused myself, went to the telephone and called up my friend Dr Eric Strauss, the head of the psychiatric department at St Bartholomew's, a very eminent psychiatrist, and a good physician. Fortunately he was at home that evening in his flat at 45 Wimpole Street. I explained Evelyn's symptoms, told him that the case was urgent and asked him to come round instantly. By the time we had moved into the lounge for coffee Eric had arrived.

'There were a few polite exchanges. Then Eric put his questions: he was a shrewd man and treated the case purely as a physician. He asked Evelyn what sleeping draughts he had been taking, how much alcohol, etc. Evelyn answered like a child, perhaps (it seemed to me) exaggerating the alcohol. Eric summed up: "The first thing you must have", he said, "is a good night's sleep." He then wrote out a prescription for a different sleeping draught, gave it to Laura, who took it to the all-night chemist in Piccadilly Circus.

'While Laura was away Eric and Evelyn exchanged recollections of post-First World War Oxford, where they had met on one or two occasions. Evelyn was more relaxed than he had been all evening. On Laura's return we all four walked to the lift. As the lift rose taking Evelyn and Laura to their room, Eric turned to me and said, 'Wouldn't it be wonderful if the voices stopped tonight!" He explained that Evelyn's malady might have been brought on by a combination of pheno-barbitone and alcohol. It had been. The voices did stop that night.

'Some time later Evelyn suggested to me that he should pay Eric a fee for his professional help. It was arranged that Evelyn, on his next visit to London, should visit Eric at Wimpole Street during his consulting hours. Eric was too wise to make the visit more than a friendly occasion. But in the course of conversation Eric suggested to Evelyn that he should write an account of his hallucinations. I never asked Eric his motive in proposing this. Perhaps he thought the exercise would stabilize Evelyn's cure, perhaps he felt that an account of his experience written by such a master of narrative as Evelyn would be of service to his profession. Whatever the explanation Eric's suggestion was the origin of *Pinfold*.

'Evelyn's account of his recovery in *Pinfold* is less dramatic than it was in fact. I find it strange that Evelyn, who always sent me signed copies of his books and showed me countless kindnesses, never sent me *Pinfold* or ever referred to the evening at the Hyde Park. The nearest he approached the subject was when I myself was finding sleep difficult. On my visits to Combe Florey at that time he would offer me his "Pinfold Mixture" (prescribed by Eric) before going to bed. Nor (I think) did he send Eric a copy of the book. If he did, it was not among his books which he bequeathed to me at his death. Evelyn at times would make enquiries after Eric whom he called "your loony Doctor friend".'

In this memorandum Father Caraman omits to mention a point which he has made to me in discussion and which I believe to be of psychological importance. Evelyn believed that he was the victim of diabolic possession, and as Catholics neither Father Caraman nor Eric Strauss looked on this as a ridiculous idea. They gave him advice as people who shared his conviction that evil was a positive force, and who respected ancient descriptions of its power and manifestation.

Eric Strauss recommended Evelyn to consult a doctor of his acquaintance, and this doctor in turn sent Evelyn to a specialist. The latter reported after examination that the 'recent hallucinations of hearing were due to bromide poisoning' and that probably 'the right antrum is infected'; finally that he was suffering from anaemia. The specialist concluded his report: 'In so far as your insomnia is concerned, my personal view is that the approach to it must be other than by narcotic drugs.' Evelyn did not follow this last recommendation.

Superficially viewed, it appeared that Evelyn's cure was immediate, but the ordeal had weakened him. I noticed this when I saw him again at Downside at the 1954 Holy Week retreat, and when he gave me his account of what he had been through. I also noticed another psychological circumstance which, I do not doubt, enabled him to achieve total recovery: he was not afflicted by the shame that often oppresses those who have temporarily lost mental balance; he was quite uninhibited about it. His description to me of his delusions may have been inaccurate here and there but it was given with no hint of embarrassment, and I remember an occasion when Simon Elwes and I were talking with him in his room and some question arose about which we asked his opinion. 'I think', he said, 'I used to know about that, but now that I haven't got a mind . . .' When he met Gaston Palewski, at that time French ambassador in Rome, and whom he knew well through Nancy Mitford, he said to him: 'I haven't seen you for a long time, but then I've seen so few people because – did you know? – I went mad.' His reserve towards Father Caraman and Doctor Strauss on the subject seems to have been an exception to his normal conduct.

Psychiatrists often recommend patients who have endured delusion to write down what they remember, as a therapeutic exercise. I have little doubt that that is why Eric Strauss encouraged Evelyn to write what ultimately became *The Ordeal of Gilbert Pinfold*. Evelyn may have quickly written a rough account soon after his last meeting with Eric, but if so it does not seem to have survived. From the evidence of his letters to Mrs Ian Fleming it is clear that he did not write the published book till much later. He began in February 1956 and finished in the following October or November. Publication was not till 1957. Though this disrupts the chronology I propose to deal with the book now, when the events on which it was based are fresh in the reader's mind.

I have assumed from the beginning of this chapter that readers of this book know *Pinfold*, as I may call it for brevity's sake, and do not need to be told the story of this literary recluse who finds himself the victim of weird delusions which he overcomes by his own inner strength, in a manner as weird as the tormenting delusions, and by reliance on his wife's homely common sense.

Few books by Evelyn have received more study, and it has proved especially fascinating to those who unprofessionally pursue the fashionable study of psychology; it is, as far as I know, the only book by Evelyn to be proposed as the basis of an operatic libretto – though for an opera that was never written. For all that, no critic can pretend that it is a neatly balanced novel. It is damaged by a fault that is commoner in musical composition than in letters: as with the wide-ranging *Chartreuse de Parme*, so in this short book the best things come first; the excellence of the first part throws the rest, including the climax of the story, into the shade. But this first part is so excellent that it can be held to compensate for every blemish; it is among the two or three best things ever written by Evelyn or to be found in modern autobiography. The first chapter, entitled 'Portrait of the Artist in Middle Age', is unashamedly a self-portrait.

'His strongest tastes were negative. He abhorred plastics, Picasso, sun-bathing, and jazz – everything in fact that had happened in his own life-time. The tiny kindling of charity which came to him through his religion sufficed only to temper his disgust and change it to boredom. There was a phrase in the thirties: "It is later than you think", which was designed to cause uneasiness. It was never later than Mr Pinfold thought. At intervals during the day and night he would look at his watch and learn always with disappointment how little of his life was past, how much there was still ahead of him. He wished no one ill, but he looked at the world *sub specia aeternitatis* and he found it as flat as a map; except when, rather often, personal annoyance intruded. Then he would come tumbling from his exalted point of observation. Shocked by a bad bottle of wine, an impertinent stranger, or a fault in syntax, his mind like a cinema camera trucked furiously forward to confront the offending object close-up with glaring lens; with the eyes of a drill sergeant inspecting an awkward squad, bulging with wrath that was half-facetious, and with half-simulated incredulity; like a drill sergeant he was absurd to many but to some rather formidable.'

The self analysis continues ruthlessly and superbly well.

The blemishes appear early on. The first one is Mrs Pinfold. Though he was more reckless in this novel than elsewhere in taking people and events from his experience, and also in owning to this direct use of experience, there is no question of Mrs Pinfold being modelled on Laura. There is not the glimmer of a resemblance. He evidently aimed at depicting an estimable but neutral person, as he had done with great success in describing Barbara Sothill. But Mrs Pinfold is no Barbara. In her different way, she is as dead as Julia. This would not matter if she had been contrived as a dim 'extra' in the background, but she is not; she is supposed to be a person of forceful goodness before whose shining virtue Gilbert Pinfold's haunting spectres fade into nothing. The end of the book is weak and sentimental. It is strange that he allowed it to be so when he had such material to draw from. Father Caraman's memorandum strikes me as far more dramatic than the end of Evelyn's novel.

In the main part of *Pinfold* Evelyn seems to have not only drawn heavily on his raw material, but to have left it raw. This is often, though not always, a literary mistake in fiction. Evelyn thought it a mistake in the case of *Pinfold* and testified to that effect. Shortly before *Pinfold* came out a first novel by Muriel Spark *The Comforters* was published in 1957. Evelyn reviewed it and owned in his article that he himself had completed a novel on a similar theme. He declared his opinion that Muriel Spark's book was better than his. Having read both books I cannot agree with this judgement; as one might expect, this first novel does not stand comparison with any of Evelyn's mature work. But in one respect *The Comforters* is distinctly superior to *Pinfold*. The delusions, voice-delusions as in *Pinfold*, are smoothly conjoined to describe experience of reality, a fine piece of craftsmanship which makes the delusions appear all the more unaccountable and all the more alarming. Evelyn's book tells two stories at the same time: that of Pinfold under the stress of his delusions, and that of Pinfold in his right mind. The second subject is much the more amusing with its vivid description of the false positions into which the unlucky hero is drawn through his belief in the reality of the overheard voices. His hopeless efforts to apologize and to explain himself are the very stuff of comedy. But these passages are a minor part of the main story, and are in the nature of 'bridge-passages'. The bulk of the book is taken up with detailed accounts of what the disembodied voices say, and throughout they talk nonsense.

'Never say: "I had such a curious dream"' was the advice of an eighteenth-century divine quoted by Logan Pearsall Smith. It was sound advice which Evelyn should have remembered. No one is more tedious than the dream-teller, a species multiplied by popular psychology. 'Behold, this dreamer cometh' reads today more than ever as a warning. It is difficult to be terrified or even disturbed by Evelyn's voices because they are such stuff as dreams are made on, and which so bored and irritated Logan Pearsall Smith's divine.

The book had a mixed critical reception. Most of the praise was concentrated, and justly so, on the fine self-portrait with which the novel opens, a miniature work of art worthy to stand with the large canvas painted with the same intention by James Joyce. Much of the attack was valid, pointing to those essential deficiencies in the subject-matter which have been indicated in the preceding paragraph, but much of it was irrelevant. Hostile reviewers felt themselves affronted by the social values implied in the best part of the book.

Of these opponents of the book the most prominent was Mr J. B. Priestley. He wrote an article for the *New Statesman*, ostensibly reviewing the book in the light of modern psychology, in effect he wrote a condemnation of Evelyn's social ideas and style of life. 'It is not Mr Waugh but Gilbert Pinfold who is the subject of this essay', he wrote at the end of his two introductory paragraphs, but the disavowal was weakened by his previous description of *Pinfold* as a 'semi-autobiographical novel'. There can be no doubt that Mr Waugh was the subject of the essay.

Mr Priestley was and is a doughty opponent. Unqualified as I am to pronounce on psychological matters, the following passage seems to me to contain an uncomfortable grain – though not more than a grain – of truth.

'They are right, these voices, when they tell him that he is a fake. It is of course Pinfold remonstrating with Pinfold; the fundamental self telling the ego not to be a mountebank. What is on trial here is the Pinfold *persona*. This *persona* is inadequate: the drink hinted at it; the dope more than suggested it; the voices proved it.'

But if Mr Priestley was a doughty opponent he was also a reckless one, a fighter who occasionally 'in rage strikes wide', taking the form, in this instance, of laying down the law not so much in accord with Socialist principles as with Socialist prejudices. In the following passage I regard it as allowable to read 'Waugh' for 'Pinfold'.

'The style of life deliberately adopted by Pinfold is that of those old Catholic landed families, whose women live for the children and the home farm and whose men, except in wartime when, like Pinfold, they are ready to defend their country, detach themselves from the national life, behaving from choice as their ancestors were compelled to do from necessity, because of their religion. Everything we learn about Pinfold fits this style of life – with one supremely important exception, the fact, the obstinate fact, that he is by profession a writer, an artist. And this is the central truth about Pinfold, who could never have achieved any distinction as a novelist if he had not been essentially an artist. He is not a Catholic landed gentleman pretending to be an author. He is an author pretending to be a Catholic landed gentleman. But why, you may ask, should he not be both? Because they are not compatible.'

'Waugh' can be read for 'Pinfold' again in the concluding passages, and 'White's' for 'Bellamy's' club. I quote an extract from the penultimate, and the whole of the concluding paragraph in which the new-style Puritan sermonizer no longer disguises his role.

'We avoid the *Cher Maître* touch. Yet I think the Continental attitude, for all its pomposity, extravagance, incitement to charlatanry, is saner, healthier, better for both the arts and the nation, than ours is. If authors and artists in this country are not only officially regarded without favour but even singled out for unjust treatment – as I for one believe – then the Pinfolds are partly to blame. They not only do not support their profession: they go over to the enemy . . .'

'Let Pinfold take warning. He will break down again, and next time may never find a way back to his study. The central self he is trying to deny, that self which grew up among books and authors and not among partridges and hunters, that self which even now desperately seeks expression in ideas and words, will crack if it is walled up again within a false style of life. Whatever Mrs Pinfold and the family and the neighbours may think and say, Pinfold must step out of his role as the Cotswold gentleman quietly regretting the Reform Bill of 1832, and if he cannot discover an accepted role as English man of letters – and I admit this is not easy – he must create one, hoping it will be recognizable. He must be at all times the man of ideas, the intellectual, the artist, even if he is asked to resign from Bellamy's Club. If not; if he settles down again to sulk and soak behind that inadequate *persona*, waiting for a message from Bonnie Prince Charlie; then not poppy, nor mandragora, nor all the drowsy syrups of the world, shall ever medicine him.'

Evelyn's reply did not appear in *The New Statesman*, in accord with the usual custom, but in *The Spectator*, a fortnight later.

It was a masterly performance and is worth some extensive quotation. He began by dealing with Mr Priestley's assertion that the roles of artist and 'Catholic country gentleman' are incompatible.

'Which of those dangers to the artistic life, I wonder, does he regard as the more deadly. Not living in the country, surely? Unless I am mis-informed Mr Priestley was at my age a landed proprietor on a scale by which my own modest holding is a peasant's patch.

'Catholicism? . . . Mr Priestley must have observed that a very large number of his fellow writers profess a creed and attempt to follow a moral law which are either Roman Catholic, or, from a Jungian point of view, are almost identical. Mr T. S. Eliot, Dame Edith Sitwell, Mr Betjeman, Mr Graham Greene, Miss Rose Macaulay – the list is illustrious and long. Are they all heading for the bin?

'No, what gets Mr Priestley's goat . . . is my attempt to behave like a gentleman. Mr Priestley has often hinted a distaste for the upper classes, but, having early adopted the *persona* of a generous-hearted, genial fellow, he has only once, I think, attempted to portray them. On that occasion, of which more later, he showed a rather remote acquaintance, like Dickens in creating Sir Mulberry Hawke. It is the strain of minding his manners that is driving poor Pinfold cuckoo. "He must," writes Mr Priestley, "be at all times the man of ideas, the intellectual, the artist, even if he is asked to resign from Bellamy's Club." Mr Priestley's clubs must be much stricter than mine. Where I belong I never heard of the committee in-quiring into the members' "ideas." It is true that we are forbidden to cheat at cards or strike the servants, but for the life of me I can't see anything particularly artistic in either of those activities.'

Evelyn next quoted Mr Priestley's penultimate paragraph which has already been referred to. Evelyn quoted it and went on to a deadly com-mentary. (The reader should be reminded that in September 1957 Mr Macmillan had been Prime Minister for a year.)

' "If authors and artists in this country" [Mr Priestley] writes, "are not only officially regarded without favour but even singled out for unjust treatment – as I for one believe – then the Pinfolds are partly to blame. They not only do not support their profession; they go over to the enemy."

'I say, Priestley old man, are you sure you are feeling all right? Any Voices? I mean to say! No narcotics or brandy in your case, I know, but when a chap starts talking about "the enemy" and believing, for one, that he is singled out for unjust treatment, isn't it time he consulted his Jungian about his *anima*? Who is persecuting poor Mr Priestley? Mr Macmillan does not ask him to breakfast as Gladstone might have done. His income, like everyone else's, is confiscated and "redistributed" in the Welfare State. Tennyson's life was made hideous by importunate admirers; Mr Priestley can walk down Piccadilly with a poppy or a lily, but he will be unmolested by the mob who pursue television performers. Is this what Mr Priestley means by unjust treatment? . . .'

The last section of the article is on the subject of Mr Priestley's activity in class-warfare.

Mr Priestley, he wrote, 'has had some sharp disappointments in the last twelve years; perhaps he would call them "traumas." The voices he hears, like Pinfold's, may be those of a wildly distorted conscience. There was, indeed, a *trahison des clercs* some twenty years back which has left the literary world much discredited. It was then that the astute foresaw the social revolution and knew who would emerge top dog. They went to great lengths to suck up to the lower classes or, as they called it, to "identify themselves with the workers." Few excelled Mr Priestley in his zeal for social justice. It is instructive to re-read his powerful novel *Blackout in Gretley*, which was written at a very dark time in the war when national unity was of vital importance. Its simple theme is that the English upper classes were in conspiracy to keep the workers in subjection even at the cost of national defeat.'

The paragraph continues with a résumé of the characters in the novel and the misdeeds of the more highly born among them. The end of this section and the conclusion of the article read as follows:

'Only two workers show moral delinquency; of these one turns out to be a German officer in disguise; the other, and more wicked, is – a Roman Catholic. Even the bad food at the hotel is ascribed to the fact that it is managed by a retired officer. "This country has the choice during the next two years", a virtuous character says, "of coming fully to life and beginning all over again or of rapidly decaying and dying on the same old feet. It can only accomplish the first by taking firm grip on about fifty thousand important, influential gentlemanly persons and telling them firmly to shut up and do nothing if they don't want to be put to doing some most unpleasant work."

'Came the dawn. Mr Priestley was disappointed. No concentration camp was made for the upper classes. Nor have the triumphant workers shown themselves generous or discerning patrons of the arts. Gratitude, perhaps, is not one of their salient virtues. When they feel the need for a little aesthetic pleasure they do not queue at the experimental theatre;

they pile into charabancs and tramp round the nearest collection of heir-looms and family portraits; quite enough to inflame the naked artist with an itch of persecution mania.'

So ended the major action in the Priestley battle. Had Evelyn scored a knock-out win? He thought so, and most of his friends were of that opinion. I thought so, and think so still. Both contestants had had re-course to class prejudice but of the two, so it seems to me, Mr Priestley had used this weapon with less scrupulousness than Evelyn. He played to a disreputable section of the gallery. He appealed to propaganda-conditioned minds in his use of the emotive word 'gentleman'. Evelyn appealed to extreme conservatism and flouted popular propaganda in his use of the emotive term 'the lower classes'. (How great the power of euphemism! If Evelyn had written 'lower income-brackets' his meaning would have been precisely the same and no one could have been upset.) The loss and the gain through these uses of prejudice were about equal. But Evelyn enjoyed one advantage which seems to me decisive. He could pack a prettier punch; he wrote better.

After 1957 the Pinfold campaign had been fought and was over. It was generally agreed or conceded that though this book might not rank among Evelyn's best novels, it certainly ranked high as a 'document' both in the personal and psychological area.


Back to 1954. After his recovery he spent most of his time working on the novel which was to appear in the next year under the title *Officers and Gentlemen*. It was the second volume of his planned Second World War trilogy, *Sword of Honour*, and was finished by November.

He went to London on short visits, less frequently than in the previous years. He lived quietly. The Pinfold experience had given him a fright. Nancy Mitford was moved to write to him in June: 'I feel rather worried about your great new goodness. I hope it's all right.' Of the great new goodness Nancy perhaps had an exaggerated idea, judging from letters written to and by him in this year.

With *Officers and Gentlemen* finished and the worst of the winter drawing on, Evelyn decided that after Christmas he must again seek warmth and sun. He discussed the matter with Ann Fleming, and the result was an invitation from her and her husband to visit them at their house Golden-eye in Jamaica. He had a few other friends there including the Brown-lows. In 1952 the delightful Kitty Brownlow had died, and in 1954 Lord Brownlow had remarried and bought a property on the island.

Here is a convenient point at which to indicate Evelyn's friendship with Ian and Ann Fleming. With Ian he was on friendly but never close terms. The surviving letters between them are few and concerned with printing business or Ian's learned bibliographical hobbies. There are no letters of

Ronald Knox at Mells with
Mrs Asquith and her daughter

Mrs Ian Fleming

Evelyn about to broadcast on P. G. Wodehouse in 1961

gossip or of literary discussion; they never wrote to each other about each other's books. (Ian had invented James Bond in 1953.) It was very different with Ann who was a cousin of Laura. Evelyn had known her since his marriage, therefore, but the great friendship only began in 1952 under what may strike many as rather odd circumstances. Evelyn's Puritanical disapproval of divorce and the remarriage of divorced persons has been noticed. After the death of her first husband Lord O'Neill (who was killed in action in Italy in 1944) Ann married Lord Rothermere. This shocked Evelyn because Lord Rothermere was a divorced man. When Ann and Esmond Rothermere were divorced in 1952 and Ann married Ian Fleming in the same year, she expected trouble from her uncompromising cousin-in-law.

To her relief and surprise Evelyn sent her a tenderly affectionate letter. He congratulated her not only on marrying a man of distinguished talent and engaging personality, but also on being once more lawfully married in the eyes of sacred authority. Since the Church refuses to acknowledge the validity of divorce or of marriages to divorced persons Ann, by the laws of the Church, was free, as the widow of Lord O'Neill, to marry the bachelor Ian Fleming. When it came to Church matters, Evelyn was always very legalistic.

The friendship which thereupon grew and flourished was similar in character to that with Nancy Mitford. Through Nancy Evelyn met a great number of people in Paris whom he would not have met otherwise; through Ann he met a great number of people in London, such as the Socialist leader Hugh Gaitskell or Lord Goodman, whom he was unlikely to get to know otherwise. Like Nancy, Ann could take him out of himself and could counter his ever-growing tendency to seclusion and melancholy. As with Nancy her ministrations were attended by occasional squalls and tantrums.

But with Ann, Evelyn found himself in relations with a less pliable character than Nancy. Neither woman was prepared to stand more than a certain amount of nonsense from Evelyn, but Ann's calls to order were more direct and merciless. It was she who brought to an end his use of an antiquated style of ear-trumpet to which he had taken with increasing deafness in his right ear.

He loved his ear-trumpet which, though uselessly antiquated in appearance, was a highly refined and effective instrument of amplification. But he cherished it also as an offensive and defensive weapon. Its use opened an infallible way to make a shy person yet more ill at ease or make the most self-confident shy; thus it could serve him in the office of a wall round his seclusion. Evelyn's use of it as a purely offensive weapon attracted some notice after this time in 1957. The occasion was a Foyle's literary luncheon, held in honour of the publication of *The Ordeal of Gilbert Pinfold*. Evelyn was the chief guest. He attended with his ear-trumpet. When the chief speaker Mr Malcolm Muggeridge began his eulogy of the book and the guest of honour, Evelyn ostentatiously laid his ear-trumpet on the table, immediately resuming it on the conclusion of the speech. Malcolm Muggeridge was to contrive a revenge, one not less open to criticism than Evelyn's offence.

The end of the ear-trumpet came when Evelyn attempted to use it as an offensive weapon at a lunch-party in Ann's house. One of the guests asked Evelyn a question. Evelyn turned his ear-trumpet to Ann saying: 'Would you repeat what has just been said?' For reply Ann gave the ear-trumpet a bang with a spoon. The noise, Evelyn told me later, was that of a gun being fired an inch away. After that Evelyn used the ear-trumpet more rarely and with more discrimination and soon abandoned it altogether.

The visit to Jamaica proved a joyous occasion. Ian was happily engaged on his third Bond novel *Moonraker*, and Evelyn making final revisions to the text of *Officers and Gentlemen*. The only social difficulty incurred was after Ash Wednesday. Evelyn kept the Lenten fasts with pedantic precision, bringing scales with him, a custom once common among old Catholic families, in order to weigh exactly the allowable quantity of food that he was to consume at every meal except his evening *cena*. This greatly added to Ann's housekeeping burden, as, to satisfy what Evelyn considered to be necessary to his religious practice, she had to put in extra fishing time so as to spear fish of the required size. Evelyn had no conscientious scruples about the extra trouble he caused. He stayed not only with the Flemings but with the Brownlows, and during this visit Evelyn ran into a fellow-writer Beverley Nichols with whom he was slightly acquainted. In the course of conversation it came out that Evelyn was staying with the Brownlows, and Mr Nichols with his friend Edward Molyneux, the famous dress-designer. The last-named was not known to Evelyn and he commented: 'I believe he makes blouses for women, doesn't he?' Mr Nichols felt this to be an unpardonably snobbish remark and did not forget it. He quoted it in a bitterly denigrating article on Evelyn written nearly twenty years later.

1955 was an eventful year in Evelyn's life. Soon after his return from Jamaica he found that he had an enemy on the staff of *The Daily Express*, not a very formidable one but dedicated. This was Nancy Spain, a 'general stunt' columnist, who on some Beaverbrook whim had been appointed the paper's principal literary critic. She was not a worthy successor of James Agate, but her noisy uninhibited knock-about journalism attracted a readership. She was an iconoclast who hoped to reduce certain reputations which in her crude opinion were over-valued. Said to be agreeable to meet, she had come to be on friendly terms with Nancy Mitford in Paris; nevertheless Nancy Mitford's reputation was one of her targets. She used to refer to her in *The Daily Express* as 'the other Nancy'.

Her main target was Evelyn. She invariably treated him in her articles as a writer who as a young man had gained an inflated reputation which had unaccountably persisted into his middle age. She confessed that as an adolescent she had loved his books until she had outgrown this raw taste. Her articles were much acclaimed and she was frequently asked to speak on the BBC. Journalistic success went to her head and in pursuing her campaign against Evelyn she grew overbold.

In June 1955 *Officers and Gentlemen* was published by Chapman and Hall an event in which Nancy Spain was to figure.

It was a far better book than *Men at Arms*, and, dealing with more dreadful subjects than its predecessor (including a haunting description of the Crete campaign), there could be no question of this being *Mrs Dale's Wartime Diary*. A host of lifelike inventions came on the scene. To Diana Cooper's great delight, Mrs Stitch was revived from *Scoop*, but given here 'treatment in depth,' and a key role.

As with *Men at Arms* the book will be more critically considered when I come to the completed trilogy.

So remarkable a fiction could hardly fail of welcome. It sold well, but the critical reception of the book in Great Britain was not as cordial as in the United States. This was not only because literary critics are especially prone to be creatures of habit, and had noted that *Men at Arms* was not 'vintage Waugh', but also because of a distressing foreword. In it Evelyn had announced that he had originally intended his 'war-book' to be a trilogy, but had changed his mind and wanted his readers to consider the work completed with this second volume *Officers and Gentlemen*. It is allowable to assume that after the effort of writing this second volume he felt that he was 'written out,' on this subject anyway. The foreword was a great mistake. If it had been a statement of the fact; if *Sword of Honour* had indeed ended with this second volume, then it would not have been a work to enhance Evelyn's literary reputation. Too many loose ends would have remained; the full intention would have been but vaguely discernible; it would have but been remembered as a minor specimen (to remember his literary idol Max Beerbohm again) among those works of art which perplex and fascinate us *quia imperfectum*. As hardly needs saying, after a long withdrawal from the subject and preoccupation with work of a quite different kind, Evelyn eventually and triumphantly finished the trilogy.

Being manifestly a largely autobiographical novel, Evelyn's friends became busy seeking to identify the invented characters with models in real life, an activity always likely to arouse Evelyn's displeasure. Some of the identifications were valid. The real life and career of Bob Laycock were dissimilar to those of the 'Hookforce' commander, the invented Tommy Blackhouse, but if Evelyn had never met Bob I think the picture of Tommy Blackhouse would have been different. As before Diana Cooper claimed with justice to be the model on which Mrs Stitch had been contrived.

Major Hound is said by some who served with Evelyn in 1941 to be a precise portrait. The rest must be guess-work; as usual Evelyn gave no clues, and as usual was easily offended when asked for them.

This was the occasion for a squall which disturbed his relations with Ann. On 4 July he wrote to her as follows:

'Dear Ann, Your telegram horrifies me. Of course there is no possible connexion between Bob and "Claire". If you suggest such a thing anywhere it will be the end of our beautiful friendship . . .' The central part of the letter is on other matters. The last part returns to the opening subject: 'For Christ's sake lay off the idea of Bob="Claire."

'Do you see the spectator? I have an awfully funny item in (I hope) the next issue about Lord Noel-Buxton.

'Just shut up about Laycock.

'Fuck you

'E. Waugh.'

Evelyn was right to protest that the character Ivor Claire owed nothing to Bob.

Ann replied on the 12th in a long letter in which she thanked him for having sent her an inscribed copy of the novel. The opening and concluding passages are as follows:

'Dearest Evelyn, Panic is foreign to your nature and you rarely use rough words. Why do you become hysterical if one attempts to identify your officers and gentlemen? The book is a great delight and I am sad I have finished it . . . Love and thank you and fuck you Ann.'

In the foregoing, the reference to Lord Noel-Buxton may puzzle some readers and revive memories in others. It concerns an incident provoked by the publication of the novel. It had occurred on 21 June, a day or two after publication when Evelyn was in the news. As a result Nancy Spain returned to the fray. The incident is best told in Evelyn's own words in the article on the subject he wrote for *The Spectator*, published on 8 July. He entitled it 'Awake my Soul! It is a Lord.' Here the opening paragraph and the central passage are given:

' "I'm not on business. I'm a member of the House of Lords." These moving and rather mysterious words were uttered on my doorstep the other evening and recorded by the leading literary critic of the Beaverbrook press. They have haunted me, waking and sleeping, ever since. I am sometimes accused of a partiality for lords; whatever touches them, it is hinted, vicariously touches me. Certainly the nobleman who tried to insinuate himself into my house half an hour before dinner that evening, has become a nine days' obsession . . .

'On the morning of the visit my wife said: "An *Express* reporter and a lord wanted to come and see you this afternoon."

' "You told them not to?"

' "Of course."

' "What lord?"

' "Noel someone."

' "Has Noël Coward got a peerage? I'd like to see him."

' "No, it wasn't anyone I had heard of."

'There, I supposed, the matter ended. But that evening, just as I was going to prepare myself for dinner, I heard an altercation at the front door My poor wife, weary from the hay-field, was being kept from her bath by a forbidding pair.

'The lady of the party, Miss Spain, has recorded in two columns their day's doings. They were on what she called a "pilgrimage." This took them, uninvited, to tea with the Poet Laureate. "Lord Noel-Buxton just walked into the house", she writes, while she trampled the hay. The poet was "silent, dreaming back in the past," thinking, no doubt, that in all his years before the mast he had never met such tough customers. He gave them oat-cake. Then he brightened, "his blue eyes danced." The old "darling" had thought of a way out. He urged them on to me. " 'See you? Of course he'll see you,' " On they came to the village where I live which, curiously, they found to be a "straggly collection of prefabricated houses" (there is not one in the place), and entered the pub, where they got into talk with its rustic patrons. I have since made inquiries and learn that they somehow gave the impression that they were touts for television. Members of the village band sought to interest them in their music, and the cordiality, thus mistakenly engendered, emboldened the two pilgrims. They attempted to effect an entry into my house and wrangled until I dismissed them in terms intelligible even to them.

'Lord Noel-Buxton seems to have been unaware of having done anything odd. "Oh, Nancy, do stop!" he is said to have cried, when I went out to see that they were not slipping round to suck up to the cook. "He's coming to apologize."

'A faulty appreciation.

'What, I have been asking myself since, was Lord Noel-Buxton's part in the escapade? He is not, I have established, on the pay-roll of the *Daily Express*. All he seems to have got out of it is a jaunt in a motor-car, an oat-cake and a novel he can hardly hope to understand. Who, in the popular phrase, does he think he is?'

Lord Noel-Buxton attempted to laugh the incident off. He sent Evelyn a telegram of congratulation on his article and then attempted a counter-attack by way of a facetious letter on the subject published in *The Spectator*. He made a mistake in taking on a leading comedian of the age on his own ground. Evelyn made rings round him. Most people who followed the incident, excepting those for whom Norfolk loyalties are unconditional, agreed that Nancy Spain and Lord Noel-Buxton came out of it defeated and mauled.

One last incident of 1955 may conclude this chapter. In the summer

Edith Sitwell became a Roman Catholic. The ceremony of reception was performed on 4 August at Farm Street. Evelyn had resumed his diary in June and thus recorded the event:

'Edith recanted her errors in fine ringing tones and received conditional baptism, then was led into the confessional while six of us collected in the sacristy – [Alec] Guinness and I and Father D'Arcy, an old lame deaf woman with dyed red hair whose name I never learned, a little swarthy man who looked like a Jew but claimed to be Portuguese and a blond youth who looked American but claimed to be English.

'We drove two streets in a large hired limousine to Edith's club, the Sesame. I had heard gruesome stories of this place but Edith had ordered a banquet – cold consomme, lobster Newburg, steak, strawberry flan and great quantities of wine. The old woman suddenly said: "Did I hear the word 'whisky'?" I said: "Do you want some?" "More than anything in the world." "I'll get you some." But the Portuguese nudged me and said: "It would be disastrous".'

Evelyn omitted one interesting detail. In her new faith he was Edith Sitwell's godfather. After this she frequently signed her letters to him 'Your loving god-daughter Edith.'

# Chapter 23

## 1956-1957

Only one piece by Evelyn belonging to 1956 is likely to be remembered, and that not for long because it was manifestly inferior. His diary tells that occasionally he was disturbed in mind by his literary inactivity, but if he had felt written out after finishing *Officers and Gentlemen*, the mood did not stay with him for long. Though there was to come a long interval before he began serious work on the third volume of the trilogy, he had started, again according to his diary, to make studies for it as early as October 1955.

By the end of that year he had reached a momentous decision regarding his private life. He made up his mind to sell Piers Court. It followed that a large part of his time in 1956 was occupied in searching for and looking at houses with Laura, sometimes accompanied by his children. The hunt for a house was to continue till the autumn.

A theme, stridently enunciated in 1955, underwent what in musical terms is known as 'development' in 1956, and did not reach its 'coda' or conclusion till 1957. The reader must again remember the name of Nancy Spain.

In *The Spectator* on 24 February, 1956, Evelyn had a polemic article against Mr John Wain. The attack was excited by a contemptuous review by Mr Wain of Mr, or, as Evelyn always said and wrote, Dr P. G. Wodehouse. In his opening paragraph he drew comparisons between literary criticism as he remembered it from his early writing days and in the fifties. Referring to Arnold Bennett in 1928 Evelyn wrote:

'I wonder whether any critic today has so large and immediate an influence. At the same period his colleague on the *Daily Express* was D. H. Lawrence, then at the height of his powers. Things have changed. The Beaverbrook press is no longer listed as having any influence at all. The *Observer* heads the poll, with the *Sunday Times* as runner-up.'

The implication that she had less literary influence than her predecessor D. H. Lawrence nettled Nancy Spain. She retaliated in the next month on 17 March.

'There is a war between Evelyn Waugh and me. He said some weeks ago in a literary weekly that *The Express* had no influence on the book trade. *The Express*, he complains, sold only three hundred of HIS novels.

He once had a book chosen by the Book Society, so that sold well. But the total first edition sales of all his other titles are dwarfed by brother Alec. ISLAND IN THE SUN (Cassells 16/-) foretold by me as this year's runaway best seller has now topped 60,000 copies as a direct result of my *Daily Express* notice. So the publishers told me yesterday . . .'

Frankie Donaldson writes of Evelyn at this time: 'It was Evelyn's practice to examine everything written about him in the newspapers in an attempt to detect grounds for a libel action. His interest in the matter was exactly comparable to other people's interest in football pools or The Irish Sweeepstake. He regarded it as the only hope of acquiring a large sum of money not subject to tax. When Randolph Churchill successfully challenged a newspaper which had described him as a "hack", Evelyn, filled with admiration and glee, was spurred on to the chase.'

On reading Nancy Spain's article of 17 March he felt certain that at last he had his quarry at bay.

The reader may not see any grounds for a legal action in Nancy Spain's words. They were boastful and vulgar, as was to be expected, but hardly libellous. But Evelyn, remembering Randolph's extraordinary success against *The People*, thought otherwise and consulted his solicitors who were of the same mind. Evelyn may have been further spurred on to action by the personal interest taken by Lord Beaverbrook in the affair. Evelyn heard about it in a letter from Ann Fleming written on 23 March. In what his admirers called his puckish, and his critics his mischief-making mood, Lord Beaverbrook attempted to use Nancy Spain's article as a means of breaking the friendship of Ann and Evelyn. He opened the campaign by sending Ann a copy of Alec Waugh's *Island in the Sun*. This part of the story is best told in the letter of 23 March from her to Evelyn.

'Lord Beaverbrook telephoned this morning, so I thanked him for your brother's book and said you were with me when it arrived. To my surprise he broke into guffaws of laughter, and said "it's a pity that story is not true, it's a most magnificent story, it's a pity it's not true." I said I was bewildered by his reaction – he chuckled some more and said "Ah no, Ann, you know as well as I do that Alec has made more money with his books than Evelyn, and Evelyn is most horribly jealous." I told him I was grateful for his gift but . . . thought there could be no jealousy as there was no comparison. He chuckled more horribly, Canadian gargling noises, and I gathered he was going to immediately telephone Nancy Spain to tell this glorious joke; twenty minutes later he telephoned again to say Nancy Spain knew how jealous you were of your famous brother and they both regretted that I had invented such an epic occasion – I am still bewildered.'

On 6 April Evelyn wrote to Ann as follows: 'The libel courts are going to be busy this year – Boofy [Lord Arran] v. Ian, the Duke of Norfolk v.

the *Sketch*, an American priest v. Graham Greene, and I, in my modest
way, am suing the *Daily Express*.'

There, under the law's delay, the matter rested till the next year.

Two religious events were the cause of deep disappointment to Evelyn
during 1956. Reference has been made to the policy of heightened, mainly
Marian devotionalism by which the Roman Catholic hierarchy hoped to
revive Catholic loyalties which had flagged in some places following the
events of World War II. A climax had already occurred in the form of the
definition in 1950 by Pius XII of the doctrine of the Blessed Virgin's
Assumption. As already related Evelyn rejoiced at the dismay caused to
many of his co-religionists by the uncompromising and fundamentalist
tone of the Pope's encyclical letter announcing the new article of faith.
Evelyn, with many others, hoped that the heightened devotionalism
would not stop at the 1950 definition. There was a movement afoot in
the Church for papal definitions of doctrines regarding two other ancient
beliefs, one in the position of Mary as co-Redemptress with Christ, the
second in a notion described as 'the mediation of Mary', meaning that all
prayers to Christ are (so to speak) automatically routed through, and
require the approval of the Blessed Virgin. Possibly because he thought
that the credulity of the faithful had been already taxed to the limit by
the 1950 definition Pius XII did not proceed with the movement. Evelyn,
who had fought with his pen for the further definitions, especially the co-
Redemptress idea, was disappointed with other enthusiasts at the Pope's
return to moderation, and his disappointment was mixed with apprehension.

For extreme Marian devotionalism was only a part of the Church's
revivalist policy. Its most striking feature was in some contrast. It lay in
an attempt at radical modernisation of the Church's practice, rule and
liturgy, described as *Aggiornamento* or *Renewal* by Pius XII's successor.
The reformation of the liturgy was the detail of *Renewal* which made the
deepest impression on the generality of Catholics. The reform had been
going forward for some years before 1956 but had been almost entirely
confined to the annual celebration of Holy Week which included the most
imposing of the regular Catholic ceremonies. They had for long been
criticized because usage in the course of several centuries had displaced
their time sequence. This was specially true of the Holy Saturday service,
originally intended to start at midnight on Saturday and to conclude with
the Easter Mass at dawn on Sunday. For the sake of convenience the service
had come to be celebrated on Saturday morning, beginning at dawn. It
followed that the first Easter Mass was celebrated at mid-morning on
Saturday, taking much away from the solemnity of Easter itself. The new
liturgy devised under Pius XII simplified the ceremonies and transferred
them to Saturday evening, concluding with a midnight Mass. The reformed celebration turned Easter into a night festival, like Christmas,

and completely lost the essential spirit of Easter as a dawn festival, a spirit vigorously expressed in the abandoned ceremonies, as much in their modified as in their original forms.

A sense of deprivation was not general among Catholics, however. The new service retained much of the beauty of the old, and the overwhelmingly impressive Maundy Thursday Mass, the 'Altar of Repose', the night offices of Tenebrae, and the liturgical masterpiece, the Good Friday 'Mass of the Presanctified', remained intact. Not for long. The belief grew that the celebration of Holy Week would be more valuable, would compel a greater corporate sense in the Church, if it was expressed in ceremonies which did not involve a keen appreciation of symbolism, if they were more easily understood by ordinary people and invited more 'mass participation' in the form of community singing from them; if they appealed less to the sense of awe they avoided the accusation of mere-tricious aestheticism, above all of excessive indulgence of the sense of the past. Nowhere did the notion of a 'Century of the Common Man' exert more fascination than on the Roman Catholic clergy. The entire edifice of the Holy Week Liturgy was swept away as being over-elaborate, and it was substituted by services of a more everyday kind. This was the beginning of a movement which was to reduce all Roman Catholic ceremonial to commonplace and to abolish the traditional order of the Mass in favour of a prayer-meeting in which only essential vestiges of the traditional cele-bration were retained.

Evelyn did not live to see the reform fully established, but he saw enough to see the way it was going and to join that multitude of his fellow-Catholics (a multitude which the reforming clergy insisted with much protestation did not exist) who saw in *Renewal* more of impoverishment than of effective religious expression. He was first confronted by the new movement in force when he went as usual to the Holy Week retreat at Downside in early April 1956. He recorded in his diary that he 'resented' the new liturgy but had nevertheless as usual found the retreat 'valuable'. But it was not long before his alarm made him intensely hostile to the whole *Renewal* movement. He only attended one or two more of the Downside retreats, after which he never went to any Holy Week services except the Easter Mass. Oddly enough Ronald Knox in this year also saw the new Good Friday service as a grave impoverishment of the Mass of the Presanctified, although he had unconsciously been one of the strongest influences towards reform in England.


In November 1955 Teresa had won a scholarship to Somerville College, Oxford, and so following family tradition she commenced scholar in the winter, in the second term of the academic year.

She was now a grown-up young woman and Evelyn and Laura decided that in 1956 she must be 'brought out' in the accustomed manner, by the giving of a 'débutante ball'. Their friends Lord and Lady Antrim had a daughter of the same age as Teresa, as had Lord Antrim's sister Lady Rose Baring, so the three families clubbed together to give a dance which was held at the beginning of July in a marquee erected in Kensington Square. Evelyn gave the following account in his diary entry for the 5th.

'After two dreary days alone at home I went to London by train for Teresa's ball. It was dark with some drizzle after a stormy night but I had sent £2 to the Poor Clares at Looe asking them to arrange good weather from 7 p.m. onwards and at 7 it cleared and remained fine throughout the night; a remarkable performance by these excellent women to whom I have sent another £3. Most days since have been wet. Rain would have ruined everything as there were far too many people for the tents & house & the square gardens were crowded. Angela [Antrim] had arranged the tents brilliantly and her painted arch was funny & clever & pretty. We were photographed in the tent in the afternoon. Angela's party dined in the square. Laura and I gave a dinner party at the Hyde Park Hotel. I sat between Maimie [Lygon] and Nell Stavordale. Ed Stanley was very jolly. The young people – except Raymond Bonham Carter – looked seedy. One dreadful youth was in a dinner jacket as were also many others at the ball – including Phil Dunne & John Marriott who should know better & have not the excuse that they wished to "jive". I spent most of the evening in the house, fairly cheerful at first but with deepening boredom. By 3.30 it was plain that the party was a great success & that no untoward incidents threatened, so I slunk away. The rest danced on until after five.'

The house referred to in the above entry was one on the square belonging to a relation of Lord Antrim. It was lent for the occasion.

Since one of the débutantes of honour was my niece I attended the ball, and I well remember seeing from the staircase Evelyn sitting on the sofa in the drawing-room of the house, glaring before him and evidently in a black humour. Laura, sitting by his side, was manifestly trying to calm him down. I was with Maimie and we instantly decided not to go into the drawing-room although I ought to have saluted my host and hostess. 'Evelyn's in a wax', whispered Maimie, 'better leave him alone and have some champenois wine with me instead.' Her advice was sound; he was in bellicose mood.

When my sister Angela asked him in the course of the evening why he seemed so depressed, he replied that he could not bear the sight of numerous people enjoying themselves. This was probably true, but on this occasion was only part of the truth. What had stirred his resentment was not the jollity of the occasion so much as the lack of tail coats. Phil Dunne and John Marriott were not, as Evelyn's diary suggests, among a minority but of the huge majority. The fact that this majority included Nancy Mitford's brother-in-law the Duke of Devonshire and other persons of the same kind did not soothe Evelyn. He felt that the wearing of dinner jackets indicated that his guests considered that their host belonged, in the dreaded phrase of old Viennese snobbishness, to the *Zweite Gesellschaft* When Evelyn wrote of 'no untoward incidents' he was unaware that a considerable number of young lady assistants from John Barker Ltd, the department store whose back premises occupy one side of the square, joined the dance, splendidly arrayed in evening frocks 'borrowed' from the store's dress department. It was thought wisest not to tell Evelyn about these lovely uninvited guests.

Evelyn's published literary output in 1956 was confined to journalism, and his only appearance 'between hard covers' was as the author of an article which he had revised for reprinting. The article (by no means one of Evelyn's best) formed part of a miscellany which was for the most part not distinguished though it enjoyed (and enjoys) some continuing fame.

The venture had had an origin two years earlier. The story is best told in the words of the eminent philologist Professor Alan S. C. Ross of Birmingham University.

'I was living in Paris in 1954, learning Tahitian for my book " *The Pitcairnese Language*". An American introduced me to Nancy Mitford and she asked me to lunch. During the lunch she asked me what I was working on and I told her about my article for " *Neuphilologische Mitteilungen*" the Finnish learned periodical. Later I sent her a proof. She took a great interest in it and asked if she might make use of it. I said of course she could, and she did.'

The Professor's title was 'U and Non-U, An Essay in Sociological Linguistics,' his subject 'class-indicators' in the differing modes of speech among English groups. (He excluded the northern and western Celts and the overseas English-speaking populations from his study.) The essay was marked by learning, observation and grasp. The subject was very much to the taste of Nancy who had touched on it in *The Pursuit of Love* in a famous passage (originally put in as padding) which made countless people afraid of using the widely accepted terms 'weekend' and 'mantelpiece'. She hastened to share her delight in Professor Ross's article with Evelyn. She described it as 'Bliss' and declared that nothing had made her 'shriek' (Mitfordese for laugh) so much for years. She also told Stephen Spender about her discovery and he commissioned an article by her on the subject for the monthly magazine *Encounter* which he was then editing. Thereafter the affair of 'U and Non-U' snowballed.

The English, who are probably the most class-conscious and class-worried people in Europe, provided a good environment for the monster's growth. *Encounter's* sales increased with the publications of Nancy's article whose matter was mostly drawn, much of it *verbatim*, from Professor

Ross's article. She added many touches of her own fantasy. Evelyn from the first had shown opinionated interest in the original article and disagreement with Nancy's views on the U and Non-U question, so, on Nancy's prompting, Stephen Spender asked him to contribute a reply to her. He entitled his article 'An open letter to the Honble Mrs Peter Rodd on a Very Serious Subject.' The massive sarcasm of the title was happily not carried into the text. Finally *Encounter* reaped the full harvest of their venture in a republication of Professor Ross's original essay which had been first published in 1954 in the aforementioned Finnish periodical. After this, the subject disappeared from the columns of *Encounter* in favour of graver matter. All this happened in 1955.

The enormous success of *Encounter*'s adventure gave Nancy's friend Hamish Hamilton a rewarding idea for book-publication. Why not, Jamie Hamilton seems to have argued, why not collect the three articles, add to them, and produce a run-away success 'slim volume'?

Jamie acted on his intuition. He obtained essays from other authors and early in 1956 produced what is usually called a 'symposium' (though in this case no drink was provided) to which six writers contributed: Professor Ross, Nancy, Evelyn, Peter Fleming, myself and John Betjeman. The resultant volume came out under the title *Noblesse Oblige*.

It did not make a good book. Nancy and Evelyn had no delusions about it and in their letters to each other referred to it as 'The Book of Shame', a reference to a fur-coat so-named donated by a much criticized Parisian admirer to Diana Cooper. Nancy took the affair light-heartedly. 'What a feast', she wrote to Evelyn just before publication in March 1956, 'what a feast it's going to be for those reviewers who loathe ONE.' But she grew impatient a month later at Evelyn's concern about the venture and its likely effects. 'How you do carry on', she wrote in late April, 'about the Book of shame. It is very funny indeed.'

Personally I never thought *Noblesse Oblige* very funny, though it was 'excellent in parts'. What merit it had, resided almost exclusively in the opening and closing contributions, those by Professor Ross and John Betjeman. The last named was represented by a short poem called 'How to get on in Society' (originally written for a literary competition) in which with dazzling skill every pretentious 'refeenment' of middle class speech was worked into a (just) coherent whole. Professor Ross excelled by his mastery of the 'dead pan' technique. His essay made one shriek, as Nancy Mitford would say, because it was quite impossible to tell at any point whether the writer was the least tickled by the preposterous conventions that he so carefully and accurately recorded. All the other contributors self-consciously aimed at being amusing, and only John Betjeman achieved originality and wit. Evelyn's reply to Nancy erred by awkwardly mixing a seriousness he could not maintain with a coyness unnatural to him. His piece had flashes of his wit but for all that was not worthy of him.

The book was denounced but enjoyed a large sale. It horrified the new Puritans, and I remember a discussion of it by the BBC literary critics one of whom took particular offence at John Betjeman's ingenious poem which he (or it may have been she) condemned as criminal snobbery which ought not to have been republished. I was reminded of the pietists of Cromwell's day who are said to have demanded public chastisement of those who made, owned, or ate Christmas puddings. Yet, paltry as the book was, I look back on it with affection. As a contributor I received royalties on its sale for a longer period than for any other book I have either written or contributed to.

'We all showed at our worst,' said Evelyn to me, 'except possibly myself.'

'*J'allais le dire.*'

On only one other occasion did I appear in a book as a fellow-contributor with Evelyn. This was in a collection of essays published by *The Sunday Times* in 1962 under the title *The Seven Deadly Sins*. Evelyn's essay on Sloth is remarkable and should not be forgotten.

Throughout the year he persisted in his search for a house and in the writing of *Pinfold*. Though Eric Strauss had probably encouraged the writing of this book as a piece of therapy, Evelyn did not face the labour in this spirit. Frankie Donaldson hints at his conviction that as a novelist he was extraordinarily fortunate in having had this peep into the world of the insane. He continued to suffer from the professional dread of the teller of tales, that his store of experience might become exhausted. He told several friends that the Pinfold experience, more outside his normal experience than even the most horrifying or bizarre of his war-time adventures, had come, like an unexpected legacy, to increase the capital sum on which he depended for safety.

As a grateful artist he worked on the book, frequently distracted by the lawyers' correspondence in connection with Evelyn's forthcoming action in the courts against Nancy Spain.

In the meantime Evelyn had solved his housing problem. On 9 July 1956 he noted in his diary: 'Laura, Teresa & I drove to see the house at Combe Florey that is for sale – cosy, sequestered, with great possibilities and slept at Pixton.' On the 10th: 'Home, stopping again at Combe Florey and another house (hopeless) lunching at Wells.'

His ultimate decision to buy Combe Florey was probably influenced by a letter from his daughter Margaret who was by now indisputably his favourite child. So early as this, when she was still a little schoolgirl she had shown some of her father's talent as a letter writer, and his chronic weakness as a speller. Some time before she had delighted Evelyn with a long letter from her convent school near Ascot, written in competition with another girl to see which of them could write the longest letter within an hour. The result contained such gems as 'I have read "Eminent Victorians" and liked it very much indeed but I got in trouble for trying to take Cardinal Manning in as a chapel book. I was told that Lytton Stratchy was, though a good writer, not very clear spiritually.' In the summer holidays she went to stay with the family of a schoolfriend who lived in Devon. Before this on 2 August she had been taken on a visit to Combe Florey. She wrote to her father: 'I am enjoying myself very much doing a lot of riding. Oh please do get Combe Florey, I liked it so much & its so nicely situated and I like it so much and I know I'd be happy there and perhaps we could keep a horse . . .' The letter continues with a refrain of. 'Please, please get Combe Florey' and ends 'Darling Papa, you have simply got to get it. Ston Easton is much too *big* and I do so love the gate house Love Meg.'

On 10 October Evelyn noted in his diary: 'This house is sold, Combe Florey is bought.' On Sunday 28th: 'My 53rd birthday . . . The house is half-empty of furniture. On Wednesday we shall sleep here for the last time. My "novel" has progressed well but is not finished. Laura has moped a little at seeing her home dismantled. I am exhilarated. We have had some rather gruesome farewell visits.'

My own reactions to the move were more in line with Laura's than with Evelyn's. Though I grew to enjoy Combe Florey, I could never love it as I did Piers Court. There was a grace and elegance about 'Stinkers' which I found absent from the Somerset house, handsome though it is. I am referring to the outsides. Within, both houses had that extraordinary and individual atmosphere given by Evelyn's taste for Victorian portraits and narrative pictures, for Victorian furniture and style of decoration, for atrocities of Ethiopian art including a large macabre wooden carving of a squatting camel, an object I could never pass without a tremor, and for *trompe-l'oeil* pictures (a taste he learned from Diana Cooper) one of which he commissioned. There was always the horrifying picture by Richard Eurich of the interior of a passenger aircraft just before the crash, to appal those on a first visit. To his collection of astonishing objects there was soon to be added an expensive and outrageous carpet, but the money to pay for it first had to be earned.

The libel case was heard before a jury on 18 February 1957. Evelyn's case, as plaintiff, was that Nancy Spain's article of 17 March 1956 meant that 'he was an unsuccessful writer who had made a false and malicious attack upon Miss Spain in *The Spectator* by reason of personal spite against her; that he was a writer whose name carried insignificant weight with the general public, the film rights and options in whose books were not worthy of purchase, and who was not worthy of consideration for the writing of articles.' Nancy Spain had put in a counter-claim based on an allegation that Evelyn's article in *The Spectator* recording her visit to Piers Court with Lord Noel-Buxton was in its turn libellous. It followed that not only the articles by Nancy Spain and Evelyn came under the scrutiny of the law, but the events of 21 June 1955.

Not knowing at the time that I would one day be Evelyn's biographer, I did not attend the court proceedings. Frankie Donaldson did, and gave a brief description in her book. (I have corrected slight mistakes as to fact and figures.)

'When the great day came Mr Gerald Gardiner appeared for Evelyn, Sir Hartley Shawcross for the *Daily Express*. The latter was called away in the middle of the case because of the illness of his mother-in-law, but not before he had cross-examined Evelyn. Evelyn gave evidence soberly and quietly – no fireworks – and admitted afterwards to a feeling of uneasiness when confronted by Shawcross. Laura, bravely, and Alec Waugh, loyally, gave evidence on his behalf. The afternoon of the first day passed with Miss Spain in the witness box denying hour after hour the undeniable. This bland effort which consisted of taking a different view of the meaning of everything, including words, from that taken by anyone else, may or may not have been prejudicial to the outcome of the case. In spite of it the judge summing up the next morning reduced the Waugh party to the depths of gloom by luncheon, since it seemed likely that Evelyn would get a farthing's damages. This would have been a serious outcome because he would have been left with costs of about £5,000. However, the jury returned to the court in the afternoon and awarded him £2,000 with costs.'

Nancy Spain did not show skill in the witness-box. According to Evelyn she 'lied sturdily on oath', but her endeavour to depict herself as the innocent and injured party only provoked ridicule. She explained that when she and Lord Noel-Buxton found that they were *only* eighty miles from Stinchcombe, they decided that they might as well call on Evelyn, since they were so close. She tried to excite the jury's pity by telling the court that during this strenuous afternoon she had had nothing to eat except an oatcake and that Mr Waugh had shamefully not offered her or her companion a drink.

Here is Evelyn's account written a few days later to Nancy Mitford: 'I had an exhilerating expedition into the Law Courts and came out two thousand pounds (tax-free) to the good. But there were anxious moments. At the end of the first day I would have settled for a fiver. A disgusting looking man called [Leonard] Russell from the *Sunday Times* gave evidence against me . . . But I had taken the precaution of telling the Dursley parish priest that he should have 10% of the damages. His prayers were answered in dramatic, Old Testament style. A series of Egyptian plagues fell on Sir Hartley Shawcross from the moment he took up the case, culminating in a well-nigh fatal motor accident to his mother-in-law at the very moment when he had me under cross-examination & was making me feel rather an ass. Sir Hartley thereafter took no further part in the case and left the rest of the cross-examination to his less celebrated and so less intimidating junior. Evelyn thus concluded his account to Nancy: I had a fine solid jury who were out to fine the *Express* for their impertinence to the Royal Family, quite irrespective of my rights and wrongs. They were not at all amused by the judge. All the £300 a day barristers rocked with laughter at his sallies. They glowered. That was not what they paid a judge for, they thought.

'So Father Collins got £200 and a lot of chaps in Whites got pop.'

He wrote a very similar letter on the case to Ann Fleming in which he recorded that after the case he sent Nancy Spain a bottle of champagne. He added this shrewd comment:

'The simple fact is that all four million readers of the *Express* detest the paper, are ashamed of reading it, & feel that any damages they can impose on it slightly exonerates themselves.'

This case was not the end of Evelyn's profitable warfare against the *Daily Express*. After he had initiated proceedings, but before the case had come before the courts, a book containing hostile comment on Evelyn and Graham Greene, had been published, and Nancy Spain reviewed it in the *Daily Express*. With inconceivable rashness she quoted the hostile comment which Evelyn saw as libellous. His solicitors were in agreement, especially in view of the fact that the offending piece had appeared while her earlier one was *sub judice*. Evelyn asked Graham Greene to join him in suing, not the author, but the *Daily Express*, but Graham declined. On the advice of their lawyers the newspaper did not contest the action which was settled out of court; the book was withdrawn from circulation and the *Daily Express* agreed to pay Evelyn £3000, with full payment of his legal expenses. From Nancy Spain's indiscretions Evelyn had reaped £5000, none of it liable to tax.

He decided to commemorate these moral and financial triumphs by an extravagance. He decided to order a carpet for his new drawing-room to be specially made for him at the famous factory at Wilton. He went there with Laura to choose a design and discuss the matter in detail with the management. He explained that he was not interested in modern but in traditional design, and soon found what he wanted: the design for a carpet which had been accorded a high-ranking prize at the Great Exhibition of 1851, a work of art of almost inconceivable hideosity. The management urged on him in vain that for the same price he could have a carpet woven on the design of one of the great French or English masters of the eighteenth century; they almost implored him to change his mind, but he was immovable. So with heavy hearts the craftsmen bent their energies to resurrecting this many-tinted horror with its staring colours and coarse adaptation of Persian motifs.

I was appalled when I saw it and when my wife and I heard from Laura the story of its making. But since then I have wondered whether our lamentations were well-judged. What would a noble carpet designed by Adam have done surrounded by pictures, every one of which told a mid-Victorian story, surrounded by the Victorian furniture of every hideous variety, and that wooden camel and the threefold picture sequence of 'Travel Then and Now'? The new-born gaud certainly struck no discord.

Evelyn, hoping to escape the English winter as soon as possible after his legal disputes, had planned to go to Monte Carlo. In the event he stayed dismally in England, the reason being one greatly to his credit, of which the memory may cancel any distaste aroused by the religiosity he showed in the cases of the Poor Clares of Looe and Father Collins of Dursley. In this instance he acted as a true Christian.

His diary and his letters of late 1956 contain references to visits to Mells where Ronald Knox had lived in the Manor House as a guest of Lord and Lady Oxford and Lord Oxford's mother Mrs Raymond Asquith since 1948. Here he had finished his translation of the New Testament and done the whole of his translation of the Old. Here the friendship of Evelyn and Ronald had become one of the closest of Evelyn's life. An uneasy note creeps into Evelyn's references to his friend at this time. He refers to his increasing unsociability, his way of avoiding the general conversation of visits, remaining preoccupied with *The Times* crossword puzzles and games of Scrabble, sometimes played alone and sometimes with Evelyn. The latter noted too that he tended to miscount the results, in his favour. 'Ronnie cooked the score' is a surprising diary entry. Neither Evelyn nor Ronald knew or suspected that Ronald's mind was becoming clouded by the onset of a mortal illness. He felt little indisposition, none commensurate with his physical state, but in January 1957 his doctor at Frome suspected cancer and an X-ray examination confirmed his fears. The disease appeared to have taken hold in a form curable by surgery, but in the course of the necessary operation another inoperable cancerous growth on the liver was discovered. Ronald returned to Mells early in February, in a state of weakness from the shock of the operation, unaware that he could never recover. He believed that sea air would invigorate him. He discussed plans with Evelyn. He had not the strength for the long journey to Brighton (which Evelyn would have enjoyed) so instead he went in March to Torquay in search of the strength which not only eluded him, but had eluded him already and for ever. Evelyn and Laura accompanied him and stayed with him at a hotel. Evelyn wrote to Ann:

'We are far from happy here. Poor Ronnie is very infirm & fretful, can't sleep, eat, drink or read. All that gives him any relief is laborious crossword puzzles. This is a bad place for invalids as one cannot move without going up or down steep paths & steps. The hotel is excessively vulgar. Not marble halls, as I had hoped, but Hollywood, glaring glass walls, cactuses, pillars painted with Mexican totems. The menu is written in Hollywood jargon "Rich golden butter fried parslied potatoes" "Minted buttered and sugared fresh garden green peas". There is a disgusting manager who goes from table to table making jokes. Laura leaves on Wednesday. We are both homesick for Combe Florey. I take Ronnie on to Sidmouth . . . Ronnie talks as though he will be on my hands for a month. I love and revere him but oh dear – '

He spent a week with Ronald in Sidmouth in a different sort of hotel, but not a more enjoyable one. From here he wrote to Ann the day before leaving: 'I am by many years the youngest boarder here. There is a disgusting old man who sits next to me in the tiny smoking-room and grunts and snuffles like an old dog.

'There is another Monsignore, also dying, in the town. He comes to see us occasionally. Poor Ronnie cannot read for long. All he likes is to smoke a stinking pipe and to make desultory comments on the news in the paper. The Times crossword, done on a peculiarly laborious system, (not reading the lights for the downs at all until we have filled them in conjecturally) lasts us from nine to ten in the evening. Sometimes I walk up and down the front for half an hour . . . Home tomorrow. I have been very home sick.'

Evelyn took him to Combe Florey for a fortnight and in the first week of April drove him back to Mells. Here Ronald remained, except for one dramatic visit to Oxford, another to London, in June 1957, for the last four months of his life. The evidence is that Evelyn met him only once more, in June. The occasion was important.

In 1950 Ronald had appointed Evelyn in his will to be his sole literary executor. This appointment carried with it the duty of choosing an official biographer. When Evelyn had once raised this question Ronald had replied with his accustomed quiet self-mockery: 'Yes, I suppose someone will want to write something.' This was long before there was any anxiety about his health.

Evelyn gave the matter of a biography no great thought until it suddenly became clear that Ronald had not long to live, and then Evelyn 'had the idea of attempting the portrait' himself. On his return from London in June, Ronald asked Evelyn to come to Mells to discuss the disposal of his papers, for he had a large accumulation of unfinished work. At the end of their talk, Evelyn, to quote his own account, 'asked for his approval of my project. He gave it. He could hardly have refused. But the next day he wrote to a friend reporting my suggestion in terms which leave me in no doubt that his acquiescence was not prompted by mere politeness.' Ronald Knox died two months later on 24 August 1957.

Immediately Evelyn started research for the biography. He was determined to erect a fitting monument to this illustrious friend who had honoured him with the dedication of *Enthusiasm*, the book which Ronald regarded as his highest intellectual achievement.

Remembering how daunting the task was, that it involved delving into the complexities of church administration and politics, and collecting information from a host of people who had known Ronald, first as a brilliant schoolboy and undergraduate, then as a High Church Anglican clergyman, then as a Roman Catholic priest, as a writer of wide versatility throughout his life; remembering all this, and that the research necessitated a journey to Rhodesia, and was interrupted by appalling family anxiety, it is surprising that he accomplished the whole task in so short a time. The book was completed within eighteen months of Ronald's death. That part of the story belongs to the next chapter.

Before August 1957 *The Ordeal of Gilbert Pinfold* had been published by Chapman and Hall. The book has already been discussed and it and its adventures need not detain the reader further. There was an odd sequel to the publication with some account of which this chapter may end. Evelyn heard from no less than six people who were suffering from delusions similar to those described in the novel and who now sought his advice. One of his correspondents was an American woman who had let her haunted apartment in her home town in the United States and had travelled to England, pursued by the haunting furies across the Atlantic, to seek his help. One odd feature of these letters is that, while seeking means of liberation from their pursuers, the correspondents insisted that their tormentors were real and not, like those of Mr Pinfold, 'a false creation, proceeding from the heat-oppressed brain'. Unhappily he left no record of how he dealt with this correspondence or what advice he gave.

I can add something from my own experience to this sequel, though it was not a matter on which I consulted Evelyn. More than a year after this time, possibly two years, I received a very odd letter from a young actress whom I had employed in several BBC productions. She told me that she was being persecuted by means of long distance telepathy by one of my BBC colleagues, a man whom I liked and respected. The details of her story were extraordinarily like those Mr Pinfold's ordeal. She was not a well-read or literary person in any way, and I think it beyond all likelihood that she had read *Pinfold* or even knew Evelyn's name as a writer. After discussion with her supposed persecutor I wrote her a long letter telling her the facts of Evelyn and the Pinfold case, but suppressing all names. I heard no more from the young woman for about six months when she wrote to say that thanks to my letter she was now cured and she offered abject apologies for bothering me with her foolish imaginings. I was glad at her news but when I described the case to a psychiatrist I knew, she replied that not only were such delusions very common, but that cures were common too, and that in ninety-nine cases out of a hundred the cure was followed by a total relapse. This happened in the case of the unhappy young actress.

It seems to me disquieting and strange that people with the very minimum in common, true I fancy of all Evelyn's *Pinfold* correspondents and certainly of the young actress, suffered from similar delusions, un-imaginable in an earlier age, and all connected with telepathy and elec-tricity.

Evelyn inscribed the copy of the book which he gave me, 'Watch out. Your turn next.' He seems to have relayed a message of this kind to most of the friends whom he honoured with signed copies.

# Chapter 24

## 1957-1961

The research for the biography of Ronald Knox was as demanding as any such toil could be. Though he had been a close friend, Evelyn knew little about Ronald's early life till his thirtieth year when he became a Catholic, nothing in any detail about his family background, nothing very much about the administrative machinery of the Anglican or the Roman Catholic Churches under which Ronald had served. He needed to master a brief for the presentation of a far from simple case concerning an area of activity in which his personal experience was slight.

In his preface to the book which ultimately emerged from his labours, Evelyn acknowledged the help of ninety people whom he named. This list probably represents much less than half the number of those whom he interviewed and with whom he corresponded. There is no diary to cover the period so one can only guess from hints in letters how he set to work. He found of course an accumulation of papers, the first and perhaps most fearsome challenge in the path of any biographer, but in this instance not so fearsome as in most, since Ronald was a man of tidy habits. He had the advantage of knowing well two of the four people who were to help him most: Mrs Asquith and Lady Acton. Before the end of 1957 he had made the acquaintance of the two others: Ronald's sister Lady Peck, and one of the last of Ronald's intimate contemporary friends, Mr Laurence Eyres.

The Actons lived in South Rhodesia and to discuss his subject with Daphne Acton, a passionately devout convert to Catholicism who had been instructed in her new faith by Ronald, and to study her large collection of Knox letters and papers necessitated a journey to Africa which Evelyn undertook in the early part of 1958. Before setting out he wrote to Nancy Mitford on 24 January. As the letter has some general biographical interest it is worth quoting in full:

'Have you seen that old Brian Howard has kicked the bucket? You will mourn him more than I (or, perhaps, than me). I must admit he dazzled me rather 25 years ago but, though I hadn't set eyes on him for 15 years or more, I went rather in terror of him in late years. I was always afraid that he would suddenly rush at me in some public place and hit me and there would be painful publicity "Middle aged novelist assaulted in West End hotel".

'Pryce-Jones wrote an obituary in the *Times*. All he could say was that poor Brian showed great promise in impersonating Bruno Hat. It was Tom, anyway, who sat in the wheel-chair as I remember it.*

'I am just off to Rhodesia so there's no need to spend all those francs in answering. I have insured my life for £50,000 for the two days of the journey (only costs a tenner) I couldn't possibly earn that sum however hard I worked in the few years of activity left to me (not with taxes) so it will be *much* the best thing for my poor children if the aeroplane blows up. In fact the only chance they have of a liberal education. But I suppose I ought not to pray for it on account of the other passengers who may not have been so foresighted.

'I'll write from Rhodesia. The snow here (and the chance of fifty thou for the little ones) reconciles me to the journey but I am sure it is a hideous and dull country. Not at all like lovely Abyssinia.

'I see that the French clergy have taken to murdering their mistresses now – and you say they are such an example to us.'

Much as he had lost his taste for travel beyond Europe, Evelyn seems to have enjoyed this journey. He spoke of it, as I remember, with relish on his return, and he took an opportunity to go to Rhodesia again. The visit had been of extreme value to the work he had in hand and moreover it had strengthened his friendship with John Acton, the grandson of the historian, and with Daphne Acton with whom a long correspondence on the subject of Ronald continued.

The story of how Evelyn toiled at this biography which took up most of his energy in 1958 is as undramatic as most other stories of research. Sufficient to say that he mastered a great mass of often wearying material, and that, judging by his correspondence of this time he in no way exaggerated when he wrote in his preface: 'I have met with none of the obstructions which biographers often suffer.' There was no one among Ronald's friends and relations who demanded an unreal portrait of an impossibly ideal man. Nor was the spirit of Evelyn one to encourage those (if they existed) who hoped he would prostitute his gifts to heap the shrine of anaemic and conventional tribute with incense kindled at the muse's flame.

---

* The 'Bruno Hat' hoax occurred on 23 July 1929 in the London house of Bryan and Diana Guinness. Bruno Hat was supposed to be an expatriate German painter for whose benefit Mr and Mrs Guinness arranged a private exhibition. In fact the artist, who appeared at the exhibition in a wheel chair, was Nancy Mitford's brother Tom (killed in Burma in 1945) skilfully disguised by a make-up artist from Messrs. Clarkson, the theatrical costume designers. Brian Howard 'impersonated' Hat in the sense that he painted the pictures. A pamphlet-catalogue entitled 'Approach to Hat' was written by Evelyn Waugh. Mr John Sutro was originally cast for the role of Mr Hat but resigned the appointment on the grounds of his imperfect German. Tom Mitford was fluent in the language, though nonetheless he was nearly caught out by one guest, Maurice Bowra. Lytton Strachey bought one of Bruno Hat's paintings.

His task was eased by the fact that there had been no scandalous occurrences in Ronald's private life; he had to skate over no ice that an honest biographer should break. But there had been two emotional attachments in his life, attachments in which the prurient could see, if they wanted, potential scandal. One of these had come into being in Ronald's days as a young Oxford clergyman. The object of his affection had been a young Etonian, much younger than himself, whose religious fervour had influenced him. In his autobiographical book *A Spiritual Aeneid* Ronald Knox had referred to this young man as 'C'. While working on the book Evelyn approached 'C' who gave him permission to use any papers relative to him, but asked for the disguise to be retained, a condition which Evelyn unhesitatingly accepted.

The other strong attachment belonged to his later years and was to Daphne Acton. Ronald first met her in the summer of 1937, when he was nearly fifty, through her sister-in-law Mrs Woodruff. This was more than attachment in the ordinary sense, it was Platonic love in the correct meaning, but, as opposed to the ordinarily accepted meaning, ardent, passionate, inspiring, a 'marriage of true minds'. In recording the life of a priest vowed to celibacy, such an attachment might seem to stand in need of explaining away. Evelyn explained nothing away; he stated the facts with frankness and left them to speak for themselves, rightly confident that there was nothing that had to be hidden for the sake of correct taste. He thus added strength to his book, and the main credit for that goes to Daphne Acton. She gave Evelyn free run of her large accumulation of papers and letters, and in the course of their long correspondence urged him, in a notable passage on her mutual relations with Ronald, to write 'as though I am dead'. Evelyn took full advantage of her generosity without any consequences that the most prudish could regret. As the book grew he sent her, for her criticism, all the chapters in which she was mentioned, which means nearly all the last quarter of the book. Her comments were invariably constructive. She asked for no suppression of fact. There were no dishonourable facts to suppress.

The foregoing stresses that Evelyn's portrait was executed with an eye to realism rather than *pietas*. So it was done, but that is not to say that he ignored the claims of *pietas*; in one respect he may have given them excessive respect, as will be shown later.

It has been mentioned that among distractions from Evelyn's intense work in 1958 there came family anxiety. This refers to June 1958 and to an event which might easily have ended in tragedy. Evelyn's eldest son Auberon had left Downside in 1956 and it was planned that he would go to Oxford, at which he had obtained an exhibition (or minor scholarship) to Christ Church, after serving his two-year term in the army in accordance with the demands of National Service, this system of conscription still being in force. He was given a commission in his father's old Regiment, the Royal Horse Guards. He served the first part of his term in England and in 1957 was sent abroad on 'peace-keeping duties' with a detachment of his regiment to British-ruled Cyprus, then in a state of uproar arising from the *Enosis* agitation. On 9 June 1958 Auberon was with an armoured transport section. At a halt he was trying to correct the movement of a machine gun when a jolt set it in action. Auberon was in the line of fire and was severely wounded, escaping death by the narrowest margin. His chance of survival was judged dubious for several weeks. As soon as his parents were informed, Laura flew out to Cyprus where the Governor, Sir Hugh Foot (now Lord Caradon) asked her to stay. Recovery was slow. In early July Auberon was flown to London and transferred to King Edward VII's Hospital. On his last day on the island, 5 July, his fellow officer in the Blues, Stephen Fox-Strangways, visited him and immediately after leaving the hospital was killed by a Greek enthusiast who later boasted of his deed. The young man was the only surviving son of Evelyn's old comrade-in-arms, Harry Stavordale. On the 11th Evelyn wrote to Nancy Mitford from Munich where he had an engagement to speak:

'Thanks awfully for your letter about Bron. It was a very anxious three weeks and painful for Laura who had to spend them under armed guard in the great heat, which she hates. But now he is back in England with good hopes of recovery. It is Harry who has been struck down. You saw? His only surviving son murdered. Tragedy doesn't seem appropriate to him & Nell. There is no conceivable human mitigation of their suffering.'

Undeterred by his anxieties, Evelyn persisted with his work in a dedicated spirit. In June he cheerfully added to his burden by raising funds for a Knox memorial to be associated with Trinity College, Oxford. This was to be in the form of an endowed travelling scholarship (despite the fact that no man hated travel more than Ronald) and a bronze cast of a terra cotta portrait bust by Arthur Pollen, which now stands by the entrance to the College Library. The plan for a scholarship was given up in 1960 in favour of a Ronald Knox prize to be awarded by Trinity to a College graduate who had shown unusual distinction in the English Literature finals.

On 2 October Evelyn wrote in a letter to Graham Greene: 'I wish we met. I never come to London for more than a night and then get bogged down in White's when I am not at the bedside of my eldest son who is still very ill. I don't somehow think you will be able to stomach my *Knox* which is getting near its end. If you ever feel like a visit to the English country side do come here. How is your liver? I have had no recurrence of hallucinations but I get crustier.'

Evelyn was right to believe that his biography would not be to Graham's taste who, in the event, admired the skill of the book while finding the subject unpleasing. He wrote a review in *The Observer* to that effect.

The biography was a labour of love, but Evelyn well knew the literary dangers attending labours of love, and so he attempted detachment. In this he was not quite successful.

He had met and corresponded with Father Cyril Martindale. He knew that Father Martindale had a low opinion of Ronald's translation of the Bible, and that he held the Knox claim to be translating the Scriptures into 'timeless English' as delusion and pretentiousness. But Evelyn did not know that both these opinions were part of a deeper disapproval and even some dislike of the man. One of Evelyn's informants was Sir Arnold Lunn who, in spite of having been largely converted by Ronald, seems to have regarded him with hostile scepticism, though Evelyn's correspondence indicates that Lunn kept these feelings and convictions to himself until after the book had been published. It was Arnold Lunn who told Evelyn later of Martindale's antipathy.

At the time of writing Evelyn did know of the vanity which unexpectedly and rather shockingly appeared in Ronald when it came to criticism of his version of the Bible. Such knowledge did prevent Evelyn writing in a hagiographical spirit, but it did not prevent him writing with something of a divided mind.

Before leaving the autumn of 1958 during which most of this writing was done, one event should be mentioned. On 11 November Olivia Greene died after a long and painful illness. From her convent nursing-home in Bath she wrote to Evelyn a letter full of affection two days before she died. So ended a long, important and strange emotional episode in Evelyn's life.

By January 1959 the book was finished in first draft. He made corrections later as a result of criticism and it came out in October. It was well received, as it deserved to be, and was helped by circumstances. Many years had passed since Ronald had been known to a large public through his detective stories, his broadcasts, his limericks, his comic sayings; his name had long ceased to be often mentioned in the popular press, but he had in 1959 a wide though smaller fame which rested on more solid grounds. His translation of the Bible had been published in its entirety and in a definitive version only two years before his death, and was regarded as an immense step forward 'in the right direction', as beneficently revolutionary. If *Enthusiasm* was only read by scholars, the opposite was true of his attractive books of popular religious instruction, *The Mass in Slow Motion*, *The Creed in Slow Motion*, *The Gospel in Slow Motion*, all of which had appeared within the last eleven years. His last eighteen years had been his most productive, and there were many people who wanted to read about the life behind a secretive personality.

Is it a good book? It can be said of most biographies, including excellent ones, that after the excitement of reading, the book is thereafter not read again but used, if at all, as a work of reference. Particular interest, apart from present necessity, has led me to read this biography again several times. I find it continuously rewarding. Nevertheless I find something continuously unsatisfying in it. The divided mind is not invisible.

Laura's sister Gabriel Dru, who also knew Ronald well, once said to me: 'What's wrong with the book is that it is founded on two assumptions, both of which are false: that Ronnie was a great writer, and that he, who could have been a bishop any day he chose, was ill-used by his superiors.' I think that this severe judgement is true. I will consider the two charges in turn.

Within the limits of Ronald's popular books mentioned above; within the limits of his gift for parody which found fine and lasting expression in his book *Let Dons Delight* (published in 1939) Ronald Knox was a superbly good writer, but always within the field of the *petit maître*. His ambitious work *Enthusiasm* has been adversely criticized by some historians and specialists in the field of learning which it explores. I can only speak of it as a general reader, and for the general reader it is stiff going (surely a grave fault) requiring for full appreciation familiarity with theological vocabulary. Far the best of his writing (so it seems to me) is to be found not in this large-scale work, but in the pamphlet which he wrote quickly in 1945, *God and the Atom*. It was little noticed at the time and is now completely forgotten. But Ronald believed that his fame as a writer would rest securely and for long on his translation of the Bible. He never recognized or suspected that he was not a great enough writer to handle so great a task. Evelyn would not face this fact because of that divided mind, and this meant that he did write the book with something of the damaging spirit of excessive *pietas*.

This almost certainly accounts for a serious omission. Though the book is the record of an eminent writer, Evelyn has nothing of literary interest to say. He quoted some of Father Martindale's scathing comments on the Knox version but he put forward no comment of his own, either of praise or the opposite. A convention has grown up that biography and literary criticism are separate activities which must never be associated. Evelyn appeared in *Ronald Knox* to go along with this new practice. 'We cannot complain', wrote Maurice Bowra in a review to be mentioned later, 'that Mr Waugh has not attempted to combine literary criticism with biography.' I think we can complain. I certainly do and believe I can also explain the blemish.

The fact was that, although he admired the clarity of the Knox version, Evelyn did not admire it as literature. He was as shocked as the most hostile critic at the philistine way Ronald had removed all poetry from his translation. He was shocked by the fact that Ronald was in large measure a philistine. This was Evelyn's *secret du roi*, never directly mentioned even to close friends, though he allowed such friends to draw the conclusion. When discussing Ronald or the biography, I often caught a look from Evelyn, if I happened to make a disparaging remark about the Knox version, which seemed to say very clearly: 'You can say that but I cannot.'

The second charge: that Evelyn wrote on a mistaken assumption that Ronald had been ill-used by the Catholic hiearchy, was effectively upheld by an unlikely protagonist, Maurice Bowra. He was asked to review the biography for *The London Magazine*, and he accepted. This was the only occasion when Maurice wrote an article about Evelyn. He took up both the questions posed in the severe judgement already quoted. Here is a relevant passage:

'His inner struggles before he took the final step of being received into the Roman Church are indeed moving in the strain which they put on his loyalties and his affections no less than in his natural hesitation to commit himself irrevocably, but other men have passed through similar struggles and not been regarded as saints. Compared with other priests of his faith Knox in his public utterances seems sometimes to lack charity and compassion, and his sheltered, regular life denied him the splendours granted to more apostolic spirits. Even his sufferings look small in the scale of what other men in like positions have endured. No doubt his years at St Edmund's Old Hall were drab and unfruitful, and the opposition in certain circles to his translation of the Bible may well have been a bitter disappointment when he had put so much of his best work into it. But Knox was transferred from St Edmond's to a congenial post at Oxford, which left him with months of every year to do what he liked in, and his translation was before long approved and welcomed with the warmth it deserved. In absorbing so unusual a convert the Roman Catholic hierarchy displayed far more insight and good nature than it had to either Newman or Hopkins.

'We must also take on trust Mr Waugh's attribution of genius to Knox. He was an extremely gifted, versatile, and scholarly writer . . . Yet in the last analysis he was not truly creative. He excelled at parody and pastiche . . .'

The book had undeniable imperfections, but when all is said, Evelyn had undertaken a task which was not one at first sight well suited to his talents, and in an astonishingly short time he had accomplished it with rare distinction. The future will owe Evelyn a special debt in this matter. Ronald Knox was happy in the time of his death, as Evelyn was in the time of publishing this biography. As the reform impetus persisted and accelerated in all the Christian churches in the West, new and more drastically untraditional translations of the Scriptures came out and displaced the Knox version. In consequence it had a very short life. Within a few years it was virtually forgotten. Today Ronald Knox is no longer a famous man and if he is not utterly obscure much credit goes to Evelyn's book which, for all its faults, is valuable.

The book never went into a second edition so Evelyn was not able to make the many corrections he wanted to, notably a misquotation of the Latin words of consecration in the now abolished order of the Mass. Douglas Woodruff pointed out that in one passage he had been unjust to the memory of Cardinal Griffin through overlooking a letter, whereat, after being convinced of his error, Evelyn publicly admitted his injustice in a letter to *The Tablet*. But, in the absence of a second edition, the error remains in available copies.

The post-publication commotions were for the most part concerned with points of scholarship in learned circles, and minutiae of modern ecclesiastical history in clerical circles, but one post-publication event caused some publicity.

The identity of 'C' had excited curiosity for a long time among the small readership of *A Spiritual Aeneid*. Among Evelyn's larger readership the use of this symbol excited a proportionately larger curiosity, and it became a matter for the competition of Fleet Street to find out who 'C' really was. Ronald had a very wide acquaintance and 'C' therefore might be anyone. In fact he was Mr Harold Macmillan, in 1959 Prime Minister. What a scoop!

If, that is to say, one could scoop it. In the course of a conversation at which Frank Pakenham (now Lord Longford) and Malcolm Muggeridge were present, the topic came up for discussion. Frank said that he had an idea that the mystery man might conceivably be the Prime Minister or his brother Daniel Macmillan. Later he saw that he had been guilty of an indiscretion. He tried to put it straight, but it was too late. Malcolm Muggeridge in the course of a telephone conversation with Evelyn's mother-in-law (who was in the secret) surprised her with a question to which her answer gave him the confirmation he wanted. She tried to put it straight, but again it was too late. The result was three paragraphs in *The New Statesman* 'notebook' column. They were a model of that familiar journalistic feat by which the action of licking one's chops over a meaty scoop is smoothly combined with the finger-wagging of disapproval. 'What interests me', wrote Malcolm Muggeridge in the superior tone of such occasions, 'is that it should have been thought expedient to hide his identity'.

Evelyn was much annoyed and let his annoyance be known. The incident seems to have aggravated the antipathy between the two men, an antipathy which, as Malcolm Muggeridge has recorded, was never smoothed over or even diminished during Evelyn's lifetime.

The story needs to go back again in time to the beginning of 1959. In January Evelyn had completed the draft of the biography and felt his perennial need to escape the horrors of the English winter. He was in doubt where to go. He toyed with the idea of India, a land 'full of splendours that must be seen now or perhaps never', but dismissed it as impractical. 'Can a man of 55', he asked, 'long endure a régime where wine is prohibited?' He recorded his decision in a revealing (if not quite accurate) note: 'I have worked eighteen months on the biography of a remarkable but rather low-spirited friend many years older than myself. I have read nothing and met no one except to further my work. Old letters, old dons, old clergymen – charming companions, but a lowering diet when prolonged.

'Last year I went to Central Africa, but saw nothing. I flew there and back and spent a month in purely English circumstances cross-examining authorities on the book I was writing. Africa again without preoccupations with eyes reopened to the exotic. That's the ticket.'

And that was the ticket he took after his friend the trusty A. D. Peters had organized financial rewards to cover expenses. Peter negotiated a contract through Leonard Russell of *The Sunday Times* for travel articles by Evelyn to be sent back to London at intervals. His goal was to revisit the Actons in Rhodesia. Throughout the journey he kept notes which have not survived; they and the articles he wrote were the basis of his last travel book published later in 1960. It was called *Tourist in Africa.*

This was the first travel book by Evelyn since the appearance twenty-one years before of *Robbery Under Law.* It does not compare in quality with its predecessors, and Evelyn knew it. He wrote to Ann Fleming while writing it. 'I can't express the horrible boredom of my African reminiscences.' He gave me a handsomely bound copy and embellished the title page so that it read: 'A Tourist in Africa A Potboiler by Evelyn Waugh Presented with shame to Christopher Sykes by the Disgraced Author Evelyn Waugh'. It was a potboiler, without doubt, and a reader who has not read it has missed little, but the book is not contemptible for all that; it was no occasion for shame. It contains some unforgettable things, such as the brief account of John Strachey's calamitous groundnut scheme and the miniature portrait of Cecil Rhodes. The following extract, describing a visit to a school in Tanganyika, is in Evelyn's best vein:

'I should have known better than to put my head into that classroom. I have been caught before in this way by nuns. I smirked and attempted to get away when I heard the fateful words ". . . would so much appreciate it if you gave them a little address".

' "I am awfully sorry I haven't anything prepared. There's nothing I could possibly talk about except to say how much I admire everything."

' "Mr Waugh, these boys are all wishing to write good English. Tell them how you learned to write so well."

'Like a P. G. Wodehouse hero I gazed desperately at the rows of dark, curious faces.

' "Mr Waugh is a great writer from England. He will tell you how to be great writers."

' "Well", I said, "well. I have spent fifty-four years trying to learn English and I still find I have recourse to the dictionary almost every day. English", I said, warming a little to my subject, "is incomparably the richest language in the world. There are two or three quite distinct words to express every concept and each has a subtle difference of nuance."

'This was clearly not quite what was required. Consternation was plainly written on all the faces of the aspiring clerks who had greeted me with so broad a welcome.

' "What Mr Waugh means," said the teacher, "is that English is very simple really. You will not learn all the words. You can make your meaning clear if you know a few of them".

'The students brightened a little. I left it at that.'

Throughout most of 1959 and 1960 Evelyn was occupied with a greater literary venture: the third and concluding volume of his War Trilogy. He had quickly recognized that to abandon the undertaking after the publication of *Officers and Gentlemen* in 1955 was a mistake, and in the four years which followed he recovered confidence in his ability to write another novel. Throughout the toil of researching and writing Ronald Knox's biography; throughout his African travels, and then putting together his articles, notes and memories for his last travel book; throughout a journey in January and February 1960 with Laura and then with Margaret to Venice, Monte Carlo, Rome and Athens (a kind of journalist Grand Tour to escape the winter organized by *The Daily Mail* in exchange for travel expenses and handsomely paid articles which were good but not worth remembering here); throughout these apparent distractions, Evelyn was still going through the mysterious and partly subconscious process from which books are made. The preparatory period had lasted long but, as so often in Evelyn's case, the actual writing took a short time. It was finished in draft by the end of 1960 and was ready for publication in 1961. Consideration of the book belongs to the next chapter. The immediate interest is in events of his private life from the appearance of *Ronald Knox* in 1959.

They were not as varied or as numerous as in earlier periods, the simple reason being that, swift writer as he was, the composition of the last volume of the trilogy *Unconditional Surrender*, the most complicated and the most successful in design of all three novels, kept him toiling at Combe Florey for more of his time than he probably would have wished. Frankie Donaldson seems to me to hit one of her numerous bull's-eyes when she writes in her book that Evelyn chose to live in the country, far from London, both at Piers Court and Combe Florey, because he knew that if he settled in a town house, superficially more to his taste, he would have wasted his time in the social round and in heavy drinking; in brief he would have ceased to be a writer, and become at best an Utinam-figure like Dylan Thomas.

The main family event in the first part of what may be called Evelyn's post-Knox period was continuing anxiety regarding Auberon's recovery which, however, was sufficiently advanced for him to commence exhibitioner of Christ Church, Oxford, in September 1959, at the beginning of the academic year, thus breaking with an eccentric family tradition. Judging by his letters to his parents he, like Evelyn, found Oxford 'a Kingdom of Cockayne'. Like his father he gave more attention to the social delights of the university than to his studies, with the result that, after failing to pass Moderations, he went down after a year and did not attempt to return to complete his course. During his long convalescence he had written his first novel *The Foxglove Saga* which was published with much success in the summer of 1960.

Evelyn's eldest daughter Teresa had become attached to a young American John D'Arms and in the course of a year or so the young couple found they wanted to marry. Evelyn and Laura wanted them to wait a while. Letters indicate that they regarded themselves as 'unofficially engaged' by the summer of 1960. They were married in the following year.

In May 1960 Evelyn lost a friend of many years; Mrs Cobb died on the 31st. In her last years Evelyn had helped her generously.


In June an event opened which was to concern Evelyn, and later myself, for more than a year. For a brief period, in 1953 and 1954, Mr Walter Taplin had edited *The Spectator* and had thus come to know Evelyn among other contributors. During their brief acquaintance they had discussed the persistent calumny of P. G. Wodehouse: the belief that the recordings he had made in the war from Germany, where he had been interned, recordings made for an American broadcasting company, were undertaken in a Naziphil and treasonable spirit. The truth had long been established and in 1944 legal authorities had advised after full enquiry that there were no grounds for prosecution because the recordings, if injudicious, were wholly free of treasonable intent or matter. The utterly innocuous texts had been published by *Encounter*. There remained not the smallest excuse for the persistence of a suspicion that was understandable enough when all that was known of the recordings had been from carefully edited extracts broadcast with commentary by Nazi propagandists.

Propaganda either collapses amid general ridicule, or it persists. In the case of P. G. Wodehouse it persisted. One reason is to be sought in the moral cowardice of former Ministers and Undersecretaries of the war-time Ministry of Information. None of them had the decency or integrity to state in Parliament or outside that the Ministry's violent denunciations of the great comic master had been (even pardonably) mistaken. People love myths, sometimes more than ever if they are baseless, and the myth of 'The Traitor Wodehouse' warmed many a breast, how many and how strongly I was to discover in the next year.

On 22 June 1960 Mr Taplin wrote to Evelyn, recalling their friendship and their common interest in the Wodehouse case. He reminded him that in October 1961 the great comedian would reach his eightieth birthday. Mr Taplin suggested that some suitable award from his country would be appropriate and, so he had reason to believe, acceptable and desired by P. G. Wodehouse. What about the Order of Merit? If not that, some other major distinction?

Would that Evelyn had not, 'through the surfeit of his own behavior', made acquaintance with T. S. Eliot impossible! Eliot's admiration of P. G. Wodehouse was only just 'this side idolatry'. The great poet had an entire collection of Wodehouse publications, items from which he lent very rarely and then only to close friends and under severe conditions. Eliot was a member of the Order of Merit, and a word from him might have had effect. Evelyn was not in a position to approach him, and further-more had disqualified himself from what Diana Cooper described as 'The Honours Rut'.

In the course of researching the life of Ronald Knox he had inevitably seen much of Harold Macmillan. The Prime Minister admired the bio-graphy. In May 1959 it was proposed in a letter from his private secretary to Evelyn that the latter should be recommended for a Commandership of the British Empire to be conferred by the Queen on her birthday. Evelyn (rightly) considered that he was worth more than a C.B.E. He did not (I think) aspire to the O.M. but he thought that he was worth a Companionship of Honour. So he refused the Prime Minister's offer. Later he regretted this. As already mentioned, he wanted honours more than one might expect, and Maurice Bowra told me that he interceded later in vain with the Prime Minister's secretariat for a Knighthood or equal honour to be recommended to the Queen for Evelyn. The official answer, according to Maurice, was always the same: if a man refuses such an offer, then the offer will not be made again.

I do not know how reliable Maurice's account was, but no further offer of an honour was made. Certainly Evelyn was in no position in 1960 to press in the corridors of power for a great honour to be offered to a widely if wrongly suspect man.

But there were other means of rectifying the injury. The Wodehouse case had originated in the mass media, and those in charge of them were as reluctant to admit a mistake as the politicians were. In a leisurely way they kept it going. The publication of texts by *Encounter* under Stephen Spender's editorship in 1954, the publication of an autobiographical account of the case in 1953 (*Performing Flea*), the support of P. G. Wodehouse by such unwoosterish figures as Gilbert Murray, had not cancelled the big mass-effect of Bill Connor, the *Daily Mirror's* 'Cassandra', and other (usually unisexual) publicists of the same kind. To defend Wodehouse was to defend escapist privilege, such had been popular reasoning in the post-war period, and educated men in power still went along with it. Such reasoning relied on publicity which it received. Evelyn decided that counter-publicity was the only answer to it.

By an extraordinary coincidence, within ten days or so of Walter Taplin's letter, Evelyn received one from the Master. In it P. G. Wodehouse enclosed a cutting from *The Evening Standard* reporting an interview. It emerges from this letter that the interviewer had interpreted P. G. Wodehouse's remarks as an admission that he found himself rejected not only by his native country but equally by the USA where he lived. He wrote to Evelyn to ask him to show the cutting to the solicitors who had served him so well in the Nancy Spain affair. 'I want', he wrote, 'to get their opinion as to whether a libel action lies.

'While on the subject of lies, there is of course not a word of truth in this blasted blithering Beaverbrook blighter's bilge. You know what happens when one is ass enough to let oneself be interviewed. On this occasion I remember saying that my books didn't sell so well in America as in England – which of course they never have – and on that he builds that stuff about Americans not liking me any more . . .

'What makes me – and my wife – boil with fury is all that "lonely" stuff. Anyone but a fool knows that an author who wants to do his work can't be always mixing with a crowd of people. I have been very happily married for forty-six years, and except for a few friends I don't need any society but that of my wife. That is a very different thing from being lonely.

'I have an idea that the tone of this interview was inspired editorially. I am a bête noire (French) at the Express, and I imagine that makes the Evening Standard hostile. I should think ye ed wrote to [the interviewer] telling him to get an interview and make it a nasty one.

'Anyways, let's see what your solicitors will say.'

The solicitors regarded the case as a strong one, and the affair seems to have been settled in P. G. Wodehouse's favour out of court. This (if I have rightly interpreted it) was a victory, but it was not enough because it received the minimum of publicity. The calumny still lingered on, and after this incident Evelyn was more than ever determined to strike a blow for this man whom he revered as an artist and liked as an acquaintance. He made no move, however, for nearly six months.

In June, the month of this P. G. Wodehouse correspondence, Evelyn came into the news for the only time during this year of withdrawal and hard work. He consented to take part in *Face to Face*, a series of interview programmes then running on BBC Television. Well-known people of the day were interrogated on their tastes, beliefs and hopes by one or other of a team of skilled questioners. It was a similar programme to the one which had sparked off the Pinfold ordeal. The questioner selected to interview Evelyn was the acknowledged master of the technique, John Freeman.

Evelyn told afterwards that he had supposed the questioning would be largely occupied with his views on current literature but found that the bulk of the questions were on the subject of his childhood (not, as he remarked, the most interesting period of his life.) His performance was well thought out and brilliantly executed. He refused to show the indignation he felt at the disregard of privacy which such a performance implies; as preposterous question followed preposterous question, he smiled indulgently, failed to rise to the questioner's bait, made his views clear in a calm manner which did not disguise his contempt. At the end of the interview Mr Freeman asked a question that, with a less skilled opponent, would have been a deadly thrust. He said something of this kind: 'How is it, Mr Waugh, that, with your strong views on the right to privacy, you consent to appear in this programme in the view of millions?' Gently smiling Evelyn replied: 'For the same reason that you do. I need the money.'

There was much admiration for the way Evelyn had acquitted himself, but within the BBC (where also he had gained admirers by his television skill), there was some resentment at what was felt to have been his haughty bearing and his propagating of unwelcome views.

The interview had been filmed and recorded at Combe Florey, not in a London studio which would have been more convenient to 'the electricians' as Evelyn invariably described all servants of the BBC, the reason being that he so rarely went to London at this time. His visits were timed in accordance with his need for a haircut. In London he would visit Diana Cooper, Ann Fleming, Lady Pamela Berry (now Lady Hartwell), the Antrims, Mary Lygon to whom he was a faithful friend in distress, and Patrick Kinross. He would spend much time in White's. His visits rarely lasted more than two and a half days. During 1960 he preferred to enjoy London society vicariously through his correspondence with Ann Fleming most of the time.

Ann's 'intelligences' (to use a pleasing old form) may have spurred him on to the accomplishment of the great literary feat he had set himself. The following extract from a letter of October 1960 may make my meaning plain. Cyril Connolly had been invited to bring Deirdre Craig (whom he was later to marry) to a luncheon in Ann's house at which the chief guest was Somerset Maugham (referred to as 'Willie'). Deirdre, Ann wrote 'had no chance to speak because Angus Wilson, Thunderbird [Ian Fleming], me, and Cyril were all shouting at Willie who is far deafer than you. It was not a totally successful occasion because Angus said you were far and away the best living writer and Willie looked frightfully cross, but I kicked Angus under the table and he bawled at Willie "the best novelist under sixty, UNDER SIXTY" – to switch the conversation I said to Cyril that you suggested I should give him some tensions so that his prose might flower once more. Cyril then looked even crosser than Willie, and said that cancelled the charming letter from you he was carrying in his pocket, and seconds later he said it was a pity your war trilogy was so dull. This annoyed me and Angus who again yelled that you were the best living writer and could never be dull but it didn't matter because Willie was asleep like the Alice doormouse: he woke up with the pudding (treacle, his favourite, the French can't make it) and refused to deny that Cyril had stolen the only Avocado Pear that had ripened on his avocado tree. Apparently Harold Nicolson wrote the story in a book and Cyril wishes to sue him for libel, but Willie remained silent except for stutter contortions, so I said that it was true, and Willie had told me himself. I find it irresistible to bully Cyril. I don't love him like you do.'

Though Evelyn refused to see in Cyril Connolly a great literary critic and thinker, and persisted in regarding him as fraudulent in large part, he remained deeply disturbed by any hostile criticism from him. He had been greatly distressed by Cyril's remark in a critical article on the subject of *Officers and Gentlemen* that Evelyn's later writing was becoming weakened by the 'benign lethargy' that sometimes accompanies advancing years. Suppose it was true? Evelyn had scoffed at the critics, Cyril among them, who condemned *Brideshead Revisited* as vulgar, and then he had come to agree with them, even dropping the excuse that it was written '*Consule Bracken*'. Was something of the same kind, some similar perversion of talent showing itself in Evelyn's work now that he was facing the onset of old age?

Evelyn's relations with Cyril were among the most ambivalent of his life, comparable to his relations with Maurice Bowra; in both cases they were sometimes admiring and sometimes contemptuous, but with a great difference which shows that Maurice was the more formidable man: Evelyn was at pains not to engage seriously in a duel with Maurice, not to go beyond such teasing as the battle of the spurs, with the sole possible exception of the Mr Samgrass affair.

It was otherwise with Cyril; Evelyn sought controversy with him in the certainty of victory; he wrote polemic articles against him; on several occasions Evelyn was rude to him to his face. Nothing of this kind occurred between Evelyn and Maurice, but at the same time nothing comparable to the reactions of affection, almost of amorous infatuation, of Evelyn with Cyril. I remember being in White's during one of these happy interludes. Evelyn burst in and asked where Cyril was: he had promised to meet him at the club – had he left? I told him that I had just seen Cyril going to the barber. Evelyn rushed to the barber to sit and talk with Cyril and so not to miss a minute of his company. Around the same time I remember dining at White's with Evelyn and Father D'Arcy. A recent article by Cyril was mentioned and Evelyn as usual demolished it, adding with a reflective sigh 'Heavens, how I love that man!' Evelyn would often dismiss Cyril as a worthless thinker, but the fact remained that he wanted Cyril's good opinion. In this odd situation it is not fantastic to suppose that Ann's gossip sharpened Evelyn's determination.

In the autumn of 1960 Nancy Mitford's last novel *Don't tell Alfred* came out. Evelyn told her his opinion that it was her best. If he was right, then she left fiction for history in triumph. Evelyn's correspondence with her in this year touched on one very odd subject. In June she heard from an American writer who wanted her help in a book he was writing about Evelyn. He had made enquiries among English literary men and women who, presumably in all innocence, had given him a misleading picture of Evelyn's life as a successful young humorist. Compared to most novelists, the seeker had been informed, 'Waugh belonged to a much gayer set, a sort of High Bohemia, centered around Lady Cunard, Lord Berners, and the Sitwells... They included such people as all "the Mitford girls"...'

The poor man's distorted idea of Evelyn's earlier life in London society appealed to something cruel in Nancy; she found she could not resist a temptation to practical joking as is shown by a letter from her of 6 October.

'I say, this book about you is going to be lovely stuff. Today's queries: Was Freddy Furneaux-Smith (sic) Sebastian?* Why didn't you (me) & Diana Cooper become Roman Catholics? Did you & Evelyn (sic) & Lord Berners & Anthony Powell plan the humour & wit of your novels in a certain way? Did Tony Last go abroad to read Dickens because he couldn't envisage life with Diana Cooper?

'We (why the royal?) have been encouraged to visit Garsington & Julian Vinogradof [Lady Ottoline Morrell's daughter] which ought to be great for us – all those places where the bright young set used to have fun! It must have been wonderful!

'Don't you die for it? I am being rather splendid in egging him on discreetly – no actual lies but I can't bear to spoil the trend.'

Nancy's labour was wasted; the book never found a publisher.

Nancy's letters also dwell on a sombre theme which was the cause of

* The family name of Lord Birkenhead is Smith. Before succeeding his father, the present earl was known by the courtesy title of Lord Furneaux. He came up to Oxford three years after Evelyn had left the University.

much grief to them both. In October 1960, though still relatively young, Maud Marriott died after a long and agonizing illness.

At the end of 1960 Evelyn decided to take action in the P. G. Wodehouse affair which had been smouldering in his mind since Walter Taplin's letter to him in June. By December he had worked out a plan for the accomplishment of which he saw in myself a useful instrument. The proposition was put to me at an annual celebration which Evelyn and I regularly attended. 'Celebration' is perhaps too formal a word to describe a regular event which had grown up in an irregular and haphazard fashion. It had been inaugurated by the chairman and main proprietor of the Hyde Park Hotel, Basil Bennet, and the hotel's managing director, Brian Franks. In a December, not long after the war, they gave a small but luxurious luncheon whose object was to try out some wine and to introduce an accomplished amateur of wine to Bob Laycock for whom this amateur had a great admiration. The lunch proved so successful and enjoyable that Basil and Brian and Bob decided to make it the foundation of an annual event. Numbers grew and by December 1960 the luncheon had evolved into an epicurean festival to which some thirty guests or more were invited. They were not asked according to any criterion, but if there was one, it amounted to friendship with Bob. Bob was the guest of honour but no one said so, and we were not asked formally to drink his health, because that would have brought with it the danger of speeches. It was a very enjoyable occasion. Evelyn gave a misleading idea of it when he described it to Ann as 'the annual vomit'. (Again one must remember Evelyn's childish delight in exaggerating his self-indulgence.)

At the December 1960 luncheon I sat next to Evelyn and presently he asked me:

'Are you still employed as an electrician at the BBC?'

I answered that I was. He then explained his purpose in asking. He wished to give a talk to celebrate P. G. Wodehouse's eightieth birthday in 1961, and to take the opportunity of refuting once and for all the odious calumny of 1941. I saw at once, as anyone with any experience of broadcasting would have done, that Evelyn's proposition was a winner. I said that I would get the proposal going and would tell him the results of the first moves when we met on another annual occasion, Evelyn and Laura's annual visit to us on Boxing Day.

As soon as lunch was over I went to Broadcasting House to see Harman Grisewood who was then in effect Deputy Director General, though to soothe the jealousy of George Barnes, he was described as the Director's 'personal assistant'. I went to Harman because I knew that he in no way shared the dislike of Evelyn prevalent in the BBC, and that to go 'through the usual channels' would offer too much temptation to too many obstructors. Harman also instinctively spotted a winner; was also aware of the obstructors. He advised me to convey Evelyn's offer directly to the

Director General, Sir Hugh Greene, Graham's brother, while keeping my departmental chief informed. I followed the advice with ultimate success, reached after many hurdles and obstacles. By 26 December Sir Hugh Greene had assured me that he was giving the proposal full support. I had also learned in the BBC that there were 'murmurs of dissent'.

The Boxing Day celebration also requires some explanation. Evelyn had a great dislike of Christmas festivity, a dislike which, true to form, he used to exaggerate, making himself out to be a child-hating Scrooge. At the time my wife and I were living near Shaftesbury about an hour's drive from Combe Florey, and Evelyn established a custom whereby, to escape from his family festivities, he and Laura came over to us for lunch on Boxing Day, it being understood that my wife provided a joint and no item of traditional Christmas fare. Evelyn's diary, which he had taken up again in December 1960, indicates that this was the first of his Boxing Day visits to us. I remember them as numerous but there could not have been more than three or four.

He arrived in furiously good spirits, in 'high fooling'. He had reason for content: he had finished the last volume of the War Trilogy. My son and his Australian fiancée let him in at the front door. When he and Laura were settled down with drinks Evelyn said to me: 'Who was the Japanese who let us in?' 'My son.' 'No, not him. He opened the door with the help of a Japanese woman.' 'That's his fiancée Miss Homewood. She's Australian.' Evelyn impatiently shook his head in contradiction and the conversation turned to other topics. In his diary Miss Homewood, whom he addressed throughout as Mrs Broadbent, is described as 'a Japanese disguised as an Australian'.

In his diary entry he did not do justice to himself on this occasion. He merely wrote: 'I felt euphoric and facetiously told a story in my absurd French.' I made a note of the story at the time. It was about the Archbishop of Canterbury who shortly before had visited the Pope to whom he was reported to have said: 'We are making history'. Evelyn, as the reader might expect, strongly disapproved of irenical inter-church activity, and was delighted with a comic story that he had heard about this famous encounter. We were a party of about ten. Evelyn sat at one end of the table next to my wife and Laura sat next to me at the other end. Presently we heard a shout of laughter at my wife's end and she saying to Evelyn: 'I am sure you made that story up as a piece of Catholic propaganda.' I asked to hear the story. 'No!', said Evelyn, 'if a story goes down well I never repeat it'. 'Well say it in French then.'

With his glaring eyes fixed on me and in his deep voice Evelyn un-smilingly complied as follows: 'Il y avait un archevêque à Rome, pas un propre archevêque mais anglican, nommé Fisher, qui se lançait dans le palais du pape en exclamant: "Nous exécutons l'histoire." Quelque temps après un autre archevêque, un archevêque anglais qui régnait sur Bombay, tout petit mais génuine, aussi se lançait dans le palais du pape pour donner homage. Le pape lui disait quand la conversation était exhaustée: "L'autre jour un autre archevêque anglais nommé Fisher se lançait dans mon palais. Il parlait tout la temps apropos de l'histoire. Est-ce que vous le connaissez? Est-ce que vous savez qui il est?"'

Before he and Laura left, I told Evelyn that Sir Hugh Greene was delighted at his proposal and that it would go through if he left matters to him and to Harman, me and Peters and kept well away himself. I promised to research into the BBC files and let him have copies of the most important documents regarding the Wodehouse scandal.

I had not supposed that in promoting Evelyn's P. G. Wodehouse proposal I was taking on a light burden. Evelyn's unpopularity in the Corporation had not been diminished by his recent appearance in the *Face to Face* series. The 'Kurkweiler' affair was not forgotten, and he was especially disliked, entirely through his own fault, in the department most concerned with the proposed venture. He had made a ludicrous fuss, a few years before, because when he was referred to in programmes of literary criticism, speakers described him as 'Evelyn Waugh' without the 'Mr'. He sent several of his complaints to me, but I never passed them on. I think Harman Grisewood acted in the same spirit of enlightened indiscipline. But this preoccupation with an obsolescent form made itself felt, as he had appealed to the Director General and his colleagues in person, and other senior functionaries, not all of whom were amused.

However this had happened some time before and though I expected to be involved in a conflict to get Evelyn's proposed talk through, I expected that the justice of the cause would win the day in the end. It did, but not easily. I was to be much surprised at the form that the opposition took. I had grossly underestimated the power of propaganda.

I had done research for Evelyn in the BBC archives while he was working on his biography of Ronald Knox, so I had a little experience of them as they were then organized. My new researches were very interesting and showed the whole P. G. Wodehouse affair in what to me was a new light. I found, as I knew, that the denunciations by the ignoble 'Cassandra' had been made at the instigation of the Ministry of Information, but I found that I was quite wrong in my belief, one generally held, that the Ministry had acted in co-operation with the BBC. On the contrary, the BBC, far better informed than the Ministry, warned the latter that scrutiny of the monitorings of broadcasts from Germany showed that the Columbia recordings by P. G. Wodehouse were wholly innocuous from a political and propaganda point of view, and that opinions to the contrary were based on clever distortions in German broadcasts to England; the BBC advised the Ministry that denunciations of P. G. Wodehouse were likely to prove unwise. But the Ministry was obdurate. It had a set broadcasting period over which the BBC had no control and this it used, in rejection and possibly resentment of BBC advice, for the broadcasting of 'Cassandra's' enduring libels. I discovered to my surprise that the BBC came out of the affair very well, and the Ministry very badly. I conveyed all my information to Evelyn and set about negotiating the talk with renewed confidence. Here was a virtually unknown story for which the BBC, if only through self-interest, would like publicity.

I was wrong. Although Hugh Greene had given it all support, by the organization of the Corporation the proposal had to make a second journey through the complex of committees on which BBC administration is founded. It was a long weary story with which I will not tax the reader's patience. I found that 'Cassandra's' propaganda had stuck. I found that it was widely believed that P. G. Wodehouse *was* a traitor, and that it would be unworthy of the BBC to pay honour to such a malefactor except in the most detached spirit of literary criticism. I found that presentation of the facts made little impression and that Evelyn's proposal was interpreted as an attempt to make the BBC offer an abject apology for having performed a necessary duty. My own championship of the cause excited suspicion, and one senior official insisted on examining my official correspondence to see whether in the course of the negotiating of contracts I had been guilty of corruption. The idea that here was an occasion of clearing the BBC of its supposed guilt in a great wrong found few followers. Above all I found an overriding concern with hurt feelings because the proposal had not at first gone through 'the usual channels'. I felt I was back again in G.H.Q. Cairo, and I remembered my witty old friend Adrian Bishop. I once remarked to him that I thought it odd to what extent a high proportion of senior staff officers remained preoccupied with their position and precedence to the exclusion of larger matters even when victory and defeat and their future as living men hung in the balance, even when enemy guns were audible in Cairo, and I wondered how they could be so short-sighted. 'Because of umbrage', he replied, 'it always comes first with soldiers. It is what they take.' But amid deepening umbrage, in spite of all efforts to relegate the talk to part of an insignificant and little-heard programme, Hugh Greene stood firm, and ultimately in June the talk was recorded. It was broadcast in July and the text later published in *The Sunday Times*.

Let it be hoped that the talk was successful in destroying a hateful myth, but it must be again remembered how much men love myths. My own hopes would be higher if the talk had been better. It was disappointing. Evelyn made his points with his accustomed vigour, but on this occasion the prose was beneath his standard. Some of the argument was clumsily worked out. But it had gone out at a 'peak listening time'. When it was all over I sighed with relief: at all events, I reflected, this was the last time when I was likely to be called on to arrange a broadcast talk by Evelyn. In fact I did arrange one other one.

(Since the completion of this chapter, P. G. Wodehouse died on 14 February 1975 in his ninety-fourth year. In the month before, the British Sovereign conferred on him the honour of Knighthood, a gesture occasioning widespread pleasure and a protesting article in the Beaverbrook Press.)

# Chapter 25

## 1961

The publication in 1961 of *Unconditional Surrender* marked the end of the War Trilogy which had been first conceived more than ten years before.

In this work Evelyn attempted to achieve a great ambition: to describe in terms of a fictional experience close to his own the significance to men and women of the ordeal of the crisis of civilization which reached its climax in World War II. Whether he succeeded; or whether, among others who tried to reflect the Hitlerian catastrophe in fiction, he merely over-reached himself, is the subject of this chapter.

Diana Cooper's witty remark about *War and Peace* and *Mrs Dale's Diary* deserves to be taken seriously. Counsel for the Defence can tellingly plead that the same could be said of Tolstoy, provided that the criticism is directed at the first part of his gigantic novel, and it must be remembered that Diana's remark was applied only to the first part of the first volume. Works on the huge scale of *Sword of Honour* (as the complete trilogy was named) are usually different in kind from compact one-volume novels. In the latter it is usually to be accounted a virtue if the first sentence agrees in spirit and style with the last; not necessarily in the former. If Tolstoy had died after writing the first fifty pages of *War and Peace*, readers of the fragment might pardonably suppose that if completed this would have been no more than a respectable example of the well-observed novel of manners, nothing more earth-shaking than that. 'It must be judged as a whole' is the often repeated protest of those harshly judged on a reading of opening chapters. In the case of most short novels the protest is irrelevant; in the case of every long work on the scale of *Sword of Honour* it is fully justified, even if the final verdict is condemnatory. This applies with particular force to the case of Evelyn. It has been noted already that publication in instalments was peculiarly apt to give a false idea of his fiction.

Like all large-scale works this one contains some blemishes and in the first paragraph of the first volume *Men at Arms* (1952), indeed in the first sentence, there occurs the worst blemish on the whole undertaking: the ineffectual hero, Guy Crouchback. He is not something new in Evelyn's writing, he is the victim as hero again, making a late though not his last appearance. He had first appeared not as farcical in himself but as an effective stimulator of farce (in the style of Buster Keaton) in *Decline and Fall* and then much later as a stimulator of unorthodox tragedy in *A Handful of Dust*. His appearances had all been successfully contrived, and they had all followed, with amazing originality, a well-worn path: that of the character who is not interesting in himself but to whom interesting (and horrifying) things happen. Here his appearance as Guy Crouchback was not successful.

Evelyn was an admirer of a book rediscovered for a younger generation by E. M. Forster and David Cecil: Howard Overing Sturgis's large-scale novel *Belchamber*. The book may be described as the last, or among the last, of those written in the direct tradition of Thackeray and Trollope, one which showed no sign of the degeneration which overcame the late products of that family. Sturgis was a younger friend and disciple of Henry James. The latter, who grew to be narrow and egocentric in his critical judgements, gravely disapproved of *Belchamber*. Time has shown his condemnation to be invalid, but nevertheless from what he said about this book there is a lesson to be learned from the master. He found a literary blunder in Sturgis's choice of chief character, a well-intentioned, weak young man who is incapable of standing up for himself. 'You cannot write a good book', Henry James is reported to have said, 'about a poor rat.' Evelyn made the same mistake as Sturgis. Guy Crouchback is Paul Pennyfeather cast for the principal role in an enormous tragedy. This is a grave blemish from which the book was never to work itself free.

Evelyn had turned against his old love *Brideshead Revisited* as related. *Sword of Honour* was to show in its late episodes the intensity with which he had replaced his love by hate. In the first volume he seems to have tried to make amends for the religiosity in *Brideshead Revisited*, to have tried to exorcize the devilish Julia and the unpleasing Lady Marchmain. The hero belongs to an ancient recusant family, the kind of 'old Catholic' family which many readers wrongly believe he attempted to portray in *Brideshead Revisited*. The hero himself is represented as conscientiously following the practice of his religion, but in a disconcertingly lifeless and mechanical way. No attempt is made to excite the reader's admiration for Guy's fidelity to the faith of his fathers; indeed the reader is given plenty of reason to regard it as repellent. Not till the concluding stages of the trilogy did Evelyn try to identify the hero with Christian virtue, and by then it was too late. But in this first volume and through most of the trilogy, the religious interest is centred not on Guy but on his father, Gervase Crouchback, an elderly widower who endures the loss of his family home and his sadly diminished wealth with noble fortitude and cheerfulness. Except for one small superstitious episode about a medal, mercifully not exploited, there is no religiosity about Mr Crouchback.

Many readers, including discerning ones, have found Mr Crouchback a bit too good to be true, have seen in him and his *sancta simplicitas* another of Evelyn's dangerous excursions into sentimentality. Such questions are largely a matter of taste. Some find a certain loftiness of mind and spirit in the quixotic Colonel Newcome, others see nothing but an old fool. The case for the defence regarding the two main charges outlined above may be stated as follows. When it is said that Mr Crouchback is too good to be true, there is an implication that Evelyn abandoned all realism for the sake of sentimental imaginings. In fact the probability is that he was working closely from a model, and that his model was Harry Scrope, the head of an 'Old Catholic' family which is one of the oldest in Europe. (In a legal case concerning coats of arms Geoffrey Chaucer gave evidence for the Scropes.) Harry Scrope was a saintly man bearing a close resemblance to Mr Crouchback in almost every detail. That he was Evelyn's model cannot be proved. (They only met three or four times.) Remembering how profoundly (and rightly) Evelyn admired him, it seems to me a strong likelihood. More than that cannot be said.

The second and similar charge that Mr Crouchback's *sancta simplicitas* is an unworthy excursion into pretty-pretty pietism overlooks the skill of Evelyn's portraiture and how he recognized the danger and guarded against it. It overlooks that though Evelyn depicts how this worthy old man's readiness to believe the best of everyone defeats the ill-doers who contrive against him, he subtly balanced the portrait by showing how his credulity could land him in ridiculous situations. Mr Crouchback becomes a characteristic dupe of publicity, and praises, louder than most, the supposed achievements of the Press-invented hero 'Trimmer'. Nevertheless it ought to be admitted that though the picture is not without the humanity and realism of that of Parson Adams, Mr Crouchback's moment does not come in *Men at Arms* but later.

It has been mentioned that a weakness of the book lies in its exclusiveness: it is alleged that it is addressed to a 'Men Only' readership. I think the accusation is true. I do not see how a woman reader, even one who served throughout World War II in the WAAFs, could get the same enjoyment through recognition as a male reader with Army experience, and even many male readers must find much of the matter wearisome. Troop movements, and the mismanagement attending them; battalion billeting in a seaside town; games of 'Housey-housey' in the Officers Mess; these are not rewarding subjects, and they are all treated in detail. Are they blemishes? That question will be answered later.

The pedestrian character of the book as a whole caused it to be received with some disappointment. People remembered the sport Evelyn had made of the essential farce of war in *Put Out More Flags*, and those who had expected a bigger and better POMF felt betrayed. Or rather, they would have felt utterly betrayed if it had not been for the amends Evelyn made to the POMF-expectants with a new farcical character, Apthorpe. When he enters the story, he is described as looking 'like a soldier. He was burly, tanned, moustached, primed with a rich vocabulary of military terms and abbreviations. Until recently he had served in Africa in some unspecified capacity. His boots had covered miles of bush trail.'

Apthorpe turns out to be a crank and, as the reader is likely to guess long before he is told in the second volume, a fraud. If the book was not a great success by Evelyn's high standards, Apthorpe certainly was. He belonged to a recognizable family of Evelyn inventions: Hooper, Atwater, Mr Todhunter, Colonel Plum, Ambrose Silk and lastly Apthorpe, each very different but each unquestionably bred in the same stud farm. Apthorpe was not only what Evelyn's readers wanted, he took hold on Evelyn himself. He became the central figure of the book whose three parts are named Apthorpe Gloriosus, Apthorpe Furibundus, and Apthorpe Immolatus.

As mentioned already, Evelyn found it necessary to kill Apthorpe at the end of *Men at Arms*, as he found that otherwise one whom he had invented as a minor character would grow out of proportion and dominate the whole work. Many readers and critics regretted Apthorpe's death and doubted the wisdom of this drastic operation. So many critics have by now called Apthorpe 'immortal' that the description has almost become a critical cliché. But Evelyn had no doubt that in contriving Apthorpe's death he had done the right thing. He always suspected the merits of any writing which the author had written with infatuation.

I think there can be little doubt that Evelyn's judgement was sound. It is strange to recall how much comic writing owes to bores. From the birth of Polonius to that of Bertie Wooster the skill of the humorist has lain, as often as not, in depicting a bore with subtle touches that make the reader long for his company in the book, as surely as he would avoid it in real life. In depicting Atwater Evelyn had shown himself a master of this art. In depicting Apthorpe he believed he had done it again. The most difficult challenge and the essence of the art is that the bore must not bore. Unless the scene with Reynaldo is cut (as it usually is for the sake of brevity) even Polonius comes dangerously near to boring. In defiance of those many critics who have found Apthorpe immortal I declare my belief that Apthorpe is a bore who bores. I think Evelyn, despite his infatuation, recognized the danger and that this led him to an ill-considered attempt to ensure that Apthorpe remained amusing.

The remedial treatment was to involve Apthorpe in some slap-stick farce, in this case revolving round the 'Thunder-Box'. Lavatory-jokes have their place in great comedy but as the most permissive must agree, unless they only want to be permissive, the place is a limited one. The idea of a crank who insists on taking a collapsible lavatory-seat or 'commode' around with him is good enough for one or at most two references and possibly one detailed incident. Evelyn gave sixteen pages to the adventure of Apthorpe's 'Thunder-Box'. The joke, even to those who relish lavatory-jokes, becomes wearisome through repetition. Diana Cooper remarked that it became 'Evelyn's *preislied*'.

Like Lord Marchmain, Apthorpe becomes most interesting on his deathbed. His end is the last incident of *Men at Arms* which finally closes with Guy being unfairly accused of responsibility for his friend's death, and the poor rat, true to form, failing to stand up for himself. Guy ends in disgrace with his beloved regiment, 'The Halberdiers', closely modelled on the Royal Marines.

The foregoing account of the book has been mainly concerned with blemishes. Has it no compensating merits? Many.

A great reward, as in all Evelyn's fiction, is the delineation of character. The minor characters, notably Guy Crouchback's brother-in-law Arthur Box-Bender, are exquisitely well drawn. (It may be noted that Box-Bender bears a family resemblance to Rex Mottram and like the latter has an ancestor in Brendan Bracken.) Even characters who only appear on a page or two, such as the Irish priest in the garrison town, remain long in the memory of an attentive reader. 'Trimmer' hardly appears in *Men at Arms* but his few seconds are so memorable that Evelyn was justified in re-introducing him without explanation in the next volume.

Of the major characters the most remarkable is not Apthorpe but Brigadier Ben Ritchie-Hook, a true-blue British *condottiere*, by no means typical of the British army but by no means as rare in it as might be thought. Evelyn's diaries leave no doubt as to where he first found the raw material for this picture of a modernized James Wolfe, but it would be absurd to suppose that his first brigade commander was his only source of inspiration. I have no evidence to allow me to boast that he was influenced by my biography of Orde Wingate, but Ben Ritchie-Hook bears a distinct caricature resemblance to Wingate. Ritchie-Hook also bears a very strong resemblance to General Adrian Carton de Wiart whom Evelyn knew, slightly but enough, as a fellow-member of White's club. Once framed in his imagination, Ritchie-Hook proved an instrument perfectly suited to Evelyn's fiction. A reader who delights in Ritchie-Hook, especially one who relishes the high comedy of this portrait in contrast with the inferior farce of Apthorpe, may regret the Brigadier's disappearance in the last section of the book, though he must welcome his sudden reappearance in the Dakar fiasco, wonderfully well described. I have heard this odd piece of construction condemned as a fault. I think that this criticism would be applicable to the book if it had been a novel purely on its own, but that it does not apply to the book judged as a part of a much greater whole. Unexpected reappearance and eclipse is of the essence of army life.

This brings me to the subject of the book's great merit, one which out-shines all blemishes. This is its picture of service life, one that can stand comparison with Kipling. If the book can be justly described in part as heavily pedestrian, the reason is that stones are heavy things. In *Men at*

*Arms* Evelyn was laying the foundation stones on which he planned to build. (That he underwent a crisis of self-confidence half way does not invalidate the foregoing: such crises, leaving no permanent mark, have been often recorded of craftsmen in all the arts.) His subject was the fate of one, still relatively young but past the prime of his age in military terms, who was caught up in the hideous process of what in its later stages was gleefully described as a People's War. (*The Awkward Age* would have been an apt title.) It was a subject, crying out for expression, staring every writer, especially novelists, in the face. Many faced the challenge, most of them unsuccessfully. Evelyn only took it up when he felt confident that he had had time to work out in his mind what the catastrophe might mean. The end of the trilogy is deliberately inconclusive. He circumscribed his area of invention severely, the central subject throughout being life seen through the eyes of an elderly junior officer. To achieve his objective, Evelyn first needed to evoke the world seen, and the point from which it is seen, and with some inevitable stumbles from having burdened himself with Guy Crouchback, he did this in *Men at Arms*.

The change in tone and spirit between *Men at Arms* and *Officers and Gentlemen* is very striking. There is a freedom and freshness about the writing which is not often found in *Men at Arms*. There are no more expositive accounts of military routine, no more troop movements: the scene has been set and the details can be taken for granted. The story gets off to a rousing start with an air-raid and a typical Evelyn challenge to the demands of good taste: 'The sky over London was glorious, ochre and madder, as though a dozen tropic suns were simultaneously setting round the horizon . . .', soon to be followed by a description of a burning club, specially written, I think, for Henry Yorke who served in the Fire Service throughout the war. 'On the pavement opposite Turtle's [club] a group of progressive novelists in firemen's uniform were squirting a little jet of water into the morning room.'

From the beginning vividly drawn characters abound, but the most interesting do not come on the scene until half way through the first part. (The book is divided into two parts, *Happy Warriors* and *In the Picture*, separated by an admirable *Interlude* set in Cape Town and concluding with an *Epilogue*.) The first character to arrest the reader's attention so that he says: 'Oh! This is something new! Not the usual stuff at all,' is a dandified fellow-officer called Ivor Claire. He is the first person whom the hero, Guy Crouchback, meets on being transferred from the imagined Halberdiers to the genuine Commandos. He only appears in this part of the trilogy. He is the *beau idéal* of British society, clever, impeccably dressed, a first-rate horseman, a born officer, the sort of man whom Evelyn was said to worship, and whom he did sometimes recklessly admire. But Ivor Claire turns out to be a man of putrefied core, only 'fair without'. He treacherously deserts his men in the hour of crisis rather than go with them into captivity. The dialogue, in which he tells Guy Crouchback of his pusillanimous decision, is among a few which can be claimed as the finest Evelyn wrote at any time.

This is to go forward to the later parts of *Officers and Gentlemen*. Early in the story there appears one of the most preposterous characters in the whole of Evelyn's invention: the former hairdresser 'Trimmer', disguised as Captain and occasionally Major MacTavish. He is compounded of fraud, artfully indicated by the fact that we never learn his real name. On this odious creature of his imagination Evelyn heaped all his scorn for 'the Century of the Common Man', a congenial task. The funniest single episode in the book is Trimmer's raid in which he leads a small Commando party in an attack on enemy installations on the north coast of France. Everything imaginable goes wrong, notably Trimmer's nerve, and the fiasco is covered up by publicity handled by the journalist Lord Kilbannock. This farce is brilliantly backed up by another. When Trimmer becomes a national hero, he turns out to be a Frankenstein's monster as well, and the sufferings of the Frankenstein Kilbannock and his friends at the hands of the monster are exploited by Evelyn with all his merciless skill.

The last part of the book, *In the Picture*, takes the story to the Middle East and is chiefly concerned with a horrifying account of the British defeat in the struggle for Crete. Two very important characters emerge. One is Mrs Stitch, last seen in *Scoop*. Evelyn, as it were, transferred Duff Cooper from Algiers to Egypt (where he must have replaced Oliver Lyttelton), transferred the Minister of State's headquarters from Cairo to Alexandria, and surrounded Diana with Maud Marriott's fashionable cosmopolitan set. As before no one, least of all Diana, doubted that the Stitches were the Duff Coopers.

But the Mrs Stitch of *Officers and Gentlemen* is a far more interesting character than her predecessor. In *Scoop* she was merely an instrument of farce. She was sketched in two dimensions. In the War Trilogy she is drawn in full perspective, drawn moreover so well and memorably that it is easy to have the false impression, after reading, that she has occupied much space.

She is no less comic in this graver book than she was in *Scoop*, but she is not a farcical figure cleverly adjusted to tragi-comedy. She is something much more, a figure essentially comic round whom the overtone and echo of tragedy can be heard.

The other character who comes to play a dominating role in the second part is possibly the most original of all Evelyn's many inventions, and certainly the most sinister. He is Corporal-Major Ludovic of the Royal Horse Guards. When Evelyn told Nancy Mitford that Ludovic was based on Cyril Connolly, he was deliberately misleading her. There is no resemblance to Cyril whatsoever except in his endeavour to become a great aphorist. Ludovic's *pensées*, which are to bring him literary fame in the concluding volume, are cruelly close in style and subject to the aphorisms published by Cyril in his book *The Unquiet Grave*. Otherwise Ludovic, who can occasionally remind a reader of Henry James's evil-minded servants, bears no relation to Cyril. He is unlike anyone else in the world of Evelyn's fiction; he is the only fully drawn Evelyn character who is a member of the working, 'socially significant' classes. He is what J. B. Priestley had asked for, but the latter may not have liked what he was given.

As mentioned already, the long descriptive passage, possibly the best of Evelyn's sustained passages, in which, in the course of an occasionally and always craftily broken narrative of nearly a hundred pages, he tells of the great reverse in Crete, Evelyn modelled the story closely on the diary he kept at the time. Fiction is firmly placed before a background of experienced reality, except in the last episode where Guy Crouchback and Corporal-Major Ludovic go through the ordeal of a long journey in an open boat from Crete to the African coast. This was not a thing that had happened to Evelyn, but had happened to many; an ordeal of which Evelyn must have heard first-hand accounts.

That *Officers and Gentlemen* is better constructed, indeed is a better book than *Men at Arms* is hardly to be denied. That the two books did not add up to a whole was not to be denied either. For all its sustained pace and well-balanced construction *Officers and Gentlemen* also had blemishes, most of which a continuation could cancel, though not all.

The story was obviously unfinished. Several characters, notably Gervase Crouchback, were as yet unachieved. A purpose in the whole undertaking was hinted at but not stated. These were the weaknesses that could be put straight if the story was continued in a third volume. But in *Officers and Gentlemen* there remain a few blemishes which could not be thus disposed of and eradicated. They are to be found in the second part of the book and are due to a literary fault to which Evelyn was not generally prone: over-subtlety. It is hinted though not clearly stated that amid the shambles of the withdrawal from Crete Corporal-Major Ludovic murdered the Brigade Major, a man called Major Hound. The last-named has been described by Professor Frederick Stopp as 'the epitome of all the most savage views of the regimental officer on "the staff".' The synopsis of the first two books, which introduces the concluding volume of the trilogy, makes it plain that Evelyn intended the reader to assume murder. But no convincing explanation is offered as to why Ludovic murdered Major Hound. Dislike? Ludovic's dislike of Hound seems merely the ordinary animosity of all regimental personnel towards 'the staff', not a thing that often leads to assassination. Ludovic, so the synopsis gives one to understand (there is no definite statement of fact), committed a second murder, that of the Sapper officer who commandeered the boat in which he and Guy drifted. Ludovic had good reason for this crime. The officer had gone mad and had only been prevented by Guy from shooting Ludovic. But the episode is so written that the disappearance of the officer in the night might as well be due to accident or suicide. The reader is not told that Ludovic knew of the officer's threat, which was whispered in secret to Guy. Until I read the synopsis six years after the book was published, I never suspected that Ludovic had committed two murders. I do not think I was the only reader to miss the second.

Over-subtlety in the treatment of Ludovic can perhaps be defended on the grounds that it helps to evoke a tortuous, cunning, psychologically diseased being. No such defence is open to the extravagant over-subtlety with which Mrs Stitch is treated in the last episode. This concerns her determination to save Ivor Claire from the consequences of his treachery and cowardice. Her only motive is friendship. She sets an intrigue on foot by which Ivor Claire is transferred to India, and Guy Crouchback, the only witness of the other's wrong-doing to escape from Crete, is ordered home. The transfer to India raises no difficulty with the reader; it is stated in direct fashion. But Mrs Stitch's intrigue to get Guy returned to England is conveyed so much by little hints and apparently insignificant remarks that the reader is likely to be unaware that Mrs Stitch is intriguing at all. The book ends with Guy leaving for England and giving her an envelope containing an identity disc, taken from a young British soldier's corpse in Crete, which he piously wishes to be returned to the boy's parents. The envelope is addressed to G.H.Q. Middle East. Guy gets a promise from Mrs Stitch that she will ask her husband to send it to the right department. Mrs Stitch suspects it is evidence against Claire. The last sentence reads: 'As he drove away she waved the envelope; then turned indoors and dropped it into a waste-paper basket. Her eyes were one immense sea, full of flying galleys.'

A reader who has detected the intrigue must find that brief terminal paragraph masterly. If he has not, and this I think must be the case with many, Mrs Stitch suddenly appears hard and unpleasant, not the author's intention.

A fine novel, not open to criticism of essentials or essential points, with merits far outweighing blemishes.

After its publication in 1955, there then occurred that long interval in the trilogy which has been indicated already. At the time Evelyn clearly felt written out on this subject, felt that he could not go a step farther with the British Army; but he did not feel written out in a general sense, and that is the important thing: the interval was not a period of literary stagnation: it contained *The Ordeal of Gilbert Pinfold* and the life of Ronald Knox, unusually contrasted subjects, and whatever literary errors these last-named books showed, literary exhaustion was not among them. After six years he returned, in the spirit of Wagner after an interval of twelve years, to the completion of his trilogy.

The theme of the last volume *Unconditional Surrender* was announced in the last chapter of *Officers and Gentlemen* when the news of the German invasion of Russia was received at Mrs Stitch's house in Alexandria. The news depressed the easily depressed Guy. He was moved to reflect as follows, referring to incidents of the now concluded second part:

'The hallucination was dissolved, like the whales and turtles on the voyage from Crete, and he was back after less than two years' pilgrimage in a Holy Land of illusion in the old ambiguous world, where priests were spies and gallant friends proved traitors and his country was led blundering into dishonour.'

The passage is very important, for this represented not only a fictitious hero's fictitious thoughts but the author's own conviction. (Evelyn was enamoured of the romantic conception of war expressed in the poems of Julian Grenfell and Rupert Brooke.) A reader may, however, protest that it is ridiculous to see in the low-spirited Guy Crouchback a spokesman of the high-spirited Evelyn. Yet that is undoubtedly what Guy was. The explanation will not surprise people who knew Evelyn well. Like most comedians Evelyn had a strong tendency to melancholy, but with him the double character of the predicament was carried further than is usual. Like many aggressive people he was liable to unworthy reactions of self-pity, and this high-spirited man went through frequent moments when he saw himself as a poor, passive, ill-used rat; saw himself not as he was but as Guy Crouchback. This dichotomy was not the most pleasing or estimable thing in Evelyn's character, but that it was a real fact in the case must be insisted upon. The tendency to melancholy was beyond disguise, and began to become dangerous as he entered on the last phase of his life in the 1960s; it was obvious to anyone who knew him at all, but the rest was hidden because he recognized its unworthiness. Only those who knew him well will recognize the fact and that in Guy Crouchback, that joyless figure, he was painting a self-portrait, as he often saw himself. In Guy, too, he gave expression to his naïve and impractical political ideas and it should not be overlooked that *Unconditional Surrender* is a political novel.

The theme is restated in a disconcerting passage in the Prologue. It occurs in a conversation between Guy and his father. The younger man is delighted at the news of the fall in Italy of the anti-British and anti-papal royal House of Savoy. The elder Crouchback speaks first.

' "Of course it's reasonable for a soldier to rejoice in Victory."

' "I don't think I'm interested in victory now," said Guy.

' "Then you've no business to be a soldier."

' "Oh I want to stay in the war. I should like to do some fighting. But it doesn't seem to matter now who wins . . ." '

The conversation provokes a long letter from the troubled elder Crouchback. In the course of it, with reference to the Lateran Treaty of 1929, which has been discussed briefly in their conversation, Gervase Crouchback makes the memorable comment: 'Quantitative judgements don't apply.' This gives a second theme to the book, one which becomes dominant later. That it does so is due to a remarkable feat of construction, one that shows with what exquisite and effective care Evelyn had written the Gervase Crouchback episodes in the first two novels. Most readers of the trilogy are left at the end with the impression that the elder Crouchback is a leading character. Nor are they mistaken. He is the only character to represent positive moral values. All the other people are morally neutral, decadent, corrupted or actively wicked. Mr Crouchback's subtle influence on those who come under it is drawn without any undue emphasis and only fully appears in the last novel of the trilogy in which he dies early in the story. Evelyn helped himself by introducing an agreeable but fatuous younger brother of Gervase Crouchback, 'Uncle Peregrine'. The latter's unenlightened Catholicism and conservatism must make any alert reader aware by contrast of 'the real right thing' in Mr Crouchback. The fully achieved portrait is a remarkable success. It may surprise many readers of the trilogy to learn that after his conversation with Guy and his single quoted letter in the Prologue, Mr Crouchback makes no further personal appearance in *Unconditional Surrender*. He is quoted and remembered only.

The book is in three main parts entitled *State Sword*, *Fin de Ligne* and *The Death Wish*; the break between the first and second parts is stronger than between the second and third parts which may originally have been composed as one.

After the slow-moving prologue with its necessary recapitulations, the story is resumed with all the vigour and impatience to be expected of a composer long separated from his work. The 'State Sword' of the first title is that civic sword, manufactured it is said by personal royal command, in 1943, and shortly after presented by grateful allies to Josef Stalin as a gift to Stalingrad to be kept as a token of admiration for that city's resistance. This public deed excited all Evelyn's scorn and prejudice. It provided him with a perfect opening subject on which he played masterly variations. He also uses it as a meeting point for characters. Among the admiring crowd queueing outside and shuffling through Westminster Abbey in order to worship the sacred object, there appears a tall recently commissioned officer promoted from the ranks. He is Captain, former Corporal-Major, Ludovic. He leads the reader from there into his murky private life and the reader learns, not with surprise, that in pre-war days he had been the Antinous of a distinguished diplomat, a relic of a past world who prides himself on his modernity, and who, partly through his affection for plebeian acquaintances made in pursuit of unorthodox sexual tastes, has become an enthusiast for the extreme Left Wing and the new Russophil fashion. He is called Sir Ralph Brompton. Pomposity is as natural to him as homosexuality, and the conjunction of the two make him unforgettably, if a little poignantly, absurd. It would be untrue to say that Sir Ralph is a caricature of Harold Nicolson, but I think Evelyn had Nicolson occasionally in mind while he was contriving the picture.

Of the minor characters who crowd the first part of *Unconditional Surrender*, one of the most memorable is Everard Spruce who publishes Ludovic's *pensées* in his monthly magazine. Spruce is manifestly based on Cyril Connolly, and his monthly magazine *Survival* on Cyril's distinguished, avant-garde, valuable and occasionally ridiculous cultural magazine *Horizon*.

Cyril was much hurt when the book came out and asked Ann Fleming to tell him candidly whether Everard Spruce was a caricature of himself. Ann candidly replied that there could be no question about it, just as there could be no question that Ludovic's *pensées* were based on his own aphorisms which had been anonymously published in *Horizon*. Cyril remonstrated with Evelyn, and Evelyn, foolishly, not only denied the charge but put the blame for his friend's distress on 'that woman in London', as he referred to Ann in his letters until his anger subsided. I was and remain on Ann's side. To anyone who knew Cyril, and to many who did not, but read *Horizon* and knew the aphorisms of Palinurus, the double identification was not a matter of guess-work or clever deduction but plain common sense.

To return to the book. The reader meets Spruce by following Ludovic's evening peregrinations in black-out London, a London often described but nowhere better than here. In Spruce's house, where he has been asked to a literary gathering, Ludovic meets Guy for the first time since 1941. The result is calamitous though not visible except to Ludovic and the reader. I do not know whether Evelyn intended subtle parallel roles for Ludovic and Mrs Stitch, but Ludovic like Mrs Stitch looks with alarmed suspicion on Guy as a sole surviving witness, in the case of Ludovic because of a baseless belief that he knows of and wishes to avenge the two murders. Mrs Stitch was moved to pursue mercilessly an errand of mercy, but Ludovic is moved to destroy evidence of his crimes by a third one. He turns into a mass-murderer in intention. Chance puts in his way the means to encompass Guy's death, not by the crude direct methods suited to the chaos of the retreat from Crete, but by the Uriah-system successfully practised by King David. His plan fails and Ludovic vanishes from the scene, unsuspected.

The book shows a return to a certain kind of cinematographic art which Evelyn first practised with good effect in *Vile Bodies*: numerous sub-plots conveyed by numerous changes of scene. It is a matchless technique for the conveying of a story which includes loosely connected incident, and Evelyn here used it matchlessly. It brings out, ironically, one blemish on the trilogy, a sub-plot concerning speciously convincing evidence given to MI6 that Guy is not politically reliable, in fact a potential traitor. As a subject for farce, spy-mania is a dangerous one as it has been used too often. On *Unconditional Surrender* the MI6 theme is something of a blot; it is not developed and from promising to become a major theme it ends up as a silly sideshow. But it would be grossly unfair and uncritical to let this small blemish influence judgement on the book, the numerous sub-plots being as finely contrived as the cinematographic technique by which they are presented, and all furnished with characters which grow, sometimes from hardly visible beginnings. Most notable among these minor characters who come to importance in the story is Guy's wife from whom he was divorced before the beginning of the events related in the trilogy. She is called Virginia Troy. She is that over-familiar figure in fiction and drama, the light-headed, loose-living woman with a good heart. Evelyn makes this stock figure of popular fiction alive, interesting, convincing and new. The sub-plot in which she is involved is a macabre comedy. In her silly way she became Trimmer's mistress for a brief spell in *Officers and Gentlemen*, and in *Unconditional Surrender* finds herself with child by the frightful little People's Hero. Virginia's search for an abortionist in war-time London is one of Evelyn's great sequences. (He got his facts from a woman friend and suggested that he should accord her a credit in his introduction!) In the end Virginia is saved by Guy's decision, on learning the facts, to remarry her. He is influenced by memory of his father's insistence on the Christian duty of selfless action. It is a truly heroic deed but coming so late in the story, and without any attempt to make Guy lovable, the reader can only see it as part of an under-dog's doom.

Above all these sub-plots the supreme one is that which centres on the inhuman Ludovic. He not only rises in stature but comes to dominate the first half of the book. He becomes commandant of a parachuting training unit and by a dramatic coincidence Guy trains under him. The trilogy has been blamed for a Dickensian excess of coincidence in the plot, but coincidence like sudden prominence and sudden disappearance is of the essence of war-experience. It is here at the parachuting school that Ludovic plans, by giving Guy an excessively favourable report for courage, to contrive his death along Uriah lines. Ludovic throughout this episode remains withdrawn in his room and never sees his intended victim Guy. The reader is purposely and cleverly left in doubt as to whether Ludovic is sane.

But for Evelyn's biographer, of far greater interest than Ludovic's homicidal tendencies and interests, are his literary aspirations, endeavours and ultimate success. He recognizes that as an author of *pensées* he cannot enjoy literary success, or be sought after by publishers, in the post-war world. To achieve such ambitions he needs to write a large-scale novel, and he decides, in his morbid seclusion in which his only companion is his

Pekinese dog, to write – *Brideshead Revisited*. Thus Evelyn described Ludovic's initial concept:

'It was a very gorgeous, almost gaudy, tale of romance and high drama set, as his experience with Sir Ralph Brompton well qualified him to set it, in the diplomatic society of the previous decade. The characters and their equipment were seen as Ludovic in his own ambiguous position had seen them, more brilliant than reality. The plot was Shakespearean in its elaborate improbability. The dialogue could never have issued from human lips, the scenes of passion were capable of bringing a blush to readers of either sex and every age. But it was not an old-fashioned book. Had he known it, half a dozen other English writers, averting themselves sickly from privations of war and apprehensions of the social consequences of the peace, were even then severally and secretly, unknown to one another, [or] to Everard Spruce... composing or preparing to compose books which would turn from the drab alleys of the thirties into the odorous gardens of a recent past transformed and illuminated by disordered memory and imagination. Ludovic in the solitude of his post was in the movement.

'Nor was it for all its glitter a cheerful book. Melancholy suffused its pages and deepened towards the close.'

The succeeding passages, which give detail of this novel about the 'Transept' family, are a 'send-up' of Evelyn's novel about the 'Flyte' family, more severe and more perspicacious and more devastating than any of which the professional critics of *Brideshead Revisited* had been capable. Ludovic's novel was entitled *The Death Wish*, the subtitle of the last part of *Unconditional Surrender*.

The new theme of the ultimate part of *Unconditional Surrender*, the Death Wish, is used in several keys and modes, and in support of or in contrast with the initial themes of the decay of idealism and of the irrelevance of quantitative judgements. The last section of the trilogy, only eighty-four pages in length but seeming more from the quantity of matter contained in it, is contrapuntal in character but, being written by a man to whom music meant nothing at all, quite unselfconsciously so.

It is as strictly autobiographical in character as was the description of the Cretan disaster in *Officers and Gentlemen*, sometimes needlessly so. The aeroplane crash from which Randolph and Evelyn so narrowly escaped with their lives is vividly described, but adds little if anything to the story. Bitter indeed is the picture of how in a Jugoslavia slowly but certainly coming under the domination of the Communist Party led by Tito, the British and American allies help in the extinction of surviving freedom, partly out of wishful thinking and partly out of blank stupidity.

One of the last inventions of the whole work is the revolting character of a young British officer, Captain Gilpin, who epitomizes the official British mood of joyous self-delusion. Gilpin and Guy occupy the last scene of the book. Gilpin gives himself airs and suggests that in befriending certain Jugoslavian Jews who are out of favour with the Communist Party, and in reporting unwelcome information about persecution Guy has put himself under suspicion. The poor rat, as usual, does not stand up for himself and so the story ends.

The book closes with an epilogue called 'Festival of Britain.' The year is 1951, the war six years behind, and Box-Bender and his wife join with another couple in giving a débutante ball. The traumatic memories of Kensington Square had not healed in Evelyn's mind, and the reader is told that some of the younger guests 'impudently presented themselves in dinner-jackets and soft shirts'. The main scene of the epilogue is Bellamy's Club where old regimental friends, including Guy, are holding a reunion dinner. Virginia was killed by a flying bomb in the war and Guy has married a suitable Catholic girl and begotten children of his own, though he is faithfully bringing up Trimmer's son as his heir. Trimmer himself has vanished, forgotten, and Ludovic has become rich through the sales of *The Death Wish*. Ritchie-Hook, who reappeared in the last part, was killed in Jugoslavia. With one exception all this comes off. The attempt to depict Guy in his new-found happiness as a jolly good fellow is wholly unsuccessful.

In my opinion *Unconditional Surrender* is Evelyn's best book. It not only worthily concluded the trilogy, it set a seal on it and made of this threefold novel sequence a satisfying whole, a fine addition to the very highest class of English fiction. The limitations are evident and Evelyn did not try to go outside them, but by admitting to them turned them to account: here is the catastrophe seen by an observer with an eye on personal events and personal reactions. Here is no imitation *War and Peace* but a record of a great event, given as only Evelyn could have done. Its only grave blemish, the unlikeability of its hero, was, by the time he reached *Unconditional Surrender*, a fault beyond correction. In its composition Evelyn ran serious literary risks. He came near to mixing mutually destructive elements, comedy with farce, and, even more perilously, black comedy with tragedy. But, to change the metaphor, he was by now an experienced navigator and he knew how to steer his craft safely through. In the perfection of its construction *Unconditional Surrender*, and perhaps the whole trilogy, is not surpassed by any other book he wrote.

With the completion of the trilogy Evelyn's career as a serious writer of fiction drew to an end.

# Chapter 26

## 1961-1966

On 4 January 1961 Evelyn wrote to Nancy Mitford: 'No, no, no. You must not think of giving up the novel. As I said in all sincerity *Alfred* positively clamours for a sequel. X has all the concealed malice of the underdog. Don't believe a word he says. Reviewers are a paltry lot.

'It has been a bad year for the old jumpers – Elizabeth Bowen, John Betjeman, Leslie Hartley down & out of the race; Tony [Powell] & you still in the saddle thank goodness, though Tony is sitting unsteady with his arms round the horse's neck & irons flying. You must collect yourself for the next fence. Graham Greene is going to have a heavy fall. I have just read his newest book about lepers [; it] is *not* what Americans call "inspirational".

'I have just been editing a little life of *la Veuve Clicquot Ponsardin* – very interesting. I had *always* vaguely supposed her a woman of the Second Empire. Did you realize she was born 12 years before the Revolution & widowed in [the] year of Trafalgar (Austerlitz to you), the daughter of a Jacobin deputy, ancestress of three dukes? Wine was at first a minor concern; her husband liked trotting round on a horse so he paid more attention to his vines than the banking & cloth-weaving which were the source of a very modest fortune. But I expect you know all this.

'I have not yet had my teeth out. The day cannot, I suppose, be far off. You can get them drawn free here but not replaced. I don't much care for Uncle Matthew's "dentures". I believe one can rub one's gums with a preparation which hardens them well enough to chew most things. Anyway I like soft food – prefer pâtés & mousses to hunks of meat.

'What do you suppose "nouvelle vague" means? According to my dictionary either "vague news" or "new waste-land". Idiot English reviewers are always using it.

'I bet you can't say "Lovely, lovely 1960!" '

Evelyn could say 'Lovely lovely 1960' because he had just finished his last and best work of fiction, but he had no impulse to do so. The melancholy which had plagued him for years more and more closed in on him.

The letter has been quoted in full because it outlines better than any of his more formal writings his preoccupations and expectations in his last years. It is worth looking at in some detail.

His hope that Nancy would 'continue novelist' was not realized, and perhaps Evelyn's wish showed faulty judgement. She had for long found it difficult to imagine the plot for a novel, and now found it impossible. This probably signalized the end of her inventive talent. If she had complied with Evelyn's passionate plea to continue with fiction the result might well have been weak and laboured work unworthy of her. She knew her limitations and that her talent, though real and interesting, was a slight one. She knew when to stop.

Evelyn's anti-reviewer goading may strike some readers as petty. It will strike no writer of fiction as petty. It is to do with the long-surviving notion (against which Jane Austen's strictures have had no effect whatsoever) that fiction is essentially trivial. The literary sections of newspapers usually have one small three-column space for fiction, the 'fiction bin' as it has been named, in which the fiction of the week or month, successful compositions and twaddle, are tossed together for the hurried consideration and judgement, not of an Arnold Bennett, but of a usually young and inexperienced or failed journalist (for with few exceptions the reviewer of long standing looks for promotion from the bin.) But the binster, as he may be called, has a grievance when the rare appearance of a distinguished work of fiction, such as *Unconditional Surrender*, is automatically taken out of his hands and given to a literary person of some standing. His grievance is genuine and a sense of justice often allows his claim, so that the writer of fiction, even such proved ones as Evelyn and Nancy, often find themselves in the humiliating position of being regularly judged by binsters, with only occasional relief in the form of a considered article by a person of deserved repute.

Evelyn affected not to read and not to bother about reviews. It was undoubtedly an affectation, one in which many writers indulge. He acutely minded Cyril Connolly's inept imputation that he was being gradually overcome by 'benign lethargy', and we may perhaps be grateful. In his annoyance was the probable origin of the unforgettable figure of Everard Spruce.

His judgement of contemporaries, Elizabeth Bowen, John Betjeman, Leslie Hartley and Anthony Powell may be left to opinion, though the reference to Anthony Powell is surprising. During 1960 his novel *Casanova's Chinese Restaurant* had been published and been admired by Evelyn. His admiration for Anthony Powell was intense, so much so that he resented any disparaging remark about his writing. The only adverse criticism he would allow was that the sequence of novels called *A Dance to the Music of Time*, of which *Casanova's Chinese Restaurant* was an item, was in danger of becoming self-defeatingly long. Evelyn would have liked the sequence brought to a conclusion after three or four volumes, and then a new one started. He was a reluctant admirer of Proust, whose influence he believed to be harmful.

The reference to Graham Greene concerns a dispute which had just opened. Graham's novel *A Burnt Out Case* had recently been published. The hero 'Querry' is a disillusioned Catholic who lost his faith not only in the Church but in God and the moral order. Evelyn was asked to review the book for *The Daily Mail*. He refused because he disapproved of the moral implications of the book and did not wish to say so in public. He wrote to Graham on the subject and a correspondence followed. It became a revival of the dispute about 'Scobie' and *The Heart of the Matter*. Graham, rightly in my opinion, protested that Evelyn's objections were, in effect, disguised prudishness; an insistence that a writer whose allegiance was to the Catholic Church should not write about a lapsed Catholic. Evelyn failed to extricate himself from the position into which he had manœuvred himself. The dispute, unlike *The Heart of the Matter* discussions, remained private. No bones were broken, and the friendship in no way faltered.

The 'little life of la Veuve Clicquot-Ponsardin' was by a friend Jaqueline, the wife of Prince Jean de Caraman Chimay. Evelyn not only edited the English translation but wrote a preface to the English edition. This was the first of the minor works which occupied his last years.

He continued to be worried about the state of his teeth. He had not neglected them but they suddenly 'went bad on him'. He postponed action till 1964. He never seems to have discovered the 'preparation' with which to strengthen his gums.

His final enquiry to Nancy on the meaning of 'nouvelle vague' shows either that he had a defective dictionary or had deliberately forgotten his French, once fluent enough for the Pope. At that time 'nouvelle vague' was a smart expression for a new fashion or new 'wave' of interest. It was used by the sort of literary journalist who likes to refer to an author's work as his *oeuvre*.

In 1961 there occurred two important family events: in early June Evelyn's eldest daughter Teresa was married to Mr (now Professor) John D'Arms; in the next month Evelyn's eldest son Auberon was married to Lady Teresa Onslow. The last occasion gave rise to a comedy which had some effect on Evelyn's life.

A press photograph appeared of Evelyn walking either to or from the church with Laura. He was appalled at the spectacle. He decided that he must do something to recapture the good looks he had once enjoyed, not so long ago. He consulted Ian and Ann Fleming about hydropathic establishments, Ian being a frequent client of such places. They recommended one of which Ian had experience, the well-known establishment Forest Mere in Hampshire. He decided to undertake a cure though he did not act on his resolve till over two years later. In the mean time the proposition stirred his inventive faculty and a hydro was the scene of his last fiction.

Benign lethargy was never Evelyn's fault, but a tendency to lethargy certainly increased. He took up his diary again in December 1960 but it contains almost no mention of activity beyond a visit to Mells to see his old friend Christopher Hollis who often came over to visit him at Combe Florey. The new diary is mostly taken up with reflections of varying merit, and ends up as something like a collection of aphorisms.

One great opportunity for comedy was missed in 1961. In March of that year the Lady Chatterley case came before the courts and Evelyn was invited to appear as a witness in favour of the lifting of the ban which was still in force against the book on the grounds of indecency. A worse choice could hardly have been made by the 'pro-Chatterley' interest. Evelyn never went along with the high admiration for D. H. Lawrence which has not been marked by sobriety as it has increased in fashion and intensity. The closure by the police of an exhibition of his allegedly indecent paintings was and still is regarded as a test-case of a man's honourable feeling: good people deplore the action of the police in 1928 as persecution of a great man and artist; nasty people rejoice at an unimaginative act of tyranny. Evelyn regarded the whole episode as glorious farce, and I dare say it influenced the customs scene in *Vile Bodies*. He used to insist that the exhibition ought to have been closed by some authority because of the extravagant incompetence of the exhibits, and he refused to see the incident in any other terms. Evelyn, who made several provocative references to it in articles, is the only man I have known who actually saw the exhibition. At that time he still hoped for a career as a draughtsman and artist, and in a state of high expectation went to the gallery early. As a writer, he regarded D. H. Lawrence as highly gifted and distressingly uneven. *Lady Chatterley's Lover* he considered a hideous failure due to Lawrence having followed a fallacious theory about how to write about sex in fiction. His views were identical with those expressed by Compton Mackenzie in an illuminating essay contained in a collection called *Moral Courage*. Not surprisingly he declined the invitation to give evidence. If he had been asked by the other side he might conceivably have accepted. The opportunity was missed, and that must be a matter for regret.

During 1961 he had not made his usual annual journey to escape the cold of January and February. To make up for the omission he made a longer journey than usual at the end of the year, from 20 November to March 1962. As before, A. D. Peters obtained a journalist contract to meet his expenses. *The Sunday Times* commissioned an article by Evelyn to be turned in on his return, the subject being a visit to British Guiana which he had not seen for thirty years, since the *Ninety Two Days* of 1932.

He was accompanied by his beloved daughter Margaret. He tried to persuade Graham Greene to come with them but he was unable to. They went by sea to Trinidad and from there flew to Georgetown. The diary which he kept throughout this journey is of no interest. He found a few elderly persons among the clergy who remembered him, or politely said they did when he had jogged their memories, but though he flew to Boa Vista where he had suffered so hideously in the old days, he never seems to have made enquiries about Mr Christie. He found life in Guiana remarkably little changed. What change he did find struck him as undesirable. I am in no position to pronounce on how sound or otherwise his later report to *The Sunday Times* was, but one change he noted was remarkable and condemned by him though not in his frequent spirit of pure conservatism: as a result of the growth of party politics through representational government, Guiana, he discovered, 'must be the only place where you can find a Negro advocating *apartheid*.'

Before leaving the subject of this journey, the last long journey of Evelyn's life, one quotation from the excellent article he wrote for *The Sunday Times* may be given. (It was entitled *Return to Eldorado* and published on 12 August 1962.) Almost in a mood of morbid curiosity he had revisited with Margaret the scene of his misery at Boa Vista in Brazil. To put it mildly, he found himself agreeably surprised. He concluded the article thus:

'Thirty years ago this settlement on the Rio Branco, four days' stiff ride into Brazil, was the desperate dead-end where the outlaws of the country came to die. There was no symbol even of law. There was no means of livelihood. Every man carried a revolver – the only man in regular employment was a gunsmith whose speciality was to file the mechanism of these weapons so as to give them "hair-triggers"; every man had malaria, and most had syphilis. They lay all day in their hammocks, hating one another and shaking with fever.

'Now, by a whim of the Federal Government, it has become a State capital. It has 15,000 inhabitants. Each of the rapidly succeeding governors (four last year) has left his mark in grand, unfinished and abandoned buildings. There is a regiment of soldiers, a busy mission school and hospital, a large hotel which has no food or (when I was there) water, and no visitors . . .

'But unlike their odious predecessors they are all smiling and welcoming. The girls are pretty and smart. Murder is comparatively rare. As long as the money arrives from the central government they are a happy people. It is too easy, with Guiana in mind, to condemn all State interference. In Boa Vista, preposterously perhaps but effectively, the State has been beneficent. It is just conceivable that something of the kind could happen in Eldorado.'

Not long after Evelyn's return to England his daughter Margaret became engaged to be married to Mr Giles FitzHerbert. Loving her as he did he could not but feel the wrench of the approaching separation. He made no secret of the intensity of his feelings to his two closest confidantes, Ann Fleming and Nancy Mitford, but he recognized his duty with cheerfulness. This called for more than ordinary courage for cheerfulness did not come to him easily at any time.

There were signs that the persecution mania which had afflicted him was possibly returning. He continued to dose himself with excessive draughts of paraldehyde while drinking far more alcohol than he should have done while using this drug. There were signs, as yet faint, that Mr Pinfold might make a return visit. Such signs concerned trifles, or rumours, but they may have included the dangerous phenomenon of imagined events. He made a great fuss about a rumour that the British Governor and his wife at Trinidad had found him boring, and refused to accept assurances that he was misinformed. In his diary for 24 March 1962 he recorded an event which he reported both to Ann and Nancy and told to several friends. The entry runs as follows: 'White's. 7 p.m. I sit alone in the hall. A member known to me by sight but not by name, older than I, of the same build, but better dressed, said: "Why are you alone?"

' "Because no one wants to speak to me."

' "I can tell you exactly why; because you sit there on your arse looking like a stuck pig".'

I was among those to whom Evelyn confided this experience. I did not believe it, but considered it as one of his many elaborations on some very different and less interesting reality. I think now it may have been a hallucination.

One event of 1962 should be remembered. Evelyn, as should be apparent by now, was not only witty in himself but the cause that wit is in others. Without his encouragement and criticism Nancy Mitford might have remained a far less remarkable writer than she was. He did something of the same kind but by very different methods for Frankie Donaldson. Some time before this, in the Piers Court days, the Donaldsons and Evelyn had had a violent argument about Herbert Samuel whom Evelyn, true to his Bellocian ideas of history, had described as one 'who lost his honour in the Marconi case.' Jack, rather than Frankie, had been roused by this, as he had a great and justified admiration for Samuel. Later, Jack Donaldson urged Frankie, who by now had a name as a writer, to research and write a study of the once famous Marconi Scandal of 1913. She fell in with the idea and found that no book had been written on it and that books about the period showed that it was not a subject that had interested historians. To find out what really happened required intense research which Frankie, goaded by Evelyn's Crouchbackian historical prejudices, undertook and achieved. The result was her admirable book *The Marconi*

*Scandal* which appeared in the summer of 1962. It remains the only book on the subject, and while it confirmed Evelyn in his low opinion of Rufus Isaacs, he felt himself bound to write to Frankie a full recantation of his errors regarding Herbert Samuel. He admired the book of which, if he was not the 'onlie begetter', he was certainly an important one.

Frankie's book may have had a wholesome influence on Evelyn's mind; it may have confirmed growing doubts about the Bellocian view of history which he had once accepted as fully as his fictional *alter ego* Guy Crouchback. That he had doubts about Belloc's history is clear from a diary entry of the year before, 1961:

'Robert Byron was like Belloc in his banging about of ideas and a few facts. Belloc represents a tradition. He thinks himself the voice of Europe. There is no personal arrogance in his slap dash manners. Robert represented nothing except his own groping follies. His march east would have taken him to communism.' (As one who knew Robert better than Evelyn in Robert's last years, I doubt the truth of the last sentence in the quotation. Robert, unlike Evelyn, had seen Communism for himself in Stalin's Russia, and had been horrified.)

Margaret was married to Mr FitzHerbert on 20 October 1962. Soon after that, if he had not done so before, Evelyn began to write his last fiction. It is impossible to say with exactness because the diary he kept ceased to be regularly dated and was rarely strictly chronological in character. Typical of it is the following entry for 1 September 1962, which deserves quotation for its own sake and also because it illustrates how much the Common-Man-Reforms in the Catholic Church were his continual preoccupation. The subject is the time-honoured *Ave Maria* or 'Hail Mary'.

'Vernacular version of the Salutation suggested by a correspondence in *The Catholic Herald*. "Hiya Moll. You're the tops. You've got everything it takes, baby, and that goes for junior too. Look Moll, you put in a word for us slobs now and when we knock out".'

There were plenty of Catholic priests then who saw nothing perverse or grotesque in such a degradation of one of the most famous of all prayers, and there remain many now.

To return to Evelyn's last fiction. The only evidence as to when it was written is in two letters to Ann Fleming; one private telling her of its completion and the other the printed dedicatory letter which prefaces the book. Both are dated December 1962. It was published in 1963 after being serialized in *The Sunday Telegraph*.

It may as well be considered now. It was called *Basil Seal Rides Again*. It is not a book likely to be remembered except by students of Evelyn's work. He himself was not proud of it and described it in the dedicatory letter as 'this senile attempt to recapture the manner of my youth.'

It is not quite as bad as that, but dealing as it does with figures he had invented and immortalized in his books from *Decline and Fall* to *Put Out More Flags*, it inevitably invites comparisons which are not in its favour. The narrative structure shows no weakening but, as with *Pinfold*, the narrative interest is not sustained. The best things come early on. Few of Evelyn's novels have a better beginning: the elderly Basil Seal and his elderly friend Peter Pastmaster attending a banquet to celebrate the award of the Order of Merit to Ambrose Silk (Brian Howard).

The central episode concerns Basil Seal's adventures at a hydro. There is no mention of a frighteningly hideous press photograph, but the circumstances in which Basil takes this step are based on Evelyn's experience. To quote the book: '[The hotel] was a place he had frequented all his life, particularly in the latter years, and he was on cordial terms with the man who took the men's hats in a den by the Piccadilly entrance. Basil was never given a numbered ticket and assumed he was known by name. Then a day came when he sat longer than usual over luncheon and found the man off duty. Lifting the counter he had penetrated to the rows of pegs and retrieved his bowler and umbrella. In the ribbon of the hat he found a label, put there for identification. It bore the single pencilled word "florid".' This really had happened to Evelyn at the Ritz. (Or was it another hallucination?)

The hydro with its dotty psychiatrist and the secret bar maintained by the venal gymnastic instructor are all in Evelyn's best vein, but thereafter the story flags and it ends in lame sentimentality in spite of a good plot. It is to be classed with *Love Among the Ruins* to which, however, it is decidedly superior.

The relation of experience to fiction is unusual in the case of this book. The vivid description of a man's experience while being in the voluntary imprisonment of a hydro ought to have come after Evelyn's experience of that state at Forest Mere. In fact it came roughly a year before. There are said to be studious authors who write reliable guide books to distant countries without leaving home. Evelyn when he wished could emulate them.

Evelyn came to his Boxing Day lunch with us as usual, and on the same conditions, but neither on the 1962 occasion nor those in the years following was there so notable an event as the Froissart-French chronicle of the *archevêque nommé Fisher*. On our Boxing Day lunch in one of these years I did insist to Laura that it was a serious omission that no biography had been written of her father Aubrey Herbert. Laura said: 'Of course it ought to be done, but it can't be till after my mother dies. She would only allow hero-worshipping twaddle.'

I answered: 'Why don't you encourage The Master to examine his papers and prepare something?', with a nod towards Evelyn.

In his deep voice, always affectedly deep when he was not quite serious, he answered: 'I never knew him and I don't want to read the papers. I think you did know him.' And I was conscious of Evelyn's glaring eyes upon me. If this was a suggestion, nothing came of it, but I believe the wrong is to be repaired by an eminently suitable author, Patrick Kinross.

Evelyn's visits to London continued to be infrequent, partly because his health was worsening, partly because in 1963 he was engaged on a new and ambitious task, his autobiography. He went for a short visit to Italy to escape the English winter, staying with Harold Acton in Florence and visiting Rome. I saw him on his rare visits to London but the time I best remember was in August when my wife and I went over to Combe Florey. The occasion was as follows: Evelyn had written to say that 'my revered friend Mr Sutro' was due to visit him in August before coming to us for a weekend in Dorset, and that it would ease his revered friend's arrangements if we drove him from Combe Florey to our house in Dorset. We went over to tea and drinks.

Evelyn, stimulated by the company of John Sutro whom he saw infrequently in these days, was in great form, as was his revered friend. Early in the visit Evelyn said to me peremptorily: 'November 14th. Put it down in your engagement thing. Fortieth anniversary of the founding of the Railway Club. Dinner. London to Brighton and back. No excuses for absence accepted.' The Profumo scandal was at high tide still and Evelyn, who always enjoyed scandals, held forth on it, comparing it to the Marconi and Robinson scandals and insisting how the invincible British taste for humbug invariably and totally obscured the main point at issue. 'The only man who talked sense in the House,' I remember him saying, 'was Lord Lambton. Supposing these relationships with these women really had been platonic – then they would have been dangerous. But what I can't get over is the expense of the women! One pound a swish! Goodness! Thank Heavens I did all that sort of thing on a conservative and stable market.' As we sat in the bow-window of the drawing-room after tea, he said:

'In October I shall reach the age of sixty. I have decided that that is the moment to enter onto a new and final phase of life. I plan to retire to a cure-place in order to change my physical appearance totally. I shall then have less difficulty in making and changing my soul before appearing before the Judgement Seat. I intend to become a totally changed being, unconnected with my present self.'

Before we left for Dorset, he gave us a letter to post. I warned him that we were driving back by the little roads and might miss the last collection. Our revered friend was thereupon inspired to improvise a song in the style of a previous age, and of which I happily made a note:

'I'm a little post box in a little country lane.
I stand in the sunshine and I stand in the rain.
Lovers come and give me their beautiful letters
And poor men seek me out when they write to their betters.'

It was one of those visits which prove unforgettable. But when we were home John Sutro told us that he had become worried about Evelyn. He felt that his health was worse than he admitted and that it could not improve while he lived as he did, never taking any exercise or even going out of doors. Later events show that John's judgement was sound, but at this time and for a little time yet Evelyn was the gayest company imaginable and life at Combe Florey was fun.

In the event he went to the Hydro in September, anticipating his climacteric birthday by more than a month. 'You did not prepare me', he wrote to Ann, 'for the great ugliness of house, furniture & scenery here. But my 50 guinea suite is spacious & the attendants civil.

'You are not one of their prize patients. They said: "You were recommended by Mr Ian Fleming." "By *Mrs* Fleming?" "Oh. *Mrs* Fleming. Well . . . but we have had Mr Fleming here. Also Godfrey Winn."

'In the last 24 hours I have had two glasses of hot lemon juice. I have sat in a "sweat-bath" & been severely massaged. I have gained ½ pound in weight. Time hangs heavy.'

I have no doubt that the Forest Mere Hydro could have done much for him and protracted his last years. To outward appearances his cure did little good. He made haste to eat all the oysters, caviare and smoked salmon he had been denied: like Randolph Churchill, who used to undergo regular cures, he found in the loss of a stone an excuse to put on a stone and a half, not a regime in conformity with the best dietetic thought. He certainly showed no signs of being under an ascetic regime on 14 November 1963 when the Railway Club held its last memorable dinner on the Victoria to Brighton line, Harold Acton, by tradition, making an oration on the return journey which lasted the whole way. British Railways entered into the spirit of the thing and issued specially printed tickets to the members. Our revered friend John Sutro was the presiding genius but Evelyn, who brought Terence Greenidge with him, was as much the party's life and soul. It was one of my last purely happy memories of Evelyn. I had urged on him and John Sutro the need for the presence of younger persons if the party was not to take on a mournful character, a proposition to which they agreed, so the last meeting of the club was held with many just-elected members.

A letter written to Nancy Mitford nearly a year later shows that Evelyn's habit of fantasy never left him and was moved by this occasion. It may be remembered that in 1964 a libel case involving the Kray brothers and Lord Boothby was settled out of court in Lord Boothby's favour for a substantial sum. Lord Boothby was a member of the Railway Club and had attended the 1963 dinner. Evelyn wrote on the case to Nancy: 'One curious point – the unnamed peer was said to have gone to an "all-male" party of licentious clergymen at Brighton. Now in November last John Sutro & I organized a party to Brighton to celebrate the 40th anniversary of the Oxford Railway Club. Bob [Boothby] was there. Clerical dress was not worn but I remember thinking how very clerical most of our voices sounded – impotent grandfathers to a man. Can that have been the origin of the rumour.'

As he had already written his book about the Hydro before he went there he had more or less nothing to tell about it. There is however one intriguing passage on the subject in a letter to Ann Fleming of 10 December.

'Did female patient at Forest Mere who took me for a woman observe me in the "treatment room"? If so she must be ignorant of anatomy.' The same letter has one other passage which should be quoted: 'I have completed first vol of life of self. It ends well with unsuccessful attempt at suicide in 1924. I have been offered large sums to write a popular history of the papacy. Shall probably accept.'

In fact he did not. *A Little Learning* was the last book by Evelyn. This record of his early life, which has been heavily drawn on in the opening chapters of this book, is a minor work but an extremely interesting one. It provided a fine *diminuendo* with which to close the literary achievement of thirty-six years. It was published in 1964 and may be briefly considered.

The witty title from Pope was not Evelyn's own. He lifted it (without acknowledgement) from a now forgotten book of reminiscence by Ronald Knox's sister, Winifred Peck. It is not a great book and was not written as such, but it is an admirable book, marred not by any serious blemish but by at least one serious omission.

The portraits of his father and mother are executed with loving care. It is allowable to suppose that in both cases he felt that he owed an act of reparation. He had caused both parents grave anxiety in his wild young days, and in later years he came, as he said in this book and often said to his friends, to understand and admire his father towards whom he had felt temporarily, as most men do as they grow into manhood, some irrational hostility. He came to see, happily long before Arthur Waugh's death, what a lovable man his father was. His relations with his mother had never been strained, but a letter he wrote to a friend when she died in 1954 shows that he reproached himself for having somewhat neglected her in her old age. Even remembering Alec Waugh's testimony, too much autobiographical importance must not be given to the references to Mr Pinfold's awkward relations with his mother. Mrs Waugh's letters to Evelyn are touching in their simplicity, affection and pride in her son's achievement. He drew his parents without excessive *pietas*, without any suspension of his sleepless critical sense, but in a way which commands respect for them.

The chapters on his childhood and adolescent years in Hampstead are finely evocative of a kind of suburban life which is very different today, or very different in places so near the centre of London. The main part of the book is concerned with Evelyn's life at Lancing and at Oxford. Of these chapters I find the most intriguing one called *Two Mentors*.

The two mentors are J. F. Roxburgh and Francis Crease, both of whom have been mentioned in earlier chapters. Many people have had Roxburghs and Creases in their young days when budding and not yet flowering imagination needs sympathetic discipline and sympathetic encouragement. To such mentors they feel an infinite debt afterwards. Evelyn was fortunate to find both at Lancing. In this book he drew the two men beautifully.

Only one part of the book shows clear signs of literary fatigue. The shortest chapter is grandiloquently entitled 'A Brief History of My Religious Opinions', but the joke fails because of the meagreness of the contents of the three and a quarter pages which follow. He makes only one point of interest, that the total irreligion of his mind between his Anglican and his Catholic days was not much induced by the rebelliousness of boyhood, but much more by the scepticism of the older Anglican generation from whom his teachers, lay and clerical, were drawn. Ten years earlier what an unforgettable twenty pages he would have written on the subject!

The book caused much interest on its appearance and was and still is widely and rightly praised. Only one condemnation of it has appeared, so far as I know. This was in a short book published in 1974, called *A Fragment of Friendship*, written by a schoolfellow of Lancing, Mr Dudley Carew. A reader may suspect an undivulged grudge.

In April 1964 Alfred Duggan died. He had by now made himself a name, but, as often happens, gratifying fame did not result in gratifying sales of his books in time to benefit him. But his fame was not brief and he has readers in larger quantities now than ten years ago. I remember meeting Evelyn soon after Alfred's death, with Diana Cooper. He told me that he wanted to do something to help the widow and Alfred's adopted son who had been left in somewhat difficult circumstances. He spoke with serious emotion, such as was rare with him. 'Alfred's story is a very edifying one', I recall him saying. 'The usual literary story is of the bright young man, with a voracious appetite for life, writing distinguished poems and novels and so on, and then the voracious appetite getting the better of him and his ending up as a pathetic old soak. Alfred kicked off as a soak and loafed round the library at Hackwood in an alcoholic haze, and then in his late years all those apparently wasted hours in the library sprouted into brilliant historical novels, and he ended up as a distinguished and sober writer.'

A little later he said to me: 'Are you still employed as an electrician?' 'Yes,' I replied, 'for a few years more.' I felt and saw Diana's blue eyes upon me. 'Are you an *electrician*?' asked Mrs Stitch, with surprise and excited hope. 'No I'm not. It's just Evelyn.' The answer needed no explanation. 'Oh the Gremlin', murmured Diana as she turned to someone else. She had a private term 'Gremlin' (old RAF slang) for Evelyn which she used to me and a few other fellow-sufferers.

But Evelyn's question had serious results. He asked me to convey to the BBC a request that he might give a talk on Alfred Duggan as a novelist in the hope that this might help sales of his books. I said I would, of course, and so, with awful misgivings about likely rows, I conveyed the request officially. It was accepted and I lived for a little in dread.

I had no need to do so. In the event, things went smoothly. Evelyn insisted as usual on the recording being made at Combe Florey, but by 1964 he had some reason for his health was manifestly weakening. I thought that I had better be present, and so I went for the night to Combe Florey, the last time I stayed there as Evelyn's guest. The 'electricians' arrived punctually from Bristol the next morning. His admirable talk ran a little short of the time allotted. The man in charge asked Evelyn if he would like to add anything. 'Certainly not', sharply replied Evelyn who had composed the piece with care. It was the only shadow, a slight one, over the occasion. Evelyn seemed to feel this too. He made himself very agreeable. He invited the young man to come to the drawing-room to have a drink, but before leaving the library he said: 'I would like to present you with one of my books, if you will accept it.' The young man thanked him and Evelyn gave him a signed copy of one of the handsomely bound copies which were regularly made for him on the publication of his later books. We moved to the drawing-room and had a drink with pleasant small talk, and then the 'electricians' drove away.

When they had gone Evelyn looked glum. 'I am afraid I have made your position as a BBC agent very difficult', he said. 'I am afraid I behaved very badly to that young man.'

'Because you were a bit abrupt about adding something? Nonsense. It was nothing.'

'No no. I mean the way I gave him a signed copy. How did I know that he wanted it? He may think I'm a very bad writer indeed. I acted presumptuously. When he gets back to Bristol he'll tell his fellow-electricians that he met a conceited beast who fancied himself as the local squire and behaved in an odiously patronizing way to him.' Laura and I laughed but said nothing to contradict him, for we knew it would be a waste of time.

Evelyn did nothing by halves.

I saw him again at the 'annual vomit' and on our Boxing Day lunch of 1964. During this winter cf 1964/1965, Evelyn had his teeth extracted. For some reason he underwent the extremely painful operation without anaesthetic. His son Auberon has told me that in his opinion he never got over the operation, though of course, true to form, he made light of it. On 27 January 1965 three days after the death of Sir Winston Churchill, he wrote to Ann Fleming:

'I own a tooth-brush but since I have no teeth it is a superfluous possession – like the tiaras of ladies who are never asked out. But I have the name of a man in London who makes false teeth & I have written to order some. I don't imagine the process can be complete in a single visit so I shall probably be in London often in the near future & hope to see you. This is the time I normally go abroad but there is nowhere I want to go. Perhaps with my new snappers I will go for a gastronomic tour. I once knew an old man who at the end of dinner buried his face in his napkin & made retching sounds & then raised a toothless face saying he could not taste port with false teeth. I have a deep horror of them.

'For the past fortnight my drive has been worn into potholes by telegraph boys bearing extravagant offers from newspapers to describe Sir Winston's obsequies. I have of course refused. He was not a man for whom I ever had esteem. Always in the wrong, always surrounded by crooks, a most unsuccessful father – simply a "Radio Personality" who outlived his prime. "Rallied the nation" indeed! I was a serving soldier in 1940. How we despised his orations . . .

'Did I tell you that I had got a lady-in-waiting to send a letter of condolence in the Queen's name to her Majesty's one-time maid in hospital. The effect has been startling. Not only has she become the tyrant of the ward but she has now convinced herself that she is a near relation of the Queen's . . .

'I suppose the editors who solicited my help in describing Sir Winston's funeral have vaguely heard I once wrote a book about funerals in California.'

Evelyn's distaste for Sir Winston Churchill has been mentioned already. Readers of earlier chapters of this book will easily recognize that his belief that it was lifelong was mistaken.

I remember being greatly surprised at the anti-Churchill impetus in *Men at Arms* when the book came out and saying so to Harry Stavordale. In his high hoarse voice Harry replied: 'Aimed at Randolph'; but now I think he was wrong. It was aimed at the Winston Churchill of 1944.

Evelyn's sense of history was defective in the same way as that of many of his father's generation. He overrated British power. It never occurred to him that Churchill had no alternative but to go along with the policies of Communism and the United States. Evelyn believed that Britain was fully capable of acting out of concert with the great allied powers at a moment of national peril. This was as absurd as Belloc's idea that the Bank of England ordained the fall of Napoleon.

On 17 April 1965 my wife and I attended the funeral of T. S. Eliot at East Coker. That lovely village is not far from Combe Florey so we had arranged to go there after the service, to lunch with Evelyn and Laura. My wife was wearing a black dress and hat and I was wearing a dark suit with a black tie. It had occurred to us that our funereal appearance might cast a gloom over the luncheon so we stopped on the way and I changed my tie and my wife replaced her black hat with a gay scarf.

We were met at the door of the house by Evelyn who was wearing a tail coat. We both presumed that he had had to attend some function in Taunton. He led us in and gave us drinks. Laura was less formally dressed, but she was never a person to put on her best clothes unless it was quite unavoidable. After we had been talking for some time, I said that I felt rather under-dressed in my suit which compared poorly with Evelyn's tails. My wife asked what function he had had to attend. Had he been elected Mayor of Taunton?

'No function at all', he replied, as though amazed by her question.

'But surely', I said, 'you don't dress like this every day?'

'Certainly not.' Then, after a silence, 'I understood you were going to the funeral of a dear and famous friend. Naturally I wished to dress in accordance with your mood. But if I had realized', he went on, in his affectedly deep voice, 'that the occasion was frivolous, so much so that Christopher puts on a garish tie, and you, Camilla, an almost indecently jolly scarf, I would not have gone to this trouble.'

Again, as with the *archevêque nommé Fisher*, it was the gravity of the manner that gave such irresistible point to the jest. I thought how Eliot would have enjoyed this elaborate piece of fooling.

The later events of that brief visit, our last to Combe Florey in Evelyn's lifetime, gave me a sad impression of Evelyn's declining health. He hardly touched his food. Several of the younger children were present and the conversation at the table was animated. I was sitting next to Evelyn and asked him something. He could not hear. I repeated my question. He said angrily, 'I can't hear with all this noise going on. Ask me afterwards.' I had often seen Evelyn acting the angry old man in jest; now he was an angry old man. He looked ten years older than he was.

Some time later that year I saw Evelyn in White's. We sat down together. I said: 'You know, for the first time I'm growing frightened of you, like poor Boots Connolly.'*

'I'd always hoped you were afraid of me. I prefer it that way.'

'Well I wasn't.'

'Why are you afraid now, of all times?'

* When she met him at Logan Pearsall Smith's house, Virginia Woolf described Cyril Connolly after as 'that smartiboots Connolly'. As a result he became known as 'Boots'.

'Because you are writing your autobiography. *A Little Learning* was all right because it was all about the years before I knew you. But Vol Two will spill over into me.'

He sighed and with a sudden change from the joking manner of our conversation he said: 'You've no reason to fear. No one has. I wish they had. My life is roughly speaking over. I sleep badly except occasionally in the morning. I get up late. I try to read my letters. I try to read the paper. I have some gin. I try to read the paper again. I have some more gin. I try to think about my autobiography. Then I have some more gin and it's lunch time. That's my life. It's ghastly.'

About the same time he told my brother-in-law, Ran Antrim, that he spent his morning breathing on his library window and then playing naughts and crosses against himself, drinking gin in the intervals between play. (He had written among the aphorisms of his later diary 'All fates are " worse than death". ')

Knowing Evelyn's tendency to exaggeration I did not take his disturbing self-revelations very seriously until one day in the late autumn of 1965 when he and Laura came to lunch with us. The occasion was the marriage of John Joliffe to Helen Eden at Wardour, about four miles from us. Although he had noted in his diary 'Punctuality is the virtue of bores', Evelyn was always on time. On this occasion he was an hour and a half late. We had almost finished lunch. He hardly ate anything and only sipped his glass of wine. He was transformed. He was looking old and had become slow in speech – a thing I had never noticed in him before. On arrival he was smoking a cigar which he threw on the carpet before sitting down, and did not seem to notice when my wife hastily plucked it up.

I drove Evelyn to the church and hurried him past the photographers at the door. During the nuptial Mass he sat by my side in a daze, until he suddenly said to me in his deepest tone: 'There's a man with a lot of lions just behind me.'

'Oh shut up', I said.

A few moments later he said: 'I tell you there's a man just behind me with a lot of lions. It's dangerous.'

I looked round and saw Henry Bath. I assured Evelyn that there was no cause for alarm. He relapsed into silence. The officiating priest whom he knew well, Dom Aelred Watkin of Downside, was wearing for the occasion a magnificent old chasuble, supposedly presented by Catherine of Aragon to Westminster Abbey. At a suitable moment I mentioned these facts to Evelyn who seemed hardly to understand. At length he said: 'Presented by whom to what?'

I repeated what I had said and he glared intently at the exquisite embroidery for a minute or so. Then he said in a voice audible to the whole congregation: 'Looks brand new to me.'

After that day it did seem to me that Evelyn had not long to live.

I saw him only once more. Against his wish but in answer to appeals from Brian Franks and Bob Laycock, he attended the annual lunch at the Hyde Park Hotel in December 1965. He sat opposite me, next to Bob. He had felt too ill to come down from his room before luncheon. He ate nothing. He drank nothing. He sat silent. I caught a glance from him which plainly said, 'You see my state.' After a quarter of an hour he left, leaning on the arm of a waiter. I never saw him again.

One of the few people he wrote to in 1966 was Diana Mosley. The letter has been quoted already in connection with *Work Suspended*. This last letter to her was written shortly before Easter. He said that he had been conscious of a certain advantage in writing the first volume of his memoirs from the fact that almost all the seniors and many of the coevals whom he needed to mention were dead, but that this was not the case with the second volume. He said that Holy Week and Easter had always been a great spiritual joy to him but now no longer, and that he now looked on his attendance at Mass on Easter day, as on all church-going, as a tedious, uninspiring 'duty parade'.

I wrote to him on some question to which I needed an answer but heard nothing, surprisingly in view of his pedantic scrupulousness about answering letters.

Easter Sunday of 1966 fell on 10 April. Harriet and the younger children were there and also Father Philip Caraman. Not far from Combe Florey there was a Catholic chapel, and it was arranged that Father Caraman would say Mass there on Easter morning. Members of the Herbert family, including Evelyn's brother-in-law Auberon Herbert, came to the Mass from Pixton. Evelyn seemed to be in good spirits, happy because he was to hear Mass said according to the time-honoured ancient rite. He had recently been on awkward terms with his brother-in-law Auberon (a usual occurence) and he seemed to go out of his way to be friendly. After Mass Father Caraman and the Waugh family returned to Combe Florey for breakfast.

What happened to Evelyn later that morning was witnessed by no one. Laura was busy in the kitchen and about the house, the children had their own interests; Father Caraman and Harriet sat in the bow-window of the drawing-room playing piquet; Evelyn retired to his library to work. No one noticed anything unusual or had reason to, until about one o'clock when Father Caraman and Harriet heard a loud cry from Laura.

It seems that some time in the morning Evelyn, went to the back parts of the house. While there he had occasion to raise his arms and this gesture brought on an instant and instantly fatal heart attack. Laura found him dead. Father Caraman administered 'conditional absolution', that is: the Last Rites on the supposition that life may not be extinct. The Church has long recognized that the moment of death is hard to define with exactness.

His death was as sudden as death can be. He was spared a long painful illness before the close, as he would have wished; he was possibly spared a second descent into that place of torment which his comic genius summed up as Pinfold, as he would have wished; he was denied conscious participation in the Last Rites of the Catholic Church, as he would not have wished.

# Postscript

Had he lived until and beyond the traditional span of life there might have been some autumnal mellowing of character. As it was there was none, indeed it can even be said that the progress of the reform-movement in the Catholic Church, a historical movement which he was at moments inclined to interpret as a final decay preceding the extinction of Catholicism, or at least an eclipse of the inextinguishable *Ecclesia Dei*, left him so open to his besetting temptation to despair as to increase his harshness. It is widely supposed that at the end of his life he had lost his faith. This is not true, as I can testify, but what is true, and is evidenced in his letters, especially his late letters to Penelope Betjeman, is that he went increasingly in fear of losing his faith; 'like one that on some lonesome road doth walk in fear and dread', on a road, one may add, that had but a short time before been crowded.

If there was no loss of faith there was some loss of confidence in his strength to survive the abandonment of a religious practice that could appeal to the heart through the imagination. He believed, I think I am right in asserting, that the Church had evolved a marvellous liturgy whereby *l'homme moyen sensuel* (as opposed to a saint) could approach God and be aware of sanctity. To thow away such a heritage for the sake of banal up-to-dateness, as was being done in his last years, struck him as not only silly but dangerous. 'Untune that string', he seems to have felt, and loss of faith will follow. The loss of faith did not follow in this case, but he lived at the end with the possibility of such a loss ever before him.

None of this anxiety for the future of the Catholic Church, nor his sharp criticism of its leaders in the '60s, made him the least more tolerant towards non-Catholic belief. Until his last days he stayed in the merciless apologist and polemicist position, in which he maintained (to his old friend Christopher Hollis, the son of an exemplary Anglican bishop) that all Anglican clergymen must by logical necessity be damned. His cruelty not only remained in him, but remained to his taste. In brief, he never mellowed.

In religion, which was the centre of his life, this cruelty, shown in his intolerance, was the authentic expression of his mind and emotional state. It was otherwise with another element in his life, close to if not

448

identical with its centre. This was his family life. He projected an image of himself as a cruel, self-centred husband and a tyrannical father. Not surprisingly, so much first-hand evidence was accepted and the story was believed. Not without reason because it contained some grains of truth. But it also contained a larger measure of fable invented by this great story-teller.

Evelyn was not an easy husband and Laura was a devotedly patient wife. But she was no 'doormat', as was sometimes believed. She could stand up for herself with great effect when Evelyn became tiresome. If she really had been a 'doormat' Evelyn would not have loved her as he did. He had many faults but there is no faint trace of evidence anywhere that he was ever unfaithful to his wife.

As a father he went against much modern tendency. He had no use for the idea of the permissive parent who never checks his offspring for fear of undesirable psychological effects. In a spirit of anti-modernism, rather than of a desire to execute an accurate self-portrait, he depicted himself as a monster rather on the lines of Samuel Butler's terrifying picture of a father in *The Way of All Flesh* (one of his favourite books). In conversation, in interviews, above all in the Pinfold self-portrait, he added to a picture which was inevitably believed to be exact.

Auberon Waugh has told me that though his three sons had to endure some difficult moments in their lives with this unusual father, his memory of his childhood is a happy one, due in large part to his father, not in spite of him. Only in one respect would he criticize him as a parent, and that is with reference to a certain emotional capriciousness in his relations with all his children except Margaret. It was, Auberon said, as though he regarded his parental affection as a gift which it was in his power to confer or to withdraw. One never quite knew where one was with him.

At the moment of writing, in 1975, eleven years after the publication of his last book, it is still hazardously early to pronounce on the position likely to be occupied by Evelyn Waugh in English letters. It is customary for a literary reputation to sink in the years immediately after an author's death, the most striking modern example being that of so great a one as Bernard Shaw's. He is only now, twenty-five years after his death, beginning to be accorded, and that tentatively, the high esteem he enjoyed in his lifetime. No such diminution of reputation is discernible in the case of Evelyn Waugh, and this suggests that his place in our literature is secure, if not for ever for a foreseeably long time.

The style and character of his work makes comparison especially difficult. He belonged to no past or contemporary school, and had he responded to appeals, such as those of Mr J. B. Priestley, to join one he would probably have thus weakened his ability. Partly his work is likely to endure because it has a certain uniqueness; partly for a somewhat

449

opposite reason. He came to manhood in a world which had been shaken to its foundations by the impact of the First World War. Its mood was consequently one of disillusion and cynicism. This mood was expressed memorably by many of the leading writers of the time and among the youngest of them Evelyn Waugh in his early novels, using the medium of black comedy. After the mid-thirties he entered wider fields with renewed trial and error.

The whole work of his literary maturity led up to a grand climax, The War Trilogy. Quite apart from its great literary merit this book is likely to be long remembered. When much of his humour is faded or has grown incomprehensible, this formidable work of imagination is likely to stand the test of time, even if only for its historical interest. It portrays a great and terrible episode in the life of 'Western Man' as he has come to be called, seen from a strictly personal point of view. The War Trilogy is a perfect example of talents deployed precisely within the author's range. It shows army life as it was lived when, possibly for the last time in history, a large British army took part in full-scale warfare on the continent of Europe. Others have done this, some with great success, but none other with Evelyn Waugh's mixture of uniqueness and grasp of public mood, with his sceptical, curious and humorous insight.

# Index